a contemporary introduction to social psychology

Lawrence J. Severy
University of Florida

John C. Brigham
Florida State University

Barry R. Schlenker
University of Florida

a contemporary introduction to social psychology

McGraw-Hill Book Company

New York   St. Louis   San Francisco   Auckland   Düsseldorf
Johannesburg   Kuala Lumpur   London   Mexico   Montreal   New Delhi
Panama   Paris   São Paulo   Singapore   Sydney   Tokyo   Toronto

Library of Congress Cataloging in Publication Data

Severy, Lawrence J
    A contemporary introduction to social psychology.

    Bibliography: p.
    Includes index.
    1. Social psychology. 2. Social problems.
I. Brigham, John Carl, date   joint author.
II. Schlenker, Barry R., joint author. III. Title.
HM251.S424   301.1   75-29052
ISBN 0-07-056330-6

a contemporary introduction to social psychology

This book was set in Helvetica by University Graphics, Inc.
The editors were Richard R. Wright, Helen Greenberg, and James R. Belser;
the designer was Anne Canevari Green;
the production supervisor was Leroy A. Young.
The drawings were done by J & R Services, Inc.

See Acknowledgments on pages 439–443.
Copyrights included on this page by preference.

Dedicated to
our families

contents

Preface xv

1 RESEARCH METHODS AND THE SCIENTIFIC APPROACH TO
SOCIAL BEHAVIOR: HOW WE CAN UNDERSTAND HUMAN
CONFLICTS 2

What Is Conflict? The Essence of Interaction 4
Unevaluated Information: Common Sense 5
Science and the Scientific Method 9
    Induction 10
    Deduction 12
    Testing 12
    A summary of the scientific method 13
Getting Evidence 14
    Observation of naturally occurring behaviors 14
Focus 1-1 Social Psychology: Science or History?
    Or, What Choices Have You Made Today? 15
    Questionnaire-interview techniques 21
Focus 1-2 A Double Standard in International Perceptions:
    It's Okay for Me but Not for You 25
Focus 1-3 Black-and-White Thinking: Misperceptions in
    International Affairs 27
    Historical analysis and content analysis 31
    Correlation: Analyzing data 33
    Gathering data in controlled settings: Experimentation 35
Focus 1-4 The Game of Life: Some Playful Ways to Study Conflict 39

Resolving Conflicts: What to Do until Armageddon   43
    Common goals: Some alternatives to invasion
       from outer space   44
    Pacifism   45
    GRIT: A lot of it's needed in conflicts   46
Summary   49

2   ATTITUDE CHANGE   50

What Are Attitudes?   52
Why We Develop Attitudes   54
    Making sense of the world   54
    Relating to others   54
    Expressing our values   55
    Protecting our threatened egos   55
Measuring Attitudes: How Do We Find Out?   55
    Self-report measures   56
    Observing overt behavior   57
    Judging task performance   57
    Interpreting ambiguous stimuli   60
    Measuring physiological reactions   60
Attitudes and Behavior: When Do They Correspond?   61
How Can Attitudes Be Changed?   63
Persuasive Communications and Attitude Change   65
    Source characteristics   65
    Message characteristics   70
    Audience characteristics   74
From Behavior to Attitudes: Or, "What Have I Done?
   Why, Something I Wanted to Do, Of Course"   76
    A bad choice   77
    A free choice   77
    A deceitful choice   78
    In search of an explanation   80
Focus 2-1 Great Expectations   81
Focus 2-2 Does Your World End If Theirs Doesn't?   82
Resisting persuasion   87
Summary   90

3   ETHNIC PREJUDICE   92

What Is Prejudice?   94
Causes of Ethnic Prejudice   96

Competition and exploitation   96
Perceived belief dissimilarity: "They" are "different"   102
Conformity and social norms   104
Cues from society   106
Focus 3-1 Of Dolls and Men   107
Focus 3-2 Charlie's Daily Racism   110
Individual Prejudice: Is There a Prejudiced Personality?   111
Authoritarianism   112
Focus 3-3 Fascism Unmasked?   113
Focus 3-4 An Example of Faulty Research   114
Dogmatism   116
Concrete versus abstract thinking   117
An important caution   120
Focus 3-5 Who Votes for Whom?   121
Ways of Reducing Ethnic Prejudice   122
Changing attitudes   122
Changing child-rearing practices   123
Changing behavior   124
Equal-status contact   127
Effects of Ethnic Separation   131
Beliefs of white separatists   131
Beliefs of black separatists   132
A dilemma   132
Summary   133

4 SEXISM AND SOCIALIZATION

SEXISM AND SOCIALIZATION   134

Is There Really a Sex Prejudice?   136
Focus 4-1 Myths and Realities for Women in a Man's World   137
Who Creates Sexism?   141
Focus 4-2 You Can't Fool Mother (Father?) Nature   142
The individual   143
Cultural forces   144
Individual agents   153
Focus 4-3 Sexism in Print   154
What Is Created?   158
Beliefs and attitudes   158
Skills   161
Motives and values   162
Knowledge   162
Ideals   164
Habits   164
How Sexism Is Created   166
The psychodynamic approach   166

The cognitive-developmental approach 169
The social learning approach 170
Summary of theoretical perspectives 175
Summary 175

5 RELATING TO OTHERS: AFFILIATION, ATTRIBUTION, ATTRACTION, AND LOVE 176

Affiliation: Why Do People Need People? 178
Instinct 179
Survival 182
Social rewards and social exchange 182
Social comparison 184
Fear and affiliation 185
Evaluating Other People 186
Generalizations 186
Implicit personality theories 188
Central traits 189
Interpreting Behavior: Ability to Evaluate Others Accurately 190
The criterion problem 190
Artifacts 191
Skill in judging others 192
Focus 5-1 How to Develop a Super Test without Really Trying 193
Making Attributions 194
Factors affecting the attributions we make 195
Other people have traits 200
Self-Attributions 201
How do you know what you feel? 201
The "juke box" theory of emotion 204
To eat or not to eat? 204
Are your attitudes your own? 205
Liking Others 206
Propinquity: The boy or girl next door 206
Similarity: To be like me is to be liked 207
Physical attractiveness: Ode to a pretty face (and body) 208
Focus 5-2 Attraction and Similarity in the Dormitory 209
Focus 5-3 Choosing a Date: Do You Go for Broke
or Seek Your Own Level? 210
Other determinants of liking 213
Focus 5-4 Playing Hard to Get 215
Loving Others 217
What is love? 217

Love as emotion   217
Liking and loving: A summary flow   219
Summary   220

6 ALTRUISM: WHERE'S THE HELP?   222

Altruism and Our Nature   225
    Reward-cost definition   225
    Moral definitions   228
    Intention descriptions   228
    Helping behavior   228
The Basics of Bystander Intervention   229
Victim-Bystander Characteristics: Or, What Is It about Me
    That . . . ?   230
    Ambiguity of victim's need   231
    Effects of group size   233
Focus 6-1 Deindividuation behind Bars   237
    Similarity   239
Focus 6-2 Sorry, Wrong Number!   244
Characteristics of the Emergency   247
    Costs and rewards   247
    Dependency   250
    Modeling   250
    Territoriality   252
    Ongoing interaction   253
The Development of Helping Behavior   253
Focus 6-3 A Theory of Why People Help   254
Personality and Helping   256
Summary   258

7 AGGRESSION   260

What Is Aggression?   262
    The nature of the beast: Aggression as a part of
      human nature   264
    The psychoanalytical interpretation of aggression   264
    Instincts and the ethological approach   265
The Way We're Wired: Genetic and Physiological Bases
    of Aggression   271
    Genetics and aggression   271
    The brain and aggression   272

The Social and Psychological Bases of Aggression 273
Focus 7-1 Brain Disorders and Violence 274
Focus 7-2 Drugs and Aggression 275
    Frustration and aggression: Damn you, I'll get you for that 276
    Social learning theory: I'll do what you do 282
Focus 7-3 The Weapons Effect: The Finger Pulls the Trigger,
  but Does the Trigger Also Pull the Finger? 283
    Violence and the mass media 288
    The social influence approach: What do you do when
      all else fails? 291
Focus 7-4 Culture and Aggression 295
Summary 296

8   CONFORMITY, COMPLIANCE, AND OBEDIENCE 298

Roles; What's a Politician Supposed to Do? 300
    Once a spy, always a spy 301
    Reelection at any cost 301
    Team players: To get along, you go along 304
Conformity 306
    Conformity and compliance 306
    Anticonformity and independence 306
Focus 8-1 It Still Moves 307
    Why conform? 308
Early Studies of Conformity 309
    The moving light 309
    Is everyone blind but me? 310
Variables Affecting Conforming Behavior 311
    Characteristics of the group 311
    Behavior of group members 312
    Personality 313
Compliance 313
    Rewards and punishments 313
    States of the individual 314
Focus 8-2 Brainwashing: Comply or Else 315
    The danger of overkill: Reactance 318
Compliance in the Extreme: Why Did They Do It? 318
Focus 8-3 If You're Guilty, You Pay 319
Roles: What Behaviors Are Appropriate? 320
    Prisoner and guard 321
    Hurting on command 323
    Other situational variables 326
    Still other variations 328

Ethical considerations 328
Watergate on campus 330
Implications 331
Is everyone a potential Eichmann? 331
The impact of the situation: There but for the grace of
God go I 332
Is There a Conforming or Obedient Personality? 333
Conformity and Compliance in Today's Society 334
Focus 8-4 Tolerance for Dissent in America 335
Summary 337

9 **GROUP DYNAMICS** 338

Groupthink: A Case Study in Group Decision Making 340
The Bay of Pigs 340
The consequences: A fiasco revisited 341
What went wrong? 342
Victims of groupthink 342
Symptoms of groupthink: The signs of faulty group
functioning 343
Factors that increase groupthink: How to generate a
poor group decision without really trying 347
Focus 9-1 Preventing Groupthink: A Little Independence, Please 348
Beyond groupthink 350
The Person versus the Group 350
Social facilitation 350
Individual versus group performance 352
Groups can do better than the average individual 353
Groups can do better than even the best individual 354
Brainstorming 354
The Social Climate: Cohesiveness 356
Cohesiveness and group members' feelings and actions 356
Looking beyond members' feelings: Cohesiveness and
performance 357
Cohesiveness and group organization 358
Cohesiveness and social influence 359
Focus 9-2 The T-Group: Learning to Communicate 360
Heretics and angels: Reactions to deviates and
conformers 361
Group Structure 363
Roles and role conflict 363
Status 365
Communication networks 366

Leadership   369
    What is a leader?   369
    Are leaders born or made?   370
    Approaches to the study of leadership   370
    Personal characteristics of the leader   371
    Personality and situation together: The contingency
       model   375
    Leadership activities   377
Focus 9-3 Authoritarianism and Democracy:
  Contrasting Leadership Styles   379
Summary   380

10   CROWDING AND THE ENVIRONMENT   382

Density and Social Behavior   385
    High density   385
Focus 10-1 Social Pathology and Population Density   386
    Low density   387
    The right number of people   389
Distribution of Persons: Give Me a Little Room!   391
    Crowding: There are too many people too close to me!   391
    Territory: That's my place!   394
    Privacy: Leave me alone!   397
    Personal space: Stand about that far from me!   399
    The influence of personal space on social behavior   400
Environmental Settings   402
Focus 10-2   Our Sociofugal Airports   403
    Natural settings   405
    Residential settings   408
    Urban settings   410
Focus 10-3 Prototype of a New Town   411
Summary   417

Bibliography   419

Acknowledgments   439

Indexes   444
    Name Index
    Subject Index

preface

To our readers—

Social psychology deals with the interactions that people engage in—parents and children, men and women, members of different ethnic groups and nations—all jostling one another on our increasingly complex and crowded planet. The problems that arise—conflict, prejudice, sexism, aggression, compliance, alienation, etc.—are issues each of us must cope with every day. We can attack these problems through protest, publicity, legislation, and the "reform" of such institutions as the penal system and the government. But underlying any action must be an understanding of the social dynamics that created the problems in the first place. Why did thirty-eight of her neighbors observe the murder of Kitty Genovese and make no attempt to help? How does the portrayal of violence in the mass media affect your own tendencies toward aggression? How did the same policy makers responsible for the disastrous invasion of Cuba at the Bay of Pigs successfully resolve the Cuban missile crisis? Why do compliance and blind obedience, such as occurred at the highest administrative levels during Watergate, happen? How can they be avoided? Why does one public housing project in New York City have a significantly lower crime rate than another project right across the street? How have the attitudes of people changed as a result of public school integration? How do parents, peers, the schools, the community, and the media create racism and sexism? How can they help abolish it?

This is a book about social psychology: life and living in the world today. As such, it takes two approaches: (1) discussion of problems of concern to students of the 1970s and (2) coverage of the research and experiments designed to analyze them. Unlike traditional textbooks, which present study after study and then give examples as to how they might apply to you, this one stresses what is happening in the world today. Social psychology as a science—the methods social psychologists use in investigating behavior—is thus presented not as an end in itself but as a tool to help you understand what is going on. Experiments and problems that merit expanded treatment are covered in special "Focus" sections. The learning objectives and major concepts that begin each chapter, and the summary that ends it, should help provide a thorough grounding in the material to be covered.

We wish to thank those who have supported and aided our efforts. On a general level, we owe thanks to both our teachers who helped us formulate our ideas and our students who responded to those ideas. On an individual level, we express our appreciation to those helpful persons at McGraw-Hill who kept us at our task; to colleagues such as Marvin Shaw for support and guidance; to reviewers who helped us see our writings in new ways, particularly Alfred Cohn of Hofstra University; to our student typists, Carla Krugman, Starr Silver, and Laurie Sistrunk in Gainesville, and Marsha Melton and Michelle Shafer in Tallahassee, for their secretarial assistance as well as their unrelenting commentary as to how the issues we raised applied to their lives; to those institutions and organizations that have funded our research (the Center for Population Research of NICHD, the National Science Foundation, and the Office of Naval Research for the three authors, respectively); to the writers and publishers who have permitted us to utilize copyrighted material (a complete listing of these sources is provided in the acknowledgments section); and most importantly to our families for putting up with us for the duration of the project.

Our late colleague, Sid Jourard, enjoyed suggesting to both students and faculty that "ideas are a dime a dozen; it's what you do with them that counts." At first, this position seems in direct opposition to American cultural and educational values, which suggest that we should value those with great ideas, "bright minds," and formal degrees. However, knowledge is most beneficial when it has practical implications for our lives. By concentrating on life in today's world, we hope that the ideas presented in this book will make a contribution.

Lawrence J. Severy
John C. Brigham
Barry R. Schlenker

a contemporary introduction to social psychology

1

research methods and
the scientific approach to
social behavior: how we can
understand human conflicts

concepts

The use of "common sense" is an ineffective way of understanding social behavior.

Scientific method provides a foundation for accumulating knowledge about social behavior.

Social psychologists use several major methods to obtain data about behavior, including observation of natural events, questionnaire-interview techniques, content analysis, and experimentation.

Social conflict pervades all social interactions and can produce misperceptions, stereotyped images, and double standards.

Conflicts increase in size as the antagonists perceive threats, prepare themselves for a confrontation, and display hostile behaviors.

Conflicts can be reduced through several techniques.

targets

After studying this chapter, you should be able to:

1 Explain the problems in using "common sense" as a basis for knowledge.
2 Describe the differences between science and common sense.
3 Discuss the chief aspects of the scientific method.
4 Describe the major ways social psychologists obtain data and state the strengths and weaknesses of each.
5 Define social conflict.
6 Summarize the typical sequence of events that leads to violence.
7 Describe the types of perceptions that accompany conflicts.
8 Discuss ways to reduce conflicts.

Almost all significant and important aspects of a person's life involve other people and society. We cultivate friends, and we make enemies. We fall in love. We develop bonds with our families and coworkers. We try to gain attention and respect. Our attitudes and beliefs are formed and affected by others, some of whom are friends and some of whom we might not even know, such as politicians or advertisers who get their messages across via the mass media.

Social institutions—governments and schools, for example—exert powerful influences on our attitudes and behaviors. The mere existence of other people affects the quality of our lives; at the extreme are the problems created by an unbounded worldwide population growth. Human life as we know it intimately involves other people, and this relationship between an individual and others captures the interest of social psychologists.

Social psychologists study the behavior of individuals or groups of individuals as it influences and is influenced by society and other people. The specific topics which interest social psychologists are so numerous that the only thing two researchers may have in common is the fact that they both call themselves social psychologists. Yet, no matter what topic social psychologists investigate, at least two common factors unite them: They share an interest in people's social nature, and they are scientists.

Social psychologists rely on theories, hypotheses, and data that bear the honorific label "scientific." Unfortunately, most people have only a slight idea of what science is. The word conjures up images of test tubes, white lab coats, sterile instruments, microscopes, and balding professors wandering to and from their ivory towers. Many people regard science with awe and wonder, recognizing that it is somehow responsible for the technology underlying our present life-styles. Others view science with fear, realizing that it propelled us into the nuclear age, where life can be ended by a social mistake—war. Still others fear that psychologists can "read" their minds and control their behaviors.

This chapter aims to describe what "science" means to social psychologists and to show why the scientific method is central to the continued development of the discipline. To illustrate how scientific methods can be applied to the study of human behavior, we'll look at some of the ways social psychologists have studied a very important topic—social conflict.

■ WHAT IS CONFLICT? THE ESSENCE OF INTERACTION

Conflict is a situation in which the goals of two or more parties are incompatible to some degree; not all parties can achieve their desired goals at one time. These clashes can involve major goals, as in the conflicting ideologies of the United States and Russia. (Many people on both sides see this conflict as ultimately involving the survival of the human race.) Conflicts also occur when the parties agree on major goals but disagree on minor ones. For example, two teenagers might agree that their goal for a Saturday evening is to have a good time, but they might disagree on the setting for it: a movie or a football game. Larger conflicts can spiral into violence and, when nations are involved, war. Small conflicts may scarcely be noticed by the participants; but when enough of them occur, they can produce serious interpersonal discord. No two people or groups ever agree totally on everything, and where differences exist, so do the seeds of conflict. In fact, it can be argued that conflict is present, at least to some degree, in all human interactions.

As conflict increases in size, the parties involved become more and more affected. They try to influence each other to change; they may misperceive one another's motives and behaviors, or try to protect themselves by stockpiling weapons, or resort to physical violence. How social psychologists obtain information about conflict, how they measure it, the kinds of perceptions and behaviors that occur, and how conflict can be resolved are some topics to be addressed.

■ UNEVALUATED INFORMATION: COMMON SENSE

Everyone has crude theories about what produces conflict and how it can be reduced. There are hundreds of unrelated, unintegrated, and untested beliefs about conflict. You might be called on to advise a friend who is fighting with a fiancé or young parents who are having difficulty with their small child. You probably feel you understand why people in other nations sometimes "misread" the motives and behaviors of the United States. You've probably never visited the People's Republic of China, yet if asked, you'd offer an opinion about what its society is like and why conflict exists between "them" and "us." Where did you get your knowledge and information about conflict?

The beliefs we hold about the world and people are formed by information from others and by our own experiences. We might learn about conflict by recalling situations in which we personally observed it and drew our own conclusions. Or we might listen to what other people say about conflict and form or change our attitudes accordingly. Together, these sources of information yield what is termed *common sense.* Commonsense beliefs are those which people accept because they seem to be correct, because many other people also believe them, and because they are useful in understanding and predicting what is happening. American society values common sense highly, but this form of knowledge is usually inadequate and inaccurate in describing things as they really are. Let's examine some problems with common sense.

1 *Since most people do not try to test their beliefs systematically, much of what is called common sense turns out to be false when analyzed.* This can be true even when everyone believes the same things, such as the once popular beliefs that the world is flat or that the earth is the center of the universe.

(a)

2 *Even when common sense does contain the germ of truth, we don't know under what conditions it is true or false.* Most people would agree that the belief "Absence makes the heart grow fonder" contains some truth. However, life is so complex that we often find ourselves accepting two opposite beliefs at one time—in this case, "Out of sight, out of mind." Since we accept both as accurate statements about human behavior, it becomes important to describe the conditions under which each is true or false. Maybe absence makes the heart grow fonder for two separated lovers who live in a small town with little social life. But perhaps out of sight becomes out of mind when the separated lovers live in a swinging city setting. Specifying the conditions under which a belief is true is important, but it's usually missing from common sense.

Similar examples abound when one considers commonsense beliefs about global conflict. One professed reason for United States involvement in Vietnam was to contain Communist aggression. The reasoning was simple: A takeover of Vietnam would reinforce Communist expansionist policies and result in aggression against other countries. Like dominoes, first Vietnam would fall, then Cambodia, then Indonesia, then Australia, then Hawaii, and finally California. American decisionmakers based their policy decisions on the theory of containment: By containing (punishing) expansion, the United States would discourage Communists from expanding further [246].* Of course, the opposite effect of containment policies also

*The numbers in brackets refer to the Bibliography on pages 419–438.

(b)

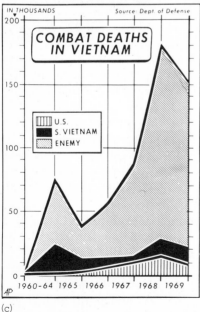

(c)

Figure 1-1. *American involvement in Vietnam began as an attempt to contain Communist expansion. American leaders, such as President Lyndon Johnson and his advisers (a), theorized that by punishing intrusions into South Vietnam, the country's government could be preserved. Other experts theorized that American involvement would be detrimental, since it would cause the North Vietnamese to become even more determined. American intervention and the resulting costs of lives, money, and prestige (b) were based on acceptance of the first theory. American leaders employed "experts" and "data" to "demonstrate" that the administration's view of the war was correct (c). Accepting the advice of even experts is risky business. Since almost no research has been conducted to test the competing theories, there is really no way of telling which theory actually was correct in this situation. But South Vietnam finally did fall to Communist forces in spring 1975.*

conforms to common sense [355]. It can be argued that containment of a nation will produce frustration and anger, increase its resolve to expand even further, and result in increased rather than decreased aggression. Thus, the same policy—containment—has been hypothesized to produce two opposite results. Given that the Vietnam conflict took 56,371 American lives, and cost taxpayers $111,600,000,000 [448], it would be valuable to know how correct either hypothesis is. Most likely, they are both correct under certain specific conditions. Yet relatively little research has been directed toward specifying these conditions.

This example illustrates that common sense is usually ambiguous. What, exactly, is meant by "containment"? Does it involve economic embargos and sanctions on the offending nation? Sending troops to stop the expansion? Threatening to send troops? Until words are defined precisely, it's difficult to examine and evaluate ideas. Commonsense beliefs usually are so ambiguous that it is impossible to tell whether they are true or false even if we do test them against evidence. For example, suppose that you cite an instance where you believe containment *increased* expansion and aggression. Your opponent might dismiss your evidence by saying that your example is faulty, since it didn't involve containment at all. To evaluate a belief against evidence, it is extremely important to define terms adequately. Only then can we tell whether a belief is supported or refuted by evidence.

3 *The opinions of others can be distorted and biased by their own interests and misinformation.* Much conventional wisdom comes from authoritative sources such as the government, the mass media, books, teachers, or friends. These sources clearly affect and shape our beliefs. For example, most of the information Americans received about the Vietnam conflict came from the United States government. But the government clearly had biases about the "correct" view of the war. The military and the executive branch wanted people to believe that we were in Vietnam to prevent Communist aggression, that the South Vietnamese were doing their share of the fighting, that we were wanted there, and that our policies succeeded in containing the enemy. J. W. Fulbright [170], former Chairman of the Senate Foreign Relations Committee, has described how military public relations men staged fight scenes in Vietnam to show that the South Vietnamese and American forces were accomplishing their objectives; these films and texts were distributed free of charge to local television stations to gain the support of the American people. Local stations usually welcomed these propaganda pieces, since they could not otherwise afford to fill their half-hour news programs. And on this supposedly correct—because authoritative—information, the opinions of many Americans were based. Accepting the opinions of experts is a risky business, especially when experts disagree. It therefore is important not to consider any belief as true or false without careful analysis of the evidence for and against it. Even "unbiased experts" have pet theories and are likely to display the all-too-human tendency to forget or underemphasize facts that do not support their views.

4 *Information obtained from commonsense or authoritative sources may lull people into the secure but incorrect belief that they already have all the answers.* A know-it-all attitude impedes further investigation and discovery. A striking example can be drawn from public reactions to a massive study entitled *The American Soldier* [432]. Commissioned by the government during World War II, this study sought to discover the attitudes, beliefs, and values of soldiers concerning themselves, the war, and life in the service. When the study finally appeared, it was soundly criticized by reviewers and by the public as having been a waste of time and money. Critics said the study revealed only what everyone already knew about soldiers. Sociologist Paul Lazersfeld [262, pp. 379–380] tried to answer the charge. In his commentary, he listed the following points about the American soldier.

a. "Better educated men show more psycho-neurotic symptoms than those with less education. (The mental instability of the intellectual as compared to the more impassive psychology of the man-on-the-street has often been commented on.)"

b. "Men from rural backgrounds usually are in better spirits during their army life than soldiers from city backgrounds. (After all, they are more accustomed to hardships.)"

c. "Southern soldiers were better able to stand the climate in the hot South Sea Islands than Northern soldiers. (Of course, Southerners are more accustomed to hot weather.)"

d. "White privates were more eager to become non-coms than Negroes. (The lack of ambition among Negroes is almost proverbial.)"

e. "As long as the fighting continued, men were more eager to be returned to the States than they were after the German surrender. (You cannot blame people for not wanting to be killed.)"

These basic descriptions of human behavior may seem obvious and cause one to wonder why psychologists waste their time. But further examination indicated that the time was not wasted. You see, as Lazarsfeld caustically noted, each of the above statements is *incorrect* and is *not* what was found in the study. Lesser-educated persons showed more psychoneurotic symptoms, and Southerners had no advantage in coping with the climate in the South Seas. The lesson is evident. Human behavior is so complex and diverse that nothing should be taken for granted. It is necessary to discover which behaviors occur when; otherwise, what we "know" will be anything but knowledge.

■ SCIENCE AND THE SCIENTIFIC METHOD

Science attempts to go beyond common sense and increase our knowledge and understanding of the world. The big difference between the scientific approach and a commonsense one is that scientists try to take into account all the pitfalls we've discussed in order to test beliefs systematically and rigorously. While scientists may get ideas about the world in the same ways that other people do, they don't stop there. A scientist defines terms precisely, specifies the conditions under which ideas are expected to be true or false, takes very little for granted, and, most importantly, *systematically tests ideas by bringing evidence to bear on them.* If one characteristic distinguishes science from other ways of acquiring and assessing knowledge, it is the use of the *scientific method* [245], which essentially is a three-step process that involves *induction, deduction,* and *testing.*

Induction

Induction is a logical process through which an investigator generalizes from a specific set of information and formulates a general statement or rule which applies not only to that situation but to others as well. This general statement is an abstract "rule" about the world. An example will clarify this. Suppose a social psychologist observes John and Dave, two college roommates, arguing about how to divide the apartment-cleaning chores. John feels each should do equal amounts of cleaning, alternating weekly on particular chores: One week, John will do all the dishes, while Dave vacuums; the next week, they will switch. Dave argues that he doesn't have time to do equal amounts since he's a premedical major, and because John owes him rent money, he feels John should do most of the housework that month. John feels the debt has nothing to do with how the housework is handled, but he reluctantly agrees to Dave's solution to the conflict. He is unhappy about the whole state of affairs, and during the month, he does a poor job of cleaning and on several occasions "forgets" to give Dave important messages.

These are the specific events which the investigator has observed. The investigator wants to explain this conflict in terms of social-psychological processes. The aim is to develop a general statement or rule which will explain not only this specific situation but other things as well. After a great deal of thought, the investigator arrives at a general statement: When an individual perceives that he or she is being treated inequitably, that person will behave in a way that restores equity. But as it stands, this proposition is vague: What is "equity"? So the investigator defines the term and specifies what equity is. In any relationship, people bring skills, time, personal attributes, and other things to bear. These inputs can be viewed as commodities—all of them are worth something. In return, people expect rewards, or outcomes, from the relationship in proportion to their inputs. More precisely, equity is defined as a condition where the ratio of one person's inputs to outcomes from a relationship are of the same proportion as another person's input-to-outcome ratio.

In the example described, John feels he is bringing the same inputs to the relationship as Dave; therefore, their outcomes should be similar. Since the outcomes aren't the same, John perceives an inequity and will take steps to reduce it. The general statement about equity goes beyond the simple descriptions of John's and Dave's behaviors. It can be applied to a wide variety of situations, such as the feelings and behaviors of employees who believe that they are receiving less than fair treatment from the boss. Or it can be applied to a husband and wife who divide household responsibilities. Or it can be applied to nations that feel they have been treated unfairly at the negotiation table. Induction, as you can see, involves a great deal of creativity, since an investigator must transcend concrete facts to develop general rules and principles.

Our statement about equity is a *hypothesis;* it is the statement of a relationship between variables. Specifically, it states that *if* certain conditions occur (that is, perceptions of inequity), *then* other conditions will follow (behaviors designed to reduce inequity). All general hypotheses have this same basic conditional form (*if* such and such occurs, *then* something else will also occur). The term *variable* should be familiar, but its meaning may be somewhat vague. Very simply, a variable is a factor or element which can change in amount or strength and which can be measured in some way. The hypothesis above relates two variables: the perception of inequity and behaviors designed to reduce it.

Given the investigator's basic idea about inequity, other, related ideas come to mind. It is proposed that equity is very important for all people in a society. By working out rules of equity, or fairness, a group can increase the chances that collective rewards to its members will be maximized. Each member of the group would contribute his or her equitable amount, and each would receive exactly what is due—no more or less. Equity norms (the rules that emerge) develop and give people a standard against which they can evaluate themselves and others to see if everyone is behaving fairly. Once developed, the norms act as a social influence to help people decide how to resolve some of their problems. Although the things that constitute equity may vary from culture to culture, each society seems to share this basic regulatory premise. Given the importance of equity to society, people try to persuade others to accept principles of equity and fairness, and they stress these principles to influence the behaviors of group members. For example, the theme of the United Way campaigns has attempted to persuade people to behave equitably and contribute to charity—"Give your fair share."

Social psychologists also could classify equity-restoring behaviors and then develop hypotheses that allow them to predict which behaviors will occur under specific conditions. People can restore equity in two basic ways: by restoring *actual equity* or by restoring *psychological equity* [480]. In our example, John might restore actual equity by decreasing Dave's outcomes from their relationship. Thus, he could forget to deliver Dave's messages, causing Dave to suffer losses. Or he could do a sloppy job of housecleaning in order to reduce his contributions to the relationship. It has been found that many employees who feel they are underpaid decrease the quantity and quality of their work, while those who feel they are overpaid will show an increase [3].

Psychological equity could be restored by distorting one's perceptions to make the inequity seem fair. For example, John might console himself by believing that the inequity will bring compensating benefits for him and/or punishment for Dave. He might convince himself that he will learn self-discipline and the ability to handle day-to-day jobs, while Dave will always be a work-shirker who will lose out later in life. Or John might "notice" things about Dave that would restore equity; for example, "Dave is the kind of guy who'll always loan me money when I need it, so I should pay him back now by doing the housework." Specific hypotheses have been proposed that allow predictions to be made about which of these possible actions will occur under different circumstances [480].

By listing all the hypotheses that describe what equity is—why it is important, when it will occur, and how it can be increased—an investigator will develop a theory of equity-related behaviors. A *theory* is a set of systematically related and organized hypotheses which allows a scientist to understand, explain, and predict a wide variety of phenomena. Several theories of equity have been proposed by social psychologists [3; 480].

Deduction

Deduction is used to generate additional hypotheses and specific predictions; it is the second step in the scientific method. Deduction is a logical process that involves taking initial propositions and placing them together in a novel way to yield new predictions that can be tested. For example, given the propositions that "Socrates is a man" and "All men are mortal," we can deduce that "Socrates is mortal." If the hypotheses about equity are correct, we should be able to deduce that in a specific setting in which people feel part of the same group and don't want to create tension and further conflict, they would rather arrive at equitable than inequitable solutions. With this deduction in mind, it is possible to test the new hypothesis. The third step in the scientific method is testing the predictions to determine if they hold true.

Testing

Lawrence Messé [300] conducted a laboratory test of the prediction that people feeling minimal tension will prefer equitable to inequitable solutions. The first step was to define operationally what equity is and what equitable solutions are. An *operational definition* is one in which a scientist specifies exactly how the concepts are being measured, manipulated, and controlled. Messé operationally defined inputs to the relationship as the amount of time subjects worked on assigned tasks. The experimenter asked some subjects to work on tasks for eighty minutes, some for forty minutes, and so on. The longer the subjects worked, the more they should have felt they contributed to the experiment and the more they should have expected in return. Messé then told pairs of subjects that he would pay them but that they had to negotiate to divide the money as they saw fit. The money represented their outcomes from the experiment. Our prediction states that subjects should desire an equitable reward—that is, pay in proportion to work. If one subject worked for eighty minutes and the second subject for only forty minutes, the first should receive twice as much money as the second. This is exactly what was found in the experiment. Thus, the evidence of the test supported the prediction that people prefer an equitable solution to an inequitable one in situations where conflict and tension are minimized.

A summary of the scientific method

The important aspects of the scientific method are summarized in Figure 1-2. A scientist begins with facts and through induction arrives at general hypotheses and theories. Through deduction, a scientist makes specific predictions about what will happen if the hypotheses and theories are correct. These predictions then are tested to determine if the facts support them. If they are not supported, the theory may be discredited, and the scientist tries to find out what went wrong. Thus, theories and hypotheses are constantly revised, and new tests are performed. Science is a continuous attempt to modify and correct theories and hypotheses according to the evidence obtained.

Several additional aspects about science deserve attention. First, the scientific method provides an *external and relatively objective set of criteria*

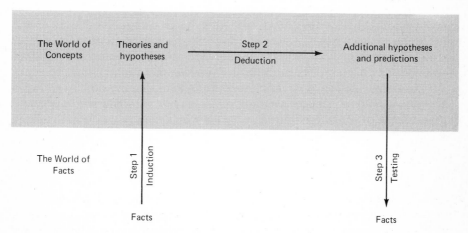

Figure 1-2. *The scientific method. A scientist begins with facts about the world. Through induction, or moving from specifics to general statements, theories are constructed. Predictions can be made on the basis of reasoning from theories. Deduction involves starting with basic propositions and drawing specific conclusions from them. These conclusions are then tested against other facts to determine if the facts support or refute them.*

for determining if and when hypotheses and theories are correct. No single individual decides on the basis of his or her subjective ideas what is true and what isn't. Since people usually can agree about when facts support or refute a hypothesis that has been carefully tested, there is an external and objective constraint on what a scientist can claim. This *consensual agreement* characterizes the scientific approach.

Second, the scientific method is *empirical* in its demand that evidence be collected to evaluate theories and hypotheses. Unlike those who hold commonsense beliefs, a scientist should not cling to a hypothesis simply because it is possible or because there is no evidence against it. A scientist is obliged to provide evidence to support a belief.

Third, the scientific method assumes that people can relate processes and events to one another. It is assumed that we can describe relationships between objects, events, and processes which will be supported by data. In other words, we assume that certain variables affect other variables: This is a *cause-effect relationship.* (The opposite view holds that the world is so chaotic and our powers of comprehension are so limited that we can't describe these relationships.)

What we've said so far describes the essence of science. It is simply a particular way of gaining knowledge. The goals of a scientist are those of anyone who wants to increase knowledge. That is, a scientist wants to *understand* what goes on and be able to *predict* in advance what will happen, given certain conditions. Focus 1-1 offers some additional aspects of social psychology and science.

■ **GETTING EVIDENCE**

Social psychologists can obtain evidence for and against theories and hypotheses in numerous ways. Some of the techniques used to obtain information, evidence, and ideas include: (1) observing behaviors in natural settings; (2) employing questionnaire-interview methods; (3) using techniques to analyze past events; and (4) controlling and manipulating environments and observing people's reactions in these controlled settings. We'll examine each of these techniques of obtaining evidence and demonstrate their strong and weak points.

Observation of naturally occurring behaviors

One basic technique for gathering evidence is to observe ongoing behaviors in natural environments. If a person wanted to find out what happens when two groups are in conflict, he or she could simply find such a conflict and systematically record what happens. The Walker Report to the National Commission on the Causes and Prevention of Violence [449] systematically described the sometimes brutal conflicts that occurred between demonstrators and police during the Democratic National Convention in Chicago in

FOCUS 1-1   SOCIAL PSYCHOLOGY: SCIENCE OR HISTORY? OR, WHAT CHOICES HAVE YOU MADE TODAY?

Social psychologists consider their discipline to be a science. But is a science of human behavior really possible? Can social psychology develop "laws" (or hypotheses) and theories about behavior comparable to the laws and theories of other scientific disciplines, such as physics and chemistry? Over the years, many have claimed that such a goal is impossible.

Kenneth Gergen [178] contends that social science is fundamentally different from other sciences and cannot yield the kinds of laws and theories about behavior that other sciences have produced. He draws this conclusion for two major reasons. First, he feels that hypotheses regarding social behavior change constantly. While Newton's laws in physics are as "true" now as when they were proposed, the behavioral "laws" of social science seem to change. Gergen contends that no laws or hypotheses can be found which apply to behavior at all places or in all times. Second, he believes that when people are told of behavioral "laws," they change their behaviors and disconfirm the laws: No one wants to seem predictable. For example, it has been found that a person who needs help is less likely to get it when a crowd is present than when only one other person is present. (The reasons for this are discussed in Chapter 6.) Knowing this fact, the next time you are in a crowd and an emergency arises, you might immediately offer assistance. If everyone does this, social psychologists would soon discover that the previous relationship is reversed. Therefore, Gergen concludes that social psychology is not really a science but the study of contemporary history. According to him, social psychologists only catalog statements about social behavior which are true now but which may change in the future and thus be relegated to history.

Gergen's conclusions are quite controversial and have been strongly criticized. Over the past several decades, philosophers of science have examined similar claims and usually found them to be lacking; they have overwhelmingly concluded that social psychology is a science. In answer to Gergen, Barry Schlenker [388] enumerates several problems in the logic of those who claim that social psychology is not a science. While the fundamental issues are quite complex, a few of them are worth considering.

The difference between a fact and a general scientific law is great. A *fact* is an interpretation of basic data which observers of the data can agree upon. For example, it is a fact that John's shirt is red, or that in a particular experiment more people help a victim when they are alone than when they are with other bystanders. A *law* or *hypothesis*, however, goes beyond such facts. It is an abstract proposition which can subsume numerous facts. Consider these two statements: (1) The Japanese people consider the neck area an erogenous zone; (2) infants who are carried on their mother's or father's back facing the neck region will later perceive that area as an erogenous zone. The first statement is a fact. However, we would hardly expect it to be true for each and every Japanese now, or possibly for any Japanese 200 years from now. The fact is limited historically and culturally. The second statement goes beyond the first. It describes a relationship between certain child-rearing practices and subsequent perceptions. It pertains not only to the Japanese but to other groups as well, and there is no reason to believe that it won't remain true 200 years from now.

Consider the bystander who will offer assistance more often when alone than when with other bystanders. This fact might be deduced from a more general proposition: A person will offer help to the extent that he or she perceives assistance to be needed. One bystander might feel help is not really needed when other bystanders are also present. Each might expect the others to help. Later, in reading that very few people come to another's aid when a crowd is present, such an individual realizes that help is most needed when a crowd is present; he or she offers help quickly the next time the situation arises. From this general hypothesis one can deduce not only when an individual will help, but also when he or she will not. And one can predict that people will be influenced by reading about social psychologists' findings. Because a "fact" changes or information affects behavior doesn't mean that general principles can't be found to explain both the facts and the changes. Gergen is incorrect in contending that general laws are impossible because things change. This is analogous to stating that general principles of evolution cannot be developed because dinosaurs are extinct and new species have evolved.

Those who feel a science of human behavior is impossible reason as follows: "People make choices and decisions. They are affected by what goes on around them in a way that inanimate objects are not. They think, they feel, and they consciously alter their fates through decisions and behaviors. Clearly, rocks can't do this. What happens to a rock may depend on laws of nature. What happens to a person does not. The laws of nature do not coerce people in the same way. People have 'free will.' Since people do make choices and don't feel constrained to obey such natural laws, no science of human behavior is possible."

There are problems with this line of reasoning. No, we aren't saying that people don't make decisions—they do. And yes, happily, people are extraordinarily different from rocks. But we are saying that it is a misunderstanding of science to state that because people make choices, no science of human behavior is possible. The problem is that many people don't understand what scientists mean by the term "the law of nature." Many people think of the law of nature as a mystical force hiding out in the universe that dictates our every action. They think it pushes and pulls us along a predetermined path. Given such a law, people become mechanistic automatons, little computers programmed by the big computer in the sky. Many people reject this and feel human choices are not simply coerced. Others view the scientist's job to be one of finding this law of nature. They see science as a search for some ultimate truth: If a scientist is lucky enough to stumble across this ultimate law, he or she will be able to say what the universe is really about.

Actually, such beliefs are unfounded. The "law of nature" is not what most people think. Simply put, it is a complete description of all that has happened and all that will happen [245]. If such a total description were possible (and it isn't), it would portray exactly what nature is about—it would be *the* law of nature. Why all these things have happened can be answered only through the human ability to *conceptualize* regularities and to develop theories. The observed regularities come from our ability to conceptualize the most useful aspects of nature. You might find these points easier to understand if we turn a popular belief around. Many people think the law of nature determines human decisions and behaviors. Actually, it is more correct to state that our decisions and behaviors determine the law of nature [245]. Thus, there is no incompatibility between believing that a science of human behavior is possible and that people make decisions.

Students sometimes come to believe that since social scientists can understand and predict behaviors, people aren't really making decisions; that people are forced to behave in particular ways because of behavioral "laws." The most sophisticated statement of this point has been made by the famed behaviorist B. F. Skinner. In his book *Beyond Freedom and Dignity* [411], Skinner argues that freedom is an illusion; that people have an illusion that they decide how they will behave, when, actually, environmental conditions and past experiences determined their behavior. Similar arguments have been cited as cases of *fatalistic determinism*, which holds that natural laws compel us to behave in particular ways and that nothing can be done to prevent or change this.

To illustrate a basic error in fatalistic determinism, let's suppose that your best friend has been invited to a party this weekend. You know how your friend feels about parties in relation to other activities, you know who will be at the party and how your friend feels about these people, you know what other things are on your friend's schedule for the weekend, etc. If you are able to predict whether or not your friend will go to the party, does it mean that your friend has no choice? Is your friend "forced" to do what you predict? Of course not. To arrive at your prediction, you developed a theory of how these things will influence your friend's decision. Social psychologists do the same thing, but more rigorously. They develop theories about how various factors will affect human social behavior and then test the theories to see how accurately they predict behavior. If the theories are accurate, our understanding of behavior is increased. But to conclude that these hypotheses or laws or theories coerce behavior, or that people don't make decisions, is silly. When we state that social psychology is a science, we do not claim that people are pushed around by forces they cannot counter; rather, we affirm that human actions are understandable and explainable. The context and methods flowing from these assertions are what we call science. Determinism in science really means that we can gain an understanding of behavior by developing theories which allow us to explain and predict behavior. Each time social psychologists discover factors that affect human decisions and behaviors, the assertion that "no science of human behavior is possible" is shown to be more incorrect.

1968. The report was pieced together from 3,437 eyewitness accounts, and the grim scenario was preserved for posterity. Let's suppose that we, as observers, could view all the events from some spot near the conflict. What transpired?

The Walker Report listed three factors that sowed the seeds for violence even before the 10,000 protesters arrived in Chicago: (1) the perception by city officials of threats from the protesters; (2) "police preparedness," which occurred in response to the threats; and (3) the "conditioning" of the police to expect that violence would be condoned and applauded by city officials.

Before the convention, a number of real and implied threats had been perceived by city officials and police. Much of the rhetoric of the "New Left" and the Yippie movement was peaceful, but pamphlets that fell into the hands of the police made violence seem a possibility. City officials were unwilling or unable to distinguish real threats from false ones, and they perceived that clear confrontations would be necessary.

The officials responded to these perceived threats in an extreme fashion. They refused permits for marches and demonstrations and made it clear that the slightest infraction of the law would be quickly dealt with. Firemen were stationed at each fire alarm box within a six-block radius of the convention site; Army personnel carriers were based in Soldiers Field; the 12,000-member Chicago police force was reinforced with 6,000 Army regulars in full battle gear, including rifles, flame throwers, and bazookas; and an additional 6,000 Illinois National Guard troopers were activated for duty. These precautions were taken even before most of the demonstrators arrived. Chicago was ready for what it felt would be a major confrontation; officials hoped to deter it through a dramatic show of armed strength.

City officials also made it clear that they intended to use the strength if necessary. Earlier in the year, Martin Luther King, Jr., had been assassinated in Memphis, and the country had been torn by riots. Ghetto riots in Chicago in 1967 and 1968 made officials even more anxious and determined. They would do all in their power not to let the presence of thousands of demonstrators touch off another riot. The superintendent of police and the police force had been cited for showing constraint and doing a good job in handling these earlier riots. However, Chicago's Mayor Richard Daley chastised the police for not fighting fire with fire and made it clear that he did not consider their constraint admirable. He defiantly proclaimed that the police should "shoot to kill arsonists and shoot to maim looters." The police got the message—not only would the city condone force and violence against the demonstrators, but it would expect it if the situation warranted.

These events set the stage for the violence that followed between police and demonstrators. Unnecessary force predominated. The conflict quickly spiraled, as initial taunts from the demonstrators drew swift retribution from the police. Demonstrators shouting "pigs, pigs, pigs" caused the police to respond with physical assaults. Protesters joined the violence. The police began to assault anyone on the street who wasn't in uniform. Newsmen received some of the more brutal attacks. Amid the beatings, each side tended to dehumanize the other. The police were viewed not as people trying to do their jobs, but as pigs and fascists, something less than human. The demonstrators were seen not as peaceful citizens with real grievances, but as protesting anarchists, revolutionaries, Communists, and troublemakers.

The picture that emerges is one of increasing conflict, or a conflict spiral. The police perceived, correctly or not, that they were confronted by a threat to the peace and tranquillity of their town. Rumors magnified the threats. To deter the demonstrators, reinforcements and additional weapons were brought in. People talked about confrontation and violence and rationalized why they would be appropriate. Incidents that would have been perceived as trivial in themselves touched off massive violence, since these events were seen against a distorted background. Both sides were convinced that the other was out to get them, and the slightest incident was taken as proof of malevolence.

Problems in interpreting data from observations. Although the evidence seems to suggest a conflict spiral in Chicago in 1968, one can't be positive that each reason cited for the violence produced the exact effects hypothesized. Consider an example. The Walker Report assumed that when a group's leaders condone violence, the intensity of the conflict will increase and lead to more actual violence. This hypothesis *seems* reasonable, since city officials did publicly condone violence, and violence did erupt. However, this commonsense conclusion is not enough; other possibilities also are reasonable. Perhaps some police officers were insulted by the city's seeming to condone the policy of "Shoot to kill." If so, the statements could have reduced the violence by making police more cautious than they otherwise would have been. In other words, if city officials hadn't condoned violence, police may have been even more violent than they were. It also is possible that many police officers were not affected by the official statements.

In order to state with confidence that the officials' attitudes and statements did increase the violence, we'd have to compare what actually happened in Chicago with what might have happened if city officials had made no statements whatsoever. That is, we'd need two different conditions; one in which city officials condoned violence and one in which they said nothing. Except for the behaviors of the city officials, all other factors would be

(a)

(b)

Figure 1-3. *The violence in Chicago at the Democratic presidential nominating convention in 1968. A conflict spiral (a) was produced. More than 60 of the 300 reporters on the scene were either injured, had their cameras damaged, or were arrested (b). The police did not want to have their behavior observed and recorded.*

alike in both situations. Then, if the police are more violent when city officials advocate violence than when they say nothing, we can claim that the data support the hypothesis. But without an adequate comparison condition, or *control condition,* one can't claim strong support for the hypothesis.

Obviously, setting up such comparable conditions in the real world is impossible. For this reason, social psychologists often construct analogous situations in the laboratory, where the events are simpler and easier to control and where appropriate comparisons can be made. Thus, a major problem with data obtained from observation of naturally occurring events is that adequate comparison conditions don't exist. This makes it difficult to draw definite conclusions from the observations.

A second problem with observation is that many events occur rapidly, and an observer may not be able to keep track of them all. The observer may overlook important details or cite events which he or she feels are important but which are actually unrelated to the conflict. Without adequate control over the events, it is difficult for an investigator to draw sound conclusions.

Unobtrusive and reactive measures. When people know they are being watched and their behavior is being recorded, they might behave differently than they normally would. The reactions of Chicago police to being photographed by reporters is a case in point. When some of them became aware that a record of their behavior was being taken, they attacked the photographers. It is possible that other policemen, aware that they were being photographed, stopped what they were doing and tried to look inconspicuous. In either event, the fact that they were being observed caused reactions which otherwise might not have occurred.

Minimizing this problem of *reactive measurement* is a major chore in any study. Some investigators try to reduce the problem by becoming acquainted with the group of people they wish to study, hoping that they will be accepted and that the group will take the investigator's presence for granted. The longer the period of time that such observations are made, the less conscious the subjects are that their behavior is being measured. Other investigators urge the use of unobtrusive measures of behavior [484]. An *unobtrusive measure* is one in which subjects have no way of knowing that their behavior is being recorded or measured. Some investigators remain out of sight and record behaviors from concealed positions, though this raises eithical questions about violating rights to privacy.

Questionnaire-interview techniques

We treated the Walker Report as information which could have been obtained by an omnipresent observer. Actually, most of the information contained in the report was pieced together by investigators through interviews with eyewitness observers. Interview techniques are extremely useful in discovering the perceptions, feelings, attitudes, and values of people. In many cases, the questions can be written down and presented to respondents in a more standardized questionnaire format.

Although questionnaire-interview techniques seem to offer unlimited access to information, there are several pitfalls associated with them. These problems include: (1) biases associated with inadequately constructed items, (2) biases associated with respondents' knowledge and motivations, (3) the interviewer's effect on respondents' answers, and (4) sampling problems.

Bias in question construction. An investigator should construct questions that are clear to an average respondent. While this might seem easy, it definitely is not. Suppose you wanted to ask some of the demonstrators about their behaviors in Chicago. If you asked, "How many times did you throw debris at the police?" you're already heading for problems. This item probably would turn respondents off, since you assume that they have thrown debris, and you'll probably antagonize them and weaken rapport. A questionnaire item should never assume an answer. Alternatively, suppose you asked, "Did you deliberately provoke the police?" This item might yield very little information, since the word "provoke" is ambiguous enough to be misperceived or misinterpreted by respondents. Here's another example of a poor question: "Do you feel that the police acted arbitrarily and illegally toward you?" This item is *double-barreled.* What would happen if a respondent felt the police had acted arbitrarily but legally? Such a respondent would want to answer "yes" to the first part of the question, but "no" to the second part. Yet respondents are only allowed to answer "yes" or "no" to the entire item. However this question is answered, an investigator wouldn't know how to interpret it.

Bias of respondents. A second problem with questionnaire-interview techniques has to do with biases associated with respondents' knowledge and motivations. Most people want to put their best foot forward when being interviewed; they are motivated to make an interviewer perceive them as intelligent, competent, attractive, moral, etc. When respondents intentionally or unintentionally distort answers to look good, *social desirability bias* affects the validity of the study. To minimize errors produced by social desirability biases, interviewers must be careful about how items are worded; respondents should not be given an impression that one answer is "better" than another.

Interviewer's effect on respondents. The third problem associated with questionnaire-interview techniques arises because of the interviewer's effect on the subjects. An interviewer's dress, sex, age, status, race, and general demeanor all can affect the answers a respondent gives. Imagine how differently a policeman might react if he were interviewed by a middle-aged, conservative man dressed in a business suit, as opposed to a bearded, beaded, sandaled, twenty-year-old. Investigators must consider the possible effects their own characteristics will have on answers from respondents.

Sampling. How does an interviewer decide whom to include in a sample of respondents? Usually, an interviewer can't question everyone who might be of interest, so he or she selects a sample of individuals and generalizes on the basis of the information gathered from this sample. But things can go awry during the sampling process.

Consider an example. As was seen in the discussion of the Chicago conflict, groups that disagree often have distorted ideas about one another. People often pay more attention to information that supports their stereotypes of themselves and the "enemy" than they do to information that contradicts the stereotypes. These distorted perceptions are quite prevalent when people from one nation gather information about people from an "enemy" nation. Take the case of an American tourist, who, on a trip to the Soviet Union, forms an opinion that the "average Soviet citizen" is dissatisfied with the government. This impression is naturally accepted, since it fits the tourist's prevailing stereotypes. But how did the tourist form this opinion? Usually tourists will say that they talked with several Russians, who all said they were unhappy with their government and would love to go to America. But how did the tourists, who do not speak Russian, begin the discussion? Most tourists reply that the Russian walked up to them and began talking. Before leaving, the Russian usually asked the tourist for books, blue jeans, or gum (all of which are valuable commodities in the Soviet Union). Clearly, the tourists do not sample a wide range of Soviet citizens. They speak only with Russians who can speak English, who recognize the tourists as American, who are assertive enough to begin the conversation, who want something in return, and who realize that a good way to gain favor with Americans is to say something negative about the Soviet Union and something positive about the United States. How well do such impressions represent the average Soviet citizen's opinion?

An atypical American tourist, Urie Bronfenbrenner, is an American psychologist who speaks fluent Russian. On a visit to the Soviet Union, he decided to learn how typical Russians view the United States and the Soviet Union [77]. As he strolled through towns, he initiated conversations. He talked with children, old people, young people, middle-aged people—anyone—in parks and on the streets. Or he entered restaurants, having decided in advance to sit at the third table on the left, and began conversations with whomever was there (it's common for people to share tables in Russia). He was treated to quite a different set of opinions than most tourists get. The majority of Russians he talked with had a genuine pride in their system and its accomplishments, and they believed that communism was the best possible system, not only for themselves but for the rest of the world.

Bronfenbrenner also found what he termed a *mirror-image* in perceptions. That is, the Russians' "distorted" view of us was "curiously similar" to our views of them. These are some of the perceptions he noticed among the people he spoke with:

1 Americans are the aggressors in the world.
2 The American government exploits and deceives its people. American elections are a farce, since candidates for both parties are selected by the same powerful economic interests and don't give the people a real choice.
3 Most Americans are not really sympathetic to their regime; given the opportunity to learn about communism, they would surely rejoice to live in the Soviet Union.
4 The United States can't be trusted to keep its agreements.
5 The policies of the United States are based on madness. They are unrealistic, designed merely to propagandize and not to produce any real understanding among the people of the world.

In addition to these mirror-image perceptions, conflict situations have other types of perceptions that make reducing conflicts difficult. Most parties to a conflict use *double standards* in evaluating their actions and their opponents' (see Focus 1-2 for an in-depth view of double standards in international perceptions).

Most parties to a conflict also engage in *black-and-white thinking;* they see the enemy as people in black hats and themselves as people in white hats (see Focus 1-3 for an in-depth look at black-and-white thinking). The essence of black-and-white thinking is that the parties to the conflict see things as "either-or," "for us or against us," with little concern for shades of gray. When neither side in a conflict trusts the other, and when each interprets its own actions positively and its opponent's actions negatively, it is difficult to get either one to move toward resolving the conflict. This is true whether the antagonists are nations, large groups like labor and management, or small groups like gangs on city streets.

Obtaining a random sample. Let's look more closely at the problem of sampling. In order to draw valid conclusions from a questionnaire-interview study, it is necessary to obtain a representative sample from the population of interest. A *population* is the group of people about whom an investigator is interested in generalizing results. If we were interested in drawing conclusions about police attitudes in Chicago in 1968, our population would include all police officers on the Chicago force at that time.

One way to get a representative sample from a population is to sample randomly. In a *random sample* every person in the population of interest has an equal chance of being included in the sample. Random sampling lies at the heart of all research. When random sampling can be accomplished, the validity of data is increased; when it cannot be accomplished, the validity of data is decreased. How would an investigator obtain a random sample? Suppose you were interested in information about police attitudes toward

FOCUS 1-2 A DOUBLE STANDARD IN INTERNATIONAL PERCEPTIONS: IT'S OKAY FOR ME BUT NOT FOR YOU

Distorted images and perceptions are common in intergroup and international relations. Besides mirror images, in which each side tends to view the other in similar distorted terms, other consistencies in how people perceive each other have been isolated. Stuart Oskamp and Arlene Hartry [336] describe the double standard that exists in American college students' evaluations of actions undertaken by the United States and by the Soviet Union. Many similarities can be seen in the behaviors of the two countries. For example, both sent supplies and military aid to opposite sides in the civil war in Laos; both began cultural exchanges of musicians and other artists; both closed large areas of their country to the other's diplomats; both announced that their armaments were for defensive, not first-strike, purposes; both established rocket bases near the other's borders; and so on. Given these similarities, questionnaires were constructed which described identical actions, without mentioning specific places, dates, or details. One questionnaire stated that the United States performed the actions; the other stated that the Soviet Union did. The questionnaires were otherwise identical in all respects. A few of the fifty items included in the questionnaire appear below.

Item	Ratings when the protagonist was described as:	
	United States	Russia
The United States (Russia) has established rocket bases close to the borders of Russia (the United States).	+1.7	−2.5
The United States (Russia) has carried on a blockade to prevent shipments of goods from entering a nearby area.	+1.9	−2.2
Some Russian (United States) citizens have fled from their country and been given refuge in the United States (Russia).	+2.2	−1.8
The United States (Russia) has warned another nation that it runs the risk of retaliation if it allows its territory to be used for Russian (United States) missile bases.	+2.0	−1.9
United States (Russian) leaders have repeatedly said that the United States (Russian) system of government will inevitably win in a peaceful		

Item	United States	Russia
competition with the Russian (United States) system.	+1.8	−1.9
Leaders of the United States (Russian) government have frequently called for the "liberation of the captive peoples" in nations allied with Russia (the United States).	+1.8	−1.7
The United States (Russia) has intercepted and interfered with Russian (United States) transportation to a foreign area.	+1.1	−2.4
The President of the United States (the head of the Russian government) has said that the United States (Russian) resumption of nuclear tests was necessary for the safety of the country.	+1.7	−1.8
The United States (Russia) has stated that it was compelled to resume nuclear testing by the actions of Russia (the United States).	+1.2	−2.1
The United States (Russia) has offered many scholarships to students from the underdeveloped countries of Asia and Africa to come for study in the United States (Russia).	+2.5	+0.2

The questionnaires were completed by 320 American college students. Some students received only the American-phrased version, while others received only the Russian-phrased version; still others filled out both versions. Subjects were asked to respond to each item in terms of how favorably they felt toward each event, and they were asked to mark the degree of favor on a scale ranging from −3 (most unfavorable) to +3 (most favorable); no 0, or neutral point, was provided, and so the subjects could check any of six points on the scale.

The results clearly indicated the presence of a double standard. Almost all the items showed that if the United States government performed the action, it was rated favorably; but if the Soviet Union performed the action, it was rated unfavorably. The only exception was the last item presented above, the one dealing with the offer of scholarships to students from underdeveloped nations. Subjects rated this action as slightly positive when performed by the Russians. However, even in this case, subjects rated the same action more favorably if it was performed by the United States.

This study demonstrates one problem which exists for those who want to reduce tension and promote peace between nations. Actions which would be praised if one's own country performed them are denounced and suspected if the "other side" performs them. The chances for peace, trust, and understanding will be much improved when people from all nations lose their double standards and are able to accurately evaluate actions taken by the "other side."

FOCUS 1-3 BLACK-AND-WHITE THINKING: MISPERCEPTIONS IN INTERNATIONAL AFFAIRS

In conflict situations, both sides tend to stereotype and misperceive themselves and their "enemy." These images provide frames of reference to interpret events, and the interpretations often serve to further the conflict.

John Foster Dulles, American Secretary of State from 1953 to 1959, believed that "Soviet Communism starts with an atheistic, Godless premise. Everything else flows from that premise." What is "everything else?" To Dulles, it meant that the Soviets could not be trusted under any conditions, that they strongly desired to destroy the West, and that they therefore must be treated with extraordinary suspicion and distrust. On many occasions, Soviet policies clearly justified Mr. Dulles's image of them. Yet his images often caused him to react in a way that seemed out of touch with actual events. For example, when the Soviets withdrew from Austria, Dulles didn't perceive them as becoming more friendly, less hostile, or less expansionistic. Rather, he perceived their withdrawal as a sign of failure in their policies toward Western Europe. And when Soviet armed forces were reduced by over a million men in 1956, Dulles felt the action was a result of industrial and economic failures within Russia, and he believed the men would be reassigned to weapons factories to increase the Soviet capacity for war. These same events might have been interpreted as signs of good faith and might have produced reciprocation and a lessening of hostilities. Instead, Dulles's preconceptions and images of the Soviet Union caused him to interpret the acts as signs of bad faith, weakness, and guile. Ole Holsti [213] performed a detailed analysis of Dulles's public statements toward the Soviet Union and found that there was no relationship between his expressed evaluation (bad versus good) of the Soviet Union and the actions taken by them. Regardless of what the Soviet Union did, Dulles interpreted it negatively.

Dulles's perceptions may have been accurate, but suppose they weren't? Joseph de Rivera [119] has raised the question, Suppose some leaders in the Soviet Union had wanted to show the Secretary of State that they really wanted to reduce hostilities and were sincere? What could they have done to convince him? His images and stereotypes were so negative that probably nothing would have changed them. His attitudes were so pessimistic that he created an atmosphere in which arms-control agreements became impossible.

Not only do preconceived attitudes lessen the chances of escaping a situation of hostility and conflict, they might actually increase the hostility and conflict. By acting in a negative way toward another person or group, one is likely to force them to reciprocate, even if initially they hadn't intended to. This illustrates a *self-fulfilling prophecy*, a belief that forces events to turn out as predicted, even if they otherwise would not have.

Several distinct images of oneself and the enemy can be found in most conflict situations. Ralph K. White [491], a social psychologist interested in understanding the psychological foundations of conflict, has listed three major misperceptions that distort the images of "us" and "them."

1 *The diabolical enemy image.* It's no fun to fight good guys. As a result, both sides in a conflict inevitably perceive the "fanatics" on the other side to be evil and immoral, with few—if any—redeeming attributes. The enemy is portrayed as a barbarian, as something less than human. People on the other side are transformed into "gooks," "chinks," "Communists," "pigs," "hippies," "anarchists," "Nazis," or whatever, and these terms carry extremely negative connotations. Dehumanizing an enemy makes it easier to attack and kill other human beings. An individual on the other side is regarded as part of a group and an agent of the devil. When war prisoners are tortured and women and children are killed (which inevitably happens on both sides), the view is reinforced that the enemy is a barbarian whose atrocities deserve severe punishment. For example, Americans were appalled by the disembowelings and beheadings perpetrated by the Vietcong. In turn, the Vietcong were outraged by such American actions as dropping napalm on villages and massive defoliation policies. In such a conflict, each side focuses on the "atrocities" committed by the other side; neither mentions their own similar actions, or they rationalize by saying that the acts are necessary means to "beneficial" ends.

The view that "everyone on the other side is evil" is hard to maintain, though. It's not easy to portray the average man, woman, child, or peasant, as diabolical, savage, and evil. So the diabolical-enemy image usually is tempered by the *black-top image.* The "common people" on the other side are viewed as basically good. But their evil leaders and fanatics mislead, dupe, oppress, and intimidate them. If the "common people" could just be "educated" which translates as "told how good we are and how bad their leaders are"—they would certainly voluntarily choose "our" side. Thus, the picture of an evil, diabolical enemy is restricted to the enemy's leaders, soldiers, and fanatics. The black-top image describes the perception of a diabolical group of people "at the top" who lead and mislead the people on the bottom. White found evidence of this perception on both sides during the Vietnam conflict, and instances of it in any conflict situation are not hard to find.

2 *The moral self-image.* The image that "we" are fighting for good, defending against foreign aggression and terror, with God on "our" side is a common perception on both sides in conflicts. No war has ever been fought in which the people believed God to be on their opponent's side.

3 *The virile self-image.* Each side during a conflict tends to portray itself as being resolved, capable, and determined enough to defeat the opponent. For example, former President Nixon's speeches during the Vietnam conflict were full of references to American "guts," "pride," "loyalty," and "strength." Former Vice-President Agnew took delight in referring to opponents of the war as "effete snobs," an obvious reference to their lack of virility. The virile self-image is fostered by the pragmatic recognition that it is not enough to be good, just, and moral; it is also necessary to be strong. In combination with the moral self-image, the line blurs between "might" and "right."

All these misperceptions are reinforced by government propaganda designed to portray its actions in a favorable light. The misperceptions are quickly grasped (both by the people and by the leaders), since they serve to maintain or enhance one's self-esteem.

Naturally, individuals differ in the degree to which they fall victim to misperceptions and in the degree to which they can empathize with the enemy and see the world from their perspective. One personality variable that has been linked to competitive, hawkish attitudes is an *inability to tolerate ambiguity*. Those who prefer immediate, right-or-wrong answers (who are intolerant of ambiguity) tend to be more belligerent than those who can tolerate ambiguity [350]. Also, people who are dogmatic and intolerant of ambiguity tend to resist compromise because they interpret it as a sign of weakness and defeat [132]. A related factor is that of *cognitive concreteness versus abstractness*. Individuals who have concrete cognitive structures tend to categorize information about the world in a limited number of cognitive cubbyholes, while those who are cognitively abstract tend to use more complex categories to store information. It has been found that cognitively abstract individuals tend to be less belligerent and competitive than cognitively concrete persons [131]. In one interesting study, the speeches of United States congressional representatives were analyzed to determine: (1) their tolerance of ambiguity; (2) their personal security or insecurity; (3) their positive or negative orientation toward people; and (4) their attitudes toward international affairs. Members of Congress whose outlooks were most nationalistic (as opposed to internationalistic) tended to be most personally insecure, most intolerant of ambiguity, and most negative in their orientation toward people in general [202].

All these images and the types of people who hold them are important in understanding the dynamics of conflict because they help to reinforce and perpetuate conflicts. The first step in conflict reduction is to find ways of minimizing the distortions in perceptions that exist on both sides and to find ways of getting each side to see itself through the eyes of the other.

the demonstrators in Chicago. You might be able to get a list of police officers who were on the force in 1968 and then randomly pick names by putting the entire list in a bowl and drawing the desired number to be interviewed. Clearly, it is not always easy or even possible to secure a random sample. If you wanted to obtain a random sample of demonstrators who participated in Chicago, how would you do it? Since no lists are available, you couldn't be sure who was in the population and who wasn't. You might advertise in newspapers, saying that you are interested in interviewing anyone at the Chicago convention protests, but this clearly would not gather a random sample. The people who respond to such an ad might be quite different from those who either never see the ad or who read it but don't respond. Those who respond may have more cooperative attitudes toward science, be more politically active and concerned with making their opinions known, be more informed about current affairs, and so on. As a result, your sample would be biased—that is, not truly representative of the population.

Let's assume you can construct a truly random sample. The next step is either to interview the respondents in person or to send them questionnaires to be returned. At this point, sampling biases can again affect the results. Suppose that when an interviewer tries to make contact, a respondent isn't home? A large proportion of a random list of respondents can be lost because an interviewer has difficulty contacting them. This makes the sample nonrandom, since people who are difficult to contact are not included. The sample might overrepresent people who stay at home. Or suppose questionnaires are sent to a group of demonstrators, and 80 percent of the sample return the completed questionnaires. The sample might be biased if the 20 percent who don't respond have characteristics that are different from those who do respond. The nonresponders, for example, may have been more violent and refused to answer for fear of getting in trouble. Data based on the sample then would underestimate the amount of violence that occurred.

Many of these sources of bias associated with obtaining a representative sample can be avoided, but some of them cannot. Researchers and consumers of research results must be aware of the problems that can arise and produce inaccurate data and interpretations.

Validity and reliability. All data are not equally "good," since many biases and errors can occur in obtaining information. A social psychologist will want to know how adequate and accurate data are before forming conclusions. Specifically, social psychologists are concerned with the validity and reliability of data.

Validity involves the degree to which data reflect what an investigator wants to measure: Is the psychologist really measuring what he or she intended? Any of the biases described can threaten the validity of data. Suppose an investigator wants to measure the degree to which police officers in Chicago felt threatened by the demonstrators. The investigator might construct some questionnaire items and administer them to a random sample of police. By adding up the respondents' scores on these items, the investigator would obtain a questionnaire index of perceived threat. Yet how would the investigator know the respondents didn't lie, distort, or misperceive their feelings, or misinterpret some of the questions? In other words, is this index of perceived threat a valid one?

The best way to assess the validity of a single measure is to compare it with other measures of the same thing. For example, the investigator might interview the spouses and friends of the police officers to learn how distressed and threatened the particular officers seemed during the confrontation. If the ratings in these interviews agree with the self-ratings of the police officers involved, we would have greater confidence in the self-ratings. When two or more different measures of the same variable agree, the validity of the measures usually is increased. For this reason, many researchers [466] urge the use of several different measures of the same variable.

A second aspect of determining the adequacy of data is its reliability. *Reliability* involves the degree to which a particular measure is consistent. There are two types of reliability: *intrapersonal reliability* and *interrater reliability.* Suppose an investigator constructs a thirty-item questionnaire to measure the amount of threat perceived by police officers. One way to determine the reliability of a measure for each respondent (intrapersonal reliability) is to arbitrarily divide the thirty items in half and see whether the scores on each half agree. If the test has high reliability, the items from each half should be answered similarly. Another way to check intrapersonal reliability is to give respondents the same test more than once—say a week apart. Again, a respondent should score about the same both times if the measure is reliable, and if nothing happened during that week to change the score.

The second type of reliability, interrater reliability, is important when two or more observers (termed "judges" or "raters") are scoring, tabulating, or categorizing a person's responses. If the responses are not scored the same way or nearly the same way by each judge, it would be impossible to interpret the data. The greater the consistency between the judges' scoring, the greater the reliability of the measure. Statistical techniques can be used to determine precisely what the reliability of a measure is.

Historical analysis and content analysis

Events of the past bear directly on contemporary problems and can help explain contemporary events. A researcher might want to determine whether a particular theory of conflict describes the events which led to World War I. Since the researcher cannot go back in time and witness the events which led to the war, and since most significant persons involved in the crucial decision making prior to the war are dead, questionnaire-interview techniques are out of the question. Must the researcher forget about trying to draw data from the past? No; historical records and other traces from the past can be scrutinized.

Consider this example. Most conflict research concludes that there are many similar patterns preceding most wars. Three basic conditions seem to precede most wars: rising tensions, rising military preparedness, and increasing hostility [355]. This is a familiar pattern; it closely resembles the situation in Chicago prior to the outbreaks during the 1968 Democratic Convention. Chicago officials perceived threats that increased their tension, which led to increased weapons and reinforcements, which resulted in increased hostility.

North and his associates [330] were interested in determining whether a similar pattern existed prior to World War I. They used a technique called *content analysis,* which consists of gathering relevant written materials from the period under study. In this case, the investigators obtained government records for both the Dual Alliance nations (Germany and Austria-Hungary) and the Triple Entente nations (France, Russia, and Great Britain), the major initial antagonists. Then *categories* were constructed to classify parts of the written materials. Since these investigators primarily wanted to measure the tension each nation perceived prior to the war, they looked for words and phrases that indicated threat perception. If a word or phrase fell into the category of threat perception, the rater increased the score for that category by 1. An investigator might want to set up dozens of categories—for threat perception, perception of friendship, perception of cooperative overtures, perception of self-weakness, etc.—and might want to scale the items that fall into each category. For example, evidence of the perception of a large threat might be given a score of 5 on a five-point scale, while intermediate and lesser instances of threat perception would be assigned lower numbers. After scoring, a numerical index shows results for each category. Since categories are established in advance, the investigator can use several judges to read and score the same material. In this way, the reliability of the scoring system can be determined.

This technique of content analysis has definite advantages over traditional ways of interpreting historical records. In the past, historians read materials and gave subjective impressions of what they contained. Not surprisingly, different historians arrived at different conclusions from the same records; it was almost impossible to determine whose impressions were "correct." One historian might cite a passage to support one interpretation, while a second historian might cite another passage to support a second interpretation that contradicted the first. Through content analysis, many of these disagreements can be avoided because the criteria used for interpretation are decided in advance. Quantitative data then replace subjective interpretation.

In their study, North and his associates found that prior to the outbreak of World War I both sides showed increased tension and perceived greater and greater threats. Figure 1-4 shows that tension increased between the time of the assassination of Archduke Francis Ferdinand, heir to Austria's throne (which historians cite as the precipitating incident for the war), and the time war was declared.

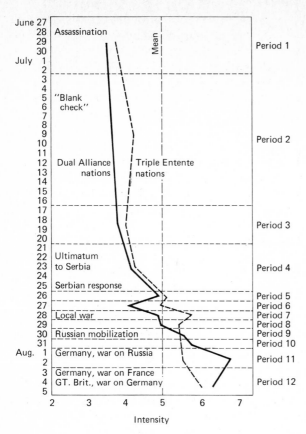

Figure 1-4. *A tension chart showing the intensity of perceived hostility in 1914. Tension rose on both sides from the time of the assassination of Archduke Francis Ferdinand of Austria to the time that World War I was declared.*

The use of content analysis is not limited to examinations of archival records. It can also be used on contemporary speeches and writings. The technique gives researchers the means to obtain data about people who might not consent to an in-depth interview or whose behavior is relatively inaccessible through observation.

Correlation: Analyzing data

Once data have been obtained by any of the methods described above—observation, questionnaire-interview, or content analysis—they can be subjected to various statistical treatments. The following example illustrates the potential uses and limitations of the important procedure *correlational analysis,* which determines statistically the degree of relationship that exists between specific variables.

Fact: During the confrontation at the Democratic Convention in Chicago in 1968, 192 policemen were injured and 49 needed to be hospitalized.

Hypothesis: When threats are perceived, weapons are built up; the greater the perception of threat, the greater the buildup of weapons.

Both these statements are relevant to the Chicago confrontation. But in addition to differences in content, the *type* of information provided by each is vastly different. The first statement, a fact, describes one aspect of the confrontation. While it may be interesting, it does not increase our understanding of the events, and it does not allow us to predict anything about other conflicts. In the second statement, a relationship is proposed between two variables: perception of threat and weapon buildups.

The second statement is a hypothesis. If it is correct, it provides several kinds of information. First, it states that two variables are related, and that they are related in a particular way: as threat perception increases, so does weapon buildup. Second, it gives us some understanding of an important aspect of conflict—we feel we understand more about conflict and weapon buildup than we would without the hypothesis. Third, the hypothesis lets us predict something about future conflicts. In a future conflict when threats are perceived, weapon buildup should follow. Understanding and prediction are possible only when two or more variables can be related to one another in some way. Our abilities to understand and predict are not necessarily increased by gathering isolated facts, though enough facts might allow us eventually to put forth future hypotheses.

As mentioned above, the correlational technique is a particular way to determine whether relationships exist between variables. In a correlational study, a researcher obtains data on two or more variables and then tries to ascertain the degree of relationship through statistical procedures.

To illustrate, let's examine one correlational study. Nancy Phillips [345] was interested in determining whether there was a relationship between people's jobs and their attitudes about conflict and war. She used a questionnaire-interview technique to gather data about men's attitudes toward the United States and the Soviet Union. Based on a number of specific questions, respondents were classified into three groups: those with belligerent attitudes toward communist countries, those with conciliatory attitudes, and those with intermediate attitudes. Phillips also recorded whether or not the respondent was employed in a defense-related job. Some respondents held jobs that were totally unrelated to the military or to national defense. The study found that people with defense-related jobs held more belligerent international attitudes than nondefense workers.

What can be concluded from these results? We know from the data that being employed in a defense-related activity is related to holding belligerent international attitudes. We might conclude that people in a defense-related job are pressured to adopt more belligerent international attitudes. The men might justify their activities to convince themselves that they are doing vital work, or because they want to be accepted by their superiors, or for many other reasons. But note that this conclusion assumes *directional influence:* working in a defense-related job *produces* attitudinal change in the direction of increasing belligerency. This conclusion is *not justified* by the data; the direction of influence could be reversed. Perhaps men who hold belligerent international attitudes seek work in defense-related jobs. Or maybe men with conciliatory attitudes seek work in nondefense jobs or quit defense jobs quickly if they are hired. A particular job may not have *changed* attitudes at all, and the men who hold particular jobs may have had different attitudes in the first place.

As this example indicates, all that can be concluded from correlational data is that the variables are related. The *interpretation* of the relationship remains unclear as long as the data are correlational. One can't tell whether the first variable influenced the second (working in defense-related jobs affected attitudes); the second variable influenced the first (holding particular attitudes led to selection of a particular job); both happened (having the job influenced attitudes, *and* attitudes affected job selection); or neither.

The last possibility—that neither variable influenced the other—might seem strange, since the variables were found to be related. But it is possible. Suppose a third variable is related to the other two. For example, people value security differently; and an individual with high security needs may be more sensitive to international threats and adopt a belligerent attitude toward other nations in self-protection. At the same time, such a person might choose a job with plenty of security, high fringe benefits, and a low risk of being fired, such as a government job or one in the military. If this were the case, an individual's desire for security would influence both attitudes and job choice, even though the latter two variables may not affect one another directly. Attitudes and job choice might be *related* to each other without *affecting* each other.

To reinforce the above points, consider a farfetched example. It has been suggested that there is a positive relationship between the number of ice cream cones sold in the United States and the number of deaths in India; when ice cream sales are high here, many people die there. No one would seriously suggest that the next time you buy an ice cream cone you are "killing" someone on the other side of the world. A third common factor accounts for the relationship. Most ice cream cones are sold during the summer months when people want something cool to eat. During the summer, droughts in underdeveloped countries produce food shortages, plagues, and numerous deaths. Hence, the weather influenced both factors, and neither is directly influenced by the other.

All correlational analyses suffer from this basic weakness. By such analyses we can determine when variables are related, but we can't tell whether the variables directly influence each other or which way the influence is exerted.

Gathering data in controlled settings: Experimentation

What experiments are. The beauty and strength of experimentation to gather data are that it allows a researcher to determine not only whether two or more variables are related, but also which variables influence other variables. None of the techniques discussed so far are experiments as the term is technically used. The term *experiment* is reserved for a particular kind of study which has two key features that the other techniques we've considered lack. First, in an experiment, the researcher *controls* and *manipulates* one or more of the variables. Variables which are manipulated are termed *causes, independent variables,* or *antecedents.* Variables which the researcher believes to be influenced by the independent variables are termed *effects, dependent variables,* or *consequents.* When investigators manipulate the independent variables of interest, they control other variables of no immediate interest by holding them roughly constant for all subjects in the experiment. The second important characteristic of an experiment is that an investigator *randomly assigns* subjects to the various conditions created by the manipulation of the independent variables.

Experiments do not have to be conducted in a laboratory, They may take place in a factory, a school, or a private home. Outside of the lab, experiments are called *field experiments.* Control over relevant variables is usually easier to maintain in the lab than in the field. But field experiments sometimes are more realistic and more involving for the subjects than laboratory experiments are.

A conflict experiment. The features of an experiment can be illustrated by describing a classic study of conflict. Morton Deutsch and Robert Krauss [124] hypothesized that when a conflict exists, the ability of the parties to threaten one another will heighten the conflict and make cooperation and conflict resolution less likely. They reasoned that if one person in a conflict situation is able to threaten the other, he or she will do so to make the other person yield. If the threatened person feels equal or superior to the threatener, he or she will feel hostility and will respond to the threat by issuing a counterthreat (given the ability) and by increased determination not to yield. Further hostility and increased conflict develop from the use of threats and counterthreats. Thus, when two people are in conflict, cooperation and conflict resolution will be most likely if neither party can threaten the other. If one of the two uses threats, cooperation will be less likely. If both parties use threats, cooperation and conflict resolution will be most unlikely.

To test these hypotheses the investigators needed to put people in a conflict situation. This is easier said than done; the situation had to be lifelike, but not so lifelike that violence and bloodshed might result. Deutsch and Krauss devised a bargaining game to create the conflict situation. Two subjects played the game, and each was asked to imagine she was in charge of a trucking company, Acme Express or Bolt Trucking Company. The subjects were told that their job was to deliver merchandise from a starting place to a particular destination. As in a real trucking company, the goal was to deliver the merchandise as rapidly as possible. The profits for each subject would be calculated by how much time they spent on the road; the less the time, the more money they made. Each subject made twenty trips, or deliveries.

The road map showing the routes each subject could take is illustrated in Figure 1-5. As can be seen, two routes lead to the destination. The longer, indirect route takes so much time that it results in a small loss of money if selected. Both subjects naturally preferred to take the short, direct road and earn a profit. But here is the catch, and the conflict. The short road has a one-lane stretch through which only one truck can pass at a time. Since the trucks are dispatched at the same time, if both truckers choose to use the short route, they will meet head-on in the middle. No accident will occur, however, since the trucks can stop in time. Instead, both trucks will stand idle in confrontation accumulating large losses until one or both go to the further expense of backing out of the one-lane route. Such confrontations can produce heavy losses; and the conflict is clear. If both parties try to earn a profit on every trip, they will lose money, since they will confront each other over and over on the one-lane road. But to avoid that conflict, one or both truckers must take the longer route and a small loss of money. The only way to resolve the conflict is for the subjects to cooperate and take turns driving on the one-lane road, thereby both making a profit over time. The apparatus for the game is constructed so that neither player knows where the other's truck is unless they actually meet on the one-lane route. Thus, players starting down the one-way route are uncertain about whether a confrontation will occur.

The next step in this experiment is to manipulate how much the subjects can threaten one another. Deutsch and Krauss operationally defined a threat as something that could block the opponent's access to the one-lane route; in this case a road gate (see Figure 1-5). If a gate is closed at the last minute, the opponent has to back out of the one-lane road and then take the longer route, and large losses. The gates therefore present a real threat.

In order to test their hypotheses, the investigators established three conditions: (1) neither party could use the threats, as no gates were provided; (2) only Acme was given a gate (unilateral threat); (3) both Acme and Bolt were given gates (bilateral threat). When gates were provided, subjects

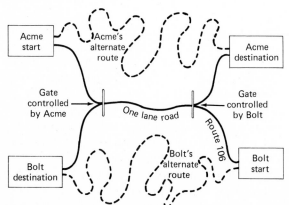

Figure 1-5. *The road map for the trucking game.*

did not have to use them unless they wanted to. If the hypotheses are correct, we should expect subjects to be most cooperative and make the greatest joint profits in the no-threat condition (1) and to be most competitive and make the least joint profits (or the highest joint losses) in the bilateral-threat condition (3).

Forty-eight pairs of female subjects were *randomly assigned* to conditions, sixteen pairs to each of the three threat conditions. Such random assignment to conditions is a vital element in any experiment because it assures that the average characteristics of the subjects in the three conditions are about equal to each other before the experimental manipulation is made.

Note how much control over variables the researcher has in this situation. All the subjects are confronted with the identical basic conflict situation. Since subjects are randomly assigned to one of the three conditions, the overall characteristics of the subjects in each of the conditions are probably the same. Essentially, *all relevant variables are held constant across all of the conditions except for the independent variable, which is manipulated.* If subjects in the three conditions do behave differently, we can have more confidence that the *differences are produced by the independent variable.* Thus, an experiment allows a researcher not only to determine if variables are related to one another, but also to state which variables affect which other variables; in this case, whether the possession of threats affects cooperation.

The results of this experiment did support the investigators' hypotheses. It was found that subjects won the most (maximized their joint profits) in the no-threat condition; they lost some money in the unilateral threat condition; and lost the most money in the bilateral-threat condition. It seems that when both parties use threats, conflict resolution and cooperation are impeded. Additionally, it was found that over time, subjects in the no-threat and unilateral-threat conditions won more and more. They seemed to be learning how to cooperate with each other and successfully resolve their differences. Subjects' profits did not improve in the bilateral-threat condition: These subjects did not learn to work out their differences and resolve their conflict.

One interesting question is, "What happened to the unarmed person when paired with the armed person?" When only one person had a gate (unilateral-threat condition), she won more than her opponent. It may seem better to be armed than unarmed. However, Deutsch and Krauss also found that if the opponent has threat capability, it is better to remain unarmed than to acquire threat capability yourself! They reached this conclusion by comparing the average winnings of the Bolt Company subjects in the unilateral-threat condition (where Bolt did not have a gate) with the average winnings of the Bolt Company subjects in the bilateral-threat condition (where Bolt did have a gate). In both conditions, the opponent had a gate. The average losses for Bolt were less when unarmed than when armed.

Focus 1-4 explores other game situations involving cooperation and conflict.

FOCUS 1-4   THE GAME OF LIFE: SOME PLAYFUL WAYS TO STUDY CONFLICT

Human beings are playful creatures. Johan Huizinga [221] has gone so far as to suggest that our species be renamed *homo ludens*—Man the player. It's a relief to play games when the tedium of everyday affairs makes us look for novel ways to pass the time. Yet life itself is a game; the rules are less formal and the situation is less structured, but the essential elements are the same. We are constantly making moves to "win" (or at least to avoid "losing"). How can Jane get Jim to like her? How can Dave get his parent to loan him the car? How can the United States reach a rapproachment with the Soviet Union and decrease international conflict without risking its own security? Each of the possible moves has a payoff associated with it. Even "luck" plays a part. A decision that looks good when it's made might be reversed by unknown factors. Many people do view life in these terms.

Conflict situations are particularly gamelike. The parties clearly have moves, each with associated payoffs. The outcome is determined by the moves each party makes, and no one knows the outcome until all the moves are made. It therefore should not be surprising to learn that social psychologists often use formal, laboratory games to study conflict. One of the most popular is *prisoner's dilemma game*, the title of which comes from an analogy described by Luce and Raiffa [281, p. 95]:

> Two suspects are taken into custody and separated. The District Attorney is certain that they are guilty of a specified crime, but he does not have adequate evidence to convict them at a trial. He points out to each prisoner that he has two alternatives: to confess, to the crime the police are sure they have done, or not to confess. If they both do not confess, then the D.A. states he will book them on some very minor trumped-up charge such as petty larceny and illegal possession of a weapon, and they would both receive minor punishments; if they both confess, they will be prosecuted, but he will recommend less than the most severe sentence; but if one confesses and the other does not, then the confessor will receive lenient treatment for turning state's evidence, whereas the latter will get "the book" slapped at him.

The essence of this situation can be diagrammed in a matrix which presents each of the possible alternatives of each prisoner and the outcomes associated with the choices (see Figure 1-6). Each prisoner has two alternatives; confess or don't confess. The numbers presented in the matrix are the number of years each prisoner would spend in jail, depending on the choices made. Naturally, the larger the number, the more negative the outcome for each prisoner; each would ideally like to spend no time in jail. If both don't confess, they each will receive one year in jail. If both confess, they each will remain behind bars for five years. But if one confesses while the other doesn't, the confessor will be freed, while the silent prisoner will get the maximum sentence of ten years.

This situation presents an interesting conflict dilemma which extends far beyond the prisoners' case. We all confront similar problems daily, though

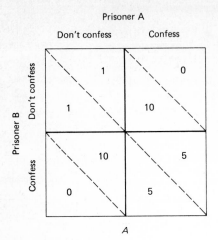
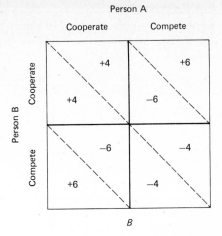

Figure 1-6. *The prisoner's dilemma game. Figure A demonstrates the dilemma for the two prisoners. Each of the numbers in the matrix stands for the number of years each person would get in jail; hence, the larger numbers represent more negative outcomes. If both prisoners confess, each receives five years in jail; if both don't confess, each receives one year in jail. If only one confesses, that prisoner gains freedom and the holdout gets a ten-year sentence. Figure B illustrates a matrix with different numbers that can be used in laboratory studies. Positive numbers represent rewards; negative numbers punishments.*

we might not recognize them. Typically, everyone wants to receive the best individual outcome. In this case, the best individual outcome is obtained by exploiting another person. But consider what happens when both players try to do this: They will both confess, and each will receive five years in jail. Each will be worse off than if they cooperated with each other (don't confess) and receive only a mild negative outcome (one year in jail). In this case, looking out for yourself also involves looking out for someone else. Both people can profit only when they cooperate. This dilemma of cooperation versus competition, trust versus suspicion, makes the prisoner's dilemma game an interesting situation.

Social psychologists have used this and similar games to study how subjects respond to the conflict of interests. Subjects are shown a matrix similar to that shown in Figure 1-6, and the experimenter records the number of cooperative versus competitive choices made. It has been found that people are very competitive in this game [358; 471], and the competitiveness increases over trials. Quite often, subjects make the competitive choice for a long time, and both lose. Neither party knows how to break the deadlock, since the first one to offer a cooperative choice is likely to be exploited and lose even more. This finding resembles what occurs in many real conflicts: Both parties know they are hurting themselves and their opponent by competing, but they are afraid to change to a cooperative stance for fear of being exploited.

There are several ways to increase the cooperation of subjects. When they can communicate with one another, their mutual trust and ability to coordinate strategies increases. Without proper communication opportunities, suspicions of treachery are increased, and no chance is allowed for clear coordination of interests. The strategy of one's opponent also affects cooperation. If the opponent reciprocates a cooperative move but remains ready to compete if competition is given, subjects will respond with a high level of cooperation. However, if the opponent consistently cooperates, no matter what the subject does (a somewhat foolish strategy), subjects will behave competitively and exploitatively. If the opponent consistently competes, subjects will compete to protect themselves. These findings indicate that flexible strategies which respond to the opponent's moves are effective in reducing conflicts and fostering cooperation. Finally, the interpersonal relationship between the antagonists also has an effect. Cooperation is much greater when the participants know and like one another than when they don't.

No one suggests that conflicts are so simple that we can learn all about them from laboratory games. And no one seriously suggests that games capture all the essential aspects of conflict. Conflict is too complex for that. But games can give us important insights into some aspects of conflict and can increase our understanding of how people perceive conflicts and respond to them.

Demand characteristics. Recall that interview subjects often want to put their best foot forward and look good to an interviewer. This social-desirability bias can distort subjects' responses and threaten the validity of a study. A comparable situation exists in experimental research. Martin Orne [332] pointed out that subjects often enter an experiment with a cooperative attitude. They feel that science is important and valuable, and they want to do their best to help the experimenter by cooperating. They try to determine what outcome the experimenter "wants" and then do their best to help fulfill the expectations. They want to be "good" subjects. The cues in the experimental situation which guide a subject's behavior in this way are termed *demand characteristics*. Since they threaten the validity of results, experimenters go to great lengths to guard against them. Deutsch and Krauss, for example, were very careful to tell subjects that they didn't have to use the gates unless they wanted to. Some experimenters try to give subjects false cues about hypotheses so that the subjects will not think about the real hypotheses. Sometimes "cover stories" are made up so that subjects believe they are doing something other than what the experimenter is really interested in. Such cover stories are particularly prevalent in attitude-change experiments and can lead to some elaborate studies. (For example, note the experiment by Festinger and Carlsmith which is described in Chapter 2, page 78.)

Not all subjects are cooperative. Some resent participating in experiments and consciously try to sabotage the experiment. Any demand characteristics which these subjects pick up will cause a different kind of effect: If the subject figures out the experimenter's hypotheses, he or she will do just the reverse. This uncooperative attitude sometimes results when subjects have previously participated in studies that involved deception and elaborate cover stories. They resent being deceived once, and they take it out on the second experimenter.

Some subjects are not as concerned with pleasing experimenters as they are with impressing them. If a subject believes a particular behavior will impress the experimenter, he or she will behave that way. It has been shown that subjects will often go out of their way to impress an experimenter and gain a positive evaluation [406]. Thus, demand characteristics should be minimized or eliminated, and much of the time it takes to design an experiment is spent trying to mitigate these different kinds of biasing effects.

Experimenter effects. Robert Rosenthal [370] has suggested that many experimenters may unwittingly affect the results of studies through their behavior. The tone of their voice, the way they interact with subjects, their nonverbal behavior, etc., may all suggest to the subjects that the experimenter wants them to behave in a certain way. This demand characteristic might have been well-concealed in the actual design of the study, but the experimenter's behavior may still communicate it.

Some critics [34] have argued that such *experimenter-expectancy effects* have not been proved. However, the mere possibility that they could occur makes it important to minimize them. In many studies, this can be done quite easily. Two ways which have been used often are (1) automating the procedure and (2) running "blind." Sometimes an experimenter can automate the entire experiment. Subjects receive instructions from a tape-recording or a videotape picture. By giving all subjects identical instructions delivered in only one way, experimenter expectancy effects are held constant in all the conditions. An experimenter might write out the instructions and have subjects read them alone. This, too, minimizes the experimenter's contact with the subjects. But when such automation is not practical, another technique can be used—the experimenter can run the subjects "blind." In a *blind* study, the experimenter does not know which condition a subject is in. One experimenter assigns the subjects to the conditions and controls the necessary apparatus, while a second, "blind" experimenter instructs and interacts with the subjects.

Just as the characteristics of an interviewer can affect respondents' behaviors, the characteristics of an experimenter can affect subjects' behaviors. The experimenter's race, sex, age, physical attractiveness, status, warmth, and anxiety level are among the many characteristics that can affect results [2; 310]. Experimenters, then, should take into account the fact that their presence alone—even if it doesn't create experimenter expectancy effects—can affect their results. Ideally, several different "types" of experimenters should be used to minimize the possibility that the characteristics of a single experimenter will affect the results.

Variety is the spice of science. Each of these research techniques supplement and reinforce one another. No single method is best for all purposes. An investigator might use observation in natural settings to get an idea which can be tested under controlled laboratory conditions. Or a test initially conducted in the laboratory might be checked against data obtained from questionnaire-interview methods or content analysis to see if the same effects are found in different situations. The techniques are best employed in conjunction with one another. Only when a coherent body of data is collected from a variety of sources, with the various techniques, and at a variety of times, can we be truly confident that we understand human behavior.

■ RESOLVING CONFLICTS: WHAT TO DO UNTIL ARMAGEDDON

The topic of conflict has been used as a backdrop for presenting some basic ideas about the scientific method and research procedures. You've seen that conflict pervades all social interactions, though people might not be aware of it. You've seen how conflicts can escalate: Threats are perceived, the antagonists become increasingly prepared for a confrontation, and a confrontation develops from sometimes minor incidents. You've seen that the antagonists often have distorted perceptions of one another which can perpetuate and intensify a conflict. You've seen that threats can increase conflict and competition and cause both parties to suffer. Now we'll turn to another aspect of conflict: How to reduce it.

Many people suggest that persuasive appeals to concepts like "brotherhood," "peace," and "harmony" might reduce conflict. Although this may sound logical, people in conflicts often don't behave logically. Antagonists usually see no discrepancy between their beliefs in brotherhood and peace and their desire to exterminate their opponent. Each antagonist views the opponent as the impediment to peace. Jerome Frank [163b] has commented that appeals to brotherhood and peace usually are ineffective ways of reducing conflict because of the kinds of misperceptions which exist in conflict situations. If one's opponent uses such appeals, they are dismissed as propaganda. If a neutral third party uses the appeals, they again are dismissed because the neutral "misunderstands the real issues." In an atmosphere of distrust and suspicion, no one listens to reason.

Conflict reduction takes place through deeds, not through words alone. Deeds must demonstrate a resolution to cooperate and compromise; they pave the way for the development of trust. In the early stages of conflict resolution, the going may be difficult. Self-fulfilling prophecies, double standards, stereotyped images, and misperceptions all make initial coopera-tive gestures suspect. However, several strategies do seem to be somewhat effective for reducing conflicts: the development of common goals, the use of pacifistic strategies, and the use of tension-reduction strategies.

Common goals: Some alternatives to invasion from outer space

Flying saucers from other worlds hover over the earth. People around the world forget their differences and work together to repel the invaders. Resources are pooled to achieve the common goal of survival against multiheaded, multilegged creatures.

Invasions from outer space and the resulting worldwide cooperation are common in science fiction books and movies. Give people a common goal where everyone needs the aid of everyone else, and they will work to accomplish it, forgetting petty differences and hostilities. Do common goals really reduce conflict, or is this science fiction also?

Muzafer Sherif and his associates [403] conducted an interesting field study which demonstrated that common goals can be effective in reducing conflict. A group of twenty-two boys, aged eleven, who previously did not know each other, were selected to go to a summer camp at Robber's Cave, Oklahoma. The boys were randomly divided into two groups and given separate but approximately equal facilities in different areas of the camp. During the first week, the groups were isolated from one another. Two co-hesive groups quickly developed; each had its own leaders, group identi-ties, and group loyalties. One group called themselves the "Rattlers," and the other called themselves the "Eagles."

During the second week of camp, the investigators tried to create conditions in which the two groups would compete and conflict with each other. A series of athletic competitions, such as baseball games and tug-of-war, was arranged complete with prizes and trophies for the winners. This competitive atmosphere was designed to produce animosity between the two groups, and it worked. The groups taunted one another, destroyed each other's flags, got into fights, cursed at each other, and even developed stereotypes of themselves and the "enemy." When asked to rate their performances in the games, each side overrated their own group and underrated the other group.

After creating this competitive atmosphere, the investigators then tried to reduce the hostilities during the third and final week of camp. They first provided the groups with opportunities to meet in noncompetitive settings in the hope that *intergroup contact* would reduce the conflict. On seven occasions the two groups met to eat, watch movies, shoot off fireworks, and share other similar activities. Intergroup contact failed to reduce conflict. Each of the groups stayed together, clearly separate from their opponents; they hurled food, taunted each other, and generally behaved in ways that would be described as anything but friendly. In a competitive, hostile atmo-sphere, contact alone is ineffective in reducing conflict.

The investigators then gave the groups of boys common goals. For example, unknown to the boys, the investigators had sabotaged the camp's water supply, and the boys had to work together to fix the damage. For six days, the groups were given similar cooperative opportunities. Both groups had to work together to help tow a truck that had broken down, both groups had to cooperate to raise money to purchase a movie for the camp, and so forth. Gradually, these common goals lessened the hostilities. The boys began to visit and eat together, name-calling decreased, they selected members of the rival group as friends, and both groups chose to ride home in the same bus rather than in separate buses.

While common goals usually promote cooperation and decrease conflict, they don't invariably and permanently eliminate conflict. Politics makes strange bedfellows, it's true, and sometimes groups work together for a short period of time only to emerge as enemies later. For example, the United States and the Soviet Union worked together to defeat Germany in World War II. But after the war, these two nations became major international antagonists. Once the common goal of defeating Germany was achieved, the divergent ideological goals of the two nations again produced conflict. Thus, so long as common goals are present, conflicts can be minimized. But during periods of cooperation, it is necessary to work out basic differences, which otherwise will reappear when the common goal is achieved.

Pacifism

Mohandas Gandhi, the great Indian leader, brought nonviolent methods of conflict resolution to the world's attention. Pacifism as practiced by Gandhi should not be confused with the word "passive." It was anything but that. It is described as "a very active effort to defeat, by means other than violence, a possessor of superior destructive power, and . . . it requires at least as much courage, discipline, and initiative as violent combat" [163b, p. 259]. Pacifism is a way of settling, even winning, conflicts by stressing and adhering to moral principles and refusing to use violence as a means to an end. Advocates of nonviolence hope to accomplish several objectives. They want to demonstrate to an opponent that they have the strength of will to suffer for their beliefs. By showing a capacity to steadfastly adhere to their beliefs, pacifists also hope to morally embarrass their opponents. Instead of stimulating further violence, this should demoralize opponents and actually inhibit violence. It becomes difficult to prolong violence when pacifists demonstrate concern for their opponents' welfare.

In this country, Martin Luther King, Jr., used many of Gandhi's methods in the nonviolent protests of the civil rights movement. But the question remains: How effective is pacifism as a means of conflict resolution? Certainly, effectiveness alone can't be used to determine whether pacifism is "good" or "bad," since ethical and moral questions are involved. However, the practical question "Does it work?" might increase our understanding of one aspect of pacifism.

It is difficult to determine how effective pacifism has been in past confrontations. It has been argued that Gandhi's use of pacifistic methods to free India from British colonial domination actually prolonged the confrontation and ultimately caused more suffering than would have resulted from a shorter, violent clash. Even those who point to the effectiveness of nonviolence in drawing attention to the plight of blacks in this country are on shaky ground. Many people argue that real gains for blacks were made because of the threat of violence from militant groups such as the Black Panthers. While credit is given to the nonviolent movement, it has been suggested that violence prompted the change. Nonviolence is credited because opponents don't want to give credit to militant groups and encourage further militancy. Such arguments about the effectiveness of nonviolent tactics could be debated at great length.

Pacifism has been studied in social-psychological laboratories [298; 405]. In these experiments, subjects played a game in which one opponent was described as a Quaker morally committed to a nonviolent position. The Quaker was part of the experiment, not a real subject. Each subject could deliver electric shocks to the other in order to force an agreement. The pacifist's strategy never allowed the use of force. Most subjects were not reluctant to use the electric shock against the simulated pacifist: By the end of the game, 65 percent of the subjects were consistently shocking the helpless pacifist. However, several conditions did increase the cooperation which the pacifist received. When the subjects received frequent communications from the pacifist, their cooperation increased, and the pacifist received somewhat fewer shocks. Also, if a "neutral" third party was present to witness the conflict, more cooperation and fewer shocks occurred. This third party caused the subjects to be more concerned with how their actions looked. However, if the subjects were given teammates who advocated continued shocks and noncooperation, the subjects behaved accordingly.

These laboratory studies of pacifistic strategies show that pacifism can be somewhat effective in reducing conflict under the right conditions: When communication between the parties occurs freely, and when observers are present who can disapprove of attempts to use violence against the pacifist. However, even in these cases, the amount of cooperation given to the pacifist was not as high as many people might hope. At present, one can conclude that pacifism is a moral strategy which is ethically satisfying and which *sometimes* can produce results, but it does not always work.

GRIT: A lot of it's needed in conflicts

Another method of conflict resolution has been suggested by Charles Osgood [334; 335]. Numerous factors act to maintain misperceptions and build up hostilities between parties in conflict. Typically, tensions rise as each side perceives the other as a threat. Each side develops mispercep-

(a)

(b)

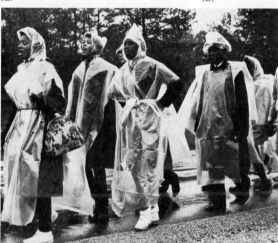

(c)

(d)

Figure 1-7. *Four ways to reduce conflict and tension. Appeals to brotherhood and other desirable values (a) are often used to try to decrease prejudice and tension. Unfortunately, when groups are in conflict, such appeals usually are ignored. Working together in a common cause, as evidenced by the blacks and whites cooperating to help starving Americans (b), is often an effective way of reducing tension and conflict. The effectiveness of pacifist strategies has been much debated, but many people view it as the only morally satisfying way to resolve conflicts. The civil rights marches of the early 1960s were typified by such resistance (c). GRIT is a conflict-reduction strategy that begins when one group announces and then makes a small initial cooperative gesture. If the gestures are reciprocated, a conflict spiral can be replaced by a cooperation spiral. A strategy similar to GRIT was successfully used by John F. Kennedy with Soviet Premier Khruschev (d).*

tions and applies double standards in evaluating actions. In this hostile atmosphere, a minor incident is often enough to trigger a violent clash. Until such an incident occurs, both sides keep increasing their armaments and draining their own resources. How to stop this armament buildup and how to halt and eventually reverse the conflict are questions Osgood sought to answer.

Osgood's plan has been called GRIT, or "Graduated Reciprocation in Tension-reduction." In essence, the plan calls for one party to announce in advance an intention to make a cooperative, conciliatory gesture. The gesture should be capable of reducing tensions—for example, a resolve to decrease the number of missiles produced. The first gesture should be relatively small; if it is exploited by the other side, no serious harm can befall the cooperator. In other words, the gesture should be reversible if the situation later demands it. Announcing the gesture in advance is important, for it prepares the other side. Without the advance announcement, the other side might interpret the gesture as a trick or trap. Having made the gesture, the first side then should provide its opponent with an opportunity to reciprocate with a cooperative overture. If no cooperative gesture is forthcoming, relatively little has been lost. However, if reciprocation does occur, the first side then has the opportunity to make another small cooperative step, which again might be reciprocated. Initially, the steps taken by each side might be viewed with suspicion. However, after several such tension-reducing steps by each side, the seeds of trust might be planted. Subsequent steps should further nurture the trust and reduce the suspicion and tension. Ultimately, large-scale acts of cooperation and disarmament might emerge.

This modest proposal, or something very close to it, was tried by the Kennedy administration following the Cuban missile crisis. The Kennedy experiment, as it has been called [144; 145], did produce some reciprocation of cooperative gestures between the United States and the Soviet Union. Unfortunately, Kennedy's assassination brought an end to the experiment. More recently, the detente policies of the Nixon and Ford administrations contained elements of GRIT. Whether these elements are enough to bring about cooperative gestures on a larger scale remains an open question.

Laboratory studies of conflict using game situations have offered support for the effectiveness of GRIT in reducing conflict. Reciprocation does occur after cooperative overtures are announced in advance, and these result in dramatic increases in cooperation [351; 443]. However, it also has been found that GRIT is most effective when the parties have equal power [444]. When the parties are unequal, the more powerful one has little reason to cooperate, since it has control; meanwhile, the weaker party can exploit conciliatory overtures to equalize the difference in power.

Social psychologists have just begun to explore the strengths and weaknesses of GRIT. But results so far certainly encourage its use as a conflict-reduction strategy. GRIT seems to appeal to more people than the other strategies we've discussed, probably because it has something for everyone. "Hawks" can tolerate it, since it offers a chance for peace without initially jeopardizing the conciliatory party. "Doves" might find it slow-moving, but it does offer the ultimate in resolutions—the reduction of tension, the production of trust, and possible disarmament. Moderates admire its apparent validity and pragmatic approach.

■ SUMMARY

In this chapter, we've attempted to demonstrate what science means to social psychologists by describing major research methods and using the topic of social conflict as an example of how social psychologists approach a research issue.

Common sense is ineffective support for knowledge because it includes unevaluated and untested beliefs. Social psychologists go beyond common sense to carefully develop theories and hypotheses. The scientific method is used as the model for gaining knowledge. First, induction is used to arrive at general hypotheses; then deduction generates specific predictions. These predictions are tested systematically by bringing data to bear on them. Researchers obtain data in several ways: by observing natural events, by questionnaire-interview techniques, by content analysis, by correlational techniques, and by experimentation. Experimentation allows researchers to formulate cause-effect relationships between variables, but data-gathering techniques are best used in conjunction with one another.

Social conflict pervades all social interactions. The descriptions of international conflict have similarities with conflicts between friends, marriage partners, and groups. As conflicts become greater, the perceptions and behaviors of participants become increasingly affected. Misperceptions, double standards, and stereotyped images occur. Tension increases, as do threats, retaliation, competition, and preparedness for confrontation. In a hostile, suspicious atmosphere, conflict resolution often is difficult. Some methods of conflict reduction include focusing on common goals, pacifism, and GRIT.

2

attitude change

concepts

An attitude is an orientation toward an object or set of objects in one's environment.

Attitudes can be measured by self-report, observation of overt behavior, judging task performance, interpreting ambiguous stimuli, and measuring physiological reactions.

Self-report measures are the most widely used measures of attitudes.

Attitudes are among the important factors that determine behavior.

People change their attitudes to function better in their environment or to obtain internal satisfaction.

The effectiveness of a persuasive communication depends on the source of the message, the message itself, and characteristics of the audience.

Large-scale attitude change can best take place as a step-by-step process.

Generally, the more fear a message generates, the more attitude change it will cause.

Persons of low self-esteem and high trust tend to be fairly easily persuaded.

The theories of cognitive dissonance, self-perception, and impression management provide different ways of interpreting the same research findings.

Ways of resisting persuasion include derogating the source, refuting or rejecting the arguments, denial, rationalization or distortion, and "defensive training."

targets

After reading this chapter, you should be able to:

1   State and describe two major definitions of attitude.
2   Identify the characteristics of attitudes.
3   Identify and describe four functions that attitudes serve.

4   Identify several types of self-report measures.

5   Discuss the important characteristics of a communication source.

6   Identify and distinguish between selective exposure and de facto selective exposure.

7   Outline cognitive dissonance theory and discuss the research findings it can explain.

8   Describe inoculation theory and its applications.

One of the most popular American television shows in recent years is "All in the Family." Developed in the early 1970s, this comedy focuses on the relationship between Archie, an overdrawn caricature of a working-class man, and his son-in-law, Mike. Archie and Mike disagree about every matter conceivable; much heat and little light are generated in their interactions, particularly when they get around to politics, social issues, and race relations. These two characters differ in age, education, and economic status. They also differ greatly in an important social area—namely, in their *attitudes.* What Archie is for, Mike is against. Issues that Mike considers crucial, Archie finds worthless nonsense. And people whom Mike likes, Archie dislikes. This basic conflict between attitudes (and between the behaviors which the attitudes represent) forms the basis for this immensely popular show.

■ WHAT ARE ATTITUDES?

As Archie and Mike demonstrate, the attitudes of people have a major effect on their lives and interactions. They influence our perceptions, the information we come in contact with, our selection of friends and partners, our political behaviors, our religious feelings, and so on. In short, attitudes are extremely important, and it's no surprise that for over half a century social psychologists have considered them one of the most central concepts in the study of social psychology. In fact, as early as 1918 social psychology was defined by some as the study of attitudes [452].

Generally, an *attitude* is an orientation toward an object or set of objects in one's environment. The range of attitudes is probably limitless; people hold attitudes toward their parents, football, the president, work, split-pea soup, nuclear disarmament, pornography, and so on. Regardless of the object, however, all attitudes share some characteristics.

1   Attitudes are *inferred* from the way individuals behave; we never see an attitude directly. Sometimes we observe a person interacting with an

object or another individual (for example, her mother) and infer her attitudes (toward her mother) from that behavior. In other cases, we might ask a person questions about the object (mother); the individual's attitude toward her mother would then be inferred from *this* behavior, that is, from the behavior of answering the questions as she did.

2 Attitudes are *learned.* We are not born with them; rather, they develop from our experiences. Since attitudes are learned, it follows that they can be relearned and that they can be *changed.*

3 Attitudes *affect behavior.* Having an attitude toward an object gives one a reason to behave toward that object in a certain way. And, in the absence of contrary information or strong situational pressures, people behave in ways that represent their attitudes.

Some theorists have proposed that an attitude be defined as "the intensity of positive or negative affect for or against a psychological object. A psychological object is any symbol, person, phrase, slogan, or idea toward which people can differ as regards positive or negative affect" [454, p. 39]. This definition considers an attitude to involve emotional feelings—that is, a person's likes and dislikes.

Other theorists [239] propose that attitudes have three components: affect, cognitions, and behavioral tendencies. The *affective component* is identical to emotional reactions. The *cognitive component* includes a person's specific beliefs, facts, and pieces of information about an attitude object. The *behavioral component* includes the behavior associated with the attitude object. To illustrate how these components interrelate, consider a student's responses to the college football team. He or she has beliefs about the players, coaches, opponents, and so forth, and holds beliefs about how well the team might do in its games; these form the cognitive component. The student also likes or dislikes the team and its players and might display other emotional reactions, especially after victory or defeat; these form the affective component. Finally, the student's behavior might include going to pep rallies and games, as well as buying programs and souvenirs. Together, these aspects of the student's reactions reflect an attitude toward the football team.

The first definition of an attitude involves only affective responses; it recognizes that a person also has beliefs and behavioral tendencies which are likely to be consonant with the affective reactions, but it doesn't consider these to be part of the attitude itself. The second definition stresses the components of an attitude; it views the parts of an attitude as being so closely related that one must consider all of them together [459]. For example, a belief ("Janet is intelligent, personable, and beautiful"), an affective response ("I like Janet"), and a behavior ("I'll take Janet to a movie tonight") may all relate to the same underlying concept. But however an attitude is defined, everyone basically agrees on how attitudes should be measured and how important they are in explaining behaviors.

■ WHY WE DEVELOP ATTITUDES

One way to judge the importance of attitudes is to ask a simple but crucial question: Why should anyone hold attitudes? What good are they? Social scientists have identified and described four *functions* that attitudes may serve [238; 414]: knowledge, social adjustment, value expression, and ego defense.

Making sense of the world

An attitude can give one a frame of reference, a way to structure the world so that it makes sense. An attitude that provides such information is said to be serving a *knowledge* function. For example, your attitudes about which political issues to support, ignore, or fight against provide you with a frame of reference for evaluating candidates in an election. If candidates support issues toward which you have positive attitudes, you are likely to respond more favorably than if they fight against those issues. The interactions between Archie and Mike in "All in the Family" further illustrate this function. It's clear that the "world" Archie sees is quite different from the "world" Mike sees. Archie views the world as a battle between the "little man" (people like himself) and big government, Communists, blacks, Jews, and various other "evil" forces. But Mike is more likely to see things in terms of underdogs (minority group members, poor people, students) trying to contend with exploitation, bigotry, and mistreatment. Such contrasting attitudes contribute to very different ways of viewing the world and, hence, serve a knowledge function.

Relating to others

Since we are social creatures, the views of certain people and groups are very important. In many cases, appropriate attitudes allow us to identify with, or gain approval from, persons and groups we consider important. In addition, the expression of certain attitudes may be rewarded directly by important people in our environment—parents, teachers, friends, etc. Attitudes that allow a person to achieve such rewards or approval are serving a *social-adjustment* function. Returning to "All in the Family," it is clear that Mike's views, however stereotyped and exaggerated, are similar to those of many college students, and Archie's are similar to those of many working people. Thus, the two sets of attitudes allow each man to get along quite well in his own life situation. If, however, Mike were to take a summer job at Archie's plant, his attitudes would probably not serve him very well. In fact, they would probably serve a social *mal*adjustment function, exposing Mike to ridicule from his coworkers. The same thing might take place in reverse if Archie were to go back to school.

Expressing our values

Think for a moment about the values most important to you. For many college students, these might include honesty, openness in personal relationships, equality, and sociopolitical liberalism, to name a few. Now think of attitudes that might accompany such values. In many cases, specific attitudes express a person's central values and self-concept. When an attitude allows such expression, it serves the *value-expressive* function. For example, many people who were active in the civil rights movement in the 1960s valued the concept of "equality" highly; their attitudes toward political figures (Martin Luther King, Jr., Rap Brown, and George Wallace) and toward various types of legislation and political activism were ways to express their commitment to "equality." Archie thinks of himself as a "red-blooded American," while Mike considers himself a "liberal." Both of these orientations reflect values, and Archie and Mike have developed many attitudes which express these values.

Protecting our threatened egos

In discussions of racial prejudice, a fourth function often is implied. We all have heard that "prejudice is a sickness," or "prejudiced people are psychologically unhealthy." These statements are, of course, overgeneralizations, but they point to another function that attitudes may serve. An attitude may reflect a person's unresolved personality problems—for instance, unexpressed aggression or fear of losing status. As defense mechanisms, attitudes allow people to protect themselves from acknowledging uncomplimentary basic truths about themselves. A white person's racial attitude, for example, may have little to do with blacks per se, but rather may reflect the white person's personality problems. In such a case, the attitude serves an *ego-defensive* function; it helps protect one's ego from threats.

The ego-defensive function of Archie's racial attitudes is sometimes evident. He feels, often with good reason, mistreated by people more powerful than he is. However, even as he sees others making more money and generally enjoying a bigger share of the good things in life, he manages to consider himself superior to an entire segment of the American population—anyone who is not a WASP (White, Anglo-Saxon, and Protestant). His ethnocentric outlook automatically elevates Archie in the hierarchy of society, since a sizable portion must, by his definition, remain "below" him. Such an orientation can be very effective in raising one's self-esteem.

■ MEASURING ATTITUDES: HOW DO WE FIND OUT?

To explore how attitudes affect social life, we must be able to measure them. This is often more difficult than one might imagine. Some problems and pitfalls connected with measurement are discussed in Chapter 1. To circumvent some of them, several different types of attitude measures have been developed. There are five general categories of measures currently used [107]: self-report measures, observations of overt behaviors, task-performance measures, ambiguous-stimuli measures, and physiological measures. Each type of measure has its own advantages and disadvantages; the best way to proceed is to use several different types together.

Self-report measures

In this, the most widely used form of measurement, a person is asked to answer various questions about an object, an event, an individual, or a group of people. The questions may ask for a simple agree-disagree response—for example, "Do you agree or disagree with the statement, 'No legal penalties should be associated with the use of marijuana'?" Or one might be asked to respond to this question on a five-category scale which includes the possibilities of "strongly agree," "agree," "neither agree nor disagree," "disagree," or "strongly disagree." This type of measure lets an individual express the strength of feeling toward a topic, and any number of categories could be used.

Another kind of self-report measure is a *social-distance scale.* A social-distance scale tries to measure an individual's attitudes toward a particular person or group of people by determining how intimate a relationship with that person or group the respondent will accept. Such a scale includes a series of situations ranging from "not at all intimate" (for example, allow him to visit my country) through "moderately intimate" (allow him to buy a house in my neighborhood) to "very intimate" (admit him to friendship or marriage). Respondents are asked whether or not they will "accept" a particular person or group of people in each of these situations. The more intimate the relationship one is willing to accept, the more positive the person's underlying attitude toward the object or group is assumed to be.

A researcher also could *interview* respondents. The interviews may be structured (a specific set of questions are asked and a specific set of answers are provided from which the respondent can choose) or unstructured (a general question is asked and respondents answer verbally or in writing, with as much detail as they want). The answers then can be coded to measure respondents' attitudes.

These self-report measures are relatively quick to develop and easy to administer, and they yield large amounts of data quickly. For these reasons, self-report techniques are the most common form of attitude measurement. However, self-report measures are susceptible to many biases, since respondents can control or change their answers. For example, in Chapter 1 we discussed social-desirability biases, in which subjects give answers they think researchers want or would approve of. For this reason, alternative methods of attitude measurement are sometimes used.

Observing overt behavior

One way to judge a person's attitudes is to *observe overt behavior* toward the attitude object. People do this all the time. Generally, we can be fairly certain of what attitudes our close friends hold, though they may never have told us about them and we may never have tested them. By observing their actions toward attitude objects, we can infer their attitudes from their behaviors. Similarly, social scientists have created behavioral situations from which individuals' attitudes can be inferred. For example, people might be asked to donate money or sign a petition to support a particular cause. Those who do so are probably more in favor of the cause than those who refuse. In one type of experiment [117; 189] white subjects were asked if they were willing to have their picture taken with a black student of the opposite sex. If they agreed, they were asked to choose which uses of the photograph they would allow. The possibilities ranged from use in laboratory experiments (a relatively anonymous use) to use in a nationwide publicity campaign advocating racial integration. It was assumed that subjects who agreed to have their picture taken and widely distributed were less prejudiced toward blacks than those who refused, an assumption that was supported by the results.

Naturally, observations of overt behavior alone don't provide a guarantee that the behavior fully represents an underlying attitude. For example, some subjects who agreed to have their pictures taken may actually have been quite prejudiced, but they might have agreed simply to avoid explaining why they would refuse. And some subjects who refused may have been relatively unprejudiced but declined because they didn't want to "embarrass" members of their family who were prejudiced. The correspondence between attitude and behavior will be considered in more detail shortly.

Judging task performance

In some tasks a person's performance may be systematically biased by his or her attitudes. Consequently, *task performance* is another indirect measure of underlying attitudes. For example, can we evaluate topics and issues accurately, regardless of our attitudes toward them? Evidence suggests that we cannot always do so. Researchers asked college students to judge the "plausibility" or "effectiveness" of attitude-related statements. The students were told to play the part of a "debate judge" and evaluate arguments impartially, without reference to their own attitudes. Nonetheless, the students' judgments were so closely related to their attitudes (arguments which a person agreed with were seen as considerably more plausible than were those the person disagreed with) that the pattern of judgments could be used as an accurate indirect measure of attitudes [70].

Self-Report Scale

Below are questions about your opinions on controversial issues.

You can state your position by checking one (and only one) of the spaces listed next to the seven answer categories. If your exact position is not given, please check the space next to the answer that comes closest to it.

Please answer every question.

You may go ahead; please *work fast*.

1. Do you believe that integration (of schools, businesses, residences, etc.) will benefit both whites and blacks?

—— I agree *strongly* that integration will benefit both whites and blacks.
—— I agree *on the whole* that integration will benefit both whites and blacks.
—— I agree *slightly* that integration will benefit both whites and blacks.
—— I am undecided whether integration will benefit both whites and blacks.
—— I disagree *slightly* that integration will benefit both whites and blacks.
—— I disagree *on the whole* that integration will benefit both whites and blacks.
—— I disagree *strongly* that integration will benefit both whites and blacks.

(a)

SOCIAL DISTANCE SCALE (completed)

According to my first feeling reactions, I would willingly admit members of each race (as a class, and not the best nor the worst members I have known) to one or more of the classifications under which I have placed a cross (x).

	7 / 1 To close kinship by marriage	6 / 2 To my club as personal friends	5 / 3 To my street as neighbors	4 / 4 To employment in my occupation in my country	3 / 5 To citizenship in my country	2 / 6 As visitors only to my country	1 / 7 Would exclude from my country
Arabs						x	
Blacks							x
Canadians	x	x	x	x	x		
Chinese						x	
Cubans							x
Danes				x	x		
Dutch				x	x		
English	x	x	x	x	x		
French	x	x		x	x		
French-Canadians	x	x	x	x	x		
Finns				x	x		

(b)

Self-Report Scale

	Agree	Disagree
1. The fact that an interracial, married couple would be socially outcast and rejected by both blacks and whites indicates that such marriages should be avoided.	——	——
2. Blacks should be accorded equal rights through integration.	——	——
3. I would have no worries about going to a party with an attractive black date.	——	——
4. I would accept an invitation to a New Year's Eve party given by a black couple in their own home.	——	——
5. I approve of the Black Power approach to improving conditions for blacks.	——	——
6. There is no truth to the idea that the black's troubles in the past have built in him a stronger character than the white man has.	——	——

(c)

(d)

(e)

Figure 2-1. *Several ways of measuring attitudes. The first three methods are all varieties of self-report techniques, in which people answer questions dealing with the attitude object. The first (a) employs a seven-point scale which allows respondents to express both the direction and the strength of their feelings about social matters. The second, a social distance scale (b), measures the amount of "social distance" the respondents want to keep between themselves and members of other ethnic groups. It is assumed that people who want to maintain a great deal of distance— that is, who are not willing to accept members of these groups in many situations—have the most negative attitudes. The third scale (c) asks respondents to agree or disagree with statements on relations between ethnic groups. Also pictured is an interview, in this case done door-to-door (d). Interviews may be structured (specific) or unstructured (more general and open-ended). The final method (e) involves the observation of overt behavior. By watching these children interacting with each other and with other children, an observer can infer what the racial attitude of each child is.*

Interpreting ambiguous stimuli

A fourth way to measure attitudes is to ask a person to *interpret ambiguous stimuli,* such as pictures, incomplete sentences, or inkblots. Since the stimuli are deliberately ambiguous and can be interpreted in different ways, it is theorized that attitudes, values, and other personality constructs will affect the interpretations systematically. The researcher can then infer what the respondent's attitude is on the basis of this systematic effect. For example, Figure 2-2 shows a white man and a black man standing near one another on a subway train. The expressions on the face of each man are rather ambiguous, but could indicate emotion. The white man holds a razor. Subjects are shown the picture for a few moments, the picture is taken away, and then they are asked to make up a story about what was going on in the picture. Many prejudiced subjects make up a story of conflict between the two men; they often portray the black man as having unjustly started a fight; they sometimes describe the white man as being dressed in a suit and the black man as being poorly dressed; and some subjects even describe the black man as holding the razor and making threatening gestures [9a]. Although ambiguous measures are commonly used to measure personality traits, they are not often used to measure attitudes. In addition to taking much time to invent, administer, and score, they are often difficult to interpret precisely.

Measuring physiological reactions

In many ways, measuring *physiological reactions* would seem ideal. Un-trained people cannot generally control their physiological responses to stimuli, and so such measures are less susceptible to conscious distortion and social-desirability biases than the other methods are. Psychologists have investigated several physiological measures to determine their relationship to attitudes. These include heart rate, galvanic skin response (GSR), and dilation (enlargement) of the pupil of the eye. Pupil dilation has fascinated many social psychologists. Eckhard Hess [204; 205] found evidence that when people view an attractive object, their pupils dilate. Male subjects' pupils became significantly larger when viewing slides of attractive female nudes than when viewing slides of the countryside. Folklore has it that the phenomenon has long been known by sophisticated vendors; sellers of wares in Middle Eastern bazaars would often watch the eyes of a prospective buyer. When the buyer's eyes spied an item which was desirable, the pupils would dilate and the vendor knew that he could make a sale with a minimum of dickering over the price. Unfortunately, investigators have not been able to reproduce this phenomenon consistently, and it is still not clear under what conditions pupil dilation will correspond to underlying attitudes [503].

One problem with physiological measures is that they are still quite crude and do not show high reliability. Also, physiological measures are

Figure 2-2. *Who has the razor? Look at this picture for a few moments, then look away and try to remember as much of the picture as you can. Who has the razor? Allport and Postman (9a) found that many prejudiced whites were very inaccurate in their recall. For instance, they remembered the razor as having been in the black man's hand. Thus, interpretation of this ambiguous stimulus, a quickly viewed picture, might serve as a measure of racial attitudes. The tendency of some whites to remember the black as holding the razor, as hostile, and threatening the white man, can be taken as an indication of a negative attitude toward blacks in these whites.*

essentially unidirectional—that is, they measure the intensity of a strong response but not the direction of it. A strong negative response yields the same physiological data as a strong positive response. Therefore, physiological measures, at least at our current level of technical sophistication, are useful only when an attitude is relatively intense and its direction is already known. In this limited situation, physiological measures of attitude may be quite useful. As the technology becomes more sophisticated, new and more useful measures may be developed [316].

■ ATTITUDES AND BEHAVIOR: WHEN DO THEY CORRESPOND?

Usually, attitudes are assumed to be important determinants of behavior. Yet, attitudes and behavior may not correspond perfectly. To understand why, consider the basic formulation proposed by Kurt Lewin, who stated that behavior is a function of a person's characteristics and environment, or $B = f(P, E)$. Attitudes are one set of a person's characteristics. They interact with other personal characteristics (motives, values, personality traits), which, in turn, interact with environmental factors to determine behavior.

Given this basic relationship, we can see that the prediction of behavior from attitudes will not always be accurate, since behavior is affected by more than attitudes alone. Prediction is most accurate when other aspects of the person and environment are consistent with each other and with the attitude, or when these other factors are irrelevant.

Other personal characteristics can make it difficult to judge attitudes from behavior. People have different learning histories and views as to what behaviors best represent particular attitudes. Consider two white college freshmen who have a positive attitude toward blacks and who want to behave in accordance with this attitude. When they arrive on campus, each finds he has a black roommate. When they meet their roommates for the first time, the two students might behave very differently. One might be afraid of appearing overly friendly and condescending and therefore might behave in a cool, detached manner. The second student might be afraid of appearing bigoted or hostile and might instead be gushy and "too" friendly. A person watching these two students might think they held different attitudes toward blacks, even though their underlying feelings toward their new roommate were really the same.

Environmental forces also exert powerful influences on behavior. In many cases, situational pressures are powerful enough to determine behavior by themselves. For example, Stanley Milgram conducted a series of studies in which adults, in the role of "teachers," were told to deliver strong, painful electric shocks to another adult, the "learner," as part of an experiment which was supposedly investigating learning techniques. During the study, the learner screamed in pain and begged to be released. But the experimenter insisted that the "teachers" continue to deliver shocks, saying the experiment would otherwise be ruined. The situational pressures on the teachers to continue to deliver shocks were so strong that most did so, even though all of them probably wanted to stop. The teachers' relevant attitudes (toward hurting people) would not have been very effective predictors of behavior in this situation because the situational pressures on behavior were overwhelmingly strong. Milgram's studies are detailed in Chapter 8.

One of the more famous studies in social psychology was carried out by LaPiere [256]. From 1930 to 1932 he traveled around much of the western United States with a Chinese couple. LaPiere carefully noted the reactions to the Chinese couple by persons in charge of restaurants and lodging places. Treatment was usually quite courteous, and they were turned away at only 1 of 67 lodging places; none of the 184 restaurants at which they stopped refused them admittance. Later, LaPiere sent letters to these establishments and to comparable establishments that they had not visited, saying he would be traveling with a Chinese couple and asking if they had any policy against accommodating Chinese. Over 90 percent of the establishments replied that they *would* object. The figures were the same for establishments they had and had not visited. This is rather startling. From his own experience, LaPiere knew that virtually every place would accept the Chinese couple, usually with great courtesy. Yet, when asked, most establishments said they would object. If we accept the response to the letter as a measure of attitude (which is questionable), then this seems to indicate great inconsistency between attitude and behavior. But is this a fair interpretation?

This study suggests that behaviors cannot *always* be predicted accurately from attitudes. But closer analysis indicates that there are a number of good reasons why the people behaved as they did. And none of these reasons involve "inconsistent" or "illogical" behavior. Psychologically, it is quite "easy" to reject a stigmatized group by letter, especially when writing to a third party. There is no prospect of contact with the rejected group, and no personal unpleasantness is likely to ensue. Contrast this with the real situation: The well-dressed, smiling Chinese couple showed up with Dr. LaPiere, and the proprietor was forced to act immediately. In this situation rejection is much more difficult; many prejudiced proprietors may have said "yes" publicly only later to say "no" privately (by letter). Rejection in person would have had immediate consequences, possibly including embarrassment, unpleasantness, and even violence. These were good reasons for not rejecting the Chinese couple.

Other factors may have been involved, too. Were the people who met the Chinese couple and behaved courteously the *same* people who later answered LaPiere's letter? In many cases, they probably were not. One cannot talk about "inconsistency" between a person's behavior and attitude when the two measures are not even gathered from the same individual. Furthermore, what mental image did the letter bring to mind among the proprietors? Do you think they were likely to expect the personable, attractive couple that LaPiere accompanied? The proprietors might have reacted to a different *stimulus* when they answered their doors and when they answered the letters.

All these factors suggest that this well-known study may not be evidence of "inconsistency" at all. They show, though, that we must be careful in predicting behavior from attitudes. In some situations, accurate prediction is likely to be difficult or impossible [493]. However, other studies have used reliable and valid measures of attitude and behavior in situations where counter-attitudinal pressures were not strong and have found a substantial relationship between attitudes and behaviors [e.g., 486]. Nowhere is this relationship perfect; Lewin's formula: $B = f(P, E)$, makes it clear that human behavior is too complex to be accounted for completely by any single factor, including attitude.

■ HOW CAN ATTITUDES BE CHANGED?

Having discussed what attitudes are, why people hold them, how they are measured, and how they relate to behaviors, it is time to ask an important related question: How can attitudes be changed?

People change attitudes for two major reasons—to function better or to satisfy internal needs. For example, in order to *function better* in the environment, a person might become convinced that a new attitude more accurately reflects the facts about an attitude object than a present attitude does. Or, someone might show a person how a new attitude will make more sense out of the world. Or, over time, one's personality structure may undergo major changes, and an attitude that used to serve an ego-defensive function may no longer be needed for defense of the improved self-concept. That attitude then becomes excess baggage and is quite susceptible to change.

Focusing on the *social-adjustment* function of an attitude, a communicator might convince an audience that a new attitude will lead to more interpersonal rewards and will reduce the likelihood of violating social norms. Several studies indicate that attitude change may take place when a communicator simply rewards people over time (with money, praise, and so on) for expressing a revised attitude. For example, Chester Insko [223] had interviewers telephone subjects and ask their opinions about a local event. (The study was conducted at the University of Hawaii. Subjects were asked about "Aloha Week," a festival held every fall.) During the interview, subjects were reinforced verbally every time they made a favorable statement about the event; that is, the experimenter gave them an enthusiastic "Good." About one week later, during their class, the subjects were asked to complete a questionnaire containing items about a number of local issues, including "Aloha Week." Subjects who had been reinforced verbally for making favorable statements on the phone expressed more favorable attitudes about "Aloha Week" than did subjects who were not reinforced. The reinforcements they had received on one occasion apparently produced a slight change in attitudes measured on another, unrelated occasion.

Simple reinforcement techniques such as this one are limited, and you can't change the attitudes of everyone you meet simply by saying "good" or by nodding your head. The studies that have been done along these lines have tried to strengthen existing attitudes, not to change attitudes. Also, the studies have used issues which are relatively uninvolving for the subjects (such as "Aloha Week"). It is another matter to change attitudes which are highly involving and resistant to change, such as racial prejudice. But stronger reinforcements received over long periods of time (from friends, family, coworkers, and so forth) can effectively shape and change more important attitudes.

A second general reason for changing an attitude is to obtain some kind of *internal satisfaction.* For example, if a communicator can show a person that a new attitude better represents important values than an old one, it should be more satisfying to hold the new attitude. This, of course, makes use of the value-expressive function. If it can be shown that a person's old attitude is inconsistent with other related attitudes, a parallel process can be expected to occur. When one becomes convinced that a new attitude is more ethically or morally right, the internal satisfaction of holding the "right" attitude might form a strong basis for attitude change.

■ PERSUASIVE COMMUNICATIONS AND ATTITUDE CHANGE

We are bombarded constantly by stimuli that provide pressure for attitude change. In some cases, these stimuli are messages explicitly designed to produce attitude change, such as advertisements, political speeches, lectures, and so forth. But pressures to change by no means stop here. Every new experience and every new bit of information provides impetus for modifying our views. (The inflexibility which many young people see in older people refers to the *loss* of this capacity. Youth sometimes claims that older people have stopped attending to the change messages that saturate our environment, and that they cling tenaciously to outdated attitudes and values.)

Not all attitude-change messages are equally effective. From both theoretical and practical viewpoints, it is important to isolate those facets of attitude-change situations which make them more or less effective. We will examine three general factors: the *source* of the communication, the *message* itself, and the *audience* to whom the communication is directed.

Source characteristics

The source, or origin, of a communication is an important determinant of whether the message will produce attitude change. Three characteristics of the source of a communication have been studied extensively by social psychologists. These include the source's credibility, attractiveness, and power.

Credibility equals expertise and trustworthiness. "He's lost his credibility" has become a devastating phrase in recent years; it means that the source of a communication has become less effective in influencing the attitudes and behaviors of others. Ronald Ziegler, former President Nixon's press secretary, lost so much credibility with the press that reporters began to believe the opposite of what they were told during news briefings. Today a "credibility gap" has emerged not only in relation to governmental statements but also in relation to statements from advertisers, older generations, and so on. What is it about credibility that makes it so important to social influence?

Credibility describes two facets of a communication source: expertise and trustworthiness. *Expertise* is the extent of knowledge that a source displays. Numerous studies have shown that the greater a source's expertise, the greater the attitude change produced in an audience [16; 219]. When a message is received from an expert source, an audience is more likely to perceive it as "correct" and as a good description of what the world is really like than a similar message from a nonexpert source would be perceived. The audience, therefore, doesn't have to think through the arguments; they can accept the expert's communications uncritically, and the message becomes effective in changing their attitudes.

Figure 2-3. *Communicators of low and high credibility. Ronald Ziegler (right), White House Press Secretary, announcing on Aug. 8, 1974, that Richard Nixon would address the nation that night on his decision to resign from the presidency. Because of Ziegler's history of deceit, misinformation, and evasion in handling questions dealing with Watergate, his credibility as a communicator was notoriously low in the eyes of most reporters. In contrast, to millions of Americans in the 1960s and 1970s consumer advocate Ralph Nader (below) was a highly credible communicator. He was seen as an expert in his field and as trustworthy and believable. In fact, Nader often appeared on lists of "most respected people" based on public opinion surveys. Thus, most people would have evaluated the same statement much differently if it were made by Nader than if it were made by Ziegler.*

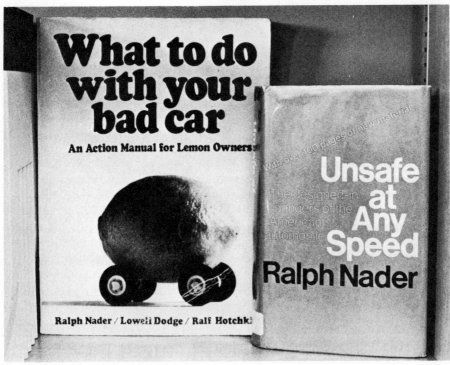

Trustworthiness refers to the intent of a source. If the source appears to have manipulative intentions and stands to gain from changing the audience's attitudes, he or she will be perceived as untrustworthy. If the source appears sincere and has no personal gain stemming from any attitude change which might occur, the source's trustworthiness will be rated high. Consider this case. You hear Gayle talking to a friend. She is enthusiastically endorsing sunflower seeds as food. She gives her friend a lot of information about the health benefits of sunflower seeds, their good taste, and so forth. Now compare this with a situation in which a person hears an advertisement by the Acme Sunflower Seed Company. Assuming that the company uses the same arguments as Gayle, which message is likely to be more effective in changing attitudes? Probably Gayle's, which seems the more sincere and impartial of the two.

Laboratory studies have demonstrated that as a source's trustworthiness increases, so does the extent of attitude change increase within an audience. It has been shown, for instance, that when people appear to argue against their own best interest (for example, when a criminal argues that police should have greater power in dealing with crime), they are more effective in producing attitude change than when they argue to support their interests (when a criminal argues that police power should be decreased) [479]. Similarly, it has been shown that "overheard" conversations are more effective in changing attitudes than are communications explicitly directed to an audience. When we overhear a communication that apparently is not meant for us, the communicator seems more trustworthy, since he or she is not trying to influence eavesdroppers. Studies [477] have shown that subjects who overheard a telephone conversation (which they apparently were not supposed to hear) were more persuaded by what they heard than were subjects who heard the same message but thought it might be designed to persuade them. For complex reasons, this effect occurred only when the issue was important and involving for the subjects, and when they tended to agree with the communicator in the first place.

Source credibility cannot be designated independently of the audience's attitudes; credibility is in the eye of the beholder. Reconsider the example of "All in the Family." Mike might view a spokesman for the American Civil Liberties Union or a college professor as highly credible. But to Archie these sources might appear worthless. Conversely, Mike probably would ridicule sources that Archie respects. No degree of sincerity or expertise by the source can overcome these basic differences in the eyes of Archie and Mike.

As we've seen, research indicates that messages of equal merit are more effective from a credible source than from a noncredible source. However, time changes all things. If an audience's attitudes are measured again several weeks or months later, a curious phenomenon occurs. Where the level of a communicator's credibility once produced vast differences in attitude change, little or no differences remain after several weeks (see Figure 2-4). Over time, the enhancing effect of a highly credible communica-

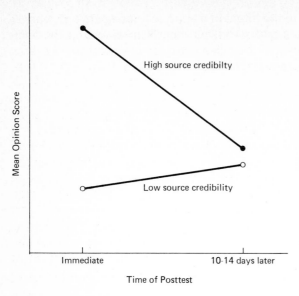

Figure 2-4. *The sleeper effect. Differences due to credibility of the source disappear over time. Several weeks after a persuasive communication has been given, the initial increase in persuasiveness due to a high-credibility source is lost. There is little or no change in the effect of a low-credibility source. (Adapted from 180, p. 135.)*

High source credibilty

Low source credibility

Mean Opinion Score

Immediate   10-14 days later

Time of Posttest

tor may be lost as the source of the message is forgotten [219]. We all have bits and pieces of information floating around in our heads for which we've forgotten the source—"Somebody said that...," "I heard somewhere ...." Some of these bits of information may have come from highly credible sources, but we've forgotten what came from where. If a person is reminded of or suddenly remembers the source of information—that is, if the identity of the communicator is *reinstated*—the differential effects of communicator credibility also reappear [244].

This phenomenon has been called the *sleeper effect:* Something happens when an audience "sleeps on" a message. However, this effect does not help a noncredible communicator; it only hurts a credible one [180]. Over time, an audience's forgetting of the credible source produces a decrease in attitude change. The noncredible source is ineffective initially, and it stays ineffective over time. Such findings indicate the difficulty of producing long-lasting attitude changes from only one exposure to a persuasive message, even if it is delivered by a credible source. Advertisers and politicians apparently recognize this, as they air the same commercial day after day, month after month, to reinstate the source of the communication. They aren't trying to put you to sleep. On the contrary, they want to ensure that a sleeper effect does not occur.

Attractiveness. A communicator's attractiveness to an audience is based on several factors, including his or her pleasantness and likeableness, physical appearance, and similarity to the audience. These aspects are closely related. For example, it has been found that we perceive people whom we like to be more similar to us than those whom we dislike. And physically attractive people are perceived as more likeable (and expert) than are physically unattractive people. Thus, each aspect of attractiveness influences perceptions of the other aspects. But despite this close relationship, social psychologists try to examine each aspect separately to determine its effects on persuasion and attitude change.

Generally, an attractive communicator produces more attitude change than does an unattractive one, and this relationship seems to hold for each aspect of attraction. An insulting, disliked communicator is relatively ineffective in changing people's attitudes. In fact, disliked individuals sometimes produce a *boomerang effect:* The audience changes its attitudes in a direction opposite to what the disliked source advocates [1]. Conversely, pleasant, likeable communicators produce large attitude changes. Those who are similar to their audience in terms of attitudes, skills, and abilities are more effective persuaders than those who are dissimilar. And physically attractive communicators are more effective than physically unattractive ones. You can see why advertisers try to pick likeable, attractive models to sell their products.

Effective communicators must walk a fine line. On the one hand, they must be perceived as experts (to some degree), or the audience will dismiss the message. On the other hand, they must not seem too dissimilar to the audience. Some experts are seen as living in ivory towers and dealing with problems far different from those of ordinary people. Consequently, an audience can reason: "Well, his ideas are appropriate for him and probably help him to function effectively in the world. But I'm in a different boat; I need to hold different attitudes in order to function effectively in *my* world." Thus, communicators must establish their expertise, but they must do it in such a way that they seem to have the same basic values, needs, problems, and desires as their audiences. Then they will seem attractive as well as expert.

Attractive communicators are more effective in changing attitudes for several reasons. First, people *identify* with them and want to be like them. One way to be like someone attractive is to adopt comparable attitudes. People imitate the accents, dress, attitudes, and behaviors of popular, attractive models. Second, attractive people frequently are considered more trustworthy and expert than unattractive people. A source who is liked is seen as having fewer axes to grind. A liked source appears to be more impartial and more concerned with the best interests of the audience. This, too, makes the source seem more trustworthy, since we don't expect people we like to mislead us or to profit at our expense. Therefore, a source's attractiveness also affects perceived credibility, and this, in turn, affects attitude change.

Power. When a source delivers a communication, a target (audience) must consider several things: "Can the source reward or punish me?" "Does the source care whether I agree?" When the answer to each of these questions is "Yes," the target of the communication is likely to be influenced. The source then has power over the target because the source can reward or punish the target, wants the target to agree, and will find out if the target did agree. The greater the source's power, the greater the influence on the target [295]. Consider the degree of conformity in a large corporation; junior executives hold opinions that are surprisingly similar to the boss's.

But is this really attitude change, or does the target merely conform to the source's opinions without privately accepting them as true? Although the behavior of junior executives may well be mere lip-service and may not indicate private agreement, evidence suggests that, over time, the ideas of those in power can become internalized and accepted privately. In the next section, we'll consider how statements that start out as "lies" come to be believed.

Message characteristics

For attitude change to occur, a communication, or message, must be delivered to an audience. A message can have special properties of its own, and these can determine the effectiveness of the message for changing attitudes.

The position advocated in a message. Of all the characteristics of a message, the one most basic is the position of the message in relation to the target's position, that is, the *discrepancy* between the message and the target's views. We saw earlier that many social psychologists define an attitude as the amount of affect for or against a psychological object. We can diagram an attitude as a point along a continuum ranging from extremely negative affect (−10) through neutral or no affect (0) to extremely positive affect (+10), as shown in Figure 2-5. Let's take the issue of the Equal Rights Amendment to the Constitution (designed to ensure women's rights) and assume that an individual's attitude toward the amendment is somewhat negative. The person feels that the amendment is unnecessary and that it allows women to be drafted into military service, a condition to which the person objects. However, the person doesn't want to return to attitudes of the Victorian age and isn't extremely negative. This person's position might be designated by −3 on the scale in Figure 2-5. Suppose a communicator wants to make this person a staunch advocate of the amendment, a person whose attitude would be near the +9 point on the scale. How should the communicator proceed? Should the communicator begin by praising the amendment as strongly as possible (a position of +10)? Or might such a large discrepancy between the target's existing attitude and the position taken in the message cause the target to dismiss the message?

Research suggests there is a limit to the amount of discrepancy which can exist between an audience's view and a communicator's. If the discrep-

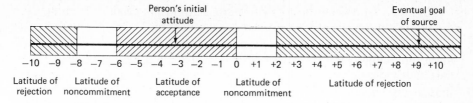

Figure 2-5. *Attitude change as a step-by-step process. Surrounding a person's attitude position (−3 in this example) is the latitude of acceptance (−6 to 0). Statements which fall within this latitude of acceptance will be seen as convincing and will lead to attitude change. Statements which fall outside of the latitude of acceptance will not lead to attitude change in the desired direction and might even cause a boomerang effect. Therefore, to change a person's attitude from −3 to +9 (in this example), the communicator would have to proceed in a step-by-step manner, with each message falling within the audience's latitude of acceptance. The first message might therefore be at the −1 or 0 point. As the attitude changes, the latitude of acceptance will change with it and previously unacceptable messages become acceptable.*

ancy is too great, the communication will be dismissed. But if the discrepancy is not great enough, the target might not notice any difference of opinion and not be motivated to change.

Muzafer Sherif and his coworkers [402; 404] have proposed that for each individual and for each attitude three distinct regions exist. Centered around one's own position is the *latitude of acceptance.* Within this range, attitude-relevant statements will be acceptable to an individual. For example, a person whose attitude toward the Equal Rights Amendment is −3 might basically accept statements judged to be from 0 to −6 and would generally agree with them. Next comes the *latitude of noncommitment.* In this range, statements are neither acceptable nor unacceptable; the person neither agrees nor disagrees with such positions. In this example, the latitudes of noncommitment fall from −6 to −8 and from 0 to +2. Next comes the *latitude of rejection,* wherein statements are unacceptable to the person. In our example, statements which were judged by the person to be +2 and above or −8 and below would be unacceptable.

The breadth of these regions varies according to an individual's *involvement* with an issue. Involving issues are those which a person considers really important. The more involving an issue is, the narrower the latitude of noncommitment and the broader the latitude of rejection. In other words, on important issues an individual will reject a greater number of positions and be noncommittal toward a fewer number. The latitude of acceptance does not seem to change as a result of involvement [404].

A communicator's credibility also affects the optimal discrepancy needed to produce attitude change. When a communicator has high credibility, it is difficult to dismiss his or her position, even if it falls within the latitude of rejection. Therefore, highly credible communicators can effectively advocate greater change than can noncredible communicators [16].

Clearly, changing attitudes in natural settings is complicated, since a communicator, to be effective, must establish high credibility and also "guess" what an audience's position is. It is thus apparent that Mike (from "All in the Family") is trying to change Archie's attitudes in the wrong way. Mike starts out with low credibility in Archie's eyes; he could produce attitude changes only by advocating positions that differ slightly from Archie's. Instead, Mike opposes Archie's position on nearly every issue, presenting him with statements that fall within Archie's latitude of rejection. Not surprisingly, Archie dismisses Mike's arguments and even moves in the opposite direction on important issues. Mike would be more successful if he tried to move Archie *a step at a time.*

As one example of the step-by-step process of attitude change, consider a study by Theodore Newcomb [320] of women attending Bennington College from 1935 to 1939, which provides clearcut evidence of such a process. At the time, Bennington was a new, rather expensive and exclusive women's college. Most students came from well-to-do families with Republican backgrounds. The faculty, on the other hand, were politically liberal and tended to support Democratic candidates and programs. A dramatic change occurred among many of the college women in terms of political ideals over their four years of college. For instance, in a straw vote prior to the 1936 presidential election, 62 percent of the freshmen but only 14 percent of the juniors and seniors "voted" Republican, while 7 percent of the freshmen and 30 percent of the juniors and seniors supported Socialist or Communist candidates. This finding may be viewed as an instance of long-term attitude change, perhaps mediated by the structures of group norms and conformity. The attitude change took place in a step-by-step manner through the four years of college.

Newcomb also investigated the relationship between sociopolitical attitudes and general knowledge. For freshmen women, there was no significant relationship between conservatism and scores on a test of general knowledge about public affairs. The information which the women had absorbed before attending Bennington apparently had not created liberal or conservative attitudes. But, for upper-level students, there was a significant relationship between scores on the general-knowledge test and liberalism. Well-informed upper-level students were more likely to hold liberal attitudes than were less well-informed students. This suggests that the information they absorbed at Bennington helped to create liberal attitudes. Newcomb also found a significant relationship between liberalism and the esteem in which women were held by their peers. Those women most frequently nominated as "most worthy to represent the college" were generally more liberal than women who were not nominated. (Of course, this evidence is correlational and does not show that liberalism *caused* popularity, any more than it shows that popularity caused women to become liberal. We can note only that these two variables were associated.)

Interestingly, a follow-up study twenty-five years later indicated that most of the college-liberalized women had retained their liberalism [323].

Most had married men with similarly liberal views. Those few who had moved back toward conservatism were likely to have married men with conservative views.

To present or not to present: The "sidedness" of a message. One message characteristic that has interested politicians and advertisers is "sidedness." When an issue has two sides, should a communicator present only the position he or she advocates, or should both sides be mentioned with the favored side stressed? The answer depends on an audience's characteristics. If an audience already agrees with the position of the communicator and the communicator's task is simply to make them agree more strongly, a one-sided message is likely to be more effective. A two-sided message might confuse such an audience, since many of them might not even be aware of the other side. But if an audience initially disagrees with the issue, a two-sided message is likely to be more effective. By presenting both sides, a communicator is apt to be perceived as more trustworthy and fair; the communicator shows the audience that he or she has considered both sides and has arrived at the "best" conclusion. In fact, merely mentioning to a skeptical audience that there are two sides to an issue (without explaining the other side) can increase a communicator's influence [235].

Similar reasoning suggests other features of the audience that are important. If an audience is relatively uneducated, a one-sided message is more effective, since it presents a position without confusion. But, if an audience is intelligent, educated, and well-versed on a topic, a two-sided communication will be more effective. Such findings have not escaped advertisers. Many advertisements in news magazines (whose readers generally are more knowledgeable on a wide variety of topics) contain two-sided messages, while ads in other magazines might concentrate on one-sided messages.

Drawing a conclusion. An issue closely related to sidedness is whether or not a communicator should draw conclusions for an audience. On the one hand, if a communicator doesn't draw a specific conclusion, he or she is likely to be considered fair and trustworthy. This increase in credibility will produce a great deal of attitude change as long as the audience can be counted on to draw the desired conclusion. On the other hand, if an audience *doesn't* draw the desired conclusion, all the credibility in the world is irrelevant, since the audience won't know what position the communicator advocates. Again, the characteristics of an audience will determine what type of message to use. When an audience is unintelligent and/or uneducated, or when a message is complex, it is best for the speaker to draw conclusions. Otherwise, the audience may not realize what the communicator wants. But when it is clear that an audience will be able to draw the desired conclusion—when an audience is intelligent and/or educated and knowledgeable about a topic, or when a message is simple—it is best to leave the conclusions unstated.

The effects of fear: How scared should an audience be? A final factor to be considered about messages is their intensity—that is, the amount of emotion they try to create in an audience. One emotion aroused by many messages is fear. For example, the television blares "Buckle up for safety," and shows a gruesome accident in which people died because they failed to fasten their seatbelts. Campaigns against smoking often include movies showing an operation on the diseased and damaged lung of a cancer patient. How effective are such attempts to scare an audience into changing attitudes?

Research indicates that fear-arousal campaigns are effective indeed. Generally, the more fear generated, the more effective the message will be in changing the attitudes and behaviors of an audience [269]. The audience is likely to pay attention to such a message and to remember what it describes. To reduce the fear aroused, a target changes his or her attitudes. This heightened attention, memory, and desire to reduce fear make fear-arousal communications effective.

But there are exceptions to this general principle, as when a communication offers an audience no clear recommendations for avoiding the fearful events, or when it is difficult to take steps to reduce the fear. For example, a message which argues that nuclear war is highly probable and shows gory scenes of nuclear destruction might not be very effective. The audience would be likely to feel powerless to avert the disaster—so why worry? In such cases, the audience will reduce the consequences by rationalizing ("It couldn't happen") or even by denying that they heard parts of the message. Thus, about one-fourth of terminally ill cancer patients who were told by their doctors that they were going to die later didn't remember having been told. Therefore, to be effective, a fear-arousing communication must give an audience some way to avoid the fearful consequences. If it doesn't, as more fear is aroused, the communication becomes less effective because the audience rationalizes and denies the message.

Individual differences also affect people's reactions to fear-arousing communications. Some people are more anxious and defensive than others. Highly anxious, defensive people are more likely to reduce fear by rationalizing or denying the communication; hence, they are less affected as fear arousal increases. Less anxious, nondefensive people, though, will act to change their attitudes and thus avoid the consequences.

Audience characteristics

In laboratory experiments, it is easy to "trap" people and deliver a persuasive communication to them. But in natural settings, it is not always easy to deliver a message to an audience. A Democratic candidate for political office may spend time and money on a special message to convince Republicans to vote for her. But when the message is aired, 90 percent of the audience is likely to consist of Democrats who have already decided that they agree with her and will vote for her. Thus, the people whom the candidate wanted to reach are never exposed to the persuasive message. Educational television programs are in a comparable situation. Many of them are designed to teach disadvantaged children what they need to know to compete; yet the children who watch such shows tend to be the ones who least need the knowledge presented.

These examples illustrate *selective exposure:* An audience tends to be exposed only to communications with which they are familiar and already agree. At first, many social psychologists felt selective exposure was a psychological process through which people (1) seek and expose themselves to information that agrees with their position because such information is comforting and reinforcing, and (2) choose to avoid exposure to information that conflicts with their position because the information shakes their views and produces tension. However, this psychological process is only part of the story. Research shows that people will seek information which is consistent with their own ideas. But people do *not* intentionally avoid information which is inconsistent with their own views: apparently, such inconsistency does not produce tension. We must look elsewhere for the complete answer.

Considerable evidence exists of a widespread phenomenon called *de facto selective exposure.* In this situation, people do not *intentionally* seek or avoid particular messages; rather, because of the subcultures to which they belong, they come into contact only with messages that support existing opinions. For example, readers of *Playboy* magazine typically are male, liberal, and young. Because they are interested in attractive women, they buy the magazine and are exposed to many advertisements and articles that support their already liberal attitudes. Similarly, conservative people in business might buy and read the *Wall Street Journal* because they want up-tó-date information about the business world. Since many of the articles and advertisements are conservative in tone, these people end up exposing themselves to ideas that support existing attitudes. Thus, behaviors that begin with another goal in mind (viewing attractive women or learning about current business trends) wind up exposing people to information that is consistent with their existing beliefs [392a].

If a communicator can get a message across, it seems logical that some people are more easily persuaded than others. Audience characteristics which have been found to be related to persuasibility include *personality characteristics* (such as self-esteem and trust), *intelligence,* and *sex.*

Personality characteristics. Individuals' personalities affect how they respond to persuasive communications. One major characteristic that has been related to attitude change is self-esteem. People with high self-esteem are less persuasible than are those with low self-esteem. People with high self-esteem view themselves as competent and have confidence in their opinions. A discrepant communication is less likely to shake their original beliefs. Also, their self-evaluation is high enough to make a credible communicator less credible; they often feel they know as much as a communicator does.

Trust also is related to persuasibility. Trusting individuals generally have been raised in situations where they learn that they can rely on the word of others. People with low trust usually have learned that others will break their word; they become suspicious and cynical about communications from others. As a result, trusting individuals are more likely to be affected by persuasive communications [180].

Intelligence. If asked, many would say that intelligent people are less persuasible than unintelligent people. However, this statement is much too simple. Highly intelligent people are not more or less persuasible than less-intelligent people; they are simply persuaded by different things. As we saw, some messages are more effective with intelligent audiences (for example, two-sided messages and messages without explicit conclusions), while other messages are more effective with unintelligent audiences (one-sided messages and messages with explicit conclusions). Similarly, intelligent individuals might be persuaded by highly complex, logical arguments, while less-intelligent individuals might be persuaded by simple, emotional arguments. Thus, persuasibility depends on the type of message used. When intelligence does influence persuasibility, it does so *indirectly* by affecting the individual's confidence in his or her opinion. If an intelligent person is confident that his or her opinion is correct, self-confidence decreases persuasibility. However, intelligence by itself does not consistently relate to how persuasible a person is.

Sex. Many researchers have found females to be more easily persuaded than males. But don't think for a moment that this relationship is inherent; it seems to result from patterns of sex-role development that exist in our society. (Sexism is explored in depth in Chapter 4.) In the past, our society presented females with a particular role to fulfill. They were taught to avoid confrontations, told that they didn't have to excel in "intellectual" matters, and informed that they didn't need to know much about anything except homemaking and "feminine" things. When presented with a persuasive message, females learned to give in—to "get along by going along." But even today, sex-role requirements in our society are changing, and females may no longer be more persuasible than males are.

■ **FROM BEHAVIOR TO ATTITUDES: OR, "WHAT HAVE I DONE? WHY, SOMETHING I WANTED TO DO, OF COURSE"**

Much research on attitudes has assumed that by changing attitudes, we can also change behaviors. But what about the other side of the coin? If behaviors are changed, will the associated attitudes also be affected? Can we legislate morality, values, and attitudes through laws that make behaviors such as segregation and discrimination illegal? And will a child learn to like spinach if gently pressured into eating it? Some experiments have provided clues to the answers to such questions.

A bad choice

Jack Brehm [67] offered eighth-grade boys a small incentive (two movie tickets or two phonograph records) if they would eat a vegetable, supposedly as part of tests for a consumer organization. Actually, the vegetable they were asked to eat was one which each boy had earlier rated as "greatly disliked." In one condition, the negative consequences of eating the vegetable were relatively small—the boy had to eat the disliked food, but at least he got his small prize. In another condition, the experimenter introduced "surprise" consequences as the boys ate. He told them that he would send a letter to their parents stating that their son had eaten the vegetable. These were high consequences indeed, since they implied that the boys might have to continue eating the nasty stuff at home. After eating, the boys were asked how much they liked the vegetable. The subjects in the surprise-consequence condition had become more positive toward the vegetable. Apparently, freely agreeing to do something which conflicted with one's attitudes (such as eating disliked foods), and then learning that the action led to dramatic *negative consequences,* produced attitude change. Evidence suggests that this change resulted from the boys' need to *justify* the behavior (eating the vegetable) to themselves. (The letters were not actually sent to the boys' parents.)

A free choice

Another experiment by Brehm [66] demonstrated how choosing between attractive alternatives could affect attitudes. Under the guise of a "market research study," college women rated eight similarly priced products, such as a radio, a coffee-maker, a watch, etc. At the end of the study, each woman was allowed to choose one of two products as a reward for her participation. Unknown to the woman, these particular two products had been selected by the experimenter specifically because she had earlier rated them as being equally attractive. In accepting one of the equally attractive products, she had to reject the other. Did her evaluations of these products change simply because now she owned one and had rejected the other? When the subjects were given the opportunity to rerate the items later, Brehm found that their evaluations did change. The products they had chosen were rated as more attractive, while the unchosen products became less attractive.

Later research has supported this finding—people tend to overvalue things they choose and to undervalue things they reject. There also is evidence [474] that a "regret phase" occasionally takes place *immediately* after the decision is made where the chosen alternative is not overvalued, and the person seems to regret his or her choice. But this phase, if it occurs at all, is short-lived and is quickly replaced by overvaluing. It should be noted that the overvaluing process occurs only when an individual has a *free choice* between the alternatives. If a person is simply given one object, or if the individual is told which object must be picked, no attitude change takes place.

A deceitful choice

Suppose a person lies. Might the person come to believe the lie? In a classic experiment, Leon Festinger and J. Merrill Carlsmith [156] found out. Males at Stanford University signed up for an experiment called "measures of performance." The experimenter brought each subject into a room and gave him several boring tasks while carefully monitoring his performance by making notes on a clipboard and checking a stopwatch. When the hour had finally passed, the experimenter told the subject that he'd like him to know what the experiment was about. "There are actually two groups in this experiment. In one, the group you're in, we bring the subject in and give him essentially no introduction to the experiment . . . but in the other, there is a student who works for us regularly . . . I introduce him as a former subject in the experiment. Then, in conversation with the next subject, he makes these points: It is very enjoyable; I had a lot of fun; I enjoyed myself; it was very interesting; it was intriguing; it was exciting. We are interested in comparing how these two groups do on the experiment—the one, with previous expectations about the experiment, and the other, like yours, with essentially none."

After further discussion, the experimenter left the room for a few minutes and then returned, looking confused, uncertain, and more than a little embarrassed. He explained that the next subject was in the other group, the group which was told that the experiment was interesting and exciting. He continued, "The fellow who usually does this [tells the lie to the subject] for us can't do it today. He just phoned in that something has come up, and we're looking for someone to do it for us. You see, we've got another subject waiting [he looks at his watch] . . . If you'd be willing to do this for us, we'd like to hire you to do it now and then be on call in the future, if something like this should happen again. We can pay you [some subjects were told the payment would be $1, while others were told $20] for doing this for us—that is, for doing it now and being on call. Do you think you can do that?" Sixty-eight of the seventy-one subjects in the experiment agreed to do it; they agreed to tell an unsuspecting person that the task was a lot of fun, when they probably thought it was terrible.

The experimenter then took the subject into another room and introduced him to a female student who supposedly was the next subject. Actually, *she* was the experimental accomplice and had been briefed on what to do. After the experimenter left, the subject struck up a conversation with the woman and began to make some positive remarks about the experiment. The woman told the subject she was surprised to hear this, because her friend had taken the experiment a week before and had told her that it was boring and that she ought to try to get out of it. The subject then had to deny that the task was dull and affirm more strongly that the experiment was fun. When the lie had been told, the female student appeared convinced. The experimenter then reentered the room and took the subject to a main office, where an interviewer from the psychology department waited to talk with him. (Subjects had been led to believe that such interviews often happen after experiments.) Actually, the interviewer was interested only in how the subject would evaluate the task.

To sum up, some subjects agreed to tell a lie (and be on call in the future) for a payment of only $1. Other subjects agreed to do it for $20. Still others—the control group—simply completed the boring task and then gave their opinions to the interviewer. (The control condition was used to see how subjects would evaluate the task when they didn't lie.) The experimenters found that subjects who were offered only a minimal incentive ($1) for lying changed their attitudes toward the task, later saying that they found it somewhat interesting and enjoyable. Subjects in the control condition and subjects who had told the lie for a large incentive ($20) said they felt the task was uninteresting and unenjoyable.

Here is evidence that counterattitudinal behavior (in this case, lying) can sometimes produce attitude change. At least two factors determine how much attitude change will follow such counterattitudinal behavior. One is the amount of *personal responsibility* felt when engaging in the attitude-discrepant behavior. People feel more responsible for their actions when they have a high degree of choice as to whether or not to perform the behavior, or, as in the Festinger and Carlsmith experiment, when they are given *very little* monetary incentive for it [188]. In these cases, subjects felt free to decline but went ahead with the behavior anyway. When personal responsibility is high, attitude change is more likely to occur. On the other hand, when people simply are told that they *must* do something they otherwise wouldn't, or when they are offered a great deal of money, they feel less responsible for the action and show little or no attitude change.

Another factor determining attitude change concerns the *consequences* of counterattitudinal behavior. If the results of the behavior seem inconsequential, they can be dismissed easily. But if the consequences of the behavior are great (if they harm or deceive someone, or if they make someone appear foolish), the behavior can't be so easily dismissed, and attitude change is more likely to occur. It has been found that people will change their attitudes to correspond with counterattitudinal actions only (1) when they feel personally responsible for engaging in the behavior and (2) when the consequences of the behavior are high [104; 387; 446].

In practical terms, such findings suggest that if you want to change an attitude by having people engage in a counterattitudinal behavior, you should apply only enough "force" to get them to perform the behavior, so that they feel free to refuse but don't (and therefore feel responsible). You then should convince them that their behavior has significant consequences [109]. Other provocative research findings that relate to these ideas are presented in Focuses 2-1 and 2-2.

In search of an explanation

When a person makes a free choice between alternatives, or when a person freely does something and learns that it produced negative consequences, or when a person is responsible for a harmful lie, attitude change will bring the relevant attitudes in line with the behavior. Why should this be so? There are several theoretical explanations.

Cognitive dissonance: How do I reduce the tension? *Cognitive dissonance theory,* a major theoretical position in social psychology, has generated more research than any other. Indeed, it stimulated the experiments described above. The theory was proposed by Leon Festinger [155], and its basics are simple and straightforward. Festinger proposed that any two "cognitive elements" (any knowledge, opinion, or belief about the world, about oneself, or about one's behavior) can exist in one of three general relationships. The cognitive elements can be irrelevant (no relationship to each other), consonant (consistent with one another), or dissonant (opposite to one another). For example, consider the cognitive elements "Cigarette smoking seems to cause serious illness and shortened life expectancy" and "I smoke." Presuming a person has no suicidal tendencies, these cognitions are dissonant. However, the cognitions "Cigarette smoking seems to cause serious illness and shortened life expectancy" and "I don't smoke" fit together nicely; that is, they are consonant. Finally, the cognitions "Cigarette smoking seems to cause serious illness and shortened life expectancy" and "I'm wearing red pants" are irrelevant to each other. Festinger proposed that when two cognitive elements are in a dissonant relationship, *psychological tension,* or discomfort, motivates a person to reduce the dissonance. The more important the two cognitions are felt to be, or the greater the ratio of dissonant to consonant cognitions that concerns a specific topic, the greater is the dissonance caused by inconsistency.

In terms of the reasons for changing attitudes which were presented earlier, cognitive dissonance theory deals directly with *internal satisfaction.* Dissonance describes a state of internal dissatisfaction. According to Festinger, to reduce dissonance an individual may change an attitude, change the disonant behavior, or seek new information or social support to strengthen one of the cognitive elements.

A cigarette smoker who must deal with dissonance created by the behavior might change his or her attitude toward medical research indicating smoking is harmful. The smoker might decide that the research is meaningless and quote an introductory statistics book to the effect that "correlation does not imply causation." Or the person might stop smoking

FOCUS 2-1   GREAT EXPECTATIONS

Suppose you have invested much time and money to gain membership in a group, such as a fraternity or a sorority. You are admitted only after undergoing a rather distasteful period of hazing—your initiation into the group. Then you discover, after finally being accepted, that you don't like the people and that the activities are tedious and boring. Your expectations of a wonderful time have been drastically disconfirmed. What do you do?

Aronson and Mills [15] carried out an experiment to see what would happen in such a situation. Female subjects were told that the experiment involved an investigation of group discussions concerning the psychology of sex—a topic that interested prospective group members. Before any prospective member could join one of the discussion groups, she was given an individual "screening test" to determine her "suitability" for the group. The *severity* of this screening test or initiation was varied. In the severe initiation condition, the woman had to read to the male experimenter a list of obscene words and two sexually vivid passages from contemporary novels. (This initiation might not seem as "severe" today as it did in the mid-1950s when this study was carried out.) In the mild initiation condition, the subject read a rather innocuous list of sex-related words. Every subject in both conditions was told that she had passed the test and was eligible to join the group. A third group of subjects was given no initiation at all.

The subject's participation in the first meeting of the group, however, was limited to listening through earphones to what was described as an ongoing discussion by the group on the aspects of sexual behavior in animals. It was suggested to each subject that overhearing the discussion without participating would give her an opportunity to get acquainted with how the group operated. What each subject actually heard was a tape recording of a discussion designed to be as dull and boring as possible. Hence, the subject's expectations that the group would be interesting and worthwhile were clearly disconfirmed.

It had been proposed that subjects who were in the severe initiation condition would experience the most disappointment at having their expectations disconfirmed, since they had "worked" hardest to gain entrance to the group. Therefore, these subjects might have to rationalize their behaviors in order to convince themselves that they had, after all, made a correct decision by joining the group. One way they could rationalize their behaviors would be to view the discussions as more worthwhile and valuable than did those women in the mild initiation and no initiation groups. And this is indeed what was found. After undergoing a severe initiation, subjects rated the group discussions much more positively than did subjects in either of the other conditions.

Apparently, subjects who underwent a severe initiation rationalized their behavior to make it appear more reasonable and intelligent. Other research [176] has shown the same pattern of results even when the subject's task and the initiation are of an entirely different sort. Therefore, it appears that severe initiation procedures, when used to gain admission to a group which turns out to be disappointing, are likely to lead to a more positive evaluation of the group than mild initiation procedures or no initiation at all. These findings have obvious relevance to the sometimes severe initiation procedures used by college sororities and fraternities, not to mention the rigors of boot camp prior to full-fledged membership in the military.

It may have occurred to you that there is another factor which might complicate things. Theorists and researchers have generally *assumed* that the people they study have reasonably high self-esteem and consider themselves reasonable, intelligent, and so forth. But what about subjects who consider themselves to be clods? Perhaps such a person would *expect* to expend a lot of energy to join a worthless group. Indeed, it is just what they would expect: "Well, I've blown it again. This group isn't worth a hoot and, as usual, I busted a gut to get into it."

This notion apparently has some validity. Research indicates, for example, that failure is not disturbing to people who truly and deeply expect to fail. For people who *do* have such negative expectations (low self-esteem), failure does not lead to rationalization and attitude change. In fact, *success* is what is troubling and needs to be rationalized [14].

FOCUS 2-2   DOES YOUR WORLD END IF THEIRS DOESN'T?

In the 1950s a woman (Mrs. Keech) in a Midwestern town apparently began receiving messages from outer space. These messages supposedly came from the planet Clarion and were transmitted by means of automatic writing. (Mrs. Keech's hand wrote out messages that apparently did not come from her mind but were imposed by external beings.) Gradually, Mrs. Keech gathered a number of followers who were interested in the messages. Some group members were college students, and one of the leaders was a doctor at a university health center. The ideas with which the group identified itself were a mixture of mysticism, science fiction, and Christianity. In September Mrs. Keech received a prediction that the world would be destroyed on December 21 by flood and earthquake.

Among those who joined Mrs. Keech's group of disciples were three social psychologists (Festinger, Riecken, and Schachter) and four graduate students, none of whom were "true believers" but all of whom were interested in the effects of disconfirmed expectancies. (They concealed their true identities and intentions from the group members, which raises ethical questions about such "infiltration.") The psychologists had read of Mrs. Keech's group in the newspapers and were very anxious to observe the progress of the group. They assumed that Mrs. Keech's prediction of doom *would be* disconfirmed; they wanted to see what would happen then. Although the regular group members varied in the depth of their commitment, the core of the group was dedicated to the extent that several members gave away all their worldly possessions, since they would no longer be needing them. Mrs. Keech's message also indicated that a flying saucer would land on the evening of December 20 to rescue the small group of faithful followers before the disaster took place.

So came the fateful night of December 20. The group, most of whom assembled at Mrs. Keech's house, expected to be picked up by the flying saucer at midnight. The hour came and went, but no flying saucer appeared. After the hour had passed and it became clear that the saucer was *not* going to arrive, shock and frozen disbelief gripped the adherents.

At 4:45 A.M., Mrs. Keech called the group together to announce that she had just received a special message from Clarion. Part of the message proclaimed, "For this day it is established that there is but one God of Earth, and He is in thy midst, and from His hand thou hast written these words. And mighty is the word of God—and by His word have ye been delivered and at no time has there been such a force loosed upon the Earth" [158, p. 169]. The rest of the message went on to describe how the powers of Clarion had decided to spare the world from the cataclysm because of the impressive faith of this small group of followers. If we look upon this message with a cold and cynical eye, we can only have the greatest respect for Mrs. Keech—what a fantastically effective way to rationalize the behavior of the group members!

But what would the group do after this disconfirmation? Assuming Mrs. Keech's message had reduced some (but probably not all) of the great disappointment or feelings of foolishness which had been created, shouldn't the group members simply slink off, trying to forget what fools they had made of themselves? This seems logical; however, precisely the opposite happened. Prior to the disconfirmation, the group had not particularly desired publicity, and had discouraged reporters and the curious. Now, however, members of the group became very active. They took turns telephoning wire services and newspapers to publicize their explanation of the prophecy and its apparent failure. They tried diligently to recruit new members. And, strange as it may seem, this is precisely the type of behavior that the psychologists had predicted.

Assuming that a good deal of tension was still present, how could it be further reduced? Perhaps, Festinger, Riecken, and Schachter argued, it could be reduced by increasing social support for their ideas. And one way to increase social support is to recruit additional members who accept those ideas. Apparently, this is what the group members tried to do.

Groups such as this are not common. About 1960, however, a group known as the Church of the True Word, consisting of 135 men, women, and children, built fallout shelters near a small town in the Southwest. The group spent forty-two days and nights in the fallout shelters in the expectation that the world would be decimated by nuclear war. Again, obviously, the group's expectation was not met. What did these group members do after emerging from their self-imposed burial?

Contrary to Mrs. Keech's group, the members of the Church of the True

Word did not immediately attempt to recruit new members. Rather, they avoided curious tourists and expressed indifference to attempts by Civil Defense officials to present them with a public service medal. Why the difference? Hardyck and Braden [196], the psychologists who observed this latter group (although they did not go so far as to join them in the fallout shelters), proposed that certain crucial differences existed. First, the church group was considerably larger than Mrs. Keech's group; hence, adequate social support may have already been available within the group itself. If so, then seeking increased membership to gain social support was not necessary. Second, the church group was not subjected to as much ridicule as was Mrs. Keech's group. Apparently, it is seen as silly to wait for flying saucers to rescue you, but fairly sensible to fear nuclear war, build fallout shelters, and take refuge in them. So perhaps, this lessened ridicule meant that the church members did not feel as much need to rationalize as the members of Mrs. Keech's group had.

Several writers (for example, Carmichael [89]), have argued that Jesus Christ predicted the immediate coming of a Kingdom of Heaven on Earth within the lifetime of his followers. If such a prediction was specifically made, or if a number of adherents *thought* it had been made, subsequent events contradicted it. Could it be that Christian evangelism in its early days was actually an attempt to rationalize disappointment in the wake of a disconfirmed prediction? This is an unanswerable question, but the analysis is an intriguing one.

---

and change the troublesome behavior. At a more devious level, smokers might change their perception of the behavior by deciding that they really don't smoke very much or don't inhale very deeply, or they may smoke a low-tar cigarette to minimize the danger. To strengthen one of the cognitive elements by adding consonant cognitions, smokers might reaffirm all the positive aspects of smoking: It offers them relaxation, social poise, and so forth. Or they might decide that they'd rather live a shorter, happy life than a longer, dull one.

Much research evidence has been gathered relating to cognitive dissonance and attitude and behavior change. One basic revision of the theory has been suggested: It makes better theoretical sense to speak not of inconsistency between two cognitive elements but rather of inconsistency between a *self-concept* and cognitions of behavior that violate the self-concept [14]. In the case of smoking, for example, dissonance arises between the self-concept, "I am a reasonable, sensible person," and the cognition, "Smoking is a behavior which is likely to shorten my life and therefore is unreasonable." This revision of dissonance theory still rests on the proposition that dissonant cognitive elements (one of which must include a self-concept belief) produce psychological tension that must be reduced.

(a)

SMOKING IS VERY SOPHISTICATED

AMERICAN CANCER SOCIETY

(b)

Figure 2-6. *Both of these messages are attempts to change attitudes about cigarettes and smoking behavior. The Newport ad (a) attempts to associate smoking with fun, excitement, and sophistication. The American Cancer Society ad (b) focuses on this same type of association, but with a drastically different intent. Which ad do you find more convincing?*

According to dissonance theory, the results described earlier were produced because subjects changed their attitudes to reduce dissonance. For example, let us return to the case of a person who makes a free choice between two equally attractive alternatives. By making the choice, the person faces some possibly negative aspects of the item chosen and some possibly positive aspects of the item rejected. (If you've ever bought a car, you know how this works.) This situation should produce dissonance, since the cognitions, "I am a reasonable, intelligent person" and "I am choosing a product that may be the poorer of the two," are potentially opposite. Assuming that dissonance is uncomfortable and motivates dissonance-reducing behavior, subjects can justify their decisions to themselves by increasing their evaluations of the attractiveness of the chosen object and/or by deciding that the rejected object was less attractive than they had thought earlier.

Consider the Festinger-Carlsmith experiment about counterattitudinal behavior. After lying to the supposedly unsuspecting women students, subjects were confronted with the cognitions "I am a moral, decent, human being" and "I just told a lie and misled someone." How could the subjects deal with the dissonance? One way would be to point to aspects of the situation that justified the decision to lie. Subjects who were offered $20 to lie had twenty very good reasons to do what they did, and this should reduce some of the dissonance. Thus, subjects who received a large incentive should have experienced relatively little dissonance and, therefore, did not have to change their attitudes. But subjects who accepted only $1 to lie did not have such good external reasons to justify their action, and they should have experienced a great deal of dissonance. To reduce it, they might convince themselves that the behavior wasn't really a lie; hence, they came to evaluate the task more positively. According to dissonance theory, when the consequences of a behavior are high and when a person has few external reasons for action (is personally responsible), a great deal of dissonance is generated, and some attitude change should occur. Dissonance theory has also been used to explain the effects of disconfirmed expectancies, which were described in Focuses 2-1 and 2-2. In these cases, group members changed their attitudes toward their group and its attractiveness in order to reduce the dissonance caused when their expectancies were not confirmed.

Self-perception: How do I look to myself? *Self-perception theory,* developed by Daryl Bem [42; 43] proposes that, just as we often infer others' attitudes by watching them behave, so we often infer our *own* attitudes by watching ourselves behave. In situations where we "see" ourselves doing something unusual (eating a disliked vegetable or telling a lie), we may use this information to revise our estimate of what our attitudes must be. Seen from this perspective, people who choose one object and reject another do not experience discomfort. Instead, they simply infer that since they chose one over the other, they must like the chosen object more than the unchosen one. In the Festinger-Carlsmith experiment, subjects who lied for $20 have an external reason for the behavior; that is, they can tell themselves that they behaved as they did to get the money, not because they liked the boring task. Subjects who received only $1, however, could not "explain" their behavior by pointing to the small amount of money. Instead, to find a reason for their behavior, they had to infer that they must have liked the task, or they would not have said what they did. This theory makes many of the same predictions that dissonance theory does, but it suggests that the *process* by which attitudes are changed is different. Instead of the state of psychological tension that dissonance theory describes, self-perception theory suggests a more neutral, passive process wherein individuals simply change their perception of their attitude. Once a behavior occurs, the individual looks around to learn what might have caused it. If an external reason for the behavior is apparent (such as a large amount of money), the person infers that he or she engaged in the behavior for that reason. If no such external cause is present, the person infers that his or her attitude must be consistent with the behavior, since nothing else could have caused the behavior to occur.

Impression management: How do I look to others? Tedeschi, Schlenker, and Bonoma [445] took a third approach to these problems. They theorized that society teaches people to behave consistently. We learn that behaving inconsistently, making foolish choices, telling lies, and harming other people will be punished by observers of these actions. Therefore, people try to avoid being "caught" behaving in these ways. When a person is caught, he or she will try to rationalize and make it appear to observers that the action wasn't inconsistent, foolish, deceitful, or harmful. In other words, subjects *manage the impressions* they create in order to look like "good," consistent people. Observers then won't punish or dislike them. The more responsible a person seems for an action, the more that person engages in impression management to rationalize the behavior. Thus, this theory explains the same data in a different way. In contrast to dissonance theory and self-perception theory, the theory of impression management views people as actively changing attitudes in order to receive rewards and to avoid punishments. Subjects are seen neither as being upset by psychological inconsistency nor as passively inferring their attitudes from their behaviors.

■ RESISTING PERSUASION

So far, we have been concerned with how attitude change may be set in motion and the theories that predict and explain such changes. What about the other side of the coin? How can we make persuasive attempts *less* effective?

Again, Archie and Mike in "All in the Family" provide us with examples of the various procedures. Imagine an argument between Archie and Mike

Figure 2-7. *Impression management at its extreme. Public figures have always been conscious of the image they project to others. This is particularly true of politicians, who depend on the approval of voters in order to gain public office and remain there. In his best-selling book, Joe McGinnis detailed the complex and somewhat devious measures employed by the media experts who worked for Richard Nixon during the 1968 presidential campaign. Their task was to manage the impression that Nixon made, to "sell" him to the public as intelligent, knowledgeable, peace-loving, and competent. There is some question as to how effective this high-powered public relations campaign really was, since Nixon enjoyed a huge lead (according to the public opinion polls) early in the campaign, but lost almost all of it by election time and achieved only a very narrow victory.*

in which each is trying to persuade the other. Research shows that one way to resist persuasion is to *derogate the source* of the communication. For example, Archie might call Mike and his friends Communists, pinko-liberals, hippies, and queers. This is an effective way for Archie to reject all arguments made by Mike and his friends. Similarly, Mike might label Archie and his coworkers Fascists, red-necks, and bigots. Again, this spares Mike the need to reply directly to Archie's arguments.

Another way to resist persuasion is to *refute the arguments* of a persuasive source. This requires a rational mode of operation and is more difficult to carry out. Persuasive communications usually are designed to resist refutation, and people usually do not have enough information to refute every type of communication. Also, even a brilliant refutation may be ineffective if the source of the communication refuses to accept it. Hence, arguments probably are refuted less often than we might expect.

Still another way to resist persuasion is to *reject* the persuasive arguments. In this case, a target does not try to refute the arguments logically or to cast aspersions on their source; instead, the arguments are dismissed absolutely as being stupid and not worthy of comment. The interactions between Archie and Mike provide many instances of such behavior. Their arguments often end with one of them, usually Archie, saying, "I don't want to talk about it anymore."

Less visible defensive procedures might also be used. The literature of clinical psychology is full of examples in which Freudian defense mechanisms such as *denial* are used to resist persuasive attempts, even when the attempts are intended to help a person regain psychological health. We often can see the operation of *rationalization* and *distortion* in people's perceptions of others' arguments. There are innumerable ways to distort, misperceive, deny, and otherwise act in a nonrational manner when faced with persuasive communications. For many people in many situations, such behaviors are common.

The characters in "All in the Family" can be seen from a somewhat different perspective. Imagine that Archie's daughter, Gloria, is about to leave home for college. Assume that Gloria has been versed in Archie's attitudes and values and that Archie knows Gloria may meet many "evil forces" at college—hippies, liberals, weird professors, and so on. Archie doesn't want Gloria's attitudes and behaviors to be changed by these sources. What can he do to make her resist attitude change? How can he increase the chances that Gloria will emerge from college still holding the attitudes and values Archie considers right?

William McGuire [294] has suggested that people can be *trained* to resist persuasion. Drawing an analogy from medical practices, McGuire proposed that just as people are most susceptible to infections against which they have not built up an immunity, they will be most susceptible to counterarguments against which they have not built up defenses. McGuire proposed, therefore, that training people to defend their positions should make them less susceptible to later attitude-change pressures. To test these ideas, McGuire and his coworkers worked with truisms about health, such as the benefits of annual chest x-rays, the merits of penicillin, and the value of frequent tooth brushing. Since these truisms are seldom questioned in our culture, McGuire reasoned that people should not have much experience in defending such practices. He then exposed subjects to one of four types of "defensive training." Training was either refutational (learning to refute persuasive communications) or supportive (creating arguments to support positions one holds); these procedures were either active or passive, depending on whether the refutations or arguments were developed by the person or provided by someone else.

McGuire's research indicated that passive-refutational training was most effective in "inoculating" people against counterarguments. It might seem that active training should be more effective than passive. But McGuire suggested that passive training was more effective because people were not very good at the task—they were not used to developing refutational or supporting arguments for these truisms. Therefore, they wasted a lot of time and came up with ineffectual arguments. The overall training was more effective in passive situations where subjects were *given* effective supporting arguments or effective refutations.

Research has measured attitudes in five major ways. Most frequent is this research suggest? To provide Gloria with passive-refutational training, Archie should forewarn her and illustrate how her beliefs are likely to be attacked, suggesting refutations and counterarguments to oppose the attacks. Besides specific training, such procedures might induce a *set* in Gloria to judge as poor *all* arguments that disagree with her present attitudes. Had Archie known about inoculation theory and practiced it, he might never have had to contend with a son-in-law like Mike.

■ SUMMARY

Attitudes form a major area of research and theory within social psychology. *Attitude* is typically defined in one of two ways: It is considered to be a positive or negative affective response toward a psychological object, or it is thought to contain three components—affective, cognitive, and behavioral. In either case, attitudes are learned, they are inferred from behaviors, they affect behaviors, and they are affected by behaviors. Holding an attitude can serve important functions for an individual, including a knowledge function, a social-adjustment function, a value-expressive function, and an ego-defensive function.

Research has measured attitudes in five major ways. Most frequent is the self-report, primarily because it is easy to administer and score. Other attitude measures include observing overt behaviors, assessing performance on objective tasks, obtaining reactions to ambiguous stimuli, and assessing physiological reactions. To ensure valid measurements, it is always best to use as many different measures of attitude as possible.

Attitudes often change when a person encounters persuasive communication. The effectiveness of persuasive communications has been studied by dividing the attitude-change process into three phases: (1) the source phase, (2) the message phase, and (3) the target phase. An ideal persuasive source is credible, attractive, and powerful. Message factors which are important include the position of a message relative to a target's views, the form of a message, and the intensity of emotion (such as fear) aroused by a message. Target factors which influence attitude change include personality characteristics, intelligence, and sex.

One way to change people's attitudes is to change their behaviors. When a person behaves in a counterattitudinal fashion, attitude change will occur to the extent that the person feels personally responsible for the behavior and the consequences it has produced.

An individual can resist persuasion in several ways: by derogating the source of the communication, by refuting the arguments in the communication, and by rejecting the arguments outright. A more elaborate method can be used to train people to resist persuasion; they can be inoculated against persuasion by having their resistance to persuasive messages built up.

3

ethnic prejudice

concepts

Prejudice is an unjustified negative attitude about groups or classes of people.

Stereotypes are unjustified generalizations.

Competition and exploitation, conformity to social norms, perceived belief dissimilarity, and the structure of society itself can all lead to prejudice and discrimination.

Authoritarian, dogmatic, and cognitively simple individuals tend to be more prejudiced than others.

Certain institutions of society tend to promote racism.

Procedures of attitude and behavior change can work to reduce prejudice.

Equal-status contact may be a very effective way of reducing prejudice.

targets

After studying this chapter, you should be able to:

1   Distinguish among the terms *prejudice, discrimination,* and *stereotype.*
2   Discuss examples of how competition, conformity, and feelings of relative deprivation foster prejudice.
3   Describe which different types of personalities are often associated with prejudice.
4   Identify different tactics for prejudice reduction.
5   Describe the aspects of a contact situation which are necessary for prejudice reduction to occur.

The concept of prejudice is familiar. It and related concepts like "discrimination" and "racism" have become a part of everyday language. But when it comes to pinpointing specific cases of prejudice, not everyone agrees. Consider these situations:

Mr. Bradley invites several acquaintances to a formal party at his country club. He then learns, much to his surprise, that one friend is Jewish. His country club has strict rules excluding Jews from club activities. Mr. Bradley calls the Jewish friend and apologetically explains that although he thinks the anti-Jewish rule is stupid, the other members support it. Therefore, he feels his friend would be uncomfortable in the hostile setting, and—for his friend's own sake—it would be better if he did not attend.

A white taxi driver bypasses a black to pick up a white passenger. When asked why, he explains that most of the blacks live in a ghetto area where the crime rate is very high and where cabbies are often robbed and beaten. He explains that he does not want to take that chance himself. He therefore avoids picking up black passengers.

These examples show *discrimination,* in the sense that people are *treated differently* because of some characteristic such as religion or race. Typically, the characteristic identifies the person as a member of an ethnic group. In the social sciences, the term *ethnic group* refers to any group defined by nationality (such as Russians, Chinese, or Americans), or by race (such as blacks), or by common cultural and religious heritage (such as Jews).

The question now becomes, Does either of the above cases represent prejudice? Typically, people disagree considerably about these examples. This disagreement extends not from the examples themselves, but from more basic disagreements about what prejudice is and how it is manifested.

■ WHAT IS PREJUDICE?

Most social scientists agree that prejudice is a type of negative intergroup attitude—that is, a negative attitude toward a group or its members. We may have negative attitudes toward many individuals and groups. Yet not all such attitudes are instances of prejudice. What seems to separate the concept of prejudice from other negative attitudes is a judgment as to its appropriateness. *Prejudice is an unjustified negative attitude toward a group or its members* [69].

A major distinction between discrimination and prejudice is one between what people *do* and what they *feel.* As a result, it is possible to discriminate without being prejudiced, as *might* be the case with Mr. Bradley in the first example. It is also possible to treat people from different ethnic groups in the same way, yet still feel negatively about representatives of one of the groups [137]. An example might be a taxi driver who treats all passengers the same, but who thinks Chicanos are worthless. More often, however, people's feelings about others are reflected in their behavior.

We said that prejudice is an *unjustified* negative attitude. There are several ways in which an attitude can be unjustified. First, it may be based on faulty or illogical reasoning. For example, the fact that many members of a group may be unemployed does *not* necessarily mean they are "lazy" or that they "lack ambition" as the prejudiced person might suggest. Second, it could be unjustified because it is an overgeneralization (not *all* members of *any* group are alike). Third, it could be based on incorrect beliefs or information (the rate of unemployment may be quite low in that group. Fourth, an attitude might be unjustified because it leads the attitude holder to engage in discriminatory treatment of group members (for example, not hiring them or paying them less for their work). Basically, then, standards for determining whether an attitude is justified can focus on the *process* through which the attitude is acquired (faulty reasoning), on the character of the attitude *itself* (overgeneralization, incorrect basis), or on the *consequences* of that attitude for the attitude object (discrimination, mistreatment).

Whenever we expect to meet and interact with someone about whom we know very little, our behavior is guided by whatever generalizations are available. We must start somewhere, and if, for example, the individual is an Italian woman, we might try to remember what others have said about Italian women "in general." These generalizations about ethnic and other groups represent our *beliefs* about the groups. Whenever they are unjustified (as defined above), they are *stereotypes. Ethnic stereotypes are unjustified generalizations about an ethnic group or its members.* Here are some examples of ethnic stereotypes: Italian men are great lovers; white Southerners are all prejudiced toward blacks; blacks have natural rhythm; Jews are all shrewd with money. The basic problem with a stereotype, as with prejudice, has to do with its unjustifiable basis and its failure to treat people as individuals. The distinction between stereotypes and prejudice is comparable to the difference between beliefs and attitudes.

Ethnic prejudice and discrimination are the subjects of this chapter. So far, we have talked as though there is one, and only one, prejudicial attitude that people have regarding any ethnic group. This is definitely not the case. A person can generate an infinite variety of unjustified negative attitudes. For example, Stuart Cook and his associates have attempted to construct a "multi-factor racial attitude inventory" of whites' attitudes toward blacks [504]. After much refinement, a number of different dimensions were found to be meaningful, relatively independent, and measurable. These dimensions concerned integration-segregation policies, acceptance of blacks in close personal relationships, beliefs about black inferiority and superiority, ease in interracial contacts, subtle derogatory beliefs, beliefs about private rights versus minority group rights, and so on. Since some of these dimensions appear to be conceptually similar, Brigham and Severy [71] analyzed the

(a)

Figure 3-1. (a) *Stereotypes in action. The radio program* Amos 'n Andy *was immensely popular in the 1940s and 1950s. The main characters—Amos, Andy, Kingfish, Sapphire—personified and reinforced the negative racial stereotypes held by many whites, whereby blacks were seen as lazy, shiftless, irresponsible, and unintelligent. Ironically, the two men who played Amos and Andy in the radio program, Freeman F. Gosden (left) and Charles F. Correll (right), were both white.*

views of white college students regarding the above topics and discovered four classifications of people. They found that one group was *status* prejudiced (disliked having blacks in positions whose status was equal to or higher than their own), another *policy* prejudiced (favored discriminatory laws and policies), and a third *contact* prejudiced (disliked personal, intimate interracial contact). A last group appeared to be relatively unprejudiced. So, it appears that there really are different types of prejudice demonstrated even when one focuses on a single target group.

■ CAUSES OF ETHNIC PREJUDICE

The important factors in the development of racial attitudes in America have been extensively studied by social scientists. The more important determinants are discussed below.

(b)

(c)

(b) *Victims of prejudice and stereotypes. Japanese-American families probably embodied the "American spirit" as much as any group within our society. Yet, when World War II broke out, 112,000 Japanese-Americans (70,000 of whom were American citizens) living on or near the West Coast were forcibly evacuated to ten "relocation centers" stretching from eastern California to Arkansas. Their property was confiscated and their constitutional guarantees were suspended. Economic losses averaged nearly $10,000 per family. Yet, not a single documented case of sabotage was carried out by a Japanese-American during the entire war! This "relocation" resulted from fear, prejudice, political expediency, and desire for economic gain by majority-group Americans.*

(c) *The plight of the true native American, the American Indian, is depicted in the wooden statues of "cigar store Indians" which used to grace many storefronts. The Indian population, estimated at 1 to 3 million when Columbus "discovered" America, had been slashed by disease and destruction to only 260,000 in 1910. It was not until 1924 that these native Americans were even granted the right to become American citizens. Once again, prejudice and desire for economic gain (in this case, land) led to the brutal mistreatment of an American minority group.*

Figure 3-2. *The changing structure of American society. Historically, American society has been structured so that many occupations were not open to women or minority group members. This black man and woman (opposite page) are in positions in the 1970s (policeman*

Competition and exploitation

The way in which competition and conflict between groups can produce intergroup hostility has been vividly demonstrated by the "Robber's Cave" study described in Chapter 1 [403]. Recall that Sherif and his coworkers set up and ran a summer camp for a group of boys (all white) near Robber's Cave, Oklahoma. After an initial period of harmony, the boys were divided into two groups and housed separately in two cabins, and a series of competitive events between the two cabins was conducted. As Sherif and his coworkers had expected, this arrangement quickly led to conflict, hostility, stereotyping, and ambushes and raids between the two groups. Recall that to reduce the hostility, the experimenters then set up a series of situations involving goals which were more important and wide-ranging than the fighting between the two groups. To achieve these *superordinate goals,* cooperation and interdependence between the groups were necessary to solve common problems. While these activities did not immediately end the hostility, they did lead to a gradual reduction in unfriendliness and conflict.

Thus competition can be one cause of ethnic prejudice between groups.

and disc jockey) which would have been almost completely closed to them less than twenty years ago. Such occupational changes may increase the likelihood of equal-status contact between ethnic groups and hence lead to further reductions in levels of prejudice.

In fact, Vanneman and Pettigrew [469] discuss only two forms of racism in their research on politics and race. These forms are competitive racism (similar to status prejudice) and contact racism (contact prejudice). An obvious demonstration of the importance of competition in prejudicial behavior can be noted in the membership levels of different minority groups in skilled and semiskilled trade unions. A U.S. Department of Labor survey conducted in four of our large cities in the middle 1960s indicated that *not one* black apprentice was employed in these cities in the occupations of plumbing, steamfitting, sheetmetal work, painting, lathing, glazing, and stone masonry [271].

Another aspect of competition is frustration which may occur. An individual may experience frustration both through actual competition and through worrying about loss of status. Certainly in "All in the Family," Frustration and fear of losing status are often apparent in Archie's ethnic attitudes. As we will discuss more thoroughly in Chapter 7, the frustration-aggression hypothesis is the notion that as a result of frustration, aggression may occur—either against the source of the frustration or against a substitute object. In the United States, for example, blacks have often served as *scapegoats* for frustrated whites. A particularly gruesome example arising from economic problems involves lynchings of blacks in the South from 1882 until 1930 [218]. It was found that whenever the price of cotton decreased, the number of lynchings increased. The economic situation may have created frustrations in the white cotton farmers that were vented on blacks.

While hostility may arise from competition and conflict, it also may serve to provide a *rationale* for ongoing *exploitative* behavior. That is, a member of a group that unfairly exploits another group may feel uncomfortable about the behavior. Further, if the person's behavior is challenged ("Why are you mistreating them?"), he or she has an embarrassing problem. One response would be to stop the exploitation. Another would be to change one's self-concept ("I do it because I'm a rotten person."). But if people cannot, or do not want to, make either of these changes, what can they do? They can try to show that the members of the exploited group *deserve* their treatment, that the ethnic group really does not merit better treatment, and, furthermore, that the exploitation actually helps them to develop in many ways. In the early 1800s, when the institution of slavery was attacked and when slaveowners and their sympathizers were forced to defend the institution, proslavery writings and speeches about blacks in America became more savagely hostile. A primary defense of slavery was to attack the character and intelligence of blacks, to try and suggest that slavery was what they deserved.

Competition can also lead to increases in intergroup hostility from minority group members because of feelings of *relative deprivation*. Deprivation exists when someone's needs are not being adequately met by the existing power structure. Clearly, though, deprivation by itself does not always cause hostility. In many countries today large numbers of starving people sit by and watch their families and friends die without protesting. Slavery existed in the United States for 200 years with only an occasional slave rebellion. The critical ingredient is the *expectation* of the people. If an individual expects to receive nothing, and considers nothing a fair and legitimate amount, then no unrest will occur. But, if one's lot in life is improving and one expects further improvement, and if these expectations are not met, then unrest and rebellion can break out. Alternatively, if one sees a reference group (to whom one can compare oneself) improving, but sees no change in one's own lot, expectations are again not met and unrest occurs.

These conditions of *relative deprivation* are illustrated in Figure 3-3. As long as actual need satisfaction grows as rapidly or more rapidly than expected satisfaction, relative tranquility and satisfaction prevail. The situation becomes dangerous when expectations exceed actual satisfaction. Then unrest and discontent occur. In one sense, this might be considered a frustration of particular goals, which produces the tendency for aggression, violence, demonstrations, and revolution.

During the period of slavery in the United States, many blacks accepted

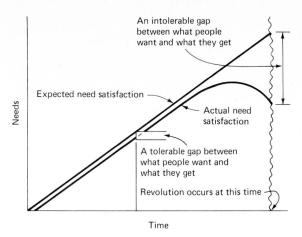

Figure 3-3. *Need satisfaction and revolution. If the gap between what people want and what they get is relatively small, as is the case in the left-hand side of the figure, there is relatively little dissatisfaction and harmony prevails. If, however, the gap between what people want and what they get becomes too great (left, above) acute dissatisfaction occurs and strong attempts will be made to change this situation. An extreme method of closing the gap is revolution.*

their lot and believed it was the natural state of affairs. Much later, during World War II, increased interracial contact meant that many blacks could compare their meager conditions with those of whites, and the comparison proved terribly unfavorable. With the advent of television, blacks became bombarded with information directed primarily toward whites: Own your own home in the suburbs; have two cars; have the latest kitchen appliances; get a better job. Yet, it was not clear why these things should be for whites only. Equality for all was preached, and finally believed by blacks. But when conditions did not improve, unrest and dissatisfaction occurred and led to the riots of the strife-torn sixties. Thus, rising expectations without equal improvement in actual conditions led to violence.

Studies of the riots of the 1960s have supported this analysis [5]. The outbreaks in ghettos were not senseless; they were attempts to change the system after other tactics had failed. The people who rioted were not the "riffraff" of the ghetto. Rather, they were the better-educated elite of the black youth in the cities. These are the individuals one would expect to be most influenced and most perturbed by an unfavorable comparison with the lot of whites. Expectations for this group would be most drastically refuted.

The interplay among black invisibility, news media, and the Los Angeles riot of 1965 has been analyzed within the relative-deprivation framework. Johnson, Sears, and McConahay [228] felt they could demonstrate that although the size of the black community had been steadily growing in Los Angeles, the newspapers were not devoting a fair share of their coverage to blacks. Figure 3-4 shows both the population growth of blacks and the relevant news coverage between 1892 and 1968. Note the similarity between these data and the earlier, theoretical curve. Clearly, the gap became intolerable; invisibility and nonattention were too preponderant.

The framework of relative deprivation can also be used to understand the attitudes of whites toward blacks. Thomas Pettigrew and his associates have studied whites' reactions to black mayoralty candidates [469]. To start,

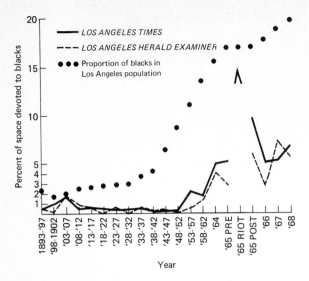

Figure 3-4. *Percentage of news space devoted to blacks in two Los Angeles newspapers. Until the 1960s, blacks in Los Angeles (as well as in other cities) had been largely ignored by the news media. Ironically, almost the only time news coverage devoted to blacks was approximately equal to their proportion in the population was during the 1965 riots in Watts. The theoretical curve shown in Figure 3-3 provides a probable explanation for this uprising.*

Pettigrew suggests that different types of relative deprivation are possible. The first is *fraternal deprivation,* which exists when one feels that personal gains are being outdistanced by the outgroup. The second is *egoist deprivation,* which exists when one feels that personal gains are being outdistanced by one's own ethnic group. (It should be clear that one could also feel doubly deprived and suffer from both of the above. Or, one could feel neither type of deprivation.) Interestingly, Pettigrew finds that both fraternal and egoist deprivation are related to contact racism, but that only fraternal is consistently related to competitive racism. Only when you feel you're losing to the outgroup do you become prejudiced because of competition for status.

Table 3-1 presents the results of Pettigrew's research in the cities of Cleveland, Los Angeles, Newark, and Gary, when various blacks were candidates for mayor. In *all* cases, whites feeling fraternally deprived were the least likely to vote for a black candidate. There is a way in which we can understand these results. The vote against a black served a *function* for fraternally deprived white voters. They thought blacks were progressing faster than they and wanted to keep another black (the mayoral candidate) from getting farther ahead.

Perceived belief dissimilarity: "They" are "different"

Consider the basis on which white college students select or reject people in controlled situations. Is the most important criterion likely to be race? No, it most definitely is not. Many studies have indicated that *perceived belief dissimilarity* is a more potent factor in acceptance or rejection of others. People tend to like others who hold beliefs and values similar to their own and to dislike those with dissimilar beliefs and values. Many Americans

Table 3-1. Racial deprivation and the percentage of whites who reacted positively to black candidates

Reactions to black candidates	Racial deprivation type, percent			
	A. Doubly gratified	B. Fraternally deprived	C. Egoistically deprived	D. Doubly deprived
Mayoralty voting				
For *Stokes* vs. *Perk*,				
Cleveland, 1969*	31	12	49	29
For *Bradley* vs. *Yorty*,				
L.A. primary vote, 1969	26	17	34	30
Run-off preference, 1969	51	30	46	46
Run-off vote, 1969	35	21	52	42
For *Gibson* vs. *Addonizio*,				
Newark, 1970	19	14	29	20
For *Hatcher* vs. *Williams*				
Gary primary, 1971	17	7	30	15
Candidate image				
(Percent favorable)†				
Stokes, 1969	57	33	64	50
Bradley, 1969	65	44	71	49
Gibson, 1970	25	18	27	36
Hatcher, 1970	35	17	36	29

Source: From Vanneman & Pettigrew, [469].

* For Democrats only, since this was a partisan final election.

†The respondents were each presented a printed card with twelve adjectives from which three were chosen as the most descriptive of the black candidate. Half of the adjectives were favorable in tone (e.g., intelligent, honest) and half were unfavorable (e.g., out-for-himself, prejudiced). The favorable percentages provided here represent those whites who chose three favorable adjectives in the cases of Stokes and Gibson, and two or three favorable adjectives in the cases of Bradley and Hatcher.

believe that the "Oriental mind" is somehow strange and different from their own. This is an example of perceived belief dissimilarity. If one must choose between persons who differ from one in race or in beliefs and values, evidence indicates that one is more likely to choose the person with similar beliefs, regardless of race [367]. Research [460; 426] suggests that differences in values usually seem to be more important in the rejection of blacks than is race per se.

This sounds encouraging. Perhaps people behave reasonably after all, and rejection on the basis of race alone is not common. But the issue is not so simple. If one asks a group of white students to predict the beliefs and values of white students and of black students, research indicates that the white students *assume* the beliefs and values of blacks are more dissimilar to their own than are the beliefs and values of whites. Furthermore, the more hostile the racial attitudes of the whites, the more "different" blacks will seem to be. Finally, the more intimate the relationship (for example, close friendship, dating), the more likely it is that any white will use race, rather than perceived belief dissimilarity, as a basis for behavior. Thus, race does have an effect in certain "sensitve" areas involving interactions of a more intimate nature—such as "invite home to dinner," "live in the same apartment house," and "date my sister" [408].

Hence, we are left with a peculiarly circular situation. Perhaps most whites do not discriminate on the basis of race alone, but on the basis of perceived belief dissimilarity, a seemingly more reasonable basis. But if the whites at the same time are *assuming* that any black person will have different beliefs and values, then we are back where we began. This is a tricky situation, but at least it suggests how general levels of discrimination might be reduced. If you can convince people that the values and attitudes of two groups are *not* as dissimilar as group members have assumed, then the overall level of mistrust and hostility between the groups might be lessened.

Conformity and social norms

It is often assumed that negative racial attitudes must serve an ego-defensive function, that racial prejudice is a symptom of "sickness" and inadequate personality development. While this is a possibility, not all cases of prejudice result from inadequate personality development. In many cases, racially prejudiced attitudes may serve a social-adjustment function. If the *norms* (standards for appropriate behaviors) of one's subculture encourage racial prejudice, then the more one conforms to these norms, the more prejudice one will show. The resulting prejudicial attitude may have little or nothing to do with one's underlying personality characteristics (except perhaps for the general tendency to conform). An extreme example of this conformity effect can be seen in a mining town in West Virginia. Above ground, in the town itself, there was rigid segregation of blacks and whites. However, down in the mines, where cooperation was necessary, black and white miners evolved a totally integrated and harmonious life-style. The norms of appropriate behavior depended on where the people were [312].

Thomas Pettigrew [343] has pointed out that conformity relates to prejudice in several different ways. One way is through the fairly superficial process of preference for the familiar, the desire to do things as they have always been done. In this case, if prejudice and discrimination are how things have "always" been done, then the prejudicial attitude would serve a knowledge function. Conformity may also stem from a more emotional commitment to a way of life or to a value system that includes ethnic attitudes. Two examples are "the Southern way of life" and "black consciousness." Finally, conformity may indicate deep-rooted insecurity, a strong need to belong and be accepted by important groups. Social adjustment and ego-defense may be most relevant to this last sense of conformity.

Norms within the black subculture for appropriate racial attitudes have undergone considerable change since World War II. The expression of antiwhite sentiments by black adults has become much more prevalent [73]. It is difficult to ascertain how much of this apparent change indicates a real change in attitudes and how much shows only an increasing freedom to express negative views which were always held, but previously were kept "private." In any case, it is clear that present norms within the black subculture are considerably different from those of thirty years ago. It is also clear that present norms are different in *segments* of the black subculture (for example, among college students or among middle-class business people).

In the American South, social norms among whites have traditionally supported hostility toward and derogation of blacks. Thus, for any individual white the acceptance of such attitudes should serve a social-adjustment function; a person with a hostile attitude will "fit in" well within the subculture. Racially egalitarian attitudes in that subculture, on the other hand, would make one *deviant* and would likely be maladjustive in terms of one's relationships with others in the subculture. Since the norms support prejudice in this situation, people with a high need to conform should adopt the norms and hence show considerable racial prejudice. People with a low need to conform should, on the average, show less racial prejudice.

In the American North, on the other hand, the situation is not as clear. *Formal* norms have been in the direction of egalitarianism and nonprejudice, while *informal* norms often have supported racial discrimination and prejudice. Hence, in this situation, an individual's attitudes will depend both on the extent of the need to conform and on which set of norms one is conforming *to.*

The magnitude of apparent attitude change among Southern whites in the past thirty or forty years has been extensive. For example, public opinion polls indicate that the percentage of white Southerners who supported school integration rose from a microscopic 2 percent in 1942 to almost 50 percent in 1970. Although the latter figure is still distressingly small, it nonetheless indicates considerable attitude change during the past few decades. Interestingly, people who have lived in integrated school districts are much more likely to approve of school integration than are people who live in segregated districts, even when they did not have a choice of which type of district to live in [73].

The public opinion polls show a decided moderation in the attitudes of whites toward blacks and toward institutions and laws which have subjugated minority group members. In recent years, whites in both the North and the South have generally become more favorably disposed toward racial integration and the ending of legal supports for discrimination and mistreatment. They have also become more positive in their attitudes toward ethnic group *members,* although this change is perhaps not as great as the change in their *policy* attitudes [73].

There is much evidence, then, that many whites have changed their expressed attitudes toward racial policies and ethnic group members. Pettigrew [343] anticipated this trend over a decade ago, when he proposed that many people should be called *latent liberals.* He used this term to describe Southern whites whose present racial attitudes were very hostile but for whom these attitudes were not serving a value-expressive or ego-defensive function. These people should be able to easily change their attitudes in the direction of reduced hostility, he reasoned, if the social norms and patterns of rewards changed. The norms *did* change somewhat in the 1950s and 1960s, and these people changed with them.

The overall implications of this view are simple. It may be possible to avoid much of the current hostility and mistreatment between various groups in our society. If the norms change so that it becomes more adjustive to hold nonhostile, nonprejudiced attitudes, then latent liberals can be expected to become "real" liberals. Later, we will discuss *why* this process takes place.

Cues from society

Symbolism. Ethnic attitudes are learned in the same ways as other attitudes. The society in which a child grows up gives cues about "appropriate" attitudes to hold toward other groups. In many cases, the cues may be very subtle. For example, in American society, white is often used to represent goodness, purity, light, and other desirable things, while black is usually associated with sickness, death, sadness, and evil. It seems likely that this societal *color-coding* could encourage a general tendency for children to perceive things labeled *white* as good and things labeled *black* as bad. Indeed, Eldridge Cleaver has stated that "white America has defined black as evil" [385, p. 55]. The series of "doll studies" undertaken by social scientists in the past four decades (see Focus 3-1) provides evidence of the effects of this orientation.

If such color-coding does occur and if it carries over into evaluation of groups of people, what can we do about it? Exploratory research [498] indicates that is possible to help children relearn so that they no longer "automatically" see most black things as bad and most white things as good. If this is done, corresponding feelings of hostility or superiority/inferiority which are associated with color may lose some of their force. Of course, far-reaching changes are needed to eliminate this association between color and "goodness" in our society.

Social barriers. Throughout the history of this country, legal and illegal societal *barriers* have impeded the social and economic advancement of minority groups. When these barriers are built into a society, they become aspects of institutional racism. On a personal level, however, consider majority-group children who look at society and see barriers and people whom they respect helping to maintain the barriers. It is unlikely that the children will conclude that all these people are unreasonable bigots. It is more likely that they would "make sense of the world" by deciding that the barriers *must* be justified, since the people manning them are intelligent and reasonable. The conclusion again would be that minority groups must

FOCUS 3-1   OF DOLLS AND MEN

An interesting line of research into racial prejudice and its effects has involved children's reactions to dolls or puppets of different colors. The situation may seem silly and inconsequential at first, but it has been argued that children's reactions to dolls of different colors may provide insight into their reactions (and attitudes) toward *people* of different colors. The first study involving dolls was conducted in the late 1930s by Kenneth and Mamie Clark, two black psychologists. They asked a large sample of black children to respond to a number of questions by choosing one of two dolls. One doll had "white" skin, and the other dark brown. The study included such questions as: "Which is the good doll?" "Which is the bad doll?" "Which doll would you rather play with?" "Which doll looks like you?" "Which is the white doll?" "Which is the colored doll?"

The Clarks [97] found that most of their sample of black children preferred to play with the white doll. The children perceived the white doll as good and the brown doll as bad. When asked to identify the "white" and "colored" dolls, over 90 percent of the children were able to do so correctly. The Clarks were disturbed, however, to find that one-third of their sample of black children chose the white doll when asked to pick "the doll that looks like you." These findings led the investigators to conclude that many black children had feelings of self-hatred and a confused sense of self-identity. In fact, these findings were cited in legal arguments during the momentous 1954 *Brown vs. Board of Education* Supreme Court case, which struck down school segregation laws.

Many later studies found the same thing. Both black and white children, when asked to pick the nice, good doll or puppet, have tended overwhelmingly to pick the white one. Also, many black children have pointed to the white doll when asked which one looked like them. Hence, these findings seem to point both to a confused sense of self-identity and to a sense of self-hatred on the part of black children.

The rise of social movements stressing black power, black pride, and black dignity in recent years in America would suggest that such findings might no longer hold. Recent research [220] indicates that black children no longer overwhelmingly favor the white doll. Instead, they tend to attribute positive characteristics to the black doll.

But while research regarding self-concept appears to reflect changes in society, the apparent problems in self-identity of black children may not have been as severe as they seemed in the first place. There was a problem in research methodology. Researchers typically used white and dark-brown dolls. What was a light-skinned black child to do when asked which doll looked like her or him? Objectively, the "white" doll's color might be closer to the child's. Yet, if the child acted on this information and pointed to the "white" doll, it was treated as an "error" in response. More recent research using a third, "mulatto" doll suggests that the supposed "self-misidenti-fication" may have resulted from such ambiguities in the research pro-cedure. Recent researchers have found that light-skinned black children and a good portion of the darker-skinned "white" children tend (accurately) to pick the mulatto doll as the one that looks most like them [189a].

Even though methodological problems such as this one have plagued the research, the trend of the past few decades seems clear. If we assume that doll choice is related to self-concept (there is recent evidence supporting this assumption [482]), then studies show a decrease in self-hatred among black children and an increase in self-pride. Apparently the vast social changes in racial matters which have characterized the past decades have contributed to this change in the self-concept of black children.

deserve separate treatment. Later, we will discuss additional evidence that people often devalue the victims of misfortune (that is, see them as deserv-ing their fate) so that they can maintain their feelings that the world is just and fair.

Institutional racism. Often, factors that lead to prejudice and discrimina-tion do not originate in individuals but are an indirect result of how the major *institutions* in a society are structured. Black activist Stokely Carmi-chael coined the term *institutional racism* to describe this indirect and often apparently unintentional mistreatment of minority groups in American soci-ety. Carmichael gives an example of the distinction between institutional racism and individual racism, or prejudice [90]:

When white terrorists bombed a black church and killed five black children, that was an act of individual racism widely deplored by most segments of society. But when in that same city—Birmingham, Alabama—five hundred black babies die each year because of the lack of proper food, shelter, and medical facilities, and thousands more are destroyed and maimed physically, emotionally, and intellectually because of conditions of poverty and discrimination in the black community, that is the operation of institutional racism.

One institution that sometimes serves to maintain prejudice is religion. Christianity in America once put strong emphasis on "civilizing the heathen" through missionary work and shouldering the "white man's bur-den" to help our "little brown brothers." Such an outlook certainly implies the *superiority* of the white Christian American culture and those who live in it.

When people try to compare cultures, the doctrine of *social Darwinism* often arises. Coming into popularity soon after the acceptance of Darwin's theory of biological evolution, this doctrine holds that "survival of the fittest" is as applicable to cultures and ethnic groups as it is to species of animals. Therefore, the ethnic group which has "survived best" and gained control of the culture—that is, the dominant group—must be the "fittest." In this view, the intricate and sometimes subtle barriers which have been placed in the way of accomplishment for minority groups are ignored, and it is naïvely assumed that the "cream" of any culture will inevitably rise to the top.

Although social Darwinism is no longer explicitly endorsed by those in power, it has been suggested that many present-day "liberal" concerns with ethnic poverty, the ghetto, and the "pathological" nature of minority group cultures may represent a more polished version of the same paternalistic orientation. For example, during the 1960s a number of social scientists became concerned over the plight of black families in America. Data showed that fatherless families were much more common among blacks than whites. Instead of asking, "What in our society is causing family structure among blacks to differ from family structure among whites?" researchers were more likely to ask, "What is *wrong* with the black family? How is it harmful for the children?" The assumption was that any institution that differed from the way white, liberal social scientists thought it *should* be was automatically wrong and undesirable.

The subtlety of societal cues as to the "natural order of things" can be seen in the simple example of "flesh-colored" bandages. As Bob Teague points out in Focus 3-2, it never occurred to the advertisers (or to most whites in the audience) that, if you're black, the bandages are definitely not flesh-colored.

Another major institution that has contributed to the pattern is our school system. In past years, textbooks have often shown minority group members in a stereotyped, derogatory manner. Blacks usually appeared only as laborers, shoeshine boys, porters, maids and butlers, entertainers, and more recently, athletes. Still another problem concerns traditional histories of America—until the past decade or so, most school history books made no mention of the crucial contributions made by minority group members. As you can imagine, use of such materials, year after year, is likely to reinforce a view of society in which it is "natural" for whites to have control.

Movies and television also offer examples of institutional racism. One has only to look at an old Shirley Temple movie to see how movies have contributed to this pattern. Blacks appear only as wide-eyed, grinning, song-and-dance men or solicitous (but not too smart) maids and butlers. Later on, the very popular radio and television show "Amos 'n Andy" gave another view of blacks—as shifty, fun-loving, irresponsible, and not too bright. In old cowboy movies, Mexican-Americans appear as jolly, rather stupid sidekicks or as cunning, vicious villains. While such obviously derogatory and stereotyped portraits have become less frequent in recent years, more subtle insults remain. The "Frito Bandito" certainly (and unfortunately) provides an updated stereotype of the Mexican-American. Focus 3-2 provides further examples of such insults.

FOCUS 3-2   CHARLIE'S DAILY RACISM

The following selections are taken from a 1968 article by Bob Teague, a black writer and newscaster.

A favorite comic theme among the "concerned and enlightened" elements of white society is "Let's Stamp Out Racial Hatred." Hoo boy! Hatred has very little to do with the central problem, Charlie. What is done to and withheld from black folk day by day in this country is based on neither hate nor horror. On the contrary, it is coldly impersonal. Like the brains of precocious computers.

Simply put, it seems to me that white folks are convinced, deep in their bones, that the way they run this melting pot—with black folk unmelted at the bottom—is nothing more than the natural order of things. . . .

And even the most militant white egalitarians are prone to compliment one another by saying, "That's real white of you, Edgar." Obviously, the notion that anything white is inherently superior to its black counterpart is built into the white American idiom, and thus into the white American mind. . . .

Consider, for example, those magazine and newspaper advertisements for "flesh-colored" bandages. The color they mean blandly ignores the color of most flesh on this planet. Mine in particular. But the top bananas who dreamed up that bit would be sorely aggrieved if someone called them racists. Some of these chaps are probably card-carrying fellow-travelers in the NAACP, and their wives probably sent food to the poor people's shantytown in Washington. Their "flesh-colored" bandages are merely a profitable manifestation of a common assumption among white folk: White skin is what human flesh is supposed to look like. Anything else—black skin certainly—is irrelevant. Sort of a whimsical goof by Mother Nature.

How else can a black man explain those ubiquitous cosmetic ads showing the pale proud beauty using the facial lotion that promises to give her "the natural look"? The joke here is that this same beauty, and those who swear by "flesh-colored" bandages, spend as much time in the sun as possible to darken their natural looks. They even buy chemical tans in bottles. And did you ever hear a commercial Goldilocks say, "Goodness gracious, my tan is much too dark"? . . .

Only last week one of my white friends—to be known here as Charlie— called my attention to one of those "flesh-colored" ads. Although Charlie is well past thirty-five and literate and had read similar ads over the years, he was seeing it clearly for the first time.

"Man, look at this," he said, wearing an embarrassed grin. "They even insult you in the ads, don't they?"

Charlie's insight is not yet complete, however. If it ever is, he'll say "we" instead of "they." . . .

Examples of how black folk are systematically misrepresented or shut out from the stuff that the American Dream is made of are virtually endless. The smiling faces on greeting cards are never black faces. Department-store manikins don't resemble anyone you are likely to meet in the ghetto. And all plastic angels who symbolize the Christmas spirit are pink.

The net effect of these deceptions is that each tailor-made reality buttresses the other in the minds of whites. This explains in large measure why so many white folk are genuinely baffled by the grumbling and violence in the ghettos. Which is the basis for the popular white joke that ends with the punch line: "What do you people want?" . . .

As for the sight gags in white society's repertoire, these too have worn thin from overexposure. How many times can an individual black be amused by the blind cabdriver routine? After the thirty-seventh time, it no longer strikes him as suitable material for a laff-in.

Did I say "individual black man"? Actually, there is scarcely any such animal as far as white eyes can see. They recognize "the first Negro who" and "the only Negro to," but not as individuals, instead, as freaks or symbols. Which is to say that white folks have a habit of arbitrarily assigning a rather standard personality to a black man. His real self is like an iceberg, deeply submerged in a sea of white assumptions. . . .

Another American institution which assists in discriminating against some ethnic groups is the immigration system. Traditionally, "quotas" have been set up, declaring how many people from each country will be allowed to emigrate to the United States. In 1962, for example, about 70 percent of the immigrants allowed by the quotas were from Great Britain, Germany, and Ireland alone. Another 25 percent were from other European countries, while only 5 percent of those allowed to emigrate were from non-European countries. Why should this be? Apparently, the government officials who established the quotas were deciding, deliberately or not, that Germans, Britains, and Irish (most of whom are white and Anglo-Saxon) were some-how *better* and should be given a greater chance to emigrate to America than should other ethnic groups.

■ INDIVIDUAL PREJUDICE: IS THERE A PREJUDICED PERSONALITY?

Despite evidence that in many cases attitude change requires only a change in norms, social scientists have spent a good deal of time searching for the components of the "prejudiced personality." Much of the work was stimulated by the events preceding World War II when anti-Semitism (prejudice against Jews) took on a new and frighteningly grim aspect in Europe.

Many people have wondered whether prejudice toward a minority group, say Jews or blacks, can exist independently of other personal characteristics. The French philosopher Jean-Paul Sartre [375] has asked whether it is likely that "A man may be a good father and a good husband, a conscientious citizen, highly cultivated, philanthropic, *and* in addition detest the Jews" (p. 8)? To Sartre, the answer is a resounding "No!" Those who are anti-Semitic are likely to be many other things also; they are afraid of themselves, according to Sartre. It is not the Jews who frighten them, but their own consciousness, their fear of responsibility and of change in themselves and the world. Hatred for Jews (or for any other minority group) is, to Sartre, a symptom of "fear of the human condition" [375, p. 54].

We see, in this light, that ethnic prejudice is not regarded as a personality characteristic that coexists in an otherwise "normal" personality. Rather, it may be a *symptom* of a much broader style or type of personality. The question then becomes, Have social scientists been able to provide any empirical support for such a notion?

Authoritarianism

During the 1940s, a team of researchers at the University of California at Berkeley carried out an in-depth theoretical and empirical investigation of the dynamics of anti-Semitism. Gradually, their theoretical focus shifted to the more general topic of prejudice toward *all* outgroups, which they called *ethnocentrism.* They concluded that ethnocentric attitudes tell far more about the people who *hold* such attitudes than they do about the outgroups being stigmatized. Adorno, Frenkel-Brunswick, Levinson, and Sanford [4] described a *type* of personality, characterized by anti-democratic tendencies, generalized loyalty to the ingroup and rejection of outgroups, rigidity, and rationalization, which they labeled the *authoritarian personality.* Because this concept has stimulated an avalanche of research in the past twenty-five years, it will be outlined in some detail here.

Nine "components" of authoritarianism were isolated by Adorno and his coworkers: emphasis on conventional behavior; support of authoritarian aggression; support of submission to authority; preoccupation with "power and toughness"; anti-intraception (impatience with subjective, or "tenderminded" phenomena); use of superstition and stereotypes; a destructive and cynical outlook (general hostility); projectivity (a preoccupation with "evil forces" in the world); and overconcern with sexual "goings on" involving other people. The *F* (for Fascism) Scale, developed to measure authoritarianism, had items specifically designed to tap each of these nine components. It was found that scores on the *F* Scale correlated quite strongly with scores on scales designed to measure anti-Semitism, general ethnocentrism, and general political-economic conservatism. Sample items from the scale and some problems with research on authoritarianism are discussed in Focuses 3-3 and 3-4.

FOCUS 3-3   FASCISM UNMASKED?

The following items are from the original version of the *F* Scale developed by Adorno and his coworkers in the 1940s [4]. Each component label is in italics while some of the actual items appear below it.

Conventionalism: Rigid adherence to conventional, middle-class values.
    A person who has bad manners, habits, and breeding can hardly expect to get along with decent people.

    The businessman and the manufacturer are much more important to society than the artist and the professor.

Authoritarian submission: Submissive, uncritical attitude toward idealized moral authorities of the ingroup.
    Obedience and respect for authority are the most important virtues children should learn.

    Young people sometimes get rebellious ideas, but as they grow up they ought to get over them and settle down.

Authoritarian aggression: Tendency to be on the lookout for, and to condemn, reject, and punish people who violate conventional values.
    There is hardly anything lower than a person who does not feel great love, gratitude, and respect for his parents.

    Most of our social problems would be solved if we could somehow get rid of the immoral, crooked, and feeble-minded people.

Anti-intraception: Opposition to the subjective, the imaginative, and tender-minded.
    When a person has a problem or worry, it is best for him not to think about it, but to keep busy with more cheerful things.

    Nowadays more and more people are prying into matters that should remain personal and private.

Superstition and stereotype: The belief in mystical determinants of the individual's fate; the disposition to think in rigid categories.
    Some people are born with an urge to jump from high places.

    Some day it will probably be shown that astrology can explain a lot of things.

Power and "Toughness": Preoccupation with the dominance-submission, strong-weak, leader-follower dimension; identification with power figures, overemphasis upon the conventionalized attributes of the ego; exaggerated assertion of strength and toughness.

People can be divided into two distinct classes: the weak and the strong.

Too many people today are living in an unnatural, soft way; we should return to the fundamentals, to a more red-blooded, active way of life.

Destructiveness and cynicism: Generalized hostility, vilification of the human.

Human nature being what it is, there will always be war and conflict.

Familiarity breeds contempt.

Projectivity: The disposition to believe that wild and dangerous things go on in the world; the projection outwards of unconscious emotional impulses.

Nowadays when so many different kinds of people move around and mix together so much, a person has to protect himself especially carefully against catching an infection or disease from them.

Most people don't realize how much our lives are controlled by plots hatched in secret places.

Sex: Exaggerated concern with sexual "goings-on," punitiveness to violators of norms.

Sex crimes, such as rape and attacks on children, deserve more than mere imprisonment; such criminals ought to be publicly whipped, or worse.

The wild sex life of the old Greeks and Romans was tame compared to some of the goings-on in this country, even in places where people might least expect it.

FOCUS 3-4   AN EXAMPLE OF FAULTY RESEARCH

Unfortunately, much initial research into the authoritarian personality was methodologically flawed. For example, since the California investigators came to the conclusion that Fascism, anti-Semitism, political and economic conservatism, and ethnocentrism *should* be related, the four scales that arose contained items which supported the relationship. By discarding items that did not fit their preconceptions of how the dimensions should interrelate, the researchers artificially *guaranteed* that the hypothesized relationships would be "demonstrated" by the interrelationships among the four scales. It is decidedly bad practice to develop measures so that they automatically support your guesses about what the world is like.

The *F* Scale has been widely used in psychology ever since its development. Yet it, too, has come under considerable criticism. For example, you may have noticed in Focus 3-3 that all the *F* Scale terms are worded in the same direction; that is, an "agree" answer is always the authoritarian one. This might not seem significant except for the fact that *response acquiescence set* may become a problem. Research has shown that some people seem disposed to agree with questionnaire or interview items, regardless of content. If people are such "yea-sayers," then their scores on the *F* Scale would be raised artificially by this tendency to agree, and they would appear to be more authoritarian than they really are.

It may appear that the problem can be resolved simply by reversing half the items. Reasonable enough; but try it with some of the items in Focus 3-3. Revise the items so that a "disagree" response would mean the *same* thing as an "agree" response now means. With many items, it's difficult to do.

Another problem with the *F* Scale is its obviousness. Reviewing the items in Focus 3-3, one can see that the answers for many of them are socially "desirable" or "undesirable." It's too easy to choose answers that form whatever impression one wants. Scores on the *F* Scale have been shown to relate strongly to both education and intelligence (which, of course, also relate to each other). While this might indicate that authoritarian people are less likely to get an education or are less intelligent, it might simply mean that people with more intelligence or education are better able to "fake" their answers and give the impression of being nonauthoritarian.

Finally, what about authoritarianism of the political "left"? As we mentioned, the California researchers were concerned with political conservatism as it related to authoritarianism. But what about far-left groups such as European Communists or radical left political splinter groups in the United States? It seems possible that they might be authoritarian also. But the *F* Scale and the sociopolitical conservatism scale were developed only to identify conservative authoritarians. Thus, those who are authoritarian but *not* politically conservative would not score as authoritarian at all on the *F* Scale.

To explain how authoritarianism develops in childhood, Adorno and his coworkers relied heavily on Freudian concepts. According to their analysis, the most central characteristic of an authoritarian-to-be child is that his or her parents are themselves authoritarian. Such parents are harsh disciplinarians and will not tolerate misbehavior or aggression from the child. This type of upbringing is likely to produce a child who will act in a similar manner when he or she grows up. Through simple learning and identification, he or she learns that this is how parents "should" act. In addition, the arbitrary and harsh parental behaviors may produce a great deal of aggression in the child, directed toward the parents. However, these aggressive feelings are repressed, since there would be dire consequences if the child dared to aggress against the parents. This hostility thus remains covert and submerged until adulthood. Finally, in adulthood, the hostility is displaced and directed instead toward groups who cannot fight back, such as minority groups. Thus, the authoritarian adult can release pent-up hostility and aggression in a more or less socially acceptable manner, onto a scapegoat. This pent-up hostility, along with other traits and approaches learned from the parents, also contributes to endorsement of the nine components of authoritarianism outlined earlier.

A particularly unfortunate event that took place during the Detroit riots in summer 1968 illustrates this concept. Three policemen were arrested for killing three young blacks they had been questioning (and torturing) in connection with possible sniping. The black men, friends, and two white women had been found in the Algiers motel with no evidence that they had been involved in the sniping [203]. The policemen clearly demonstrated their zeal for duty and felt they were "taking care" of the populace. As Nevitt Sanford [374], one of Adorno's original associates, writes:

The three policemen most directly involved were, as personalities, strongly disposed to take their roles in the drama. Not only were they prejudiced against Negroes, but, because of their inner conflicts (they were each backward in their relations with women and had been overenthusiastic in their work as members of the vice squad), they were unusually aggressive, particularly toward people perceived as violators of moral standards.

These individuals appear to be rather "good" examples (unfortunately) of the authoritarian personality.

Brown [81] proposed that the single characteristic which would best distinguish authoritarians from nonauthoritarians is the kind of evidence needed to change their attitudes toward a given object. For highly authoritarian people, the simple say-so of a respected authority figure should be enough to cause attitude change. "If that's what George Wallace (or Edward Kennedy) says, then, by God, that's the way it is!" Such attitude change involves no real consideration of the issues; it's a case of authoritarian submission. Such submission and attitude change would seem to be as characteristic of people on the political far left as of those on the political far right.

Dogmatism

Other social scientists have tried to develop measures of concepts similar to authoritarianism. Concerned about the "right bias" of the *F* Scale, Rokeach [366] developed the concept of *dogmatism*. Rokeach defined dogmatism as "(a) a relatively closed cognitive organization of beliefs and disbeliefs about reality, (b) organized around a central set of beliefs about absolute authority which, in turn, (c) provides a framework for patterns of intolerances toward others" [366, p. 195]. Note that this definition says nothing about a dogmatic person's position toward political ideology. Logically, it would be expected that although dogmatism may not be related to any particular ideology, it should be related to the *intensity* with which one holds whatever position one takes. Therefore, looking back at our initial definition of prejudice, dogmatic people should be those who are *rigid* in their attitudes and quite resistant to change.

It is clear that the concepts of authoritarianism and dogmatism considerably overlap. But evidence also indicates that they are not identical. For example, a small study in England in the 1950s of college-student members of five political groups found that Communists scored lowest on the *E* (Ethnocentrism) and *F* Scales but highest on the dogmatism scale. It could be argued that Communists are dogmatic in adhering to a nonconservative nonethnocentric ideology [366].

Concrete versus abstract thinking

A third related way of looking at people and prejudice is in terms of the concreteness or abstractness of their thoughts and conceptual systems. Harvey and his associates [197] identified four general levels of conceptual functioning, ranging from very concrete to very abstract.

People who are most concrete in functioning, called *System 1,* would be expected to score highest on measures of authoritarianism and dogmatism. Such people are characterized by conventionalism, ethnocentrism, dependency on authority-related cues as guides for thought and action (recall Brown's definition of authoritarianism), intolerance for ambiguity, simpler cognitive structure, and a relative lack of empathy for others.

People who function at the next higher level of abstractness, *System 2,* are characterized by rebellion against society, avoidance of dependency, distrust, low self-esteem, and relatively high authoritarianism (although not as high as System 1). These people dogmatically *oppose* the same societal institutions that System 1 people support. The next level of abstractness, *System 3,* includes people who have a generally positive view of others, a need to depend on others as well as to have others depend on them, and are generally very person-oriented. They are likely to place considerable emphasis on friendship and the avoidance of loneliness. Representatives of the most abstract and highly developed system, *System 4,* are theorized to have had freedom as children to explore all aspects of their environments and establish their own values. As adults, System 4 people are flexible and creative; they tend to base values and behaviors on internal rather than external standards. They are cognitively abstract, open to change, and able to see things from many perspectives.

Thus the three different approaches—focusing on authoritarianism, dogmatism, and level of conceptual functioning—all suggest that there is a *type* of person who is more likely to be prejudiced. We will discuss an additional set of findings related to this area and then note some dangers in the kind of assumptions that people sometimes make.

The theoretical relationship between level of conceptual functioning

(a)

(b)

(c)

(d)

(e)

Figure 3-5. *Men who seemed to embody many characteristics of the authoritarian personality: Nazi Führer Adolf Hitler (a), Russian Premier Josef Stalin (b), former U.S. Senator Joseph McCarthy (c), Fascist Italian Premier Benito Mussolini (d), and former head of the American Nazi party George Lincoln Rockwell (e). Many of the components of authoritarianism— emphasis on conventional standards, support of authoritarian aggression and submission to authority, preoccupation with power and toughness, and a generally destructive and cynical outlook—are visible in the lives and actions of these men.*

and ethnic prejudice is clear: The higher (more abstract) the level of one's conceptual functioning, the less likely one is to be ethnically prejudiced. Focus 3-5 illustrates how two variables—level of conceptual functioning and racial attitude—were related to voting behavior during the 1968 and 1972 presidential elections.

An important caution

All the approaches we have discussed identify one *type* of person (high authoritarianism, high dogmatism, concrete level of conceptual functioning) who would be most likely to be racially hostile and prejudiced. Again, however, let us keep in mind that to propose that all such people would be prejudiced or that all prejudiced people have these characteristics would be an overgeneralization. As our previous discussion has indicated, social norms and standards play an important role in determining ethnic attitudes.

A further example of this is provided by a small study of ultraconservatives in Dallas in the late 1960s. On the surface, we might expect ultraconservatives to be authoritarian, dogmatic, conceptually concrete, and ego-defensive. But no such evidence was found in this small study. These ultraconservatives simply were people whose lives were involved and intertwined with other ultraconservatives. In their particular subculture, ultraconservatism was the norm. Therefore, they simply were adapting to the norm. They did not show the other personality characteristics theoretically associated with racial prejudice [140].

To many college students, conceptions such as authoritarianism make sense, particularly since many college students like to consider themselves liberals, and the conservatives in these conceptions are most often depicted as the "bad" people. But it is precisely this factor which should make us cautious. Our caution should center on the potential roles that our *own* values may play in *biasing* our descriptions and conceptualizations of others. An example follows.

In the late 1930s, psychologist E. R. Jaensch reported the identification of a consistent human type which he called the Anti-type. According to Jaensch, such people tended to make ambiguous, indefinite judgments, to be weak and effeminate, to take childish pleasure in being eccentric, and to think (incorrectly) that environment and education were the determinants of behavior. The contrasting personality type, the J-type, was characterized by tough, masculine, stable behavior. These people would make definite, unambiguous perceptual judgments and would stick by them. They recognized that human behavior was fixed by blood, soil, and national tradition [81].

These typologies may sound familiar. To a great extent, they are the authoritarian and nonauthoritarian viewed from a different perspective. Here the J-types (authoritarians) are "good." How could this be? It will add some perspective to note that Jaensch proposed that Jews and others of

FOCUS 3-5   WHO VOTES FOR WHOM?

A number of studies since 1940 have suggested that personality and attitude variables are not particularly strong predictors of voting behavior. This may be surprising, since the concepts of authoritarianism, dogmatism, and level of conceptual functioning would seem to translate rather directly into voting behavior, especially when there is a choice between a conservative and a liberal candidate. We thought so too; Severy, Brigham, and Harvey [396a] set out to assess the relationships among level of conceptual functioning, racial attitudes, and voting behavior in the 1968 presidential election. We found that both variables *did* predict voting behavior to some extent. White college students who were at higher levels of functioning and had more positive racial attitudes were more likely to vote for Humphrey. Students with more concrete levels of functioning or who showed more racial hostility were more likely to vote for Nixon or Wallace.

Brigham and Severy [72] decided to look at this relationship again in the 1972 presidential election. As in the 1968 election, one candidate was clearly considered liberal and the other conservative. We obtained measures of racial attitude, level of conceptual functioning, and commitment to the electoral process from 320 white college students in colleges and universities in 7 different states, one week before the election. Students were also asked to rate themselves as to "general social-political orientation" (liberal to conservative). Finally, each student was asked to evaluate how good a job each candidate would do if elected and to state separately the probabilities that he or she would vote for McGovern or for Nixon.

As expected, several of the measures related quite strongly to self-rated probabilities of voting for Nixon or McGovern. In brief, students at more concrete levels of conceptual functioning and with more hostile racial attitudes were more likely to intend voting for Nixon. Furthermore, students showing a greater commitment to the electoral process were more likely to be Nixon supporters. Those with high commitment to the electoral process were more likely to be at concrete levels of conceptual functioning.

It is hard to say whether this latter relationship results from a close relationship between the two concepts measured or whether it is due to the fact that people at abstract levels of functioning—who were more likely to be McGovern supporters anyway—had seen the writing on the wall and were anticipating McGovern's massive defeat. If so, this could have reflected disenchantment and low commitment to the electoral process. So it's possible that this particular relationship is limited to this election.

Such results suggest that meaningful personality variables, such as level of conceptual functioning and racial prejudice, may be important in predicting behaviors of crucial import, such as voting. They suggest further that such factors may bias or affect people's reactions to other aspects of the political process. One would expect, for example, that reactions to the Watergate scandal were very different among people who differed in level of conceputal functioning and, perhaps, among those who differed in racial attitude.

"racially mixed" heredity were Anti-types, while people of North German heritage were likely to make good J-types. As you probably have figured out by now, Jaensch was not only a psychologist but a German and a Nazi. The J-types he described would probably have made excellent members of the Nazi party.

Jaensch's bias is obvious. We only wish to warn you that the same kind of value-related bias may characterize how you categorize people, even if you do it in ways similar to those described by (liberal?) social scientists.

■ WAYS OF REDUCING ETHNIC PREJUDICE

Changing attitudes

Mass media campaigns. In Chapter 2 we discussed how attitude change may be induced by persuasive communications. In these days of electronic wizardry, communications can reach millions of people, and in America private organizations and (sometimes) the government have mounted enthusiastic persuasion campaigns to reduce intergroup hostility and preju- dice. Despite their money and manpower, these campaigns have not been particularly effective. While there undoubtedly has been some attitude change resulting from the campaigns, it appears to have been minimal.

One problem is that of de facto selective exposure (see Chapter 2, page 75); often messages don't reach the intended audience. This is particularly likely to be the case with messages designed to reduce ethnic hostility. People who are most hostile are most likely to miss such messages or to mis- interpret them.

Another problem centers on the importance of the attitude. Ethnic attitudes often are very important to those who hold them, and important attitudes are least likely to change. There is a reduced latitude of accep- tance for contrary arguments, and such attitudes are likely to be closely interrelated with other important attitudes and values. Hence, it is unlikely that a "mass-produced" attitude-change message would fall within the appropriate zone (latitude of acceptance) and lead to attitude change for large numbers of individuals. The message might be more effective with people for whom these attitudes are not as important—for example, "latent liberals," for whom the attitudes may serve knowledge or social-adjustment functions. But here again, the norms of the immediate situation and the patterns of reward and punishment are probably more important than any single attitude-change message.

Individual therapy. For persons whose prejudicial attitudes serve an ego-defensive function, some sort of therapeutic experience would seem necessary to reduce prejudice. And such therapeutic experiences would most likely occur on an individual, one-to-one level. There are many individual case histories which show that therapeutic experiences have resulted in reduction of prejudice along with other personality changes. But there is relatively little research on therapeutic programs designed specifically to reduce prejudice.

Researchers have tried to achieve attitude changes regarding ego-defensive attitudes through the arousal of self-insight. Insight into the causes of one's attitudes is presumed to lead to control of the ego-defenses. Control, in turn, can lead to reduction in the prejudice that stems from these defenses. McClintock [291], for example, demonstrated a reduction in prejudice toward blacks in some ego-defensive subjects by virtue of carefully explaining and talking about case studies that illustrated the dynamics of repression and projectivity. This is not a simple process, however.

Group therapy. Recent interest in T-groups, encounter groups, sensitivity groups, and so forth suggests a powerful means by which racial attitudes and prejudice might be reduced through increases in self-insight, self-acceptance, and honesty in communication. Thus far, however, little is known about the results of such groups. Available data suggest that sensitivity groups involving both blacks and whites may lead to considerable reduction in prejudice and hostility on the parts of both blacks and whites. However, in such situations, attitude measurement is susceptible to bias. On the one hand, people who participate in such programs may be quite different from the average person; that is, those who are least prejudiced may be most likely to participate. On the other hand, people who invest time and energy in such programs may feel the *need* to report beneficial results such as prejudice reduction, whether or not such results have actually occurred. Finally, we do not yet know whether such change—if accomplished—is lasting, or whether it dissipates over time.

Changing child-rearing practices

Earlier we outlined parental behaviors that might lead to authoritarianism and, hence, to ethnic prejudice. If this formulation is accurate, then changes in child-rearing practices should drastically reduce both authoritarianism and ethnic prejudice. First, if parents behave so that children do *not* need to suppress hostility they feel toward them, the later tendency to displace hostility onto ethnic group members may be correspondingly lessened. Second, less authoritarian parents may simply teach children to be more egalitarian. As we noted earlier, racial attitudes among whites are becoming

(a)

Figure 3-6. *Possible ways of reducing integroup prejudice. Large-scale campaigns to change racial attitudes by utilizing written materials (a), and radio and television, have had only limited impact, for reasons described in the text. Equal-status interracial contact, such as that found in encounter groups (b) and in some preschools and grade schools (c), provides opportunities for the reduction of prejudice if the contact situation has the important characteristics identified by Allport and by Cook.*

less prejudiced. It seems reasonable to expect that changes in general child-rearing techniques that have occurred in recent years may be one significant factor in this change. Since "expert" advice regarding appropriate measures of child rearing seems to go in cycles over the years, however, it is risky to predict future trends in child-rearing practices.

Changing behavior

At first, it may seem strange to propose that changing behavior will lead to a change in prejudice. We are accustomed to thinking of things the other way around: Changed attitudes lead to changed behaviors. Around the turn of the century, sociologist William Graham Sumner said, "Stateways cannot change folkways." Sumner was saying that you can't legislate morality; that is, no matter what behaviors a new law might require, people will continue to feel as they always have. Hence, passing laws to change behavior will have no effect on the attitudes, beliefs, and values that underlie the behavior.

This position is reflected in the attitude of American courts toward racial matters. In the historic 1896 Supreme Court decision of *Plessy v. Ferguson,*

(b)

(c)

which set the precedent for the separate-but-equal doctrine, the Court said, "Legislation is powerless to eradicate racial instincts or to abolish distinctions based upon physical differences, and the attempt to do so can only result in accentuating the difficulties of the present situation. . . . If one race is inferior to the other socially, the Constitution of the United States cannot put them on the same plane." The Court was saying that it could not affect the "racial instincts," prejudice, and "social inferiority" characterizing relationships among blacks and whites. The thought that laws might *cause* whites and blacks to feel less prejudice seemed ludicrous.

But racial attitudes *have* changed dramatically during the twentieth century. One major influence has been the increased level of education. Another is legal change. The force of recent legal decisions (such as the 1954 *Brown v. Board of Education,* which struck down school segregation laws) has been to ignore whether racial attitudes can be changed and to concentrate on eliminating discriminatory behaviors. It has become clear, however, that when behaviors change, attitudes often change too.

How may changes in the law result in attitude change? Both cognitive dissonance and self-perception theories suggest how such changes may occur. A new behavior may be inconsistent with old attitudes. To reduce the inconsistency, one might change old attitudes. Further, changes in behavior may lead to new and different experiences and information, which themselves lead to attitude change.

Let's take a specific example. Suppose a white child's parents believe in racial segregation, yet their child is legally "forced" to attend an integrated school. Suppose also that, though a financial hardship, the parents *could* afford to send their child to a segregated private school. They have decided, however, to save the money for the child's college education. Therefore, they feel that they had at least some choice in the matter.

Seen from the perspective of dissonance theory, two cognitive elements are in conflict: belief in segregation and knowledge that they have chosen to send their child to an integrated school. Hence, the parents should be in a state of dissonance. Since parents cannot usually change the racial makeup of a school, the easiest route to dissonance reduction may be to change their beliefs ("Well, maybe integration isn't so bad after all"). If this occurs on a large scale, parental attitudes should show an appreciable change. Nationwide public opinion data suggest that this is the case; parents whose children attend integrated public schools are more open to integration than are parents with children in segregated public schools [73].

Self-perception theory suggests a similar process. In this example, the parents think that they are rigidly opposed to racial integration; yet they see themselves sending their child to an integrated school. Rather than thinking "What a hypocrite I am," the parents' evaluation of their attitudes toward integration may change. That is, they may think, "Well, since I'm sending my child to this school, I must not think that integration is so bad." Once again, such a process on a large scale could lead to attitude change, not only toward the *policy* of school integration but also toward the minority groups themselves.

Such processes might operate in the opposite direction, too. If people are "forced" to act in a hostile or discriminatory manner, they may develop attitudes that justify the behavior. For example, if a white person is forced to discriminate against blacks because of local norms or subtle pressures of society, his or her attitudes may become more negative as a result. Or, if a black person is forced to behave in a hostile manner toward whites because of the norms of a subculture, he or she may develop negative attitudes to justify the discriminatory behavior. Hence, attitudes may follow behavior; and attitude change may occur either in a positive or a negative direction, depending on the nature of the preceding behavior.

Equal-status contact

Many people have said, "If we could only get blacks and whites (or Jews and Gentiles, or hippies and hardhats) together and let them interact, then hostility, prejudice, and discrimination would end." This may be true. Evidence shows that *contact situations* sometimes lead to considerable attitude change.

For instance, during World War II, the U.S. Army was in part racially segregated and in part integrated. When white soldiers were asked whether or not they approved of integration in the Armed Forces, their opinions varied depending on prior experiences. Among white soldiers who had had no experience with integration in the service, only 38 percent favored integration. Among those whose regiment or division was integrated but who had served in a segregated company, 78 percent accepted integration. Finally, among white soldiers who had served in integrated companies, 93 percent approved of integration in the Armed Forces. These are dramatic differences. Since the men had no choice as to which type of company they served in, we can assume that initial attitudes of the three groups toward integration were approximately the same, but were changed through interracial contact [431].

Low-cost government housing projects built after World War II provided another field in which the effect of interracial contact could be investigated. Some projects were racially integrated; some were racially segregated; and some were building-segregated (or "checkerboard"), where both blacks and whites lived in the development but each building was either all-black or all-white [122; 499]. Investigations of whites' racial attitudes in such developments indicated that the opportunity for contact significantly affected attitudes. Whites who had shared neighborhood activities with blacks held more favorable attitudes toward them.

A second important factor was social climate. Investigators were able to identify groups of whites in integrated projects who happened to live so far away from the few black families that their contact with them was no greater

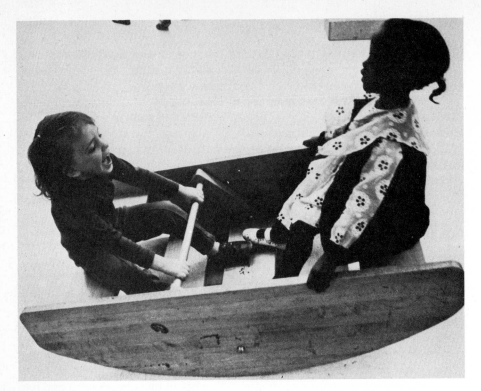

Figure 3-7. *Equal-status contact between ethnic groups. The fun and experience these playmates share with each other can be expected to have powerful effects on their racial attitudes as they grow up. It is only recently that such valuable interactions have become possible. Many children are still denied the opportunity to make friends with children from other ethnic groups. Such missed opportunities may be intentionally caused by parents, or may simply result from the way society (e.g., schools and neighborhoods) is structured.*

than that of whites in the "checkerboard" and segregated developments. Nevertheless, racial attitudes among whites in integrated projects were more favorable than among whites in the other two types of developments. The researchers hypothesized that this reflected the influence of the social climate; in the integrated development, it was communicated to residents that integration was desirable, since the development was integrated. In the checkerboard and segregated projects, on the other hand, the organization of the development strongly implied that integration was not desirable. Residents of these developments apparently used such information as a basis for their own attitudes.

Many investigations like this one demonstrate that interracial contact *can* lead to reduced prejudice. But close contact does not *necessarily* lead to reduction in prejudice. For example, in Hitler's Germany, Jews had lived in close contact with Gentiles for almost a century. Or, for another example, 300 years of relatively close contact between blacks and whites in the United

Figure 3-8. *The harsh reality of legal racial segregation. This black freedom rider debates whether to enter the whites-only waiting room at the Jackson, Mississippi, bus station in 1961. Although the civil rights movement beginning in the late 1950s led to the eradication of most laws and rules which explicitly supported racial segregation, many more subtle barriers to true equality for all in America remain.*

States has not ended racial prejudice. Writers have suggested that the degree of interracial contact has been greater in the South, even though whites' racial prejudice has remained higher there than in the North. Of course, the type of relationship, particularly in the South, has usually been one of unequal status: master-slave, householder-servant, prostitute-customer, foreman-laborer, and so on.

Studies of school segregation and racial attitudes generally yield no consistent results about whether racial attitudes improve or deteriorate with desegregation and increased contact. Some have found increased prejudice, some have found reduced hostility, and some have found no change. So other important variables must interact with contact to determine whether a situation will lead to reduced prejudice, increased prejudice, or no change. In the schools, both Clark [96] and Pettigrew [343] have argued that violence and disruption occur in desegregation whenever ambiguous or inconsistent policies are apparent.

The conditions which would make a contact situation ideal for fostering positive attitude change have been outlined by Gordon Allport [8] and Stuart Cook [106]. (1) Probably the most important condition is that the participants in the contact situation be of *equal status,* with neither superior to the other. In many interracial contact situations in America this has not been the case. (2) The situation should be structured to encourage mutual interdependence and *cooperation.* Moreover, the cooperation should lead to a *successful outcome.* Recall how competition and cooperation increased and reduced hostility among the boys in the Robber's Cave Study (Chapter 1). (3) Social *norms* applicable to the situation should *encourage interracial association.* The housing studies described above demonstrate how important this factor is. (4) The situation should *promote personal relationships* and the formation of friendship. (5) The *attributes* of participants should *contradict* prevailing negative ethnic stereotypes. For example, in interracial situations, whites should not be insensitive racists. Similarly, blacks should not fit the stereotype of either the "lazy Uncle Tom" or the "violent black racist." (6) The situation should *encourage* participants to *generalize* their changed attitudes to other situations and ethnic group members.

Stuart Cook [106] created a situation which met all of these conditions. It involved groups of three female college students—a black, a nonprejudiced white, and a prejudiced white—and two experimenters, one black and one white. The first two women were experimental confederates; the prejudiced white woman was the only real subject. The experiment consisted of a complex game that was played two hours a day for four weeks, and the results are encouraging. About 40 percent of the subjects changed their racial attitudes significantly on three separate attitude measures when these were given in a completely different setting a month or more after the experiment had apparently ended.

Cook also wanted to learn whether personality factors could account for the fact that some women changed their attitudes drastically, while others did not. It was found that a group of measures that assessed positive attitudes toward people and low cynicism effectively differentiated "changers" from "nonchangers" [108]. Women who became less prejudiced were those who had the most positive attitudes toward people and were the least cynical. They also tended to have lower self-esteem and a higher need for social approval than nonchangers—two measures that probably indicate general *persuasibility,* as discussed in Chapter 2. Subsequent research by Cook and his associates involving military groups has indicated that success on a group task leads to increased liking for *all* group members, black and white [61a], and that the perceived competence of the black member of the group was of major importance in determining whites' reactions to him [61b].

Still another recent study [163] looked at the way in which racial attitudes of men admitted to a "tough" state prison changed during imprisonment. Some prison units closely approximated Cook's optimal conditions, but others did not. Results were similar to Cook's original findings. When units appeared to support interracial contact and people were treated as equals, prejudice was reduced. Further, attitudes toward people in general were the best personality predictor of change. These findings applied to both blacks and whites.

■ EFFECTS OF ETHNIC SEPARATION

We have discussed the potentially beneficial effects of equal-status interracial contact. But what about the opposite situation? Some writers suggest that the most reasonable course in America is to increase racial isolation. This point has been made not only by segregationist whites but also by some black leaders. As analyzed by Pettigrew [342], the separatist position is based on several assumptions.

Beliefs of white separatists

The first assumption of white separatists is that whites and blacks will be more *comfortable* apart than together. There is some validity to this. There is often a good deal of awkwardness and discomfort in initial phases of interracial contact. But as contact increases, discomfort lessens. In terms of social cost, initial discomfort is small indeed when compared with the potentially negative effects of continued racial separation.

Continued separation can prevent blacks and whites from learning that their beliefs and values are not really so dissimilar. We discussed earlier the role that perceived or assumed belief dissimilarity plays in ethnic prejudice and discrimination. Further, separation may lead to *real* differences in beliefs and values; if so, the differences that evolve will make future contact situations more uncomfortable and potentially nonproductive. In addition, separation leads to the growth of vested interests—people and institutions that favor the separation for their own economic, social, or political gain. As Pettigrew points out, racial separation is the cause of, not the remedy for, awkwardness in interracial contact situations.

White separatists also make what Pettigrew calls assumptions of *racial inferiority*—that whites are biologically, intellectually, and culturally superior to blacks. Such racial-inferiority assumptions are becoming less frequent among whites, however. A third white-separatist assumption, the *racial-conflict* assumption, holds that situations of interracial contact must inevitably lead to conflict and unpleasantness. In one sense, this is correct. American history reveals that in periods when the traditions of white supremacy have gone unchallenged—such as from 1895 to 1915—there has been a good deal of *apparent* racial harmony. In contrast, periods of racial change have seen racial conflict. If there is change, and if large segments of the population oppose it, some conflict seems inevitable. But conflict is perhaps a necessary by-product of progress toward interracial harmony.

Beliefs of black separatists

According to Pettigrew, black separatists base *their* case on three main assumptions. First, like white separatists, they believe that the races are more *comfortable* apart. Another assumption often made by black separatists is that racism is a white problem and that, hence, *white liberals should eradicate racism* and not depend on blacks to do the dirty work. This idea appears rational and fair, but it's not likely to work. We have already seen that most mass media campaigns have been unable to reduce prejudice. And we have described the effectiveness of interracial contact in producing change. Obviously, interracial contact cannot produce attitude change unless both racial groups participate. Hence, even though it probably is unfair, it seems crucial that blacks participate in interracial contact if meaningful change is to occur.

A final assumption often made by black separatists is that blacks should achieve social and economic *autonomy before interracial contact increases.* This, too, has logical appeal. It could be argued that since blacks and whites presently are not equal economically and (in the eyes of many whites) socially, further contact should be postponed until blacks have gained equality so that the contact that follows will be on an equal footing.

A dilemma

But how can economic equality be achieved, and what will happen in the meantime? Since blacks are presently underrepresented in politics, projects designed solely for and by blacks are not likely to receive significant funding. Furthermore, black politicians, even when successful, are not likely to have access to a large part of the tax base; they lack the financial clout needed to build economic strength. And even if they had it, in the time that economic strength was being built, racist institutions would go unchallenged and probably grow still stronger. The negative effects of continued isolation in terms of belief dissimilarity and growth of vested interests who profit by maintaining segregation also make this assumption damaging and unfeasible.

Pettigrew believes society can achieve "true integration," wherein personal and group autonomy are maintained along with racial togetherness. No one would be forced to associate with others, but the barriers would be down and the doors would be open. The tough question is, How can we best achieve this goal?

▣ SUMMARY

We have suggested that equal-status interracial contact may lead to attitude change, partly because of learning on the part of the participants, partly because of the realization that beliefs and values are quite similar, and partly because of the rationalization associated with counterattitudinal behavior. But how likely is such interracial contact in America? Many writers, both black and white, have suggested that, though small, the likelihood is increasing.

One way to approach this dilemma is to modify the institutions which foster prejudice and racism. We discussed several ways in which institutional racism has been supported. If these institutions were changed, the racism associated with them might also change. But who is to do the changing? The people who are in the best positions to do so are naturally those who hold power within those institutions. However, they might be those *least* expected to be aware of ethnic bias or racism in "their" institutions. Since they have worked within the institution for so long, institutional biases may go completely unrecognized or, perhaps, be rationalized effectively.

It is clear that to make meaningful progress toward achieving a truly egalitarian society, massive changes must take place on at least two fronts. The ethnic attitudes, beliefs, and behavioral inclinations of the American majority (and to some extent, of the minority, too) must undergo major changes. Equal-status interracial contact and massive reeducation programs may have an effect here. At the same time, the ways in which society and its institutions oppress minority group members must be fully recognized, and effective measures must be taken to eliminate societal barriers. Only then will "true integration" be possible, with all ethnic groups enjoying equal freedoms and opportunities in American society.

4

sexism and socialization

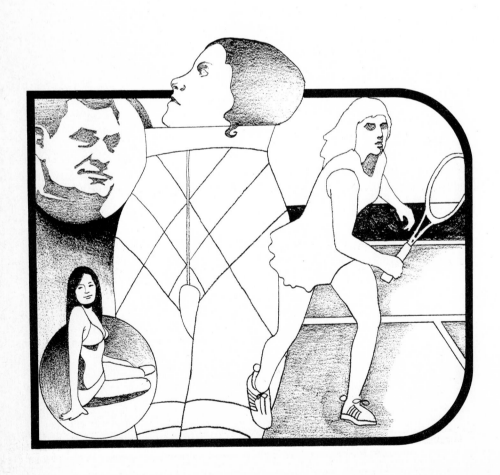

concepts

Sexism, a prejudice based on gender, operates like ethnic prejudice.

Sex-role behavior is behavior that is perceived to be characteristic and appropriate for one's gender.

Sexism can be understood as a result of being socialized into one's culture.

The study of socialization involves: (1) the groups that influence and shape behavior, (2) the products of that influence, and (3) the processes involved in that influence.

The socialization process can be seen both to have caused sexism and to be involved in alleviating it.

targets

After studying this chapter, you should be able to:

1   Identify several characteristics of sexism.
2   Describe differences between sexism and the development of sex roles.
3   Discuss the influence of others (and groups of others) in the development of sexism.
4   Identify how sexism affects females' self-concepts and sense of value.
5   Identify the major theoretical explanations of how individuals are socialized into their culture.

In Chapter 3, we discussed ethnic prejudice. The term *sexism* refers to a special kind of prejudice; it is an unjustified attitude relating to someone's gender, or sex. Theoretically, both men and women can be discriminated against and subordinated because of their sex, but in our culture most sexist attitudes and acts are directed against women. Even Aristotle suggested that "we should regard the female nature as afflicted with a natural defectiveness."

Sexism is widespread in American society today. It is also clear that Women's liberation and activism have brought recognition to this problem, and changes are being made. The more blatant aspects of sexual discrimination—unequal pay for equal work, failure to hire or promote women, differential credit practices for men and women—are being fought in the legislatures and in the courts. The effort will affect men as well as women.

But what about more subtle manifestations of sexism? Like racial prejudice, sexism is supported and taught by people and institutions in our society. (Try the quiz in Focus 4-1 to discover your own awareness of sexism.)

In this chapter we shall discuss sexism, how sexism is affected by conceptions of what are appropriate and inappropriate roles for men and women in our society; and how these conceptions of roles are developed.

■ IS THERE REALLY A SEX PREJUDICE?

To what extent do people guide their interpersonal behavior on the basis of sexual identity—being a woman or a man? Consider that there are relatively few women in public office and that politics appears to be almost exclusively a man's world. When Governor Ella Grasso of Connecticut assumed office in January 1975, she became the nation's first woman to be elected governor without benefit of a husband's prior incumbency. Suppose you are a woman who wants to be elected to a head-of-state position, such as mayor or governor. Who might vote for you? Do people make judgments primarily on the basis of sexual identity? A 1973 run-off election in Gainesville, Florida, gave an opportunity to investigate some of these areas. In the primaries for two seats on the city commission the two leading candidates for each seat were a man and a woman. Voters were interviewed in an attempt to discover whether sexual identity would be a major determinant of the voting behavior which they exhibited at the polls.

The interviews indicated that voters seemed to forget specific issues, differences in personalities, and differences in political ideology. Instead, they considered primarily the sex of the candidates. As one might expect, more women than men stated they would vote for the woman candidate. Not all women did, however. Those who felt they were "falling behind" their sisters tended not to vote for the woman candidate. On the other hand, men who felt women were improving their status more than men tended to

FOCUS 4-1 MYTHS AND REALITIES FOR WOMEN IN A MAN'S WORLD

The following questions come from a game devised by Tavris and Wexo [440]. Its intent is to increase our understanding of the sex-role myths by which we live. Find out where you stand.

Multiple-choice Questions *(Choose the best answer.)*

1 In Denmark, what percentage of the dentists are women?
  A—3%. B—46%. C—75%.
2 How many hours a week does the average housewife work in the house?
  A—40.3 hours. B—66.7 hours. C—99.6 hours.
3 Why was the word "sex" added to Title VII of the Civil Rights Act of 1964?
  A—It was a joke, put in as a last-minute attempt to get the bill defeated.
  B—Legislators were concerned about discrimination against women.
  C—Women's rights pressure groups had lobbied successfully in the House of Representatives.
4 Compared to female lawyers with ten years' experience, male lawyers with the same length of practice earn:
  A—20% more. B—50% more. C—200% more.
5 What percentage of women in professional and technical occupations are either nurses or teachers?
  A—50%. B—70%. C—90%.
6 In a 1970 study by the American Association of University Women, what percentage of men agreed that women are denied equal opportunity in business?
  A—27%. B—52%. C—77%.
7 In which country is this true? "Men are expected to show their emotions . . . they are sensitive and have well developed intuition and . . . are not expected to be too logical. Women, on the other hand, are considered to be coldly practical."
  A—Iran. B—Poland. C—China.
8 According to Freud, which of the following is a consequence of penis envy in women?
  A—A sense of inferiority. B—Contempt for other women. C—Low moral character. D—Desire for a male child. E—All of the above. F—None of the above.
9 The Supreme Court upheld a Texas law declaring that a married woman did not have the capacity to enter into a binding contract. This decision came in:
  A—1966. B—1926. C—1886.

True-false Questions

10 In the United States, only 1% of the engineers are women. True or false?

11 Black men were granted the right to vote fifty years before women were. True or false?

12 In 1900 the typical woman worker was 26 and single; now she is 41 and married. True or false?

13 In childhood, males are more likely than females to have severe psychological problems. In adulthood, the reverse is true. True or false?

Check your answers to learn how well you understand the nature of sexism. If you get eleven to thirteen, you understand a bit of the problem. However, if you get less than half right, you are a victim of what has been called the "nonconscious sexist ideology."

Answers

1. C	6. C	10. True
2. C	7. A	11. True
3. A	8. E	12. True
4. C	9. A	13. True
5. B		

---

vote for the man. We might say they were trying to "keep women in their place."

Some assume that there is "a place for women" and that the forefront of politics is not that place. What about people with more positive, liberal attitudes toward the recent aspirations of women? Are they also reluctant to vote for women? No. In fact, the strongest determinant of voting for women is a liberal conception of women's roles. This is true for both males and females. The more liberal (unbound by tradition) the voters were about women's roles, the more likely they were to vote for female candidates [473].

We have seen that a candidate's sex is a major consideration of some people's voting behavior. We have also seen that this may be a result of attitudes toward sex roles. What characteristics do most people identify as typical of each sex? Inge Broverman and her associates asked about one hundred undergraduates to list the characteristics, attributes, and behaviors by which they thought men and women might differ [80]. From these lists the researchers chose all items that were suggested at least twice and entered them in a questionnaire; other men and women were then asked to indicate the extent to which each item characterized an adult man (masculinity response), an adult woman (femininity response), and themselves (self-response). Since the concept of a *sex-role stereotype implies extensive agreement about characteristic differences between men and women,* only items with at least 75 percent agreement were considered "stereotypic." The result was a set of forty-one items that described masculine and feminine sex roles. These forty-one items appear in Table 4-1.

Since it was devised, the questionnaire has been administered to over a thousand adults. The findings can be summarized as follows:

1   General agreement exists about the different characteristics of men and women in various groups despite differences in sex, age, religion, marital status, and education level.
2   Characteristics descriptive of men are more highly valued than are characteristics descriptive of women. The positively valued masculine characteristics may be grouped together to form a profile which includes *competence, rationality,* and *assertiveness.* On the other hand, the positively valued female characteristics may be grouped together to form a profile which includes *warmth* and *expressiveness.*
3   Differences in sex-role characteristics exist, and they appear to be accepted and incorporated uncritically into the self-concepts of *both* men and women. The researchers suggest that sex-identity differences are considered "desirable" by college students, "healthy" by mental health professionals, and "ideal" by both men and women.
4   Individual differences in sex-role self-concepts result from differences in family situations and learning experiences. For example, daughters of employed mothers tend to perceive women as more competent than do daughters of homemaker mothers.

These findings suggest that there is a fairly extensive group of characteristics generally ascribed to females and males. Further, these characteristics appear to reflect our judgment of the quality of work men or women can accomplish in various areas [80].

We know that sexism exists and we know that there are sex-role stereotypes. But must it always be the case, however, given our physiological makeup, that society will end up along the lines that we have described? Evidence from the cross-cultural work of Margaret Mead and others with various New Guinea societies suggests that it need not. The society of the Tchambuli is organized like our own insofar as different sex roles are assigned to males and females. However, the roles are largely reversed. The Tchambuli female is an aggressive business manager and the dominant member of a marital relationship. The Tchambuli male, on the other hand, is closely attached to his children and fulfills a role similar to a mother's in our society. His mate considers him dependent and subordinate. The Tchambuli believe this arrangement follows the natural order of things and stems from the biology of males and females. Females, the Tchambuli note with confidence, are stronger than males. When Tchambuli females give birth to

Table 4-1. Stereotypic sex-role items

Competency cluster: masculine pole is more desirable

Feminine	Masculine
Not at all aggressive	Very aggressive
Not at all independent	Very independent
Very emotional	Not at all emotional
Does not hide emotions at all	Almost always hides emotions
Very subjective	Very objective
Very easily influenced	Not at all easily influenced
Very submissive	Very dominant
Dislikes math and science very much	Likes math and science very much
Very excitable in a minor crisis	Not at all excitable in a minor crisis
Very passive	Very active
Not at all competitive	Very competitive
Very illogical	Very logical
Very home oriented	Very worldly
Not at all skilled in business	Very skilled in business
Very sneaky	Very direct
Does not know the way of the world	Knows the way of the world
Feelings easily hurt	Feelings not easily hurt
Not at all adventurous	Very adventurous
Has difficulty making decisions	Can make decisions easily
Cries very easily	Never cries
Almost never acts as a leader	Almost always acts as a leader
Not at all self-confident	Very self-confident
Very uncomfortable about being aggressive	Not at all uncomfortable about being aggressive
Not at all ambitious	Very ambitious
Unable to separate feelings from ideas	Easily able to separate feelings from ideas
Very dependent	Not at all dependent
Very conceited about appearance	Never conceited about appearance
Thinks women are always superior to men	Thinks men are always superior to women
Does not talk freely about sex with men	Talks freely about sex with men

Warmth-expressiveness cluster: feminine pole is more desirable

Feminine	Masculine
Doesn't use harsh language at all	Uses very harsh language
Very talkative	Not at all talkative
Very tactful	Very blunt
Very gentle	Very rough
Very aware of feelings of others	Not at all aware of feelings of others
Very religious	Not at all religious
Very interested in own appearance	Not at all interested in own appearance
Very neat in habits	Very sloppy in habits
Very quiet	Very loud
Very strong need for security	Very little need for security
Enjoys art and literature	Does not enjoy art and literature at all
Easily expresses tender feelings	Does not express tender feelings at all easily

Source: From Broverman et al., 1972.

their young, the males enter confinement, are attended by midwives, and have sympathetic birth pangs symbolizing the new birth.

On the other hand, there are not always distinct differences between the sexes. The Arapesh are a mountain-dwelling tribe; Arapesh men and women are characterized by their mild, passive, domesticated, and gentle approach to sharing the care of the children as well as the home and other duties. In the Arapesh culture, division of labor is hardly recognizable. The Mundugumor culture is another example of minimal differences between the sexes. But unlike the Arapesh, Mundugumor men and women are ruthless, aggressive, and violent.

These cross-cultural data suggest that our physiological makeup simply can't explain why we become the social animals we do. In some cultures sex roles are reversed from our own, and other cultures are structured so that men and women are more similar than different in their social behavior. What is it about being human, about interacting with others, that creates behaviors and attitudes about "appropriate" or "inappropriate" things for a man or a woman to do? In "Woman as Nigger," Naomi Weinstein maintains that women do what the social environment causes them to do; that women do what is expected of them, what different authorities tell them to do. (We would add that the same is true for men.) Ms. Weinstein suggests that until we change the structure of society so that it expects women to succeed and does not program them into tailor-made slots, we will have sex differences. She summarizes by suggesting that "except for the genitals, I don't know what immutable differences exist between men and women . . . probably there are a number of irrelevant differences. But it is clear that until social expectations for men and women are equal, until we provide equal respect for both sexes, answers to this question will simply reflect our prejudices" [487, p. 58]. For a further look at the theory that "anatomy is destiny," see Focus 4-2.

Given that sex-role stereotypes do exist, it is not surprising that sexism and differential treatment are evident. We have to question whether sex-role stereotypes are necessary. Since anthropological evidence suggests that other cultures have other patterns, the answer appears to be *no*! To understand how sexism develops in the first place, this chapter will discuss *who* creates sexism; precisely *what* is created; and *how* it is created.

WHO CREATES SEXISM?

The process of bringing an individual's social behavior into line with the culture is known as *socialization*. Sexism and sex-role stereotypes result from socialization. We have modified Elton McNeil's [296] socialization scheme (Figure 4-1, p. 144) to identify the roots of sexism. McNeil's scheme describes the socialization process through several major aspects. They include: (1) The *individual* and the dimensions along which socialization will occur; (2) *who* socializes, including cultural forces as well as specific

FOCUS 4-2 YOU CAN'T FOOL MOTHER (FATHER?) NATURE

Many in our society defend the current male-dominant–female-submissive orientation by pointing to what they call the "natural order of things." According to this reasoning, human males are dominant because humans are animals and the "facts" suggest that males in other animal species are the "top-dog." However, it is worth pursuing the facts about other species.

First, we must recognize that when we turn to biology to explain social behavior, we are including ourselves as part of nature. Can our new understanding of genetic codes, of reproductive and other hormonal systems, give a clue to the explanation of our more stable and recurring social patterns? Can we reexamine the role of evolution as described by Darwin and others to discover what might stimulate regularities in human social behavior? Scientists who favor this approach propose that we consider the possibility that biological structures set the stage for patterns of social interaction like those described in connection with sexism.

Research in this area has considered the social behavior of primates, which are closely related to humans in the evolutionary chain. Descriptions of the social behavior of most primates are similar. Consider baboons, as described by Jane Van Lawick-Goodall. Baboons live in groups, or clans, and have a rather clear social structure. The males enter clearly established status or power hierarchies, depending on numerous fights or simulated threats and withdrawals. The power structure in such a "family" can be observed. Offspring are nursed by their mothers and cling to them physically for mobility during early stages of life. During early weaning, the young baboon makes male and female friends, and although it retains close family ties, it sometimes adopts adult friends from within the clan. As a young male nears adolescence, he starts to fight his way through the power hierarchy, but, generally speaking, he must leave his clan and wander until he finds another clan to join if he is to achieve a really powerful position in a clan's hierarchy. Male and female baboons are attentive toward one another as evidenced by their grooming of one another, a practice common among primates. The total picture is clear: Whenever there is intrusion from outside, the male becomes the dominant force, and older patriarchs totally dominate the clan's social behavior.

One does not have to study only primates to find this behavior. The social behavior of American Wapiti (elks), closely parallels what we have just described. Herds of Wapiti roam together, and whenever there is danger, the male must ultimately engage the intruder in combat and protect the herd. There has been recent concern as to whether this phenomenon of male dominance is real or simply a group's utilization of the strongest—usually a male—for defensive purposes. Researchers have also questioned whether the old matriarchical females might really be the leaders in primate groups; they might "allow" the powerful males to act in defense by nodding their heads. All we want to suggest is that even in cases which appear clear, controversy remains.

Nor is the story entirely one-sided. Some species offer examples of female-dominated interaction patterns (bees, ants, etc.). We know, for example, that the female black widow spider typically devours her male mate. And consider the following description of the praying mantis [59, p. 28].

> Imagine yourself perched on the stem of a flower. Your bright green skin matches the leafy background beautifully. You are a male praying mantis. Several inches ahead of you on the stem, looking very much like you *but nearly twice your size*, is a very appealing female mantis. Your problem is to achieve copulation with her. What will you do? Be careful. You must leap upon her and clasp her firmly, but if you are slightly off target, she will turn upon you and bite your head off. You can't blame her really: after your head has been munched off, your body jerks convulsively in a very effective imitation of copulatory behavior, and the job gets done. You may in fact, be a better lover when you have lost your head.

A male praying mantis must either figuratively or literally lose his head to achieve copulation with a female. While this is a rather violent social interaction, it leaves no doubt about which sex in this species is dominant.

Another, less violent example is provided by sea horses. A female sea horse does not devour or kill the opposite sex. But she does lay her eggs in his pouch and leave. The male must hatch the eggs and care for the young.

These examples show that the "facts" about the "natural" order of things are two-sided. Whichever side you want to prove can probably be supported by natural examples.

"agents"; and (3) *what* results, including certain specific acquisitions as well as the final personality of the individual.

The individual

Throughout history people have held different conceptions about the nature of a human being. Some have thought that a child's mind is a *tabula rasa*, or "blank tablet," to be formed (written on) by meaningful events in life. Other philosophers have taken the opposite side, suggesting that each individual is predetermined to accomplish certain things in specific ways according to preplanned patterns. The middle ground probably makes more sense to twentieth-century thinkers. Today we have evidence both that there are genetic determinants of particular abilities and predispositions (for example, intelligence) and that certain experiences can affect the learning and performance of different behaviors.

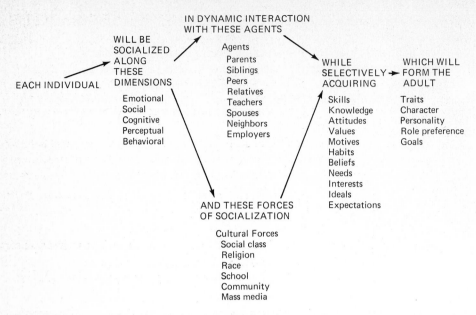

EACH INDIVIDUAL → WILL BE SOCIALIZED ALONG THESE DIMENSIONS

IN DYNAMIC INTERACTION WITH THESE AGENTS

WHILE SELECTIVELY → ACQUIRING

WHICH WILL FORM THE ADULT

Emotional
Social
Cognitive
Perceptual
Behavioral

Agents
Parents
Siblings
Peers
Relatives
Teachers
Spouses
Neighbors
Employers

Skills
Knowledge
Attitudes
Values
Motives
Habits
Beliefs
Needs
Interests
Ideals
Expectations

Traits
Character
Personality
Role preference
Goals

AND THESE FORCES OF SOCIALIZATION

Cultural Forces
Social class
Religion
Race
School
Community
Mass media

Figure 4-1. *According to this schematic of McNeil's socialization framework, each individual is socialized along a number of dimensions by virtue of dynamic interaction with certain agents and cultural forces of socialization. One selectively acquires a number of characteristics which form the adult personality.*

Figure 4-1 suggests that socialization is accomplished along several dimensions: emotional, social, cognitive, perceptual, and behavioral. All these different aspects of a person will be affected by processes that socialize. For example, socialization processes affect how we perceive a certain situation, how we think about it, how emotional we are in it, our interpersonal behavior, and even our behavior when alone. The effects of socialization are comprehensive indeed. Now let's look at who is responsible for these widespread effects—first, in terms of the global influence created by culture and, second, in terms of the specific important people in our lives.

Cultural forces

Margaret Mead has described cultures that seem to have sex-role patterns opposite to our own. Every culture has prescriptions and ideas about "correct" behavior for men and women. These ideas of appropriate behavior have much to do with what is valued in a society. In many primitive cultures, special emphasis is placed on fertility. In some cases, a woman's proven fertility determines her value as a marriage partner, and in other cases, a barren wife can be returned to her parents as a *defective* product [63].

Anthropologists identify five different types of cultures, depending on

(a)

Figure 4-2. *The effect of developing sexism can be seen in these two scenes. At early ages (a), in preschool and grade school, boys and girls appear to have equal opportunities to participate and learn. However, male domination is clearly evident in later life, as shown by this scene at the Chicago Mercantile Exchange (b). Note the two female clerks standing next to the "Eggs" sign, the lowest position in the entire stock exchange.*

(b)

their source of food and other needed items. These types clearly differ in patterns of male or female dominance. In *hunting and gathering* cultures, males and females appear to be equally important. Both have functions to serve in getting food. Men hunt but often are unsuccessful, and so it is important that women be able to find food in gathering activities. The second type of culture is known as the *horticulture group;* in these societies, domestication of plants and animals is most important. These groups tend to wander into new areas when the land being used cannot support sufficient crops and livestock. In the horticulture societies, females are dominant, since they supervise and are responsible for agricultural activities. The third type of culture is *agricultural;* it is characterized by the use of mechanical energy (such as plows) to get more from the soil and supply food for larger groups. In agricultural societies, land must be defended, and males are dominant. A fourth type of culture is identified as *pastoral* and is characterized by its specialized dependency on a particular group of animals—say, cattle. In the societies, males are supremely dominant, and the status of females is lower even than that of the all-important animal. These cultures tend to produce militant, aggressive individuals. The last type of society is described as *industrial* and is characterized by production of consumer products. According to this classification of cultures, an industrialized society should tend toward equalization of roles between males and females. In other words, as societies become less primitive, sexism should become less evident. We've seen, however, that this is not always what happens.

Concern for achievement cuts across the interplay between appropriate sex-role behavior and society's values. It is described by Margaret Mead in *Male and Female* [297, p. 168]:

In every known human society, the males' need for achievement can be recognized. Men may cook, or weave or dress dolls or hunt hummingbirds, but if such activities are appropriate occupations of men, then the whole society, men and women alike, votes them as important. When the same occupations are performed by women, they are regarded as less important. In a great number of human societies, men's sureness of their sex role is tied up with the right, or ability, to practice some activity that women are not allowed to practice. Their maleness, in fact, has to be underwritten by preventing women from entering some field or performing some feat.

Mead is suggesting that although males and females may perform different sex-role behaviors in different cultures, it may be that more often men enjoy the rights of choice, status, and prestige.

In addition to these general comments about the influence of culture on developing sexism, McNeil has identified six different cultural forces that influence socialization: social class, religion, race, school, community, and the mass media.

Social class. Social class has been found to affect sex-role behavior [356]. Lower-class children tend to identify themselves with interests appropriate to their sex sooner than do middle-class children. There are several possible explanations for this finding:

1. Perhaps stronger pressures are brought to bear at an earlier age in lower-class homes for engaging in appropriate behavior for the particular sex.

2. It may be that a clearer distinction is made between male and female roles in the lower classes.

3. There is the possibility that lower-class parents may be less tolerant of deviation from a stereotyped norm [229].

Although social-class differences may influence the approach to socialization, the problem is more complex than may first appear. Most measures of social class include such characteristics as education level, income, amount of money inherited, etc. These may be appropriate measures for males. But for females, social status depends more on whom they marry than on what they personally achieve or have been accustomed to since childhood [208].

Religion. A review of religious thought of four different persuasions demonstrates the widespread view that men are superior to women [45].

First, from Genesis (1, 2, 3).

In the beginning, God created the heaven and the earth . . . and God said, let us make man in our image, after our likeness; and let them have dominion over the fish of the sea, and over the fowl of the air, and over the cattle, and over all the earth . . . and the rib, which the Lord God had taken from man, made he a woman and brought her unto the man . . . and the Lord God said unto the woman, what is this that thou has done? And the woman said, the serpent beguiled me, and I did eat . . . unto the woman He said, I will greatly multiply thy sorrow and thy conception; in sorrow thou shalt bring forth children; and thy desire shall be to thy husband, and he shall rule over thee.

Second, from Saint Paul:

For man . . . is the image and the glory of God; but the woman is the glory of the man. For the man is not of the woman, but the woman of the man. Neither was the man created for the woman, but the woman for the man.

Let the woman learn in silence, with all subjection. But I suffer not a woman to teach, nor to usurp authority over the man, but to be in silence, for Adam was first formed, then Eve, and Adam was not deceived, but the woman, being deceived, was in the transgression not withstanding, she shall be saved in childbearing, if they continue in faith and charity and holiness with sobriety. (1 Tim., 2)

Third, from the morning prayer of the Orthodox Jew:

Blessed art Thou oh Lord our God, King of the universe, that I was not born a woman.

And lastly, from the sacred text of Islam, the *Koran:*

Men are superior to women on account of the qualities in which God has given them preeminence.

Given such religious thought and writing, it should be no surprise that sexism develops. Male dominance in religious thought is probably exemplified in its most extreme form when people react to the possibility that God may be a woman! Heresy!

Race. In comparison with white families, black families are more often described as being mother-dominated (as noted in Chapter 3, this "finding" is not without opposition). If black males are less used to depending on a father figure, the absence of a father might have a less disruptive effect on sex-typing among black males than among white males (wherein the father typically dominates). This reasoning has been confirmed in part [206]. More competitive and aggressive play occurs among father-absent blacks than among father-absent whites. These traits are generally promoted for males, and the white males lacked them. There is also ethnicity information about sex difference on school performance and conformity, and about perceptual judgments [224; 227; 462]. For instance, school-age black males and white females have found adult goals to be only minimally relevant to school performance. With regard to conformity behavior, black males and white females appear to be more likely to be influenced by others than are white males or black females. In all these studies, black males and white females appear to be similar in some behaviors. Since these two groups share neither hormones nor race, the similarity seems to be based on shared environmental handicaps [208]. Although ethnicity does seem to affect sex-role identification, the phenomenon has not been well studied.

School. The school's influence on sex-role concepts and sex-typing is significant [313]. Comparing children from traditional, middle-class schools and homes (stressing socialization toward conventional standards) with children from more modern middle-class schools and homes (stressing the development of the individual rather than conformity to a norm) suggests that conventional sex-role attitudes are more characteristic among children from traditional settings. Unequivocal commitment to one's own sex role, to sex-typed play, and to aggressive expression in boys and family orientation in girls are more consistent among children from traditional backgrounds. It can also be noted that girls, more than boys, depart from conventional expectations when placed in modern school settings.

The school setting is a complex situation for females. During the elementary years, success and excellence in school are rewarded with love and approval by parents, teachers, and peers. The love-and-approval orientation of elementary schools is a by-product of their effort to confront the child with as little break from family life as possible, so as to ease entry into the education process. Since females traditionally are socialized toward family orientation, the elementary school gives an opportunity to compete and excel while remaining consistent with the feminine orientation. However, changes occur at higher levels of education, particularly in college and professional pursuits. "Driving home a point, winning an argument, beating others in competition, and attending to the task at hand without being sidetracked by concern with rapport require the subordination of affiliative needs" [208, p. 137]. These qualities, which adults need for sustained top performance, are typically not part of the feminine sex role defined by our culture. As a result, a discrepancy is created between achievement and characteristic "feminine" behavior.

Community. The concept of community is particularly interesting to social psychologists. Some of us live in more well-defined neighborhoods than others; some live in rural, others in urban, settings. But each community has certain basic social institutions that affect socialization, such as health care, government, and transportation systems. The criminal justice system is one which touches us in many ways. Whether primitive or sophisticated, each community has people who are in charge of preventing crime and apprehending individuals who break the law, a judicial system, and a penal or rehabilitation system. Although this is just one social institution that reflects a community, the functioning of most criminal justice systems demonstrates the community's socializing influence on sex-role identity. Although there is recent evidence that females are beginning to commit more "white-collar crimes" (victimless crimes, such as embezzlement and fraud), historically there have been distinct differences between the types of crimes committed by males and by females.

The President's Commission on Law Enforcement and the Administration of Justice reported in 1967 that more than one-half the girls referred to juvenile courts in 1965 were referred for conduct that would not be criminal if it were committed by an adult. The offenses included running away from home, incorrigibility, truancy, sexual delinquency, waywardness, ungovernability, or simply being a person in need of supervision. On the other hand, only one-fifth of the boys were referred for such conduct. Boys usually are charged with larceny, car theft, burglary, and other adult offenses. There are no differences between male and female juvenile-delinquency rates when samples of students are asked about actual behavior; however, official police and court records show large differences like those described. The initial difference is in referrals. Our social system appears to select for punishment girls who have transgressed sexually or who have defied parental authority. In singling out such females, our social system defines a narrow range of acceptable behavior for girls, and courts interpret even a minor deviation as a substantial challenge to family authority. Official police and court data suggest that girls who have committed noncriminal offenses are overrepresented in court populations, and they tend to receive harsher treatment than boys who have actually broken laws.

In another way, boys are also discriminated against. Police tend to release a larger proportion of girls apprehended for actual violations than

(a)

(b)

(c)

Figure 4-3. *Changing representations of the female role in the mass media can be noted in the comparison of the 1943 Ginger Rogers film* Lady in the Dark *(a) with* The Mary Tyler Moore Show *(b). The message of the 1940s appeared to be that career "girls" inevitably became neurotic. Such is not the case in the 1970s. In fact, note the total reversal in the two photographs. In the film, the male is holding the note pad, listening to the female with the faraway look in her eyes, seemingly unsure of herself. Thirty years later, it is the female who holds the note pad, jotting down ideas and looking confident, while the male has that faraway, indecisive appearance. The changing view of women in publications can be seen in this mailing piece for* Ms. *magazine (c), the first magazine to present a nonstereotyped view of women. And in advertising (d), the increasing professionalism of women is now being recognized.*

(d)

boys. It appears that police have a paternalistic attitude. Girls should be treated chivalrously and released, unless they need protection. So girls escape punishment for adult offenses and receive harsh treatment for minor offenses. Males, on the other hand, appear to be released by officers for minor offenses but are prosecuted for real adult crimes [93].

Parental referrals are also different for girls and boys. Parents do not tend to call the police if their sons are somewhat truant, but the opposite applies with daughters. A large proportion of original referrals for running away from home, incorrigibility, waywardness, truancy, etc., are from parents—most often from the mothers of the girls.

The story does not end with differential arrest rates. After an arrest, there is a clear difference in how boys and girls are treated by correction officials and the judicial system. As soon as they are placed in detention homes, females far more often than males are given physical exams (often pelvic exams) with the intent of identifying evidence of sexual behavior (to find out if girls "carry" venereal disease). This reflects the courts' equation of female delinquency and sexuality.

Once in custody, girls are detained longer than boys. In Honolulu in 1964, for example, girls averaged 19.3 days in pretrial detention, while boys averaged only 8.9 days. In Hawaii from 1970 to 1971, nearly 70 percent of girls in the state training school were committed for juvenile offenses, compared with only 12.9 percent of boys. Similar data are available from other states, such as Pennsylvania, where 83 percent of imprisoned girls were held for juvenile or sexual offenses [93].

Mass media. The mass media, including television, radio, movies, books, magazines, and newspapers, have a very strong effect on our social behavior. A good example of sexism in the mass media is provided by sex-segregated employment ads in the newspapers. In the early 1970s, several human-relations commissions became concerned with the effects on employment patterns of separate job listings for males and females. The question became: Do sex-segregated ads discourage women from seriously considering jobs that might be classified as "male" in interest? Researchers had women rate thirty-two jobs advertised in Sunday editions of the *Pittsburgh Press* as to their desirability as a job setting. The results indicate that sex-segregated ads do discourage women from considering jobs that otherwise interest them. When the same jobs appeared in the integrated, alphabetical listing, 81 percent of the women preferred "male interest" to "female interest" jobs. When the jobs were listed separately, only 46 percent were as likely to apply for a "male interest" job as for a "female interest" job. The job of newspaper reporter is a case in point. Its popularity fell from seventh place in the integrated listing to nineteenth place in the segregated, "male interest" listing. As a result, employers could effectively discourage female applicants from positions by placing them in sex-segregated listings [41]. In response, the U.S. Supreme Court decided on June 21, 1973 that sex-segregated listings are illegal.

An example of sexism in public broadcasting comes from Dr. Edgar Berman, a Baltimore physician, in a speech on July 25, 1970:

If you had an investment in a bank, you wouldn't want the president of your bank making a loan under these raging, hormonal influences at that particular period. Suppose we had a President in the White House, a menopausal woman president, who had to make the decision on the Bay of Pigs, which was, of course, a bad one; or the Russian contretemps with Cuba at that time.

These examples only hint at the overwhelming impact of the media on sexism. Historically, bias can be found even in comic books of Superman, Batman, etc. The potential effects of "women's magazines," advertising, popular song lyrics, and even language style are large. However, just as media have kept sexism alive, they also can be used to fight it; consider this chapter and McGraw-Hill's instructions to authors in Focus 4-3.

Individual agents

Besides the cultural forces representing large groups of people, McNeil [296] indentifies various individuals who are extremely important during socialization. These "agents" of socialization are parents, siblings, peers, relatives, teachers, spouses, neighbors, and employers.

Parents. In our culture, parents have more influence on our developing personalities than any other socializing agent. Their sex-typing of boys is somewhat different from the sex-typing of girls [319]. The most crucial determinant of the development of "masculine" traits in boys is the nature of the father-son relationship. "Appropriate" sex-role preference in boys is found to be directly related to nurturant, affectionate relationships with the father. In general, the boy who sees his father as a highly salient and powerful person is likely to develop sex-appropriate responses. Maleness is valued highly in our culture, and therefore is something the boy wants anyway.

On the other hand, the acquisition of "feminine" traits by young girls is not so simply determined. Again, a positive mother-daughter relationship is of paramount importance. Girls who have affectionate, warm relationships with their mothers find it easier to adopt "sex-appropriate" behavior. However, in addition to this factor, it appears that parents' personalities are very important. Both parents must be highly self-confident, and the mother must display behavior that indicates she likes herself. Further, the father's personality and behavior are very important in the daughter's development. The more his interests and attitudes are masculine in nature, and the more he encourages his daughter's participation in feminine-typed activities, the more likely she is to develop "appropriate" sex-role preferences. The process of female typing, while directly related to mother-daughter relationships, is thus fostered by (1) a highly adequate mother as a female model and (2) a father who is aware of the behavior expected of a young girl and

FOCUS 4-3   SEXISM IN PRINT

The language one uses to communicate often reflects sexism. As we wrote this book, the McGraw-Hill Book Company supplied us with a set of guidelines for the treatment of the sexes in its publications. Excerps from these guidelines follow:

a.) In descriptions of women, a patronizing or girl-watching tone should be avoided, as should sexual innuendoes, jokes, and puns.

no	yes
the fair sex; the weaker sex	*women*
the distaff side	*the female side or line*
the girls or *the ladies* (when adult females are meant)	*the women*
girl, as in: I'll have my girl check that	I'll have my *secretary* (or my *assistant*) check that. (Or use the person's name.)
the little woman; the better half; the ball and chain	*wife*
female-gender word forms, such as *authoress, poetess, Jewess*	*author, poet, Jew*
female-gender or diminutive word forms, such as *suffragette, usherette, aviatrix,*	*suffragist, usher, aviator* (or *pilot*)
libber (a put-down),	*feminist; liberationist*
sweet young thing,	*young woman; girl*
housewife	*homemaker* for a person who works at home, or rephrase with a more precise or more inclusive term

b.) In reference to humanity at large, language should operate to include women and girls. Terms that tend to exclude females should be avoided whenever possible.

no	yes
mankind	humanity, human beings, human race, people
primitive man	primitive people or peoples; primitive human beings; primitive men and women

no	yes
man's achievements	human achievements
the best man for the job	the best person (or candidate) for the job
manmade	artificial; synthetic, manufactured; constructed; of human origin

c.) Occupational terms ending in *man* should be replaced whenever possible by terms that can include members of either sex unless they refer to a particular person.

no	yes
congressman	member of Congress; representative (but Congress*man* Koch and Congress*woman* Holzman)
businessman	business executive; business manager
fireman	firefighter
mailman	mail carrier; letter carrier
salesman	sales representative; salesperson; sales clerk
insurance man	insurance agent
statesman	leader; public servant
chairman	the person presiding at a meeting; the presiding officer; the chair; head; leader; coordinator; moderator
cameraman	camera operator
foreman	supervisor

Source: From *Guidelines for Equal Treatment of the Sexes in McGraw-Hill Book Company Publications.* Reprinted with permission from McGraw-Hill Book Company.

who actively encourages his daughter to act in "feminine" ways. In effect, young males need one model (a father), while females need two (both a strong mother and strong father). Apparently, since "femaleness" is not valued so highly in our culture, more effort is needed to "appropriately" sex-type females.

Other studies of parental influence suggest that parental warmth and dominance are also important variables in appropriate sex-role identifica-

Figure 4-4. *Do girls really like to help their mothers wash the dishes? Do boys really like to help their father change the oil in the car? Or, rather, do children learn which tasks are traditionally "appropriate" to learn, which toys to play with, and which parents to imitate? Parents play a crucial role in supervising all these activities.*

tion [207]. Dominance appears to be important for appropriate imitation by boys, while maternal warmth is more effective for appropriate identification for girls. In short, parental behaviors differ according to the sex of the child and, in turn, reaffirm the potential for sustaining sexism.

Siblings. Sisters and brothers—siblings—are also very influential agents of socialization in the family. Different-sized families with different sex compositions affect developing masculinity and femininity in several ways. In two-child families, boys with a brother develop significantly more masculine behavior than do boys with a sister. Similarly, girls with a sister show more feminine behavior than do girls with a brother. The sibling may act as a model. But in larger families, a *counteractive phenomenon* also occurs. Boys with two sisters and no brothers score higher on scales of masculinity, not femininity. In families with two or more sisters, a boy appears to react against (or counterbalance) the femininity and adopt an excessively masculine profile. Interestingly, the same is true for a father: The more daughters he has, the more masculine he acts. Conversely, the more sons there are in a family, the more feminine the father's score. That is, fathers of two or more sons are relatively more willing to express sensitivity, anxiety, and so on, behaviors traditionally regarded as feminine. It is as though the father tries to "balance" the family in one direction or the other. As a result, siblings affect not only a child's socialization regarding sex-role behavior, but that of the parents as well [437].

Peers. We all have seen the influence of peers on sex-role development. Boys are forever challenging and daring their playmates to games of football, contests of athletic prowess, war games, etc. At the same time, young girls seek playmates for games with dolls, to play house, and to be nurses. At older ages, the picture is not much different. In the early teenage years, the peer group is as important as it ever will be. During the years immediately following puberty, many sex-role ideas are learned. Just when the peer group is most influential, the physiological events of puberty draw attention to sexual functioning. As a result, the peer group can have a dramatic influence on sex-typing.

It should be noted that these descriptions of socialization practices occur in Western cultures. However, in an analysis of child rearing in the Soviet Union, it has been noted that there, too, the peer group is the chief source of values, rewards, and discipline, especially in school [78]. Children in a given row within a classroom are jointly responsible for one another's actions, so that if one child falls behind in learning fractions, the row leader will provide tutoring or have another math expert in the row do it. This system is not unlike the child-rearing practices of the Israeli kibbutz (collective farm), in which the peer group gains in importance at the expense of adult agents of socialization [420].

Relatives, Teachers, Spouses, Neighbors, and Employers. Although we could continue with a description and examples of the influence of each of these agents, the picture should be clear by now. Each of these individuals is, at one time or another, in a position to model, teach, or in some way influence and make more complete the process of socialization.

■ WHAT IS CREATED?

Having seen how different cultural forces and agents affect sexism, it is time to ask how widespread their effects are. Table 4-1 (see page 140) suggests that we selectively acquire skills, knowledge, attitudes, values, motives, habits, beliefs, needs, interests, ideals, and expectations regarding appropriate sex-role behavior. These acquisitions, or results, are fostered by the different agents. For instance, because of socialization by agents such as parents and teachers, young females may not develop an interest in science and, as a result, may not take enough science courses to learn much about the topic. Later, if they decide to become physicians, they may not have developed the skills necessary to get into a premedical program, even though medical schools now accept more women students. Although we have implicitly (and explicitly) discussed the results of socialization throughout this chapter, a more systematic description of the results of sex-role socialization is necessary.

Beliefs and attitudes

In our introduction to this chapter we said that prejudice on the basis of sex exists, as do certain stereotypic characterizations about sex roles. Such stereotypes affect our self-concepts and our sense of self-esteem. For women, this process may incorporate certain negative beliefs, such as the *fear of success.*

Martina Horner [215, 216] suggests that in competitive achievement situations women are often caught in a double bind. They not only fear failure, they fear success. The idea is that the dominant societal stereotype views competence, independence, competition, and intellectual achievement as qualities that are basically inconsistent with femininity. A woman then comes to expect that success in achievement-related situations will have negative consequences. This expectancy arouses fear of success, which tends to inhibit performance. This is a two-pronged fear. First, there is concern that, in achieving, a woman may not be perceived as feminine; and second, there is fear that success may actually have negative results. In other words, the men and women, friends and strangers, who interact with a successful woman may change their behavior toward her in a way that is unpleasant. For example, they may not ask her to go to lunch with them and may even wish not to work with her.

Horner's research required both females and males to tell a story based on the following introduction: "After first term finals, John (Ann) finds himself (herself) at the top of his (her) medical school class." Females wrote

Figure 4-5. *During adolescence and at older ages, the influence of peers becomes very important in all that we learn. The formalities and customs surrounding dating help to solidify our ideas regarding "appropriate" behavior for both males and females.*

about Ann, while males wrote about John. Afterward, all stories were scored for motives to avoid success. Three general types of response were noted.

1 The most frequent stories about Ann reflected strong fears of social rejection as a result of success. The stories depicted anxiety about loneliness, popularity, and unmarriageability. For example, "Ann doesn't want to be number 1 in her class—she feels she shouldn't rank so high because of social reasons. She drops down to ninth in the class and then marries the boy who graduates number 1." "Ann starts proclaiming her surprise and joy. Her fellow classmates are so disgusted with her behavior that they jump on her in a body and beat her. She is

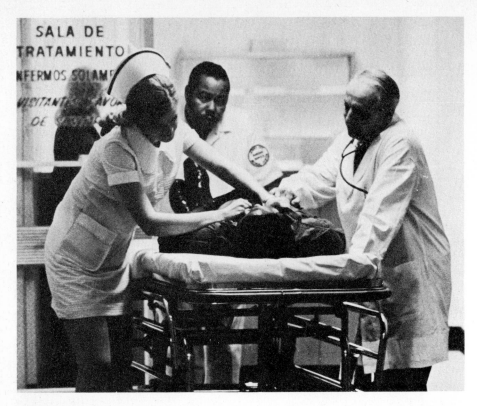

Figure 4-6. *An unfortunate result of the socialization of sex roles is that, often, competent individuals come to believe that certain occupations hold no opportunities for them. A very real example is provided by the medical profession. Traditionally, women have been the nurses and men the doctors. Recently, however, the admissions of women to medical school and men to nursing school have been on the increase, and scenes such as this from an inner-city hospital may change in time.*

maimed for life." These examples reflect the first category's social rejection and fear of losing friends as a result of success.

2   Other females seem much more worried about their definitions of womanhood than about rejection. Their stories expressed fears and negative feelings about success and doubts about Ann's femininity and normality. For example, "Unfortunately, Ann no longer feels so certain that she really wants to be a doctor. She is worried about herself and often wonders if perhaps she isn't normal. . . ." "She didn't even want to be a doctor. She is not sure what she wants. Ann says to hell with the whole business and goes into social work—hardly as glamorous, prestigious, or lucrative; but she is happy."

3   The third type of response is even more bizarre. These stories seem to deny the fact that Ann is at the top of her class, or they show such

hostility that the stories don't make sense. For example, "Ann is a code name for a non-existent person created by a group of medical students. They take turns writing exams for Ann. . . ." "Ann is talking to her counselor. Counselor says she will make a fine *nurse.*" These stories don't logically follow the premise of the story but seem to be an attempt to cope with what must be an inconceivable situation.

Over 65 percent of the females' stories fell into one or another of the above categories, but only 8 percent of the males' stories showed evidence of similar motives to avoid success. In short, the differences between the stories of males and females were enormous. Do women really fear success? Some probably do; but Horner may have stacked the deck too much. What was found may really have been fear of "sex-role inappropriateness" rather than of success [458]. In other words, women may want to succeed as much as men, but society channels their achievements into homemaking, etc., rather than professional success. That is, they may want to succeed in these areas, not in "inappropriate" ones. As outlets for feminine achievement expand in range, fewer women should devise stories like those described above.

Skills

A similar result of socialization appears in women's evaluations of their skills and competency. In one study, female subjects judged the technical competence and artistic future of a series of artists on the basis of slides showing examples of the artists' work. Investigators wanted to learn whether ideas about competency are so deeply embedded that they would be demonstrated in the ideas and judgments of the very group being studied. Half the paintings were by male artists, and half by female artists. In addition, half the paintings were described as recognized winners in "The Annual Cleveland Competition." The remaining paintings were represented as having been "entered . . . in a museum-sponsored young artist contest." The results are intriguing. Since it would be hard for inexperienced judges to disagree with art critics who have actually made awards, ratings of the technical competence and future artistic promise represented by the winning paintings were similar for male and female artists. However, the paintings which were only "entries" allowed more freedom to the subject-judges. In this case, the females rated the male artists as more competent and promising [344].

These results do not reflect the fact that one or two of the works really were better than the others, since pairs of artists and their works were randomly reassigned among the subjects. Why did these women evaluate men as more competent? It is possible that—self-defeating as it is—members of a group who feel themselves the target of prejudice may come to accept the attitude of the dominant majority—that is, that they are inferior.

Thus, the "prophecy" of the majority group comes to be accepted by the minority group. This "self-fulfilling prophecy" is dangerous: When you say, "I can't do it," you don't do it; and everyone then agrees that you can't.

Motives and values

One might expect successful women to be at the forefront of efforts to create change. But several psychologists have described a "queen bee" syndrome [422]. The queen bee is a woman who has fought her way up in a man's world and achieved success, who then tacitly *opposes* the aims of feminism. This response can be expected. Such a woman has achieved success as an individual. She has accepted the system enough to fight within it, has learned to work and succeed within the system, and now might even be responsible for promoting the system. It's not surprising that she would be the last to give up the system and the first to attribute her success to her own skills rather than to some social or environmental push. Consequently, as Table 4-2 suggests, queen bees tend to be more likely than feminists, radicals, or other women to favor individual initiative, to shun atonement for discrimination, and to reject some basic assumptions and goals of feminist organizations. They seem to believe, "I made it, and so could any woman who really tried."

Knowledge

By simply being alive and being either a male or a female, we are exposed to many opportunities to learn what is appropriate or inappropriate sex-role behavior. In being socialized, we acquire a vast amount of knowledge about what is acceptable and unacceptable behavior for each sex and the situations which make the behavior appropriate or inappropriate. This makes it possible for some individuals to display *either* masculine or feminine behavior, depending on the situational appropriateness of various behaviors [44]. Such *androgynous* individuals tend to display sex-role adaptability across situations, engaging in situationally effective behavior without regard for its stereotype as more appropriate for one sex or the other. Androgynous subjects of both sexes display "masculine" independence under pressures to conform and "feminine" playfulness when given an opportunity to interact with cuddly kittens. On the other hand, nonandrogynous people tend to display appropriate sex-role behavior when their own situation calls for it, but appear to be lost in situations that are traditionally appropriate only for the other sex. For example, a nonandrogynous male may feel comfortable in the pursuit of athletic competition but quite uncomfortable when discussing sewing patterns. An androgynous male would be comfortable in both situations. This suggests that masculinity and femininity may not be an either/or situation. If there are feminine and masculine traits, and feminine and masculine situations, it may be that some individuals will display either or both

Table 4-2. Attitudes of women toward the concerns of feminism

Percent who:		Feminist groups			
	"Queen Bees" (professionals)	Nongroup women	Consciousness-raising groups	NOW	Radicals
Agree that "women have only themselves to blame for not doing better in life"	54	51	37	36	24
Favor preferential treatment for women to make up for past discrimination	20	19	30	54	64
Think women can best overcome discrimination by working *individually* to prove their abilities	51	48	44	20	20
Think the women's movement will improve their lives	40	41	73	88	95
Think the "special courtesies extended to women keep them feeling helpless and in their place"	28	33	53	83	88

Adapted from *Psychology Today*, January 1974.

behaviors, depending on a situation and its rewards. It's clear that socialization provides these individuals with enough knowledge to act.

Ideals

Sandra and Daryl Bem suggest that, consciously or not, we have been training women to know their place. They give examples of how sexism operates as an insidious and unconscious ideology in our society [45]. The following is a paraphrase of a "liberated" marriage description:

Both my wife and I earned Ph.D. degrees and I turned down a superior academic post in Oregon, and accepted a less desirable position in New York, where my wife could get a part-time teaching job and do research at one of the other colleges in the area. Although I wanted to live in a suburb, we purchased a home near her college so that she could have an office at home, where she would be when the children returned from school. As my wife earns a good salary, she can easily afford to pay a maid to do her household chores. My wife and I share all the tasks around the house equally. For example, I do the laundry for her and help her with many of her other household tasks.

This example shows how widespread sexism is. Why is it *her* maid, instead of their maid? Why is it *her* laundry? Why *her* household tasks? Why must the wife consider the part-time position, and why does the husband's career mostly determine the alternatives? The Bems suggest that if this marriage really is egalitarian, the descriptions should retain the same flavor if the roles of the husband and wife are reversed. Again paraphrasing, it would then read:

Both my husband and I earned Ph.D. degrees and I turned down a superior academic post in Oregon, and accepted a less desirable position in New York, where my husband could get a part-time teaching job and do research at one of the other colleges in the area. Although I wanted to live in a suburb, we purchased a home near his college so that he could have an office at home, where he would be when the children returned from school. As my husband earns a good salary, he can easily afford to pay a maid to do his household chores. My husband and I share all the other tasks around the house equally. For example, I do the laundry for him and help him with many of his other household tasks.

Perhaps society is changing; but we are not yet at a point where many families think this way.

Habits

When we address individual habits, an infinite number of behaviors surface for discussion. One way to characterize behavior generally is to discuss psychological health, or freedom from behavioral disturbance. Recent information suggests that although there appears to be little difference in the

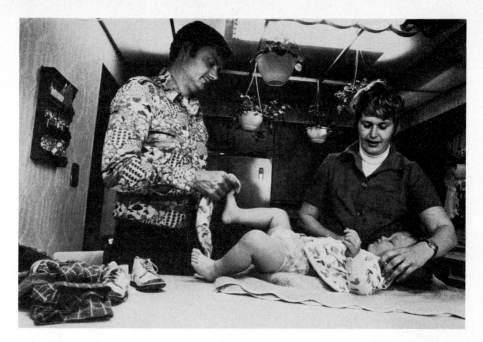

Figure 4-7. *The contemporary ideal seems to be an egalitarian marriage, wherein the division of tasks is not assigned solely on the basis of sex-role "appropriate" or "inappropriate" tasks. The husband can now change the diapers, vacuum, and wash the dishes without feeling threatened, while the wife can handle the checking account and fix appliances that need repair. Hopefully, tasks will be shared on the basis of competencies rather than prejudices.*

psychological health of male and female youngsters, things change with age [92]. For a number of reasons, women seem more likely to have problems than men, and these problems tend to be of a self-destructive nature. According to statistics of the National Institute of Mental Health [223] 268 more women than men were hospitalized in state and county mental hospitals from 1950 through 1968. Similarly, 125,351 more women than men were either psychiatrically hospitalized or treated on an outpatient basis between 1964 and 1968. Second, most female neuroses "are a result of societal or sex role demands and discrimination" rather than the individuals' supposed mental illness. Chesler suggests that most husbands and therapists encourage a woman to accept blame for this unhappiness and be "cured." Further, she suggests, "the therapist-patient relationship reinforces a system of beliefs and attitudes that are psychologically damaging to the patient, and psychologically rewarding to the doctor" (p. 18). The situation is complex in that 90 percent of the therapists in the country are male (and a few of the female therapists may be queen bees). Female patients have looked up to males as protectors, advisors, and competent authorities over various matters, and it is very hard, when in trouble, for them to go to another woman for help. At the same time, however, male therapists may tend to worsen the problem by holding the traditional view of women as submissive, fragile, etc. They therefore may intensify their patients' problem.

A different example of how behavior is affected by sex-role socialization is presented in *The Male Machine*, by Marc Feigen Fasteau [147]. He suggests that the traditional male credo of maintaining "a stiff upper lip, being tough and strong all the time" is directly responsible for some of the United States foreign policy during the Vietnam war. Male toughness and the refusal to give up are supposedly evidenced in the Pentagon Papers and by at least three Presidents and their advisors regarding policy on Vietnam. Fasteau quotes a 1965 memo from Secretary of Defense Robert McNamara's assistant (John McNaughton) listing United States aims in Vietnam as "70 per cent—to avoid a humiliating U.S. defeat (to our reputation as a guarantor). 20 per cent—to keep South Vietnam . . . from Chinese hands. 10 per cent—to permit the people of South Vietnam to enjoy a better, freer way of life." Many lives were sacrificed to reputation. In addition, Fasteau argues that other traditional male attributes are responsible for the endless competition in our society, strokes and heart attacks, and many mangled lives.

This socialization process is widespread. We have discussed who is involved and what the results are. We will now turn to a discussion of how socialization works and the acquisition of sex roles. The process that has created sexism and allowed it to continue will also be the process that creates change.

■ **HOW SEXISM IS CREATED**

The three major theoretical orientations to socialization and the acquisition of sex roles are (1) the psychodynamic approach, (2) the cognitive-developmental approach, and (3) the social-learning approach. These approaches differ widely in their views of human nature. For instance, some see children as passive products of socialization, and others view them as active creators of their own development. All three approaches give considerable attention to the development of sex roles.

The psychodynamic approach

Freud's psychoanalytic model is the classic theory regarding the development of personality [25]. One fundamental concept of Freud's approach is that of instinctual drive. Supposedly, each individual has a store of vital energy that is sexual in nature and serves to energize the drive toward pleasure. This basic energy has been termed *libido*. Freud believed that the difference between an adult and a child is a difference in how the libido is regulated. Both adults and children seek pleasure, but adults achieve it in a different, more socially acceptable fashion. Freud describes three structures of personality that help this process: the *id*, the *ego*, and the *superego*. Basic and present at birth, the *id* functions according to the pleasure

Figure 4-8. *Unfortunately, sex-role stereotypes are slow in changing. Tough, strong, stiff-upper-lipped John Wayne represents the male machismo of myth and legend. Richard Benjamin's spoiled, neurotic husband in* Diary of a Mad Housewife *represents one form of male dominance today.*

principle—"I want what I want when I want it." As soon as the goal of the id is achieved, a child is happy for a while. The *ego* develops out of the id and acts to control it. It responds to the outer world as well as to inner drives, and it controls the id by delaying, inhibiting, and retraining pleasure-seeking into socially acceptable forms. Drives are satisfied, but according to a principle of social reality. The *superego* can be thought of as one's conscience. It is the moral aspect of personality and consists of cultural values, parental strictures, etc., that have been accepted by an individual. In terms of the interrelationships among the three structures, the id is the source of motivation for all systems and represents instinctual and pleasure-seeking drives; the ego represents a happy medium, providing and patterning behavior in such a fashion that the desires of the id are achieved, but within the restrictions of the superego.

A second maturational process described by Freud is the staging of psychosexual development. He felt that psychosexual development occurs as the primary center of gratification shifts from the mouth to the anus and then to the genitals. In other words, at different stages of life, different body zones become the centers of pleasure. Changes in these zones are important.

The first psychosexual stage follows birth, and is called the *oral stage.* The primary source of pleasure and gratification comes from stimulation of the mouth region. After the oral stage (at some time during the second year), a child enters the *anal stage,* when the predominant source of pleasure becomes the anal region. This shift is believed to be a universal maturational process. An important concept in Freudian theory is that a person can be arrested at one stage of development. One who smokes cigarettes and pipes, is overly appreciative of mountains, chews on pencils, or has a breast fixation might be said to be an oral personality. And one who is miserly with valuables and possessions might be described as anal, since the person "holds things in."

At about age four, a child's primary source of libidinal pleasure shifts to the genital region. During the *phallic stage,* sex-role identification becomes important. Now the child is curious about anatomical differences between the sexes, the origin of babies, what sex is, and what the father and mother do to create babies. Freud believed that during this stage, both boys and girls learn to place particularly high value on the penis. It becomes a valued possession for males, and females' lack of a penis is supposedly viewed as either a defect or a result of someone's taking it away. An attempt by females to win success in masculine terms would be seen as a manifestation of "penis envy" and a desire to "get even." A major aspect of the phallic stage is the *Oedipus complex.* In the Greek tragedy, Oedipus becomes king by murdering his father and marrying his mother. Freud felt that—like Oedipus—all boys, out of love, develop a desire for sexual relations with their mothers. The thought of taking their father's place in sexual encounters with the mother would, of course, be compounded by a child's inadequate understanding of sexual behavior. A boy loves his mother and feels hostile toward his father but is afraid of potential retaliation via castration by the father. He "knows" that castration occurs; females, after all, don't have a penis. This conflict between desire for the mother and fear of castration is the Oedipus complex. Castration anxiety (fear of castration) finally makes the boy give up sexual wishes for his mother. He turns to the aggressor and winner—his father. By aligning himself with his father's power, he turns his back on the feminine orientation. This identification with the aggressor solidifies his masculine interests and values.

Freud didn't work out female development through the Oedipal situation so completely, but he did think the process was similar. According to Freud, a girl's sexual desire for her father and rivalry with her mother is usually resolved by repression of all sexual desire. Then a girl identifies with her mother which leads to the adoption of feminine characteristics and values.

The difference between Freud's developmental schemes is that for boys the Oedipal complex *ends* because of the castration complex; for girls, the *Electra* complex *arises* because of the castration complex. (Mother cut off my penis; therefore, my dad is nicer, and I want to be like him.) As there is less anxiety involved in this process for females than for males, Freudians theorize that females have weaker superegos and less solid or improper sex-role identification. The weak superego supposedly causes high deviance rates, as well as nontypical sexual behavior, such as homosexuality. Later, during adolescence, the genital stage is relived, but with a different emphasis. Now the love object shifts from the family to someone outside it. Also, by adolescence, one's concept of love has become more tender and altruistic. With this, the psychosexual development of a child is complete.

A basic criticism of the psychodynamic approach is that it focuses primarily on speculation and offers little direct supportive data. In fact, the only premise found to be true in almost all cultures is the incest taboo. It is a tremendously rich theory with sparkling metaphorical possibilities, but it does not generate directly testable propositions.

The cognitive-developmental approach

Another approach to the development of sex differences is provided by cognitive theorists, who concentrate on people's capacities for thinking and their styles of thinking. Jean Piaget has suggested that children pass through four different stages of development that vary according to cognitive style, from the most concrete operations (such as knowing that objects have permanence) to the most abstract conceptualizing. Piaget's theory has been applied to many areas, such as game playing. Children in beginning stages cannot understand the rules to games. During the concrete-operations stage, children understand the rules completely and are unwilling to deviate in any way from them. Lastly, during the formal-operations stage, children can understand that people make the rules and, therefore, can modify them to make the game more exciting.

Larry Kohlberg [250] suggests that the development of sex-role concepts, like the development of intellectual skills, is a form of growth that occurs in all children. According to this view, sex-role concepts become permanent and stable when ideas about physical objects become stable— between ages three and seven. The implication of this approach is that the process of forming a sexual identity is not a unique process determined by instinctual wishes and identifications; it is seen, rather, as part of a general process of conceptual growth. This multiple-stage growth process involves the following sequence:

1 The child labels itself as either a boy or a girl, based on the physical reality of genital differences.
2 Masculine-feminine values develop out of the need to value things that are stereotypically consistent with the self (e.g., liking a doll because Carmen is a girl and girls like dolls).
3 The child then identifies with and imitates like-sex parents by virtue of the desire to be either masculine or feminine.
4 While identifying with the like-sex parent, the child translates the parent's behavior into sex-typed preferences and values.
(Kohlberg [250] calls these preferences and values sex-role identification.)

The social learning approach

Social learning theory is concerned with how people acquire and then perform different social behaviors. The learning of interpersonal behavior may take many forms. In this section we'll look at three major aspects of social learning: reinforcement, coaching, and observational learning.

Reinforcement. Practically all social learning theories distinguish between acquisition and performance. Acquisition is thought of as the learning phase, when we acquire what we know. Performance is thought of as the acting out of a particular behavior that has been learned. Rewards (and punishment) affect both the acquisition and the performance of behavior.

According to social learning theory, sex-role behaviors may be defined as behaviors that typically elicit different rewards for one sex than for another. In other words, sex-role behaviors have consequences that vary according to the sex of the performer, or acquirer. Sexism and sex-typing occur as an individual learns (1) to distinguish between sex-typed behavior patterns, (2) to generalize from the specific learning experiences to new situations, and (3) to perform sex-role behavior. Clearly, reward and punishment are important aspects of all three steps.

Since parents are often the dispensers and withholders of rewards and punishments, it can be expected that children quickly learn differences in parental expectations regarding appropriate sex-role behavior. Appropriate sex-role behavior refers to the extent to which a child behaves in a way considered typical for that child's sex. Researchers have shown pairs of pictures involving appropriate and inappropriate sex-role activities to five-year-old children of both sexes. The children were asked which activity of each pair the mother and father would prefer for boys and for girls, and which activity each child would prefer herself or himself. It turned out that boys chose "masculine" activities more than girls did, and children of both sexes thought parents preferred appropriate activities for the child's sex [148].

We know that parents pressure children to adopt appropriate sex-role behavior by selectively distributing rewards. They give toy soldiers, trucks, and footballs to their sons, toy kitchens and dolls to their daughters. There is also evidence that parents perceive the behavior of their sons and daughters differently. Consider the responses provided by fathers who were asked to describe their two- and three-year-old daughters: "She's seductive, persuasive, knows how to get me to do things she can't get her mother to let her do." "She loves to cuddle, she's going to be sexy—I get my wife annoyed when I say this" [184]. Similarly, when males and females are punished, they are punished in different ways. Males receive more physical punishment than girls. In one study, four-year-olds tried to solve puzzles while researchers observed the mother-child interaction as the parents attempted to "teach" their child how to complete the problem. The children were from middle- and lower-class environments and two different racial groups. In each of these four subgroups, boys received more punishment than girls [150]. Clearly, direct reward or punishment for social behavior will influence the kinds of behavior that are learned, and the kind of behavior that is performed. This is as true of any social behavior (for example, ethnic prejudice) as it is of the acquisition and performance of sex-role behavior.

In discussing reinforcement, we described how parents often operate as teachers, trying to get their children to perform particular kinds of behavior. In addition to controlling the reinforcement of their children's behavior, parents also can provide "hints" about what they think is appropriate. But teaching involves more than reinforcement.

Coaching. In a coaching relationship, one individual guides a second through a series of situations designed to form behavior. For example, a mother may guide her daughter through a series of situations designed to create a perfect "little woman." The steps in this process are not fixed. The coach must be prepared to predict, indicate, and explain the events involved to the pupil. For example, a father may decide that he wants his daughter to become an excellent cook, and he may arrange a series of experiences that will give the daughter an opportunity to learn about cooking, to experience cooking, and to taste the results. Throughout the process, the coach stimulates current desires and also seeks to create new desires and aims [433]. The coach, of course, hopes that the child will acquire (1) new knowledge about the range of behaviors that the coach thinks are appropriate, (2) new skills and responses, and (3) greater motivation from enjoying the experiences that foster a particular behavior. As a result, a mother who spends most of her daughter's summer vacation teaching her to cook would be particularly pleased if the daughter developed a desire to be a skilled chef.

There are other aspects to coaching. One involves the importance of challenges or dares. A father who "dares" his son to ski down a particularly rough slope, or to tackle a hefty fullback, is asking the child to assert his "masculinity." The effect of a challenge is complex. The challenge itself probably raises anxiety in the child. In accepting the challenge, the child makes a commitment to behave in a particular fashion and will probably do so. Failure to follow through would make the child appear foolish to himself (herself) and others. If the child successfully meets the challenge—which is generally the case, when a coach is wise—the child feels good and is thus rewarded. The child then becomes more committed and more motivated to maintain that behavior.

Observational learning. People do not always have to be taught directly how to behave in a particular situation. They need only observe the behavior of others in similar situations and then act similarly when it is their turn. This process is called *observational learning.* The basic notion is that a person is *exposed* to some behavior or attitude and may, in turn, become disposed to act similarly. Observational learning differs from other contemporary learning interpretations in its view of the role played by cognitive functions (the processing of additional information, developing and testing hypotheses, and establishing rules and strategies for behavior). According to proponents of observational learning, or *modeling,* as it is popularly called, much social behavior is learned—either deliberately or inadvertently—through the influence of examples provided by meaningful others.

Albert Bandura [29, 30] proposes that three different effects result from exposure to modeling stimuli. In the *first* of these, observers may *acquire response patterns* not previously within their behavior repertoire. For example, a young girl may imitate her mother's behavior in interactions with the father. So Daddy enters the room and hears, "Well, hello there, honey," from his three-year-old daughter. *Secondly,* one can *strengthen* or *weaken certain existing responses* by attending to what happens to the actor as a result of engaging in that behavior. For example, a female student who may not like to flirt sees a classmate get higher grades by engaging in such behavior. Bandura suggests that she may learn that such behavior pays off in this particular instance and decide not to inhibit it but to engage in it herself. The student has not learned new behavior. She has learned that by flirting she can get what she wants in this situation. The *third* effect of exposure to modeling stimuli has to do with helping one to *distinguish among stimuli.* Having observed a few women actually enter the fields of law and medicine, more and more women now perceive it to be a real choice and are entering these fields to achieve success and financial security. Therefore, exposure to modeling stimuli can provide new behavioral skills and abilities, information about the probable outcome of engaging in a particular behavior, and knowledge about the situation [29, 30].

Modeled behavior is affected by whether or not the model receives reward or punishment for the behavior. For example, Maria may acquire the knowledge that it is unladylike to be aggressive if she sees other females acting in a passive fashion and being rewarded for submissive behavior.

Figure 4-9. *Models are an important part of social learning. Traditionally, women have done the majority of teaching in the earlier grades, especially preschools. One excuse for this classification of jobs was that the child's transition from home to school would be easier if both authority figures were women. As males feel freer to engage in the education of young children, different models will be provided than have historically been valid in this country.*

But, the *performance* of observationally learned responses largely *depends upon the nature of the reinforcing consequences to the observer.* Maria may never choose to engage in submissive behavior herself. If she never has occasion to perceive rewards for acting in a nonaggressive fashion, it is unlikely that she will behave in such a manner.

Suppose yourself a citizen of a small town with one major industry. Most people in town work for the same company. By observing the behavior of the man in charge of hiring, you become convinced that he is a male chauvinist. You have watched his behavior with others, how others respond to him, and what happens to them when they engage in certain behaviors. You saw one young woman play up to him while seeking a traditional feminine job. He rewarded her with a good position with high pay. At the same time, another woman who sought an engineering position was not hired, while a male seeking the same position was. (To complete the four possibilities, we can imagine that a male who applied for a job as secretary to this personnel manager would find himself out on the sidewalk in an instant.) You are seeking a position with this firm and have learned much by

Figure 4-10. *Just as women's groups and men's groups have served to perpetuate traditional ideas of "appropriate" sex-role behavior, social learning goes on in groups today with different purposes. These women are not interested in knitting. Their assertiveness is clearly evident, and new "appropriate" behavior is being learned.*

observation. Given that you have the skills needed for different positions in the company, and given what you know about the personnel manager, your approach will be determined by the interplay of the kinds of rewards you want and your personality. If you are a female who really needs money, you may choose to flirt a bit and ask for a secretarial position. Given other circumstances, you might be quite businesslike. If you are a male and need money, you choose to present yourself as competent, independent, highly motivated for advancement, but willing to start at any level.

An aspect of modeling that has been studied most often by sociologists is the concept of *differential association.* The thrust of this work is that when you spend more time with one group of people than another, your behavior will become similar to the first group's. You simply have more time to model the first group. One aspect of differential association is that people are passive about choosing associates. For instance, a child is reared in a particular family that lives in a particular neighborhood largely because of its income and desires. This environment for learning continues to affect the behavior of the child, whether desired or not. Girls spend most of the time with their mothers, and (when both parents are present) boys spend it with their fathers—sometimes by necessity (such as in public restrooms), but other times only by custom. And, until serious dating begins, most children spend the majority of their time in same-sex peer groups. Nor is it uncommon to find even adults splitting many social functions into groups characterized by clusterings of men around the bar, women in the kitchen, etc. Very clearly, this involves differential association, and there is high potential for a different kind of social behavior to be picked up in these same-sex groups.

The real thrust of observational learning is that there are different aspects of the modeling situation, all of which affect acquisition and performance of social behavior. Such learning is probably a very important aspect of our developing personalities. Whether through direct reinforcement, coaching, or modeling, individuals develop expectancies and values that vary according to sex and the particular social setting.

Summary of theoretical perspectives

The psychoanalytic, cognitive-developmental, and social-learning perspectives of sex roles are clearly quite different. Freud concentrates on instinctual drives and the anxiety arising from taboo relationships to account for sex-typing. Kohlberg suggests that changing capacities for problem solving and thinking are closely related to understanding masculine-feminine concepts and the values associated with each. Lastly, the social learning theorists suggest that sex-role conceptions develop as a result of meaningful interactions with others; the child either observes "appropriate" behavior or is reinforced and taught it. These theoretical approaches, as well as the rest of the chapter, apply to much more than sexism. Socialization occurs for a broad range of social behavior and sexism is just one example.

■ SUMMARY

An unjustified attitude relating to one's sex (gender) is known as sexism. One tragedy of sexism is that often women themselves adopt certain beliefs and behaviors that promote it. This adoption illustrates the process of socialization, by which an individual's social behavior is brought into line with that of the culture at large. Sex-role behavior is, then, behavior which is perceived to be characteristic and appropriate, depending on one's sex. Skills, knowledge, values, attitudes, habits, and ideals can all be affected by socialization.

Cultural forces and larger groups of people, as well as individuals (agents), can be identified as responsible for sexism. Social class, race religion, school, and the mass media are some of the major forces of socialization. Parents, siblings, peers, relatives, and teachers represent the individuals who create sexism. How groups and agents accomplish the task of socializing individuals is a matter of theoretical interest. We have discussed the Freudian psychosexual framework, the Kohlberg cognitive-developmental approach, and the social-learning perspectives.

5

relating to others: affiliation, attribution, attraction, and love

concepts

Fear can increase the desire to affiliate with others.

All of us have implicit personality theories regarding how personalities are structured.

The ability to judge others accurately depends on both stereotype accuracy and differential accuracy.

The attributions we make to another person based on their behavior depend on the strength of environmental forces, how expected the behavior was, and how much the behavior affected the observer.

People tend to explain their own behavior in terms of the situation but others' behavior in terms of the others' personalities.

Self-attributions of emotion depend on both physiological arousal and cognitive cues in the environment.

Overweight persons tend to be more stimulus-bound than normal-weight persons regarding feelings of hunger.

The most important determinants of liking are propinquity, similarity, and physical attractiveness.

targets

After reading this chapter you should be able to:

1 Discuss the possible causes of affiliation.
2 Outline the basics of social exchange theory.
3 Identify four steps in friendship formation.
4 Explain the importance of central traits.
5 Outline the underlying structure of attribution theory.
6 Describe the effects of believing in a "just world."
7 Explain the "juke box" theory of emotion.

8 Identify situations where complementarity is a stronger determinant of liking than is similarity.

9 Outline how the two-factor theory of emotional arousal can explain love.

10 Describe the Romeo and Juliet effect.

Absence makes the heart grow fonder.

Out of sight, out of mind.

Opposites attract.

Birds of a feather flock together.

I never met a man I didn't like.

Beauty is in the eye of the beholder.

Love is merely the exchange of two fantasies and the contact of two skins.

All these bits of folk wisdom refer to *interpersonal relationships,* the interactions between two or more people. Whether we talk about togetherness or loneliness, friendship, love, or hate, we are talking about how people relate to each other.

This chapter explores several aspects of interpersonal relationships. The first question we'll deal with involves why we interact. Why do people establish relationships with others? The second question involves how we make judgments about others and form impressions of them. Our impressions of others will determine whether we want to interact with them at all, and, if we do, the impressions will affect the type of relationships which develop. Finally, we'll consider what causes us to like or dislike others, what determines attraction, and when attraction develops into love.

■ AFFILIATION: WHY DO PEOPLE NEED PEOPLE?

Most of us sometimes want to be alone, away from the madding crowd. Some people expend a great deal of effort to get away for a day or a weekend at regular intervals. A few people (for instance, hermits) isolate themselves from other people for long periods of time. Yet the facts that a recluse is often seen as strange and that it often takes a good amount of effort to maintain isolation point to a basic characteristic of modern society: *Most of our waking hours are spent in interaction with other people.* The range of possible types of interaction is vast. Talking, making love, working cooperatively, arguing, listening, playing competitively, and fighting are just a few. People are truly social animals. But why do we affiliate? Several answers have been proposed, including explanations based on instinct, the need to survive, the desire for rewards, and a need for social comparison.

Figure 5-1. *A frustrated desire for affiliation. This baby's reaction shows how powerful and terrifying loneliness can be. We may learn to handle loneliness more skillfully as we grow older, but the desire for affiliation, for the presence of others, remains a powerful motivating force.*

Instinct

Speculating on the nature of people, Aristotle concluded that people instinctively affiliate with others. We are "political animals," and because of inborn characteristics, we seek out others, form families, and organize societies.

This instinct position on the nature of affiliation was further elaborated in 1908 in the book *Introduction to Social Psychology,* by William McDougall [293]. (This was the first social psychology text written by a psychologist.) McDougall defined instinct as "an inherited or innate psycho-physical disposition which determines its possessor to perceive, and to pay attention to, objects of a certain class, to experience an emotional excitement of a particular quality upon perceiving such an object, and to act in regard to it in

(a)

Figure 5-2. *Varieties of affiliation.* (a) *The quiet interaction between the man and his son probably satisfies many needs for both of them. The couple by the lakefront* (b) *satisfy some of the same needs for each other, but their interaction has other costs and rewards as well. The group of people at a party* (c) *are also satisfying their desire to affiliate, but in a quite different atmosphere. The types of rewards and costs which are most important may be considerably different for people in differing age groups.*

a particular manner, or, at least, to experience an impulse to such action" (p. 30). For McDougall, instincts were the ultimate basis for, and units of, behavior. He eventually listed eighteen instincts, one of which was *gregariousness,* the tendency to affiliate with others.

According to the instinct position, we do not seek out others because we need them or because others are rewarding; we do so simply because our biological nature impels us in the direction of others. Although there may be some truth to this position, it is impossible to test. The testing problem arises because it is impossible to prove that affiliation doesn't occur as a result of rewards that occur during interactions. In other words, if affiliation occurs to obtain rewards, then there is no reason to assume that it is instinctive. Also, a researcher would have to show that a person who has never seen others since birth (and therefore couldn't have learned to affiliate) would suddenly affiliate if given the opportunity. Because we cannot

(b)

(c)

test the instinct position, other views have dominated the field in recent years.

Survival

Plato, Aristotle's mentor, taught that people affiliate because they have to in order to survive. An infant enters the world helpless and would die quickly if not cared for. Even after the child has left this stage of helplessness, other people are needed for it to survive in an often hostile world. Society rests on the continual interaction of people. Major societal institutions which so vitally affect our lives—government, business, education, religion, etc.—are all based on interaction. Without affiliation, such institutions, and hence society, would topple. And without society, people might cease to exist.

Social rewards and social exchange

Social scientists and philosophers have long known that many of the prime motivators of human beings—need for approval, for love, for power over others, for goods, and so forth—are based on human interactions. Without others, rewards could not be achieved. Approval, praise, love, and friendship can be "delivered" to a person only by another person. But receiving rewards is only part of the story; one has to give as well as receive.

We often speak of conversation as an "exchange of ideas." But human interactions involve the exchange of many things in addition to ideas. Social scientists [459; 214; 62] have proposed a way to analyze human interactions that focuses on what is exchanged; logically, this approach is called *social exchange theory*. Any activity that leads to the gratification of a person's needs can be described as "rewarding." The "cost" of engaging in an activity then depends on the degree of effort, unpleasantness, and difficulty involved, and on rewards from other possible activities which are rejected in order to participate in the present activity. Applying such economic analysis to human interactions, one can speak of the *outcome* of an interaction in terms of overall rewards and costs. An activity provides one with a *profit* if the outcome is rewarding or a *loss* if the outcome is negative.

Comparison level: What we expect. We can all think of many relationships which have had positive outcomes for us, and many which have had negative ones. But the *proportion* of outcomes which have shown profits or losses differs among us. Some people have had high success interpersonally, with many profitable relationships. Others have received less overall profit. Based on these differences, people develop different expectations about the kind of outcome they are likely to receive from a particular relationship. Social scientists have described this expectation as a person's *comparison level* [459].

Individuals' comparison levels depend on their past experiences in relationships with others and their judgment of what outcomes people like

Figure 5-3. *Social exchange in action. These men and women at a singles bar are estimating the rewards and costs associated with continuing to talk to each other. They may now either change partners or become involved in the bargaining process, trying to elicit greater and greater social rewards from each other.*

themselves generally receive. One attribute of a person with high self-esteem is a relatively high comparison level for interpersonal relationships—people with high self-esteem expect to have relationships that provide a good profit level. People with low self-esteem and a lower comparison level, on the other hand, may be satisfied with relationships that show little profit or even a loss, if that is what they are used to receiving.

Comparison level for alternatives: The next best thing. A closely related concept is termed *comparison level for alternatives* [459], which refers to the value of the next best alternative interaction a person could enter. For example, if a student is stopped by an acquaintance after class and trapped into a conversation, the length of time spent talking will depend on what alternative activities are possible. If the person was going to the library to study for a test when the acquaintance popped up, he or she might spend a long time in conversation (assuming that studying in the library is not a very appetizing alternative activity). The comparison level for alternatives is low. If, on the other hand, he or she was going to meet an important date and go to a movie, the interaction with the acquaintance would be quite brief, since the comparison level for alternatives would be high. The comparison level for alternatives determines a person's *dependence* on a particular relationship, since it affects whether the person will sustain a particular interaction or reject it for an alternative.

Social exchange theory can be applied to analyses of why we need others (we need them to obtain rewards), and how we develop bonds with others. Consider, for example, what might transpire at a "friendship mixer" dance where few of the people there knew each other beforehand. According to social exchange theory, the relationships one would form there may develop in four general steps. The first step involves *sampling and estimation* of the rewards and costs likely to arise from a given interaction with another person. A person who seems interesting promises high rewards, a dull or cloddish person low rewards.

The second step is *bargaining.* This is a mutual attempt to maximize rewards and minimize costs from a relationship. If both participants try to do this and are successful, a kind of spiral effect may take place, with each person successively receiving higher levels of rewards. We've all seen this happen many, many times, most often in the search for common interests and common acquaintances ("Oh, you're from Kalamazoo. Do you know Elmer Glotznik?").

If the bargaining process is successful and both participants feel they are getting rewards that match or exceed their comparison level, the stage of *commitment* may take place. This means simply that for some period of time the two participants commit themselves to each other and stop (or minimize) sampling and estimating the rewards available from other people.

Finally, if all continues to go well, the level of *institutionalization* may be reached. This refers to the recognition by others of the legitimacy of your relationship. There are expectations shared by you, by your partner, and by others about the exclusiveness of the relationship. Examples would be when you are recognized as "good friends," "his girl" or "her guy," and so forth. Society provides us with many ways of formalizing heterosexual relationships in their ultimate form: marriage.

Social comparison

Another function of affiliation is to allow us to assess the appropriateness or validity of our thoughts and feelings by comparing ourselves with others. In describing the importance of this process of *social comparison,* Rollo May has said: "Every human being gets much of his sense of his own reality out of what others say to him and think about him" [169a].

Leon Festinger [154] developed a theory about the processes of social comparison. He proposed that people need to evaluate themselves, their ideas, their attitudes, and their feelings. When *physical reality* can't serve as a standard against which to evaluate the accuracy of beliefs, a person turns to other people, to *social reality.* The "truth" of some beliefs can be tested quickly against physical standards. For example, if you believe it is raining, the quickest test is to look out the window or step outside. But many beliefs can't be dealt with so simply. For example, are you friendly? No physical standard can evaluate friendliness. It is necessary to compare yourself with others to arrive at a conclusion. Thus, other people often are used as an index of reality for evaluating ourselves, our ideas, our attitudes, and our feelings.

Fear and affiliation

In researching the area of affiliation, social psychologists have sought to discover conditions which increase or decrease the tendency to seek others out. One major condition that affects affiliation is *fear*.

Stanley Schachter [379] noted a common element in the autobiographical reports of religious hermits, prisoners of war, and castaways—a devastating dread of social isolation. Some reports described conditions of "profound disturbance, anxiety, and pain" produced by isolation. The anxiety increases with time until it reaches a maximum; then, after long periods of isolation, it decreases, and the person becomes extremely apathetic, withdrawn and detached from the environment (conditions which resemble schizophrenia). The state of apathy is so severe that prisoners in solitary confinement often have to be dragged from their cells, and it is so frequent in religious orders that "the Church recognizes the state of acedia (or sloth, one of the seven deadly sins) as an occupational disease of hermits" [379, p. 8]. An additional effect of prolonged isolation is the tendency to think, dream, and hallucinate about other people.

Schachter reasoned that if isolation produces such severe attacks of anxiety, fear, and finally retreat, then the arousal of fear might lead to increased affiliation. To test this hypothesis, he conducted an experiment in which female students were told that the experiment was investigating the effects of electric shocks. Subjects were told that the shocks, to be realistic, must hurt. A control group was told to expect mild shocks. The experimenter then left the room, giving the subjects the option of waiting alone in a spacious room equipped with books and magazines, or in a classroom with other women who were also participating in the experiment. Of the subjects in the high-fear condition, 63 percent chose to wait with others, 28 percent didn't care, and only 9 percent wanted to wait alone. In the low-fear condition, only 33 percent of the subjects chose to wait together, while 60 percent didn't care, and 7 percent wanted to wait alone. The results clearly indicate that high fear leads to an increased tendency to affiliate with others in the same predicament, who might provide assurance and help reduce your fear.

However, seeking out others to obtain the reward of fear-reduction may not be the only reason affiliation occurs. Social comparison theory also provides an understanding of affiliation in stressful situations. In high-fear conditions, subjects experience feelings of arousal and anxiety. Are such feelings "normal"? Do others react the same way? Am I more afraid than I should be? All these questions, and others, may occur to subjects. To determine whether their reactions are "normal," subjects can seek out others to see how they are reacting. Together, the individuals can compare their feelings and discover if their own reactions are appropriate. In low-fear conditions, few such feelings of apprehension and dread exist, and subjects have little reason to compare reactions.

Clearly, not all other people can serve as valid standards for social comparison. We generally compare ourselves only with those who are similar to us in some respects. For example, "average" students do not compare their progress in a course with that of the "class genius"; rather, they use other average students as their yardstick. In the same vein, if other people are in a completely different predicament from your own (such as waiting for a faculty advisor while you are waiting to receive electric shocks), there is little reason to seek them out to discover how they are feeling and reacting. The reactions of these dissimilar others could not be used as standards to help evaluate one's own feelings. Thus, "Misery loves *miserable* company," because only miserable company is in a comparable situation. This principle of similarity works in the opposite direction, too. Just as we don't want to affiliate with others who are much less fearful than ourselves, we don't want to affiliate with others who are much more fearful than ourselves. It has been found that subjects in these experiments do not choose to wait with people who are described as being extremely fearful [357]. Waiting with extremely fearful others would only increase one's own fear. Thus, affiliation is increased when one has the opportunity to interact with similar other people.

■ EVALUATING OTHER PEOPLE

We have pointed out that people often want to be with other people, and that people usually don't want to be with just *anyone.* Rather, they prefer being with others who may provide social rewards or who allow social comparison to take place. All of this presupposes that people make judgments about what others are like so that they can decide whether they want to affiliate with them or not. Social psychologists have devoted a great deal of time and effort toward finding out how we perceive and judge other people.

Generalizations

Consider the following statements:

College students enjoy rock music.
Athletes are not very intelligent.
Politicians are crooked.
White Southerners are bigots.

Figure 5-4. *Affiliation by necessity. These wartime refugees are huddled together in the ditch, apparently for safety's sake. However, Schachter's research suggests that in a fear-producing situation (such as war), people still wish to be with others, even if such affiliation is dangerous.*

Anyone over thirty can't be trusted.

Pretty women are conceited.

Hippies are immoral and promiscuous.

Blacks are lazy and happy-go-lucky.

All these statements are *generalizations;* that is, they make some general statement about a category of people (college students, or politicians, or blacks, etc.). Previous learning enables us to use generalizations as part of *concepts* about people, so that we can simplify and codify the world. These concepts distinguish groups of people by factors such as sex, age, ethnicity, occupation, religion, and region.

Thus, when we meet another person for the first time, we already have some expectations about what that person is probably like, based on whatever concepts we hold and believe to be relevant. This is all well and good; without such concepts we would have to spend a great deal of time with every person we met, just to establish the groundwork for future interactions. However, while concepts (and the generalizations about people which they include) are necessary and valuable for human interactions, they can also serve a very negative function, permitting or encouraging mistreatment of others. In Chapter 3 we described how generalizations which are seen as *unjustified* are called *stereotypes.* Several generalizations in the above list might deserve such a label.

Implicit personality theories

Not only do people make generalizations about what groups of others are probably like, they may also make assumptions about what particular personal characteristics go together *within* a person. For example, if one knows that a certain man is sociable, friendly, and jovial, one may also be likely to make assumptions about that person's sense of humor and generosity ("He is probably humorous and generous."). But if one knows that he is uptight, withdrawn, and unfriendly, one will probably make different predictions about his sense of humor and generosity ("He is probably humorless and stingy.").

This suggests that people have *implicit personality theories;* that is, they hold unstated (and perhaps unrecognized) assumptions about how others' personalities are structured. Given that we know another person has certain traits (say, friendliness), we will *assume* that the person also has other traits (say, a sense of humor), even though we have never seen direct evidence of the other traits. We assume that clusters of traits are related. These implicit personality theories have a major impact on how we view other people, on how we treat them, and on how we structure our world. If one's implicit personality theory is a fairly accurate reflection of the world, there will be few problems. But if one's theory misrepresents and incorrectly describes how traits are related, a person may continually mislabel and possibly mistreat others. Recent research indicates that such theories are often somewhat valid [434].

Central traits

The notion of implicit personality theory recognizes that if an observer learns a person being observed has one characteristic, the observer may *assume* the person to have other characteristics, too. Research has identified some traits that are more likely than others to lead to such assumptions.

For example, suppose a friend of yours is describing two roommates. One is described as intelligent, warm, skillful, industrious, determined, practical, and cautious; the other is characterized as determined, cold, cautious, skillful, practical, industrious, and intelligent. What is your overall reaction to these two persons? How would you expect them to score, for instance, on measures of generosity or sense of humor? Who sounds more likeable?

The above two descriptions are identical except for one pair of traits— *warm* and *cold.* Soloman Asch [18] used descriptions like these and asked people to rate such hypothetical persons on a number of other personality dimensions, including generosity and humor. Asch found that when the hypothetical person was described as cold, only about 10 percent of the subjects stated that the person was also generous and humorous. When the person was described as warm, however, about 90 percent of the subjects also expected him to be generous, and over 75 percent described him as humorous. Hence, this difference on a single pair of *central traits* has a significant effect on perceptions; their existence modified the meaning of other traits. Asch tried varying other pairs of traits, such as "polite-blunt," but found that these did not have nearly the effect on evaluations that the "warm-cold" distinction did. Other traits were not as central.

This effect also occurs in evaluations of people in everyday situations. Harold Kelley [240] arranged to have a new instructor lead a twenty-minute classroom discussion. Students were told that they would be asked to evaluate the instructor at the end of the classroom period. A biographical sketch about the instructor was passed out to each student before the new instructor arrived. Unknown to the students, two forms of the sketch were used. One form read:

Mr.—————————is a graduate student in the Department of Economics and Social Science here at MIT. He has had three semesters of teaching experience in psychology at another college. This is his first semester teaching Economics 70. He is twenty-six years old, a veteran, and married. People who know him consider him to be a rather warm person, industrious, critical, practical, and determined.

The other sketch was identical except that the phrase "a rather cold person" appeared instead of "a rather warm person." Half the students received one biographical sketch, and half received the other.

Kelley found that, as he had anticipated, the prior description of the instructor affected the students' perceptions of him. Students who had been informed that the instructor was "a rather warm person" rated him as considerably more humorous, sociable, good-natured, considerate, and informal than did students who had been informed that he was "a rather cold person," even though both sets of students had heard precisely the same class discussion. In addition, most of the students who had received the "warm" description participated in the classroom discussion (56 percent), while less than a third (32 percent) of the students who had read the "cold" description participated.

Studies such as these show that a single trait can have considerable influence on our overall impressions of people. Of course, the centrality of a trait will depend to some extent on the context in which it appears. If you're describing students, traits such as "intelligent" and "industrious" might be particularly central; if you were describing businesspeople, on the other hand, traits such as "honest" and "responsible" might be more central.

Another way in which one set of traits influences others has been labeled the *halo effect.* Suppose you have to make a judgment about someone when you have relatively little information about him. In such cases, your impression of the person may be a generally favorable or unfavorable "blur." This "blur" may cause you to make judgments about other traits solely on the basis of the person's estimated position on the general "good-bad" dimensions. Thus, all other judgments would result from the "halo" that accompanied the original judgment of goodness or badness.

■ INTERPRETING BEHAVIOR: ABILITY TO EVALUATE OTHERS ACCURATELY

Some people seem to be consistently good judges of others, quickly learning what other people are "really" like. Others seem continually to misjudge the people they meet, often ending up deceived by them. Although these differences in ability to judge others have been noted for centuries, social scientists have had a surprisingly tough time pinning down what makes some people better judges than others [99; 439].

The criterion problem

Part of the difficulty stems from the *criterion problem.* Suppose you are a researcher who wants to find out whether one group of people (say, psychology majors) is better or worse at judging others than is another group (say, physics majors). You could have both sets of majors judge other people, and then see how accurate the judgments are. Sounds simple enough, doesn't it? But how will you decide how accurate each group is? You have the predictions made by each group of majors, but with what do you compare them? How do you determine what the target person's *true* characteristics are, so that you can see how accurate the others were in their judgments? What criterion (standard for comparison) do you use?

Although there is no easy solution, the best way to proceed is by using criterion instruments (psychological or other tests) which have been validated under rigorous conditions and are quite sensitive to individual differences. Furthermore, one would want to use more than one measure of the same criterion characteristics, preferably measures which employ different methods. Then, even though each measure might be susceptible to a specific kind of bias, the different biases might tend to cancel each other out and give a valid overall measure of the criterion.

Artifacts

Let us assume that one was able to obtain a valid criterion based on several related measures (say, of honesty). We want to see which of ten introductory psychology students does best at predicting the characteristics of a stimulus person (*P*). Each of these ten students observes a videotape of *P*'s behavior and estimates *P*'s honesty. We find that five observers were apparently quite accurate in their evaluations of how honest *P* is (based on the criterion measures given to *P*), while the other five were much less accurate.

The conclusion to be drawn from such results probably seems simple enough—the first five subjects are better judges than are the second five. But this conclusion is not necessarily justified. Research has shown that most raters are likely to *assume* that the people they observe are *similar to themselves* [198]. This assumed similarity can lead to a research *artifact*—a finding which is not what it appears to be. For example, suppose none of the raters really had any insight whatsoever into how honest *P* really is. When asked about *P*'s honesty, subjects might simply describe *their own* level of honesty. Further, suppose five of the raters just happened to be about as honest as *P* was. These five people will appear to be very accurate, when, in reality, their responses were no better than those of the five people who completely missed. In all ten cases, the ratings were based on the *raters'* characteristics instead of on those of the person rated. Because some subjects happened to have characteristics like *P*'s, these raters appeared to be more accurate than did those who happened to have characteristics unlike *P*'s. Thus, the fact that people often assume others to be somewhat similar to themselves can produce research results which are not what they appear to be.

Skill in judging others

Despite many research complexities like those described above, social psychologists have been able to gather evidence on the skills involved in judging others accurately. These skills seem to be composed of at least two components which may be fairly independent of one another [111; 439]. The first component is what has been called *stereotype accuracy,* the ability to know or sense what the *average* person is like with respect to any characteristic. A person who has this skill would be good at judging what most people are like. However, one could still have this general sense of what *most* people are like but "miss" badly on judgments of unusual or atypical individuals.

The second component relates to the judgment of specific individuals. This has been called *differential accuracy,* or sensitivity to interpersonal differences. This involves the ability to tell where each person stands in relationship to others.

A good degree of stereotype accuracy has considerable implications for the way your judgments of others are likely to be regarded. If you are able accurately to assess what *most* people are like, then you're less likely to be off in your evaluation of a single individual. This information is well-known to fortune-tellers, palm readers, and the like. They provide clients with general descriptions, and the clients interpret it as a specific description of themselves. If you have developed a high degree of stereotype accuracy, then you are likely to appear quite insightful, perhaps even mystical, when you describe other people. Focus 5-1 describes a situation in which this knowledge was utilized to provide "accurate" feedback from psychological tests—tests *which had actually not even been scored!*

Stereotype accuracy and differential accuracy seem to be independent; the fact that a person is good at one of them does not always mean that he or she will be good at the other. Clearly, the factors which make a person a good judge of others are complex. But based on the research, some general characteristics of good judges have been described, and it has been suggested that these characteristics apply to being good, at least to some degree, at both stereotype accuracy and differential accuracy [9]. The general characteristics of a good judge of others include: (1) broad personal experience; (2) high intelligence; (3) good social skills and personal adjustment; (4) an aesthetic attitude; (5) detachment (such as might be evidenced by a physicist or other specialist in the physical sciences); and (6) cognitive complexity (the ability to see the world in terms of shades of gray rather than as black or white).

Perhaps surprisingly, when psychologists and psychology students are compared with other groups, they do not seem to do any better (and sometimes do considerably worse) in judging others. Psychologists and psychology students are likely to *overdifferentiate* others. That is, they are so conscious of individual differences that they overestimate the degree to

FOCUS 5-1 HOW TO DEVELOP A SUPER TEST WITHOUT REALLY TRYING

If you can figure out what traits and characteristics usually apply to *most* people, then you may be able to convince *some* people that you have particulary good insight into their own personality structure. Hence, high *stereotype accuracy* can sometimes lead to an impression of high accuracy in assessing specific individuals.

Three psychologists, Ulrich, Stachnik, and Stainton [463], have demonstrated this phenomenon. They administered two standard psychological tests, the Bell Adjustment Inventory and the House-Tree-Person (HTP) Test, to their classes. In one class, students filled out the tests and were told that the tests would be scored and interpreted by a psychologist and returned to them at a later date. About a week later each student received an interpretation with his or her name on it. After reading and thinking about the evaluation, each student was asked to rate the interpretation in terms of the following scale:

I feel that the interpretation was:
   Excellent   Good   Average   Poor   Very poor

In the second class, students were given instructions for administering the test to one other person, such as a roommate or neighbor. They were to tell this person that they were studying personality testing and needed a subject for practice. These "practice" persons would also be given an interpretation of the test results and would be asked to rate the accuracy of the interpretation on the same scale.

Suppose you had been a member of the first class. You have taken the two tests, they have been scored, and the following evaluation is given back to you, based on your test performance:

> You have a strong need for other people to like you and for them to admire you. You have a tendency to be critical of yourself. You have a great deal of unused capacity which you have not turned to your advantage. While you have some personality weaknesses, you are generally able to compensate for them. Your sexual adjustment has presented some problems for you. Disciplined and controlled on the outside, you tend to be worrisome and insecure on the inside. At times you have serious doubts as to whether you have made the right decision or done the right thing. You prefer a certain amount of change and variety and become dissatisfed when hemmed in by restrictions and limitations. You pride yourself as being an independent thinker and do not accept others' opinions without satisfactory proof. You have found it unwise to be too frank in revealing yourself to others. At times you are extraverted, affable, sociable, while at other times you are introverted, wary, and reserved. Some of your aspirations tend to be pretty unrealistic.

How well does this fit? How would you rate this as an interpretation of your own personality characteristics?

Ulrich, Stachnik, and Stainton gave this *same* personality description (adapted from [163a]) to every one of the people who took the tests. In reality, the researchers did not even score the tests at all. What did the respondents think about these "individual" interpretations? If the interpretation had a great deal of stereotype accuracy, then most of the respondents should have thought it was very accurate. Indeed, this is exactly what happened. Furthermore, students thought that it was accurate whether the tests had been given by a psychologist or by another student for practice.

It would appear that the unscored test works remarkably well; fifty-three out of fifty-seven students rated the psychologists's interpretation as good or excellent in spite of the fact that the students were admittedly inexperienced and doing it for practice.

The researchers also asked for additional comments from the respondents. Among the comments were:

On the nose! Very good. I wish you had said more, but what you did mention was all true without a doubt.

The interpretation is surprisingly accurate and specific in description.

I shall take note of many of the things you said.

It appears to me that the results of this test are unbelievably close to the truth. For a short test of this type, I was expecting large generalizations for results, but this was not the case and I give all the credit to the examiner, whose conclusions were well calculated.

Notice that these people fully believed that the test focused directly on their specific personality attributes. What happened, apparently, was that most of those tested were unaware of how similar their worries and weaknesses were to those of most other people. *Most* of us have strong needs to be liked, are sometimes self-critical, have some problems with sexual adjustment, sometimes feel insecure, and so on. But often we are not aware of how many other people share these characteristics. And this lack of awareness keeps fortune-tellers and palm readers in business.

---

which an individual differs from the average person. Therefore, their estimates for any one individual may not be very accurate [438a].

■ MAKING ATTRIBUTIONS

Up to now, we have described impressions from the observer's point of view. We haven't discussed how the behaviors of the other person affect the impressions which we form. Under what conditions will an individual be confident that he or she knows what another person is like? What factors allow us to assert that another person intended to behave in a particular way? *Attribution theory* deals with the inferred *cause* of an action or behavior; was the action produced by the person's attitudes and dispositions, or was it produced by something outside the person?

Fritz Heider [200] proposed that any human action is determined by two classes of forces: *environmental forces* and *personal forces.* Environmental forces are the external pressures and constraints on a person which cause him or her to behave in a particular way. Personal forces include two factors: the person's *ability* to perform an action and the amount of *effort* expended to perform the action. If a person has the ability to perform an action but doesn't try to perform it, or if the person tries very hard to perform the action but has no ability, personal forces will be minimal. When an observer makes attributions about why a particular action occurred, he or she will be able to find the cause in either the environmental conditions or the personal forces of the actor.

Factors affecting the attributions we make

How strong are environmental forces? Most of the research on attribution theory has looked at how the strength of environmental forces causes an observer to make different types of attributions to an actor. Environmental pressure can be examined directly by having an observer view the behavior of an actor under conditions where a great deal of external pressure is placed on the actor, or where very little external pressure is placed on the actor. In a recent experiment, Jones and Harris [232] did exactly this. They had subjects observe a student delivering a speech about Fidel Castro. The student was described as a debater, and his speech took a position which was either pro-Castro or anti-Castro. Environmental pressure was manipulated by informing some subjects that the debater had been free to choose which side of the topic to present, while other subjects were told that the debater had been assigned to one or the other side of the topic. Subjects then were asked to describe the debater's true attitudes toward Castro.

It was found that subjects tended to attribute favorable attitudes toward Castro to the debater who delivered a pro-Castro speech and unfavorable attitudes toward Castro to the debater who delivered an anti-Castro speech. This is a very interesting effect. Even when under strong environmental pressure in the no-choice condition, subjects still inferred that the person's behavior was at least somewhat representative of his private attitudes. This effect has been termed *behavior engulfing the field,* since the behavior itself influences an observer's attributions even when the behavior has been forced.

It should be added that environmental pressure also played a role. Subjects attributed a much more favorable attitude to the pro-Castro debater who *chose* that side of the topic than to the debater who was *assigned* the topic. But people who observed the anti-Castro debater saw him as having an unfavorable attitude toward Castro, regardless of the amount of choice given the debater. These results illustrate some rather intriguing points. Why did environmental pressure have very little effect on the attributions made by the subjects who observed an anti-Castro speech? The reason seems to lie in the fact that most Americans in the 1960s were anti-Castro. When the subjects observed an anti-Castro speech, they simply assumed that the debater was like most people, and therefore would hold an unfavorable attitude toward Castro. Making it appear that the debater had very little choice in his anti-Castro comments had no effect on this attribution, since it was based on what the subjects thought most people would do. However, when the debater took a pro-Castro viewpoint, the effects of environmental pressure were much greater. Being pro-Castro is an unusual stance in our society, so when the subjects saw that the person had a choice about expressing his views, they assumed he must be *very* favorable toward Castro. When they saw that the debater had little choice, they assumed he must be pro-Castro only to a somewhat limited degree.

These results illustrate the following points. First, there is a tendency for behavior to engulf the field, that is, for observers to assume that an actor's behavior is at least somewhat representative of the actor's personal viewpoints. Second, when an action is predictable and expected, such as when the debater delivered an anti-Castro speech, environmental influences have only a small effect on attributions. The observers seem to feel that most people would behave in the predictable manner anyway. Third, when an action is somewhat unexpected and unpredictable, such as when the debater delivered a pro-Castro speech, environmental forces play a very large role in determining the observer's attributions. The observer assumes that when environmental factors are minimal, the actor's behavior represents underlying personal characteristics.

How expected was the behavior? When an action is expected, it tells us less about the actor than when the action is unexpected. Two factors that affect such expectations are the degrees to which the behavior is *role-related* and *socially desirable*. Each person occupies certain roles, or positions, which are appropriate for a particular kind of individual. We often assume that because a person is a politician, he or she will act in the ways that most politicians act (for example, dignified and tactful), thereby fulfilling the role of politician. If one behaves in an out-of-role (inappropriate) fashion, it is unexpected and is likely to provide a good deal of information about what the actor is really like.

For example, traditionally in our society one acceptable role behavior for females has been crying, even under minimal provocation. But crying has not been acceptable role behavior for males. If a male cries, it is out-of-role behavior and may be used by others to infer that he is effeminate or is extremely sensitive. In March 1972, Senator Edmund Muskie, then the heavily favored frontrunner for the Democratic nomination for President, burst into tears on the steps of the Manchester, New Hampshire, courthouse, during the campaign for the New Hampshire Presidential primary. Muskie was responding to a hostile editorial written by William Loeb, arch-conservative editor of the *Manchester News-Leader.* Many political analysts believe that the attributions which voters made to Muskie because he cried (that he was weak or unstable) began a process that culminated in his loss of the nomination.

The *social desirability* of an action and its consequence is a second situational factor which affects how expected an action is. Socially desirable actions are those which most people approve of and perceive to be appropriate and correct in a particular situation. People are *supposed* to behave in a socially desirable way; it is expected of them, and there is a great deal of environmental pressure placed on all of us to behave in these ways. When someone resists this pressure and behaves in a socially undesirable fashion, such as belching loudly at dinner without saying "Excuse me," observers will quickly attribute a personality trait, such as rudeness, to the actor. Ironically, the "good" effects of a series of "good" acts may be completely wiped out by the effect of one "bad" act. Fair or not, a socially undesirable action carries far more information and is weighed more heavily than a desirable one in reaching conclusions about what the actor is really like [231].

Does the action affect the observer? The degree to which an observer is somehow involved with or affected by an actor's behaviors will also affect the type of attribution made about the actor. Two aspects of this involvement are termed *personalism* and *hedonic relevance* [231]. Hedonic relevance describes the degree to which an action is gratifying or disappointing to the observer of that action. Personalism is closely related to hedonic relevance and refers to the degree to which an observer perceives that action as directed specifically toward him or her. When an action is hedonically relevant, it affects the observer, but when it also contains the element of personalism, it is perceived as being *intentionally* directed toward the observer.

For example, consider how a psychology professor might react to the news that salaries of auto workers were going to be cut by 10 percent. This action has no hedonic relevance to the professor, since it does not affect him one way or the other. If the professor was trying to infer something about the personality of the company president who ordered the cut in workers' salaries, it might be difficult. The president might be stingy, unfeeling, or fiscally responsible. However, suppose that the dean of the professor's college announced salary cuts of 10 percent for all college employees. This action is hedonically relevant. The professor might be much less charitable in making attributions about the dean and might narrow the field

(a)

Figure 5-5. *Events of high hedonic relevance. The threat of unemployment (a) and inflation (b) are events which can affect all of us; the stronger the effect, the greater the hedonic relevance involved. Those people most affected by these events are likely to make strong attributions about the people they feel are responsible for causing these conditions.*

down to his being either stingy, or unfeeling, or both. But he still might not be sure that his conclusion is correct. However, suppose that the dean walked into the professor's office and announced that only that professor's salary would be cut. This action is not only hedonically relevant, it contains a high degree of personalism since it is directed specifically at that professor. In this instance, the professor's charity in making attributions might be nonexistent. He might perceive the dean to be several rather negative things. And, he would probably feel *confident* that these characteristics really apply to the dean.

As these examples illustrate, when the hedonic relevance and personalism of an action increase, the degree to which an observer will make personal attributions to an actor will also increase, as will the observer's

(b)

confidence that he or she has made the "correct" attribution. The fact that the observer is being affected by the actor's behaviors increases the observer's willingness to infer the personal characteristics of the actor.

An observer's beliefs about the world also seem to affect the attributions he or she makes about others. Most people believe that the world is a fairly sensible, orderly place where people get what they deserve. This belief in a "just world" [265] leads them to make certain attributions. In April 1968, shortly after the murder of Dr. Martin Luther King, Jr., a sample of American adults were asked about their strongest reaction to the assassination. About one-third of the respondents chose the response "He brought it on himself" [368]. These people took the view that Dr. King must have deserved it, apparently based on the assumption that in a just world people would not be shot unless they deserved to be shot. A similar belief may apply to police treatment of rape victims. Much has been written about the response of police officers to rape victims, a response often bordering on disbelief and harassment. If in a just world "innocent" women would not be raped, then the police officers may be assuming that this violent act must have been encouraged by the victim. She must have acted in a provocative manner, encouraging her assailant, or she would not have been raped, the officers may feel. Thus an application of this "just world" hypothesis causes a good deal of additional *unjust* mistreatment for the victims.

Other people have traits

We've examined some factors that affect the attributions people make about the personal dispositions of others. Interestingly, it appears that people are not quite so willing to infer dispositions about themselves as they are to make such dispositional inferences about others. Consider the following example.

When a student who is doing poorly in school discusses his problem with a faculty adviser, there is often a fundamental difference of opinion between the two. The student, in attempting to understand and explain his inadequate performance, is usually able to point to environmental obstacles, such as a particularly onerous course load, to temporary emotional stress, such as worry about his draft status, or to a transitory confusion about life goals that is now resolved. The faculty adviser may nod and may wish to believe, but in his heart of hearts he usually disagrees. The adviser is convinced that the poor performance is due neither to the student's environment nor to transient emotional states. He believes instead that the failure is due to enduring qualities of the student—to lack of ability, to irremediable laziness, to neurotic ineptitude [233, p. 79].

These tendencies for an actor to attribute the causes of behavior to the environment and for an observer to attribute the causes of behavior to personality traits have received some empirical support. For example, a list of personality-trait descriptions (reserved–emotionally expressive, lenient–firm, etc.) was presented to college students, who were asked to judge how each trait applied to five persons: oneself, one's best friend, one's father, an age peer who was liked but not known well, and a prominent newscaster. It was found that college students were quite willing to assign personality traits to others but were very likely to use a "depends on the situation" category for themselves [328]. It appears that in each person's mind, personality traits are things that affect *other people's* behavior very much, but that affect *one's own* behavior to a far lesser degree. We recognize the influence that situational forces may have in determining our own behavior, but we tend to forget this when judging others and deciding why they do what they do. This tendency is particularly relevant to situations in which we are trying to determine why someone committed a terrible act. To the perpetrator, the explanation "I had to do it; I had no choice," (high situational forces) may seem extremely reasonable. To the observer, however, this rationale may seem completely unacceptable. We will discuss this issue further in Chapter 8.

◼ SELF-ATTRIBUTIONS

How do you know what you feel?

All of us experience many different emotions: fear, love, hate, jealousy, joy, and so forth. How do emotions arise? How can you tell whether you are experiencing joy or sorrow, love or hate?

During childhood, parents and other observers teach us to label many emotional states. A boy may be furious at a big brother for taking his truck, and while the child is screaming, his mother comes by and says, "Now, now, don't be angry." After many similar events, the boy learns to associate the term *anger* with the psychological and physiological states he was experiencing at the time. Labels for other emotions might be learned in identical ways, as socializing agents provide the child with labels for behaviors.

Although this process of labeling certain emotional behaviors does occur, it does not tell the whole story. This explanation assumes that a person is able to physiologically differentiate emotions such as anger and joy. That is, after a person learns that the behaviors which accompany a certain physiological response are called "joy" by observers, he or she can later identify that response when it recurs. However, there are simply not enough different physiological states to account for all the emotions we say we feel. In addition, the same visceral (internal) states may exist in emotional states which are very different from each other [87]. Under conditions of strong emotion—any strong emotion—physiological changes occur which are associated with the sympathetic nervous system. In all cases, there is a slowing down of digestion, a diversion of more blood to the head and the extremities, pupil dilation, deeper breathing, and a higher pulse rate. Since there are more labels for emotion than there are different physiological states, why don't we get confused about what we feel?

Stanley Schachter [380] proposed that the way we label our emotional states depends on two factors: (1) the existence of a general state of physiological arousal, and (2) cognitive cues in the environment which tell us how we should be feeling. In most everyday situations, these two pieces of information go hand in hand. We feel physiologically aroused, and it is obvious to us what caused the arousal. For example, consider a letter carrier who walks into a yard and suddenly meets a large, growling, ferocious dog. Physiological arousal will occur; the letter carrier's heart pounds, his hands sweat, and his pupils dilate. What caused this arousal? The dog, of course. The environment provides a clear cue for the arousal, and the letter carrier quickly labels the state "fear." Or, consider a young woman who is enjoying a drive-in movie with her date by not watching the movie. Again, we should note deep breathing, a high pulse, etc. And again, we have a very clear cue which allows the young woman to explain her arousal—her date. The state will be labeled "passion" or, perhaps, "love."

In these cases, the state of physiological arousal and the cues are closely associated. In fact, they are so closely associated that most people would never consider them separate aspects of the process. However, under some conditions of arousal, the environment may be ambiguous and provide no clear cues for why arousal occurs. What do we do then? Schachter and his associates tried to find out [382].

In an experiment supposedly examining the effects of a "vitamin supplement" on vision, subjects were injected with the vitamin supplement. Unknown to them, some of the subjects actually received an injection of epinephrine (a synthetic form of adrenalin), which leads to physiological arousal. While in the waiting room, their hearts began to pound, their faces flushed, and their breathing became deeper. How could they interpret these reactions?

The researchers assumed that if the subjects were given *cues* about how to interpret these emotional reactions, the cues themselves would significantly affect these interpretations. Two types of cues could be provided. The subjects could be led to *expect* that the vitamin supplement would produce such effects. If they were told this, then they would have a simple explanation for their arousal and would not have to search further. Or they could be placed in the situation of *inferring* their emotional state from the behaviors of others in the same situation. The investigators did both. One group of subjects was led to believe that the drug would produce arousal; the other group was given no such expectation.

Each subject was placed in the waiting room with another student (who actually was an accomplice of the experimenter and was instructed about how to behave). In one condition of the experiment, the student acted euphoric, happy, and silly during the waiting period. Soon afterward, the subjects were asked by the experimenter how they felt. When subjects had no simple explanation for the arousal experienced, they stated that they were very happy. The label they applied to their own emotion was influenced by the behavior of the other person. However, subjects who had been told that the drug would produce such arousal states had explanations for their arousal. When asked how they felt, they expressed much less happiness. They didn't need the cues provided by the confederate to label their arousal, since they had already used the cues provided by the experimenter. Another group of subjects had been initially injected with a placebo substance (one which had no physiological effect). When later asked how they felt, they expressed intermediate degrees of happiness.

This experiment supports the view that two factors, physiological arousal and cognitive cues, are important in labeling emotions. When physiological arousal is minimal or absent, no emotion is experienced. However, when physiological arousal is present, the emotional label applied to the arousal will be determined by a person's cognitive interpretations of environmental cues.

This process is not limited to euphoria. In another phase of the experiment, different subjects received injections of adrenalin or placebo substances and waited with another subject (again, an accomplice). This time, subjects had to fill out an annoying personal questionnaire while waiting. Two sample questions were:

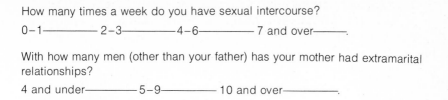

How many times a week do you have sexual intercourse?
0–1————— 2–3—————4–6————— 7 and over————.

With how many men (other than your father) has your mother had extramarital relationships?
4 and under————— 5–9————— 10 and over—————.

The accomplice became furious, ripped up the questionnaire, and stormed out. Subjects in this condition acted quite angry; furthermore, the subjects who had received the injection of adrenalin and who were not told what physiological reactions to expect acted angrier than those who had received only the placebo injection.

Stuart Valins [466] had male college students look at slides of naked women in a study supposedly concerned with "physiological reactions to sexually-oriented stimuli." The students were told that the experimenter was interested in their heartbeat rates, which would be recorded as they looked at various slides. Subjects were told that because of a malfunction in the machinery, they would be able to hear their own heartbeat rate amplified, but were told to pay no attention to it. Students watched a series of slides and were then asked to rate the slides in terms of overall attractiveness.

Imagine yourself in this situation. The women are all reasonably attractive, and you hear your heatbeat thumping along in a fairly regular manner. Suddenly, in response to the fourth slide, it increases dramatically. It slows down again for the next slide and stays at about the same rate until the seventh slide, when it increases again and slows down once more. Here is an interesting bit of information for you to ponder: Why did your heart rate increase when viewing those two slides? When asked to rate the attractiveness of the slides and allowed to take some slides home as a "reward" for participation in the study, students rated as most attractive, and were most likely to take home, those slides toward which their heartbeats had "reacted" and increased.

Reasonable enough, it would seem—but the students were *not* really hearing their own heartbeats. Rather, it was a tape-recorded heart rate timed to increase in speed when certain slides were viewed, completely independently of how the subject's own heart actually reacted. In other words, the feedback was completely false. Nevertheless, this bogus feedback had a distinct effect on the subjects' patterns of rating attractiveness. This was true not only for cases where the heart rate increased; Valins ran another experiment in which subjects' heartbeats apparently slowed down in response to certain slides. Here again, subjects rated as most attractive and were most likely to take home those slides toward which their heartbeats had reacted, this time by slowing down.

The "juke box" theory of emotion

These findings have led to what has been labeled the "juke box" theory of emotion. People in a state of physiological arousal will label that state in terms of the cognitive factors available in the situation. If there is an appropriate explanation for what they are feeling, no evaluative needs will arise. But if the situation is ambiguous, individuals may look to others or to additional information to determine the correct label for the emotional state. The physiological arousal has been likened to inserting a coin into a juke box, thereby activating it, while cognitive perceptions of the situational cues may be analogous to selecting a particular song to play. Both are necessary, but neither may be sufficient for feeling an emotion.

Even such seemingly clearcut states as pain or fear can be manipulated similarly. For example, one study [327] had college students undergo electric shocks. Some of them were told to expect "side effects" from a pill they had taken prior to the shocks. Actually, the "drug" was a placebo with no physiological effects. The side effects they were told to anticipate were all symptoms of anxiety. Those subjects who could attribute their anxiety reactions to the pill rated the pain of the actual shocks as significantly less severe than did another group of subjects who were not told to expect side effects from the pill. Furthermore, several persons who expected the side effects were willing to take a higher shock than the machine could deliver; none of the persons in the control condition were willing to do this. Hence, if a person can attribute anxiety to a pill rather than to fear of shock, the shock becomes less feared and (apparently) less painful.

Clearly, what we believe affects how we feel and how we act. Individuals who believe they are fearful will label an arousal state as "fear" in an ambiguous situation. Individuals who believe they are brave but somewhat excitable will label an arousal state as "excitement," not fear, in an identical situation. The behaviors of these two persons will be quite different simply because of how they see themsleves. Cognitive processes can exert tremendous control over our emotions and internal states. To a large extent, it's all in the mind.

To eat or not to eat?

How hungry are you right now? Very, some, or not at all? In deciding how to answer this, you probably did one of two things: checked out your stomach reactions or looked at a clock or watch. Chances are that if you are overweight, you looked at the clock; but if you are underweight or of normal weight, you checked out your stomach. It appears that even for such a mundane state, individuals differ widely from each other in the *ways* they attribute hunger to themselves.

In a series of studies, Schachter [381] and his students have investigated how obese persons (14 to 75 percent overweight, according to insurance charts) and normal-weight persons react in various situations involving food and hunger. It appears that these two types of people often react in very different ways. For obese persons, the internal state (an empty or full stomach) seems largely irrelevant; eating behavior is determined chiefly by external cues, such as the amount of time remaining before dinner or the amount of food on the table. When food is in sight, obese persons will eat more of it than will normal-weight persons; when food is out of sight (say, in a refrigerator), obese subjects are actually less likely than normal-weight subjects to go and get it and eat a great deal. Similarly, when food tastes good, obese subjects are likely to eat more than normal-weight subjects; when it tastes bad, they are likely to eat less. When a good deal of effort is involved in eating, such as removing the shells from nuts or using chopsticks at an Oriental restaurant, obese people eat less than normal-weight subjects.

Other studies have found that obese subjects' hunger is significantly affected by the apparent time of day, while normal-weight subjects' hunger is not. In all these cases, the obese subjects appeared to be more *stimulus bound*, basing their self-attributions on external stimuli. Hence, the way in which we *use* internal stimuli in making self-attributions apparently depends on factors which are also somehow related to obesity.

Are your attitudes your own?

The previous discussion may lead you to question how "real" are any of the states you feel. A similar point might be made about the attitudes we hold. How susceptible are these to external factors? Consider: A good friend hears you talking about what a clod you consider one of your classmates to be. He looks you in the eye and says, "You know, I don't buy that. I don't think you feel nearly as negative toward her as you say you do. I've watched you interact with her and seen the way you look at her, and I really think you kind of like her, even if you don't know it yourself." How is this external information likely to affect your attitude?

You may initially deny it and question your friend's judgment, but later, might you be likely to reconsider what your "true" attitude really is? We suggest that this may indeed take place. In making a self-attribution about attitudes—especially in a situation that is at least a little ambiguous—cognitive cues in the situation, including your friend's impression, may be used in the self-attribution process. The outcome of this might be a change in your attitude or in your *perceived* attitude toward your classmate.

In practical terms, this suggests the existence of another attitude-change process in addition to those discussed in Chapter 2. Perhaps one way to change people's attitudes might be to ignore the issues involved and simply to suggest that the attitudes are not what they think they are. That is, one may try to convince them that their attitudes are more favorable or unfavorable than they believe. If you are convincing, this may produce attitude change in the direction you wish [74].

■ LIKING OTHERS

So far in this chapter, we have considered why people affiliate with each other, how people make judgments about others, and the way in which people interpret the behavior of others, as well as their own. With this basic information, we now can turn to an analysis of those situations in which two people concern themselves directly with each other. We can analyze *interpersonal attraction,* the determinants of liking and loving. Attraction is an attitude toward another person, group, or object that represents an evaluation along a like-dislike continuum. Interpersonal attraction is defined as a tendency to evaluate another person positively or negatively. When we are attracted to people, we evaluate them positively, tend to approach them, and tend to behave positively toward them. To begin an examination of interpersonal attraction, we will highlight those factors which have been shown to affect the degree of attraction between people.

Propinquity: The boy or girl next door

Suppose you live in an apartment house or dormitory and a team of social psychologists arrives to give everyone a series of questionnaires asking about personality characteristics, attitudes, values, and so forth. Suppose also they ask each of you to name your best friends within the dorm or apartment. What factors do you think would predict most accurately the friendship patterns in the apartment or dorm?

A major characteristic from which friendship can be predicted in a situation like this is *propinquity,* or nearness. One can most accurately predict whom you will say you like best by knowing who lives nearest to you. The same goes for other persons' opinions of you; those liking you the best are likely to be those living near you. Clearly, we all can think of specific cases for which this is not true, as in lengthy feuds between neighbors. Nevertheless, this general finding has been noted again and again [159]. There are several reasons why propinquity influences the development of attraction.

1 *Availability.* People who live close to us are more available, and there are more opportunities to get to know them. In terms of social exchange theory, the "costs" of getting to know each other (in terms of time and effort) are relatively small when a person lives close by. The factor of lowered costs is pointed out even more dramatically by findings which indicate that physical distance is not as important as is the ease of crossing distance. For example, suppose a person lives on the first floor of an apartment house and there is an equal distance between his or her door and the doors of two neighbors, one on the first floor and one on the second. When asked, such a person usually picks the individual on the first floor as a better friend than the individual who is the same

distance away but one flight of stairs away [159]. Thus, the importance of distance depends on how much effort is necessary to traverse it.

2 *The expectations of continued interaction.* People expect to interact more often, whether they want to or not, with those living nearest to them. Since this is the case, people tend to accentuate the positive and minimize the negative aspects of the relationship so that future interactions will be pleasant and agreeable.

3 *Predictability.* As you get to know your neighbors you are better able to predict how they will react. Hence, you are better able to elicit positive reactions from them if you want to, and to arrange rewarding situations. If another person is too unpredictable, he or she usually is disliked. On the other hand, some people can be so predictable as to be boring. It appears that high levels of predictability, but not too high, do increase attraction [65].

4 *Familiarity.* By itself, familiarity may lead to increased liking. People develop more positive feelings toward objects and individuals they see often [509]; they dislike the unfamiliar and the unexpected. Those "comfortable" people and things with which we are familiar elicit positive feelings and attraction. The more people are exposed to objects (such as unusual patterns, letters from foreign alphabets, and so forth) or other people (including photographs of others or actual contact with others), the more attracted toward them they will become [509]. This effect is strongest when somewhat positive feelings toward the stimulus already exist [436].

Believe it or not, this tendency has been found even among rats! Several researchers [112] exposed newborn rats to a steady diet of classical music. One group of rats heard selections from Mozart for twelve hours a day for fifty-two days, while another group of rats heard the music of Schoenberg for the same period. A third group of rats heard no music. After a fifteen-day break, the rats' musical preferences were assessed over a sixty-day period. Sure enough, the rats who had been raised on Mozart preferred Mozart—they learned to activate switches to turn on the Mozart selections. The rats raised on Schoenberg preferred Schoenberg, although the tendency was not as strong. Finally (probably to the relief of many music lovers), rats who had previously heard no music tended to prefer Mozart over Schoenberg.

Similarity: To be like me is to be liked

And they are friends who have come to regard the same things as good and the same things as evil. . . . We like those who resemble us, and are engaged in the same pursuits. . . . We like those who desire the same things as we, if the case is such that we and they can share the things together.

(*Aristotle,* Rhetoric)

FOCUS 5-2   ATTRACTION AND SIMILARITY IN THE DORMITORY

Theodore Newcomb [322] carried out several studies at the University of Michigan in the mid-1950s to assess the relationship between similarity and attraction in "real-life," nonresearch settings. On each of two occasions, seventeen men who did not know each other accepted invitations to live rent-free in a cooperative house. In return for the free rent, they agreed to devote several hours each week to providing experimental data for Newcomb and his colleagues. All subjects were males who were transferring to Michigan as sophomores or juniors; all were white, and their average age was twenty.

Newcomb had control over room assignments and also gathered data on attitudes and values. Based on these data, he assigned some men to roommates who were similar to them in attitudes and values and others to roommates who had dissimilar attitudes and values. One purpose of this study was to learn whether these pairs of men would get along equally well. (The men had no idea of why they were assigned to particular roommates.) Measures of attraction were taken several times during the men's stay in the house.

Newcomb found a strong relationship between preacquaintance attitude similarity and level of attraction at the end of the semester. For those men whose initial attitude similarity to each other was high, 58 percent reported at the end of the semester that they and their roommates were good friends. On the other hand, for those groups in which initial attitude similarity was low, in only 25 percent of the cases did the men report a high degree of attraction to their roommates. This is quite a difference.

This similarity-attraction relationship was not stable from the start. Only after several weeks did the relationships become strong; they remained so for the remainder of the semester. Apparently, it took a while for roommates to find out how similar or dissimilar they were. After this had been established, the similarity apparently had a strong effect on later attraction and liking for each other. From the data, we would expect that knowing how similar or dissimilar in attitudes and values two people are will not help us much in predicting how much they will like each other immediately; it is only after they have gotten to know each other over time that this information will serve as a strong predictor of attraction.

One important factor here is how well an individual can *predict* the attitudes and values of others in order to assess their similarity to his or her own. Newcomb found that individuals who felt strongly attracted tended to overestimate their similarity to each other. On the whole, *perceived* similarity of attitudes and values was more strongly related to interpersonal attraction than was *real* similarity.

FOCUS 5-3 CHOOSING A DATE: DO YOU GO FOR BROKE OR SEEK YOUR OWN LEVEL?

Recent research has illustrated the importance of physical attractiveness as a determinant of liking in dating situations. But what about one's *own* social desirability (which includes assessing one's own physical attractiveness)? Shouldn't this influence one's perception of the probability of attaining any particular social object (such as a lover)? If so, we would expect a kind of "matching" process in which people tend to pair off with others who are at about the same level of physical attractiveness as they are.

This is a reasonable hypothesis, but one that is not strongly supported. Most studies looking at this variable have focused on computerized dance situations in which strangers are brought together and paired with one another for an evening. If the experimenters have access to personality test scores (presumably used in making computer matches) and are able to make physical attractiveness ratings of the participants at the dance itself—and if they also happen to be the people running the entire show—they can match couples on any criteria they deem appropriate (physical attractiveness, attitude-value similarity, or whatever).

The first few studies conducted in this framework found strong relationships between physical attractiveness and date preference. However, little or no evidence of matching could be found. This led later researchers [61] to propose that the matching principle might reveal itself when an individual is required to actively *choose* a dating partner, rather than to evaluate one who has been preselected. The first study involved a computerized dance situation; a second involved an "undergraduate dating study." In each study, participants (college students) were secretly rated by several undergraduates as to physical attractiveness and were given the opportunity to choose potential dates from a series of photographs (which varied in physical attractiveness from high to low). For some students the choice situation was realistic (the man or woman chosen by the subject could refuse to go out with him or her), while for others it was idealistic (the man or woman chosen *had* to go out with the subject as part of the study).

As in other studies, the results showed that physically attractive dates were preferred by everyone, regardless of their own physical attractiveness. Within this general trend, however, Berscheid and her coworkers [61] did find evidence for some matching; less physically attractive males and females tended to choose somewhat less physically attractive dates for themselves than did more physically attractive subjects. Contrary to what the experimenters had expected, this tendency held for both realistic and idealistic choice situations.

Additional analyses indicated that one's own physical attractiveness (as rated by others) is related to dating popularity for both men and women but that this relationship is considerably stronger for men than for women. There was a tendency for physically attractive males also to have more close friends of the same sex than less physically attractive males had, but this relationship was not found for women.

As Aristotle suggests, an important factor in determining liking is similarity, particularly similarity in attitudes and values. Research has clearly indicated that, all other things being equal, people tend to like others whose beliefs and values are similar to their own [85]. It is rewarding to have others agree with us; it indicates that our attitudes and values are correct, since they are shared by others. Those who disagree with us present a threat to our attitudes and values, and therefore dissimilarity in attitudes and values can be punishing. (We discussed one instance of the effects of similarity-dissimilarity in the more specific context of ethnic prejudice in Chapter 3. Prejudiced whites tend to assume that the beliefs and values of blacks are far different from their own.) Focus 5-2 describes an in-depth study of the relationship between similarity and attraction.

Physical attractiveness: Ode to a pretty face (and body)

Suppose you were asked to list those characteristics which you find most important in rating the attractiveness of a member of the opposite sex. Take a moment and think about what you would list. If you are like most college students, you may have thought of things such as sincerity, intelligence, honesty, sensitivity, and perhaps even similarity in values and attitudes [472]. But recent evidence suggests that there is one factor which you probably have not mentioned and which often far outweighs all these others in determining your reaction—*physical attractiveness.* This may sound like a simple overgeneralization; surely educated persons have gone beyond the level of judging a book by its cover; certainly we all have heard that "beauty is only skin deep." We have all heard this, but, judging by Focus 5-3, very few of us really believe it.

The studies described in Focus 5-3 are part of a considerable body of research into the effects of physical attractiveness on preferences. They suggest that physical attractiveness is very important. Berscheid and her coworkers did find evidence that "matching" according to physical attractiveness may take place and that people may seek others whose level of attractiveness is like their own, but they found that overall attractiveness was still more important in interaction situations. There is also evidence of matching in ongoing relationships. Photographs of ninety-nine couples who were engaged or going together were rated for physical attractiveness, and these ratings were compared with ratings for a control group of couples formed by randomly matching pictures of ninety-nine men and women. The similarity in attractivenss of the engaged-dating couples was significantly greater than that of the randomly matched couples [318].

Why should physical attractiveness be such a powerful determinant of initial liking? There appears to be a series of reasons.

1   There is a *physical attractiveness stereotype* which assumes that "what is beautiful is good." Much evidence demonstrates that when college students are asked to predict what others are like, their predictions will vary according to how physically attractive the other person is. The more attractive the other person, the more likely students are to assume that the person has attractive personality characteristics as well. This holds for both male and female stimulus persons and male and female judges.
2   The assumption exists that attractive people are *better able to reward you* and may like you better. Although this may sound whimsical, there is some research evidence that people act as though they believe this. Physical attractiveness also appears to interact with belief and value similarity. While both factors are determinants of attraction, they are not necessarily independent in the eyes of observers [248]. That is, there is some evidence that people will *assume* that those whom they consider physically attractive hold beliefs and values similar to their own. Thus, these two characteristics can affect each other in determining overall attractiveness.
3   If a physical attractiveness stereotype is widely shared within a culture, it may come to have validity as a *self-fulfilling prophecy* (a generalization which comes to be true precisely because people have acted *as though* it were already true). If we assume that physically attractive people are good, and if we treat them as if they are good, such positive, warm treatment could conceivably lead them to be good people as adults, and hence, appear to support the existence of the stereotype. (And then, if the generalization now is true, perhaps it no longer is unjustified and, hence, should no longer be called a stereotype.)

There is some evidence that the first half of this hypothetical process does take place—people do treat physically attractive children differently than unattractive children. For instance, it has been found that the physical attractiveness of a child who commits a transgression influences adults' evaluation of the child. Adult observers were less likely to attribute a chronic, antisocial personality style to attractive than to unattractive children who committed transgressions. Furthermore, the same transgression was rated as less undesirable when committed by an attractive child than when committed by an unattractive child [126].

Physical attractiveness may influence teachers' evaluations of children, too. Fifth-grade schoolteachers were asked to examine the information

Figure 5-6. *Physical attractiveness rewarded. Events such as beauty pageants and contests for college homecoming queen have institutionalized the importance of physical attractiveness in our society. Although such events may also supposedly involve popularity, personality, and talent, in the past these factors have generally been secondary to appearance.*

given on a student's report card and to give their professional evaluations of the student's IQ and likely future educational accomplishments. The teachers, who represented 400 different schools in Missouri, all received the same report card to evaluate. The only difference between report cards was in the student's picture—either one of six attractive boys and girls or one of six unattractive boys and girls—which was pasted on the corner of the report card. Researchers found that the more attractive the child (whether male or female), the higher educational potential and IQ teachers assumed the child to have [98]. This is a striking finding, particularly since evidence shows that a teacher's attitude toward a student can have a significant effect on the student's performance [371].

Such findings suggest that since physical attractiveness affects some ways that people behave toward others, it might in turn affect the kind of person one becomes. The evidence is not clear, however. There is at present no strong evidence that physical attractiveness is related to self-concept or to "goodness" on various personality dimensions [60]. Hence, this does not seem to be a prophecy which fulfills itself completely.

Other determinants of liking

Ability: If you're competent, I'll be your friend. As social exchange theory suggests, when other people are rewarding, we affiliate with them. Similarly, the more rewarding others are, the more we like them [85]. People who are *able, competent,* and *intelligent* can provide many rewards. They can help us solve problems, give us advice, help us interpret world events, and so forth. Therefore, competent, intelligent people are liked more than are incompetent, unintelligent people [65].

This proposition has a major limitation, though. If a person is *too* perfect, we may feel uncomfortable or threatened. A too-perfect person also may be viewed as very dissimilar to oneself in terms of attitudes, values, etc. This perceived dissimilarity also might decrease their attraction for us. This suggests that persons who are extremely competent and intelligent might be liked more when they show a few human frailties than when they appear to be perfect [17]. This may explain why President John F. Kennedy became more popular with the American people after his blunder in sponsoring the attempt to invade Cuba at the Bay of Pigs in 1961. Most research has indicated, however, that a blunder decreases attraction for even the highly competent person [116; 301]. If the blunder makes one appear to be not only highly competent, but also somewhat more similar to the audience, the increased-liking effect may occur. Otherwise, the blunder will simply decrease one's appearance of competence and thereby decrease attraction.

Reciprocal liking: I'll like you if you'll like me. When we know another person likes us, we can expect to be rewarded by the other, since we generally assume that those who like us will help us and those who dislike us will harm us (or at least offer little help). Therefore, knowing that you are liked is a powerful reward. We can expect that the other will help us in the future, and we also will feel good about the fact that another person thinks enough of us to be a friend (increasing our self-esteem). Therefore, liking begets liking. Friendship given usually means that friendship will be returned.

Naturally, the reward value of a compliment from another person greatly depends on *who* gives it, and *why* they seem to be giving it. If a person who compliments you seems to have ulterior motives and to expect something in return, the compliment will not be worth much. In fact, receiving a compliment under such circumstances could even decrease your liking for the ingratiator [234]. Therefore, effective compliments are those which appear to have no strings attached. For this and other reasons, compliments received from people who have high status, who are very popular, who are powerful, and so on, are usually much more effective in increasing liking toward them than are compliments received from low-status, powerless, unpopular subordinates. The subordinate may have something to gain from the compliment, while the high-status person probably has much less to gain and hence appears more sincere.

The "reward value" of a compliment also may differ greatly depending on how often one has been praised by that person before. If you are used to receiving compliments from someone (say, your spouse or boyfriend/girlfriend), those compliments may lose much of their reward value for you. If, on the other hand, you receive a compliment from someone who has previously been neutral or negative toward you, this compliment may mean much more and may significantly increase your liking for the person who gave it. Praise from a stranger is much more effective than praise from a friend, and criticism from a friend is much more effective than criticism from a stranger. The reward value of approval also can depend on how often one appears to spread it around. Focus 5-4 presents an interesting demonstration of this "playing hard-to-get" effect.

Complementarity: The sadist and the masochist are good friends. As we've seen, similarity of attitudes, values, beliefs, and so on leads to increased attraction. But what about the sadist and masochist? On the surface, these two appear to be quite dissimilar—one likes to inflict pain, while the other likes to receive it. However, there really is a great similarity between them. Each has similar attitudes about how their relationship should proceed. They should become good friends, since they need each other to satisfy their desires.

This rather extreme example illustrates the principle of *complementarity.* Complementary relationships are those in which the needs of each party are fulfilled. For example, an individual who has a domineering personality would not get along very well with another dominant person. The dominant individual requires a submissive partner who will fulfill both their needs. Many types of close relationships, particularly marriage, may require such complementarity of need systems to be successful [500]. Even though the needs are different (one has dominance needs, the other submission needs), this can still be viewed as a special case of similarity, since both partners agree on the roles each will fulfill.

In the case of dominance-submission needs, complementary needs are opposites. However, in other cases, identical needs turn out to be complementary. For example, a warm, accepting person will get along best with another warm, accepting person and would be unhappy with a cold, critical one. Thus, the greater the complementarity on a wide spectrum of needs (some of which require the same needs and others opposite needs), the greater the attraction in relationships.

FOCUS 5-4 PLAYING HARD TO GET

It is well established in our folklore that the woman (or man?) who plays "hard to get" will be seen as more desirable and presumably have more success than the "easy" woman. Indeed, the Roman poet Ovid, writing about two thousand years ago, argued that:

> Fool, if you feel no need to guard your girl for her own sake, see that you guard her for mine, so I may want her the more. Easy things nobody wants, but what is forbidden is tempting. . . . Anyone who can love the wife of an indolent cuckold, I should suppose, would steal buckets of sand from the shore.

Walster, Walster, Piliavin, and Schmidt [481] have enumerated some reasons why this should occur, based on interviews with college students who were asked to explain the relationship. The students pointed out that a woman can afford to be choosy and hard to get only if she is popular, and that a woman is usually popular for some good reason. Furthermore, men are intrigued by the challenge offered by an elusive woman. Since her desirability is well recognized, the man can gain prestige if he is seen with her.

According to the students, an easy-to-get woman, on the other hand, spells trouble. She may be desperate for a date and is probably the kind of woman who will make too many demands on a man and might want to get serious immediately. Even worse, the students pointed out, she might have a "disease." Walster and her coworkers carried out a series of studies to gather evidence about these impressions.

One study was unique in that it used a prostitute as an experimenter. After the prostitute's customer had arrived and had a drink, she delivered the experimental manipulation. In the hard-to-get condition, she stated, "Just because I see you this time, it doesn't mean that you can have my phone number or see me again. I'm going to start school soon, so I won't have much time, so I'll only be able to see the people that I like the best." In the easy-to-get condition, on the other hand, she did not say this. Walster and her coworkers tell us, "From this point on, the prostitute and the customer interacted in conventional ways" (481, p. 116).

The client's liking for the prostitute was determined in two ways. The prostitute herself estimated how much the client had seemed to like her, based on such factors as conversation and amount paid. In addition, the experimenter recorded how many times within the next thirty days the client arranged to have sexual relationships with the prostitute.

This unique study failed to confirm the hypothesis that playing hard to get would lead to increased attractiveness. Walster and her coworkers report that clients who were told that the prostitute did not take just anyone (and, hence, was somewhat hard-to-get) were actually less likely to call back and liked the prostitute less than did the other clients. So it would appear that things are not as simple as we might have imagined. (Of course, one could question how hard-to-get *any* prostitute could be. Perhaps, in this case, her remarks simply seemed like an insult to her customers.)

It seems that it is not simply being hard-to-get that determines how attractive someone will appear. Perhaps, Walster and her coworkers reasoned, it is being *selectively* hard-to-get—hard for others to get but easy for *you* to get—that will make someone particularly attractive to you. A second study supported this contention. As part of a project supposedly designed to determine whether computer-matching techniques are more effective than random matching, male college students were invited to the dating center on the University of Wisconsin campus to choose a date from a set of five candidates. The student looked over and chose from five folders, each of which described one potential date.

The experimenter also explained that some of the women had already been able to come in, examine the background information of *their* "matches," and indicate the first impressions of them. Three of the women had already come and evaluated the subject along with her four other matches. This information allowed the experimenters to describe (via the folders) five different "types" of women. One of the five women had indicated that though she was willing to date any of the men assigned to her, she was not enthusiastic about any of them. The experimenters label her the uniformly hard-to-get woman. A second woman appeared to be uniformly easy-to-get, since she indicated that she was enthusiastic about dating all five men assigned to her.

One woman appeared to be easy for the subject to get but hard for anyone else to get. This selectively hard-to-get woman had indicated only small enthusiasm for four of her date choices but extreme enthusiasm for the subject. The remaining two women had not filled out the forms. The subject then was asked to consider the folders, complete a ."first impression questionnaire" for each woman, and then decide which one of the women he wished to date.

Walster and her coworkers found that, as expected, men were much more likely to choose the selectively hard-to-get woman than any of the other four types. Forty-two of the seventy-one men made this woman their first choice. Furthermore, according to the ratings on the "first impression scales," the men expressed greater liking for the selectively hard-to-get woman than for any of the other four. Personality ratings also indicated that the selectively hard-to-get woman was rated similarly to the uniformly hard-to-get woman in terms of two positive characteristics: selectivity and popularity; but she was rated similarly to the easy-to-get women in terms of three other positive characteristics: friendly, warm, and easy-going. Therefore, the selectively hard-to-get woman appears to represent the best of both possible worlds—popularity and niceness.

◾ LOVING OTHERS

What is love?

A recent edition of Bartlett's *Familiar Quotations* lists 769 references to "love," second only to the 843 references to "man." This remarkable number of quotations is superficial evidence of human interest in, and puzzlement about, the nature of love. There are as many definitions of love as there are philosophers and poets, and space does not permit even a brief overview here. However, psychologist Zick Rubin [372] has surveyed the descriptions of love provided throughout the centuries by philosophers, poets, and (lately) social scientists.

Rubin suggests that the concept of romantic love has three characteristics. (1) There is a physical and emotional need for another person, the passionate desire to possess and be fulfilled by that person. This feeling of *attachment* is similar to what the ancient Greeks called *eros.* (2) Love involves giving oneself to another person, a kind of ultimate altruism. Rubin refers to this dimension as *caring,* similar to the Greek conception of *agape.* (3) Love involves an intense bond between two people, which Rubin labels *intimacy.* When a relationship has all three of these qualities—attachment, caring, and intimacy—we can call it love. Note that this is a different kind of relationship than liking or simple interpersonal attraction, which we have been discussing up to this point. It seems possible that while we can certainly like someone we do not love, we may also love someone we hardly like.

Love as emotion

How do you know when you are in love? If you "feel it," what exactly do you feel? Writing in the *Art of Love,* the Roman poet Ovid suggested that an excellent time to arouse passion in a woman was while she was watching gladiators fight. Centuries later, in the late 1800s, Horwicz (cited in [372, p. 6]) suggested that "Love can only be excited by strong and vivid emotion, and it is almost immaterial whether these emotions are agreeable or disagreeable. The Cid wooed the proud heart of Donna Xiemene, whose father he had slain, by shooting one after another of her pet pigeons." Thus, Horwicz proposed, by taking one's date to a place where strong emotions of repulsion or fear would probably be aroused (such as by watching gladiators), the arousal of love might be facilitated as well. Why might this be?

Recall our earlier discussion of *self-attributions,* or how people go about deciding what emotions they are feeling. The research of Schachter, Valins, and others led to Schachter's *two-factor theory* of emotional arousal. He proposed that the particular feeling of an emotion is dependent on (1) a state of physiological arousal and (2) cognitive cues available in the environment as to what that arousal represents. We pointed out that in most cases, these two items of information are very clear; that is, we feel physiologically aroused, and what the arousal represents is obvious to us. But in cases where the cognitive cues are somewhat mixed or ambiguous, a person may be uncertain about what emotion he or she is feeling. In these cases, arousal of one sort (say, fear or repulsion) might be interpreted as representing an emotion of a quite different sort (love).

Social psychologists Elaine Walster and Ellen Berscheid [476] have suggested that the physiological arousal necessary for feeling an emotion such as love could stem from many causes. Obviously, sexual arousal is one. But it has been suggested that other seemingly irrelevant emotional states, such as anxiety, guilt, loneliness, hatred, jealousy, or even confusion, may also lead to physiological arousal and, hence, to the increased probability of labeling one's state as love. Thus, following Ovid and Horwicz, it can be predicted that if a state of emotional arousal exists *for any reason,* and if the cognitive situation suggests that passionate love would be an appropriate state to be feeling, then feelings of passionate love may actually increase [475]. If this is so, then even negative experiences can induce love, since they still would intensify arousal. Love does not exist unless the lover defines it as such; therefore, if the appropriate cognitions are present, almost any form of arousal may lead a person to label the emotion as love. As poets have said, love may not be very different from hate after all.

Although research is far from complete, some evidence supports the application of this theory of emotion to the area of love. For example, very passionate love affairs appear particularly likely to occur during wartime. Perhaps part of the passion is associated with the heightened general levels of emotional arousal that characterize such periods.

Countless dramas and poems have been written about the effect of parental interference on young love; *Romeo and Juliet* is probably the most well known. In many cases, both in drama and in real life, the effects of such parental interference appear to be precisely the opposite of what the parents intended; that is, although they hoped to destroy the bond of love, their resistance seems to strengthen it. There are at least two good reasons why this might occur.

1 Parental interference may cause frustration and anger in the lovers. If so, the emotional arousal associated with anger might be interpreted as love, in line with the two-factor theory of emotion.
2 Research has shown that when a person feels that freedom of choice is threatened or restricted, he or she will be motivated to reestablish that threatened freedom. This tendency to reestablish freedom has been labeled *reactance* [68]. When people are told that they are not allowed to do something or to see someone, then in order to reestablish their freedom to do what they wish, they may feel even greater desire to do the forbidden thing or see the forbidden person.

The likelihood that parental interference will intensify feelings of romantic love has been called the *Romeo and Juliet effect,* since this is apparently what happened to Shakespeare's hero and heroine. Parental interference is likely to be perceived by the couple as frustrating and as threatening their freedom of action, their freedom to see each other as they please, and their freedom to decide what future courses of action to take. Reactance theory predicts that as such perceived threats to freedom are felt, action will be taken to reduce the threats. One way such action could be taken is for feelings of love to intensify and the couple's determination to defy or ignore attempts at interference to increase.

Some recent research appears to support this contention. One study found that couples who felt their parents were interfering with their romance tended to be those who claimed to feel the greatest amount of romantic love for each other. When measures were readministered six to ten months later, it was found that changes in degree of parental interference correlated positively with changes in the extent of romantic love felt. Thus, the hypothesis that parental interference intensifies feelings of romantic love was supported [130].

Liking and loving: A summary flow

Experiences with others can be described in terms of the degree of relationship which exists between the parties [270]. As shown in Figure 5-7, these *levels of a relationship* can be represented in terms of the amount of contact parties have with each other. Before a relationship begins there is a stage of *zero contact;* the parties have no contact at all and are strangers. At the first level, *unilateral awareness,* one person knows the other exists, forms an impression of the other, but has not yet interacted with the other. At this level, the person gathers information about the other and, if the information is favorable, may try to obtain a higher level of relationship.

At the second level, *surface contact,* interaction begins between the parties. However, the interaction is restricted, and the relationship is somewhat shallow. Now each person begins to probe the relationship more intensely to determine whether to go further. At this stage, surface characteristics are important, as are any factors that ease further contact. Thus, propinquity, physical attractiveness, perceived competence, and reciprocal liking will all be important to the relationship. These are instances of the periods of sampling and estimation, and of bargaining, described in social exchange theory.

At the final level, *mutuality,* there is an intersection between the parties. At this level, they turn their attention away from surface traits and look more deeply at one another. Similarity of values and attitudes becomes more important, as does complementarity of needs. Mutuality, interdependence, intimacy, and possibly love, can result.

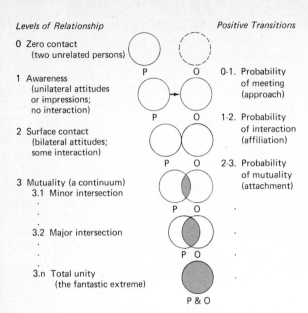

Levels of Relationship

0 Zero contact
   (two unrelated persons)

1 Awareness
   (unilateral attitudes
   or impressions;
   no interaction)

2 Surface contact
   (bilateral attitudes;
   some interaction)

3 Mutuality (a continuum)
   3.1 Minor intersection
   .
   .
   .
   3.2 Major intersection
   .
   .
   .
   3.n Total unity
        (the fantastic extreme)

Positive Transitions

0-1. Probability
      of meeting
      (approach)

1-2. Probability
      of interaction
      (affiliation)

2-3. Probability
      of mutuality
      (attachment)

Figure 5-7. *Levels of relationship. The levels of relatedness between two persons (P and O) can be considered as a series of stages. People typically engage in lesser degrees of contact (top) before developing greater relatedness (bottom).*

■ SUMMARY

We have explored various aspects of interpersonal behaviors and relationships. The first question we raised concerned affiliation: Why do people seek one another and want to be together? Several explanations for affiliation were proposed, including an affiliation instinct, the necessity of affiliation for survival of our species, the rewards which can be obtained and exchanged during affiliation, and the need to evaluate ourselves (social comparison theory). Each explanation focused on a different aspect of togetherness, and each may contain at least some truth. Fear and anxiety are closely related to affiliation. Prolonged isolation raises anxiety to high levels and then results in withdrawal and apathy. Conversely, as fear increases, so does one's tendency to affiliate: "Misery (or joy) loves miserable (or joyful) company."

Once people come into contact with each other, they begin to form impressions, evaluations, and judgments. Each of us has concepts (generalizations) about what certain other types of people are like. These generalizations help determine whether much interaction will occur. We also carry implicit personality theories with us; these theories tell us what traits seem to be associated with other traits in people. Based on observations of people's behaviors, we make attributions about what they are like. The tendency to make dispositional attributions increases when (1) external pressures on the other's behavior are minimal; (2) the other's behaviors are unexpected; and (3) the other's behaviors are hedonically relevant or are intended to affect us.

We also often make attributions about our own internal states based on environmental cues. The two-factor theory of emotion suggests that the labels we apply to our internal states are determined by a condition of physiological arousal plus cognitive cues which allows us to label the arousal state.

Finally, as contact is increased between people, liking and disliking become important. Factors which increase interpersonal attraction include: propinquity (nearness), similarity, physical attractiveness, ability, reciprocated liking, and complementarity. Love goes beyond mere liking to feelings of attachment, caring, and intimacy.

6

altruism: where's the help?

concepts

Altruism is helping behavior motivated by another person's being in need.

Bystander intervention involves noticing and interpreting an event as an emergency as well as assuming the responsibility to respond according to one's ability.

Emergencies become ambiguous when witnesses fail to act, thereby allowing others to infer that there is no need to help.

The more people there are in social settings, the more likely there is to be a lessening of social restraints.

An analysis of helping behavior involves characteristics of the victim, the bystanders, and the situation.

targets

After studying this chapter, you should be able to:

1   Discuss different views of the nature of humanity.
2   Distinguish between altruism and helping behavior.
3   Identify characteristics of the victim that increase the likelihood for help.
4   Identify bystander characteristics that are associated with increased helping.
5   Describe the effects of deindividuation.
6   Discuss a theoretical model regarding why people help.
7   Discuss the development of helping behavior.
8   Identify the several personality attributes related to helping behavior.

John Harrington, a forty-nine-year-old laborer, walked down a street in Miami Beach late in 1973. Before he realized it, he was shot in the chest and robbed of $1. Realizing that he was in serious trouble, he took some change from his pocket and boarded a city bus for a Miami hospital; he crossed the causeway from Miami Beach to Miami and got off the bus, looking for medical assistance. After staggering three blocks, he slumped onto a bench. A woman sat beside Harrington for almost half an hour before noticing his collapsed state, observing the bleeding, and notifying authorities. So, John Harrington wandered around Miami for almost an hour after being shot without getting help. After undergoing emergency chest surgery, however, Harrington survived. He's one of the lucky ones, and his case is by no means unusual.

Perhaps the best-known incident of this type concerned Kitty Genovese, who lived in Kew Gardens, New York. At three-thirty A.M. on the morning of Mar. 13, 1964, Ms. Genovese was returning home from her job as manager of a bar. She parked her car in the parking lot and headed toward her apartment. She noticed a man at the far end of the parking lot and, becoming nervous, headed toward a nearby police call-box. She got as far as the streetlights before the man grabbed her. She screamed, "Oh, my God! He stabbed me. Please help me! Please help me!" It later turned out that thirty-eight of Ms. Genovese's neighbors went to their windows to see what was happening. One, in fact, shouted, "Let that girl alone!" However, moments later, the killer returned to Ms. Genovese and stabbed her once again. Lights went on again in many apartments, and the murderer got into his car and drove away. However, the assailant returned again. It was now 3:35 A.M. By then Kitty had crawled to the back of her building, looking for safety. The killer found her there, slumped against the stairs. He stabbed her a third time, this time fatally. One half hour and thirty-eight witnesses later, Kitty Genovese was dead. At 3:50 A.M. the police received the first call and were at the scene in two minutes. It later turned out that the neighbor who made the call had first crossed the roof of the building to the apartment of an elderly woman to ask her to make the call. Before he had even done that, he had phoned a friend in Nassau County for advice. When questioned, he simply said that he didn't want to get involved [325].

In an incident reported by United Press International on Feb. 23, 1973, a group of young men tied a screaming woman to a lamppost in a Protestant area of West Belfast, Ireland, and savagely beat her while residents watched silently from their windows. Police said that the woman was left hanging on the post for more than an hour in subfreezing weather without anyone coming to her aid, although her screams were heard several blocks away. One officer reported, "Not a single person living on the street said they heard anything when we questioned them, but people living three streets away said they did." When finally cut down from the post, the woman was in deep shock and unable to say anything about the attack.

Events such as these cause us to wonder why people don't help. Are people so self-centered and callous that they really don't care if others are in need? Or is there a natural tendency to be concerned for our brothers and sisters? The concept of *altruism* comes from the Latin word *alter,* meaning "other," and generally connotes an orientation toward others rather than toward the self. But there is a basic question about whether or not altruism really exists.

■ ALTRUISM AND OUR NATURE

Philosophers have argued about the existence and nature of altruism for several centuries. The argument in favor of self-interest is a popular one. It states that in a conflict between one's own interests and those of another person, it seems unreasonable to prefer anyone else's interests to one's own. Machiavelli, for instance, held that people were always self-interested. He stated in the *Discourses* that we "must start with assuming that all men are bad and ever ready to assume to their vicious nature" [283, p. 117]. This position provides little room for being concerned with others. Similarly, well-known philosophers such as Hobbes and Nietzsche have stressed humanity's self-interest and lack of altruism. But not all philosophers agree with this outlook.

Plato was one early thinker who implied that our self-centered nature can be changed by proper education and remolding human nature. In *The Republic,* Plato suggests that a philosopher-king "will take society and human character as his canvas, and begin by scraping it clean—he will rub out and paint in again this or that feature, until he has produced, so far as may be, a type of human character that heaven can approve" [352, p. 209]. Plato suggested two reasons why altruism must exist. The first one is really another theory of self-interest; people help others because not to help would pain them and cause them to lose the credibility and respect they need from society. Therefore, in their own self-interest, they help others. A second, later argument developed by Plato and his student, Aristotle, emphasized that the only way a person can achieve individuality is through aesthetic, intellectual, and affectionate union with others. Since this union is necessary, altruism is allowed to develop.

Such differing views of human nature have led to varying conceptualizations of the meaning of altruism. They can be divided into three categories, discussed below.

Reward-cost definition

A definition stemming from one reward-cost framework, discussed in Chapter 4, suggests that altruism exists whenever someone helps but gets far less in return for helping than the cost involved. An example of this would be trying to stop a mugging and getting stabbed in the process (an extremely high cost). A more common example is stopping to help someone pick up a book, only to be late for class and in trouble with the professor. There are

Figure 6-1. *The murder of (a) Catherine (Kitty) Genovese on Mar. 13, 1964, is often identified as having initiated the research on bystander apathy. Although later information regarding her personal life (such as probable lesbian behavior) has tempered her story as a "typical" or "model" case, the fact remains that thirty-eight of her neighbors failed to help as her attacker, Winston Moseley, (b) returned three times to finally complete her murder. Some research has focused on characteristics of the environmental*

(a)

(b)

(c)

(d)

setting of the incident (Kew Gardens in New York City), which is displayed in this aerial photo (c). Ms. Genovese parked her car at (1) and was attacked at (2), (3), and (4), where her body was finally found. (d) A closer view of location (4) shows the spot where Moseley looked up the staircase and saw one of Genovese's neighbors, who witnessed the last act of murder and closed his door. (Ten years later, in 1974, another woman was also killed here, and again people heard her scream and ignored it.) Moseley later escaped from prison and created an opportunity for more social science research after terrorizing hostages, who later sued the State of New York for not protecting citizens from such persons. He is shown here surrendering to the FBI.

obvious problems with this formulation. First, who determines how much the costs must outweigh the rewards for an action to be labeled altruism? Second, what is rewarding or costly for one person may not be for another. Picking up a book might give you the opportunity to finally introduce yourself to someone you have been wanting to meet for several months. And a stabbed hero or heroine might be the kind of person who gets tremendous satisfaction in gaining attention from others. The point is that internal rewards might be substantial and far outweigh any costs. So, although this definition does sound fairly viable, we can never be sure when someone's behavior is altruistic or not.

Moral definitions

Some philosophers have suggested that it is our *duty* to help others. For example, one is being altruistic if, even unwillingly, one runs into a burning building to rescue a child out of a sense of duty. By definition, the rescuer acted both altruistically and morally. In this formulation, there is no difference between moral behavior and altruistic behavior. But surely not all the things we *should* do are examples of altruism. For example, we should all be open and honest. Yet to do so in some situations might create, rather than solve, problems. There must be something else that distinguishes altruism from other concepts.

Intention descriptions

Using this approach, altruism is identified on the basis of *why* people act. An altruistic act (1) is an end in itself (not directed at any gain); (2) is performed voluntarily; and (3) accomplishes good [264]. For example: You are walking along the beach and hear someone screaming in the surf. You realize the person is in trouble and swim to the rescue. Or, if you can't swim, you call a lifeguard. According to the intention definition of altruism, we now would explore the reasons for your behavior. If your first thought was of ego enhancement or publicity, or if you felt morally compelled to act, or recognized the victim as the child of a wealthy banker, then we could not say that you were being altruistic. An intention definition of altruism, we now would explore the reasons for your behavior. If your first words, *altruism is helping behavior motivated by the other person's being in need* [396]. The problem with this approach is that intentions are also difficult to measure.

Helping behavior

These different conceptions of altruism relate to human nature and how we see ourselves. However, it is also clear that the person in need (John Harrington, Kitty Genovese, the Irish girl) could not care less about these distinctions. The only important consideration to the victim is whether he or she has been helped. As a result, we will use the more general term *helping*

Figure 6-2. *Some people do help—and at a high cost. These six children were left without parents when widower Frank Walker went to the aid of a New York City policeman and lost his life. Police, from patrolman to captains, launched a fund drive which collected hundreds of thousands of dollars to care for the children.*

behavior throughout this chapter. *Helping behavior is behavior designed to aid another individual regardless of reason.* Who cares if the helper makes money after the fact? The victim has been saved! Most social scientists have concentrated on identifying factors which tend to decrease or increase the amount of helping behavior. If Kitty Genovese had been helped, for any reason, she might be alive today. Notice that the measurement problem is not as large for helping. Rewards, costs, and intentions need not be attended to.

■ THE BASICS OF BYSTANDER INTERVENTION

The studies social psychologists have conducted to investigate incidents like those described at the beginning of this chapter have been labeled studies of *bystander intervention.* Do people standing by intervene? These studies are all designed essentially the same way. The subjects are persons who, either by design or by accident, have happened upon a staged or real emergency; the social scientist is interested in their response to the situation. One way of analyzing the bystander-intervention process is to focus on the *sequence of decisions* a bystander must make. This is the approach taken by John Darley and Bibb Latané [114]. They felt that when faced with an emergency, one must make a series of rapid decisions. First, one must *notice,* or pay attention to, the event. Second, having become aware of the event, one must *interpret* it to decide whether it is an emergency. Therefore, in addition to noticing an event, a bystander must be able to recognize that the situation calls for action. This sounds simple enough, but we all know that there are situations in which both children and adults do not recognize dangers. Third, having decided that an event is an emergency, one must determine one's personal *responsibility* to act. (We will return to this shortly.) Two further decisions are required. They involve determining *what kind* of aid to give and how best to act according to one's perceived *skills and abilities.* Darley and Latané differentiate between *direct* and *indirect* aid in emergencies. For example, if you see someone break a leg in an automobile accident, direct intervention would mean rushing to the scene and trying to provide aid, medical assistance, or comfort. Indirect intervention, on the other hand, would mean calling for an ambulance or the police—in other words, calling on those whose responsibility or function it is to aid emergency victims. Lastly, of course, one could decide not to intervene.

Another way to structure the bystander-intervention situation is to recognize that there are three different factors involved: *the victim, the bystander,* and the event or *emergency* itself. It should be evident that a victim may provide cues which partially determine the outcome. Is the victim visibly bleeding and suffering from severe injury? Is the victim a small woman or a football linebacker? Considerations such as these will obviously affect a bystander's response. Characteristics of a bystander also will affect the nature of the response—a physician will react differently to another's broken leg than will a child. The nature of an emergency also plays a part in determining bystanders' responses. Helping a child fix a toy, helping a stranded motorist fix a flat tire, saving a swimmer who is about to drown, and stopping a stabbing are very different emergencies. Each will present different problems for a potential helper.

With these analytical frameworks in mind, we now will turn to a discussion of the circumstances and characteristics that tend to enhance or reduce helping. And, although we can identify different components of the bystander phenomenon, it is important to remember that the situation is basically a social one. That is, beyond the characteristics of each of these components, we are concerned with how the people in the situation *interact.*

■ **VICTIM-BYSTANDER CHARACTERISTICS: OR, WHAT IS IT ABOUT ME THAT . . . ?**

Probably hundreds of characteristics of bystanders and victims could be related to helping behavior. In fact, some people believe there are "victim traits" which consciously or unconsciously invite attack. How else, they argue, can we account for the fact that some individuals (such as twenty-two-year-old Dolores Perez of the West Bronx, who has been mugged an extraordinary six times to date) appear to always be victimized [324]? We shall try to focus on some of the more basic characteristics: ambiguity of the victim's need, effects of group size, similarity of bystander and victim, and mood.

Ambiguity of victim's need

As you read about John Harrington's trek around Miami while gravely injured, it probably occurred to you that others might not have known he was in trouble. Recall that, according to the sequence of decisions proposed by Latané and Darley, an individual must notice an unusual situation and then decide that the situation is an emergency. Further, they suggest that, in making these decisions, *an individual will be heavily influenced by the decisions that other bystanders appear to be making.* If everyone else concludes that the situation is not an emergency, one's own perception may be altered and the response changed accordingly. Latané and Darley [258] tested these ideas by asking subjects to sit in a small waiting room and fill out a questionnaire while supposedly awaiting their turn to participate in an interview study. While they were seated, a stream of smoke began to pour into the room through a wall vent. The condition was manipulated as follows: The subject was either (1) alone in the room, or (2) with two other students who had earlier been told not to respond, or (3) with two other students who were also naïve. The researchers were interested in determining how much time would elapse between noticing the smoke and reporting it.

As the researchers had predicted, subjects who were alone would glance up from their questionnaires, notice the smoke, become slightly startled, and then undergo a period of indecision, perhaps returning briefly to the questionnaire before again staring at the smoke. Soon most of the subjects would get up from their chairs, walk over to the vent and investigate it closely, sniffing the smoke, waving their hands in it, feeling its temperature, etc. They then left the room and reported the smoke within a median time of two minutes. In all, 75 percent of the twenty-four subjects who were alone reported the smoke before the end of the six-minute experimental period.

When subjects sat with nonreacting research confederates, the results were dramatically different. Of the ten subjects run in this condition, only one reported the smoke. The other nine remained seated, working steadily on the questionnaires as the room filled with smoke. Because there were three subjects (instead of just one) in the third condition, Latané and Darley used the speed of the first subject in a group to report the smoke as the dependent variable. However, since there were three times as many people available to respond to the problem, at least one person would be expected to report the smoke much more often than in the one-subject groups. However, of the eight groups of three subjects, only one person reported within the first four minutes and only three reported within the entire experimental period. This constitutes 38 percent of the groups. Latané and Darley interpreted these results to mean that social influences affect the interpretation of an ambiguous situation. In other words, when others are present and do not react, an ambiguous situation is seen to be less serious than when one is alone.

Because the above study is clearly not the same kind of situation as the one involving Kitty Genovese, a second study was undertaken to investigate more precisely how the actions of others color our perception of an emergency situation. A situation was constructed in which subjects (waiting either alone, with a friend, with a confederate stranger, or with another naïve subject) heard a young woman in the next room (whom they had previously met) climb on a chair and then fall with a loud crash [257]. The crash was followed by screams and moans as the victim tried to free herself from the weight of a bookcase which had supposedly fallen on her legs. Again, the dependent variable was whether or not the subject took action, and if so, how quickly. This study allowed the subject to choose either direct intervention (going in to help) or indirect intervention (reporting it to the experimenter or calling out to the victim). This type of laboratory setting is more similar to the Genovese incident than the study with the smoke-filled room because it was a single person that required aid.

When subjects were alone, it was found that 70 percent either called out to see if they were needed or went in to help the victim. The same percentage of subjects helped when they were waiting with a friend. However, when two naïve strangers were together, only 40 percent intervened. And when the subject was waiting in the presence of a nonreacting research confederate, only 7 percent offered to help the victim. The difference between the "friend" and "stranger" conditions was attributed to the fact that friends discussed the situation and possible courses of action, thus arriving at a joint decision, while strangers did not. Further, friends were probably less likely to misinterpret each other's initial responses as showing a lack of concern and were therefore more likely to express their alarm openly. On the other hand, consider what happened with strangers. The longer each sat and did nothing, the more information was indirectly provided for the other that the situation was not really an emergency. This condition is known as *pluralistic ignorance.* Because no one is helping, others are cued in that there is apparently no need to help.

A question that arises in studies of bystander intervention is: What would happen if there were a clearcut emergency, with no opportunity for pluralistic ignorance to develop? This question of ambiguity can be demonstrated by a routine described by the Smothers Brothers comedy team. Tom tells of a friend who had died in an unfortunate accident when many people were around who could have helped. Dick asks how this could possibly have happened. Tom procedes to make matters worse by saying that his friend had screamed out and no one helped. Dick continues to appear incredulous and asks for a description of exactly what happened. Tom then tells the entire story. His friend was working at a candy factory and at an inopportune moment fell into a large vat of chocolate. He couldn't swim and kept screaming, "Chocolate! Chocolate! Chocolate!" until he died.

Although this story may be humorous in entertainment settings, the point is that if a victim can make a situation less ambiguous, he or she is more likely to receive help. Empirical verification of this point has been provided by Clark and Word [94, 95]. They exposed single persons and two- and five-person groups of subjects to an unmistakable emergency. Another set of subjects in similar groups were confronted with an ambiguous emergency. Subjects overheard an identical fall, but some did not receive verbal cues indicating that the victim was injured. In the clear emergency, 100 percent of the subjects offered help; in the ambiguous situation, only 30 percent offered help. Clark and Word noticed that in the ambiguous situation, subjects who were alone were more likely to help and responded faster than either the two- or five-person groups. In the clearcut emergency, no subjects misinterpreted the event or tried to explain it away, and their behavior was not affected by the presence of others. So, if you are the victim in an emergency, clearly shout out that you need help.

Unfortunately, describing an emergency to some bystanders might frighten them off or alert them to the dangerous possibilities that exist if they intervene. However, clarity is still the best advice. When you need assistance, it has been suggested that you scream, "Fire!" instead of "Help!" If, in fact, some people have learned to ignore a cry for help, it is still true that people respond quickly to a cry of "Fire!" As can be seen in Figure 6-6, groups such as the Governor's Crime Prevention Committee in Florida suggest similar tactics for women who are attacked. The point is: When you need assistance, call out but try not to frighten away possible helpers.

Effects of group size

Two areas of study are relevant to the effects of group size on helping behavior: diffusion of responsibility and deindividuation.

Diffusion of responsibility. Continuing with Latané and Darley, their model suggests that, in situations where an emergency occurs, the offers of help will decrease as the number of others believed to be present increases. This seems reasonable when we ponder that if responsibility is to be taken in an emergency, the more people who are present, the more the responsibility can be shared. In effect, then, no one person was responsible for Kitty Genovese's death; rather, each of the thirty-eight was partly to blame. Latané and Darley call this phenomenon the *diffusion of responsibility*.

To test their hypothesis, Darley and Latané [114] designed a study in which female subjects could see neither the victim nor other bystanders. The cover story for the experiment was this: Each subject entered a small room equipped with a communication system that allowed verbal exchange with other participants. Each subject was allowed to express her views on a personal problem (with her microphone on and all others turned off) while all the other subjects listened to what was being said. One of the subjects (who was a confederate) mentioned early in the conversation that she had a history of epilepsy. Later in the study, subjects were led to believe that they were overhearing her undergo an epileptic seizure and that the seizure was also being heard by the other subjects. The major independent variable in the study was the number of other people the subject believed to be listening; in some cases it was none, in others one, and in still others, four. The dependent variable, again, was the time it took the subject to help the victim after the seizure began.

The results showed clearcut differences depending on the number of other people present. To start, 85 percent of the subjects who were alone helped in some way very quickly. On the other hand, 65 percent of the subjects who thought another subject was listening responded, while only 31 percent of the subjects responded when they thought four other bystanders were listening. A popular adage is that there is safety in numbers. This study demonstrates that for the victim, such may not be the case.

The original work on social behavior as affected by large groups or crowds was done by the sociologist Gustave Le Bon. Le Bon suggested that when an individual is caught up in a crowd, the "group mind" tends to take over and each individual's behavior is affected by what the crowd wants to do. "Whoever be the individuals that compose it, however like or unlike be their mode of life, their occupations, their character, or their intelligence, the fact that they have been transformed into a crowd puts them in possession of a sort of collective mind" [263, p. 27]. Clearly, it would be extremely hard for anyone to resist a crowd set on a particular course of action. For example, consider yourself a member of a vigilante group in the Old West. A desperado has been hunted down and is about to be lynched. You may strongly feel that you want to prevent the lynching, but to question the group's behavior at that point would be very difficult. It is likely that screaming "no" would have the immediate effect of making you stand out from the crowd and possibly land you next to the desperado on the nearest tree. Early researchers in bystander intervention indicated that a similar process was occurring. To stand out from the crowd and assume responsibility for intervention would have the effect of clearly pointing out to an attacker or to others watching that you were the next victim—or, at least, that you were different from the rest of the group.

Although some of the above ideas seem reasonable, not all studies have demonstrated the group-size effect. Irwin Silverman [408] had to try several situations before he found one in which the number of people present affected the speed of helping. The situation he did find "successful" was one in which a person appeared to have lost a contact lens. This is a situation which clearly does not expose the bystander to much danger. Other, more systematic attempts to replicate the diffusion effects have turned up an interesting finding. It may be that the effect of group size on helping holds only for female subjects [267; 392]. Most of the subjects in the study done by Latané and Darley were female, and most other studies on diffusion of responsibility have also involved female subjects. So, it may not be appropriate to generalize that this is true of all individuals. (We shall return later to a more extensive discussion of how the sex of participants affects bystander intervention.)

Deindividuation. On Sept. 26, 1973, a twenty-seven-year-old woman in Dania, Florida, climbed to the top of a 110-foot tower, intending to jump to her death. Three days earlier, another would-be suicide had been talked down from the same tower by fire fighters. In the second incident, a crowd of about 300 clustered around. However, rather than try to help, they pelted police with rocks and stones as they tried to rescue the distraught woman. The fire chief reported that the two officers who helped the woman down were risking their own lives in the attempt. The rock throwing increased as the trio climbed down the ladder, and the crowd finally booed when they realized that the woman would not jump. The police chief said, "There is something wrong in a society when a crowd has no feeling for human dignity" [21]. People have gone beyond not helping in such an instance; they have actually tried to prevent help from being given.

Festinger, Pepitone, and Newcomb [157] coined the term *deindividuation* to refer to the loss of inner restraint that occurs when an individual is submerged in a group where "individuals are not seen or paid attention to as individuals." More recently, Zimbardo [511, p. 251] expanded these ideas, suggesting that

Deindividuation is a complex, hypothesized process in which a series of antecedent social conditions lead to changes in perception of self and others and thereby to a lowered threshold of normally restrained behavior. Under appropriate conditions what results is the release of behavior in violation of established norms of appropriateness.

It should be clear that such violations would permit the expression of all kinds of behavior harmful to human welfare. A naturally occurring crowd, where people can easily lose their individual identities, can be found at sports stadiums and arenas. In recent years the high emotionalism that is part of sports and the increasing anonymity of groups of fans acting as a unit have created some of the deindividuated conditions described by Zimbardo. The classic example of hysterical behavior is that of soccer fans attending a match in Lima, Peru, about fifteen years ago. In a riot over the outcome of the game, 293 were killed and 500 were injured. More recently, fans on the American sports scene—especially in football, hockey, and baseball—have become alarmingly violent, as the following example from Cincinnati [421, p. 11] shows:

. . . the Houston Astros' outfielder, lay stunned. . . . [H]is sunglasses had shattered when he had crashed into the fence . . . he was bleeding from facial wounds. . . . A group of spectators . . . leaned over the railing. . . . Then as Watson's teammates, who had run over to help, backed off in astonishment, fans began to rain beer down . . . and to pelt him with ice cubes. . . .

It is unlikely that these fans would have responded this way if they had not been part of an anonymous crowd. What is it about deindividuating situations that creates such behavior?

In one study, groups of male college students were asked to comment about their parents. In the control situation, discussions were held under ordinary conditions. In the deindividuated situations, subjects were dressed in gray laboratory coats, and the discussions were held in dimly lit rooms [157]. The intent was to create a condition in which people would not be able to identify exactly who made certain comments. The researchers' prediction was supported; in the deindividuated situation, restraints were lowered, leading to many more negative comments regarding parents than were given by the group meeting under ordinary conditions. It has been demonstrated that deindividuation (created in a similar fashion) will also lead to greater use of obscenities when describing pornographic material [409]. Both of these studies indicate that when a subject cannot be identified and is in fact lost in the crowd, there is a lessening of inner restraints and more violation of what we would call typical appropriate behavior.

Zimbardo contends that deindividuation is not just a condition but rather an entire process. By this he means that there are many different social conditions which, when combined in certain ways, lead to both (1) changes in how people perceive themselves and (2) lowered restraints. These two changes, in turn, can be expected to cause an increase in antisocial or unusual behaviors. Zimbardo's representation of conditions in the deindividuation process is summed up in Table 6-1. Not all of these conditions can be studied at any one time. An interesting Zimbardo study described in Focus 6-1 investigates the possibility that some of society's institutions unfortunately are structured to promote deindividuation and antisocial behavior. Are all the conditions described by Zimbardo really necessary to create the kind of nonresponsible behavior we have been talking about? An interesting cross-cultural finding shows a direct relationship between a tribe's warring and aggressive behavior and its costuming to achieve anonymity [483]. Further, the degree of hostility or aggressiveness the tribe plans for any particular occasion is directly related to how carefully each warrior covers himself with paint (and becomes more anonymous). It may be that anonymity alone can create deindividuated behavior.

Table 6-1. Adapted version of Zimbardo's deindividuation process

When one finds oneself:	One will experience a lessening of:	Which will result in:
Anonymous	Self-observation	Impulsive and overemotional behavior
With shared responsibility	Concern for what others think	
In group action	Controls based on guilt, fear, shame, etc.	Intense behavior
Confused about time	Inhibitions	Repeated behavior
Overly aroused or drugged		Forgetfulness
In a new situation		Insensitivity to others
Acting emotionally		A "liking" for the crowd
Being physical		Destruction of traditional and cultural norms

FOCUS 6-1   DEINDIVIDUATION BEHIND BARS

Athough our description of deindividuation and the kinds of antisocial behavior it seems to create might appear unusual or rare, it may be more common than we would like to think. In fact, even though no one knowingly would design social programs or social institutions to create such an atmosphere, recent work suggests that prisons, for example, promote deindividuated behavior. The evidence comes from a study known as the Stanford Prison Experiment [513]. In this study, the experimenters were concerned with the psychological consequences of prison life. Now, there are two roles in prison: inmates and guards. Half of the volunteer subjects in this study were randomly assigned roles as prisoners, the other half as guards. All subjects were paid $15 a day, and before the study could begin, all subjects participated in extensive clinical interviews and personality testing to ensure that only "normal" participants would engage in the experiment.

Instead of using an existing prison, the researchers did their best to psychologically *simulate* the characteristics of a real prison, since the entire experiment was designed to make the event as real as possible. The subjects designated as prisoners were rounded up from their homes by city police officers in squad cars, then taken to a police station, where they were processed in a normal fashion (that is, searched, handcuffed, fingerprinted, and booked) and taken blindfolded to the "prison" (the basement of the psychology building at Stanford University). Prisoners were manipulated so as to deindividuate them as much as possible. They were stripped and deloused, as real prisoners are. They were identified by numbers, rather than being allowed to keep names. They were made to wear identical hospital gowns, which stripped away another aspect of identity. Lastly, they had to wear stocking caps or bags on their heads to reduce identifiability and distinctiveness from hairstyles. Everything was done to remove the "prisoners'" individuality and make them anonymous and invisible.

At the same time, subjects serving as guards also were fitted for their new roles. All "guards" were dressed in identical khaki uniforms. To reduce their recognizability and then increase anonymity among the prisoners, all guards wore reflecting sunglasses. They were given billyclubs, whistles, keys to the cells, and handcuffs—all of which, again, added to the costume and represented power. Both prisoners and guards could hide behind their uniforms and lose their individuality. The study was designed as a two-week experiment; guards were instructed to maintain "law and order" and take responsibility for whatever problems arose. They were also given sixteen prison rules, which were designed to keep the two roles separate.

What happened? To start, the manipulations appeared to work. In fact, one prisoner stated, "I began to feel that I was losing my identity. The person that I call (own name) . . . was distant from me, was remote until

Figure 6-3. *Sing Sing Prison, and most others like it, are big, old, and dehumanizing. The death house (A) is even more confined. What kind of behavior is created in such settings? Is it really rehabilitation?*

finally I wasn't that. I was number 416 . . . I was really my number" [513, p. 12]. The guards, too, seemed to fall into their roles. They became more aggressive and abusive; generally, their interactions with the prisoners became appallingly bad. Unfortunately, the prisoners responded the way most real prisoners respond. They became passive, helpless, and depressed. In fact, several of them had to be released within the first few days of the experiment. The experience was, in fact, too real; after six days, it had to be terminated. Several of the prisoners had already been released early, one because of a psychosomatic rash over his entire body, and four because of extreme emotional problems. The guards were in an equally bad state. Their role identification was complete, their brutalization swift.

The strangest aspect of this experiment was that the effects were obtained in a group of normal, average college students participating in a simulated study. In six days, they had reached a point that was no longer tolerable. What about real prisons? Things are not much better. Even though people in positions of authority may not act deliberately, they can and do allow programs to continue which foster deindividualized, antisocial behavior. Not only in the laboratory, but also in the real world, loss of personal identity and feelings of self-worth have dramatic impact on behavior.

Laboratory evidence on anonymity and deindividuation also exists [38]. An attempt was made to differentiate between (1) a lowered sense of identifiability or individuality and (2) anonymity. This was accomplished by manipulating subjects' distinctiveness and also their anonymity from the victim and the experimenter. The results suggest that anonymity, not the loss of individuality, causes lowered restraints. But a final piece of evidence adds a bit of complexity to the story. Researchers took advantage of the customs of Halloween trick-or-treating to study the effects of anonymity on children's behavior. Half the children met at the door of a house were carefully identified; the other half were allowed to remain anonymous, hiding behind the cover of their costumes. The investigators were interested in what would happen when the children were left alone in the foyer of the house, with a bowl of candy and a bowl of pennies in clear view. They found that the second, anonymous group was more prone to take the money and candy. However, the investigators contend that anonymity alone does not always lead to increased antisocial behavior. They propose that this occurs only when anonymity is combined with the presence of a group [165]. Being anonymous does not itself create the behavior displayed on that Cincinnati ball field (see page 235). Being anonymous and hidden in a crowd, however, does create a tempting situation for inappropriate behavior.

Similarity

A number of aspects are involved in describing the basic ways in which people can be seen as similar. We shall discuss perceived similarity, ethnic identity and race, sex, and social class.

Perceived similarity. One thing that determines the relationship between bystanders and victims is perceived similarity. Two types of similarity must be considered: similarity among the bystanders themselves and similarity between the bystanders and the victim. Interestingly, these two types of similarity create different results. When several bystanders at an emergency perceive themselves as extremely similar, they tend to interact with one another. They are busy talking, for example, and since they perceive themselves to be similar, there is a heightened possibility that the victim in the emergency is not like them. They see themselves as the "in-group" or "us"; the victim becomes "the other." In this situation, help would not be given very quickly. Therefore, it has been noted that similarity between bystanders has the effect of decreasing helping behavior [415]. On the other hand, when bystanders are dissimilar, they are interacting only tentatively, if at all.

(a)

Figure 6-4. *Deindividuation is a condition or process in which individuals lose their uniqueness and often engage in behavior unthinkable to them under normal social conditions. Two situations in which this may happen are seen here. In (a), a meeting of the Ku Klux Klan takes place in broad daylight. The crosses and the American flag, which add religious and patriotic overtones, are attempts to legitimize the Klan's behavior.*

As a result, when an emergency arises, each is looking for different relationships, and thus, each is in a position to be more responsive. As these results differ from the finding that friends help faster, it must be that perceived similarity is not the same thing as friendship.

As this discussion suggests, when a bystander perceives a chance to interact pleasantly with a victim, he or she is more likely to help. In studies where the victim and bystander were alone and the bystander perceived a similarity with the victim, response was much quicker in terms of both direct intervention and indirect offers of help [e.g., 496]. A similar finding is that the more a bystander "liked" a victim, the more readily and willing the bystander was to help [341]. It's possible that perceived dissimilarity and dislike directly affected Kitty Genovese's situation. Her neighbors knew her to be a lesbian. They may have perceived her to be unlike themselves, or further, disliked her for such behavior. Each reaction lessens the potential for help.

This might suggest that we tend to help friends faster than we help

(b)

A completely different setting is that of sports scenes, where deindividuation has led to violent audience reaction. Fans fight in (b) after Manchester United defeated Cardiff City in a soccer match in Cardiff, England. Because of particularly violent mob action, English police arrested scores of people involved in fights at the soccer grounds and in the town.

strangers. Most people probably would agree with this. However, research measuring self-sacrifice in children's choice of toys to be given to a friend or a strange child has indicated that children are more generous to a stranger than to a friend. A similar reaction can be obtained when children are asked whether it is better to be kind to a stranger than to a friend [25]. It appears that children are more open to strangers, and, with age, people learn to draw back.

So far, we have discussed how perceived similarity between a bystander and a victim affects willingness to help. However, there is another side to this matter—namely, the victim's reaction to aid. It should be evident that when we accept help from someone, we are, in a sense, admitting that we can't do what is required ourselves. We are, therefore, admitting that the other person is better than we are, at least in this particular situation. It is not easy either to ask for help or to receive it. Perceived similarity also affects a victim's reaction to aid. Receiving aid from someone similar to ourselves has the effect of damaging our self-esteem and self-confidence. On the other hand, if a bystander is noticeably different, receiving help increases a victim's self-esteem and self-confidence. However, it should be noted that in one study, *all* helpers were rated more favorably than nonhelpers [162]. We can conclude that even if one is not too happy about having to be helped, one would rather be helped than ignored in a serious emergency.

We have now described how perceived similarity affects both direct and indirect help. And even though you might not feel as good about having to ask for help from someone who is similar to yourself, your chances of being helped are better if you do.

Ethnic identity and race. Some evidence shows that white people are more prone to help white victims than black victims. However, there are several possible reasons, and we should question whether this behavior is true for all whites. There seem to be three reasons why a white bystander might not help a black victim. First, people may recognize that help is needed but consciously decide to withhold it because of the victim's race. A prejudicial attitude directly influences this decision. Second, discrimination may occur unwittingly. Race may affect the recognizability of a helping situation. Bystanders may be unsure whether help is needed or desired. As noted before, if a bystander does not perceive a situation to be an emergency, there is no need to help. Third, a bystander may recognize that help is needed but lack the motivation to give it. As a result, he or she may reinterpret the situation as one in which help is unnecessary. This possibility clearly involves an interplay between the first two ways that race may affect helping behavior.

To clarify these possibilities, Samuel Gaertner [171] reran the injured girl, loud crash study, this time with a black victim for half the trials and a white one for the other half. He found that black victims were helped as frequently as white victims when a white bystander was alone, but less frequently when white bystanders were together. This suggests that whites may be more inclined to diffuse responsibility for black victims than for white victims. And if that is the case, since diffusion of responsibility can occur only when a bystander has defined a situation as one in which help is needed, it may be that the attitude toward the victim is leading to prejudicial behavior. Gaertner offers a second alternative, however. A white person may be influenced by social norms to ignore black victims more easily than white victims. This explanation suggests that the bystander recognizes help is needed but is concerned about being viewed as a deviant. One doesn't mind helping if the victim is white, but may if the victim is black.

The results of this study are somewhat similar to those of a study carried out in the New York City subway system (discussed fully later in the chapter), which indicated that whites helped blacks who were perceived to be ill as quickly as they helped whites, but that they helped blacks more slowly than whites if they thought that each was drunk. In another study, subjects found themselves in a position to help or not help a young black or white female whose bag of groceries had just broken in front of a supermarket [502]. Overall, results showed that blacks offered assistance without regard to race more than whites did. However, it was also noted that women tended to be less helpful toward women of their own race than are men. These findings are similar to those discussed in the telephone study in Focus 6-2.

Not all studies have suggested that ethnicity affects helping, however. Quite different findings were obtained when 800 addressed, unstamped letters were "lost" at various locations in different cities [280]. Half the letters were addressed to someone with a Spanish surname (Gonzalez), the other half to someone with an Anglo surname (Garrison). A total of 260 letters were picked up and mailed; exactly half were labeled Gonzalez, half Garrison. In this study of helping there did *not* seem to be an ethnicity effect.

In a similar study the researcher avoided identifying a social or ethnic group while at the same time varying similarity and dissimilarity. In this way, he could make the most general test of whether or not ethnic differences affect rates of helping. The cover story for the investigation is rather interesting and different [217, p. 32]:

Figure 6-5. *A wallet on the street—what are you going to do with it? Most wallets contain enough information to allow you to return them. Research suggests that the nature of the information will affect your response. Does the owner of the wallet sound similar to yourself, someone whose good opinion is important to you, or is it someone you'd probably dislike?*

FOCUS 6-2 SORRY, WRONG NUMBER!

There are many reasons to believe that subjects of laboratory studies do not
respond in "real" ways but, in fact, are suspicious, and that their
relationships both with the experimenter and with other subjects are
strained. So researchers try to devise ways to successfully manipulate the
phenomena they wish to study in "real-life" (field) settings. An example
of this approach is provided by a study by Samuel Gaertner and Leonard
Bickman [172] of how helping behavior is affected by race.

It was their intent to investigate both white racism and antiwhite
discrimination by blacks. If antiblack sentiment existed, they expected that
blacks would not be helped as often as were whites by whites. If there was
antiwhite sentiment by blacks, blacks would not help whites as often as they
would blacks. The study was conducted by contacting approximately 1,100
residents of Brooklyn, New York. The entire study was to be conducted over
the telephone, and names were chosen from the Brooklyn telephone
directory. People were contacted at home and asked for help; they did not
have to leave their home, did not have to be suspicious about an
experiment, and did not have to confront either the "victim" or an
experimenter in deciding whether or not to help. Also, they did not have to
worry about being evaluated by a crowd or a group of peers.

Each subject (from nearly equal numbers of black and white subjects)
received only one phone call. Seven black males and seven white males
did the calling. When the caller (victim) was to seem black, the black caller
used a modified "Southern Negro" dialect and identified himself as George
Williams. When the caller was to seem white, a white caller used a typical
New York dialect and again identified himself as George Williams. The
content of the messages given by both the black and the white callers was
precisely the same. Only the pronunciation of the words was different. Each
call was designed to proceed as follows:

Caller: Hello! . . . Ralph's Garage? This is George Williams. Listen, I'm
stuck out here on the parkway, and I'm wondering if you'd be
able to come out here and take a look at my car?

Subject: [*Expected response:*] This isn't Ralph's Garage. You have the
wrong number.

Caller: This isn't Ralph's Garage! Listen, I'm terribly sorry to have
disturbed you, but listen: I'm stuck out here on the highway, and
that was the last dime I had! I have bills in my pocket but no
more change to make another call. Now, I'm really stuck out
here. What am I going to do now?

Subject: [*Might volunteer to call the garage.*]

Caller: Listen: Do you think you could do me the favor of calling the garage and letting them know where I am? I'll give you the number. They know me over there.

If the above conversation was not successful, two different prods were used to try and increase the potential for help.

Prod A: Oh, brother. Listen, I'm stuck out here. Couldn't you *please* help me out by simply calling the garage for me [pleading]?

Prod B: Listen: If *you* were in my situation, wouldn't you want someone to help you? [172, pp. 219, 220].

If the subject still refused to help after receiving the second prod, the "stranded motorist" tried to alleviate the tension by suggesting that he was beginning to see a police car, which would probably help him.

If the subject agreed to help, the caller provided a telephone number that was set up by the experimenters. The measure of helping that the experimenters were looking for was an actual call to what the subject thought was a garage. Results from field studies such as these tend to yield data which are quite plausible. In this particular case, Gaertner and Bickman found that white subjects helped white victims 12 percent more frequently than they helped black victims. As they point out, this 12 percent difference may be statistically significant, but it is really rather small. The odds for being helped, black or white, are just about the same. Interestingly, blacks helped whites and blacks with almost equal frequency.

If one ignores both the subject's and the victim's race, "stranded motorists" were assisted by 67 percent of the male subjects and by 58 percent of the female subjects. Although only a 9 percent difference, again it was statistically significant.

In this study, it appears that whites gave some preference to whites, while blacks gave equal help to both. Gaertner and Bickman concluded that the race of the victim, at least as inferred from the dialect, has therefore a small but detectable influence on the helping behavior of white residents in New York City.

The basic procedure was to deposit an envelope on the ground at a pedestrian thoroughfare. Protruding from the envelope was a man's wallet. Wrapped around the wallet was a type-written letter which led the finder to believe that the wallet was lost not once, but twice. On the first occasion, it was found by the person who addressed the envelope to the wallet's owner and wrote a letter describing his feelings about returning the wallet. This well-intentioned person then lost the wallet himself, along with the envelope and his letter. Our subject had to decide whether to emulate the previous finder's behavior by returning the wallet or to keep it for himself.

In the "similar" condition, the letter started: "I found your wallet, which I am returning. Everything here is just as I found it." In the "dissimilar" condition, the letter began: "I am visit your country, finding your ways not familiar and strange. But I find your wallet which I here return. Everything is here just as I find it." No particular ethnic group can be identified in the "dissimilarity" letter, but it is clear that the writer is probably different from the person picking up the letter and the wallet. At any rate, almost twice as many wallets were returned intact (with all the money present) in the "similar" condition as in the "dissimilar" condition.

It is clear, then, on the basis of all these studies, that although we cannot be sure when helping will occur or when it will not occur, racial differences do appear to be important. Further research seems required to delineate the other factors that must be influencing the race effects.

Sex. We have already noted that diffusion of responsibility seems to occur more frequently with females than with males. Second, we have discussed that females may respond less frequently than males in studies regarding the effects of race on helping behavior. Both of these effects may be the result of the way men and women are socialized in our society (see Chapter 4). Women are brought up to receive help, and men are raised to give it in a Sir Galahad fashion [497]. But there are other basic issues regarding the effects of sex on helping behavior. Consider the sex of the victim and that of the bystander. Most research suggests that there exists something like a "pure stimulus" effect [191]. This means that in our society, merely being female generates more aid from potential helpers, since we are socialized to believe that females are more helpless. On the other hand, there is consistent evidence that both sexes prefer to help a member of the opposite sex rather than someone of the same sex. This tendency is labeled an "ingratiation effect." Some have noted that the ingratiation effect becomes much stronger if the emergency occurs after the victim has offered a bystander a favor [201]. The reasoning is that receiving a favor from a stranger of the opposite sex is an unusual and pleasant event and, therefore, would produce a favorable reaction toward the stranger who did the favor. On the other hand, when a favor comes from a member of the same sex, the intention may be seen as strange, leading to a negative, unfavorable reaction. All the studies suggest that females tend to help less often than males. However, females are helped more often than males, and both males and females, given the appropriate conditions, seem to be more efficient and speedy at helping persons of the opposite sex.

Social class. It has been suggested that self-employed middle-class people are more concerned with a balance of exchange in helping than are bureaucratic middle-class or working-class people. Research has found that self-employed subjects were likely to provide help only when they themselves had received it. On the other hand, the working-class and bureaucratic subjects gave help regardless of their own personal experiences [55].

Mood

If you've ever had to ask someone for something, you probably made a quick assessment of the person's mood. If you found the person in a bad mood, you probably decided—unless it was an emergency—to wait a while before making your request. As it turns out, your decision was probably correct. It has been shown that happy children will donate more money to a children's fund, in the experimenter's absence, than children who are sad [464].

Another way in which a bystander's mood affects the amount of helping concerns sympathy and empathy. Obviously, the more we "feel for" others, the more we understand their problems and worries. If we understand their troubles, the situation is less ambiguous, and we are more likely to help. In being able to put yourself in another's place, you're asking if you would like to be helped. The answer, of course, is, yes. So, if you want to increase your chances of being helped, pick someone who is happy and empathetic.

■ CHARACTERISTICS OF THE EMERGENCY

The characteristics of an emergency situation involve more than just the characteristics of victims and bystanders. Clearly, some emergencies are more "crucial" than others (a broken leg versus a flat tire); and some are more dangerous than others (interceding in a mugging when weapons are involved versus interceding when weapons are not involved). The characteristics of emergencies that we shall discuss are cost-reward considerations, social-responsibility norms, modeling, and territoriality.

Costs and rewards

Often, helping others means donating money. But that may not be the only *cost* involved. Three other cost categories are evident in helping situations. The first is *time.* When you decide to help someone, you are also deciding to forego some other activity. A second cost has to do with *physical well-being.* Most help is costly in terms of energy. Helping to fix a tire on a hot afternoon or moving furniture can be physically exhausting. But certain emergencies are also dangerous; you may be injured if you intervene. The ultimate cost in such a situation would, of course, be your life. A third cost is *emotional cost.* Many emergencies involve mental anguish and stress, which are costly to both mind and body.

We must not consider costs alone, however. In some situations we receive both physical and psychological rewards, and the possibility of viewing bystander emergencies as a cost-reward situation has appealed to many researchers. In this approach, social interaction is regarded as being similar to financial exchange [451]. People give help to others mainly to receive benefits in return. They typically act as they do because they believe the action will benefit them—as long as the rewards seem greater than the costs. However, one must take into account the possibility of alternative interactions. For example, we often maintain a losing relationship as long as it's the best one available. So, even though it may cost to help, we sometimes feel we have no choice.

The importance of costs in determining bystander behavior is indicated by a study carried out during a number of 7½-minute express runs on a New York subway [349]. For each trial on a different trip on the subway, a male confederate played the part of either a collapsed invalid with a cane or a collapsed drunk. He remained on the floor looking at the ceiling until one of the passengers came to his aid. (If no passenger helped after a period of time, another confederate did.) The researchers assumed that passengers would perceive helping a drunk as more costly (he might embarrass you, insult you, assault you, become sick, etc.) than helping a sober person with a physical handicap. They found that passengers did help the invalid more often and more rapidly than they helped the drunk. (This study is complicated by one problem, however; another reason for not helping a drunk might be that subjects feel he does not deserve help.)

This problem was bypassed in a second subway study [347]. In this case the researchers noted the reaction of bystanders to invalid victims who were or were not bleeding from the mouth. They thought that approaching someone who was bloody would be more costly than approaching someone who was not; and a bloody person would certainly not be less worthy or less needy than an unbloody victim. Yet, findings are clouded. As we have already noticed, helping is more likely in unambiguous situations. The sight of blood would clearly signal an emergency (unambiguous) and would supposedly require more help. However, the researchers found the predicted results: Help was *slower* in coming and *less frequent* to the bloody victim. The more costly the situation, the less often people help.

The analysis of what one gets out of a situation in relation to what one puts into it is known as the study of *equity*. Unfortunately, we don't always get what we give, and this is known as an inequitable relationship. People usually dislike situations in which they feel they are getting less than their fair share. Instead, we tend toward something like *distributive justice* [214], in which everyone receives awards appropriate to costs. If distributive justice is not achieved in the real world, people may engage in behaviors to ensure that the world is "psychologically" just. This concern for a *just world* [265] can result in three different attempts to restore psychological equity. Consider, for example, the possibilities open to a bystander who has not helped. First, a bystander who does not help a suffering victim can rationalize that the victim does not deserve help. This makes the bystander's

IF ATTACKED,

What kind of resistance can and should a woman use against a rapist? Think. Don't panic.

Most women escape a rapist by talking their way out of it.... few escape by fighting. Tell him he doesn't really want to hurt anybody...that he doesn't want to upset his family. Getting him to talk may give you the opportunity to escape.

Your first defense is noise— long and loud screaming. Scream FIRE! ... not HELP! People will react to a scream of FIRE more than to anything else. It is not recommended that you physically resist your attacker. Your life is too important.

If instinct should force you to resist, don't hold back! You must try to hurt him! At the first opportunity—run! Remember, the objective of your resistance is to get away.

Violence is seldom far from the surface of the rapist's mixed-up mind. Rape is much more a crime of violence than of sex. If persuasion and resistance do not work, many authorities advise the victim to concentrate on identity—age, race, height, hair color, eye color, distinguishing characteristics (scars, tattoos, a limp, etc.),clothing, complexion, speech accents and patterns.

Figure 6-6. *Research on bystander intervention has led to practical applications in a number of areas. One example is provided by this section of a pamphlet on potential rape, widely circulated by the Governor's Crime Prevention Committee in the State of Florida. It suggests several actions open to women in danger of rape. All the suggestions are designed to encourage others to help.*

position more reasonable. Second, a bystander can minimize the victim's suffering. In this way, the bystander redefines the situation as a noncrisis and, again, can reasonably decide not to help. Third, a bystander can deny responsibility for the victim's suffering. Then the bystander-victim relationship becomes equitable. The bystander who is convinced that he or she is not supposed to help incurs no cost in ignoring the victim. This bystander uses energy either to reevaluate the situation or to explain away certain behavior by relying on justification techniques to reduce stress. These avoidance responses may not actually restore equity, but they can make us *feel* better by helping us forget that we have behaved in a nonresponsible fashion [478].

It seems rather logical that the more "costly" it becomes for a bystander *not* to help, the more likely he or she is to feel motivated to offer aid. There are two different potential costs that can be incurred when a victim receives no aid. First are costs that might reflect directly on the bystander. By not helping, he or she is giving up potential feelings of competence, praise from others, thanks from the victim, and perhaps fame and fortune. An unhelpful bystander also takes on the stressful costs of self-blame for not acting, possible public censure, and even prosecution as a criminal in some situations and states. A second cost involves the stress that results from knowing a victim will continue to suffer. When we know someone is continuing to suffer, increasingly unpleasant stress occurs. The conclusion appears to be that bystanders who help a victim are also helping themselves.

The interplay between costs for helping and costs for not helping has led Jane and Irving Piliavin to develop a model to account for why people help. The model is briefly described in Focus 6-3 (pp. 254–256).

Dependency

When people feel that certain behavior is appropriate in certain settings, or that certain behavior "should" take place, it may be that a cultural norm is operative. Leonard Berkowitz has suggested that one such norm is a *social-responsibility norm*. This means that individuals are "supposed to" help others who are dependent on them in some way and who need their assistance. When one learns that another needs help, one recalls the norm and feels obligated to help. Evidence for such a position comes from a study wherein one student was assigned the role of supervisor to a second student "worker" who was supposedly dependent on the supervisor in one condition and not dependent on the supervisor in the second. The game was conceived so that the supervisor could help the worker attain prizes not available to the worker when working alone. The supervisor exerted greater effort in helping win prizes for the dependent workers. This help continued when neither the person helped nor the experimenter could learn of the assistance. When asked why they gave help, many subjects suggested that they felt obligated [54]. It was also noted that the amount of help given was increased even more when subjects had previously been helped by the dependent peer. In other words, when we are helped by someone who depends on us, the social-responsibility norm becomes even stronger.

The question then becomes: Is helping behavior affected by a social-responsibility norm or a more specific responsibility to those who are dependent on us for help? Although it would be more optimistic to think that people feel responsible to all others, there is not much evidence to suggest that this really happens. So if you want to increase the amount of helping you can get, try to make people feel that you are *depending* on them.

Modeling

It appears evident that if we see others engaging in a lot of helping behavior, we would tend to imitate them. Such learning by observation is called modeling, imitation, or observational behavior (see Chapter 4). As we have noted throughout, people may simply be learning what is appropriate behavior given the circumstances. This is borne out by a study involving fourth- and fifth-grade children. Those who observed a helpful model donated gift certificates to charity, whereas children who had no model to imitate made no donation when given an opportunity [369].

In another study of donation behavior among children, it appeared that there are two kinds of observational learning regarding helping behavior [289]. In the first, children *imitate* and donate exactly the amount given by the model. This is an example of learning what is appropriate in a given situation. Second, some children donate more than the model. It can be argued that these are children who really have learned the essence of helping or altruistic behavior. It also appears that learning through modeling is not solely restricted to laboratory findings. When children four to five and one-half years old were exposed to television programming that emphasized positive social behavior, they were observably less aggressive in play activities than were those who had not viewed the prosocial programs [425]. Thus the media can affect the kinds of people we become.

Although most studies of helping behavior and situational modeling have dealt with children, it is clear that adults also are affected by models. Recall the study in which supposedly lost wallets were deposited near pedestrian thoroughfares. All the lost wallets had letters wrapped around them which were designed to lead subjects to believe that the wallets had been lost twice. In addition to studying ethnicity, the researcher was interested in whether a positive or negative model would affect the rate of returned wallets. In the positive-letter condition, the writer included the following line: "I must say it has been a pleasure to help somebody in the small things that make life nicer. It's surely been no problem at all and I'm glad to be able to help." And in the negative condition, the letter said: "I must say that taking the responsibility for the wallet and having to return it has been a great inconvenience. I was quite annoyed at having to bother with the whole problem of returning it. I hope you appreciate the efforts that I have gone through" [217, pp. 32–33]. As can be expected, a much higher percentage of wallets was returned with the positive model.

Another interpretation regarding the effects of modeling on helping behavior is provided by James Bryan and H. A. Test [82]. They suggest that most people like to think of themselves as charitable and helpful, and seeing a model simply reminds people of how they would like to be. Bryan and Test state (p. 405):

The results hold for college students, motorists and shoppers, in the university laboratory, city streets and shopping centers. When helping is indexed by aiding others solve arithmetic problems, changing flat tires, or donating money to the Salvation Army . . . the presence of helping models significantly increases subsequent behavior.

What this means is that if we want to increase the amount of helping behavior in society, we might engage in a little helping behavior ourselves.

If helping behavior can be modeled to be appropriate for certain situations, can such behavior also be reinforced? An answer is provided in a study of the sharing behavior of two groups of young children. One group consisted of white children from a private nursery school, the other of black children in a welfare center for dependent and neglected children. Initial testing showed that there were differences in the sharing behavior between the two different groups. However, when researchers devised special learning trials using the incentive of social reinforcement (such as, "I think it would be very nice if you would share your dogs with Jimmy"; "That would be a very nice thing to do"), both groups increased the amount of sharing [128]. The choice of social reinforcement or social approval was a particularly good one, for people tend to donate more in public settings when others are watching than they do in private settings, when they have to deal only with their conscience [376]. Consequently, we can increase helping behavior not only by modeling it, but by rewarding it when it occurs.

Territoriality

Although environmental effects are discussed more fully in Chapter 10, it seems reasonable to suggest here that more helping takes place in situations where people feel responsible for territory—for example, if someone breaks a leg in someone else's house. In fact, several researchers have suggested that Kitty Genovese was not helped more rapidly because Kew Gardens is not well known for having a solid "neighborhood" feeling [187; 495]. There are several reasons why help might occur more rapidly in neighborly settings. When an accident takes place in "our" territory, we usually feel a heightened sense of responsibility. Another reason may have to do with the fact that there tend to be more friends in our territory. And some experiments suggest that friends do help rather quickly [257]. The conclusion seems clear: Do not have an emergency in no-man's-land.

Ongoing interaction

Another way a social setting may affect the outcome is described by Piliavin [346], who suggests that there are two different types of bystander settings. In the first and most common setting, subjects actually face other subjects in an emergency setting. They can read their facial expressions, observe their behavior, etc. In the second type of setting, although one is led to believe that others are present, they cannot be observed; one can only hear, their voices over communication systems, or assume that they are nearby. This situation is analogous to that of the different individuals who watched the Genovese murder from their windows without knowing the behavior of their neighbors. Most of what we have discussed would lead to the prediction that higher rates of helping would occur when participants are already involved in face-to-face, ongoing activity.

Table 6-2 and Focus 6-3 provide a quick review of the bystander, victim, and situational characteristics that enhance or reduce helping behavior.

■ THE DEVELOPMENT OF HELPING BEHAVIOR

The preceding section identified different characteristics that tend to increase helping behavior. Some of the findings we discussed were based on studies with children, others with adults. However, children and adults often behave differently, and with this in mind, we will now consider how helping behavior develops. We'll look at three different kinds of studies on the relationship between age and helping behavior. Most of the studies with children have investigated how donating money and material goods relates to age. The results are quite consistent. For children in preschool through the sixth grade, the amount of donations increases with age. Also, children tend to share more as they grow older.

A different kind of result is obtained when we are interested in children's willingness to provide help to strangers. Two such examples are aiding a child in distress, as in the adult bystander studies [423], and giving more typical help in free play activities [397]. In the first study, children in kindergarten, first, second, fourth, and sixth grades heard sounds of a child in severe distress from an adjoining room. There was a curvilinear relationship between grade level and various forms of behavioral help. In other words, an early increase in helping behavior was followed by a decrease later. Erwin Staub suggests that as children grow older they become increasingly concerned with what peers think, which sometimes can keep them from acting. Peers are not the only source of concern regarding increasing fear of disapproval. Children's helping behavior can be inhibited by concern over what an adult might think. To test this, Erwin Staub [423] constructed a situation wherein it appeared that a·child needed help. One-half of the children who were confronted with the emergency received

Table 6-2. Circumstances and characteristics that enhance or reduce the probability of help

	Enhances help	Reduces help
Bystanders	Identifiable	Anonymous
	Alone, relaxed	In groups
	Similar to victim	Dissimilar to victim
	Just granted a favor	Just denied a favor
	Have plenty of time	In a hurry
Victim(s)	Female, child	Male, adult
	Similar to helper	Dissimilar to helper
	Dependent, asks	Self-sufficient
	Ill	Dirty, bloody
	Asks	Doesn't ask
Emergency	Riskless	Dangerous, unpleasant
	High probability of rewards	High probability of costs
	Someone's place	No man's land
	Cooperative	Competitive

FOCUS 6-3   A THEORY OF WHY PEOPLE HELP

The model developed by Jane and Irving Piliavin of why people help is probably the most comprehensive available. We will summarize it here and reflect on some of the incidents described in this chapter. The model is concerned with emergencies involving people who are unknown to each other. The first aspect of the model has to do with the motivation for helping.

Proposition 1: Observing an emergency occurring to another person arouses a bystander physiologically and emotionally. Arousal supposedly increases with the perceived severity of the emergency, the similarity of the bystander to the victim, the length of time the observer is exposed to the emergency (given that no one else intervenes), and the closeness of the bystander to the victim.

Proposition 2: The arousal described above becomes more unpleasant as it increases. The bystander is motivated to eliminate or reduce the stress.

Proposition 3: Special circumstances and specific personality types will create rapid, impulsive, "irrational" helping.

Proposition 4: Under conditions other than the type noted in proposition 3 (rapid, impulsive helping), a bystander will respond so as to reduce the arousal most rapidly and most completely, with as little cost as possible.

The model is a drive reduction model; that is, people act to *reduce* the stress and arousal they feel. It is also a *phenomenological* one. In other words, the costs and rewards are those *perceived* by the bystander—things that could happen, such as personal danger, effort expenditure, time lost, embarrassment, exposure to disgusting experiences, and feelings of inadequacy if help is ineffective. The final cost is that of foregoing one's own activities and pleasures by taking time to help the victim. These are the costs of helping a victim.

A second dimension of costs results from not helping a victim. These include rewards that one might *forego*—such as feelings of competence, thanks from the victim, and so on. Costs that one might *incur* include self-blame for inaction, public censure, or the disapproval of others. With these two different concerns for costs, it is possible to develop the scheme shown in Table 6-3.

In cell A the costs for directly helping are low, while the costs for not helping are high. An example of this situation would involve a drowning swimmer and a bystander lifeguard who has excellent swimming skills. The prediction here is that the lifeguard will directly intervene. (Except for the sight of blood and the possibility that John Harrington might have died in your arms (see page 224), we would probably place this particular situation in cell A. Not being helped would involve a high cost for Harrington. On the

Table 6-3. Predicted modal responses of moderately aroused observer as a joint function of costs for direct help and costs for not helping victim. (Adapted from Pilliavin & Piliavin, 1975.)

		Costs for direct help	
		Low	High
Costs for not helping victim	High	(A) Direct intervention	(C) Indirect intervention or → Redefinition of situation, disparagement of victim, etc., which lowers costs for not helping, allowing ↓
	Low	(B) Variables will be largely a function of perceived norms in situation	(D) Leaving the scene, ignoring, denial

other hand, calling the police or an ambulance would not have taken much effort on the part of others. This may have been why he was eventually helped and why he is alive today.)

In cell B, both costs are low; the emergency is not serious, and the bystander's cost of involvement is not too high. In this case Piliavin and Piliavin suggest that bystander response will be largely determined by the situation itself. An example might involve someone who has dropped some books; a bystander knows that help is not really needed, but on the other hand requires little effort. Since there might be some embarrassment in offering help, the bystander cannot decide what to do. However, if bystanders notice that the person needing help is rather similar to themselves, is attractive, or appears to depend on their help, these characteristics may influence the decision.

In cell C we have a more typical situation. Piliavin and Piliavin suggest that there are two possibilities here. If the cost for direct help is not too high, and a bystander does not feel enough stress and anxiety to be polarized, the bystander may help indirectly. In fact, when someone did offer assistance to Kitty Genovese, even though it was too late, it was not by directly going downstairs and helping her; it was by calling the police. The other possibility for such a situation (when the psychological costs appear to be too high) is that people will try to restore psychological equity be redefining the situation. They will decide that the victim is not really worth helping, that the victim is responsible for getting into trouble, etc. Carried to an extreme, this may account for the strange behavior of the crowd that stoned the potential suicide victim and her rescuers in Dania, Florida (see page 235). Psychologically, the mob may have decided that she was not worth the trouble she had caused them (the arousal she had created) and therefore deserved to be punished for her behavior.

The last possibility is cell D, in which a victim will not be further injured if he or she is ignored by bystanders. A cut finger is an example. Yet the cost of helping may be very high, if, for example, the sight of blood is sickening.

The bystanders will probably leave the scene so as to avoid seeing the blood.

The final appraisal of any model, of course rests on its usefulness for describing real behavior. Future research and observation will tell us how applicable this model really is.

indirect permission to engage in helping behavior. The other half received no such information. The first group was much more helpful. It appears, then, that all children might *want* to help, but older children are inhibited because they feel their efforts will be frowned upon.

A similar possibility is that older children are being socialized into other norms which might conflict with helping. The two norms which are most likely in this regard are the norms of achievement and independence, which promote competitiveness among growing children. This line of reasoning suggests that the reason for the failure to observe greater helping among older children is that, although their ability to recognize the need for help (and their ability to help) has grown, independence, achievement, and competition may be more important than helping [397]. For example, we often hear someone suggest that we do not help a child because the child needs to learn to do things independently. The implication is that we can "help" the child "grow up" by not helping. Consequently, it may be that older children can help, but that competing social values tend to inhibit their response, as they do with adults.

The fact that helping behavior does not automatically increase with age (at least, as studied within the age ranges described here) should not be surprising. If helping behavior *did* increase with age, we would all know what to do in an emergency: simply call for the oldest person around. But that's ridiculous; we would not expect ninety-year-olds to be the most responsive in incidents like the Kitty Genovese case. We must conclude that characteristics of the situation and of the person are more important than age alone in determining helping response. Therefore, let us turn to a discussion of personality differences in helping behavior.

■ PERSONALITY AND HELPING

We can look at personality as it relates to helping behavior in a number of ways. A major consideration is: What kinds of people are altruistic? What personality dimensions can we use to describe someone who tends to be helpful in various situations? Children who are helpful tend to be better adjusted socially than others and are not hostile, competitive, quarrelsome, or aggressive. Similar characteristics of emotional stability are found in

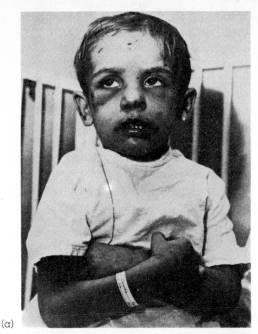

(a)

(b)

Figure 6-7. *The need for help knows no age bounds. This battered child (a) and this fifty-five-year-old potential suicide (b) both cry out for our help. An infinite variety of situations can become emergencies. Why do neighbors avoid involvement when parents abuse children? Why do people only stand and watch from eighty feet below the girder?*

adult helpers. Good relationships with others and a good grasp of social standards also enhance helping behavior. It has further been found that helping behavior is negatively associated with dominance. People who enjoy dominating others are not very helpful [361]. It appears, then, that sociable people who do not wish to dominate others tend to be more helpful.

In one study, researchers attempted to identify a group of college-age helpers. After deciding that they had identified both females and males who were quite helpful, the helpers' personalities were investigated. The female helpers tended to be *socially oriented*—that is, they had social values rather than values dependent upon political or economic foundations. They appeared to want to nurture others while having low needs for achievement and dominance. Male helpers were also socially oriented and tended to think that they controlled their own fates. They seemed to be well liked by others, slightly conservative, and possibly authoritarian [252]. The suggestion that people who help tend to view themselves as in control of their own fate has been well documented [179; 303]. In other words, people who feel they can accomplish something by acting are much more likely to help than people who feel things are pretty much determined by chance. These findings are buttressed by the fact that people who feel they are personally responsible for the consequences of their behavior also tend to believe that their behavior has an impact on others. And clearly, feeling that your behavior has an impact on others would lead you to be more helpful.

One personality characteristic potentially related to helping was suggested by Irwin Silverman [408]. He provocatively hypothesizes that we help because we all want to be heroes. The only reason people sacrifice for others, whether a little or a lot, whether in time, goods, or energy, is that we need to and prefer to. This implies that people are more self-centered than we often wish to admit. Possibly, then, we don't help more often—especially in crowds—because there seems to be an ethic against being a hero. We all want to be heroes, but we're all afraid of looking foolish if we behave heroically. Consequently, Silverman suggests that most people are ambivalent. They want to be heroes, but at the same time, they want to maintain their public images.

■ SUMMARY

The existence of, nature of, and rationale for altruism (as opposed to self-interest) has been a longstanding argument. However, there do appear to be times when people help others simply because it is needed. Social psychologists have concentrated on studies of helping behavior (behavior designed to aid another regardless of the reason). The basic paradigm for such studies is that of bystander intervention. In order to intervene, bystanders to an emergency must notice the event and interpret it as an emergency. This must be followed by decisions regarding whether or not to help and how to help.

Characteristics of bystanders and victims, such as the ambiguity of the victim's need, the size of the bystander group, similarity of the people involved, and the bystander mood can be seen to determine the amount of helping. Emergency characteristics, such as costs and rewards, norms, situational modeling, and territorial responsibilities may also increase helping. By making it more costly for not helping, while at the same time making the emergency perfectly clear to the bystanders, speed of response should be increased. And, if you're going to have an emergency, have one in the territory of people who are in a good mood. While this advice may sound flippant, these factors definitely increase your chances of being helped.

Helping behavior can be increased by modeling and direct learning. Therefore, if children are not overly trained with competing norms such as independence, they become more helpful. Lastly, people whose personalities are socially oriented tend to be better helpers.

7

aggression

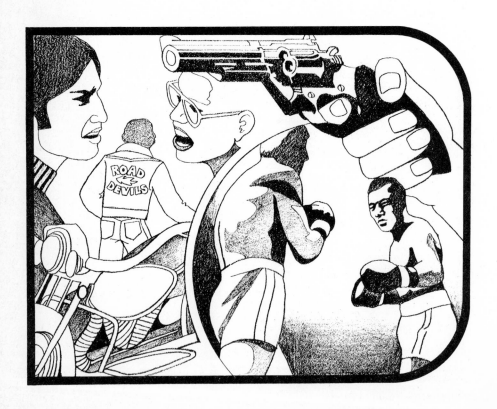

concepts

Aggression is often defined as the intentional attempt to harm or injure others, although many other factors are involved before an action can be labeled aggression.

Three major perspectives have been taken to explain aggression: These positions emphasize instinctive, biological, and environmental factors.

The instinct position views aggression as being an innate response inherent in all species.

The biological position stresses genetic and physiological factors associated with aggression.

The environmental position stresses how aggression is produced by frustration, social learning, and attempts to influence others.

targets

After studying this chapter, you should be able to:

1 Describe when an action will be called aggression.
2 Discuss the implications of aggression as a part of human nature; for example, if aggression is instinctive, how can it be controlled?
3 Explain why many social psychologists don't feel that aggression is instinctive.
4 Explain how physiological and genetic factors are related to aggression.
5 Summarize each of the environmental positions on aggression, including the frustration-aggression model, social learning theory, and the social-influence approach.
6 Explain what effects the mass media have on aggressive behaviors in viewers.
7 Cite examples of how culture affects aggression.
8 Discuss how you would try to control and minimize aggression.

Stories of violence and aggression monopolize today's headlines. All indices of crime reveal drastic increases in street violence [186]. In the years since President John F. Kennedy's assassination, gun casualties in the United States have included 100,000 murders, 700,000 wounded, and 800,-000 suicides [173]. Since the turn of the century, more than 800,000 murders by firearms have been recorded in the United States (not counting deaths in wars). Although political violence has always occurred, many people believe it has spiraled in recent years. Assassinations and assassination attempts are commonplace: John F. Kennedy, Martin Luther King, Jr., Robert Kennedy, Malcolm X, Medgar Evers, and George Wallace.

Harm is not confined to such physical assaults. Zimbardo [511, p. 243] reports an interesting type of psychological aggression which has evolved from that "age-old destructive technique, the 'Dear John' letter." Compared with letters sent by wives and girlfriends of servicemen during World War II, letters ending relationships increased during the Vietnam war. What's more, the content of the letters changed. "Some wives and girlfriends send photographs of themselves with other men in compromising positions. Some send tape recordings of intimate exchanges with another man" [511, p. 243]. The resentment felt by being left at home while the serviceman is away overseas is often evident in these attempts to sever relationships.

At a more organized level, violence and the potential for violence abound. It is estimated that during the period from 1820 to 1946, at least 59 million people were killed in wars, attacks, and other violent episodes [363]. The world spent over a *trillion* dollars on weapons between 1964 and 1970 [299]. The Vietnam war has produced a toll of over 1.5 million killed, most by American arms. Two and one-half times the number of bombs dropped during World War II were unleashed on the Vietnamese people, mainly within South Vietnam, the country we were "defending." While international leaders talk about their desire for peace and report that international hostilities are lessening, budget allotments for the military reach all-time highs. In 1976, the United States federal government will spend about 100 billion dollars on weapons, a figure which would be much higher if we were not at "peace."

In this chapter, we'll examine how social scientists view what most people consider the seamier side of human behavior—aggression.

■ WHAT IS AGGRESSION?

What is aggression? Think about the incidents described and try to determine whether they have some commonality. If you consider the problem of defining aggression for more than a few seconds, you will probably run into difficulties. Yet the answer to this question is more than just a semantic riddle. It not only will determine what you think aggression is, but also may reveal what you feel causes aggression, how you would try to reduce aggression, and how you would go about studying aggression.

Several definitions of aggression have been offered by psychologists. The simplest is a behavioral one that defines aggression solely in terms of a behavior and its consequences, without considering the motives of the actor [84]. According to this definition, aggression is an action that produces harm or injury to another person or persons; the harm can be either physical, like hitting someone, or psychological, like name-calling and verbal abuse. Thus, if harm occurs, the actor can be called aggressive, and the action can be called aggression.

Although the simplicity of this definition is appealing, problems arise in accepting it. Suppose you accidentally step on someone's toes. You've done harm, but would you really consider this action aggressive? Or suppose a young boy throws a dart at a dartboard but misses it and hits his sister. These actions show that it is important to consider the *intentions* of the person who does harm. Was the action accidental, or did the actor intend to produce the harmful results? Another problem with the behavioral definition arises in cases where harm is intended but doesn't occur. If a sniper takes aim at a prospective victim but misses, one would want to call the action aggressive even though no harm results. A sniper clearly has aggressive intentions. So it is not enough simply to observe the behavior and its consequences. The motives, intentions, and goals of an actor also must be considered.

One popular definition of aggression captures both the behavioral and the intentional aspects of aggression. It defines aggression as *an action whose intention and goal is to inflict injury and harm to another person or persons.* The intentional component of this definition is important, since it does not matter so much whether an action actually produces intended harm. According to this definition, an unsuccessful sniper can be defined as aggressive. If you feel this definition is useful, be careful. Intentions and goals themselves are difficult to define. For instance, a doctor might cause momentary pain in giving an injection of penicillin. Clearly, the action was intended, and the doctor knew pain would result. But the doctor's goal was to reduce pain and suffering in the long run, and one would not label the action aggressive because the pain was instrumental in producing a beneficial long-term health goal. Thus, the *ultimate goal* of an action is also important in deciding whether or not to call an action aggressive. For this reason, almost any action can be rationalized by its perpetrator to justify it and show that the long-term goal was beneficial.

Official statements by the United States labeled the North Vietnamese as aggressors during the Vietnam War; the rationale: we felt that our goal was the protection of the South Vietnamese, and that the harm done to the North Vietnamese was merely instrumental to a beneficial long-term goal. Similarly, the North Vietnamese justified their actions by claiming the beneficial goal of reunifying an arbitrarily divided country. This distinction between means and ends, between actions and goals, is important when you consider the conditions that would have to exist before you could label an action "aggression."

As can be seen, calling a particular action "aggression" depends on the perspective taken. "Aggression"—like many labels—may really be in the eye of the beholder; it may not describe any single action or class of actions. For our present purposes, though, we will discuss aggression as *an action which involves the intentional attempt to harm or injure another person or persons,* recognizing that to label a particular action as aggressive depends on many factors.

The nature of the beast: Aggression as part of human nature

William Golding's novel *Lord of the Flies* is a fictitious story of the violence and savagery that developed among a group of English schoolboys shipwrecked on an island. The boys divided into factions; the group was finally rescued after they had killed one boy and while they were hunting another, dressed in primitive outfits with painted faces chanting, "Kill the beast! Cut his throat! Spill his blood!" A movie was made from Golding's book, and the young actors became so involved with their roles that they displayed violence and hatred similar to those described in the book. The director of the movie, Peter Brook, described what he felt [79, p. 23]:

Many of their off-screen relationships completely paralleled the story, and one of our main problems was to encourage them to be uninhibited within shots but disciplined between them. . . . My experience showed me that the only falsification in Golding's fable is the length of time the descent to savagery takes. His action takes about three months. I believe that if the cork of continued adult presence were removed from the bottle, the complete catastrophe could occur in a long weekend.

This view of human nature as basically savage is not new. In the seventeenth century, social philosopher Thomas Hobbes professed a pessimistic view of our constitutional nature. He contended that life was "solitary, poor, nasty, brutish, and short." He felt that unconstrained human nature would selfishly exploit and harm others. Humans would exterminate themselves were it not for organized societies, which act as an external control to keep people in line. The basic view that aggression and violence are part of human nature is represented in some modern theories of aggression.

The psychoanalytical interpretation of aggression

Sigmund Freud believed that aggression is instinctive. Freud's early writings held that there is one basic instinct: *eros,* the life instinct. This life instinct revolves around sexual drives and keeps our species alive. During World War I, Freud was both intrigued and depressed by the organized human destruction. He could not understand how killing could fit into his view of human nature if people were motivated by eros alone. So Freud added the concept of *thanatos,* the death instinct. Death instincts aim to destroy life. If turned inward upon a person, these destructive impulses would produce self-injurious actions and/or suicide, and would account for masochism. If these destructive impulses are turned outward, they would discharge themselves in the forms of violence, aggression, and war. The life and death instincts were, according to Freud, two opposing sets of instincts which underlie all actions.

Freud's pessimistic view of people essentially holds that nothing can alter our basic level of aggression, since this level is fixed by human nature. Similarly, nothing can completely abolish the discharge of aggressive energies; they exist, and must be discharged periodically. Particular behaviors which reflect this discharge, however, can be modified. Instead of discharging aggressive impulses through socially unacceptable channels, they can be sublimated—that is, discharged in acceptable ways. This drainage might occur in athletic contests like football or boxing. Or a doctor might sublimate aggressive impulses by performing surgery and thereby saving, rather than taking, lives. Thus, aggression is part of human nature, and nothing can be done to eliminate it, although it can be controlled by rechanneling destructive impulses.

Freud's view has been largely rejected by scientists. Freud never satisfactorily worked out his concept of the death instinct, and it remains completely untestable and unclear. Also, the phenomena which he sought to explain by the death instinct can be explained by other, simpler and less mystical, concepts.

Instincts and the ethological approach

A sophisticated variant of the "aggression as part of human nature" theme has been offered by some ethologists—scientists who study animal behavior, usually in natural habitats. The renowned ethologist and Nobel Prize winner Konrad Lorenz [277] has popularized an approach to the study of aggression which has become known as the ethological position, although it should be noted that many ethologists disagree in whole or in part with his contentions. In his best-selling book, *On Aggression* [277], Lorenz contends that aggression is produced by instinctive energies; that is, the energy or drive for aggressive behavior is innate. An innate response is one that is not learned but rather derives from one's biological heritage. Aggressive energy builds up in an organism until it is finally discharged in aggressive behaviors.

While Lorenz views aggressive energy as instinctive, he feels that aggression usually occurs only when instinctive energies are triggered, or released, by external *cues.* For example, a male wolf might notice another male wolf in his territory and begin an attack. But had the second wolf not

(a)

Figure 7-1. *Photo (a) is a scene from the movie* Lord of the Flies, *which deals with a "descent into savagery" when children are left without societal control. According to the theory that aggression is a part of human nature, aggression is viewed as both natural and unavoidable. However, aggressive actions can be sublimated—that is, channeled into socially acceptable behaviors. Such might be the case for the boxers (b), surgeons (c), and artist (d) shown here.*

(b)

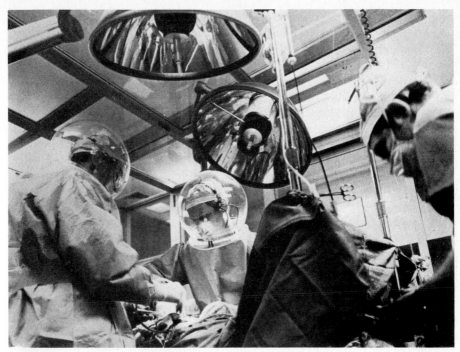

(c)

(d)

served as a cue, no aggression would have occurred.[1] Presumably, cues that trigger aggression also are innate in many species.

Lorenz's model of aggression is hydraulic, since the basic energies exist and are just waiting to be released by appropriate environmental triggers. Like a pressure cooker, if too much "energy" builds up in the system, it may overflow and be discharged even without an appropriate trigger. For example, an animal might attack its young (an inappropriate target) if aggressive energies build up and overflow. However, in most cases aggressive instincts are set off by environmental triggers. Upon discharge, aggressive energy again slowly builds until it is again released.

Unlike Freud's view, this model does not see instinctive energies as diabolical and destructive. Rather, Lorenz [277, p. 48] contends that they are "an essential part of the life-preserving organization of instincts." Aggression serves a useful biological function in the animal world; it operates to ensure the survival of the species. Fighting occurs within species for several reasons. First, it occurs when animals fight to secure *control* over a particular territory. By so doing, they spread themselves over a relatively large area and obtain access to a wide variety of food sources. If animals did not spread out in this way, a particular area might quickly be stripped of food, and many members of the species might die. Thus, by securing territorial control, the chances of finding enough food are increased.

Second, animals fight to establish *dominance hierarchies*—that is, clear patterns of the stronger and weaker members of the species. For example, dominant males have first choice of females and access to the most females. This ensures that the characteristics necessary for survival are passed from these dominant males to future generations. Dominance hierarchies also allow the dominant animals to eat first after a kill, thereby increasing the chances of survival for stronger animals. For these reasons, Lorenz views aggression as an evolutionary asset.

Logically, aggression would not be useful if it produced a mass slaughter of members of the species. To prevent such slaughter, Lorenz contends that animals have developed instinctive *inhibitions* against killing members of their own species. When a fight reaches the point where a combatant could be killed or mortally wounded, the potential loser engages in behavior which serves as an instinctive cue to stop the attack. For example, Lorenz noted that the apparent loser in a fight between two wolves would suddenly stop fighting and bare his jugular vein to the victor (if the jugular vein were

[1] Biologists avoid using the term *aggression* to explain animal behavior. Instead, they use terms like *predatory behavior* and *agonistic behavior*. Predatory behavior is aimed exclusively at the goal of obtaining food. Predatory animals kill members of a *different species,* and the attack is methodical and angerless, much as a human would go about cutting and eating a steak at dinner. Agonistic behaviors involve *intraspecies fighting*—that is, threats and attacks on members of one's own species. Agonistic behaviors are those which writers generalize to human behavior when they discuss aggression. Generalizations about human behavior on the basis of predatory interspecies killing are considered totally improper. Similarly, generalizations from predatory to agonistic behaviors, and vice versa, also are improper, since these behaviors are quite different.

attacked, it would mean instant death); this submissive action triggers a stop in the fighting. The victor would stop the attack long enough for the loser to run away. Both animals live to fight again.

Human aggression. Lorenz generalizes his entire model to human behavior—with one exception. Humans *are* viewed as being instinctively aggressive and as having aggression triggered by appropriate environmental stimuli. However, the major difference between humans and other animals is said to be that humans are almost unique in the animal kingdom in having no inhibiting mechanisms against killing other humans. In fact, Lorenz contends that only humans and rats possess no innate inhibitions against killing; they are the only scoundrels in the animal kingdom. He believes that humans failed to develop such inhibitions because primitive people didn't need them. Unlike other animals, humans were ill-suited for killing. They did not have long, dangerous incisor teeth or nails that could inflict severe damage; nor were they physically strong enough to kill larger animals with their bare hands. For food, primitive people may have been scavengers, living off already killed remains. Thus, they had no need for inhibitory mechanisms. Their physical characteristics served that function well enough. Their descendants invented weapons, and now humans are the most dangerous animals on earth. We are intelligent enough to have created weapons systems capable of exterminating all life on the planet, yet we lack the now-necessary inhibiting instincts that evolution warranted unnecessary. The attack will instinctively start, but it will not instinctively stop.

This theory of aggression and its extension to human behavior have been popularized by the former playwright Robert Ardrey in his books *African Genesis* [12] and *The Territorial Imperative* [13], and by Desmond Morris in *The Naked Ape* [315]. Because of its popularity and familiarity, the theory warrants further discussion and more than a little critical appraisal.

Criticism of Lorenz. The theory has been soundly criticized by many social scientists. Noted anthropologist Ashley Montagu [314, p. xiv] puts the case bluntly: "Certainly the views of Ardrey and Lorenz concerning man's nature have no scientific validity whatever." There are many reasons for this statement:

1 Lorenz often failed to present evidence to corroborate his major statements; many of them sounded like facts, but Lorenz did not provide support.
2 While Lorenz is considered a brilliant observer of animal behavior, many of his personal observations have been questioned. For example, it has been noted that what Lorenz believed was the instinctive response of baring the jugular vein to inhibit fighting among wolves may actually be a challenge by the eventual victor (not by the loser, as Lorenz assumed), which the victor might use to signal an impending attack [cf. 31]. Hence, the gesture might serve just the opposite function.

3   Lorenz believed that only rats and humans made uninhibited aggressive attacks that resulted in death to members of their species. But evidence opposes this. Fights to the death have been observed between members of the same species in several careful studies of animal behavior, including intraspecies killings by lions, chimpanzees, lizards, elephants, hippopotamuses, rodents (such as hamsters), and many others [cf. 230].

4   Evidence makes it doubtful that aggressive energies build up over time and demand release. When an animal is deprived of food or water for long periods, its drive increases, it becomes increasingly hungry or thirsty, and it will work to supply its needs. Yet, when an animal is deprived of the chance to aggress, it does not become more aggressive, nor does it work to gain the opportunity to aggress [468, 230]. According to Lorenz's theory, Gandhi, the admired pacifist who made nonviolent protest a worldwide political art, should have been uncomfortable after all those years of nonaggression. In fact, the opposite was true; Gandhi was proud of his methods and did not lash out at others, even with extreme provocation.

5   The final criticism of Lorenz's position concerns how he and others indiscriminately generalized from animal to human behavior. Humans are unique among animals. They can learn from their culture and transmit that culture to later generations through abstract symbols like speech and writing. Humans can think abstractly and contemplate the past and future as well as the present. It has been contended that everything uniquely human has arisen because of society and culture. Given these unique capacities of humans, it is improper to assume that we behave in the same ways and for the same reasons that lower animals do. While similarities may exist, the differences may far outweigh them.

Similarly, it is difficult to understand how instincts alone (in either Freud's or Lorenz's terms) can explain complex human acts such as war. War is not caused because all individual soldiers suddenly want to kill. War is caused by complex economic, social, cultural, political, and psychological factors. Knowing about aggression in lower animals or even about aggression in an individual tells little about when and why war occurs. Society and human institutions cause it.

Why are these people smiling? Given these criticisms of the theory of aggression as part of human nature, why has the position become so popular? Probably for several reasons. First, Lorenz, Ardrey, and Morris are excellent writers. The beauty of their prose often hides problems in their logic and evidence. Second, the notion of an aggressive instinct is probably the simplest and easiest explanation to understand. When someone asks why aggression occurs, one can answer, "Because it's instinctive, and that's how humans are." It is too easy to rationalize crimes, killings, and wars this way; people are absolved from the responsibility to change society and minimize aggression. In 1912, the German General von Bernhardi stated, "War is a biological necessity . . . it is as necessary as the struggle of the elements in Nature . . . it gives a biologically just decision, since its decisions rest on the very nature of things" [cited in 314, p. 10]. Many militarists rationalize their "business" in similar terms.

■ THE WAY WE'RE WIRED: GENETIC AND PHYSIOLOGICAL BASES OF AGGRESSION

Genetics and aggression

Secretariat, 1973's wonder horse, was sold for $6 million, yet the buyers have no intention of letting the horse race again. Why pay so much for a racehorse that won't race? To breed him, of course. Horsebreeders have known for generations that by selecting superior parents, they can increase the chances that offspring will inherit certain abilities—in this case, to streak around the track. An unproved colt sired by Secretariat will be worth more money than a colt that looks as good but doesn't have such a regal parent. Dog breeders also know the value of pairing superior dogs to produce a superior show animal. It is assumed that characteristics which create desirable behavior can be passed genetically to offspring.

The link between this thought and aggression should be clear. If certain characteristics predispose an animal or a human being to aggressive actions, and these characteristics can be passed on genetically, it should be possible to breed a creature with the ability of a superaggressor—or, for that matter, a creature that is docile and peaceful.

Scientists have taken up the challenge and shown that they can do just that. By selecting two aggressive rats and mating them, then mating the most aggressive offspring with each other, then mating these offspring, and so on through about twenty generations, an extremely aggressive rat can be bred: an aggressive superrat. This aggressive strain of rat can be counted on to fight with minimal provocation, and it will usually emerge victorious from a battle. But if one selects two docile, gentle rats and successfully breeds them and their offspring for as many generations, a pacifistic strain of rat will emerge. Will the same hold true for humans? Can aggressive tendencies be transmitted genetically? Can a "bad seed" predispose one to a life of violence and crime? Unfortunately, for those who want a simple answer, the evidence is unclear and generally negative.

Several studies have tried to link genetic factors with human criminal behavior. The results have been ambiguous, and the methodologies have been criticized [cf. 31, 230]. There is no strong evidence to link human violence, criminality, and aggressiveness *exclusively* to genetic factors.

To understand the difficulties in the view that aggression can result exclusively from genetic factors, it's necessary to understand something about genetics. Social scientists long ago abandoned the view that behavior is a function *either* of genetic influences *or* of environmental and social influences. Instead, they view behavior as a complex combination of both determinants.

Genes do not directly "cause" behavior. Rather, they lay the biological foundation for the organism and might affect behavior indirectly. Genes act by producing enzymes which, in turn, affect biochemical processes and therefore the physical development of the organism. These biochemical and developmental changes may or may not produce differences in behavior. In themselves, though, genes can only directly affect the kinds of enzymes produced. They can't *directly* influence behavior. For example, genetically bred "aggressive" mice typically are more active and less emotionally upset by stress and threat than are "average" mice [254]. Because of their high activity level and because they are not paralyzed with fear or overcome with anxiety, these animals might become good fighters if the environment permits. In this case, the genes seem to have acted not by "forcing" the mice to fight but by giving them biological characteristics that allow them to be successful if they do fight. Reinforced by success, they become more likely to fight in later situations.

As an example of this capacity, what do you think would happen if one such supermouse was taken from its aggressive mother and raised by a mother bred to be docile and gentle? Evidence indicates that the "aggressive" mouse will be influenced by its upbringing and become less combative and more docile [cf. 31]. The influence of early upbringing was indicated clearly in a classic study by Z. Y. Kuo [253]. We all know that cats "instinctively" kill rats and mice, right? It's in their genes, isn't it? Kuo doubted it, and raised kittens in three different environments. Some never saw rats during their upbringing. Others were raised in an environment where they watched their mother kill rats. And still others were raised with rat "friends." Kuo found that about half the cats that were raised in isolation (nine out of twenty) killed rats when they grew up. Almost all (eighteen of twenty) of those that watched their mother kill rats also killed rats when mature. However, cats that were raised with rat companions didn't kill a single rat while growing up with them, and only a few (three of eighteen) killed rats in adulthood. Clearly, environmental influences drastically modify genetic dispositions.

The brain and aggression

Aggression does not seem to be an instinctive part of human nature, nor is it affected by genetics alone. What if one takes a more direct route to a basic biological source that might control aggression—the brain? Everyone knows that the brain controls and directs all our complex behaviors. Could it be that an "aggression center" lies hidden in the brain? If so, humans may be "wired" to behave aggressively at times, and little would stop this action short of removing the area surgically. The notion of an aggression center is popular among many laymen. Unfortunately, it too is a misunderstanding and simplification of the causes of aggression.

Popular claims for an aggression center in the brain have been drawn from animal studies concerning the effects of electrical stimulation and surgical removal of certain brain areas. It has been found that when certain areas of the brain are electrically stimulated, rage and violent attack behaviors occur. It is as though the guiding center for aggression has been touched off and the controlling agent for aggression has been isolated. Such regions also have been linked with other motivational processes, such as hunger, thirst, and sex. Stimulation of other brain areas produces an opposite effect—the cessation of aggressive actions and the production of docility.

One might think that with this information, all we need to learn is what sets off these "centers" naturally; the explanation of aggression will follow. But the picture is not so clear. First, it has been found that several sites in the brain will produce aggressive reactions [230]. Second, even when these portions of the brain are completely removed from an animal, it can display aggressive reactions [139]. It seems that the entire brain produces aggression in one way or another. Third, the reaction obtained from stimulating such an area depends on numerous factors. For example, imagine a monkey that is caged with another monkey which the first has successfully beaten many times in fights. If electrical stimulation is applied to a particular brain area of the dominant animal, it will attack the submissive one. However, if the first monkey meets another monkey that has beaten it in past fights, it will turn and run when the same brain area is stimulated [118]. Thus, one brain area produces both fight and flight, depending on the submissiveness of the target at hand.

A complex interplay of environmental and physiological factors again seems to determine whether or not aggression will occur. The conclusions to be drawn from these studies are similar to those drawn from the examination of genetics and aggression. The brain is organized, and it does provide the capacity to behave aggressively. However, whether or not this capacity will ever be exercised depends on many other factors. The fact that the capacity exists does not mean that it must be exercised, nor even that it is natural to exercise it. For a look at other aspects of the brain and aggression, see Focuses 7-1 and 7-2.

■ THE SOCIAL AND PSYCHOLOGICAL BASES OF AGGRESSION

The preceding views of aggression have focused on human nature, instincts, or physiology and genetics to explain aggression. In contrast, many theories of aggression rely heavily on the examination of social and psychological factors that determine when aggression will occur and when

FOCUS 7-1 BRAIN DISORDERS AND VIOLENCE

Some forms of aggressive behavior are so bizarre that many people think something must be "wrong" with the aggressor. As we'll see later when we discuss how people label aggression, this conclusion is not necessarily true. What looks bizarre to a person in one culture may be quite normal for another person in another culture.

Nevertheless, some evidence suggests that violent behavior may be produced by certain types of brain damage. An interesting case is that of Charles J. Whitman. On the night of July 31, 1966, Whitman killed his mother and wife, and then climbed to the top of a tower at the University of Texas at Austin. In an hour and a half, he gunned down thirty-eight people, killed fourteen, and even hit an airplane. Earlier that day, Whitman had written about his feelings:

> I don't really understand myself these days. I am supposed to be an average, reasonable and intelligent young man. However, lately (I can't recall when it started) I have been a victim of many unusual and irrational thoughts. These thoughts constantly recur, and it requires a tremendous mental effort to concentrate on useful and progressive tasks. In March when my parents made a physical break I noticed a great deal of stress. I consulted a Dr. Cochrum at the University Health Center and asked him to recommend someone that I could consult with about some psychiatric disorders I felt I had. I talked with a Doctor once for about two hours and tried to convey to him my fears that I felt overcome by overwhelming violent impulses. After one session I never saw the Doctor again, and since then I have been fighting my mental turmoil alone, and seemingly to no avail. After my death I wish that an autopsy would be performed on me to see if there is any visible physical disorder. I have had some tremendous headaches in the past and have consumed two large bottles of Excedrin in the past three months.

> It was after much thought that I decided to kill my wife, Kathy, tonight after I pick her up from work. . . . I love her dearly, and she has been as fine a wife to me as any man could ever hope to have. I cannot rationally pinpoint any specific reason for doing this. I don't know whether it is selfishness, or if I don't want her to have to face the embarrassment my actions would surely cause her. At this time, though, the prominent reason in my mind is that I truly do not consider this world worth living in, and am prepared to die, and do not want to leave her to suffer alone in it. I intend to kill her as painlessly as possible. . . .

After killing both his wife and mother, Whitman wrote:

> I imagine it appears that I brutally killed both of my loved ones. I was only trying to do a good thorough job.

> If my life insurance policy is valid please see that all the worthless checks I wrote this weekend are made good. Please pay off all my debts. I am 25 years old and have never been financially independent. Donate the rest anonymously to a mental health foundation. Maybe research can prevent further tragedies of this type.

An autopsy performed on Whitman's body revealed a walnut-sized malignant tumor in his brain [438]. Could the tumor have produced his behavior, or was it just a coincidence? If it was not coincidental, would Whitman have behaved as he did anyway, and did the tumor merely hasten the process? If the tumor affected his behavior, did it directly cause him to become violent? Or might it have indirectly influenced his behavior in other ways? For example, the tumor may have distorted Whitman's perceptions of the world to such an extent that he truly felt his and other people's lives were worthless. Thus, he was doing a "favor" for his wife, mother, and others, since he would free them from their human bondage. Answers to such questions await future research.

FOCUS 7-2   DRUGS AND AGGRESSION

One of the most widely held attitudes among middle-class Americans is the notion that "drugs" are directly related to violence. According to this view, the mind-altering effects of drugs somehow compel people to behave against their own wills and consciences, and produce violence and anti-social behaviors. Is this popular attitude correct? Are "drugs" associated with aggression?

The first question to ask anyone who holds this view is, "What type of drug are you talking about?" Different drugs have drastically different effects on the central nervous system and on behavior. Some drugs—for example, barbiturates—produce a general relaxation effect. Barbiturates are often used to kill pain, to put people to sleep, and to tranquilize them to reduce hyperactivity. Given these tranquilizing effects, barbiturates decrease the incidence of aggression and violence.

Other drugs, such as amphetamines, are stimulants. In large doses, they heighten activity, increase muscular tension, and produce excitability, irritability, and impulsiveness. These symptoms increase the chances that a person will overreact with violence and emotion to a suspected threat or insult. If an amphetamine user is in a calm, tranquil environment where threats are minimal or absent, there is no reason to believe that the drug will be associated with violence. However, a person's mood when ingesting the drug and factors in the surrounding environment could affect the aggression exhibited.

According to the President's Commission on Law Enforcement and Administration of Justice [353], the only drug *directly* related to aggression and violence is alcohol. After drinking, individuals become impulsive and less concerned with the norms of conduct they usually obey. The distortions of judgment produced by alcohol may explain why many bars are closed on Election Day, and why bars are among the first stores to be closed when a riot threatens.

The effect of alcohol on the tendency toward violence can be interpreted in many ways. Individuals who assume aggression to be part of human nature feel that when alcohol dulls social control, aggressive energies are given free reign and can be discharged in antisocial ways. Social control is removed, and a Pandora's box of evils is opened. On the other hand, many social scientists don't see it this way. Under the effects of alcohol, normal judgmental processes are distorted. While sober, for example, we might estimate that we have only one chance in ten of beating up a threatening bully, and therefore we refrain from provoking him. But when drunk, we may feel we're undefeatable, and therefore we accept the challenge and begin the fight. Thus, alcohol may affect social judgments and decisions without releasing aggressive energies and impulses.

One of the most widely discussed drugs, marijuana, typically produces a pleasant, euphoric state; consequently, it is rarely associated with violence. The 1971 report from the National Institute of Mental Health [286] clearly indicated that no evidence was found to link marijuana with violence. Some studies have even shown that marijuana reduces aggression [230].

As this discussion of the relationship between drugs and aggression indicates, the concern over drug-caused aggression is probably misplaced. The only direct causal link that has been established involves the only drug that is legal—alcohol. Relationships that associate drug use with crime really indicate more about our social system than about the drugs themselves. Since most drugs are illegal, their users often are forced to operate in a criminal subculture. They must associate with criminals to get drugs, and they constantly are exposed to pressures to use more powerful drugs. A heroin user, for example, must spend between $75 and $100 a day to support the physically addicting habit. One of the few ways such prices can be met is through crime: prostitution, robbery, burglary, etc. If drugs like heroin were controlled, their price would be reduced drastically, and withdrawal might occur in a controlled setting. You can understand why many social scientists feel the way to minimize problems caused by drugs like heroin is not to place more severe penalties on users, but to consider ways of changing the system to remove them from the criminal subculture they are forced into.

people will call a particular action aggressive. The following sections examine these perspectives.

Frustration and aggression: Damn you, I'll get you for that!

Mary was watching a television show. It was a mystery, she was totally engrossed, and the end of the movie was near. Her baby started crying. He always seemed to do this whenever she was enjoying herself. She shouted at him to shut up. His response was intensified crying. Mary got angry and slapped his face. The baby cried even louder. The movie ended, and Mary missed it. Angrily, she struck her son again, breaking his arm. Another situation: you've got an important date with someone you've wanted to go out with for months. You're ready to leave, but your father won't let you use the car. You want to shout a few obscenities, but you refrain. You go to your room, and your younger brother comes in and laughs. You push him out and slam the door in his face.

In both of these situations, the central person pursued some goal— seeing the end of a television show or going on a date. But something unexpected happened, and the means to the goal was blocked. The person was frustrated, anger built up, and aggression occurred.

The frustration-aggression model. These situations capture the key elements of one of the first psychological approaches to the study of aggression. This approach, developed by John Dollard, Leonard Doob, Neal Miller, and several colleagues at Yale in 1939, is called the *frustration-aggression model.* Many social psychologists reject the view that aggressive energy is innate and that violence is inevitable. Yet, people often are made to feel angry, and such an internal state seems to "push" them toward behaving aggressively. Dollard and his coworkers felt that internal states do have such a push, or drive effect, but are not innate aggressive impulses; rather, they are reactions to frustration. *Frustration* is the blocking or interference of a goal response which would otherwise have been achieved; frustration is thus a state of being thwarted. The central hypothesis in this theory of aggression is that "aggression is always a consequence of frustration. More specifically, the proposition is that the occurrence of aggressive behavior always presupposes the existence of frustration and, contrariwise, the existence of frustration always leads to some form of aggression" [129, p. 1]. Note the two times that the word "always" occurred. Frustration *always* produces aggression, and aggression is *always* the result of frustration. These are key words—they inextricably link frustration and aggression.

According to the theory, frustration produces a drive state, comparable to other drive states such as hunger or thirst. This drive is an arousal that eventually produces aggressive thoughts or actions.

Displaced aggression. Aggression is not always directed toward the original frustrator. For example, consider a businessman who has a hard day at the office. His boss belittled him for blowing a big deal. On the way home in his car, the frustrated commuter blows his horn angrily at a car ahead when it doesn't pull away fast enough from a stoplight. As he enters his home, his dog jumps up on him, only to receive a quick kick. He shouts at his wife during supper. All these aggressive behaviors are assumed to be instances of *displaced aggression.* In many cases, it would be dangerous for an individual to aggress against the person who caused the original frustration. In this case, swearing at the boss or physically assaulting him for his frustrating actions would prove impractical and could cost the employee his job. When the original frustrator has high status or is powerful, aggression may be displaced onto a weaker target who may have little in common with the original frustration. According to this theory, the more similar a substitute target is to the original frustrator, the more likely the aggression will be displaced. Admittedly, though, we find it much more satisfying when we can aggress against the original source of the frustration rather than a substitute [209].

Catharsis. Once an aggressive action occurs, the frustration-aggression model proposes that it reduces the aggressive drive state and thereby lessens the drive available for further aggression. This discharge, or purging, of an aggressive drive is termed *catharsis.* The notion of catharsis is important and has much in common with Freud's and Lorenz's views. Both Freud and Lorenz assumed that energies produced by aggressive instincts could be discharged through an aggressive action. This reduces the likelihood that further aggression will occur, since the energy that caused it has been drained. Similarly, the frustration-aggression model hypothesizes that once catharsis takes place, aggressive drives are reduced. Thus, to drain off the frustrations of the day, you might pin a picture of your professor on a dartboard and fantasize wildly as you hurl darts. Or you might watch a violent television program and similarly reduce the aggressive drive.

Evidence supporting the frustration-aggression model. The frustration-aggression model has been supported by many interesting studies. If the theory is correct, one would expect to find that conditions which produce frustrations should also increase aggression. One early study was conducted with children [37]. One group of children was taken to a room filled with attractive toys, which they were forbidden to enter. They were frustrated by being made to stand outside, looking at the toys through a window. A second group of children was shown the toys and allowed to play with them immediately. For them, it was an enjoyable experience. When the frustrated children finally were allowed to play with the toys, they behaved destructively, throwing them against the walls and floor.

Evidence has been gathered on a wider scale, as well. Several investigators examined historical data to determine whether frustrating periods of history evoked increased aggression. They discovered, for example, an inverse relationship between the price of cotton per acre and the number of lynchings of blacks in the South from 1882 to 1930 [218]. Presumably, when the price of cotton was low, white Southerners suffered economic hardship and frustration. Their aggression was displaced onto the black community.

Evidence undercutting the frustration-aggression model. Much evidence also fails to support the frustration-aggression theory. It didn't take long to find that some people do not aggress following frustration; indeed, anthropologists hold that in many cultures aggression is not considered an appropriate response [cf. 31]. It also has been shown that aggression can occur

Figure 7-2. *According to the original frustration-aggression model, frustrating experiences always lead to aggression. When the frustrator is unknown or powerful, aggression might be displaced onto a substitute target, or scapegoat. It has been hypothesized that many lynchings of blacks in the South were the result of such displacement of aggression.*

even without earlier frustration [cf. 31, 32]. Such findings weaken the statements that frustration *always* produces aggression and that aggression *always* follows frustration.

Additional nonsupport for this model has been found in studies that investigated catharsis. They show that once an aggressive action occurs, it does not always produce a cathartic effect [cf. 31; 53; 447]; that is, an aggressive act does not always lessen the likelihood of later aggressive acts. In fact, aggressive behavior often increases the chance of later uncontrollable aggression. Zimbardo [511, p. 244] recounts the story of an American soldier involved with questioning Vietcong prisoners, who stated: "First you strike to get mad, then you strike because you are mad, and in the end you strike because of the sheer pleasure of it. This is the gruesome aspect of it which has haunted me ever since I came back from Vietnam." Similarly, during the Democratic National Convention in Chicago in 1968, demonstrators sometimes begged not to be hit by police. The more they begged, the more they met with fury and violence [511, p. 244]. Brutality spread and begat more brutality.

Studies that have investigated the relationship between aggression and athletics also have found no support for the catharsis hypothesis. There is no evidence to indicate, for example, that playing football decreases aggressive behavior in other settings [53].

Where does the frustration-aggression model stand today? Although its basic notions turn up constantly in newspaper and magazine columns, the model contains only an element of truth. It clearly does not account for all aggressive behaviors. The model has generated research which has shown that frustration *can* be an important antecedent of aggression. However, frustration alone is not the complete answer.

Frustration-aggression revisited. Jack has argued with his wife, whom he suspects of seeing another man. His anger is building, but he controls it. He's always been relatively mild-mannered, and would never normally consider striking a woman. He broods for a few hours, and after dinner, the argument begins again. His wife is washing the dishes, happily planning to go out "with the girls." Jack thinks that she has things on her mind other than bridge. His anger builds again. Seeing a knife on the kitchen counter, he seizes it and stabs his wife to death.

The original frustration-aggression model is too simple to account for a wide variety of human aggressive behaviors. Leonard Berkowitz [50, 51, 53] has modified it and added some unique elements to explain aggression. Berkowitz feels that frustration doesn't always produce aggression (early in the evening, Jack was clearly frustrated and annoyed, but he broods rather than act). Instead, Berkowitz feels that frustration produces arousal and the "readiness" for aggression. Aggressive actions will occur primarily when this readiness is followed by an aggressive cue (for example, the sight of a gun, knife, blood, and so on). Such a cue can either exist in the environment or be brought into play by one's thoughts. Jack's rage was released at the sight of the knife. If such a cue did not occur, aggression would have been much less likely.

This approach has some similarities to Lorenz's instinctive model of aggression. Both models propose that aggression is usually the result of some type of arousal or energy, plus an aggressive cue. However, the theories differ in their specifics and in the recommendations each would make for the societal control of aggression. Lorenz proposes that both aggressive energy and many aggressive cues are instinctive. Society has relatively little control over either. All that can be done is to redirect the aggressive energies into socially acceptable channels. Berkowitz proposes that arousal is the result of frustration, and that aggressive cues are learned through their past association with aggressive actions. Aggression can be reduced either by changing social conditions to minimize frustration or by minimizing the number of cues associated with aggression. If these controls fail, aggression can still be channeled into socially acceptable activities. Since Berkowitz proposes that neither of the components of aggression is instinctive, society has much more leeway in the control of aggression.

Berkowitz and his colleagues [cf. 50, 51, 53] have conducted some interesting experiments to explore this model. In a typical experiment, a subject is either insulted or treated in a neutral manner by a paid experimental accomplice (whom the subject believes to be another subject participating in the experiment). The actions produce anger and frustration toward the accomplice in some subjects and neutral feelings in others. After this initial encounter, subjects are shown excerpts from movies. The movie some subjects see is unassociated with violence and aggression—for example, a track meet or English canal boats. Other subjects see excerpts from violent films, such as a prizefight scene from the movie *The Champion,* starring Kirk Douglas. These clips from violent films gave some subjects an opportunity to see aggression, possibly associate it with their anger, and then associate the person who angered them with the person in the film.

After viewing the aggressive or nonaggressive film segments, subjects were given a chance to administer electric shocks to the accomplice as part of a learning task. The experimenters were interested in how subjects would react when given the opportunity to hurt the accomplice.

In one experiment [52], the accomplice was described either as a physical-education major interested in boxing or as a speech major. Presumably, the "boxer" label would associate the accomplice with the boxers in the film and serve as an aggressive cue. The "speech major" label presumably would have more neutral associations. As predicted, subjects who were angered (and thereby felt a readiness to aggress) and who then saw *The Champion* delivered more shocks of higher duration when the accomplice was described as a boxer rather than as a speech major. This finding supports the prediction that following arousal, the aggressive cue value of a person will affect the amount of aggression directed toward him or her. It was also found that the boxer elicited more aggression than the speech major even when subjects had seen the innocuous, nonaggressive film. Berkowitz suggested that this might have occurred because boxers are so closely associated with aggression anyway, the label itself might provoke aggression. Or, subjects might have perceived that the boxer was better able to tolerate the shock and, hence, didn't feel they were administering an inordinate amount of pain.

Such findings strongly suggest that associations with violence can elicit aggression, particularly from people who are frustrated and angry. How do you think these findings relate to reactions toward a police officer (who typically is associated with violence) in a big-city ghetto?

In another study, the above procedure was followed. However, instead of varying the accomplice's major, the accomplice's name was changed [56]. The aggressive film of the prizefighter starred *Kirk* Douglas. The experimenters felt that a person named Kirk might be more strongly associated with violence than a person with another name. So, when the accomplice was introduced to the subjects, he was called either Kirk Anderson or Bob Anderson. In support of predictions, it was found that the angered and aroused subjects who saw the aggressive film delivered more shocks to Kirk than they did to Bob. A rose by any other name clearly does not elicit the same reaction as far as aggression is concerned.

These findings support the hypothesis that following arousal, aggressive cues in the environment will increase the likelihood of aggressive behavior. For an interesting further demonstration, see Focus 7-3.

Social learning theory: I'll do what you do

Johnny sits in front of the television spellbound as Matt Dillon shoots another villain. Then he watches the Six Million Dollar Man hurl a telephone pole at subversives. Then a movie commercial shows a Kung-fu master chopping, hacking, and kicking his way through the bodies of ten enemies. While all this TV action goes on before his eyes, Johnny sees his sister being slapped by their father and sent off to bed for getting bad grades on her report card. Just before Johnny goes to bed, he hears his parents having an angry conversation, complete with name-calling, about the household budget.

Johnny is learning, by observing what goes on around him, the ways people in society handle conflicts, enemies, and problems. Will he learn that verbal and physical aggression are good ways to resolve such difficulties? Or will he be turned off by aggression and adopt a different approach himself? Unfortunately, the evidence indicates that Johnny will probably imitate.

Social learning theorists, most notably Albert Bandura and his associates [e.g. 29; 31; 32], have stressed the importance of learning, particularly *observational learning,* in accounting for a wide variety of human behaviors. Much of the important information people get about the world comes from watching others and then modeling, or imitating, their behavior. Both adults and children model the behaviors of others and develop behavior styles based on what they observe.

A nursery school child is playing with toys in a corner of the room. An adult enters the room and begins playing with toys in another corner. In some cases, the child observes the adult assemble Tinker Toys and play in a constructive manner. In other cases, the child sees the adult attack a large, inflated "Bobo" doll. The model strikes the doll with one hand, knocks it over, plunks it with a mallet, and while doing all of this, says things like "Sock him in the nose," "Pow," and "Kick him." After observing either the constructive or the destructive model, the child is taken to another room and shown some attractive toys. Then the child is frustrated; as soon as he or she begins to play, the experimenter says that the toys are too good to be played with. The experimenter then explains that the child can play with some toys in another room, to which they go. Some of the toys in the second room are nonaggressive (crayons and coloring paper, a tea set, a ball, some dolls, bears, cars and trucks, and plastic farm animals). Other toys are aggressive (a three-foot "Bobo," a mallet and pegboard, dart guns, and a tether ball with a face painted on it which hangs from the ceiling). For twenty

FOCUS 7-3   THE WEAPONS EFFECT: THE FINGER PULLS THE TRIGGER, BUT DOES THE TRIGGER ALSO PULL THE FINGER?

Proponents of gun-control legislation argue that the easy availability of firearms allows people who would impulsively use them to do so. Without the availability of cheap hand guns, or "Saturday night specials," many tragedies might be avoided. Tighter controls on guns could decrease violence by giving frustrated individuals time to calm down and think about their actions. The association between the availability of guns and crime has often been noted by law enforcement officials. J. Edgar Hoover strongly believed that the availability of firearms has a powerful inducing effect on violence. These arguments stress that if guns are available, they will be used. Given sufficient or even insufficient causes, a gun owner will pull the trigger.

Leonard Berkowitz has noted an even more subtle influence of firearms on aggression. He asked: Do guns act as aggressive cues which are so intimately associated with violence that they produce aggression in angered individuals merely at the *sight* of them? In other words, does the trigger also pull the finger?

To study this question, Berkowitz and Lepage [57] conducted an ingenious experiment. Subjects were given either one (low arousal) or seven (high arousal) electric shocks by a paid experimental accomplice. Subjects believed that the accomplice was another subject like themselves. They were given the shocks as part of a procedure in which the confederate was supposed to "evaluate" their laboratory work by "grading" it through punishment. After being shocked, subjects were given a chance to administer shocks in return. As some subjects approached the shock apparatus, they observed a rifle and a revolver lying on a table. Some were told that the firearms belonged to the other subject (the accomplice), who had left them there. Other subjects were told that the firearms belonged to one of the experimenters and were being used in another study. Thus, the firearms were either associated or unassociated with the person to whom subjects would shortly administer shocks. Other subjects approached the shock apparatus and saw no firearms but only nonaggressive cues, a badminton racquet and some shuttlecocks, lying on the table. Finally, with still other subjects, the table was bare.

Not surprisingly, the experimenters found that subjects who received seven shocks paid back the accomplice by giving more shocks than subjects who only received one earlier shock. More interesting were the effects of the weapons on the subjects' behaviors. In the high-arousal condition (seven shocks), the presence of weapons elicited more shocks to the accomplice than the presence of either the nonaggressive cues or no cues. Thus, given arousal, aggressive cues can increase the aggression exhibited. This occurred regardless of whether or not the guns "belonged" to the accomplice. In the low-arousal condition (one shock), the cues did not affect the number of shocks delivered. These data support the contention that the combination of arousal plus an aggressive cue significantly increases aggressive behavior. If either variable is low—that is, if either arousal or aggressive cues are absent—aggression will be minimal.

These results have not gone unchallenged. Page and Scheidt [340] and others have tried to replicate the experiment and found it difficult. They could obtain similar findings only when subjects were sophisticated about psychological experimentation and had guessed that the guns were in the room to produce more aggression. In other words, subjects may have wanted to cooperate with the experimenter and therefore acted more aggressive to support the hypothesis. These findings certainly suggest that more research is needed before one can conclude with reasonable confidence that "the trigger pulls the finger." Nonetheless, the Berkowitz hypothesis is intriguing, and if supported by future research, it could affect social policy decisions.

minutes, the experimenter records which toys the child plays with and how they are treated.

This experiment clearly demonstrated the effects of modeling on children's aggressive play behaviors [33]. As compared with children who observed the constructive model or children who observed no model at all, the children who observed the aggressive model displayed a great deal of aggression in playing with the toys. They imitated many of the statements the model had made in knocking over the Bobo doll, they hit things with the mallet, tossed the Bobo doll in the air, punched it in the nose, and sat on it.

The children also displayed many forms of aggressive behavior that the model did not demonstrate. For example, children in the aggressive-model condition, as compared with children in the other conditions, played more roughly with the toys and said things like, "Shoot Bobo," "Cut him," "Stupid ball," "Knock over people," and "Horse fighting, biting."

Many factors determine whether imitation will occur after an aggressive model has been observed. Imitation is not simply indiscriminate or all-inclusive. For example, a child watches a TV western in which a character robs a bank, shoots three people, and rides off with his ill-gotten gains. How do you think this child's behavior would differ if (1) the robber were apprehended by the sheriff, brought back for trial, and hung, or if (2) the robber escaped with the loot, rode off into the sunset, and lived happily ever after with a lovely señorita in Mexico? As one might guess, the *consequences* of a model's behavior play a vital role in determining whether aggression will be imitated. In the first case, the moral tells us that crime doesn't pay; in the second case, it tells us that crime pays rather well. The consequences to the model are termed *vicarious consequences*. If the model is rewarded for the

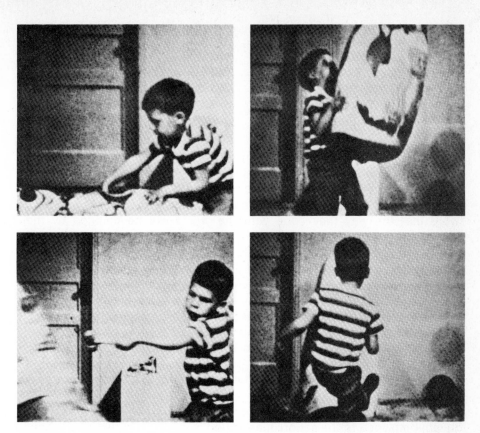

Figure 7-3. *Bandura and his associates have demonstrated the powerful effects of observational learning, or modeling, on aggression. Children exposed to an adult model who behaves in an aggressive manner will imitate the model's exact behaviors and also go beyond them, demonstrating new aggressive actions that the model did not display.*

behavior, vicarious reinforcement occurs; if the model is punished for the behavior, vicarious punishment occurs. Numerous studies [cf. 31] indicate that vicarious punishment inhibits modeling behavior, while vicarious reward often increases it. The effects of vicarious reinforcement and punishment explain why the Motion Picture Producers Association approves only films in which crime and murder are not glamorized and rewarded. Unfortunately, though, in many films the villains are not punished until the final few seconds. Throughout the rest of the movie, their antisocial behavior is well rewarded. To what extent are children or even adults able to separate the immediate rewards of aggression from the long-range punishments? Future research clearly is needed to answer this question.

The characteristics of the model also affect whether aggression will be modeled. If an aggressive model has high status, and is respected and admired, considered to be an expert, attractive, and powerful, the model will be more effective in influencing the actions of observers [cf. 31, 445].

Imagine the difference in your own reactions and modeling behavior if the Sundance Kid had been played in the movie by Don Knotts rather than by Robert Redford.

These important characteristics of a model help to explain why parents exert such tremendous influence on their children's development. Young children view their parents as experts, as having high status, as being respected, powerful, and very attractive. Thus, an aggressive father or mother who demonstrates to a child that aggression is an appropriate and acceptable response in many different situations will have a drastic impact on the child's development. Considerable evidence indicates that children who are raised by aggressive parents are themselves more aggressive than children reared by less aggressive parents [e.g. 393]. Parents should be aware that the way they cope with the world will be imitated by their children.

A child also learns a great deal about life from what parents don't do. What do you think would happen if Johnny saw his sister strike a friend while their parents merely sat in their chairs, watched, but didn't react? Johnny would learn that aggression pays, that it is an effective way to get what one wants, and that his parents consider it appropriate behavior. Parental permissiveness has been found to be positively related to aggressive behavior in children [393]. This research indicates that extremes in parental behavior—either extreme punitiveness and aggressiveness or extreme permissiveness—can have important effects on a child's aggressive behaviors.

Another important factor that affects modeling of aggression concerns the *label* attached to the action. If an action is viewed by other observers as "immoral," "unethical," and "unjustified," it is less likely that an individual will imitate it [302]. Such a label clearly indicates that an action is "bad" and socially disapproved, and it is a form of vicarious punishment associated with the action. On the other hand, if aggressive actions are labeled as "justified," "legitimate," and "ethical," imitation becomes more likely. Aggression then becomes a socially accepted way of dealing with others. Sergeant York, the most decorated hero of World War I, entered the army as a conscientious objector. His religious convictions held that all fighting and killing were wrong. His battalion commander cited chapter and verse from the Bible to show that killing was sometimes justified, ethical, and Christian. During a long prayer session, York finally decided that his commander's arguments were correct, and he became the most effective fighting machine of the war, killing several of the enemy and capturing many.

Such considerations have awesome implications. They suggest that we should be more concerned (as far as imitated aggression is concerned) about the aggressive actions that our society condones—such as wars and capital punishment—than about aggressive actions that are seen by most people as illegitimate and evil. The labeling of a model's behavior affects modeling in other ways as well. Many violent episodes reported by the mass media are portrayed as fictional; it is clear to many people that the behavior

(a)

(b)

Figure 7-4. *The real Bonnie and Clyde (a) and their movie counterparts, portrayed by Faye Dunaway and Warren Beatty (b). It is often difficult for moviegoers to differentiate between reality and fantasy in Hollywood productions about violence. Notice the striking differences between the photos. Unlike the real Bonnie Parker, Faye Dunaway is attractive, with a contemporary hair style and plunging neckline. Compared to the real Clyde Barrow, Warren Beatty looks like a model, with an immaculate, tailor-made suit and stylish shoes. To what degree does the line between fact and fiction blur, and the romanticized characteristics of the criminals produce modeling behavior?*

is not real, but is simply fantasy. If aggression and violence are perceived as fantasy and not fact, how will this affect imitation? To test this question, Seymour Feshbach [151] showed children between the ages of nine and eleven a film clip of a campus riot. Some children were told that the film portrayed an actual event; others were told that the event had been staged by actors. After watching the film, the experimenter gave the children an opportunity to aggress by delivering loud noises to an adult whenever the adult made incorrect guesses in a game. The children who were told that the violence was real were more aggressive than were those who had not observed the film; the children who had been told the violence was unreal were the least aggressive of all.

These results are encouraging in some ways, since they suggest that violence which is clearly labeled as fantasy might actually decrease aggressive behaviors. Yet, other studies have found that even violent cartoons can produce increases in children's modeled aggression, and most people would clearly label a cartoon unreal. Also, if Feshbach's results are valid, why would college students increase their use of electric shocks after seeing a fictional presentation, such as the film clip from *The Champion?* The data are somewhat unclear, although it does make sense to think that "unreal" violence has less impact on behavior than "real" violence.

Even more dangerous is the fact that it is difficult to tell just how many children, or even adults, can really distinguish between programs that depict real and unreal violence. Some people identify so closely with movie characters that the line between fact and fantasy becomes blurred. For example, how many people know to what extent *Bonnie and Clyde* depicted events as they actually happened? How much was glamorized and idealized? Do children realize that no one is really hurt when a law officer shoots the bad guy on television? Or do children realize that people are actually hurt when the evening news depicts shootings, robberies, and war? These questions raise some interesting and currently unresolved problems. Another possibly dangerous effect of fictional violence has not received adequate attention: the degree to which fiction dulls people's reactions to actual violence. People are exposed to so many fictional killings on television and in movies that it's hard to realize that the tragedies and suffering on the evening news are real. Often, the carefully edited versions of real violence that are shown on the news programs look like the lulls in the action in a fictional movie such as *Dirty Harry.* If thresholds for violence are raised to such a point that only sensational and bizarre events evoke reactions, unfortunate consequences may await our society.

Violence and the mass media

Learning by imitation is a powerful determinant of behavior. It has been estimated that an average child spends 1,200 hours a year watching television; between the ages of five and fourteen, a child watches over 13,000 people killed. Children observe, on the average, one television act of violence every sixteen minutes and one murder every thirty-one minutes [391]. How does all this violence affect children?

Three positions have been taken on the effects of media violence on behavior. The social learning position holds that media violence should result in an increase in imitated aggression. A second position has been taken by those who believe that catharsis occurs. (Recall that catharsis is the draining off of aggressive energies or drives by engaging in or fantasizing about aggression.) According to the catharsis hypothesis, observing violence should actually decrease aggression, since it discharges a viewer's aggressive energies and provides a harmless outlet. A third position, taken primarily by the television industry, holds that the effects are so complicated that behavior should not change much one way or another.

There is relatively little support for the catharsis position and a great deal of evidence against it. Only a very few studies support the position that watching media violence decreases aggression [152], and these studies have been criticized for poor experimental procedures. In addition, when other investigators try to replicate these few experiments, they find no support for the catharsis position [488].

Most current evidence supports the position of social learning theory. Studies conducted both in the laboratory and in field settings find that televised violence increases verbal and physical aggression among viewers, particularly among males [cf. 31; 273; 142; 143]. One study showed that early exposure to violence on television can affect behavior years later [143]; the amount of violence children watched on television when they were eight years old was directly related to the amount of verbal and physical aggression they displayed at age nineteen. The National Commission on the Causes and Prevention of Violence states: "It is reasonable to conclude that a constant diet of violent behavior on television has an adverse effect on human character and attitudes. Violence on television encourages violent forms of behavior, and fosters moral and social values about violence in daily life which are unacceptable in a civilized society" [138a].

Leonard Berkowitz and Jacqueline Macaulay [53] examined crime statistics in this country to determine whether a relationship could be demonstrated between the occurrence of an infamous event and subsequent rises in crime. They examined the records of the Federal Bureau of Investigation from 1960 through 1966 for each of forty cities. In particular, they wished to determine if crime increases could be observed after the dramatic assassination of President John F. Kennedy in November 1963 or after the infamous Speck-Whitman murders during the summer of 1966. As shown in Figure 7-5, they found a significant rise in crime after each sensational event. They also cited the FBI's report that it did not know of any widespread changes in police procedures which might account for the data.

Consider some specific examples of crimes illustrated by the above statistics. In November 1966, an eighteen-year-old boy walked into an Arizona beauty school and shot four women and a child. He later stated that he got the idea from the Richard Speck's murder of eight nurses in Chicago

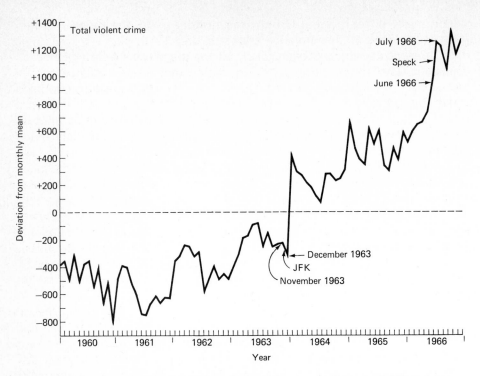

Figure 7-5. *Deviations in violent crime from the monthly mean for the sum of violent crimes, 1960–1966. This data, obtained from the FBI, suggests that increases in crime occur shortly after an unusual, well-publicized act of violence. Violent crime increased dramatically in the months following John F. Kennedy's assassination, and also after the Richard Speck and Charles Whitman incidents in summer 1966. Violence carried by the mass media does appear to affect the amount of modeled aggression.*

and from Charles Whitman's shootings of passersby from a tower at the University of Texas; both tragic events had occurred during the summer of 1966 [53]. A jealous husband finally shot his wife's admirer when he lost his fear of killing after watching Jack Ruby shoot Lee Harvey Oswald on television. He later commented, "I saw how easy it was to kill a man when Oswald was shot on TV" [quoted in 31, p. 107].

Fictional television programs also produce widespread imitation. The much publicized Sharon Tate murder by Charles Manson's "family" was partially instigated by an idea that Susan Atkins, one of the assailants, got from a television program. Robert Beausoleil, another member of the Manson "family," had been arrested for a previous murder that was actually committed by Atkins. Atkins felt that if more murders were committed, the police would realize that they were holding the wrong man and release Beausoleil. She stated: "I saw a movie on television like that once. They arrested a man and then there were eight more killings before the police realized they had the wrong man" [230].

NBC once televised a show entitled "Doomsday Flight," involving an extortion attempt in which a bomb was planted aboard an airliner and was set to explode at a particular altitude. In the movie, the pilot outwitted the would-be bomber by landing at an airport above the critical explosion altitude. Before the program had ended, a real bomb threat had been called into one airline, and within twenty-four hours after the telecast, four more bomb threats occurred [31; 230]. Every time the program was rerun in different cities around the country, in Canada, and in Australia, such incidents occurred. The Federal Aviation Administration finally asked television stations to refrain from further showings of the film.

From such evidence, should one conclude that violence must be banished from the television screen? This question will be hotly debated for years to come. Should news clippings be edited to remove all references to violence and crime? Clearly, total censorship would be intolerable in a free society. To what degree should the government control what can and cannot be shown in non-news shows? This question again raises the issue of censorship. Another ramification to be considered is the type of individual that should exist in this or any society. If the total elimination of aggression is our goal, then surely bans should be imposed on the amount of violence shown on television and in movies. On the other hand, is the complete elimination of aggression desirable? Most people feel that aggression and violence are necessary under some conditions to defend ourselves against unjust impositions of others. Thus, a fine balance must somehow be struck between completely eliminating violence in the mass media and allowing such violence to overflow.

The social influence approach: What do you do when all else fails?

So far we've explored two major psychological approaches to aggression: the frustration-aggression model and social learning theory. A third approach to aggression takes a slightly different perspective and illustrates that people influence one another's attitudes and behaviors through aggression. Some examples will clarify this.

Johnny wants a classmate to play baseball after school. He says, "If you don't play with me, I'll beat your brains out," and he's ready to do it if compliance doesn't follow. H. Rap Brown once advocated nonviolent, peaceful demonstrations to improve social conditions for blacks. After several friends were killed in bombings and children were beaten and stoned, Brown changed his tactics and advocated militancy and the use of violence. A frustrated, debt-ridden businessman was tired of his wife, children, and job; he decided that if he only had some money, he could escape to another country and start over. Since embezzlement from his company's funds was difficult, he called an airline and threatened to detonate a bomb on a plane unless $100,000 ransom were paid. The United States seemed hopelessly entangled in Vietnam, with discontent mounting at home and no real military victories abroad. President Richard M. Nixon decided to undertake massive bombings of North Vietnam to beat them to the conference table. In all of these cases the aggressive action can be viewed as *instrumental* to the accomplishment of other goals, usually involving the influencing of other people.

One way to influence others is to use persuasion—that is, to try to appeal to logic or emotion to get them to comply. Another way is to cajole them with flattery and subtly manipulate them into doing what is wanted. Still another way is to promise some reward if they comply. A final way is through the use of threats of punishment or actual punishment. One way to stop a bully from hitting you is to hit him first. One way to make children eat spinach is to threaten them with a spanking.

Almost all of what people commonly call aggressive actions are ways of influencing other people through threats and punishments. Yet all threats and all uses of punishment are not labeled aggression. We saw earlier that defining what we mean by "aggression" is a very difficult endeavor. The label "aggression" is used only for certain actions which involve threats and punishments [31; 447].

Three major conditions must exist before a threat or punishment will be called aggression [447].

1 The action must be perceived as *intentional* rather than accidental. This condition has already been discussed.
2 The action must be *offensive* rather than defensive. A would-be victim knocks a robber cold. Would you call the victim aggressive? Probably not, because the action was in self-defense. Thus, punishments and threats in defense are considered justified by norms and are not labeled aggression. This point is important in examining the actions of countries involved in international disputes. The United States was careful during its Vietnam involvement to label its actions defensive; we were protecting South Vietnam against the *aggressive* invaders. The North Vietnamese naturally pointed out that we were the invaders and the aggressors, while they were trying to unify their country and protect themselves against foreign invasion.
3 The action is perceived as *illegitimate* and *antinormative* rather than as legitimate and normative. The concept of legitimacy is complex. Legitimacy exists when an action is seen as justified by the circumstances and approved by the existing social norms and rules in the society. This is why the United States tried to justify its involvement in Vietnam by pointing out that commitments and treaties had dictated our presence there. We were bound by duty not to break our commitments. Many of the euphemisms that evolved during the Vietnam War show how the administration wanted to portray its behavior as legitimate and defensive. Bombing raids on villages were called "protective reactions," while the right to shoot down anyone in a particular area was justified by the label "free fire area."

The social influence approach makes it clear that groups of people will disagree over whether any single action is or is not aggressive. The perpetrator of the action often sees the harm done as legitimate, justified, and defensive. The person harmed will probably perceive the action as illegitimate, unjustified, and offensive and, therefore, will characterize it as aggression. Since the term "aggression" has negative connotations, it usually is in people's best interests to see that the label is not applied to them or to a group to which they belong. Many white, middle-class Americans saw the ghetto riots of the 1960s as outrageous instances of aggression, since they viewed these actions to be against the law and offensive. Blacks, on the other hand, pointed to a "higher law" which demands justice and equality for all. For them, the riots were justified and legitimate. Also, the riots could be seen as defensive rather than offensive, since they were reactions against previous injustices perpetrated by the existing (white) system. Thus, many blacks perceived the aggression to be perpetrated against them and not by them. The label "aggression" is largely in the eye of the beholder.

The social influence position stresses that aggression is a behavior that people use to accomplish goals. Actions which appear on the surface to be senseless and purposeless forms of violence become easier to understand when they are viewed as influence techniques. This position causes one to examine aggressive acts from the perpetrator's perspective. What did the perpetrator want? Why did the perpetrator feel that he or she could not achieve the goal through other tactics, such as persuasion?

Many individuals, for one reason or another, cannot satisfy their needs through other influence tactics; they are almost compelled to use threats and violence to get what they want. For example, who would you expect to commit more violent crimes, those from upper occupational brackets (professionals, managers) or those from lower occupational brackets (the unemployed or semiskilled)? Your answer is probably the latter. Why? The answer partially lies in the alternatives available to the upper occupational and educational groups. If people from these brackets needed money, they might take out a loan; if a family dispute created tension, a divorce would occur; if they wanted freedom from their children, they might hire a babysitter and go out every night. In other words, they have alternative behaviors to reduce the stresses and strains of life. They can fulfill their needs without resorting to armed robbery, fights, and other forms of violence.

Often, however, only violent forms of behavior are available for settling conflicts and fulfilling needs in lower occupational and educational levels. Such people often don't have the knowledge, self-confidence, or money to find more acceptable ways of reaching their goals. This is why people who have a tendency toward fistfights are usually deficient in the verbal and other social skills necessary for coping with provocative situations in more "legitimate" ways [456]. Given these considerations, it makes sense that violent crime is concentrated in large cities, particularly in slums and ghettos [186; 230]. This is precisely where one finds low income, low status,

Figure 7-6. *A Bengali soldier proudly displays the head of a victim. During wars, the opponent is perceptually dehumanized and becomes a mere trophy whose killing can confer status.*

poor education, high unemployment, poor health care, overcrowding, and misery. Also, homicides and assaults occur most often among relatives, friends, and acquaintances. This makes sense if aggression is viewed as an action designed to satisfy needs and resolve interpersonal conflicts when other techniques fail. People get into more conflicts with those they know that with strangers.

Aggressive actions often are performed to achieve status in certain groups, particularly in street gangs and in the military. During wars, status and rewards are meted out in direct proportion to the amount of destruction perpetrated upon the enemy. Bandura [31] reports the way one particular United States infantry battalion conferred status during the Vietnam War. For each enemy killed, a soldier was rewarded with rest and recreation; the lucky soldier received a "kill Cong" emblem that let others know of his accomplishment. To qualify for such treasures, it was necessary to supply proof of the kill; the proof consisted of the victim's ears. A string of ears was displayed proudly at headquarters to give soldiers an idea of what was expected and appropriate.

Similarly, many street gangs establish norms of aggression and make aggressive behavior a prerequisite for membership and status. In one city gang, each physical assault upon a stranger was worth 10 points if observed by another club member, and 100 points were required for club membership [31]. In another example, a boy involved in a gang killing later told authorities, "If I would of got the knife, I would have stabbed him. That would have gave me more of a buildup. People would say, 'There goes a cold killer'" [506, p. 8]. Clearly, in some groups, aggression achieves status and rewards. The degree to which aggression is normatively controlled and affected by culture is discussed in Focus 7-4.

FOCUS 7-4   CULTURE AND AGGRESSION

People are not equally aggressive the world over. The rate of gun homicide in the United States is 214 times higher than it is in Japan. In Tokyo, with a population of about 9 million people, only 3 murders were committed by guns in 1970, and only 414 robberies occurred; in New York City in the same year, over 500 people were murdered by handguns and 74,102 robberies were committed [230]. By many standards, the United States could be rated the most violent nation in the world.

Differences in the amount of aggression demonstrated in different cultures are produced by drastically different learning experiences. People derive values and attitudes toward others from these learning experiences. These values and attitudes determine whether and when it is appropriate to use aggression. In some societies, aggression is viewed as the normal way to handle interpersonal disputes. In other societies, aggression is prohibited and censured. In the Western world, for example, wars are fought because of conflicts in ideology, land, goods, resources, etc. In contrast, anthropologist Ruth Benedict [47] observed that the Aztecs engaged in wars only to obtain captives for their religious sacrifices: wars over land and goods were unthinkable to the Aztecs.

The entire range of the pacifism-aggression spectrum can be found in different societies. In North America, the Eskimos, Hopi Indians, and Zuni Indians are peaceful people who abhor violence and raise their children to be gentle. In Tahiti, aggressive behavior is not rewarded by parents or peers, and children learn that it is an ineffective form of social influence. Parents "punish" aggression indirectly. Instead of physically punishing their children for aggressive actions, the parents tell them that ancestral spirits will punish them. In this way, the child is unlikely to behave aggressively when the parents' backs are turned. Children believe that the spirits, which are watching and evaluating them wherever they go, will cause accidents and problems if they behave aggressively. As a result, Tahitians are described as "affable people who are slow to anger, who quickly get over any ill feelings, and who lack vengefulness and hostile aggressiveness. They are disinclined to create anger-provoking situations, and when they show aggression, it is generally expressed in words rather than physical fights" [31, p. 109].

In contrast, other societies, such as the Dani of New Guinea, organize social life around aggression and fighting. Their children grow up accepting aggression as a way of life and must learn the appropriate ways for bands of warriors to conduct their frequent battles. Unlike the Tahitians, who use the spirits of the dead to punish aggressive actions, the Dani use spirits as instigators of battles. The people believe that a fallen warrior's ghost will cause accidents, crop damage, and other problems until the spirit is avenged by the killing of an enemy. Dani women goad the men into battle, and status is conferred upon the best fighters. Dead spirits can be further placated by amputating and then burning the finger of a little girl, and so most adult females are missing numerous fingers [31].

Culture exerts a powerful influence on how a person sees the world, and it will drastically affect how a person behaves.

■ SUMMARY

Aggression has received a great deal of attention by social psychologists because of its importance to society. Social psychologists have been interested in why aggression occurs and how it can be reduced. Several general perspectives have been taken: aggression as part of human nature, aggression as produced by genetic and physiological factors, and aggression as affected by social-psychological factors.

The first position, aggression as part of human nature, sees aggression as being produced by instinct. The position has a long history and was popularized by Sigmund Freud. A modern version has been elaborated by ethologists, particularly Konrad Lorenz. Essentially, aggressive instincts which produce energy are presumed to exist. The energy builds up over time and is triggered by innate reactions to certain stimuli. Nothing can be done to alter the basic level of aggressiveness, but the energy can be redirected to socially acceptable channels. Although this position is popular, there is no conclusive evidence to indicate that such aggressive energies are instinctive, and many social scientists prefer to explain aggression in other ways.

Aggression is related in complex ways to genetic and physiological factors. Strains of aggressive or passive animals can be bred, and stimulation of certain areas in the brain produces aggressive actions. However, genetic and physiological factors don't cause aggressiveness by themselves. There is a complex interplay between biological factors and environmental, learned, factors. One's biological endowment might help to make one a successful fighter should the opportunity arise, or make one restless and irritable and hence likely to react aggressively when annoyed. However, simply because one has the capacity to be aggressive doesn't mean that aggressive behavior will follow.

Social-psychological positions on aggression have stressed how environmental frustration, social learning, and the necessity to influence others account for a wide variety of aggressive behaviors. These positions explain how aggressive behaviors are learned, when aggressive behaviors will occur, and when observers will label an action as aggressive. Each of the positions assumes that through proper learning and in proper environments, aggressive behaviors can be controlled and reduced. If we observe models who respond to frustration and life's problems in nonaggressive ways, if we learn that aggression and violence are unacceptable in virtually all situations, and if we provide people with the skills and abilities to settle their differences without resorting to violence, then aggressive actions will be reduced.

8

conformity, compliance, and obedience

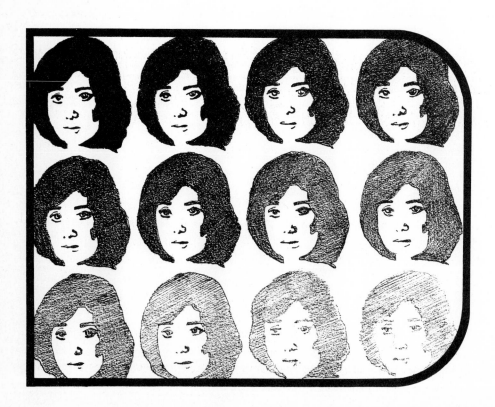

concepts

A person's role is the set of behaviors associated with the position he or she has in a group.

Conformity means yielding to group pressure.

Compliance exists when behavior is changed to fit the expressed expectation, request, or demand made by someone else.

The likelihood that an individual will conform to an incorrect group opinion depends upon the characteristics of the group, the behavior of group members, and the individual's personality attributes.

Individual states, such as guilt or desire to restore equity, may influence the likelihood of compliance.

Research suggests that characteristics of the situation are often powerful determinants of behavior.

Some analysts believe that general levels of conformity and compliance to arbitrary power within our society have decreased in recent years.

targets

After reading this chapter, you should be able to:

1 Discuss how the concept of role helps us to understand complex events, such as the Watergate scandal.

2 Identify the distinctions between conformity and compliance.

3 Discuss the concepts of anticonformity and independence.

4 Describe the early research on conformity carried out by Sherif and Asch.

5 Describe the notion of reactance and how it may affect compliance behavior.

6 Enumerate the reasons why so many "normal" individuals delivered the highest shock in Milgram's experiments.

7 Describe the many variations made by Milgram on his basic research paradigm.

8 Discuss the ethical questions raised by research such as that carried out by Milgram and by Zimbardo and his coworkers.

9 Discuss whether each of us is a "latent Eichmann."

10 Outline the results of research which has tried to identify characteristics of the "conforming personality."

11 Describe the most important characteristics of the Communist Chinese "brainwashing" tactics.

I have never been a quitter. To leave office before my term is completed is abhorrent to every instinct in my body. But as President, I must put the interest of America first. America needs a full-time President and a full-time Congress, particularly at this time with the problems we face at home and abroad.

To continue to fight through the months ahead for my personal vindication would almost totally absorb the time and attention of both the President and the Congress in a period when our entire focus should be on the great issues of peace abroad and prosperity without inflation at home.

Therefore, I shall resign the Presidency effective at noon tomorrow. Vice President Ford will be sworn in as President at that hour in this office. . . .

With these words, on Aug. 8, 1974, Richard M. Nixon declared his intention to resign as President of the United States, less than two years after he had been reelected by the largest margin in history. The Watergate scandal revealed an astonishing network of chicanery, deceit, complicity, and deception, which led directly to the criminal prosecution of many high officials in the government and in the Committee to Re-Elect the President (CREEP). Finally, it had culminated in the resignation of the President himself in the face of almost certain impeachment and conviction by Congress.

Many thoughtful Americans, regardless of political leanings, found themselves asking: "How could such actions take place in this day and time in America? What kind of atmosphere must have existed to allow such things to happen?" Even though all the details will probably never be learned, the next two chapters will discuss research findings about several factors: conformity, compliance, and group processes, which can help shed light on how and why events like these can take place.

■ ROLES: WHAT'S A POLITICIAN SUPPOSED TO DO?

Like members of any organization, campaign committee members divide up the tasks that have to be accomplished. The set of behaviors associated with each member's position in the group is termed the person's *role*. One role might be to coordinate the candidate's travel schedule, another to write speeches, another to solicit donations to the campaign fund, another to guarantee that large, friendly crowds turn out to hear the candidate's speeches, while still another might be to report what the opposition candidate is saying and doing. Each committee member would be engaged in behaviors associated with the role he or she held.

During the 1972 presidential campaign, the Committee to Re-Elect the President had an overall structure like any typical national election committee has, with roles such as director, deputy director, finance chairperson, treasurer, committee counsel, political coordinator, security chief, and so forth. But the "unofficial" roles of some campaign workers included behaviors that were anything but typical.

Once a spy, always a spy

E. Howard Hunt, Jr., was one of the burglars caught inside the Watergate complex. A White House "consultant" at the time, Hunt had left the Central Intelligence Agency in 1970 after twenty-one years of carrying out clandestine operations. Hunt had relished his role as a spy. According to a friend, "He couldn't get over the fact that he'd been a C.I.A. agent. You couldn't have a conversation with him for 10 minutes without him bringing it up some way or another. This was a romanticist who couldn't get over the fact that he had been a spy" [326, p. 839]. Hunt's perception of his role led him to organize the break-in at the office of the psychiatrist who had treated Daniel Ellsberg (Ellsberg had earlier "leaked" the so-called Pentagon Papers); his role led him to consider breaking into the safe of a Las Vegas newspaper publisher in search of presumably damaging evidence on Senator Edmund Muskie (at the time a leading candidate for the Democratic presidential nomination); and his role led to his involvement in the Watergate break-in. After Hunt's conviction, he proclaimed: "I cannot escape the feeling that the country I have served for my entire life and which directed me to carry out the Watergate entry is punishing me for doing the very thing it trained and directed me to do" [326, p. 839].

Reelection at any cost

Many of Nixon's campaign workers seemed to accept their "unofficial" role as people who must ensure the reelection of President Nixon at any cost, by any means necessary. Thus, for example, White House Special Counsel Charles Colson pledged that he would "walk over my grandmother" if it would help him better serve Richard Nixon. Given such an orientation, ordinary standards and norms concerning fairness and legality, which usually regulate behaviors, seemed largely irrelevant. The standards used to decide whether or not to do something often were entirely practical: Will it work? Will we get caught? Do we have enough money? Will it get us valuable information? The overriding goal, again, was to reelect President Nixon.

Figure 8-1. *All the President's men. Some of the high government and campaign officials who were involved in the mushrooming Watergate scandal of the early 1970s: (a) White House "consultant" E. Howard Hunt; (b) White House Special Counsel Charles W. Colson; (c) Attorney General and later Campaign Director John N. Mitchell; (d) Acting FBI Director L. Patrick Gray; (e) Counsel to the President John W. Dean III;*

(a)

(b)

(e)

(f)

(f) Deputy Campaign Director Jeb Stuart Magruder; (g) Assistant to the President for domestic affairs John D. Ehrlichman; and (h) White House Chief of staff H. R. (Bob) Haldeman. The roles which these men saw themselves occupying, the unusual norms which they applied to their situation, and their personality makeup, may all have contributed significantly to the pattern of behaviors which they engaged in.

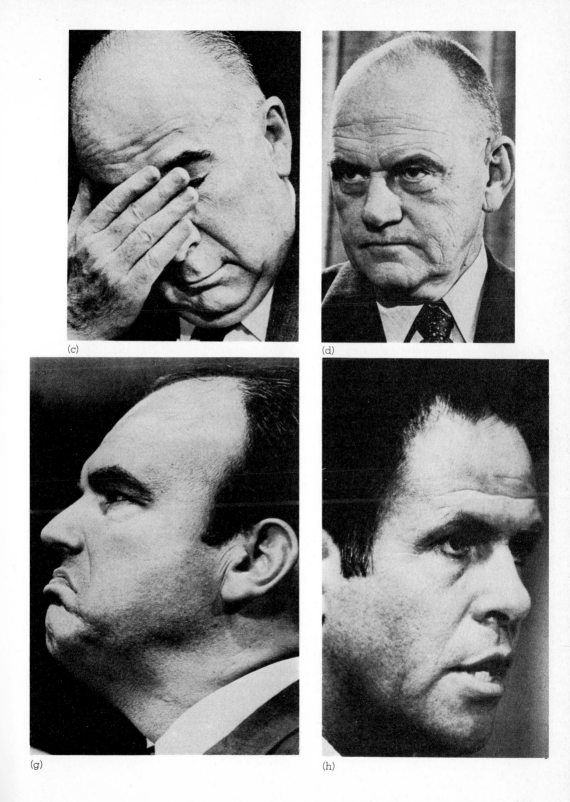

(c)

(d)

(g)

(h)

Former Attorney General John N. Mitchell was asked repeatedly during the Senate hearings in July 1973 why he had concealed his considerable knowledge about Watergate matters from President Nixon during the campaign. Mitchell's reasoning, as illustrated in these excerpts from the hearings [326, pp. 390–392], clearly shows what role Mitchell thought he occupied, namely, protector of the President.

Mitchell: I was sure that, knowing Richard Nixon, the President, as I do, he would just lower the boom on all of this matter and it would come back to hurt him and it would affect him in his re-election. And this is the basis upon which I made the decision not to tell Nixon. And apparently, others concurred with it. . . .

Senator Herman Talmadge: Am I to understand from your response that you placed the expediency of the next election above your responsibilities as an intimate to advise the President of the peril that surrounded him? . . . all around him were people involved in crime, perjury, accessory after the fact, and you deliberately refused to tell him that. Would you state that the expediency of the election was more important than that?

Mitchell: Senator, I think you have put it exactly correct. In my mind, the re-election of Richard Nixon, compared with what was available on the other side, was so much more important that I put it in that context.

In testimony the next day, Mitchell and Senator Howard Baker had this exchange:

Senator Baker: You understand, I am sure, what an enormous premium you put on success [the reelection of the President]? I suppose all politicians put a great premium on success. But do you care to weigh that any further and tell me that the concealment from the President of facts such as you have described as the . . . White House horrors and the break-in to the Watergate on June 17, that all of those things were inferior in importance to the ultimate re-election of the President?

Mitchell: I had no doubt about it at that time and I have no doubt about it now.

Team players: To get along, you go along

Even though Howard Hunt may have relished his role as spy, and John Mitchell his role as protector of the President, other important officials who did not see themselves in such roles were also drawn into the morass of Watergate. As time went on and the Watergate "cover-up" grew, they were compelled to participate in more and more shady or illegal activities, such as obstructing justice, destroying records, lying under oath, making "hush money" payoffs to families of the convicted burglars, and so on. Many of the officials were terribly uncomfortable and unhappy with the way things were going, yet they kept quiet and often intensified their illegal activities. How could such people—successful, intelligent, politically powerful—let themselves sink deeper and deeper into the quagmire?

Perhaps part of the answer lies in the kind of people they were. Many of these officials were accustomed to carrying out others' orders. Acting FBI

Director L. Patrick Gray, for example, had spent twenty-six years in the Navy as a submarine commander, legal officer, and military assistant. Such a background may have predisposed Mr. Gray to accept orders from "above" without question. "Mr. Gray conceded that he sent raw FBI reports to the White House, for example, but explained that he had been acting on the belief that there should be a 'presumption of regularity' about the men close to the President, and that he had simply followed their orders, which had come to him 'down the chain of command'. It was the old submarine captain speaking" [326, p. 625]. At another point during the FBI's investigation of Watergate, Gray was given two boxes of files by presidential advisors John Dean, III, and John Ehrlichman, and was told that they were "political dynamite" and should be destroyed. Gray kept the files for about six months and then burned them. When asked at the Senate hearings why he hadn't refused to do this, Gray replied, "I don't think the thought ever entered my mind to do that. . . . I was receiving orders from the Counsel to the President and one of two top assistants to the President and I was not about to question these" [326, p. 632].

Presidential Counsel John Dean, III, one of the men who told Gray to destroy the files, had as his credo, "To get along, you go along" [324, May 21, 1973, p. 28]. In a similar vein, an aide to Deputy Campaign Director Jeb Stuart Magruder commented, "If you are conformist oriented you go along. Jeb didn't like to be a pain in the ass" [455, May 7, 1973, p. 18]. So Dean, Magruder, and others went along and got along.

Perhaps the clearest evidence of the general atmosphere in which these things took place is revealed in the testimony of Herbert L. Porter, an official on the Committee to Re-Elect the President [326, p. 227]:

Porter: I was not the one to stand up in a meeting and say that this should be stopped, either. . . . I kind of drifted along.
Baker: At any time, did you ever think of saying "I do not think this is quite right, this is not the way it ought to be?" Did you ever think of that?
Porter: Yes, I did.
Baker: What did you do about it?
Porter: I did not do anything.
Baker: Why didn't you?
Porter: In all honesty, probably because of the fear of group pressure that would ensue, of not being a team player.

Here, then, we see a situation where a number of bright, talented people found themselves in a situation (obviously at least partly of their own making) which seemed to say: *Go along with it.* And most of them did. Why? Partially because of the *roles* they saw themselves occupying. Partially because of the perceived *norms* of the situation, which seemed to make ordinary concepts of legality and fair play irrelevant. And perhaps partially because of the kind of people they were, persons who had *learned* that "to get along, you go along." For the remainder of this chapter, we will consider the factors that lead people to conform to social pressures such as these and to comply with the wishes and demands of others, even when compliance may cause harm to others and, eventually, to themselves.

■ CONFORMITY

Conformity and compliance

Mark Smith, a volunteer campaign worker, hears his coworkers talk about sneaking a look at the financial books of the opposition, to see whether they have received any illegal donations. Privately, Smith thinks this would be unwise, since it would be both morally wrong and a political disaster for his candidate if they were caught. Nevertheless, all his coworkers express their enthusiasm for the "raid," and one asks his opinion. Mark agrees that it sounds like a good idea. He later accompanies the raiders on a nighttime foray to the opposition party's headquarters.

Smith's behavior is an instance of *conformity:* He has *yielded to perceived group pressure.* He undertook behavior (agreeing that the project was wise, going on the raid) which coincided with the expressed group norms but which was contrary to his private opinions and behavioral preferences.

Suppose, however, that Smith had instead expressed strong disapproval of the raid when it was first mentioned and that his boss told him: "Look, I don't care whether you approve or not; we need your help on this project. Now, you'll go with us tonight or you won't be working with us anymore." If Smith reluctantly agreed to take part in the raid but continued to voice objections to it, his behavior would not be considered conformity. Rather, we would call it *compliance:* He *changed his behavior to fit the expressed expectation, request, or demand made by someone else.* Compliance, then, refers to a reaction to a specific demand, while conformity involves changing one's attitudes and behaviors as a response to direct or subtle group pressure and going along with the group.

Looking back at the Watergate scandal, John Dean's philosophy, "To get along, you go along," is the epitome of a conforming approach. Similarly, Herbert Porter's desire to be seen as a "team player" is an expression of conformity, of modifying behavior to match the group's ("team's") norms. The destruction of files by L. Patrick Gray, on the other hand, was an instance of compliance. He received a specific order from a source he respected, and he complied with it. Focus 8-1 describes an important instance of compliance that happened several centuries ago.

Anticonformity and independence

During the Korean war, from 1950 to 1953, approximately 3,600 American soldiers were captured by the North Korean and Communist Chinese forces and imprisoned in China. While in prison, they were subjected to constant

FOCUS 8-1   IT STILL MOVES

The heliocentric theory of the solar system, which says that the earth and other planets move around the sun, has a long and interesting role in the framework of scientific theory. The controversy surrounding this theory and its antithesis, the geocentric theory, also provides an interesting example of compliance.

The followers of Pythagorus, a Greek philosopher and astronomer of the sixth century B.C., were the first to propound the heliocentric theory. Later, Aristarchus, another Greek astronomer (living about 310–250 B.C.), advanced the theory in a systematic manner. The geocentric theory, the belief in a stationary, nonrotating earth as the center of the universe, was proposed during the second century A.D. by Ptolemy, an astronomer and mathematician in Alexandria. This second (geocentric) orientation dominated astronomy for many centuries.

Toward the end of the Renaissance, Polish astronomer Nicholas Copernicus resurrected the heliocentric theory by publishing (in 1543) his book, *Concerning the Revolution of the Heavenly Bodies*. Although Copernicus endorsed the heliocentric approach, he had little direct evidence for it. (The telescope was not developed for several decades.)

Half a century later, Italian physicist and astronomer Galileo Galilei came to support the Copernican view. Galileo was the first to use the newly invented telescope for astronomical observation; he discovered four of Jupiter's moons, the irregularities on the surface of our moon, and the fact that the Milky Way was composed of countless stars. In 1615 Galileo was denounced by the Holy Office in Rome for teaching and publishing letters supporting the heliocentric approach. Then in 1632 Galileo published a book of dialogues on the Copernican and Ptolemaic systems. He placed some remarks that had been made by the Pope into the mouth of a character named Simplicius; as you might imagine, the Pope became furious at this sacrilege. Galileo—at the time seventy years old, very ill, and going blind—was summoned to Rome to meet the Inquisition.

The sentence of the Inquisition read, in part [quoted in 373, p. 31]:

1. The proposition that the sun is in the center of the world and immovable from its place is absurd, philosophically false, and formally heretical because it is expressly contrary to the Holy Scriptures.

2. The proposition that the earth is not the center of the world nor immovable, but that it moves, and also with a diurnal action is also absurd, philosophically false, and theologically considered, at least erroneous in faith. . . .

Galileo was required to renounce his earlier work and never undertake it again. His abjuration, in part, read:

> With a sincere heart and unfeigned faith, I abjure, curse, and detest the said errors and heresies, and generally every other error and sect contrary to the said Holy Church; and I swear that I will nevermore in the future say or assert anything, verbally or in writing, which may give rise to a similar suspicion of me. . . .

It is clear that Galileo's renunciation was compliance; he continued to hold his "heretical" ideas but was forced to live in seclusion for the rest of his life and to not express them publicly. The strained nature of his compliance is also illustrated by the well-known story that, after reciting his abjuration, Galileo muttered: *"Eppur si muove"*—"it [the earth] still moves." It is questionable whether Galileo actually said this; Bertrand Russell assures us that he did not. "It was the world that said this—not Galileo" [373, p. 32]. But whether he said it or not, Galileo probably was indeed thinking it.

---

pressure to change their attitudes and behaviors and adopt the standards and group norms repeatedly stressed by the Red Chinese (see Focus 8-2). Most of the American war prisoners resisted these attempts and did not conform. But evidence indicates that there were at least two different reasons why they resisted the pressures to conform [386].

One group of men resisted because they simply felt it would be wrong to collaborate with the enemy. These prisoners held to the standards they believed in. This is an example of *independence*, behavior which ignores group pressures and norms. Another group of resisters were characterized by a long history of unwillingness to accept *any* authority; they had not conformed well to the norms of the U.S. Army and neither did they obey their Red Chinese captors. These men were showing *anticonformity*, an active attempt to contradict group pressures. In a sense this second group was just as sensitive to group norms as were the few soldiers who conformed (and collaborated with the enemy), since their behavior was also influenced by the norms, but in the opposite direction.

In the mid-1960s, right after the Beatles first became popular, many American high schools became battlegrounds over the proper hair length for male students. Typically, school administrators (and many parents) wanted the boys' hair kept short, while the boys wanted to wear their hair long. Some students conformed to group pressure and kept their hair short. Others let their hair grow longer. Some did this because they thought it looked better or was easier to care for (independence), while others let their hair grow mainly to spite their parents and school officials, to show that they couldn't be pushed around (anticonformity).

Why conform?

When a person conforms, two quite different processes might be operating [123; 241]. One is *normative influence*, which occurs when an individual conforms to the expectations of another person or group because of the satisfying feeling this generates. Conformity to group norms is likely to gain one acceptance and liking by the group; conversely, disagreeing with group norms may lead to one's being seen as a deviate and rejected. Furthermore, agreement with group norms is likely to contribute to the attainment of group goals and to help ensure the continuation of the group. Disagreement might lead to intragroup fighting, arguments, and eventual disintegration of the group. In the political situation which led to Watergate, the danger in not being a "team player" was emphasized repeatedly.

Most people want to be right most of the time. The behaviors and views of others are one source of information about the world, particularly in ambiguous or unfamiliar situations. In such cases, others' behaviors can have *informational influence.* An example might be when one is traveling in a foreign country and knows little or nothing about local customs. If we do not want to insult the citizens by behaving inappropriately and making social blunders, we are likely to pay attention to what local people and experienced travelers do, individually as well as in groups. If they belch after a good meal, we do (or we at least consider the possibility of doing so); if they take off their shoes before entering a building, so do we. The actions of others provide valuable information about the norms of the culture, and we are likely to conform to those norms.

■ EARLY STUDIES OF CONFORMITY

The moving light

If a person looks at a stationary pinpoint of light in an otherwise completely dark room, the point of light will appear to move. This *autokinetic effect* stems from a complex combination of perceptual processes [282] and was noticed by astronomers long before the birth of modern psychology. (One reason that aircraft have blinking lights instead of constant lights is to counteract the autokinetic effect.) Muzafer Sherif [401] used this phenomenon to investigate how others affect a person's responses.

Sherif was interested in a very simple question: If a person hears someone else make judgments about the movement of this same pinpoint of light, will these judgments affect his or her subsequent judgments? To find out, Sherif had college students view and make judgments alone and then in pairs.

Sherif found that if a subject was alone while making judgments, he or she developed a stable frame of reference rather quickly. All judgments of the light's movement were within a relatively small range. Sherif compared this situation with the two-person group to see whether one member's report of the light's movement would affect the other member's report. Not surprisingly, it did—presumably because there were no other sources of information except for the subject's own perception and knowledge of what the cosubject said. The responses of the cosubject had *informational influence.* Interestingly, though, most subjects claimed that their judgments had *not* been influenced by the other subject. The changed frame of reference that developed from the other's influence was very stable; when subjects returned the next day to make judgments alone, the influence of the other subject was still apparent in their responses. Indeed, one study found that this changed frame of reference persisted for as long as a year [365].

Is everyone blind but me?

Solomon Asch [19] set up another situation to study conformity. Imagine yourself to be a male college sophomore participating in a visual perception experiment along with six other male subjects. You all are seated at a circular table with the task of judging which of three lines on one board appears to be the same length as a single line on another board in front of you. The task is actually quite easy and, individually, well over 90 percent of subjects make correct judgments. An example of the problem Asch used is given in Figure 8-2 (the correct answer is *B*).

All subjects are instructed to state their choice out loud, one at a time. You are next to last in sequence. On the first few trials, everyone makes the correct response on each trial, and so the seven of you are in complete agreement. By the end of a few trials you are probably thinking that this task is rather easy and quite dull. Suddenly the first subject makes an incorrect response. The second agrees with the first, and so does the third. By the time it's your turn, all five subjects speaking before you have already made the same incorrect response.

What's going on? The other subjects obviously are not kidding. Are your eyes deceiving you? Is there some trick to the situation which they see but which you have missed? What do you do? Do you agree with the other subjects, hence *conforming* to perceived group pressure and making a response which you know, or think you know, is incorrect? Or do you remain independent of the group judgment and give the answer which you think—which your eyes tell you—is correct? As you can imagine, this is a very stressful situation. (The other "subjects" are accomplices of the experimenter and gave the incorrect answers intentionally.)

In a series of studies, Asch [19, 20] found that about one-fourth to one-third of his subjects never conformed; these people kept on giving the answer which their eyes told them was right, even though it disagreed with the responses of the other subjects. None of the subjects conformed to the incorrect group responses on *every one* of the 12 "critical" trials (where the others gave the incorrect answers), although a small number (about 15 per cent) conformed on three-fourths or more of the critical trials. Thus, the typical subject conformed on at least one trial but "stuck to his guns" and resisted conformity pressures on the majority of critical trials. Averaging across all subjects, conforming responses were given about one-third of the time.

Notice that we have said nothing about the subjects' private judgments, but only about conforming *behaviors*. There are at least three ways in which

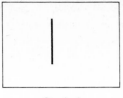
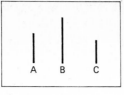

Standard   Comparison

Figure 8-2. *Stimulus cards like those used in Asch's conformity experiments. The subjects' task is to judge which of the three lines on the right is exactly the same length as the line on the left. Conformity pressures are set up when the rest of the subjects (who are secretly accomplices of the experimenter) unanimously give an incorrect answer (in this case, say, line A) and the actual subject must either discount what his eyes tell him (i.e., that B is the correct answer) or publicly disagree with the rest of the group.*

a conforming response might develop in this type of situation. First, *distortion of perception* might take place. A subject actually comes to perceive the incorrect answer as correct—that is, to perceive the shorter line as longer. This process demands rather extreme perceptual distortions and apparently did not happen often in these experiments. In such cases, the group's responses would be a source of informational influence, telling the subject which response really *is* correct.

Second, *distortion of judgment* could take place. A subject knows that his perception disagrees with the majority but concludes that he must be wrong; therefore, he verbally agrees with the majority. This appears to be the most common type of conformity to occur in these situations. A third type of conformity would be *distortion of action.* A subject could feel certain that the group is wrong but go along with their incorrect answer anyway. This type of conformity is most clearly a case of normative influence; it was relatively infrequent in the experiments.

■ VARIABLES AFFECTING CONFORMING BEHAVIOR

Characteristics of the group

In a series of studies, Asch and later investigators looked at the effects of a number of situational and personal variables affecting the amount of conforming behavior that occurs. One variable is the size of the group. As group size increases up to a point (still with only one person being the real subject), the average amount of conforming behavior also increases [177]. However, groups larger than six or eight people tend to induce an equal or somewhat lesser amount of conformity than smaller groups [20]. The status, similarity, and apparent expertise of group members also affect the amount of conformity. Findings in this area suggest that the higher the status of other group members or the more expert or similar to the subject they appear to be, the more conforming behavior is likely to occur [247]. We usually treat information from "experts" as more valuable and therefore can be more easily persuaded to follow their lead. Looking back at the Watergate scandal, we can see that in many situations lower-status members of Nixon's campaign organization (such as Herbert Porter) were faced with conformity pressures from others who were of high status (important officials in the government or on the reelection committee); who were somewhat similar to them (they were all Republicans interested and involved in politics, working for Nixon's reelection); and who were seen as experts in politics. Hence, it is not surprising that Porter and many coworkers went along.

Behavior of group members

Recall that in Asch's basic study, the rest of the group is unanimous against a lone subject. What happens when a second group member also disagrees with the majority? This makes a drastic difference. In Asch's study, when there was a second "deviate," the amount of conforming behavior by the real subject was cut to about one-fourth [19]. Interestingly, the other dissenter need not be correct in his responses. Research indicates that even when another dissenter gives an incorrect answer (line C in Figure 8-2), the likelihood of conformity by the real subject is reduced [6]. Here the other dissenter would *not* be serving as a source of informational influence (since he or she was wrong, too) but would be providing evidence that it is all right to *disagree* with the rest of the group.

The recent performance histories of the individual and the group also have an effect. If the group began by agreeing with the subject for many trials and then suddenly disagreed, the average subject was more likely to conform than if the group began by disagreeing. Also, subjects who have evidence that they did *well* on the task individually are more likely to resist conformity pressures in a group situation [290].

Asch [20] set up another situation in which a confederate initially agreed with the subject (and disagreed with the group) and then "defected"—started agreeing with the incorrect group response. The amount of conformity shown by the real subject in this case was nearly as great as it had been in the initial study, in which he did not have a supporter. More conformity is also likely to occur when the response must be made publicly (stated aloud) than privately (written down and not shown to others) [123].

The amount of discrepancy between a subject and the group is an important determinant of the amount of conformity. Using techniques in which the *degree* of discrepancy could be varied, researchers have found that the greatest amount of conformity occurs with *medium* amounts of discrepancy. This is easy to understand: with small discrepancies, subjects probably can continue to feel free to give their original responses, while with very great discrepancies the situation may be so unbelievable or stressful that subjects revert to their original responses. Finally, the easier the problem or the more competent the person feels, the less conformity is likely to occur [212].

Looking again at the Watergate situation, the behavior of group members often encouraged conformity. Disagreement with prevailing opinions was not encouraged (good team players don't disagree). Since all the participants were from the same political party and most shared similar political philosophies, the amount of discrepancy was probably only moderate between what individuals may have wanted to do and what the group pressure suggested was appropriate.

Personality

The Watergate scandal also suggested that there may be a particular *type* of person who is most likely to conform. However, psychological research has identified few personality characteristics that seem related to conformity in different situations. There is some evidence that people with lower intelligence or lower self-esteem are more likely to conform [329]. Such people may feel less competent and less expert than others. Studies conducted during the 1950s and 1960s indicated also that females tended to conform more readily in experimental situations than males. These findings may represent differences in sex-role training; that is, women in our society have traditionally been trained to be relatively passive and agreeable. If so, then as sex-role training changes, such sex differences in conformity may change or disappear also (see Chapter 4). In addition, research suggests that the nature of the task may make a big difference. A recent study found that when the conformity task was more familiar and interesting to women than to men, women conformed significantly *less* than men did [410].

■ COMPLIANCE

Recall that we defined compliance as changes in behavior to fit the expressed expectation, request, or demand of someone else. We all get such requests and demands—from parents, friends, bosses, teachers, advertisers, politicians, and so forth. While no one complies with every request, all of us comply with some. Now we'll look at factors which may increase the likelihood that a person will comply.

Rewards and punishments

Rewards and punishments are used constantly to achieve compliance. Many parents search for the most effective rewards and punishments to make children comply and be obedient to parental expectations and desires. In politics such punishment is often straightforward, as Watergate Special Prosecutor Archibald Cox learned on Oct. 20, 1973. When Cox refused to comply with President Nixon's order that he drop legal actions aimed at obtaining tapes of White House conversations, Nixon fired Cox, abolished the position of Special Prosecutor, and ordered the FBI to seal off the offices of Cox and his staff. As this case illustrates, some rewards for compliance and punishments for noncompliance are quite direct (e.g., firing); in other cases they may be more social and less tangible (praise or censure, approval or disapproval). In addition, compliance may be increased through reasoning and justification. If people are given good reasons for complying, then compliance is more likely to occur.

States of the individual

When we are experiencing certain states—certain emotions or self-percep-tions—we may be more likely to comply with a request. In an early speech on Watergate (Aug. 29, 1972), President Nixon commented, "What really hurts in matters of this sort is not the fact that they occur, because overzeal-ous people in campaigns do things that are wrong. What really hurts is if you try to cover it up." Implicit in Nixon's statement is the idea that in the heat of the campaign people may be more likely to comply with unreasonable or illegal requests than they ordinarily would be. But heightened emotions felt during a political campaign are not the only states which may encourage compliance.

Salespeople have long known that if a person can be made to comply with a small request, the chances are improved that he or she will later comply with a larger request. The effectiveness of this "foot-in-the-door" technique was demonstrated by Freedman and Fraser [166]. Their experi-menters went from door to door asking housewives to sign a petition sponsored by the Committee for Safe Driving, which asked their senators to work for legislation to encourage safe driving. Almost all the housewives signed the petition. Several weeks later, different experimenters went from door to door in the same neighborhood asking housewives to agree to put a large, unattractive sign which said, "Drive Carefully," in their front yards. More than half the women who had previously agreed to sign the petition (the small request) agreed to post the sign (the larger request). In contrast, only 17 percent of the women who had not been approached earlier (with the petition) agreed to post the sign. Thus, the likelihood that a housewife would agree to post the sign was over three times as great if she had previously agreed to sign the petition.

A chilling example of this same technique, used during the Korean war, is provided in Focus 8-2. The "pacing of demands" technique used by the Chinese Communists is an application of the foot-in-the-door technique.

Another way to increase the likelihood that someone will comply with a request is through concerns for social justice and reparation. For instance, it seems reasonable that if someone does you a favor, you will probably be more likely to help in return. If that person asks you to do something, you will be more likely to comply with the request. Research indicates that this commonsense notion is valid; people will tend to "restore equity" by return-ing favors and complying with requests [360]. The tendency to comply is particularly strong when the original favor seems entirely voluntary [185]. Interestingly, although people are more likely to comply with the request of someone who has done a favor for them, it is apparently not because of any increase in liking for the favor-doer, but rather in order to restore equity or pay the person back [266; 360; 390].

FOCUS 8-2 BRAINWASHING: COMPLY OR ELSE

While a truce to end the Korean war was being negotiated, a prisoner exchange, labeled "Operation Little Switch," was carried out in April 1953; 149 American prisoners of war (POWs) were released. However, only 129 were sent home; the whereabouts of the remaining 20 POWs became a mystery. Finally, the Defense Department announced that "having succumbed to Communist indoctrination," the missing prisoners had been flown to a military hospital for medical and psychological treatment. At the time, a commentator [75, p. 108] suggested that this reflected "a story of deep and shocking importance to the American people. It is the story of an effort, as finely organized as any battle plan, to capture the minds of American prisoners and send them back to the U.S. to spread Communist doctrine." An Air Force Lt. Colonel who had been a POW commented [103, p. 25]: "It's not pretty to see your GI buddies go over to the Communists—this one for a warm room, that one for a few cigarettes, someone else for rice instead of millet." Was it this simple? Did many prisoners "go over" to the Communists?

It had been known for several years that the Chinese Communists had developed a technique of "thought control" which had come to be known in China as *hsi nao*, "washing the brain." Now it was being used on American soldiers. Popular hysteria at the time made it seem as though a diabolical new technique had been developed by the Communist Chinese, a technique through which anyone could be made to comply with the wishes of the "brainwasher" and which, hence, threatened the entire free world. Was this really the case?

First of all, we should note that the brainwashing techniques were not as effective as popular hysteria made it seem. Actually, few POWs were apparently sincere in their "conversion"; only 21 of approximately 3,600 American prisoners chose to remain in China or North Korea after repatriation to America became possible. It was estimated that another several hundred POWs had cooperated with their Communist Chinese captors to some degree while imprisoned (these men were labeled "progressives" by their captors).

The Chinese Communist indoctrination program, designed to induce compliance for propaganda purposes, was based on four major factors [386]. The first centered on the *removal of supports* for beliefs, attitudes, and values. All the prisoners' accustomed sources of information about daily events on a local, national, or international level were cut off by the Chinese. They substituted their own heavily biased newspapers, radio broadcasts, and magazines for sources of information.

The prisoners were segregated by race and rank. The rank segregation was a systematic attempt to undermine the internal structure of the group by removing its leaders. When any effective organization appeared among the men, the Chinese would usually immediately remove and segregate the leaders or key figures. Emotional isolation prevented prisoners from validating any beliefs, attitudes, and values through meaningful interaction with others at a time when these were under heavy attack from many sources and when no accurate information was available.

A second phase of the indoctrination involved *direct attacks* on beliefs, attitudes, and values. Although the anti-American material in daily lectures was naïve and often incorrect, the constant hammering at certain points, combined with other techniques—and in a situation where prisoners had no access to other information—made it likely that many Chinese arguments did filter through enough to make many prisoners question former points of view.

According to interviews with former POWs [386], the most effective attack on beliefs, attitudes, and values was the use of testimonials by prisoners who apparently supported Communist enterprises. Such testimonials had a double effect; they further weakened group ties while at the same time presenting pro-Communist arguments.

A third procedure used *indirect attacks* on beliefs, attitudes, and values. Most lectures, for example, ended with a series of pro-Communist conclusions. Often the prisoners were then required to break into squads to discuss the material for periods of two hours or more and provide written answers to questions handed out during the lecture.

A second means of indirect attack was interrogation. The Chinese tried to create the impression that they could obtain *any* information from *anyone*. If a prisoner refused to answer a question despite great fatigue and continued repetition of the question, often the interrogator would pull out a notebook and give the complete answer to the question, sometimes in astonishingly accurate detail. The interrogator then would move on to a new topic and the same procedure would be repeated, until the prisoner was unable to decide whether there was indeed *anything* that the Chinese did *not* know.

Another effective technique of getting prisoners to question their own beliefs and values was to make them confess publicly to wrongdoings and to "criticize" themselves. When a prisoner broke one of the strict camp rules, he was urged to write a "confession" of his misdeed. While such trivial confessions seemed relatively harmless, eventually a prisoner would break another camp rule, leading to increased hostility from the Chinese and correspondingly greater demands for confession and self-criticism.

Sometimes the men found ways to obey the letter but not the spirit of the Chinese demands for self-criticism. Schein [386, pp. 159–160] provides an example:

> During public self-criticism sessions they would often emphasize the wrong words in a sentence, thus making the whole ritual ridiculous. "I am sorry I called Comrade Wong a *no-good-son-of-a-bitch*." Another favorite device was to promise never to "get caught" committing a certain crime in the future. Such devices were effective because even those Chinese who knew English were not sufficiently acquainted with idiom and slang to detect subtle ridicule.

Encouraging collaboration by the direct use of *rewards and punishments* was still another method in the indoctrination program. Medication, clothing, better and less crowded conditions, and promises of early repatriation were powerful incentives. Perhaps the most important privilege was freedom of movement; the "progressives" had free access to Chinese headquarters and could go into town or wherever they wished at any time of day or night. At the other extreme, threats of death, nonrepatriation, torture, reprisals against families, reduction in food and medication, and imprisonment were all used. There was no evidence that the Chinese used drugs or hypnotic methods or offered sexual rewards, however. Some cases of severe physical torture were reported, but their incidence was difficult to estimate.

There were several general principles in all phases of the Chinese indoctrination. The first of these was *repetition*; the Chinese were immensely patient in whatever they were doing. They were always willing to make their demand or assertion to the prisoner over and over again. A second characteristic was the *pacing of demands*. In the various kinds of responses that were demanded of the prisoners, the Chinese always started with trivial, innocuous ones and, as the habit of responding became established, gradually worked up to more important ones. Thus, after a prisoner had once been "trained" to speak or write out trivia, statements about more important issues were demanded. (This is an example of the foot-in-the-door technique.) *Active participation* was another principle constantly used. It was never enough for prisoners to listen and absorb; some verbal or written response was always demanded. In addition, the Chinese made considerable efforts to insert their new ideas into old and meaningful contexts. In general, this was apparently not very successful, although it worked for certain prisoners who were already not content with their lives.

It is difficult to assess the overall effectiveness of this massive program, in terms of either active collaboration or true ideological change. We might note that neither of these necessarily implies the other; it was possible for a prisoner to collaborate with the enemy without altering his beliefs, and it was equally possible for a man to be converted to communism to some degree and still not collaborate. Nevertheless, some degree of compliance was achieved in some prisoners.

Compliance may also be increased through the arousal of *guilt* in an individual. If we feel guilty because we have done something we consider wrong, it's likely that we will try to do something good to reduce the guilt. We may perform a good act to "balance" the bad (guilt-inducing) act, we may let ourselves in for some unpleasantness and thereby punish ourselves for the bad act, or we may try to minimize the negative aspects of the guilt-arousing situation by making the original act seem less bad. The first two of these techniques might make a guilty person more likely to comply with an appropriate request than a nonguilty person would be. Focus 8-3 describes several studies in which this was indeed found to be the case.

The danger of overkill: Reactance

We have been discussing techniques by which people can set up external pressures or induce emotional states in individuals to make it more likely that these individuals will comply with requests. Things are not always that simple, however. What if the person *knows* you are trying to force compliance? What if this knowledge makes him or her feel manipulated, and feel that freedom of choice is under attack? *Reactance,* mentioned earlier in Chapter 5, may occur in such situations. When one feels that freedom of choice is threatened or restricted, one is motivated to reestablish the threatened freedom. Therefore, a person will be very *un*likely to comply with a request in this situation, since compliance requires one to give up even more freedom.

FOCUS 8-3   IF YOU'RE GUILTY, YOU PAY

It has been hypothesized that people who feel guilty should be more likely to comply with a request than people who do not feel guilty. Researchers have investigated this possibility, with interesting results. In several experiments, college students have been led to believe that through carelessness they damaged or broke expensive research equipment. Students who thought they had broken the equipment were more likely to comply with a request to volunteer for another experiment than were students who did not think they had broken the equipment. Similarly, subjects who thought they had done a great deal of damage to the equipment (resulting in a great amount of smoke and noise) were more likely to volunteer for a future experiment than were students who thought they had done a small amount of damage (a small puff of smoke) to the same equipment [76].

In another experiment, students were induced to deliver electric shocks or loud buzzes to another subject (a research accomplice) in a learning experiment. When the learning trials were completed, the person who had been shocked asked the real subject to do a favor (calling people to enlist support for a campaign to "Save the Redwoods in California"). Subjects who had delivered shocks complied with this request significantly more often than did subjects who had delivered only buzzes. A second study showed that this did not simply result from sympathy for the shocked confederate, since subjects who had watched him get shocked but had not delivered the shocks themselves complied significantly less than subjects who had actually administered the shocks [88].

The research demonstrates that the arousal of guilt can be a very effective way to induce compliance without direct social pressure. But there are several qualifications to this relationship. It has been suggested [168] that a guilty person is torn between two considerations: (1) reduction of guilt and (2) a desire to avoid confronting the person who has been harmed. If this is so, the greatest compliance should be obtained when adherence to the request *does not* require further interaction with the victim. And this has been found. If the request requires a person to work closely with the victim of the guilt-inducing action (an uncomfortable situation, certainly), guilty persons are no more likely to agree to participate than are nonguilty ones [88; 168].

Finally, another important factor is the ease with which one can make reparations to a victim. If the guilty person cannot repay the victim fully or if the "cost" of repaying is too great (in terms of time, inconvenience, money, discomfort, etc.), the guilty person may react in other ways. In such a situation, the guilty person might get the greatest satisfaction by *devaluing* the victim ("Well, he deserved it; it was his own fault for letting it happen") or the amount of harm done ("Besides, nobody was badly hurt, and it builds character"). Similarly, a guilty person might justify the behavior by deciding that the harm was caused for good reason, such as for the sake of science or because it was ordered—he or she had no choice. Hence, in these situations guilt is reduced by changing the perceptions of the victim or of the act itself.

■ COMPLIANCE IN THE EXTREME: WHY DID THEY DO IT?

Field Marshal Keitel, on trial for murder in the Nuremberg War Crimes Trials in Germany, in 1946 stated [324, Sept. 9, 1946, p. 53]:

It is tragic to have to realize that the best I had to give as a soldier—obedience and loyalty—was exploited for intentions which could not be recognized and that I did not understand the limit which is set even for a soldier in the performance of his duty.

Adolf Eichmann, Nazi leader who was tried and convicted of murder (in Israel in 1961) for his acts during World War II defended his actions in the following manner [455, Jan. 14, 1961, p. 25; 324, Jan. 17, 1961, p. 42]:

I have regrets and condemnation for the extermination of the Jewish people, which was ordered by the German rulers, but I myself could not have done anything against it. I was a tool in the hands of the strong and powerful and in the hands of fate itself. . . . Where there is no responsibility, there can be no guilt. . . . I was only receiving and carrying out orders.

First Lieutenant William Calley, while on trial for the murder of 104 civilians in the Vietnam hamlet of My Lai in 1968, commented [324, Mar. 8, 1971, p. 51]:

I felt then and I still do that I acted as I was directed. I carried out the orders that I was given and I do not feel wrong in doing so.

An anonymous Vietnam veteran called a radio talk show in Boston in 1972 and commented on the devastation and horrors of the Vietnam situation [455, Oct. 23, 1972]:

I was there a year, and I never had the courage to say that was wrong. I condoned that. I watched it go on. Now I'm home. Sometimes I, my heart, it bothers me inside, because I remember all that, and I didn't have the courage to say it was wrong. . . .

You say it's right because they are the enemy, and then when you come home, you can't believe that you didn't have the courage to open your mouth against that kind of murder, that kind of devastation over people, over animals.

Historian C. P. Snow has written [416, p. 24]:

When you think of the long and gloomy history of man you will find more hideous crimes have been committed in the name of obedience than have ever been committed in the name of rebellion.

All the quotations above refer to obedience, compliance, and the maintenance of order in situations where such behavior led to hideous massacres during wartime. Obviously, not all cases of obedience or even overobedience are associated with such atrocities. Nevertheless, many people have agonized over how such atrocities could possibly take place. Social scientists have attempted to find out how and why such things occur.

■ ROLES: WHAT BEHAVIORS ARE APPROPRIATE?

In Chapter 1 we described the notion of *demand characteristics* and how they may invalidate research results. We noted that in some cases people's behaviors may reflect what they think they are *supposed* to do in an experimental situation rather than what they *would* do in such a situation if it were not an experiment. The characteristics of the situation ("This is a psychological experiment") may produce considerable pressure for people to behave in a certain way (in this case, as a "good subject"). Hence, subjects might comply with virtually any request that was made.

One way of looking at this issue is in terms of roles. When we are in the role of research subjects, we may behave appropriately (as we think a research subject should). But people occupy many other roles, and there is increasing research evidence that roles may be strong factors in determining behavior, much stronger than most people have assumed. There are, in particular, highly structured institutions in society (such as the military or the prison system) in which roles (soldier or prison guard) may be especially powerful in determining behavior.

Prisoner and guard

In Chapter 6 we discussed a study in which the basement of the psychology building at Stanford University was briefly turned into a prison [195; 513]. The "guards" and "prisoners" were male college students selected randomly from a group of emotionally stable, physically healthy, mature students. Both prisoners and guards were paid for their participation, and individuals were randomly assigned roles as either guards or prisoners.

Zimbardo and his coworkers found that both prisoners and guards became totally involved in their roles. The guards became increasingly callous and arbitrary in their use of power, and the prisoners grew increasingly passive and helpless. The following incident provides further chilling evidence of how thoroughly the participants got into their roles [513, p. 14]:

Prisoner 819, who had gone into a rage followed by an uncontrollable crying fit, was about to be prematurely released from the prison when a guard lined up the prisoners and had them chant in unison, "819 is a bad prisoner. Because of what 819 did to prison property we all must suffer. 819 is a bad prisoner," over and over again. When the superintendent realized 819 might be overhearing this, he rushed into the room where 819 was supposedly resting, only to find him in tears, prepared to go back into that prison because he could not leave as long as the others thought he was a "bad prisoner." Sick as he felt, he had to prove to them that he was not a "bad" prisoner. He had to be persuaded that he was not a prisoner at all, that the others were also just students, that this was just an experiment and not a prison and the prison superintendent and his staff were only research psychologists.

The simulated experiment had been scheduled to continue for fourteen days and nights. However, the intensity with which the roles were enacted and the increasing frequency of situations such as that described above forced researchers to end the experiment after only six days and nights. Even by this time, they had released five of the nine prisoners because of extreme emotional depression or acute anxiety attacks.

Zimbardo and his coworkers carried out a full-day debriefing session at the end of the simulation. Since the study had worked "too well" in simulating the intense oppressiveness of prison life, the researchers were naturally concerned that they might have caused psychological harm to some participants. They found in year-long follow-ups by questionnaires, personal inter-

Figure 8-3. (a) *U.S. Army First Lieutenant William Calley (right) convicted of murder for his part in the "My Lai massacre" in Vietnam in 1968 where 104 civilians were killed by American troops. The massacre was not generally known for several months until Ron Haeberle, an Army photographer who had accompanied Calley's patrol, made public his photographs of the carnage (b). Calley's trial, like the Nuremburg trials of former Nazi officers after World War II, highlighted the enormously complex issue of the extent of an individual's responsibility for acts committed while "under orders" from someone else. (c) Participants in the "Congress of the Greater Germany" in Nuremburg in 1940 signal their allegiance to their Fuhrer Adolf Hitler. Millions of German civilians denied any personal responsibility for massive atrocities they had witnessed or heard about. But whether or not the civilians were literally following orders, the basic question remains: How far does personal responsibility extend?*

(a)

(b)

(c)

views, and group discussions that the mental anguish of the participants was transient and situationally specific, but that the self-knowledge gained in the experiment persisted. This study vividly illustrates the drastic effect that role requirements may have on human behavior and interactions. "Normal" college students performed some pretty brutal and "abnormal" behaviors in the situation. What would you have done? Can you be sure?

Hurting on command

The above study tried to reproduce one of several situations which seem to *demand* obedience from at least some participants. Obedience is also demanded in the military chain of command. Stanley Milgram [304; 306; 307; 309] carried out a series of studies to investigate the effect of obeying orders in a situation somewhat similar to the military. Milgram's basic experimental setup was fairly simple: try to imagine your own reactions if you had taken part as a subject.

Having seen a newspaper advertisement that they could earn $4.50 by participating in a one-hour study of "memory and learning" at Yale University, male adults arrived individually at the Yale Interaction Laboratory. There, each met a second "subject" who arrived at the same time. Neither was a college student; the second subject was a mild-mannered man, forty-seven years old, who was an accomplice of the experimenter.

The experimenter, an impassive and rather stern man, remarks that it is not known how much punishment is best for learning or how much difference it makes as to who is giving the punishment. Subjects are told that in the present study they are asking people to be teachers and learners to investigate the effect of punishment. The experimenter asks whether either subject has a preference about whether he will be the teacher or the learner; neither subject states a strong preference. The experimenter then lets each draw a slip of paper from a hat to determine who will assume which role. The drawing is rigged and the real subject becomes the teacher.

The experimenter explains that the punishment will be electric shock of increasing intensity. The subjects are taken into an adjoining room, where the learner is seated and strapped into an "electric chair" apparatus. An electrode is attached to his wrist, and electrode paste is applied "to avoid blisters and burns." The experimenter declares, in response to a question from the learner: "Although the shocks can be extremely painful, they cause no permanent tissue damage."

The learning task itself involves paired-associate learning. The teacher reads a series of words to the learner, and the learner must press a button to indicate, for each word, which of four other words had earlier been associated with that word. After the learner is strapped in to the "electric chair" and the situation is explained, the teacher is led back into the main room and seated in front of a shock generator. This impressive machine has thirty levers in a horizontal line. The levers range from 15 to 450 volts in 15-volt increments. In addition, signs clearly indicate each group of four levers: *Slight shock, Moderate shock, Strong shock, Very strong shock, Intense shock, Extreme intensity shock,* and *Danger: severe shock.* The last two levers after this point are simply marked *XXX*. When a lever is pressed, a red pilot light is illuminated, an electronic buzzing is heard, a blue light labeled "Voltage Energizer" flashes, a dial on the voltage meter swings to the right, and various relay clicks are sounded. In order that he may have some idea of the intensity of shocks he will be delivering, the teacher is given a sample shock of 45 volts. The shock is delivered by pressing the third lever on the generator, and it stings considerably.

The teacher's task is to administer a shock to the learner each time the learner gives a wrong response; moreover, he is told to move one level higher on the shock generator each time the learner makes a wrong answer. He is also told to announce verbally the voltage level before administering a shock. After a trial run to get familiar with the machinery, the teacher is given a list of word pairs and is told to go through it with the learner. He then goes back through the list, giving shocks until the learner can pair all words correctly. Each shock should be 15 volts stronger than the previous one.

Initially the learner does not do very well, missing about three-quarters of the items (performing at a chance level). More bothersome, he doesn't seem to be improving. He keeps missing three-quarters of the items, and the teacher has to deliver stronger and stronger shocks. When the teacher pushes the 300-volt lever, the learner pounds on the wall of the room but doesn't respond at all. In many cases, the teacher may ask the experimenter what to do, since the learner is no longer responding. The experimenter tells him to treat the absence of a response as a wrong response and to shock the learner according to the usual schedule. On the next item, the 315-volt level, the learner again pounds on the wall but doesn't press any of the answer buttons. For the remainder of the experiment, the learner is not heard from at all.

What would you do if you were the teacher in this situation? Would you continue to deliver increasingly severe shocks until the 450-volt (*XXX*) level is reached? Or would you, at some point, refuse to comply with the experimenter's instructions to continue?

Milgram described this procedure in detail to forty psychiatrists at a leading medical school; they predicted that less than 1 percent of the subjects would deliver the highest shock possible (450 volts). A sample of college undergraduates made similar predictions [307]. So the general expectation was that only the most sadistic or unusual subjects would deliver shocks until the most powerful level was reached.

But Milgram's findings showed otherwise. In his original study, twenty-six out of forty subjects (65 percent) went all the way to the 450-volt level. This does not imply that subjects enjoyed their participation or remained cool while delivering punishment to the learner. On the contrary, most subjects indicated that they wanted to end the experiment and spare the learner further pain. But the experimenter would not "let" them. If the subject suggested or pleaded that they stop (this often happened at the 300-volt level), the experimenter would reply, "Please continue," or "Please go on." If the subject continued to protest, the experimenter would say, "The experiment requires that you continue," or, "It is absolutely essential that you continue." If protests continued or recurred, the experimenter might say, "You have no other choice, you *must* go on." (Of course, the subjects *did* have a choice; they could have walked out at any time.) If the subject asked who would take the responsibility if serious injury occurred, the experimenter assured the subject that he, the experimenter, would take all responsibility. If the subject asked if the learner was likely to suffer permanent physical injury, the experimenter said, "Although the shocks may be painful, there is no permanent tissue damage, so please go on." These "prods" and assurances from the experimenter were powerful factors in increasing obedience from the subjects.

What happens after the experiment? Either the teacher quits and refuses to continue at some point in the experiment, or he delivers the highest shock possible. In either case, after this point he is told that the experimental setup was not what it seemed to be. He is shown that the shock generator is not real and that the sample shock he received was actually delivered from a battery hidden in the fake machine. He is also shown that the learner was not actually receiving any shocks and was really an accomplice of the experimenter. The learner emerges from the room smiling and relaxed, and discusses the experiment with the teacher. What would your reaction to this information be? We will return to this issue a little later.

But *why* would any subject continue to deliver shocks after it was clear that he was giving pain to another person, a person who was doing nothing worse than failing to learn a list of word pairs?

Perhaps one point of considerable importance is that it's an *experiment.* We mentioned earlier the widespread findings that people will do some pretty unusual things "for the sake of science." And the "teacher" had been assured in this case that he was helping to obtain scientific knowledge about the effects of punishment. Perhaps an additional factor is that the experiment was conducted at Yale, a prestigious institution, in the very impressive Yale Interaction Laboratory. The fact that the designations of teacher and learner were (supposedly) random may have made it easier for the teacher to justify his behavior. The financial payment does not seem to have been important, though. All subjects were paid before the experiment began; they were told that the money was theirs for showing up at the laboratory, whether or not they actually completed the experiment. Certainly the prods and assurances from the experimenter played a major role in eliciting maximum cooperation.

But why shouldn't subjects (teachers) stop? The money was theirs anyway, and since they were not students, there was no way people at Yale could retaliate against them for leaving. In addition, most subjects probably didn't have much interest or involvement in the issue of punishment and learning. Furthermore, the learner himself obviously did not want to continue to participate, had pounded on the wall twice to be let out of the experiment, and had refused to respond beyond the 300-volt level. Yet, remarkably, these reasons were not sufficient to motivate people to quit the experiment in most cases.

Other situational variables

There are several ways in which a situation like the one described above could be modified to assess the effect of other variables on the amount of obedience which occurred. In a later series of experiments, Milgram [306; 307] varied the following four major aspects of the experimental situation to see how they would affect the degree of obedience: (1) closeness of the victim, (2) immediacy of the authority figure, (3) prestige of the sponsoring institution, and (4) amount of group pressure.

Closeness of the victim. Milgram used four levels of proximity in his studies. In the *remote-feedback* condition the victim (learner) was in another room and could not be heard or seen by the subject until, when the 300-volt level was reached, the victim pounded on the wall. After 315 volts, the learner no longer answered or made any noise. (This is the basic experimental setup described above.) The second condition, the *voice-*

feedback condition, was identical to the first except that the learner made vocal protests that could be heard through the wall and through a slightly open doorway between the rooms. In the third, or *proximity,* condition, the learner was placed 1½ feet from the subject in the same room. Thus both visual and audible clues to the victim's pain were available to the subject. Finally, Milgram carried out a *touch-proximity* condition. This condition was identical to the proximity condition except that, beyond the 150-volt level, the victim momentarily refused to put his hand on the shock plate. Thus, on every subsequent trial, the experimenter ordered the subject to *force* the victim's hand onto the shock plate. A plastic shield prevented the teacher from receiving the shock. The learner in these last two conditions was a trained actor.

A different set of forty adult males participated in each of the four conditions. The percentages of men who obeyed the experimenter (administered the highest shock) were as follows: remote-feedback, 65 percent; voice-feedback, 62.5 percent; proximity, 40 percent; and touch-proximity, 30 percent. Thus, when the victim is closer, more subjects refuse to obey. As many soldiers have reported, it is much easier to drop bombs on an unseen enemy than to have to kill an individual enemy soldier, even though the amount of death and suffering caused may be much greater in the more remote (bombing) situation.

Immediacy of the authority figure. Milgram completed additional studies in which he varied the closeness of the authority figure to the subject. In one condition the experimenter sat only a few feet from the subject. In a second condition the experimenter was present at the beginning to give initial instructions but then left the room, using a telephone for further instructions.

Obedience was almost three times more frequent when the experimenter remained physically present. Moreover, when the experimenter was absent, several subjects administered shocks of a lower voltage than they were supposed to. This response clearly violated the stated purpose of the experiment (the effect of punishment on learning), but perhaps it was easier for the subject to handle conflict in this way than to openly defy the experimenter.

Prestige of the sponsoring institution. As we suggested earlier, a large part of the obedience might be accounted for by the fact that the research took place at Yale University, in Milgram's words, "an institution of unimpeachable reputation." To check this factor, Milgram conducted the experiment again, this time in downtown Bridgeport, Connecticut. The sponsor of the study was supposedly Research Associates of Bridgeport, and the three-room office suite was in a "somewhat run-down commercial building located in the downtown shopping area" [307, p. 70]. Subjects again were paid $4.50 for their participation. Even under these conditions, almost half (48 percent) the subjects delivered the maximum shock possible. This is not quite as many as had done so at Yale, but it is close enough to suggest that the prestige of the sponsoring institution was not crucially important.

Effects of group pressure. To assess the effects of group pressure, Milgram ran two additional studies with three accomplices instead of one. Of course, the real subject believed that he and the other three participants were all real subjects. The experimenter explained that three teachers and one learner would be utilized. The (real) subject "by chance" became teacher 3; two of the accomplices became teachers 1 and 2, and the other became the learner. Teacher 3 was the person who actually pushed the shock level each time. In one study both accomplice-teachers were *obedient;* they followed the experimenter's commands and neither showed sympathy for the victim nor commented on his apparent discomfort. Such obedient models did not strongly affect the number of real subjects willing to deliver the maximum shock. In this experiment twenty-nine out of forty subjects went all the way to 450 volts; this proportion is not significantly greater than the twenty-six of forty found in Milgram's original study.

In a second variation, the two teacher-accomplices were *defiant.* One accomplice refused to continue after the 150-volt level, and the other refused to continue past the 210-volt level. In contrast to the findings in the "obedient" condition, the defiance of the accomplices apparently had a major effect on real subjects. In this study only 10 percent (four out of forty) of the real subjects continued all the way and eventually delivered the maximum shock. Yet interestingly enough, three-fourths of the thirty-six subjects who refused to go all the way claimed that they would have stopped even *without* the other teachers' (accomplices') example. The results of Milgram's other studies strongly suggest that this is not so, although the subjects may have honestly believed that it was.

Still other variations

Milgram carried out still other variations of these obedience studies [309]. One study used women as subjects; the obedience rate was precisely the same (65 percent) as it had been with men (the learner was still male). In another study, the teacher could *choose* the level of shock to deliver; only one of forty subjects used the 450-volt level at all.

Perhaps the most important findings occurred where the real subject was assigned to a subsidiary role, where he did not have to press the shock levels himself. In this situation, over 90 percent of the subjects (thirty-seven out of forty) stayed with the experiment through the 450-volt level. So most adults seem to be quite willing to participate in a situation which involves pain as long as *they* are not the ones who inflict it.

Ethical considerations

We have described the prison study and the obedience studies in some detail so that you might imagine what it would have been like to take part.

We did this first because from only a brief description of the study you might find it unbelievable that "ordinary" people would have done such things. Second, we want you to give some thought to the research ethics involved with such studies.

Participation in such studies is obviously a very powerful experience, much more powerful than the average psychology experiment. What were subjects expecting? Whatever it was, it probably was much less, emotionally, than they received. Subjects in the prison experiment were given a description of what to expect—namely, that they would role-play prisoners and guards. But they (and apparently the experimenters, too) were utterly unprepared for the intensity of the experiences that followed. The framework of Milgram's experiment was not described to subjects until they had arrived at the laboratory and had accepted money for their participation. In both cases it could be argued that the experiments were unfair to the participants because they got far more than they had been led to expect, whether or not they wanted it.

As we mentioned earlier, college students and psychiatrists thought that virtually no one (presumably including themselves) would go all the way in the original Milgram experiment. Probably few if any of the "guards" in the prison experiment expected that they would engage in abusive, sadistic behavior. These conceptions are alien to a "healthy" self-concept. But what about after participation? The guard in the prison experiment knows that he *did* engage in abusive, hostile, sadistic behavior. Many of the subjects in Milgram's experiments found out that they *would* continue to obey the experimenter and deliver apparently severe electric shocks to a helpless cosubject. What is likely to be the effect of such knowledge on one's self-concept? Perhaps devastating. The subject finds out that he is perhaps not so different from others whose behavior he has condemned utterly. He finds that he is not a pillar of strength and not as resistant to pressure as he thought he was.

Milgram, Zimbardo, and many other psychologists have argued that such knowledge is valuable. Perhaps it gives the subjects a greater understanding of human behavior, particularly of their own. To illustrate, in October 1970 a young man who had been a subject in one of Milgram's studies wrote to Milgram [309, p. 200]:

When I was a subject in 1964, though I believed that I was hurting someone, I was totally unaware of why I was doing so. Few people ever realize when they are acting according to their own beliefs and when they are meekly submitting to authority. . . . To permit myself to be drafted [into the army] with the understanding that I am submitting to authority's demand to do something very wrong would make me frightened of myself. . . . I am fully prepared to go to jail if I am not granted Conscientious Objector status. . . .

The young man later wrote that although his draft board did not seem very impressed with the effect of his participation in the experiment, he was granted status as a conscientious objector nonetheless. But, then again, subjects did not bargain for such self-knowledge when they entered the experiment, particularly Milgram's experiments. They were not asking for drastic and perhaps depressing insights into their own psyche. Some have argued that, because this was not part of the original bargain, it was unfair to the subjects [40]. The letter quoted above suggests, on the other hand, that such self-knowledge might be the most valuable that could be received. Zimbardo [512] reports that some participants in his study later volunteered vacation time to work in local prisons, and most have become advocates of penal reform as a result of their "prison" experience.

We mentioned that Zimbardo and his coworkers carried out a thorough debriefing process. Milgram also carried out an extensive follow-up study to see whether participation in the experiments had any long-lasting effects on subjects. Of the subjects contacted after participation, 84 percent indicated they were glad to have taken part in the research, 15 percent reported neutral feelings, and only 1 percent reported they regretted having taken part. Four-fifths of the subjects felt that more experiments of this sort should be carried out. Some caution should be used in interpreting these figures, however. People who have done something unpleasant (such as administering shocks to others) may be motivated later to justify their behavior to themselves, regardless of what they first thought of the experiment. Therefore, to make themselves feel better about what they have done, ambivalent or neutral subjects may decide that it was a worthwhile, valuable experience (both for them and for the learner). A university psychiatrist also interviewed a sample of people who had taken part in Milgram's studies and was unable to find evidence of any injurious effects resulting from participation [305; 307].

Watergate on campus

While the Milgram and Zimbardo studies have shown how normal persons may injure or mistreat others in some situations, another recent study provides evidence that normal college students may also be quite susceptible to pressures like those that stimulated the break-ins which precipitated the Watergate scandal.

College students were contacted individually by a local private investigator, who told them that he had "a project you might be interested in" and got them to agree to meet at his home or a restaurant. There the investigator outlined elaborate plans for breaking into a local advertising firm. The plans (which included blueprints, aerial photographs, and lists of city and state police patrol cars and their routes and times) involved a four-person "team"; the student was asked to be the fourth member of the team. The private eye stressed that the plans were "foolproof," and he and his assistant put considerable pressure on the student to join them.

Some students were told that the burglary was secretly sponsored by the Internal Revenue Service. The advertising firm had been keeping illegal financial records, they were told, which defrauded the government of $6.8 million. The "team's" task would be to microfilm those records; this would enable the government later to obtain a search warrant and subpoena. The student's specific task would be to serve as the inside lookout and to actually microfilm the records. Students were told that the government promised them total immunity from prosecution if something went wrong and they were caught. This situation was designed to parallel the Watergate situation as closely as possible. A second set of students were given the same explanation except that no mention of immunity from prosecution was made.

The break-in was described to a third set of students as sponsored by another advertising firm, rather than by the Internal Revenue Service. In this case, students were told they would get $2,000 for participating. Finally, a fourth group of students was told that the break-in was the private investigator's own idea and was merely to see whether his plans would really work. Nothing would be stolen or disturbed.

The situation was designed to elicit as much cooperation as possible. Each student was first induced to commit himself or herself to attending the meeting (foot-in-the-door), and was faced with a unanimous majority (the private eye and his assistant) which had great expertise (the detailed plans and knowledge). Faced with this pressure, 20 percent of the students who were told to expect payment of $2,000 agreed to participate; 10 percent agreed to participate when the break-in was merely to test the plans. Only 5 percent agreed when the break-in was sponsored by the IRS but no immunity was mentioned. However, when immunity was promised, almost half of the students contacted (45 percent) agreed to take part. There were no differences between sexes in willingness to participate. After each subject had either agreed or refused to take part, the entire experiment was explained to them and the reasons for the deception were discussed. Thus, no one actually engaged in illegal activities [489; 106a].

These results provide further evidence that in a situation which encourages compliance, many presumably law-abiding citizens can be induced to actively participate in illegal activities when the activities are apparently sponsored by the government *and* immunity from prosecution is promised. This suggests that it might not be difficult to find many people, even on a college campus, who would agree to take part in illegal, Watergate-type spying activities.

■ IMPLICATIONS

Is everyone a potential Eichmann?

The quotations from Eichmann, Keitel, and Calley all speak of "following orders" as a reasonable explanation for their behavior. Historically, such explanations have usually been rejected by others as self-serving rationalizations. The evidence we have presented suggests that such rejection may not be entirely justified. Perhaps these men *were* just following orders. And perhaps, furthermore, many of us might have done the same kinds of things if we were in a situation which seemed to demand such behavior. This might be particularly likely if we have been brought up in a culture where strict obedience to authority was stressed, such as in post-World War I Germany.

These quotations focus on situations of military-related atrocities. Indeed, Milgram [304, p. 371] has commented:

Gas chambers were built, death camps were guarded, daily quotas of corpses were produced with the same efficiency as the manufacture of appliances. These inhumane policies may have originated in the mind of a single person, but they could only be carried out on a massive scale if a very large number of persons obeyed orders.

Some researchers have proposed that Milgram has identified the "latent Eichmann" residing in most of us [146]. The shocking atrocities apparently committed by "ordinary" American soldiers in the late 1960s provide compelling evidence of the possible relevance of Milgram's findings. For example, columnist Stanley Karnow [237] has suggested that Milgram's original experiment was "remarkably prescient. He demonstrated in the laboratory what Lt. William Calley and his unit would later dramatize at My Lai—that man's behavior is almost invariably dominated by authority rather than by his own sense of morality." Karnow quotes Milgram as commenting: "If we now recoil at our own conduct it is because we are just as capable as the Nazis of committing crimes in the name of obedience." Is this so? Is your behavior "almost always" dominated by authority, and are you and the people you know "just as capable as the Nazis" of committing such crimes?

H. V. Dicks [125] interviewed a number of former officers from Nazi concentration camps and Gestapo units. He felt that there were clear parallels between their reasoning and the reasoning of subjects in Milgram's obedience studies. Dicks noted similarities in the need to devalue a victim and see him as deserving his fate and the adoption of a "helpless cog" attitude as a moral defense (the claim that they were "just following orders" while being convinced of the wrongness of what they "had" to do). Dicks believes that Milgram's work indicates that some of the same ego defenses used by the SS and Gestapo men were used as justifications by Milgram's "ordinary" subjects in the U.S. twenty years later.

The impact of the situation: There but for the grace of God go I

The research findings we have discussed illustrate the tremendous impact of situational forces—forces leading to obedience to authority or forces that place people in specific roles—on human behavior, yours and ours, as well as that of military officers and Watergate burglars. The studies above, and others like them, suggest that situational pressures are far more important than most of us like to think.

Although we all like to think of ourselves as free souls and independent of situational restraints, this is often not the case. Zimbardo, Haney, Banks, and Jaffee [513, p. 21], have proposed:

Therefore, it is time psychologists stopped offering legislators, lawmen and lay people "traits," "dispositions" and "individual differences" as reasonable solutions to existing problems in our society. To change behavior we must discover the institutional supports which maintain the existing undesirable behavior and then design programs to alter the environments.

■ IS THERE A CONFORMING OR OBEDIENT PERSONALITY?

The personality variable of authoritarianism was the only one (of the many which were measured) that predicted whether or not prisoners would be "successful" in lasting the entire six-day period in Zimbardo's prison study. Those prisoners who scored high on authoritarianism were more likely to have lasted the six days. Milgram also gave a number of personality measures to persons who participated in his obedience studies. Of all of them, only a measure of authoritarianism, once again, was able to predict the amount of obedience shown. People high in authoritarianism were more likely to complete the experiments than people low in authoritarianism [141]. A second study contacted a few subjects who had taken part in Milgram's experiment and administered a scale of moral development to them [249]. It was found that of the subjects in the middle stages of moral development, over 85 percent had complied and gone all the way in the Milgram setup. Of the subjects at the highest levels of moral development, only 25 percent had gone all the way. Although this study was unfortunately based on a relatively small number of people (thirty-four), the results are intriguing. Nevertheless, with the exceptions of these relationships, researchers have had little success in predicting such compliance behaviors on the basis of personality characteristics.

We outlined a little earlier the personality characteristics which tended to accompany conformity in several experiments: low intelligence and low self-esteem. Yet the above findings of the prison study and Milgram's studies seem to suggest that personality characteristics are of little value in predicting conformity or obedience. Is that really the case? Can we identify something called the "conforming" or "obedient personality"? In discussions of the Watergate scandal there were many suggestions that some of the participants had such conforming personalities.

Richard Crutchfield [113] extended Asch's work by assessing conforming or nonconforming responses from a large group of men on twenty-one different conformity-related tasks of various types. The degree of conformity he observed was not an all-or-none picture; virtually no one conformed all the time or none of the time. The amount of conformity observed varied widely with the nature of the task. For example, only 2 percent of the subjects made the conforming response on a task requiring an aesthetic judgment, while the conforming response was observed 79 percent of the time for one of the tasks requiring a logical judgment. Summing up both tasks and people, conforming responses were observed about 40 percent of the time. Only a modest degree of cross-situational consistency was found. Subjects who conformed on one type of item tended to be more likely to conform on other items than did nonconformers, but the relationship was not very strong.

Crutchfield found evidence that subjects who conformed least were likely to be high on intellectual effectiveness, ego-strength, leadership ability, and maturity of social relations, and low on authoritarianism. This sounds almost too consistent to be true, a notion that the nonconformers are the "good guys" in all respects. Counteracting this trend somewhat, no overall difference in degree of psychological adjustment was found between those who tended to conform and those who tended not to conform.

■ CONFORMITY AND COMPLIANCE IN TODAY'S SOCIETY

Many analysts have suggested that the general levels of conformity and compliance to arbitrary power within our society have decreased in recent years. This is despite vivid evidence that our governmental structure may still react arbitrarily and oppressively to "activists" of various sorts (blacks, Indians, women, homosexuals, students, etc.) who attempt to "rock the boat." Governmental responses in terms of wire-tapping, bugging, surveillance, and "preventive detention" make it clear that freedom to dissent is by no means desired by many Americans. The studies discussed in Focus 8-4 provide evidence on the inconsistency between American ideals and practices with regard to the toleration of dissent. Note that, contrary to general expectations, governmental officials were actually *more* tolerant of dissent (at least verbally) than was the "average" American in these surveys.

Despite these troubling findings, it has been proposed that pressures for conformity and compliance are probably less today than in the past. M. Brewster Smith [413] has suggested that four general characteristics stand out in the social-historical analysis of compliance and conformity in American society. The first characteristic is a general *decline of authoritarianism.* There is a lessening tendency to unquestioningly obey arbitrary authority such as family, church, and state. Accompanying this tendency has been a *waning of the "Protestant Ethic"* [485], less commitment to the values of self-sacrifice, hard work, reliance on inner authority, self-denial, and asceticism. In the Protestant Ethic, ideal persons would be devoted to their work, postponing gratification to the future, conserving assets and belongings, and saving surplus wealth in order to extend (capitalistic) economic enterprise.

A third characteristic of modern society, according to Smith, is what he calls a *failure of community.* This refers to the relative absence of common experiences, interests, and values, and the lack of a sense of common fate in our present society. Large gaps exist between persons differing in race, age, education, nationality, political orientation, and other characteristics.

FOCUS 8-4   TOLERANCE FOR DISSENT IN AMERICA

Among the cornerstones of American democracy are an emphasis on freedom of speech and behavior and maintenance of the rights of all Americans, both minority and majority group members. And, in theory, the American public supports such tenets: Prothro and Grigg [354] reported that over 95 percent of the people they asked agreed with the statement: "The minority should be free to criticize majority decisions." Similarly, McClosky [292] found 89 percent agreeing to "I believe in free speech for all, no matter what their views might be."

But when things become more specific, tolerance for opposing viewpoints becomes fragile. The same atmosphere which led to the legal abuses of the Watergate affair also contributed to a frighteningly narrow view of what is acceptable dissent. You may recall that an "enemies list" was discovered in 1973, containing the names of many prominent Americans who had questioned some of the policies of the Nixon Administration. In the view of those people who created and maintained the list, dissent was *not* to be tolerated; rather, anyone who dissented with administration policies was an "enemy."

Survey research has demonstrated that tolerance for minority viewpoints is not generally acceptable to many Americans. In a 1954 survey of community leaders and the general public [430], it was found that only 27 percent of the general public answered yes to the following question:

Suppose an admitted Communist wants to make a speech in your community. Should he be allowed to speak, or not?

Interestingly, a considerably greater portion of community leaders (51 percent) answered yes to the question than did the general public. Hence, community leaders appeared to be more protective of freedom of speech than was the general public. Comparing the responses of the general public with those of delegates to the 1956 national political conventions, McClosky [292] found that the convention delegates' responses were more likely to be protective of the "rules of the game" and of minority rights than were the responses of the general public.

The first ten amendments to the American Constitution, the Bill of Rights, have been viewed as an exalted document, a statement of values basic to the sociopolitical standards of our country. One researcher [284] drew up a list of questions which asked about all ten amendments in the Bill of Rights and then asked college students whether they agreed or disagreed with the items. At one extreme, about 95 percent of the students agreed with the principle of the Sixth Amendment, that a person should be informed of legal accusations made against him or her. Over 82 percent of the college students agreed with the principle of freedom of speech and the press. But agreement with some other aspects of the Bill of Rights was less widespread. Only six of the fourteen items were able to muster a two-thirds majority among college students. Interestingly, there were no differences in extent of agreement with the Bill of Rights between students labeling themselves as Democrats or Republicans, or between students labeling themselves "liberals" or "conservatives."

After reading the fourteen statements, fewer than 10 percent of the college students realized that they had been evaluating the Bill of Rights. The significant findings of this study, in the researcher's eyes, are: "The considerable body of disagreement and indecision regarding what had been considered basic civil rights, and the impressive ignorance of educated people regarding the constitutional provisions for these rights" [284, p. 268]. Indeed, if we are living in a time where the Bill of Rights goes unrecognized and unlamented, the atmosphere which encouraged the "White House horrors" of the Watergate scandal becomes a little more imaginable.

There is considerable evidence that such gaps have widened, psychologically as well as actually, in recent years.

This failure of community, coupled with the decline of authoritarianism and of the Protestant Ethic, leads to the fourth characteristic proposed by Smith, which he calls the *exposure of the individual*. He is referring to the individual's moral exposure; in today's world we are on our own, without benefit of customary supports and guidelines for appropriate or required attitudes, values, and behaviors. While such exposure is indeed a kind of freedom, it is a freedom that is difficult to handle, as many modern philosophers and social scientists have noted in some detail.

More than fifty years ago, Harold Laski [259] wrote:

Civilization means, above all, an unwillingness to inflict unnecessary pain. Within the ambit of that definition, those of us who heedlessly accept the commands of authority cannot yet claim to be civilized men.

Our business, if we desire to live a life not utterly devoid of meaning and significance, is to accept nothing which contradicts our basic experience, merely because it comes to us from tradition, or authority. It may well be that we shall be wrong; but our self-expression is thwarted at the root unless the certainties we are asked to accept coincide with the certainties we experience. That is why the condition of freedom in any state is always a widespread and consistent skepticism of the canons upon which power insists.

The lessons from war and Watergate, as well as from the psychological laboratory, point to a basic facet of human behavior: We are all quite susceptible to pressures, direct or subtle, to conform or comply with the wishes of others. The choice of whether to accede to these pressures is still ours, but it is often a terribly difficult one.

■ SUMMARY

Concepts of conformity, obedience, and compliance 'all relate to social-influence processes, the effect that roles, norms, and the expectations or demands of another person may have on an individual's behavior. Conformity has been defined as yielding to group pressure; the antithesis of conformity can be viewed either as anticonformity or independence. Conformity may occur as a response to normative influence or to informational influence.

The work of Sherif, Asch, and others has demonstrated some of the conditions under which conformity may occur. Research has indicated that characteristics of the group—such as group size and the status, similarity, and expertise of group members—will affect the amount of conformity that will occur. In addition, the behavior of group members will influence the degree of conformity.

Compliance has been defined as changing behavior to fit an expressed expectation, request, or demand made by someone else. Social scientists have been most concerned with situations in which compliance has led directly to harm or death to other people, such as atrocities during wartime.

Research has indicated that rewards and punishments, as well as certain individual states such as guilt and desire to restore equity, may increase the likelihood of compliance. Even more powerful as determinants of compliance are roles and situational pressures. Both the prison study carried out by Zimbardo and his coworkers and Milgram's studies about hurting on command have vividly demonstrated that ordinary, well-adjusted people may behave in seemingly cruel ways when the situation seems to demand it. Milgram's many additional studies show the importance of the closeness of the victim, the immediacy of the authority figure, and group pressure, in increasing or decreasing the amount of compliance likely to occur.

Attempts to identify components of a conforming or obedient personality have indicated that such a simplified picture is perhaps not appropriate. A measure of authoritarianism was the only one which was related to behavior in both the Zimbardo and Milgram studies. Persons scoring high in authoritarianism were likely to have lasted the entire six days as prisoners; persons high in authoritarianism were more likely to go all the way and deliver the highest shock in Milgram's studies. None of the other personality measures used in these two sets of studies was able to consistently predict behavior.

It has been proposed that pressures for compliance and conformity are less powerful today than in the past. Smith has proposed that this results from a general decline in authoritarianism, coupled with a waning of the Protestant Ethic, a failure of community, and the consequent "moral exposure" of the individual.

9

group dynamics

concepts

A group exists whenever two or more people interact and influence each other's behavior; groups are unitary entities, are organized, and are held together by the common interests and goals of the members.

Groupthink can occur in highly cohesive groups and can produce a deterioration of mental efficiency, reality testing, and moral judgment.

Groups can perform at better levels than those of the average individual; a pooling of abilities sometimes occurs wherein groups perform even better than the "best" group member would alone.

The social climate of a group affects its interactions, the feelings of its members, and conformity to its norms.

The structure of a group, in terms of status distributions and communication networks, affects its satisfaction and productivity.

Leadership is best viewed in terms of the interaction between a leader's personality and the group situation.

targets

After studying this chapter, you should be able to:

1   Give examples of groupthink from group experiences you've had.
2   Describe how to minimize groupthink.
3   Explain how the presence of others affects one's motivation and performance.
4   Cite examples of problems which you would prefer to work on when alone and when in a group.
5   Summarize the effects of cohesiveness on group activities.
6   Discuss how you would structure an "ideal" group in terms of status distributions and communication patterns.
7   Discuss the concept of leadership.

Groups exert a profound influence on our lives. At any particular time, we consider ourselves members of numerous groups of different sizes and types—say, a fraternity or sorority at college, a group of friends who get together informally but consistently for weekend parties, groups in the community. Many kinds of social influences originate in such groups. Usually, we obey the rules and submit to social pressures, yet we often perceive our behaviors to result from personal preferences, not from external influences. We also tend to view many group rules (such as the rules of a religious group) as indicative of the "right" or "appropriate" way for *everyone* to live, not just of the ways people within the group should behave. Many rules which were developed to ease the functioning of a particular group at one point in time are perceived by group members to be applicable to everyone, everywhere, at all times.

We will consider a *group* to exist whenever two or more people interact with each other and influence each other's behavior [400]. This definition is useful because it allows us to consider many different kinds of situations which most people would describe as examples of group behavior. Having defined a group in this way, though, it is important to add that many social psychologists consider other aspects and qualities of groups essential in understanding group behavior.

1 We perceive a group to be a single, *unitary entity,* even though we recognize that it is composed of numerous separate individuals. The individuals in a group may come and go, enter and leave, and yet the group norms and rules may remain very much the same. This is another way of saying that a group is more than the sum of its parts, since its nature may stay very much the same despite changes in membership.
2 Groups are held together by *common interests and goals* of group members. People join groups for a reason, and these reasons are important in understanding how a particular group functions.
3 Groups are *organized* to a greater or lesser degree. Each member has specific duties and roles to fulfill in order to ensure the group's survival.

These different aspects of groups will be examined throughout this chapter.

■ GROUPTHINK: A CASE STUDY IN GROUP DECISION MAKING

The Bay of Pigs

To begin our examination of group behavior, consider how one particular group, President John F. Kennedy's Executive Committee in 1961, went about solving a problem it faced. The problem happened soon after Kennedy's inauguration, when the group was still evolving and discovering how to attack problems as a unit. The members of the group respected one another and felt honored to be included in the elite body. Each member's credentials were impressive, and each member had certain jobs to perform and particular areas of competence. The group was highly organized; its leader was clear—President Kennedy. By examining how this group functioned in one instance, many aspects of group dynamics will be illustrated.

In the early 1960s, American friendship toward Fidel Castro had cooled, and Communist influence in Cuba was viewed with great dissatisfaction in Washington. In March 1960, Vice President Richard M. Nixon had requested that the CIA look into the feasibility of sending an armed and trained group of Cuban exiles to Cuba to lead a resistance movement and possibly overthrow the Castro regime. When Kennedy took office in January 1961, the CIA's plan had been completed; Kennedy's Executive Committee had to decide whether or not the United States should support the proposed Cuban invasion. The Committee acted quickly, and on Apr. 17, 1961, the invasion was launched. It has been said that the results of this decision rank "among the worst fiascoes ever perpetrated by a responsible government" [226, p. 14].

The consequences: A fiasco revisited

The consequences of the Committee's decision were disastrous in terms of lives lost, money spent, and the subsequent threat to United States security and its loss of credibility. Of the 1,400 Cuban exiles who were trained, equipped, and sent on the invasion mission, 200 died. The remaining 1,200 who landed at the Bay of Pigs spent seven months in Cuban prison camps before being ransomed by the United States for food and drugs worth $53 million.

The incident had enormous international repercussions. Feeling even more threatened than before, Castro was pushed into closer rapprochement with the Soviet Union. Within eighteen months, Soviet Premier Krushchev sent nuclear weapons, missiles, and technicians to Cuba, claiming that Castro needed such "defensive" weapons (which actually were quite offensive) to protect Cuba from future United States invasions. The missiles precipitated the Cuban missile crisis—the "13 days" in October 1962, when the world waited on the brink of nuclear war as a result of the confrontation between the United States and the Soviet Union.

The credibility of Adlai Stevenson, the respected and trusted American Ambassador to the United Nations, was shattered when he denied (under orders) that the United States had been involved in the Bay of Pigs invasion. It eventually was learned that United States frogmen were the first to land on Cuban shores (against Kennedy's orders), that American B-26s stripped of United States markings were used in air attacks, that CIA agents recruited dissident Cuban exiles in Miami and trained and equipped them in Guatemala, and that Nicaragua had agreed to allow the United States to use its air bases to launch air attacks.

What went wrong?

The Executive Committee made dozens of mistakes in reaching its final decision to support the invasion. It made assumptions that could have been refuted easily if anyone had checked relevant information and spoken out in the group; yet Committee members failed to gather the relevant information. For example, the Committee assumed that even if the invasion failed, the exiles could retreat to the Escambray mountains and join up with small bands of rebels who were fighting against Castro. Yet the original site of the invasion was changed from a spot near the mountains to the Bay of Pigs, a place that was 80 miles away from the mountains, separated by a tangle of uncrossable swamps. If the Committee had taken the time to study a map, they would have realized that retreat was impossible. They also did not go out of their way to learn what experts in Cuban and Latin American affairs thought of the plan; the Committee seemed so secure in their belief that the decision was a good one, that they excluded outside experts (who would have pointed out major flaws in the plan). For example, the Committee assumed that a large-scale popular uprising against Castro would be touched off by the invasion; yet experts in Latin American affairs were aware of opinion polls that indicated general satisfaction with Castro's leadership and little desire to overthrow him. The group also overlooked details, and as all planners know, a plan will succeed or fail depending on its details.

Even more generally, the Committee failed to consider alternative courses of action. Their discussions focused only on whether or not to launch the invasion. Whenever a group (or person) fails to consider many alternatives, an artificial limitation is imposed on their flexibility, and the ultimate results are likely to be of lesser quality. This group also failed to reconsider its initial decisions to see whether they looked different the next day.

In sum, the method by which the Committee reached its decision was poor. They closed themselves off from the outside. They failed to consider alternatives and to gather information. They overlooked important details. They had a false sense of security which lulled them into carelessness. In all, their decision was shoddy.

Victims of groupthink

Irving Janis [226] studied documented accounts of numerous domestic and foreign group decisions, some of which produced fiascoes like the Bay of Pigs or the escalation of the Vietnam War and some of which produced successes like the resolution of the Cuban missile crisis. Janis concluded that the bad decisions were produced, at least in part, by *groupthink,* and that groupthink was avoided in successful group decisions. Groupthink is a process that occurs in highly cohesive groups; the group members' striving for consensus is so strong that it jeopardizes independent, critical thinking. Group members fail to check information; they become blind to moral concerns; and they can't see beyond the secure boundaries of the group situation. In short, an atmosphere is created in the group that results in deterioration of mental efficiency, reality testing, and moral judgment.

Groupthink can have disastrous consequences for a group's decision-making abilities, but it occurs for a reason. When a challenging, important decision confronts a group, it presents a potential *threat to the self-esteem* of the members. Group decisions can cost lives and money; at the very least, a bad decision can produce great embarrassment for group members. Groupthink is a defense mechanism which allows group members to protect themselves from such threats. By striving for consensus and unanimity, the group members can feel more secure in a decision; they can reason, "All the other group members feel the same way, so we must be correct." By going along, and by convincing themselves that they are conforming not simply because of pressure but because the group is correct, they minimize threats of social disapproval and self-disapproval. They derive "collective strength" from the group and share the responsibility for potential failure.

To gain consensus, though, group members often blind themselves to contradictory information; they conform unquestioningly to the group; they minimize their own doubts about the group's decision; they seal themselves off from the outside; and they rationalize.

Symptoms of groupthink: The signs of faulty group functioning

Janis listed eight *symptoms of groupthink:* these are the trouble signs which indicate that a group may be headed toward disaster. All groups may display one or more of these symptoms at one time or another, but groupthink is evidenced only when most or all of them occur together.

1 *Illusion of invulnerability.* On the day of the Bay of Pigs invasion, Robert Kennedy stated, "It seemed that, with John Kennedy leading us and with all the talent he had assembled, nothing could stop us. We believed that if we faced up to the nation's problems and applied bold, new ideas with common sense and hard work, we would overcome whatever challenged us" [193, p. 88]. Clearly, the decision makers felt that luck and invincibility were theirs. They perceived that they were unbeatable and that even if they did make one or two "minor mistakes," everything would work out in the end. Unfortunately, such perceptions can spell disaster. They give a false sense of security and cause one to minimize or overlook minor problems which may actually be major ones, or may become major. Caution is thrown to the wind, and one walks steadfastly down the barrel of a cannon. This illusion is similar to that of the virile self-image discussed in Chapter 1.

2 *Illusions of morality.* During the Committee's deliberations, it was implicitly recognized that the United States was helping democracy and ridding the Western world of the evils of communism. There was an unquestioned belief in the group's inherent morality and "goodness."

(a)

Figure 9-1. *The "best and brightest"—key members of John F. Kennedy's Executive Committee, who made the decisions that resulted in the Bay of Pigs fiasco. Many of them would later help make policy on the war in Vietnam. Pictured are: (a) President John F. Kennedy; (b) Attorney General Robert Kennedy; (c) Secretary of State Dean Rusk, who had been head of the prestigious Rockefeller Foundation and who had served in the State Department during the Truman administration; (d) Secretary of Defense Robert McNamara, an expert statistician who had been President of the Ford Motor Company and, earlier, had been a member of the Business Administration faculty at Harvard; (e) McGeorge Bundy, Special Assistant to the President for National Security Affairs, who had been Dean of Arts and Sciences at Harvard University; and (f) Arthur Schlesinger, Jr., a Harvard historian who had been asked to attend all the meetings.*

(b)

(c)

(d)

(e)

(f)

No one questioned whether it was moral for a large country (the United States) to back an invasion of a small one (Cuba). Similarly, during the Vietnam war, the Johnson and Nixon administrations gave little consideration to the morality of bombing innocent men, women, and children. By assuming self-righteousness, a group does not have to consider the consequences of its actions. This group illusion is similar to the moral self-image discussed in Chapter 1.

3 *Stereotyped views of the enemy as evil, weak, and stupid.* Castro was not given much credit in the Executive Committee meetings; they clearly underestimated him. He was viewed as *evil,* the embodiment of communism on our doorstep. He was viewed as *weak,* as having a dissension-ridden army and air force (which was not true), and as being unable to fight back. He was viewed as *stupid*—for example, as not even having the intelligence to be tipped off by the air attacks twenty-four hours before the invasion and then rounding up subversives on the island to quell a popular revolt. These stereotypes allowed the Committee to take risks which otherwise would have been unacceptable. Again, this stereotype is similar to the evil-enemy image discussed in Chapter 1.

4 *Illusion of unanimity.* A curious illusion of unanimity existed within the Executive Committee. Each member assumed that all the other members were in complete agreement with one another. Insiders indicated that almost no dissent toward the faulty initial plan was ever raised, and that if dissent had existed, the plan probably would have been discarded [389; 419].

5 *Self-censorship of dissenting ideas.* The illusion of unanimity allowed Committee members to suppress personal doubts about the plan. They seemed to assume that since there was a consensus of opinion, it would be silly to object. In his book *Kennedy,* Theodore Sorenson [419] related that "doubts were entertained but never pressed, partly out of a fear of being labelled 'soft' or undaring in the eyes of their colleagues." Each individual felt group pressure to silence objections. This process went even further, in that the group members not only failed to object, but also began to convince themselves that their personal doubts were not valid.

6 *Social pressures of conforming.* Pressures were placed on the Committee members to go along with the presumed consensus, and deviation was quickly chastised. For example, President Kennedy allowed CIA representatives (who strongly favored the plan) to dominate the meetings. When slight criticism was raised by a group member, Kennedy called on the CIA representative to refute the criticism and silence the critic, instead of asking if other group members had the same doubts and encouraging independent thinking. Thus, the meetings were organized to reduce dissent and replace independence with conformity.

7 *The existence of mindguards.* A *mindguard* is someone who protects other group members from ideas that might shake their confidence in the correctness of group solutions [226]. These self-appointed mind-

guards place additional social pressure on the slightest form of deviation from group consensus. For example, on one occasion, Robert Kennedy was informed by Schlesinger of some doubts the latter had about the group's decision. Kennedy took Schlesinger aside and stated, "You may be right or you may be wrong, but the President has made his mind up. Don't push it any further. Now is the time for everyone to help him all they can" [quoted in 226, p. 42].

8 *Rationalizations of warnings.* The Committee members tried to discount or rationalize any warning signs which would indicate that their decision might be a bad one or which would deter them from their favored course of action. For example, the group assumed that a popular uprising would occur in Cuba. They held this assumption despite evidence to the contrary. Another assumption made by the Executive Committee was that no one would discover that the United States was responsible for the invasion. The decision makers did not want the world to learn of United States involvement, fearing it would damage America's image. When newspapers got hold of the story before the invasion, the decision makers began to rationalize away the potentially damaging effects. They reasoned, "Well, if we deny it, our friends will believe us, and our enemies wouldn't have believed us one way or the other, so it doesn't really matter."

Groupthink and its symptoms can be found at one time or another in most groups: discussions between a husband and wife, the student senate at a college or high school, the local PTA meeting, the state legislature, higher branches of government, and so forth. It is not an isolated phenomenon.

It is important to note that the faulty decision making typified by groupthink does not always occur in groups. A short time after the Bay of Pigs incident, Kennedy's Executive Committee faced the momentous decisions which resolved the Cuban missile crisis. It is generally agreed that the way they arrived at decisions during the crisis was singularly impressive. Thus, groupthink can be minimized. Focus 9-1 presents ways in which a group can avoid groupthink. Many of these methods were used by President Kennedy during the Cuban missile crisis—he and his Executive Committee having learned from the Bay of Pigs incident what can go wrong in groups and how to take preventive measures.

Factors that increase groupthink: How to generate a poor group decision without really trying

Janis specifies four factors that increase the tendency for a group to engage in groupthink.

1 The prime condition for groupthink is the *cohesiveness* of the group. Cohesiveness refers to the degree to which members are attracted to a

FOCUS 9-1   PREVENTING GROUPTHINK: A LITTLE INDEPENDENCE, PLEASE

The consensus-seeking of groupthink can be prevented with effort from group members. Irving Janis [226] has discussed several techniques to minimize groupthink. At present, none of these suggestions have been tested, but all are reasonable and appear able to decrease the likelihood that a group will fall victim to groupthink.

1. The leader of a group should avoid making initial statements that reveal his or her preferences and expectations for a solution. If the leader opens meetings with explicit recommendations for a solution and limits the types of suggestions offered, many good ideas may never be expressed. Although it is difficult to avoid communicating biases and preferences, it should be attempted. Otherwise, a leader sets in motion pressures for conformity that will sacrifice openness.

2. A leader should encourage group members to express doubts and objections to the ideas presented. Members should be encouraged to become critical evaluators, and dissent should be held in high regard rather than stifled. Naturally, leaders must be willing to consider criticism; otherwise, they will increase the group members' fears of disapproval and produce the conformity they might wish to avoid.

3. In conjunction with point 2, a different group member should be assigned the role of *devil's advocate* at each meeting. In this context, a devil's advocate plays the unpopular role of attacking premature consensus and challenging existing ideas. During the Cuban missile crisis, President Kennedy assigned his brother Robert the role of devil's advocate and instructed him to challenge any idea, no matter how good it might initially appear to be. The result was the consideration of numerous alternative courses of action and a thorough examination of all the relevant details and ramifications of each. Although a devil's advocate can produce tension and bruised egos, the viewpoint so expressed is in the best interests of the group. Any hostility directed toward the devil's advocate can be minimized if (1) it is recognized that such challenges are expected and (2) the role is rotated among members to ensure that everyone shares the hotseat. If correctly implemented, the critical evaluation of ideas should produce a comforting feeling, for group members will realize that all aspects of the problem have been considered and all voices and options heard.

4. The group occasionally should divide into smaller subgroups that discuss the same issue under different temporary leaders. When the subgroups reach solutions and arrive at specific recommendations, they can re-form into one group and try to resolve differences in strategies and plans. Although this technique is time-consuming and often produces

duplicated efforts, it should be used when practical if the consequences of a decision are important. It increases the likelihood that a wide variety of opinions will be sampled; and even if groupthink occurs within the subgroups, their solutions may differ, and the differences then can be resolved. During the Cuban missile crisis, the Executive Committee frequently formed subgroups, and it has been suggested that this strategy increased the group's overall effectiveness. In addition, the subgroups met without President Kennedy, thereby ensuring that members would feel free to talk.

5. Outside experts and qualified individuals should be asked to provide facts and interpretations that might not be known to group members and that might present dissenting views. Also, group members should discuss their deliberations with trusted associates to obtain different views. During the Bay of Pigs deliberations, experts were excluded from top-level meetings to keep word of the invasion from leaking out (it did anyway). However, experts were consulted during the Cuban missile crisis.

6. When possible and when time permits, a second-chance meeting should be held before implementing the group's decision. This allows second thoughts and last-minute doubts to be raised. All too often, groups decide on a course of action and never look back. Although this "damn the torpedoes, full speed ahead" attitude might be effective sometimes, it does not improve overall performance.

7. In situations where a rival group, organization, or nation is involved, sizable amounts of time should be spent putting oneself in the other party's shoes, checking out warning signs, and considering alternative actions available to the other party. The importance of role-playing and considering the other's viewpoint was dramatically observed by President Kennedy immediately following the Cuban missile crisis. Kennedy recognized that Khrushchev would be forced to toughen his stance if the Soviet Union were made to look foolish, soft, and conciliatory. Therefore, Kennedy took pains to avoid any possible humiliation of the Soviet Premier. When Secretary of State Rusk remarked to the press, "Remember, when you report this—that eyeball to eyeball, they blinked first," Kennedy demanded that no other member of the government make statements that could be interpreted or misinterpreted as claiming a United States victory. Robert Kennedy concluded, "A final lesson of the Cuban missile crisis is the importance of placing ourselves in the other country's shoes."

On some occasions a group may want to promote consensus and conformity, such as when little is at stake or when a decision must be reached rapidly. In these cases, the above recommendations should be implemented in reverse (except for number 7, which is always useful). But when groupthink can produce serious negative consequences, these recommendations, or at least some of them, should be tried.

group (it will be considered more fully in a later section). The greater the cohesion of a group, the more likely groupthink will occur. In highly cohesive groups, members can get support easily from one another. They are more likely to conform to each other's statements. Therefore, the atmosphere in a cohesive group lends itself to group unity, but it also produces conditions under which members strive for consensus. As we'll see shortly, cohesive groups are "better" than noncohesive groups in many ways, but they must follow recommendations described in Focus 9-1 to prevent groupthink.

2 The more a group is *isolated,* the greater will be its tendency toward groupthink. Isolated groups, free from external pressures and criticism, are also free to use stereotypes and engage in behaviors characteristic of groupthink. The more open a group is to outside influences, the greater the pressure will be to consider alternatives and seek relevant information.

3 The presence of a *strong, directive leader* who exerts pressure to concur with his or her preferred solution will increase the tendency toward groupthink. Few people want to challenge a firmly implanted leader, and so group members "get along by going along."

4 Finally, the *importance of the decision* may increase (at least up to a point) the tendency for groupthink to occur. When the consequences of a decision are trivial, little or no threat exists to the self-esteem of group members. But as the consequences of a decision increase, group members will feel more threatened and might engage in groupthink to protect their self-esteem. Ironically, when a great deal is at stake, a group becomes most vulnerable to the dangers of groupthink.

Beyond groupthink

After learning about the existence of groupthink, some people might conclude that individuals working alone can produce better solutions than groups do. However, this is not always the case. In the next section we will explore issues concerning the *person versus the group.* The discussion of groupthink points to aspects of the group experience that demand further examination. How does the *social climate* of a group (for example, group cohesiveness) affect group behavior? How does the *structure of the group* (its degree of organization) affect group behavior? What is *leadership?* Each of these questions will be explored in the following sections.

■ THE PERSON VERSUS THE GROUP

Social facilitation

The most basic question to be asked when comparing individuals with groups is: "What happens to a person in the presence of other people?" Does a person's behavior change when (1) simply being observed by others or (2) knowing that others are nearby and engaged in similar activities?

The question of how the presence of other people affects behavior produced, in 1897, the first experiment conducted in social psychology [461]. Triplett, a cycling enthusiast, noted that the recorded times for bicycle races were much faster when a rider was competing against others than when riding alone paced by a fast multicycle; both times were faster than when a rider raced alone (and unpaced) against the clock. Triplett wondered whether the presence of others really improved performance. To test this, he conducted a simple experiment. Children were given a fishing-reel device which, when turned, moved a little silk band around a course in front of them. The children worked (turning the device) either alone or in the presence of another child who worked independently. The times for children working in each other's presence were much faster than those for children working alone.

Since this initial experiment, several studies have replicated the finding and have shown that the presence of an audience or coactor often enhances task performance (called a *social facilitation effect*); other studies have found that the presence of others decreases task performance (called a *social debilitation effect*); and still other studies have found no differences between these conditions. This puzzling and contradictory set of results existed for years.

Robert Zajonc [508] tried to explain the contradictions with an ingenious theory that borrowed heavily from learning theory. Zajonc hypothesized that the presence of other people increases a person's motivation and general arousal. This will either improve or impede task performance, depending on the type of task. Learning theorists have found that as arousal increases, so does an individual's tendency to perform well-learned, *dominant responses.* Dominant responses are those which have been practiced a great deal and are almost habitual, occurring with a high frequency. Arousal decreases the frequency of occurrence of nondominant responses (those which are not strong habits and which may be novel and inventive in a particular situation). Imagine a student who has studied for an oral history quiz and has overlearned and overpracticed one piece of data, "America was discovered in 1492." The next day, his anxiety level is very high as he stands to answer the teacher's question, "Who discovered America?" His rapid reply is, "1492." For this student, the date was a dominant, well-learned response and was emitted under high arousal. Unfortunately, it was the wrong response to the question. If the student had been less aroused, he might have given the appropriate, nondominant response.

Thus, Zajonc hypothesized that (1) the presence of other people increases arousal; (2) arousal increases the tendency to emit dominant responses and decreases the occurrence of novel, nondominant responses; and (3) whether these dominant responses are appropriate or inappropriate for the task will determine whether performance will increase or decrease. If an individual is working on a very simple or boring task, dominant responses may be perfectly correct. For example, turning a spinning reel or performing some other simple motor task are cases where dominant responses are likely to be correct, and so the presence of an audience or set of coactors will improve performance. Complex tasks and those requiring the use of higher mental processes (complex reasoning) are ones which require nondominant, novel responses, and so the presence of an audience or set of coactors is likely to decrease or have no effect on performance.

Consider an actress who has overlearned her lines in a play to the point where she can say them backward and forward, and who has performed the part for thirty weeks, night after night. The task is simple for this actress, and if she had to say the lines to herself when alone at night, her motivation might be so low as to make it difficult for her to get into the role. The presence of an audience, however, will bring out her best, since her motivation will be increased. Even though her behavioral flexibility may be limited, her dominant behavior is "correct" for the situation. On the other hand, an actress who went over her lines only a few times might be paralyzed in front of an audience. For her, dominant behavior might be the script of her last play, rather than the present one. When on the stage in front of an audience, she may find herself stuttering and repeating the lines from a past play. This phenomenon also helps explain the "Why didn't I say that?" or "Why didn't I think of that?" situation, in which we come up with a novel and ingenious reply to someone else's comment only when we're alone later. Similarly, it's easier to answer questions on television game shows when sitting alone at home than when in a studio with an audience and coactors. Thus, it's good to have an audience or coactors when we've overlearned and extensively practiced the appropriate behaviors, but when new, novel, and complex behaviors are required, it might be better to be alone.

Individual versus group performance

When a hundred clever heads join a group, one big nincompoop is the result, because every individual is trammelled by the otherness of the others.

Carl Jung

Madness is the exception in individuals but the rule in groups.

Nietzsche

These statements clearly indicate that a phenomenon like groupthink has been observed for years by psychologists and philosophers. One might be tempted to conclude that it is better to attack problems alone than in groups. Naturally, the question of whether groups or individuals alone are superior in performance is an important one for government, business, community groups, and so forth. Many novelists, scientists, and technologists prefer to work alone, virtually in isolation. They feel that ability and hard work will allow them to solve problems without the delays, social courtesies, inferior suggestions, and distractions that may occur in a group. However, perhaps Thomas Edison (a loner) would have been even more creative if he had met with a group of other able individuals.

Groups can do better than the average individual

Most early studies comparing the performances of individuals with those of groups found that groups produced solutions of better quality than those given by most individuals [192; 398]. The problems used in these studies ranged from answering multiple-choice tests to solving puzzles.

It was eventually realized, though, that the results of such studies are questionable and might not indicate that groups are superior to all individuals. Typically, the studies compared the performance of groups with the average performance of a comparable number of individuals working alone. For example, performance on a multiple-choice quiz would be computed for a four-person group, and this score would be compared with the average performance of four individuals, each of whom answered the problems alone. What if the most capable member of the group solved all the problems? He or she might easily convince the other group members of the correctness of the solutions, and the group would get the problems correct. In this case, all that is happening is that the group is performing at the level of its best member and is doing no better than would the best member working alone. Group performance then would appear to be better than "average individual" performance, since the individual average might consist of the scores of one capable individual and three low-ability individuals.

When the results of some of the earlier studies were reanalyzed [278], such an effect did seem to occur. Groups performed better than the average individual but no better than the best member of the group working alone. Further analyses indicated that certain types of tasks are most likely to produce this "no better than the best" effect. When a task requires very few steps for a solution (such as the right or wrong answer on a multiple-choice problem), and when the solution will be clear to the group members once the answer is presented by one of them, the group usually does no better than the best member would have done alone [242]. For this type of task, the most capable group member simply arrives at the correct answer and then (through self-confidence and influence) persuades the others to agree.

On other types of tasks, groups may not even do as well as the most capable member working alone. Suppose the solutions to a problem are not obvious, and several steps are required to solve it. In such cases, the most capable group member may encounter difficulties persuading the group that he or she is correct. The performance of the best member is then weakened by the mediocrity of the group [115].

Groups can do better than even the best individual

Other types of tasks bring out the best in group members and produce an atmosphere where members can cooperate and where the combination of individuals will allow them to do better than would any of them working alone (including the best group member). Some tasks are complex and require remembering, manipulating, and dealing with a lot of information. In such cases, group members can correct errors made by each other which might be unnoticed by any one person working alone. Additionally, such a situation allows division of labor; each group member can apply unique skills and abilities to different facets of the task. Examples of such tasks which have been used in experiments include anagram tests (forming words from a long series of scrambled letters) and intelligence tests. These tasks permit members to pool abilities and add to the strengths of one another; something one person might not know, another will (one member might concentrate on the verbal-reasoning portion of an intelligence test, while another works on mathematical reasoning), and when one person makes a mistake, someone else can correct it.

In such cases, a *pooling-of-abilities* effect can occur: The group does better as a whole than any single member would do alone. However, there is a catch. Both the difficulty of the task and the abilities of group members will affect what, if anything, gets pooled. Suppose a task fits the characteristics described above but is very easy, such as an intelligence test for beginning high school students which is administered to college students. In this case, groups comprising members with low ability will do better than any of the low-ability people alone [183]. The low-ability members pool their strengths (what few they have) and do very well. However, persons with high ability do just as well alone as they would in groups. The high-ability person knows all the answers to the problems and cannot be helped by another person.

Suppose we increase the difficulty of the task and administer an advanced intelligence test to college students. Now persons with high ability do even better in groups than they would alone [261]. They pool their talents, divide the labors, correct each other, and excel. Unfortunately, persons with low ability seem to do just as poorly in groups as they do alone. This suggests that a group must have something to pool in the first place; when encountering difficult problems, unintelligent persons are just as unintelligent in groups as they are alone.

Brainstorming

During the past several decades, many people have felt that groups could be used to great advantage to generate novel, creative, and radical solutions to traditional problems. A technique called *brainstorming* evolved to fulfill this goal [333]. The major guideline for brainstorming is that group members must *withhold criticism* and evaluation of ideas. Quantity of ideas (rather

Figure 9-2. *A brainstorming session. Brainstorming is a type of group free association in which members spontaneously jump into a discussion with their ideas, and criticisms of ideas are withheld until all aspects of a problem have been presented. Brainstorming is effective in generating novel solutions to problems when the group is cohesive and the members have been trained in brainstorming techniques.*

than quality) is stressed; members are encouraged to express as many ideas as possible, no matter how unusual. Members also are encouraged to "freewheel" and jump into a discussion whenever a thought strikes them, thus adding as much as possible to the ideas of others. Basically, then, brainstorming is a kind of group free association where everyone contributes and suspends criticism until all suggestions are made.

Initial studies found that brainstorming sessions produced creative solutions to traditional problems, and this early success made the technique very popular in business and government. However, later work dampened the enthusiasm [136; 441]. These later studies compared the performances of groups that used brainstorming procedures with the performances of the same number of people who worked on the same problems alone. The performances of individual subjects were then added and compared with the performances of the groups. It was found that when their solutions were combined, the individual subjects produced nearly twice as many novel solutions as brainstorming groups did.

However, the superiority of individual subjects may be somewhat tempered by the fact that brainstorming group members had not worked together before. Perhaps the discomfort associated with getting to know new people produced distractions that undermined the brainstorming groups. It has been shown that when brainstorming groups are selected for compatibility, receive training to work together effectively as a group, and like one another, they are much more productive than are the average performances of individuals working alone or even the performances of brainstorming groups in which the members are neutral or hostile [102]. Thus, brainstorming groups can be extremely effective, but only when the members are trained and enjoy working together.

■ THE SOCIAL CLIMATE: COHESIVENESS

For most people, one important consideration in joining or remaining in a group is the social climate: Is the group attractive? Do the members get along? Does the group have unity and solidarity? The term *group cohesiveness* has been used to refer to these social aspects of group membership. Cohesiveness is rather broadly defined as the sum of all forces that act to keep people within a group [153]. These forces can be of several different kinds. *Liking* for other group members is a major determinant of cohesiveness. Groups whose members care for and like one another are more cohesive than groups where little love is lost between members. The *prestige* associated with group membership is important, too. People usually feel more drawn to groups that have high prestige than to those with low prestige. Another force that keeps people within a group is the group's ability to let its members *achieve goals* that they might not accomplish without the group's aid. (And so, a lonely introvert would be drawn to the local "Lonely Hearts" club.) Finally, the *lack of a viable alternative* to the group also can act to increase cohesiveness. Our lonely introvert would probably be much more attracted to the Lonely Hearts club if it was the only one in town. In all these cases, pressures are exerted on group members which make the group seem attractive to them.

Cohesiveness and group members' feelings and actions

Naturally, the atmosphere in a cohesive group is different from the atmosphere in a noncohesive group. A major surface difference is that more communication and interaction occur among group members in cohesive groups [23]. Some laboratory studies of groups are difficult to terminate because the members of cohesive groups want to continue talking to one another. The *content* of communication also differs within cohesive and noncohesive groups. The communications sent by members of cohesive groups are more positive and friendly [121]. The general positive state of belonging to a cohesive group generates greater attendance at group meetings; cohesive group members take more responsibility for the functioning of the group; they remain group members longer; and they work longer toward group goals [105].

Figure 9-3. *Cohesive groups are different from noncohesive groups in many ways. Cohesiveness produces more conversations, friendlier conversations, greater attendance at meetings, greater effort at working toward group goals, increased self-esteem, greater compliance to group norms, and more democratic group organization.*

Belonging to a cohesive group also comforts group members. Since the social climate is positive and supportive, such groups provide personal security for members, which reduces anxiety and can heighten self-esteem. Workers in cohesive groups are less nervous on the job, feel freer to communicate with others (have less fear of being embarrassed by saying the wrong thing), and report a higher level of self-esteem [105]. Ironically, this last phenomenon, when carried to extremes, can produce the consensual strivings of groupthink. Members feel so secure, and are so comforted by each other, that they can get carried away with congeniality and lose their independence.

Looking beyond members' feelings: Cohesiveness and performance

From our earlier discussion of groupthink, one might conclude that noncohesive groups (where groupthink does not occur) are better than cohesive ones (where groupthink sometimes can occur). But the conclusion is not justified. First, groupthink can be prevented. Second, some benefits of cohesive groups are noted above, and these characteristics are desirable from the standpoint of maintaining a group over time. Third, evidence does not indicate that noncohesive groups are superior in performance to cohesive ones.

When performance on tasks is considered, research evidence is mixed. Some experimental studies have shown that cohesive groups perform better; others have shown that noncohesive groups perform better; and still others show no difference [91]. When conflicting results are found, it often means that other factors produce the differences, and one major factor involved is the normative structure of the group.

Suppose you are part of a group working on an assembly line to manufacture a particular product. You get a message from some coworkers that asks you to slow down because you're going too fast. Would you be more likely to decrease production if you liked the others or if you disliked them? Given these conditions, workers in cohesive groups show inferior performance to workers in noncohesive groups (that is, they slow down production). This effect has been demonstrated in laboratory studies which captured the essentials of this example [49; 383]. In some factories, cohesive groups of workers disagree with the policies of management and agree among themselves to keep productivity and quality down. In places where workers establish expected rates of production, "rate-busters" are censured and excluded from interactions with other workers. (This happens quite often to overenthusiastic college students who take summer jobs in such places.) Conversely, members of cohesive groups are more productive than members of noncohesive groups when urged by other group members to increase productivity [49].

Thus, members of cohesive groups are more affected by group norms and other group members' opinions. This can affect the group members' motivation. When the group urges productivity, motivation and performance increase in cohesive groups; when the group urges nonproductivity, motivation and performance in cohesive groups decline.

Cohesiveness and group organization

Since members of cohesive groups are sensitive to one another's feelings, such groups tend to display more democratic patterns of organization than do noncohesive groups [91]. The members of cohesive groups participate more in setting group goals and in establishing group policies. Noncohesive groups, on the other hand, tend to be more authoritarian and/or bureaucratic in structure. They tend to establish rigid organizations; group decisions are handed down to the group, not discussed by the group.

These principles appear to work in reverse as well. In bureaucracies (where there is rigid group organization) cohesiveness is low; but when group members have a significant hand in establishing group policy, cohesiveness is higher [91]. A spiraling effect is created in many groups. For example, noncohesiveness leads to bureaucratic group structure, which leads to even further decreases in cohesiveness. This presents many real problems for large companies and government agencies, since the morale of group members may be low and there may be little group unity. Some companies have been concerned with morale problems and have devoted more and more time and money to finding ways of increasing the cohesiveness among workers. By so doing, they hope to ensure identification with the company and the establishment of norms which lead to increased production. One way that businesses and agencies have tried to increase cohesiveness is by bringing employees and supervisors together to discuss self-perceptions, their coworkers, and the group as a whole. It is hoped that such T-group sessions will improve group communications and, ultimately, cohesiveness and productivity. Focus 9-2 explores T-groups.

Cohesiveness and social influence

One of the most consistent findings of social psychology is that when people get together, their opinions begin to converge [320]. Each person tends to accent areas of agreement and avoid areas of disagreement. This process occurs to a much greater extent in cohesive than in noncohesive groups. In fact, in cohesive groups the members help the process by attempting to influence one another's attitudes and increase the amount of agreement. Thus, cohesive groups include more compliance and more attempts to influence than do noncohesive groups [cf. 446].

A classic study of social influence in groups was conducted by Leon Festinger, Stanley Schachter, and Kurt Back [159]. They investigated social pressure in informal groups—in housing projects for married students at the Massachusetts Institute of Technology. Two married-student housing complexes existed, Westgate and Westgate West, and applicants for housing were randomly assigned at the beginning of the year to apartments in one or the other. During the year, a controversial issue about the merits of a tenants' organization developed within the projects. In Westgate, the tenants' organization had existed for some time, and people in the project differed markedly in attitudes toward the organization. Westgate was constructed so that sets of apartments opened onto courtyards, providing natural groupings of residents. The investigators interviewed residents and asked which people in the community they had most contact with. This information was used to compute an index of cohesiveness within each court. The more contact residents had with others in their court, the greater the cohesiveness of a court unit. Investigators found that the greater the cohesiveness of a court, the fewer residents deviated from the majority opinion on the issue of tenant organization. Thus, where cohesiveness was high, residents conformed more and deviated less. Interestingly, people who did deviate from majority opinions tended to be more physically isolated from the rest of a court because of the location of their apartments.

The other housing project, Westgate West, did not show this pattern of influence. Westgate West consisted of seventeen two-story buildings and, hence, did not provide natural groupings of people, as did Westgate. Additionally, residents of Westgate West had only recently been invited to join

FOCUS 9-2   THE T-GROUP: LEARNING TO COMMUNICATE

The *T-group* (T stands for "training") movement has taken the country by storm. In more radical forms, it has been termed the *encounter group movement* and has been popularized in movies such as *Bob and Carol and Ted and Alice*. Some people claim T-groups are the universal panacea for all interpersonal ills, while others feel the movement is led by charlatans who do more harm than good. Everyone knows the kind of religious fervor that is often associated with such groups, yet not everyone knows what T-groups are and what they try to accomplish.

A T-group is supposed to be a unique environment for new learning experiences. But unlike traditional learning techniques, it doesn't involve force-fed lectures or the learning of more information about the world. The learning is personal, and consists of learning by doing and experiencing rather than by simply being told.

Traditionally, the goal of a T-group is *to gain valid communication* with others. To communicate validly, people must be sensitive to their own feelings, perceptions, and behaviors and to those of others. It is necessary to discover how you yourself behave, and how others' behavior and perceptions affect you. Since the focus of many groups has been on this process of sensitivity to oneself and others, the term *sensitivity group* also has been associated with the movement.

Bennis and Shephard [48] were two early leaders in the T-group movement. They felt that the two major areas of interpersonal concern and uneasiness in groups are one's *relationships with authority* and one's more *intimate relationships with peers*. Authority relationships concern questions such as, How do we react to the boss? How do we perceive our own use of power? Intimacy relationships involve questions such as, How should we react to the presence of peers? Should we behave acceptingly or critically, warmly or coldly?

To focus attention on these two areas of concern, certain rules and patterns were established for T-groups. The leader of a T-group tries to maintain a nondirective manner. He or she refuses to take a dominant role or to lead the group. The leader leaves it to group members to display unique ways of behaving in this unstructured setting. It is hoped that the members therefore will display their own ways of relating to authority. In this nondirective climate, many T-group members feel ill at ease. They can't relate well to situations where the "authority" does not behave in a directive fashion. When members do begin communicating with one another, they might gain insight into how they have reacted to authorities in the past. Members then can begin to discuss how they see people, particularly others in the group, and can display their own assumptions about human behavior. What results can be an experience in learning how others react to our assumptions and behaviors.

Why is this important? Don't we know how others react to us just from our normal, everyday experiences? Unfortunately, often we don't. Have you ever tried to compliment someone you liked and found out later that he or she took the intended compliment as an insult? Or have you ever wanted to criticize your teacher or boss, but when the time came, you minced words, hemmed and hawed, and made a statement that was anything but critical? The problems caused by these invalid and faulty communications can threaten our interactions with others and our own self-perceptions.

Do T-groups work? Are they effective in producing these end results? T-groups have drawn both praise and criticism. The critics point out that valid communication might be momentarily established in the new social climate of the T-group, but once members reenter the "real world," all the gains are lost, and they behave as they always did, with little real insight and no change in behavior. The data gathered from studies of people who participated in T-groups, however, generally support the claims of the advocates. Studies have indicated that as a result of T-group participation, people perceive themselves and are perceived by others as more sensitive and considerate, as more interpersonally oriented, as more open-minded and less prejudiced, as more accepting of themselves, as more understanding of self and others, and as having improved their leadership skills. While there also is some evidence that is not so encouraging, even many former T-group critics [e.g., 134a] have been swayed and now feel that T-groups hold a real promise for improving interpersonal understanding.

the tenants' organization, and so the issue was new to them. Thus, attitudes toward the organization were determined largely by personal preference and less by group influence.

Thus, where there is an important issue among natural groups of people (and where group members have had time to form opinions and discuss the issue among themselves), social pressures seem to be exerted on group members to go along with the majority opinion. The greater a group's cohesiveness, the greater the compliance with the majority opinion.

Heretics and angels: Reactions to deviates and conformers

It's comforting to know that others agree with your opinions. This provides social support and security, and it increases confidence in the correctness of your opinions. People who disagree, however, might shake one's confidence and produce dislike. As we saw in Chapter 5, we like people whose attitudes are similar to our own.

It is more important to have members of one's own group agree than to have someone from a different group agree. People identify with the groups to which they belong, and they look to those groups to provide standards and agreement. On the other hand, someone from a different group might be expected to hold different opinions, and therefore disagreement is not as threatening.

The greatest threat to one's opinions comes from someone who once was a member of one's group but has left for an alternative group with alternative viewpoints (such as a defector from one's country who adopts an opposing ideological stance). Such people are called heretics, and reactions to them are usually quite negative. In one study, divinity-school students listened to a speech that attacked the motives and values of their religious group [225]. Some subjects were told that the speech was made by a law student (who obviously had a dissimilar background and thus was a member of an outgroup); other subjects were told that the speech was made by another divinity student (the heretic). When asked to evaluate the speakers, the students stated that they had more in common with the law student than with the divinity student, and then rated the law student as much more likable, pleasant, and warm than the divinity student. The heretic was rejected soundly.

In most group situations, an opportunity exists for group members to try to reconvert a deviate into the fold. Do such influence attempts occur, and what happens if a deviate remains deviate? Stanley Schachter [378] tried to answer these questions and to examine how group cohesiveness affects reactions to deviates. Subjects in the experiment were assigned to groups which were either very attractive and high in prestige (high cohesiveness) or very unattractive and low in prestige (low cohesiveness). The groups then were given a problem to solve which was either relevant or irrelevant to group goals. Schachter added paid experimental accomplices to each group and thus could control the degree to which these confederates went along with or deviated from the group's ideas about solving problems. In some conditions, the confederate consistently conformed to the group's ideas (the conformer); in other conditions, the confederate initially deviated from the group's ideas but then changed his opinions and conformed (the slider); in still other conditions, the confederate deviated from the group throughout the task discussion (the deviate).

Schachter found that the number of communications sent to the deviate first increased and then decreased. At first, groups communicated with the deviate to try to bring him back into the fold. But once it became obvious that he would not go along with the group, communications were cut off. This was particularly true when the group was high in cohesiveness and when the issue was relevant to group goals.

It also was found that the group's rejection of the deviate was most intense when cohesiveness was high and when the topic was relevant to group goals. Specifically, when group cohesiveness was high, the deviate was disliked more than when cohesiveness was low. And when the topic was relevant rather than irrelevant to the group's goals, group members assigned the deviate to unimportant and uninteresting jobs. The conformer and slider did not receive such harsh treatment as the deviate did.

These findings are reminiscent of some aspects of groupthink. Recall that groupthink occurs more in high—than in low—cohesive groups, and it occurs more when a problem is important to the group. It is precisely these conditions which Schachter has shown will produce the greatest rejection of people who don't go along with majority opinion. Knowledge of this pressure probably makes many well-intentioned individuals conform. When a group is noncohesive or when a topic is irrelevant to a group, one can disagree with greater impunity.

▪ GROUP STRUCTURE

Roles and role conflict

Some groups develop rigid, formal structures. For example, in large corporations and government bureaucracies, organization charts specify who has responsibility for particular jobs, who can communicate with whom, and so forth. In other groups, organizational structures are less firmly established and are not put down on paper; but it is clear that some group members have higher status than others, that they have different jobs to perform, and that they each can influence some individuals but not others.

Whatever its organizational style, a group sets out to achieve some goal, and group members divide the tasks that have to be accomplished. The set of behaviors associated with the position each member is given or assumes in the group is termed the person's *role*. Each person has many roles. There is a different role for each group to which an individual belongs, and even within the same group there are different roles for different occasions. In school, your perceived role might be that of the student, and you see yourself as having to engage in certain behaviors (such as studying) to maintain that role. A female college student also might see herself in the role of the young adult who acts independently and makes her own decisions. Yet at home, she might also see herself in the role of "obedient daughter," deferring to parental judgment.

As this example indicates, roles frequently can be in conflict. At home during vacation, a college student might question whether to act independently or comply with what appears to be a silly parental request. Many college students are rebellious during the early days of a vacation and try to assert individuality; but after several days, they begin to fill the more accustomed role of son or daughter (and therefore get along better in the family group). Back at college, they again revert to the independence of the young adult role (and therefore get along better with peers).

This example points out that roles change with time and that it is very difficult to revert to what we might perceive as an earlier, outmoded role. Returning home is difficult. When a successful individual (say, an artist, writer, or scientist) returns home, an awkward situation is produced. Parents and old friends react in terms of old roles rather than new ones, and *role conflict* results. (This has been the theme of many television comedy shows.) Role conflict troubles many women today. Women are feeling conflict between the traditional roles of wife, mother, and housekeeper and new roles dictated by chosen careers.

(a)

(b)

(c)

Figure 9-4. *Deviance from group norms can produce rejection, especially when a group is cohesive and when the issue is important and relevant to the group. Early suffragettes were ridiculed (a) and arrested (b) for their deviance. Alexander Solzhenitsyn (c) was forced to leave the Soviet Union because of his criticism of police state actions.*

Status

Each role within a group is accorded greater or lesser value by group members. Some roles, such as group president, are usually evaluated positively by group members; other roles, such as loading-dock worker, are evaluated much less positively and are seen as contributing less to the group.

People's *status* is defined as the worth or value of the role positions they occupy in a particular group. Two types of status can be distinguished: achieved status and ascribed status. *Achieved status* is earned through hard work and ability. A man who works his way up from the role of delivery boy to company president has (usually) earned the status received. *Ascribed status,* on the other hand, is received through no fault or effort of one's own. For example, being born black or poor in America automatically gives a person low ascribed status, while being born the son or daughter of a millionaire gives a person high ascribed status. Needless to say, achieved status is usually more legitimate and fair than ascribed status.

Status determines to a large extent how other group members will react to a person and how he or she will react to them. People with high status are given prerogatives not afforded to those lower in the status hierarchy. For example, a high-status person usually is given a better position and opportunities within a group, such as a seat at the head of the table. People are so accustomed to associating status with such prerogatives that the person sitting at the head of a table is seen by newcomers to the group as the individual with highest status [279]. Similarly, how two people treat one another lets an observer infer the status of each. In one study [417], subjects viewed films of different interactions. In one film, a man knocked on the door of an office, opened the door, and stepped just inside. In another film, the man knocked on the door, opened it, and walked all the way to the desk of the person who occupied the office. The person who walked all the way to the desk was viewed as having higher status than the one who stopped just inside the door. Clearly, greater "daring" was perceived as demonstrating greater prerogatives in the social situation.

Status strongly affects the type and amount of communication within groups. The flow of communication within groups is up the status hierarchy; people of low status try to communicate with people above them, while those of high status tend to communicate with each other [274]. Even rumors seem to spread upward in a status hierarchy, rather than downward [24]. Thus, a person with high status is likely to have much more information about what is happening within a group than is a person with low status. However, the information which the high-status individual receives is often biased. Low-status individuals are not as likely to criticize high-status individuals because of fear of retaliation. Therefore, the content of communications directed toward high-status persons tends to be much more positive than is the content of communications directed toward those of low status [450]. The high-status person may have a lot of information, but much of it consists of things which the high-status person wants to hear, and not necessarily the truth.

Status not only affects who talks to whom, but also influences how much a person is listened to when he or she does talk. Torrance [457] dramatically demonstrated that it's not what you say, but who says it, that counts in groups. Torrance gave military airplane crews a series of problems to solve which were irrelevant to the larger goals of the group and did not pertain to the military at all. Despite the irrelevance of status to the problems, status affected how influential each crew member was in having a solution adopted by the group. It was found that when the high-status pilot gave the correct answer, it was always accepted by group members. But when the lowly gunner gave the correct answer, it was accepted by the group only 40 percent of the time. Clearly, the same words take on different meanings when used by persons with high or low status.

Communication networks

In most small groups, individuals have face-to-face contact with each other, and members can communicate freely. However, as groups become larger, communication can become restricted. In a large organization, a typist from the secretarial pool cannot walk into the president's office and sit down to chat. A secretary must talk instead to an immediate superior, who then relays information to another superior, who then relays this information, and so on; finally, if the secretary is lucky, the information may reach the top level of the organizational hierarchy. Similarly, as a college student, you would find it difficult to meet with the president of your university. If you had information to convey to the president, you'd have to go through proper *channels.*

Most organizations formalize communication channels (which usually correspond closely to the status structures of the groups), and employees know whom they can talk to directly and whom they can communicate with only indirectly. Groups typically become organized in this way in order to allocate time for high-status individuals. These restrictions on communication do serve an important function in groups, since individuals throughout the group deal largely with information suitable for their levels of competence. This saves everyone time and maximizes efficiency. However, the lack of free-flowing communication also can cause difficulties in the group, since communication problems may develop. Information may not reach its intended source, or, if it does, it may become distorted as it is passed along. People at different ends of communication chains may have little or no idea of what is going on in the rest of the group, and they may lose contact with each other.

It could be expected that communication patterns within a group would have major effects on the behavior of group members. Consequently, the topic of communication networks has received much attention from social psychologists for several decades. A communication network represents the communication opportunities within a group. As such, it depicts the direct and indirect lines of communication between group members and describes how limited or unlimited communication opportunities are.

To study communication networks in small groups, several simple group structures have been devised and studied. Some such networks for a five-person group are shown in Figure 9-5 (the circles represent group members, and the lines represent open channels of communication). The first two types, the wheel and the Y, are termed *centralized communication networks.* In these, group members must communicate through one or more persons in central positions (person *A* in the wheel and persons *A* and *B* in the Y are in central positions). Peripheral members cannot directly communicate with each other but must communicate through the central intermediaries. The remaining three networks—the chain, the circle, and the concom—are relatively *decentralized communication networks.* In these, all or almost all group members can communicate with others to the right or left, and no single person has a central role. The concom is the most decentralized of all the networks, since each member can communicate directly with all other persons.

The effects of these communication networks can be studied quite simply in laboratory settings. Investigators can place subjects in individual cubicles, each of which is separated by partitions. Slots in the cubicles let subjects send notes (transmit information) between cubicles. By blocking and opening slots, various communication networks can be simulated in the laboratory. Then, each group of subjects can be given different tasks or problems, and measures can be taken of how efficiently a group performs

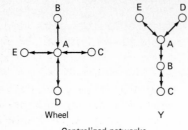

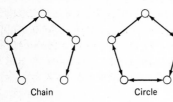

Wheel   Y

Centralized networks

Chain   Circle   Concom

Decentralized networks

Figure 9-5. *Communication networks. The circles in each diagram represent persons, and lines connecting the circles represent open channels of communication. Communication opportunities are greater in decentralized than in centralized networks.*

the tasks, how satisfied group members are with the group, and how leadership patterns develop.

One major concern for a group is the amount of *satisfaction* members receive. Recall the numerous positive effects that result from membership in satisfactory, cohesive groups. Communication networks affect how satisfied group members feel. A number of studies [399; 400] indicate that group members are more satisfied with roles in decentralized communication networks than in centralized ones. Group members like to communicate directly with as many people in the group as possible. When communication opportunities are restricted, members often feel left out and unimportant. Although this holds true for the group as a whole, it is not surprising that the central person in a centralized network (for example, person *A* in the wheel) is very satisfied with that dominant position [400]. A central position makes a person feel important to the group, and satisfaction is quite high. Peripheral members, however, tend to be dissatisfied with their roles.

Another reason to feel high satisfaction in the central position of a centralized network is that the central person usually emerges as the group leader [399]. When group members are asked who they feel is the leader of their group, members in centralized networks usually name the person with the central position. Thus, being placed in the right spot in a communication network (regardless of one's talents) will affect how much one is seen as a leader. In decentralized communication networks, leadership patterns do not emerge as readily, and almost any member can become the leader.

Another important consideration for a group is how effective it is in completing tasks. Logically, it would be reasonable to predict that both centralized and decentralized networks would be effective on tasks, but for different reasons. One might expect decentralized networks to be effective because of the free communication flow within the group. Members can exchange information quickly and directly, correct one another's errors, and get to the root of a problem, solving it accurately. On the other hand, centralized networks also offer strengths. Group members can channel all information to a central person, who then can scrutinize it, sort the important from the unimportant, and provide a solution.

As this reasoning implies, both networks are effective, but under different conditions. When a group works on a simple problem—to compile information, after which the solution becomes obvious—a centralized network has been shown to be better in terms of both time saved and number of messages sent. However, when a complex problem confronts a group—information must be collected, and then group members must manipulate it to produce a solution—a decentralized network is more efficient. In decentralized networks, members can communicate directly, manipulate information, and arrive at a correct solution. Centralized communication networks can become *saturated* when dealing with complex tasks [399]. The central person can be overwhelmed and overloaded by all the information he or she must handle; one can't see the forest for the trees. Such flooding of information at the central position can cause centralized networks to perform poorly on complex problems.

■ LEADERSHIP

What is a leader?

Until now, we've used the term *leader* without defining it or exploring just what it is about a person or a person's position that makes him or her a leader. Everyone "knows" what a leader is; but when asked to define the term, many people hem and haw. "Why, a leader is someone who leads," is a common reply. Or someone else might state, "A leader is someone who occupies a leadership position, such as President." Such answers are not very satisfying and raise other questions. What does it mean when one says "to lead?" How does a person attain a position of leadership?

Generally, a leader is someone who can do two things. First, a leader must successfully influence the direction of a group by influencing its attitudes and behaviors. An individual who cannot influence other group members is not likely to emerge as leader; and the more influence a person can exercise, the more likely he or she will be to reach a position of leadership. Second, a leader must maintain the image of having the group's best interest—not his or her own—in mind. Group members usually rebel against individuals who use a group for their own advantage and who don't appear to be concerned with the general welfare of all members. When an individual is perceived as exploiting a group, he or she will be rejected. For these reasons, politicians' speeches are filled with references not only to what they have done to influence legislation, but also to how they have done it for their constituencies and have not personally profited.

Are leaders born or made?

We've all heard it said that someone is a "born leader." Usually, the phrase refers to the fact that an individual has certain qualities that suit a position of influence in a group. However, few people seriously suggest that these qualities are genetic and inherited. Rather, individuals are shaped by their experiences, and these experiences provide abilities which can be used to advantage by a group. For example, studies of Woodrow Wilson trace his important personality characteristics back to his childhood [175]. His father, a preacher and former professor of rhetoric, was a stern task master who drilled his son for hours to make him try to excel. The boy was never allowed to use an incorrect word or phrase. When he made a mistake, his father belittled him with jokes. Young Wilson held his father in awe and was so afraid of him and overcome by the tension of his upbringing that he didn't learn the alphabet until he was nine and couldn't read until he was eleven. These experiences instilled a sense of unimportance, inferiority, inadequacy, and weakness in Wilson; yet he felt he had to excel. Historians have viewed his life as a constant attempt to compensate for perceived weaknesses, which probably accounts for his later hard work and idealism. Wilson became President of Princeton University and eventually President of the United States. Naturally, such characteristics as hard work, idealism, and overcompensation don't guarantee that one will assume a position of leadership, as we'll see shortly. But in Wilson's case, the characteristics for which he was most admired were developed during his early life.

An individual can profit from experience in other ways, too. John F. Kennedy learned a great deal about leadership from the Bay of Pigs fiasco. Recall that he used this failure as a lesson which aided his handling of later events and crises. It is quite possible that everyone needs a failure like the Bay of Pigs to teach them how to function effectively as a leader.

Approaches to the study of leadership

The "great man" theory. Many people feel that leaders are systematically different from followers, that they have personality characteristics which set them apart from the crowd, and that no matter what the situation, they would emerge in positions of dominance. Thomas Carlyle, the famous historian and biographer, felt that historical events are the result of the actions of great individuals, who are as different from the masses as day is from night. To Carlyle, only great persons are important in history; all other situational and social forces are inconsequential by comparison.

This approach to leadership has been termed the *great man theory*. It takes the position and if Napoleon had been John Doe, if Cleopatra had been Jane Smith, and if Lincoln had been Sam Snurd, history would have been quite different. The great person forces events to occur and molds the world in his or her image.

The social forces theory. At the opposite extreme, many think that people, even so-called great ones, are molded by their times, rather than the reverse. People are forced by the social, economic, and political conditions of their age to behave in particular ways. If Hitler had never been born, someone else would have risen to power in Germany and precipitated World War II. (There is evidence for this view. After World War I, Winston Churchill and others predicted that the damaging "peace accords" forced on Germany would ruin its economic structure and cause it to seek vengeance.) In essence, human beings are pawns moved by forces around them. They behave in ways that almost anyone would, given the same conditions. It is not so much the right person in the right place at the right time as it is any person in a particular place at a particular time. History is shaped by the *Zeitgeist* (spirit of the times) of a period.

Neither the great man theory nor the social forces theory is completely correct. Yet neither is completely incorrect. The personality characteristics of leaders are important to how they will react under novel conditions and how they will interact with group members in various situations [127]. But personality characteristics alone don't explain all leadership actions. Social forces and other situational influences affect behavior as well [181; 211]. A mixture of the approaches is needed, and this is the direction current research is taking. However, before examining approaches which combine personality and situational factors, let us consider in more depth some personal factors associated with leadership.

Personal characteristics of the leader

Stirred by the great man theory, researchers between World War I and World War II began searching for characteristics which great people possessed. These can be broken into three categories: *physical characteristics, intelligence,* and *personality traits.*

Physical characteristics. Generally, leaders of groups are bigger (both taller and heavier), healthier, and more attractive physically than an average group member [181; 285]. However, although these physical characteristics are slightly associated with leadership, the relationship is not strong. It is not hard to think of a small leader (Napoleon) or one with health difficulties (F. D. Roosevelt was confined to a wheelchair by polio during most of his political life). Similarly, the relationship between physical appearance and leadership is not all that strong and varies considerably with what a group regards as attractive. Thus, slovenliness and misconduct are related to leadership in gangs of juvenile delinquents.

And though height and weight are slightly related to leadership, more is involved—a leader must be similar to other group members. A six-foot-tall leader is unlikely to emerge among a group of pygmies, even though the person will stand out in a crowd. Similarity to the group was illustrated in a study of voters' preferences for candidates in the 1969 mayoralty election in

(a)

(b)

(e)

(f)

(h)

(c)

(d)

(g)

Figure 9-6. *The characteristics of prominent leaders are many and varied. The personality style of a leader must be compatible with the group situation for the leader to function effectively. The leaders shown here include (a) John F. Kennedy, (b) Golda Meier, (c) Richard M. Nixon, (d) Franklin D. Roosevelt, (e) Winston Churchill, (f) Adolf Hitler, (g) Mohandas Gandhi, (h) Dwight D. Eisenhower and Lyndon B. Johnson, and (i) Indira Gandhi. Considering their varied personalities, is it any wonder that generalizations about leadership are hard to make?*

(i)

New York City [58]. The opposing candidates were John Lindsay (six feet, three inches) and Mario Procaccino (five feet, six inches). It was found that (holding constant other factors, such as ethnic group) voters generally preferred the candidate who was more similar to themselves in height; shorter voters favored Procaccino, and taller ones supported Lindsay.

Thus, although physical attributes are related to leadership, the relationship is not strong. At best, physical attributes make a person stand out from other group members and thereby gain recognition. Physical attributes must be considered not by themselves, but in relation to the rest of the group.

Intelligence. Leaders do seem to have the edge over followers in intelligence and ability. For example, scholarship, general knowledge, insight, verbal facility, and adaptability have been associated with leadership [181]. Leaders must be sufficiently competent to accomplish the tasks required. General competence and past success are highly associated with leadership [210]. Once again, though, these statements must be tempered with the recognition that similarity to other group members should be high. Thus, a group leader tends to be more intelligent than other group members, but only slightly more so. If a leader is perceived as too intelligent (a genius, egghead, etc.), he or she might have difficulty communicating with the group and might be perceived as not really understanding what the "average person" thinks. This balance between overall intelligence and similarity was demonstrated in the 1952 and 1956 American presidential elections, in which Democrat Adlai Stevenson was regarded by most intellectuals and academicians as the person best equipped to handle the duties of office, but was defeated by Dwight Eisenhower, an army general who was regarded as the man of the people.

Personality traits. It has been very difficult to pin down specific personality traits associated with leadership. Mann [285] noted that over five hundred personality measures have been studied by social scientists to determine their relationship to leadership. However, a slightly different list of traits seems to appear in every study, and there is only a minimal degree of overlap between traits across studies. No traits were associated with leadership in every study. It appears that the particular personality traits of a leader vary from group to group; some traits seem appropriate in one situation, while others seem appropriate in another. None appear absolutely necessary or absolutely related to leadership.

Having pointed out that the relationship between personality traits and leadership is not invariant, it can be noted that three factors do appear more frequently than others. These seem to be associated with leadership, at least to a small degree, across many situations.

1   *Self-confidence* and *self-assertiveness* are two personality traits which appear frequently as characteristics of leaders. Individuals who have these traits speak frequently in groups, express their ideas, influence

others' attitudes, and are less influenced by others. High self-confidence also is necessary if a leader is to survive the challenges of opponents. Although self-confidence and self-assertiveness seem to be related to being selected as leader by group members, some leaders are appointed rather than elected. In such appointive cases, self-confidence and self-assertiveness may be less important for the job, and other characteristics (such as loyalty) may be more important.

2 In groups where leaders are selected by the group members, any personality trait that enables an individual to either *contribute to the group* or *become popular with its members* would increase the chances of being chosen a leader. Thus, personality adjustment, low anxiety, extroversion (outgoingness), sensitivity to the feelings of others, taking responsibility, cooperativeness, and dependability have all been found to be related to leadership in some groups [91; 181; 400]. However, many exceptions also can be noted for each of these traits.

3 In many groups, leaders must win election to a leadership position. In such cases, the aspiring leader must work hard to get votes, campaign, put up posters, give speeches, raise money for campaign expenses, and so forth. To engage in these kinds of activities, an aspiring leader must have *motivation and drive*. This would appear to explain why leaders are generally healthier than other group members; good health is usually a prerequisite for the activities required by those with high motivation and drive. Two aspects of such motivation are the *need for power* and the *need for control over others* [470]. For example, budding politicians who were running for office in their college student governments were found to have much greater need for power than other students [470].

Mentioned above is the fact that some studies found personality adjustment to be related to leadership. However, as a leader's power increases, so does his or her tendency to score abnormally high on needs for power and control. The World Health Organization Expert Committee on Mental Health has gone so far as to suggest that the stresses and strains on people who are in high positions in government are often too great for the average, well-adjusted person. Consequently, persons who have psychopathic personality tendencies (who exploit power and have little concern for social values) have a greater chance to become powerful leaders because they fill the vacuum left by the better-adjusted people who don't want the job and the pressure [505].

Personality and situation together: The contingency model

A successful leader in one group might not be successful in another group, or even in the same group under different conditions. As the situation changes, so do the demands placed on a leader. Personality characteristics that help a leader to gain power might actually make it difficult for a leader to retain power. Ideally, an approach is needed that (1) specifies the characteristics of a group situation which affect leadership and (2) relates personality characteristics which are most helpful to a leader under these different conditions. Personality and situational factors must be combined into one coherent model.

A first step in combining personality and situational aspects of leadership was taken by Fred Fiedler [160; 161]. Rather than deal with all possible personality characteristics associated with leadership, Fielder focused on one very important dimension: a person's orientation toward a group. People differ along a dimension which is labeled at one end *relations-oriented* and at the other end *task-oriented.* A relations-oriented leader is nonanxious, nondirective, and concerned with maintaining warm, pleasant relationships with other group members. In a leadership situation, such an individual will try to reduce tensions within the group and keep everyone satisfied. A task-oriented leader is more anxious and directive and is less concerned with maintaining pleasant group relations. Such an individual focuses on the task that confronts the group and views successful completion of the task as the major goal.

Fiedler reasoned that in some situations, a relations-oriented leader would be more successful in a group, while in other situations, a task-oriented leader would be more successful. Three situational variables were deemed important: the leader's position power, the task structure, and the leader-member relations in the group. *Position power* refers to how much the role (or position) of a leader allows him or her to influence group members. Position power is also related to a leader's legitimacy or authority. Some leaders have leadership positions in name only and actually can exercise little influence within their groups (for example, the Queen of England); the positions of other leaders give them a great deal of power (the President of the United States).

Task structure refers to the clarity of the task facing the group. Some tasks are ambiguous, and group members are not sure what their goals really are or how to devise tactics to achieve the goals. Other tasks are highly structured, and it is apparent to the group members what the goals are and how to devise tactics to achieve the goals. Research has indicated that when the path to a goal is unclear, group members display more anxiety, are less satisfied and motivated, and are less efficient than when the means to a goal are clear [101; 359]. Thus, a leader's job is more difficult when tasks are poorly structured than when they are highly structured.

The final situational variable reflects the *leader-member relations* within the group. In some situations, members like their leader, accept him or her, and are loyal; in other situations, tensions can exist between the leader and other group members.

By combining these three variables, Fiedler classified situations according to their favorableness for a leader. The most favorable situation is one in which the leader's position power is high, the task is clearly structured, and the leader-member relations are good. The least favorable situation is one in which the leader's position power is low, the task is poorly structured, and the leader-member relations are bad. Intermediate degrees of favorableness also can be derived.

Fiedler's *contingency model of leader effectiveness* is so named because it predicts that leader effectiveness depends on, or is contingent on, the orientation of the leader and the favorableness of the situation. The model makes two major predictions.

First, when the group situation is either very favorable or very unfavorable for the leader, a task-oriented leader will be more effective in managing the group and allowing it to reach its goal. When the situation is very favorable, the task-oriented leader can concentrate on the task at hand, guide the group, solve the problem, and get on to other matters. The group is rewarded with success. A relations-oriented leader is not needed in this situation and might actually sidetrack the group. When the situation is very unfavorable, a task-oriented leader is again more effective. The group is near the point of falling apart, and the task-oriented leader can provide firm guidance and direct the group toward task completion. Under unfavorable conditions, the group needs a take-charge person in control.

Second, a relations-oriented leader is more effective under conditions that are either moderately favorable or moderately unfavorable. In these intermediate conditions, the group needs someone who will maintain morale and satisfaction. A directive, harsh, abrupt, task-oriented leader could produce bitterness and deter the group from reaching its goal.

The contingency model has been tested in several situations, including the military, high school athletic teams, and business. Generally, the data support the major predictions of the model [160; 161], although the support is far from perfect. The model should be regarded as an interesting first step, but not a final product, since only one personality variable, the leader's orientation, is included, and many situational factors (such as group cohesiveness and the group's organizational structure) are left out.

Leadership activities

Fiedler's contingency model suggests two major activities that leaders engage in during group interactions—maintaining pleasant, positive relations within the group and guiding the group toward task completion. Robert Bales [27] has devised a classification scheme for behaviors which occur within groups; this technique is termed *interaction process analysis.* After studying hundreds of small groups, Bales found that behaviors can be classified into four major categories, with each category having three minor subcategories (see Figure 9-7). The major categories include: showing positive reactions, attempting to solve problems, questioning, and showing negative reactions. Observers can record the behaviors of group members and classify all behaviors into one of these categories. By so doing, a picture of the activities of group members and group leaders will emerge.

In a series of studies, Bales and his associates [26; 27; 28] have found that individuals do emerge in groups who tend to score higher on one of these dimensions than another. In fact, he found that two different leaders, each with unique behavior patterns, emerge in many groups. One is termed a *socioemotional specialist* and is concerned with eliciting positive reactions from group members. This is comparable to what Fiedler would call a relations-oriented leader. The other is termed a *task specialist* and engages primarily in problem-solving attempts. This is comparable to Fiedler's task-oriented leader. Unlike Fiedler, who suggests that groups have one or the other type of leader, Bales suggests that groups frequently develop both types of leaders *at the same time.* During group interactions, the task specialist frequently generates tension and hostility within the group because of his or her constant prodding and striving for task completion. This tension is most likely to be generated when the task specialist is not fully accepted by the group and when the group is not firmly committed to particular goals [83]. When tension and hostility occur, a second leader emerges who is socioemotionally oriented and who attempts to reduce the interpersonal hostilities produced by the demanding task specialist. Once these two leaders emerge, they can work together successfully to attain group goals and to keep group cohesiveness high. Each leader has separate sets of activities and a particular domain within the group. This should sound familiar, since families in Western society seem to develop this structure. A father typically assumes the role of task specialist, while a mother assumes the role of socioemotional specialist. Other types of leadership activities and styles are presented in Focus 9-3.

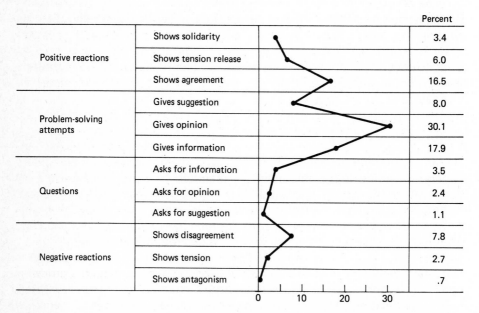

		Percent
Positive reactions	Shows solidarity	3.4
	Shows tension release	6.0
	Shows agreement	16.5
Problem-solving attempts	Gives suggestion	8.0
	Gives opinion	30.1
	Gives information	17.9
Questions	Asks for information	3.5
	Asks for opinion	2.4
	Asks for suggestion	1.1
Negative reactions	Shows disagreement	7.8
	Shows tension	2.7
	Shows antagonism	.7

Figure 9-7. *A technique for analyzing the types of social behaviors that occur in group situations is called interaction process analysis. A social behavior can fall into one of four major categories: displaying positive reactions, attempting to solve problems, asking questions, and displaying negative reactions. Each of these can, in turn, be broken down into three subcategories. In a laboratory study of group behavior, the actions of 96 groups of subjects were classified as they discussed social relations problems. The results of this study are presented in above. Over 56 percent of the subjects' actions were classified as problem-solving attempts, and very few negative reactions were displayed.*

FOCUS 9-3 AUTHORITARIANISM AND DEMOCRACY: CONTRASTING LEADERSHIP STYLES

Stirred by the rise of Nazism in Germany in the 1930s, Kurt Lewin, Ralph White, and Ronald Lippitt [492] became curious about how particular leadership styles affect group behavior. It seemed to them that an autocratic leader (who is directive, domineering, and critical) would produce a much different group climate than would a democratic leader (who is concerned with members' opinions, nondirective, and noncritical). To study this question, they formed several after-school hobby clubs for ten-year-old boys. They then trained adult group leaders in three styles of leadership. The *autocratic leadership style* provided the leader with a directive role. The leader personally determined all group goals, dictated what tasks the group would work on, and dominated the interactions by praising or criticizing group members. The *democratic leadership style* provided the leader with the role of general guide and leader of group discussions. The leader openly discussed with the boys what goals they wanted for their group and what tasks they wanted to work on; the leader allowed the group to vote on its activities. The third role was termed a *laissez faire leadership style*. In this type, the leader gave almost no direction to the group. He tried not to participate in discussions and to minimize his role in the group. The group was essentially left on its own. These different leadership styles were alternated within the groups. Some groups first worked with an autocratic leader; six weeks later they worked with a democratic leader; and then six weeks later they worked with a laissez-faire leader; other groups received different orderings of these styles.

The different leadership styles clearly produced different patterns within the groups. Under democratic leadership, group members were more open-minded, more friendly, more efficient in their work, and more individualistic. Under the autocratic climate, a great deal of hostility and aggression was observed, particularly when group members were not being watched by the autocratic leader. The boys demanded more attention, blamed other group members for failures in the group, were submissive and obedient, and were relatively inefficient in their work. The products of the autocratic group were inferior to the products of the democratic group. The group members also liked the democratic leader more than the autocratic leader. Under laissez faire leadership, the group rapidly deteriorated. The boys did very little work, and the work they did was poor. Group meetings were characterized by play and activities unrelated to goals.

Although these results may be comforting to those who favor a democratic style of leadership and group organization, one should bear in mind that the study was conducted in the United States. It would have been interesting to learn how German children during World War II would have reacted to the three styles. Perhaps they would have preferred the autocratic leader to the democratic one, and the results would have been reversed. Without further research, it is impossible to determine just how culturally specific these results are.

Under some conditions, people actually prefer an autocratic leader to a democratic one. As Fiedler's leadership model indicates, when paths to a goal are unclear and when a situation is quite unfavorable, a task-oriented, directive leader is more effective; he or she also is preferred by group members. Whenever a group experiences a strong threat to survival or undergoes a great deal of stress, an authoritarian leader is likely to emerge. To demonstrate, one study examined the behaviors of an organized group of Dutch grocers who ran small shops in Holland [317]. The investigators planted a rumor in the group that a large supermarket chain was going to open near them in the immediate future. Naturally, such competition posed a direct economic threat to the survival of this group of small storeowners. It was found that cries soon rang out in the group for strong, directive leadership.

Korten [251] has suggested another refinement of this basic relationship between group threat and authoritarianism. Based on numerous studies, it was concluded that when group goals assumed greater importance than individual goals and when ambiguities obscured the paths to the goals, authoritarianism was preferred. This process clearly reflects what occurred in the United States in the late 1960s. Troubled by a "permissive" society, the apparent decay of law and order, rising crime rates, campus revolts, and city riots, voters pushed the team of Nixon-Agnew into power. Their election was based largely on promises that they would be strong, directive leaders; permissiveness would not be tolerated, and laws would be enforced. Hitler's rise to power in Germany was similar in many ways. Germany was near the point of economic collapse produced by the harsh peace treaty accepted after World War I. Crime was rampant, and the society was troubled. Hitler promised a strong, directive leadership. He guaranteed law and order. He blamed the country's troubles on a scapegoat, the Jews. He even helped his campaign along by bombing buildings and then blaming the destruction on the Jews. Clearly, democratic societies must be vigilant, especially in times of strife, to protect themselves against the natural rise of authoritarianism during troubled periods.

■ SUMMARY

Prior to this chapter, our emphasis has been on the social behavior of an individual or the behavior of two individuals in interaction. We've now expanded the scope of discussion and considered processes that occur in small groups. Groups comprise two or more individuals who are interacting and influencing each other's behaviors. Typically, groups are perceived as units, rather than as made up of independent individuals. Group members have common interests and goals, and groups are organized to some extent.

To illustrate some processes that occur in groups, a case study of groupthink was presented. Groupthink refers to a process which occurs in cohesive groups where the members' striving for consensus interferes with the group's ability to function successfully and deal with important problems. Groupthink is most likely to occur when a group is cohesive, when a strong leader states preferences for solution of a task, when a group is insulated from outside advice, and when the problem facing a group is important. Luckily, numerous techniques can reduce the likelihood that groupthink will occur.

Simply because groupthink can occur does not imply that individuals perform better alone than in groups. Groups usually are better at solving problems than an average person is. However, whether a group will be superior to, inferior to, or equal to the performance of the most capable group member is determined by the type of task that confronts the group. When tasks are complex and division of labor can occur, group members can pool their abilities and perform better than even a capable individual could alone.

Group cohesiveness has major effects on group functioning. Although groupthink can occur in cohesive groups if no precautions are taken, cohesiveness is superior to non-cohesiveness on most counts. Members of cohesive groups enjoy their association, follow group norms, assume responsibility within the group, and work hard to achieve group goals.

All groups are structured to some degree. Members assume different roles within a group which permits division of labor. Evaluation of these roles will determine a person's status within a group, which will affect how he or she is treated by the group and how he or she will act toward the group. Groups also sometimes limit the amount of communication between group members, and communication networks affect members' satisfaction, leader emergence, and group performance.

A group leader is someone who exerts influence on the group members' attitudes and behaviors and appears to have the group's best interests at heart. Historically, two general perspectives on leadership have emerged: the great man theory and the social forces theory. The great man theory contributed to the search for personality characteristics associated with leadership. Unfortunately, only a few characteristics seem related to leadership, and none applies to every situation. The social forces theory contributed to the examination of how environmental and situational influences affect leadership. Currently, the most useful models of leadership combine the two approaches and describe how personality and situational factors interact to determine leadership effectiveness.

10

crowding and the environment

concepts

Population growth continues while the world's resources diminish.

Social pathology appears to be related to crowded living conditions.

We develop ideas about what the "right" number of people is for various social settings.

Crowding exists when one's desire for space exceeds what is available.

People develop attitudes about appropriate distancing from others.

Some factors in the environment promote social interaction, while others seem to force people apart.

Different living conditions seem to affect one's personality.

People seem to adapt to urban living.

targets

After reading this chapter, you should be able to:

1   Discuss predictions of population disaster.
2   Describe the effects of both too-high density and too-low density on social behavior.
3   Differentiate among the concepts of crowding, personal space, territory, and privacy.
4   Describe how personal space is measured and how it influences social behavior.
5   Identify different ways to characterize various environments.
6   Discuss the reasons people give for spending time in recreation.
7   Explain the idea that urban environments create cognitive overload for people.

As the world's population continues to increase rapidly, scientists from many disciplines are making predictions about the future of humanity. These predictions take two different forms and answer two different questions. The first involves projections of population growth, both for specific countries and for the world. Social scientists who engage in this research are called *demographers,* and they typically use information from public records, such as birth, death, and census surveys. An example of this work is provided by Figure 10-1. As can be noted, even if a trend toward two-child families were begun immediately in the United States, another 130 million people would live in this country in 100 years. Alarmists such as Paul Erlich, author of *The Population Bomb,* claim that unless something is done, the earth simply won't be able to provide what is needed to sustain life. An example of the effects of decreasing resources for individuals in recent years has been provided by the petroleum industry, which is involved with a variety of energy problems. When computer projections are developed up to the year 2100—mapping resources, food, pollution, industrial output, and population—they often predict disaster. In the *Limits to Growth Report* [100], the year 2030 (only about fifty years away) would be the doomsday year. Supposedly, food and resources will not be sufficient, but the population will still be growing. It's obvious that our environment will be quite different with such growth. We will be a country of about twenty-five large urban centers. All the area from Boston, New York, and Washington to Chicago will be one large, sprawling city. Most of Florida and California will also be citylike.

These findings highlight the importance of the second form of predictions—those dealing with the effects of such crowding on human beings. The important questions for social scientists become: What will be the

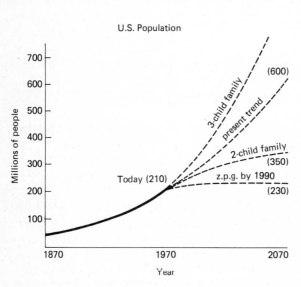

Figure 10-1. *The population growth in the United States (and the world) is sometimes hard to imagine. The numbers are simply too large and the problem does not seem as dramatic as it is when displayed in graphic form. Consider that the current United States population, which is slightly over 200,000,000, would rise to 350,000,000 in less than 100 years, if a two-child family were to become typical. And almost 1 billion people would crowd the country in 100 years if a three-child family were to become the norm. Many think that the United States is crowded now. What does the future hold?*

effects of high population density? Will our interpersonal behavior change because of these different living conditions? To offer a few answers, we will consider evidence from a variety of sources. Community surveys, crime-rate statistics, natural history, and experimental studies provide information about future possibilities. One classic work on the effects of crowding, conducted with rats, is described in Focus 10-1.

■ DENSITY AND SOCIAL BEHAVIOR

High density

Early studies of the effects of population density on social behavior were performed by demographers. And, although variables utilized in census surveys are not usually precise measures of social behavior, a relationship between social disturbances and population density appears quite evident. Working with 1950 census data from 75 community areas in Chicago, it has been found that the more people there were in a given area, the more frequent were sickness, delinquency, infant mortality, and needed welfare assistance [501]. This finding parallels evidence from crime-rate statistics. It has been found that across the United States, in cities of sizes varying from 10,000 to 1 million people, not only does the amount of crime increase with size, but so does the rate of crime. Again, crime rates are only crude measures of social behavior, but the picture appears consistent.

Many factors might account for these findings. For example, high-density areas tend to be poverty areas. When people are poor, health problems arise, and the push toward crime is stronger. So the census study of Chicago's 75 community areas was redone with 1960 data to identify more precisely the relationship between population density and social disturbances. Galle, Gove, and McPherson [174] reasoned that they should distinguish between simply having a large number of people in an area and having a large number of people with whom one must interact. They called the first condition *structural density;* it would be high if there were a large number of buildings in a given area. They called the second condition *interpersonal density;* it would be high if many people were forced to live in the same room or building in a given area.

In other words, one can differentiate between the number of people who live in a community area and the potential and probable number of social contacts for an individual. Galle and his coworkers proposed that the latter would be more closely related to disturbances in social behavior. That is exactly what was found. Very strong correlations existed between the number of persons per room and lowered fertility, higher mortality, child abuse, and increased asocial and delinquent behavior. Further, increased mental hospital admissions seemed to be the most closely related to the number of rooms within any housing unit—the other measure of interpersonal density. Galle, Gove, and McPherson suggest three possibilities for these results:

FOCUS 10-1   SOCIAL PATHOLOGY AND POPULATION DENSITY

The best-known animal study regarding increasing population density and social pathology is that of John B. Calhoun [86]. Calhoun was interested in observing the social behavior of Norway rats as their populations were allowed to grow until they were clearly crowded. Each population group began with thirty-two rats; in all cases, the animals were just past weaning; half were males, and half females. By the end of the year, all populations had multiplied to comprise eighty adults. At this point, Calhoun held the population constant at eighty by removing the infants that had survived birth and weaning. The physical setup of the experiment is described by Calhoun as follows:

> The males and females that initiated each experiment were placed in groups of the same size and sex composition. In each of the four pens that partitioned a ten by fourteen observation room, the pens were complete dwelling units; each contained a drinking fountain, a food hopper, and an elevated artificial burrow, reached by a winding staircase and holding five nest boxes. A window in the ceiling of the room permitted observation, and there was a door in one wall. With the space for a colony of twelve adults in each pen—the size of the groups in which rats are normally found—this setup should have been able to support 48 rats comfortably. At the stabilized number of 80, an equal distribution of the animals would have found 20 adult rats in each pen, but the animals did not dispose themselves in this way.

Calhoun had structured the environment so that the rats could not make a complete circle by traveling through the adjoining pens. This arrangement immediately created a mathematical probability of a higher population density in the middle two pens. And the rats did tend to congregate in the middle. At the end of the first year of the study, the rats developed *behavioral sinks* in the two middle pens—Calhoun's term for extreme behavioral disturbances. The most severe behavioral abnormalities were observed among females. Many were unable to carry pregnancy to full term, or even to survive delivery of their litters. An even greater number, after successfully giving birth, did not perform maternal functions. The males, on the other hand, developed abnormal sexual behavior and cannibalism, with the dominant rats taking over possession of the outer pens. Some males reacted by adopting severe withdrawal and would emerge only to eat, drink, and move about when other members of the community were asleep. In other words, both sexes displayed severe social disorganization. Interestingly, some regular biological activities were transformed into social activities in which it appeared that the principal satisfaction was derived from interaction with others. For example, individual rats would rarely eat except in the presence of others. Further, this pathological "togetherness" tended to disrupt other activities involving vital modes of behavior, such as courting of sex partners, building of nests, and nursing and care of the young. In fact, infant mortality in the behavioral sinks ran as high as 96 percent among the most disoriented groups in the population.

Supplemental evidence from Calhoun's studies suggests that these effects are truly long-lasting. Recall that the young who did survive were withdrawn from the population to retain a stable size of eighty. At the end of the first series of experiments, Calhoun allowed the four healthiest males and the four healthiest females to survive. These animals were six months old at the time, and in the prime of life. Although they no longer lived in overpopulated environments, when mated, they produced fewer litters in the next six months than would have normally been expected, and *none of their offspring survived to maturity*. Quite clearly, the effects of the population density are strong in this species.

1   It's possible that as the number of social obligations increases, so does the need to inhibit individual desires. When others are around, one can't do what one wants.
2   There may be too much social stimulation to respond to each person appropriately.
3   Interpersonal conflict may grow as one's territory is infringed upon.

We shall return to each of these possibilities throughout this chapter. The point, however, is that evidence suggests that social behavior is affected by the number of other people present.

Although problems result when high interpersonal density exists, psychologists insist that not all people respond in the same ways. In fact, Filipino men residing in a crowded section of Manila demonstrated three clearly distinct patterns of psychosocial behavior associated with high interpersonal density. In response to the crowding, the men developed one of three different types of personalities. The first was characterized by alienation anxiety (a fear of not being included in what was going on). The second was characterized by withdrawal behaviors designed to isolate the individual from the situation. And the third was characterized by violence and attempts to strike out at the system [287]. This is our first indication that different people respond in different ways to crowding.

Low density

The above discussion suggests that the most optimal environments would be those in which people did not have to interact with a large number of others. Architects have actually tried to construct entire housing developments wherein walls, barriers, partitions, and shrubbery are situated to limit interpersonal contact. This approach is a natural response to the concerns

Figure 10-2. *An example of differential crime rates in two different types of housing is shown here. The older Brownsville, a low-rise project, has a much lower crime rate than the high-rise Van Dyke project directly across the street. Van Dyke has not only a higher crime rate but also a higher maintenance cost. Urban design does affect social behavior.*

we described. A classic example of this type of "new city" has been described by architect Carl Feiss [149]. A town named Albertslund was built in the mid-1960s outside Copenhagen, Denmark. Albertslund was a town of about 10,000 people, and every attempt was made to construct housing that would provide the minimum perception of crowdedness. The floor plans for apartments were developed to be very attractive. Apartments had several bedrooms, a kitchen, living room, and several bathrooms, and were arranged in an L shape around a private patio. The apartments appeared comfortable, well-designed in terms of traffic flow, separated from the other apartments, and had sliding glass doors to the patio. To secure privacy for occupants, the apartments' only windows overlooked the patio. In addition, the patio was bordered by high decorative fencing.

What happened to the social behavior of the families living in Albertslund? The opposite of what was desired. Many family disturbances occurred, similar to those noted in the social behavior of the crowded living conditions in Chicago and the Philippines. Further, among couples who had no children, the suicide rate for wives far exceeded the national norm. The planners had gone too far in psychologically separating these people. In trying to provide privacy for the families, the designers had isolated them. The wives who committed suicide saw no one between 8 A.M. and 5 P.M. (while the husbands were at work), unless they left their apartments explicitly for social stimulation.

Although it has been demonstrated that too many people can create disturbances in social behavior, the results at Albertslund suggest that too few people also can pose problems. In fact, early research on affiliation was generated by the observation that whenever people lived in isolation—such as in wolf-child incidents—they developed behavior dominated by fear.

The right number of people

If both high interpersonal density and low interpersonal density are associated with aberrations in social behavior there must be a middle ground, a "right" number of people with whom to interact. And proponents of ecological psychology suggest that no behavior can be analyzed independently of the setting, the environment, in which it occurs [36]. Consequently, Allan Wicker [494] suggests that we consider the *manning* of an environmental setting. An *undermanned* setting would be one in which more individuals are needed to maintain the social functions of the setting. For example, a baseball team without a pitcher would be undermanned. The extreme of undermanning would be the isolation created in Albertslund. Alternatively, *overmanned* settings have too many people for social behaviors to be appropriately managed, such as three people in a two-seater sports car. In this case, the extreme of overmanning would be the crowding occurring in the Chicago studies. As Figure 10-3 shows, any setting might be undermanned, adequately manned, or overmanned.

Now the question becomes, What are the characteristics of a setting that determine what is felt to be the "right" number of people present? The first set of characteristics has to do with the design of the environment, and the second set concerns the nature of the ongoing social situation. Both sets of characteristics were studied in a unique investigation [120] which presented subjects with scaled-down rooms and human figures, and asked them to place as many people as possible in different rooms without overcrowding them. The architectural design and the kinds of activities that were being conducted were varied for the rooms. One researcher hypothesized that any architectural feature that reduced interpersonal perception (interpersonal density) within a space would reduce the level of crowding. Designs that

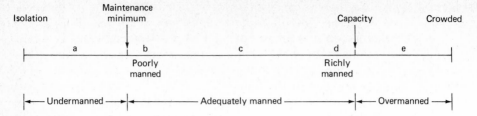

Figure 10-3. *There is a continuum of degrees of manning in any social situation. A situation is adequately manned if more than a minimum number of people for maintenance are present and if that number does not surpass the capacity of the situation. A football team is adequately manned with 11 players, a baseball team with 9, and a basketball team with 5. If fewer than a minimum number are present, the situation is undermanned; if the capacity is surpassed, it is overmanned. The extreme ends of this continuum are termed "isolation" and "overcrowded."*

included partitions and sound-absorbing walls and ceilings, and that minimized the number of mirrors, doors, and windows, had the effect of reducing cues that other people are nearby. Subjects placed many more "people" in the same area if partitions and walls were included that did not allow each "person" to see all the "others."

As mentioned, the nature of the ongoing social activity also affected the number of "persons" placed in the settings. A cocktail party, an airport waiting room, and a library situation were included as different social events. Clearly, the greatest number of "people" were placed in the cocktail party and the fewest in the library situation. These findings emphasize Wicker's idea that different social settings suggest an appropriate number of people.

We have mentioned Kurt Lewin's [272] field theory several times. Recall that he held human behavior to be caused by an interplay between a person and the environment. This proposition is generally denoted symbolically as $B = f (P, E)$, where B represents behavior, P represents the person, and E represents the environment. This position includes several important aspects. First, a person's social behavior is affected both by characteristics of the person (wants, knowledge, abilities, attitudes, etc.) and by characteristics of the social environment. Lewin emphasizes behavior to be the result of current expectations, situational characteristics, and personal feelings, abilities, and desires. So even though the usual desire would be to have many people at a cocktail party, variations in the appropriate size of the party may result from the personalities of the host and guests. A party-giver with amorous intentions might not want much competition, while a host who enjoys confusion might pack the place to the seams.

A second important aspect of Lewin's approach is that it is clearly psychological. Behavior is described in terms of the psychological field as it exists for a person. For Lewin, the situation should be analyzed in terms of how any person *perceives* the world, rather than how the world actually is.

Since it appears that the "right" number of people depends on both the people involved and the social environment, the rest of this chapter discusses first, factors related to the distribution of people in an environment, and, second, different types of social environments. Finally, by putting all the pieces together, we may be able to answer some questions about what the future holds.

■ DISTRIBUTION OF PERSONS: GIVE ME A LITTLE ROOM!

Four concepts are important to a discussion of the distribution of people in social settings. Research on *crowding, territory, privacy,* and *personal space* all bear on individuals' perceptions of whether or not one has enough room.

Crowding: There are too many people too close to me!

Although early work with animals and high density has produced consistent findings, and although demographic correlational work from large urban settings appears to replicate the animal research, very little work was done on human social response to crowding until the early 1970s. Part of the reason for this stems from lack of agreement about what constitutes crowding. Perhaps the most comprehensive conceptual framework is provided by Daniel Stokols [428; 429]. The essence of Stokols's analysis is that "*crowding exists* and is perceived as such by an individual *when the individual's demand for space exceeds the available supply* of such space" [428, p. 75; italics added]. In other words, we are crowded when we want more space but can't have it. Stokols differentiates between the concepts of density and crowding. Density denotes a physical condition involving limitations of space, whereas crowding is an *experiential* state wherein a person perceives a spatial restriction and experiences physiological and psychological stress. In some situations we may desire high density and, therefore, would not feel crowded, such as at a party. Further, it may be that some people who live in high-density areas (possibly subjects in Galle, Gove, and Mc-Pherson's Chicago study) do not feel crowded because they are used to having many others around. On the other hand, some might feel real stress in such a situation—causing the social pathologies mentioned—mental hospital admissions, family disturbances, etc. Stokols further differentiates nonsocial from social crowding. In nonsocial crowding, a person's supply of usable space is restricted to an inadequate level by purely physical factors, such as not having a large enough room in which to conduct one's work or having too many boxes, desks, file cabinets, etc. On the other hand, social crowding denotes an individual's awareness of spatial restriction as it relates directly to the presence of other people as well as to the individual's relationship with these people. Social crowding exists when there simply

Figure 10-4. *People usually don't like to be crowded; they prefer to have some room of their own. When such space is not available, pushing and shoving usually results. In this group it would be difficult to get from the center to the outside, where one could breathe easily. Often such pushing and shoving becomes quite aggressive if more space isn't provided.*

are too many people around in a particular social context. This formulation is analogous to the suggestion made by Galle, Gove, and McPherson that high density leads to problems when people receive excessive stimulation from social sources.

In early studies of human crowding, researchers brought subjects into laboratory and field settings, had them engage in different tasks, and noted changes in their social behavior and performance while engaging in such tasks in one of two conditions. For the first condition subjects were dense; in the second condition they were not. Some of these tasks (such as the joint solution of a giant erector-set problem) involved cooperation and competition; others concerned the individual alone (such as individual problem solving of puzzles). Also, some of the experiments allowed an individual to have a personal work space; others required all subjects to share the same facilities. For example, some research allowed each individual to sit at a chair throughout the experiment. The studies in which the subjects must share and compete for use of blackboards are probably more like real life.

Bearing these distinctions in mind, it is not surprising that the results have proved to be inconsistent.

Several such studies of crowding with children have indicated that density does affect social behavior. In one study, four- and five-year-old children were allowed to play with toys of their own choosing in a rather large room. After a while, group size was increased until the room was crowded (and toys were more scarce). The children became more aggressive and less interested in being friendly with others [222]. Another way of investigating the response to crowding would have been to take the original, smaller group and simply place the children in a much smaller room. When this is done, children seem to withdraw, play in solitude, and not develop interaction with others. They become much less interested in all forms of interpersonal behavior[276].

Some feel that crowding does not lead to a decrease in the ability to perform appropriately. When adults are given paper-and-pencil tasks to perform, puzzles to solve, and so on, and are seated in comfortable wooden chairs with desklike arms, it does not seem to matter if there is a small or extremely large number of people in the experimental room [167]. When subjects are thus allowed to "cocoon themselves" from others in the experimental setting, performance and social behavior do not change. Unfortunately, everyday life does not allow such cocooning; there is competition for goods and space. What about settings in which one must share? More research is needed to answer questions such as these that reflect real life situations.

As a result of the complexity of such research, there is developing interest in "real world situations," such as different living conditions, and their effects on social behavior. For example, do differences in social behavior result from living in crowded or uncrowded apartment complexes? A few answers are provided by the research of Stuart Valins and his colleagues regarding residential environments, social interaction, and crowding [39, 467]. At the State University of New York at Stony Brook, first-year college students are randomly assigned to one of two different residential environments. One is a traditional corridor dormitory with seventeen double-occupancy bedrooms on each floor. The other dormitory is constructed of suites made up of two or three double-occupancy bedrooms, a lounge area, and a small bathroom, with each dorm unit housing thirty-four to thirty-six students in four-, five-, or six-person suites. Valins found that 58 percent of the subjects in traditional living arrangements reported that their dormitory was crowded, whereas only 10 percent in the suite-designed dormitories reported their dormitory to be crowded.

Valins asked his subjects to place miniature figures in fixed-space model rooms under varying conditions of social or nonsocial activity. When the activity was social, such as a party, those from the crowded living arrangements did not place many "people" in the room. However, when the activity was nonsocial, such as business teams, they tolerated more people. It seems that subjects living in the crowded form were beginning to protect their space, and when the situation demanded a large number of people, it was acceptable. However, if it was a social situation, even though subjects *could* tolerate people, they would rather not. These results suggest that crowded residents learn to avoid social interaction. However, there is more to the story. When the researchers wanted the subjects to solve problems and complete tasks, they found that the crowded residents did better when competition rather than cooperation was stressed. It may be that the residents were adopting competitive orientations as they reacted to excessive social stimulation. How are your dormitories designed? Are you crowded? Is the design affecting your personality?

Territory: That's my place!

Results such as these and the earlier work on the effects of social behavior in laboratory settings of different density suggest that an important aspect of feelings of crowding is the concern for one's *territory*. *Territory* is generally defined as an area than an organism will protect and defend against intruders, again depending on the situation. In various animal species such behavior is necessary for protecting the young, determining mating patterns, and promoting the ecological system. Human beings also like to have a "home turf," a physical location to consider their own. Street gangs prefer to fight on their turf, since they feel it gives them an advantage over their opponent. They know the territory, while their opponent does not. They feel comfortable, while their opponent is the intruder. Similarly, football coaches and teams prefer to have the home-field advantage, and most teams are likely to win more often at home than on the road. Naturally, for a football team, the home field offers a psychological edge over opponents, since they know the field and have their screaming fans in the stands.

The benefits of holding meetings in one's own territory were strikingly demonstrated in a study of negotiation processes [288]. Pairs of subjects were asked to negotiate the solution to a mock jury case, in which they were asked to decide the length of a prison term for a criminal who pleaded guilty to a crime. Some subjects were assigned the role of defense attorney and preferred to reach a solution that drew their client a minimum sentence. Other subjects were assigned the role of prosecutor and preferred to negotiate a long sentence for the criminal. Half the time, negotiations were held in the dorm room of the defense attorney; the rest of the time, negotiations were held in the dorm room of the prosecutor. The results of this study indicated that the person who was on his own turf held the floor and talked much longer than did the visitor and was much more effective in achieving the preferred solution. The home participant "won" the negotiation twenty-one times, while the visitor "won" only nine times. These results dramatically demonstrate why attorneys prefer to use their own offices in negotiations with the opposition. They also explain why it takes so long for international negotiators to decide on an appropriate site for treaty negotiations.

Once the location of a group meeting is established, the physical

(a)

(b)

Figure 10-5. *Most people like to personalize the areas in which they work. In (a), an office worker has used this windmill, name card, and distinctive coffee cup to put a little of herself into her work space. Increased space (b) provides an opportunity for a much more elaborate statement of personality. For this executive, opulence and elegance take the place of the windmill, name tag, and coffee cup.*

arrangements of the meeting place can affect what happens in the group. As you may remember, the Paris peace negotiations to bring an end to American involvement in the Vietnam war were held up for months while negotiators tried to decide on an appropriate shape for the negotiating table. Most people's immediate reaction to this apparent nonsense was to wonder why there was so much cause for concern. What difference could it possibly make if the table was rectangular, circular, square, hexagonal, or whatever? Robert Sommer [417] showed subjects a variety of different seating arrangements for different activities. When a rectangular table is used, people prefer to sit next to one another when cooperating on a problem; they prefer to face one another across the table if they are competing; and they like to sit corner to corner or across from one another when engaged in conversation. It therefore appears that the shape of the table and the places where chairs are set can make a great difference. (Whether the difference is great enough to hold up negotiations to end a war is another question.)

After being seated at a table, one's placement will affect which people one will converse with. At a round table, people talk to those seated across the table, rather than to those seated next to them [427]. At a square table, people also prefer to talk to those across from them *unless* a strong, directive leader is present [199]. With a strong leader present, people tend to talk to those seated next to them, rather than to those across the table. This makes the individual less conspicuous at the table; he or she doesn't stand out as much when talking to a person on the side as when talking across the table.

These effects indicate that if you are in a high-status position and want to dominate a conversation, you would do best to choose a square or rectangular table with yourself at the head. In fact, in one study of jury deliberations, it was found that jurors from professional or managerial backgrounds (those who had high status) usually took the head seat at the jury table [435]. If you have high status and want to ease group conversation, you would be wise to use a round table. Legend has it that King Arthur chose a round table because he didn't want status distinctions to affect the meetings of his knights. This lesson has not been lost on contemporary leaders and their spouses. Mamie Eisenhower enjoyed the role of First Lady and relished the status that the position afforded. Consequently, she used rectangular tables in the White House dining room with herself and President Eisenhower at the heads. Jacqueline Kennedy, who wanted a more egalitarian atmosphere during dining and more relaxed conversations, moved the rectangular tables out and brought round ones in.

Another aspect of the importance of territoriality in human group behavior is reported in an observational study of nine coworkers in a large insurance company. These employees made up the voucher check unit and spent most of their time filing. For a number of years the work area assigned to this unit in the company building had a built-in barrier system. Enclosed steel mesh walls reinforced with filing cabinets surrounded the workers' desks, and the area soon became known as "the cage." A real *esprit de corps* developed among the workers, who regarded the materials within "the cage" as their own. The group was cohesive and had decision-making privileges not given to others in the company. Workers could go out during the afternoon when in the mood and bring snacks back to the unit. Unfortunately, the company had to relocate the unit to another floor. With relocation, several small changes occurred in the physical arrangement. First, the territory was slightly reduced in size. Second, the protective file-cabinet barrier was removed. Third, control over company property was taken out of the unit's hands, and desks within the territory were altered. The changes in social behavior resulting from these minor changes in physical setup were catastrophic. There was a perceived loss of status for the entire group, a loss of an area to identify with, generally decreasing morale, and reduction in work efficiency [362]. Changes in the size, shape, and boundaries of the territory created a state of confusion and a sense of personal loss for the employees.

A possible explanation for these profound effects is that people may use territories to establish and maintain a sense of personal identity. This seems plausible. Often people describe themselves in terms of a place, rather than in terms of their personalities. For example: "Hi, I'm Rico Brown from South Philly; went to Kennedy High School, and now live in Chicago." In studies of socially isolated pairs of sailors, men laid claim to particular places, beds, and chairs, not only to guarantee social needs and biological satisfactions but also to preserve a sense of identity [11]. In observations of the aquanauts involved with the underwater Sealab projects, it has been noted that the men with collapsing upper berths displayed less than optimal social behavior (such as aggression) during the day, when their beds were folded away [453].

Another social behavior we have discussed is helping behavior. It is possible that territory plays an important role in determining response to emergencies. Kitty Genovese may not have been aided in the infamous Kew Gardens incident (see Chapter 6) because the attack took place in a setting outside anyone's territory. If the attacks had occurred inside an area that someone laid claim to and felt responsible for, then the person might have been stimulated to help [496]. This may have been an example of *interstitial* behavior. An interstitial area is defined as a crackline area falling between other well-defined areas. Alleys, interstate highways, etc., are areas which clearly belong to no one, and increased antisocial and decreased prosocial behavior seems to occur in these settings. The fact that another murder of exactly the same nature took place ten years later in the same area as the Genovese attacks indicates that the area may be a place in which no one takes responsibility to act [325].

Privacy: Leave me alone!

Another concept closely linked to crowding and territorial behavior is that of privacy [10]. In fact, it would seem that privacy is the exact opposite of crowdedness. The most common definition of privacy is Alan Westin's [490]. He suggests that privacy is "the claim of individuals, groups or institutions to determine for themselves when, how, and to what extent information about them is communicated to others." Westin goes further to suggest that there are four basic states of privacy. (1) *Solitude* is the state of privacy in which a person is alone and free from observation of others (Leave *me* alone!). (2) *Intimacy* refers to the type of privacy sought by a couple or the members of a larger group to achieve maximal personal relationships between or among its members (Leave *us* alone!). (3) *Anonymity* is a state in which an individual seeks and achieves freedom from identification and surveillance in a public setting, for example, in the street, in the park, on the subway, or at an artistic event (I hope no one figures out who I am). And (4) *Reserve* means not revealing certain aspects of oneself that are either too personal, shameful, or profane (I don't think I'll tell anyone that). Whether one is trying to achieve intimacy, solitude, or whatever, it is clear that one is being sensitive to the number of other people in one's environment.

Recent research has focused on the development of privacy. Researchers have interviewed 840 children and teen-agers between the ages of four and nineteen, half from New York City and half from a rural district outside of Milwaukee [260]. The children were evenly divided by sex and socioeconomic background, and the sample was further subdivided by ethnic background (white, black, and Spanish-speaking). Preliminary results suggest:

1 Children as young as four years of age have an understanding of what privacy is.
2 The perception of privacy grows in complexity with increasing age and increased language efficiency.
3 The most important elements of the concept of privacy—for example, being alone—are present at the earliest ages and remain critical over time.
4 Frequency and importance of some elements, however, change with age. Younger children most often reported being alone as very important to privacy, whereas older children think that keeping one's thoughts to oneself is at least as important.
5 Concern for possession of objects is more prevalent at younger ages, whereas older children replace such a concern with *controlling* who uses them. For example, instead of being concerned with having one's own bicycle, a concern develops for having one's own room or apartment (rented—but still one's own).
6 The meaning of privacy seems to change from just being alone or doing something by oneself to a concern for the freedom to choose such settings.

It appears, then, that privacy is a concept which is with us during the formative years and which seems to have a lot to do with the formation of attitudes regarding how many people (under what circumstances) one would like to interact with. Further, it appears that this concept changes with age, with increasing importance being given to the aspects of freedom and choice.

Personal space: Stand about that far from me!

Throughout this chapter we have described the interdependency between the environment and social behavior. We have seen how the human environment affects interpersonal behavior and have noticed how projections of population growth and increasing urbanization will probably result in feelings of crowdedness and needs for privacy. A concept which may underlie these phenomena on the social-psychological level is that of *personal space.* Personal space can be defined as *the area that individuals would like to have between themselves and others in different situations.* Given the importance of this concept, we shall briefly review several theoretical orientations, the methods used, and typical findings in studies of personal space.

What is it? Psychologist Robert Sommer [417] suggests that personal space is an area surrounding a person's body into which intruders may not come. A slightly different interpretation is that personal space refers to the area immediately surrounding an individual in which most face-to-face interactions occur [275]. E. T. Hall, an anthropologist, suggests that personal space is a learned phenomenon and that there are four personal-distance zones surrounding each individual which are concentric and fluctuate depending on the situation [194]. According to Hall, the first zones represent *personal* space and describe the distance usually found between individuals who are familiar with one another or family members. The outer zones are labeled *social* space and refer to distance between individuals who may be strangers. These conceptions of personal space suggest that there may be a zone around each of us which we feel is appropriate to have between ourselves and others in various situations.

Research has suggested that these zones are not circular and that they vary with the type of social behaviors involved. For instance, we know that people can stand or sit closer to one another if they are back-to-back or side-by-side rather than face-to-face. Notice that seating in most classrooms is arranged in a side-by-side fashion to allow the greatest number of people to listen comfortably to a discussion leader. What would happen if the chairs were just as close, but you had to directly face your classmates? A second point is that our behaviors change with the setting. It is appropriate for a nurse to stand very close to a male patient to take his temperature, but it may be that if the same two people met in a social setting, both would want more space between them.

Practically all theorists make a distinction between personal space and individual distance. Individual distance can be measured in physical units. We can observe any two people and measure how far apart they are in feet and inches (individual distance), it may or may not be the distance the people would like to have between themselves (personal space). For instance, you may want to have someone closer to you, especially if the person is highly attractive. However, the social situation may suggest that it is not appropriate at this time. On the other hand, you may wish to have more space between yourself and others, but you may tolerate them inside the boundary as long as the situation demands it (say, on an elevator). Notice that when we don't have the space that we want, we feel crowded (see the earlier discussion of Stokol's ideas on crowding).

How is it measured? Three general methodological strategies have been used to study personal space. The earliest approach was that of simulation. Subjects were presented with dolls, cut-out figures, or symbols representing people and were instructed to move or place these figures in various positions. Often the situation was varied (such as a cocktail party versus a library table), and subjects were asked to place dolls as close to each other as would be appropriate in that particular environmental setting. In this approach, the researcher simply measures the distances between the figures and notices the direction in which the subject has faced them.

A second approach is more behavioral and provides an index of space indicative of both individual distance and personal space. Specifically, subjects are asked either to approach someone else until they think they wish to stop, or to watch as other people approach and tell them when to stop. Characteristics such as sex, size, ethnicity, and the beauty of the approaching individuals are varied, as are characteristics of the environmental setting. The general idea, however, remains the same: subjects indicate when they start to feel uncomfortable or inappropriate. Another behavioral measure is derived from field research in naturalistic settings. In these situations the individual distance between different persons serves as an index of personal space. For example, a waiting room for subjects may be structured with various chairs in different positions. As subjects are brought into the room, they are asked to sit wherever they would like to wait for the study to begin. Notice is made of which chair a subject uses and its relationship to another individual in the room, who, in most cases, is a confederate of the experimenter.

A third measure which has been applied to the study of personal space is more reminiscent of the attitude survey or attitude questionnaire approach. One version of this approach has been to show subjects pictures of various individuals in different settings and to have them rate how appropriate the physical spacing is. A second version asks subjects to mark on a piece of paper how close they would like individuals to approach, given that they (the subjects) were represented at a particular point on the piece of paper to start with [133]. It is clear that these various methodologies could result in slightly different findings. However, the few studies which have compared them indicate substantial agreement. Now that we have an understanding of what personal space is and how to measure it, the question is, In what ways does personal space affect social behavior?

The influence of personal space on social behavior

There is considerable evidence that there are crosscultural or ethnic differences in personal spacing behavior. Germans appear to have larger personal space requirements and are much less flexible in them than are

Americans. On the other hand, Latin Americans, French, and Arabs seem to be much more tolerant of close quarters and have smaller personal space requirements. Similar findings have been obtained on subcultures within the United States. It appears that Chicanos stand closer together than whites, who in turn stand closer together than blacks [41]. This would suggest that if two people from different ethnic backgrounds were talking, one of the two might be very uncomfortable simply because of the space between them. This discomfort might affect the quality of the interaction. As a consequence, there is an indication that mixed-race groups have larger space requirements than same-race groups. It is, of course, possible that such differences are more attributable to socioeconomic differences than to ethnic differences [236]. In other words, ethnicity may not be as important as whether a person is from the upper, lower, or middle class, and therefore familiar with different spatial experiences (such as bigger houses).

As there are subcultural variations in personal spacing behavior, it is likely that personal space concepts are acquired through learning at early ages. Girls apparently develop adultlike perception in management of personal space much earlier than boys, which in turn reflects the fact that girls generally develop social maturation at earlier ages. It appears, however, that males have more definite personal space boundaries when compared with females. Males keep the same distance regardless of whom they interact with, whereas females are a bit more adaptable. This would seem perfectly consistent with American cultural values. Further, it has been found that females interacting with females exhibit smaller personal space zones than males interacting with males [268].

It appears that the "other" person in an interaction has meaning for children as they develop personal spacing behavior. It has been found that children will place themselves closer to relatives (in the simulation games) than they will to other authority figures, such as school principals. Clearly, the other person and the social setting are important in the spacing response [134; 331]. Children learn early that there are appropriate interaction distances, and, therefore, if someone violates those distances, children might resist the attempt to interact.

One way of demonstrating the fact that personal space concepts are acquired via social learning is to study the influence of modeling. Researchers had models (confederate children of the same age as the subjects) either approach or stay away from object-persons (also confederates) in an experimental setting. Both boys and girls tended to stay close or far from the object-person as a function of the model's behavior when given an opportunity to walk around in the experimental setting [24a].

Evidence from studies with college students indicates that personal spacing behavior is related both to interaction styles and to personality. Consider the kind of person who would be bold enough to come a little closer to people than others might. Such individuals probably think highly of themselves, like to control or dominate others, feel that they are the master of their fate, and are not afraid to open up to others. Subjects who demonstrate close personal spaces have been found to have high self-esteem, high dominance, feel internally rather than externally controlled, and tend to be self-disclosers [164]. It makes sense that individuals who like to keep themselves separate from others physically are those who do not like to disclose information about themselves.

Another social behavior that is related to personal space is aggression. In Chapter 7 we discussed the fact that in lower species animals display aggression when other animals trespass into the first animal's territory. The person who gets too close can be said to be *invading* another's personal space. A typical response is to be on the defensive. In fact, when it appears that someone is purposely getting too close (and not with amorous intentions), we usually view the behavior as an unstated challenge. We tend to perceive the invader as someone who is trying to dominate. Our social response to such a perception might be aggression, or it might be flight.

Lastly, if in fact personal space behavior is a basic building block in our understanding of the human response to high population density and crowding, there should be some indication of an empirical relationship among the variables. In one study, both males and females, black and white subjects, of ages ranging from four through nineteen provided information about their personal space behavior as well as developing attitudes toward population growth and environment. It appeared that individuals who had larger personal spaces were concerned with potential population problems [395].

Very clearly, people have different personal space requirements in different social settings—usually depending on norms of appropriateness. Now that we know how these different aspects of interpersonal spacing behavior operate, the question becomes, What different kinds of social behavior does one find in different environments? We shall turn to an analysis of different settings and the behaviors one finds in each.

■ ENVIRONMENTAL SETTINGS

Contemporary life is complex; each of us spends some time in many different environments. After briefly describing several characteristics that differentiate among environments, we shall describe the social behavior found in the following environments: natural settings, residential areas, and cities.

One can look for *sociofugal* or *sociopetal* factors in any environment [337]. Sociofugal factors are characteristics of the environment that serve to discourage or prohibit social interaction. Sociopetal factors, on the other hand, are characteristics that have the potential to foster and improve the quality of social interactions. For example, it was noted in Chapter 9 that certain seating and communication patterns fostered cohesive interaction (sociopetal), while others did not (sociofugal). Unfortunately, as is discussed in Focus 10-2, too many designed environments, such as airports, are sociofugal.

FOCUS 10-2   OUR SOCIOFUGAL AIRPORTS

Throughout this chapter we have discussed how certain environments promote social interaction, whereas others seem to negate any possibility of meaningful interaction with others. An investigator who has studied the interplay between the design of our physical environment and our social behavior is Robert Sommer. In his book *Tight Spaces* [418], Sommer discusses the nature of our modern airports. He suggests that although they are technically and architecturally impressive, the effect they have on social behavior is an outrage.

To start, Sommer suggests that airports are not designed for most people, but for a relatively small proportion of those who use an airport. Second, they are designed in such a way that—almost a conspiracy—passengers are driven to the concessions to spend money. The reason for this, he suggests, is that airport designers labor under several misconceptions. The first of these is that people spend very little time in airports—which hardly applies to the delayed, overbooked, cancelled, security-checked cross-country and international flights today. Each individual spends at least an hour per trip at a major airport, and this estimate is probably low. Some passengers want to be left alone, and their wishes should be respected. "The sociofugal (or personal-contact discouraging) layout of airports suits these passengers quite nicely, but the situation is different for passengers who would like to wait in a reassuring and comfortable environment. The terminal atmosphere does nothing to calm people who have latent fears about flying" [418]. The fact that airports can give a sense of loneliness and alienation has been demonstrated by several movies, such as *The Graduate*, in which Dustin Hoffman rides alone on a seemingly endless passenger conveyor belt in a convincing demonstration of this silent vigil.

Sommer suggests that in some sense, airports are designed like turkey coops. Biologists have discovered that when turkeys are forced to face outward from their coops, they avoid eye contact and therefore minimize their aggressive responses. This situation seems similar to the social situation in modern airports. Windows provide psychological refuge, passengers are encouraged to retreat into newspapers and magazines, and chairs are bolted to the floor, facing one direction, again minimizing eye contact. (Note, also, that there seems to be an assumption that all people are the same size and shape, and that, therefore, all chairs should be identical.) The point is that these architectural features curb, first, creative use of the environment and, second, conversation and social interaction. The lone businessperson may easily adapt to the isolating arrangement, but the elderly, the young, and gregarious individuals who wish to talk are discouraged. Sommer suggests [p. 14] that

The children are restricted to a few rote responses such as playing with the insurance machine, walking up the down escalator, turning on the water fountain, riding the conveyor belt in the baggage section when the attendant isn't present, inspecting the candy machines, checking out the waste baskets, and pulling the levers on the cigarette machines. . . . The exploratory urges of the child propel him to the only movable, manipulable objects available—and these are likely to be the cigarette machine and the stainless steel ashtray.

The only place where one can find chairs not lined up in such an antiseptic fashion is in the special lounges or club facilities available only to corporation executives and others who can afford luxury. The rest of us simply have to suffer.

Not only is the airport itself consciously or unconsciously designed to be sociofugal; interactions with airline personnel do not particularly help the situation. Consider the following passage from Sommer (p. 13):

After an arduous trip to the airport, the arriving passenger, like the departing one, is left to his own devices, and treated as a non-person by all the uniformed personnel chatting with one another. Assuming he finds the right sequence of lines in which to wait, and walks down the right tubes, he eventually arrives in a sterile room in which all the black chairs, facing in a single direction, are bolted together, and he is again ignored by the uniformed individuals who converse with one another and occasionally make announcements in the microphones. When the passenger finally boards the plane by entering a smaller tube, and then straps himself into position inside a larger tube, the uniformed people suddenly become aware of his existence. Coffee, tea, or milk; cocktails, magazines, three course dinners, films—there is no end to what is done for him. Ignored at the terminal, he reigns as king of the long tube, he assumes. He is on his way across the country. The spatial experience of flying is nil, and the social environment is as bad. The stewardess waits on each passenger individually, and there is very little possibility for interaction between them. Very few passengers . . . have ever made a friend during an air trip.

Consequently, the only place you are made to feel at all human and can engage in any social interaction—as bad as it might be—is while sitting on the plane. This only serves to contrast with the airline terminal itself, thus making it a thoroughly sociofugal place.

One can also talk about just how much social behavior takes place in a given environment. Without regard to the type of behavior, some places can be described as "busy," while others are "slow." Clearly, Manhattan at 5 P.M. is busy when compared with most other environments. It is also possible to describe the potential for different kinds of activities occurring in a particular environment. For example, in some settings a limited variety of activities occur (cocktail lounge), whereas other settings are characterized by tremendous flexibility (such as the Astrodome, where bullfights, dances, and basketball games are held). The frequency of different kinds of activities describes the *activity profile* of a place. In some sense, the real impact of an environment is described by the different social behaviors it promotes, rather than by characteristics such as size, shape, color, and so on. With these thoughts in mind, let's review how social behavior varies in several different environments.

Natural settings

Do people respond to different natural environments and geographic areas in different fashions? We know that people are different and often appreciate different things. Some people would not leave the big city regardless of the inducement. Yet some take their vacations at the seashore, and others go to the mountains. Still others want to spend their entire lives working and living in the desert, the mountains, or by the sea. So we know that people are not all interested in the same natural environments.

One way to study the interplay between the natural environment and social behavior is through an analysis of the differential uses of recreational areas. There are two aspects of such studies. First, it is interesting to ask what kinds of *expectations* different individuals have regarding different types of recreational facilities. It is not surprising to find that people with different interests use different recreational facilities. Some look forward to boating, fishing, and swimming, while others enjoy hunting, skiing, and mountain climbing. Different areas have different *functional utilities* for the users. In other words, we tend to like things that are useful or provide us with something we want. Consequently, one should have a positive attitude toward a seaside campsite if the reason for going camping includes water activities. Second, one could ask about the characteristics of people who prefer to spend their vacation time in different settings. For example, it has been demonstrated through the use of attitudinal data that campers vary on how "wilderness oriented" they are.

We have been suggesting that different behavioral settings (in this case, natural settings) carry with them different expectations for social behavior. It is commonly assumed that the reason people seek wilderness areas is that they are seeking physical, aesthetic, and educational experiences while at the same time trying to isolate themselves from other individuals. The first three components of such reasoning may be valid. However, it appears that less than 5 percent of all hikers hike alone; more than 75 percent hike in parties of at least three persons. Finally, only 5.9 percent of all respondents have suggested that the most important thing they enjoyed about wilderness recreation was to be alone [384].

Another aspect of social behavior expectations in different settings is the concept of desired change. How many times have you seen people change their interpersonal behavior as they change their environment? For fifty weeks of the year a hard-driving businessman interacts aggressively and with aloofness. When his vacation comes up, he travels to a serene mountain location. He drapes a camera from his neck and scans every

(a)

(b)

(c)

Figure 10-6. *Different kinds of social situations suggest different distributions of people. In a library (a), we want freedom from intrusion in order to concentrate and read. People disperse uniformly throughout a library room to avoid interacting with others. (b) It is also possible to wish to be alone with someone else. While still desiring privacy and tranquility, we wish to share them with another. At still other times (c), we are in the mood to be with many other people. Parties and other social events satisfy this need.*

scene with the hope of taking a dramatic, sensitive picture. He smiles wherever he goes and acts carefree. This is the same person; he is simply in two different settings, and different social behaviors are appropriate to each. His knowledge of the differences in expectations probably played a large role in choosing this vacation area.

In addition to discussing why people choose one site over another, it is possible to address the characteristics of people choosing a particular kind of natural environment. Most of such research has been conducted in federal "wilderness areas." It appears that more males than females (77.6 percent to 22.4 percent) utilize wilderness locations. Wilderness areas also appear to be popular with younger individuals (66.4 percent of the users are under age forty); and the majority of the users come from professional occupations (55.6 percent) or are students (15.8 percent). To pursue this idea further, visitors to such recreation areas tend to be better educated. One report suggests that as many as 80 percent hold doctoral degrees [338]. As only 1 or 2 percent of our population have such advanced degrees, these individuals probably have expectations (or values about these expectations) regarding the experiences to be found in such settings that are different from the population in general.

Residential settings

When most people are asked to describe their environments, they do not think of the mountains, the seaside, or the kinds of natural environments discussed above. Rather, most individuals tend to think in terms of their neighborhood. The term *neighborhood* has several different connotations; it can be thought of in terms of physical dimensions or social parameters. For our purposes, a neighborhood should be identified as a place in which an individual physically resides and that may, in turn, carry implications for social behavior.

A key to understanding the importance of social behavior for neighborhoods is to identify what determines neighborhood satisfaction. Recall, from the work on affiliation, that friendships develop as people live close to each other. In turn, studies suggest that the best prediction of neighborhood satisfaction is whether or not individuals report that their neighbors are friendly. In addition, subjects are more inclined to be satisfied with their neighborhood when they have greater privacy, decreased density, and less noise than others [255].

Recently, neighborhood satisfaction was compared in four different communities—two "new towns" (Columbia, Maryland, and Reston, Virginia) and two suburban communities (Norback, Maryland, and Southfield, Michigan). These communities are all middle class in nature. After a rather detailed and sophisticated analysis, it appears that five factors are related to neighborhood satisfaction. (1) The "maintenance level of the neighborhood" was correlated with neighborhood satisfaction and reflected how well-kept and maintained the buildings, sidewalks, grounds, and lawns were in an area; (2) "friendliness"; (3) the "perceived similarity between the neighbors in the area"; (4) the "neighborhood noise level"; and (5) the "accessibility of various community facilities" [510]. (The last factor was the least predictive.) Therefore, it seems that, at least in these middle-class areas, the most important parameter relating to how one feels about residing in an area is the perception of how clean, neat, and physically appealing it is. And, the next most important parameters are aspects of social behavior.

Another investigation of similar scope has been conducted in a completely different setting, the West End urban-renewal project in Boston. Instead of studying satisfaction with in neighborhood, investigators questioned residents about their perceptions of why people were committed to living in the area. Three factors seemed to have special importance to the inhabitants of West End: (1) residence was highly stable; (2) the entire area seemed to carry a connotation of "home"; and (3) commitment to the area derived from the meaningful relationships maintained there [169]. Within this type area one is bound to find strong kinship and friendship ties. Lowered potential for residential mobility due to economic reasons creates the strong possibility that one's family will be found in the same area. Second, again due to the low potential for movement, it is obvious that one would have an increased opportunity to develop firm and lasting friend-

(a)

Figure 10-7. *Here, two very different sites, Reston, Virginia, and the West End of Boston, have both created a neighborhood feeling. The "new town" of Reston (a) has walkways, and a blend of high- and low-rise structures beautifully orchestrated in an extremely pleasant, well-planned community. Wooded areas and pathways wind gracefully throughout the town. The West End (b) is obviously quite a different setting. However, when family ties are extremely strong and there is little movement away by family or friends, this setting, too, can breed an intense feeling of neighborhood.*

ships. Another characteristic of interpersonal ties in West End was a degree of "localism." Localism is something like exclusivity; not only are a person's best friends in an area, but practically all of one's friends are in the area. It is easy to understand why one would continue to identify with such an area and make strong commitments to maintain and be satisfied with it.

There is reason to believe that social activity patterns are affected by and dependent on both ethnicity and social class. The social relationships found among neighbors in the middle class are different from those in the lower class. While neighboring is popular in both classes, it is suggested that the intensity of such interaction tends to be stronger in the working class and weaker for upper-income-bracket residential areas [507]. In other words, lower-class respondents seem more closely tied to and spend more time with their neighbors. There also seems to be evidence that within working-class neighborhoods, blacks appear to engage in more neighboring behavior than whites. This may result from different senses of territoriality, or from different senses of what neighboring involves.

In Chapter 5 we mentioned that the "closeness" of neighbors affects the development of friendships. Such findings led psychologists [159], when talking about the role of architects in planning, to suggest that:

The architect who builds a house or designs a site plan, who decides where the roads will and will not go and who decides which directions the houses will face and how close together they will be, also is, to a large extent, deciding the pattern of social life among the people who will live in those houses.

Of course, another possibility is that social relationships develop because people who live in a neighborhood tend to have similar personalities and interests. This is very likely. Unfortunately, there is no evidence about which personality characteristics need to be similar to promote interaction. We do know, however, that a buyer or renter of a house knows that his house will probably be similar to most in the neighborhood and usually finds a high degree of similarity in background to the neighbors.

Social networks and social behavior are not the only components of residential planning. Physical aspects of housing, recreational opportunities, and the general environment are also factors in good planning. Extensive systematic work is being done to plan new towns with regard to all such dimensions. Focus 10-3 provides a schematic representation of a proposed development. Such attempts, obviously, involve much more than concern for social networks and social activity patterns; they demonstrate, just as clearly, that the social environment must be included in the planning of any new town.

Urban settings

The percentage of United States population living in small towns is decreasing at a steady rate. If more and more people are living in cities, the question becomes, What effect does living in an urban setting (versus a rural setting) have on an individual and social behavior? At least three different aspects of the response to urban living have been studied: (1) the amount of incoming

FOCUS 10-3 PROTOTYPE OF A NEW TOWN

The prospect of designing an ideal new town, with all its complexities, is truly awesome. Aware of the problems, the Rockefeller Foundation funded a project entitled, "Man and His Urban Environment." This group, headed by a social psychiatrist, an anthropologist, and a business executive, spent three years traveling throughout the world in search of useful ideas regarding the development and design of new communities. They paid particular attention to four different aspects: services, housing, transportation, and industry. As a result, they designed a town of approximately 21,500 acres, with a mature population of 150,000 people.

The proposed scheme is designed to carry out the following of specific tasks (adapted from [412]):

1 Make possible a balance of population and industry, so that people can live and work in the new town, preventing insofar as possible the draining out of existing cities the middle- and upper-income families, forcing the new town to deteriorate into a bedroom community.
2 Accommodate population at all income levels, including the redistribution of 35,000 low-income people from an existing city.
3 Provide devices to control land use far into the future so that total management and construction plans can be carried out successfully and permanent development programs can be maintained.
4 Lay the groundwork for the development of new types of governing procedures in institutions, including the possible restructuring of public services, such as medical, welfare, law enforcement, and educational systems.
5 Provide a "research and development" project to assist in developing a formula for workable cities in which people can live successfully and with a reasonable degree of satisfaction.
6 Provide a practical system for continuous federal-state-local cooperation under carefully structured local leadership and wide citizen participation.
7 Make it possible to take advantage of important technological advances now available to provide better and more reliable urban services, (power, water, sewage, and solid waste disposal), at the least cost and with minimum environmental damage.
8 Provide ample communication and travel in and out of the new town, without excessive highway development and without creating other transportation-induced environmental problems.
9 Reduce the need for automotive and truck traffic to the absolute minimum within the new town.
10 Provide ready access to essential services and cultural amenities from the outset, without waiting for the new town to "mature."

These are goals that have been decided upon as beneficial to the development of new towns. However, the project leaders also faced the fact that in designing a human environment, they were in some sense creating or generating a new society. The researchers felt there were nine fundamental person-environment relationships which, depending on how they were handled, would determine whether human nature was going to control the city, or whether humans would be doomed to remain at the city's mercy.

These social scientists suggested that a new town can be viewed as a source of social innovation and that there are nine different dimensions along which changes could be created:

1 *The ethnic and cultural makeup of the population.* Traditionally, American cities have been heterogeneous, with strong social pressures encouraging integration of ethnic groups. In recent years, these pressures have been reversed, and current trends suggest more isolation and independence. Is the gain of political power by close-knit ethnic groups an appropriate price to pay for the failure of integration?

2 *The nature of economics, and its relationship to human requirements.* New and constructive systems must be devised to involve (not simply subsidize) certain citizens. The researchers suggested that this can be done only if we conceive of partial unemployment as normal, an integral part of our overall economic system. In other words, we can't just have the employers, employed, and unemployed, with the last being a social burden.

3 *The relationship of the consumption of goods to human nature.* Although people in all social systems seem to have a desire to possess goods, is it possible to create an environment which would curtail excesses of consumption and growth?

4 *The relationship of recreational facilities and services to the needs of urban dwellers.* What kinds of facilities should be provided for the kinds of individuals we are becoming in different environments?

5 *An assessment of justice as a factor in social management.* "Contrary to our finest rhetorical traditions, we are not all born equal, nor are we likely to achieve equality, though our systems of justice are clearly founded upon the mistaken idea that democracy produces equality" [412, p. 47].

6 *The nature of mounting health problems and effective services.*

7 *The educational system and its impact on society.*

8 *The function of culture's institutions and activities.*

9 *The relationship between individuals and the corporation.*

Consequently, although these researchers set out to design a new town, they soon realized that they also were designing a new society. Each one of these dimensions, if changed, would have a dramatic impact on human life.

information which might be responded to; (2) anonymity and the desire to stay in one's apartment; and (3) the effects of noise.

Cognitive overload: To what do I respond? The first writer to comprehensively review the experience of living in cities from a psychological perspective was Stanley Milgram. Milgram recognized that cities are indispensable in complex societies but that there are some negative aspects of such life. He points out that an office worker in mid-Manhattan can meet a quarter of a million people within ten minutes of his or her desk. Clearly, such potential is different from that of a farm worker in Kansas, and it has real implications for a person's social behavior. The concept of *cognitive overload* was developed by Milgram [308] to describe what happens in social settings confronted by an urban dweller. *Cognitive overload occurs when an individual receives too many stimulus inputs.* Buses whizzing by, a quarter of a million people every ten minutes, and vehicles filling the air with noise involve perhaps too much to process and respond to appropriately. Remember that Galle, Gove, and McPherson, in their high-density study of Chicago, also talked about excessive social stimulation. In response to overload, the individual must give less time to each input. Milgram suggests that there are several other possibilities for adapting to the overload: disregard low-priority inputs (things you care little about); assign to others responsibility for some task (let the police help people in need); cut down on the orbit of behavior to block others from having access to you (don't go out of your office or apartment); and, lastly, develop specialized institutions to absorb inputs that would otherwise fall on an individual (have a secretary intercept people). In other words, Milgram suggests that, by living in a city, an individual is faced with too many things happening, and, in response, adapts and structures life along lines that would simplify and restrict the complexity of the situation.

As examples of this attempt to restructure and simplify the social life of urban dwellers, Milgram refers to a number of ways that social behavior is affected. It has been found that the amount of prosocial behavior, as indicated by rates of bystander intervention, is substantially less in urban settings than in rural settings. Further, the help that does occur in urban settings seems to be affected by variables such as race. This would be an example of an individual's drawing back along lines of higher priority and excluding low-priority inputs. Milgram also discusses the exercise of civility among urbanites. Examples such as bumping into each other and not apologizing, or appearing grumpy and disinterested, are common among city dwellers. He suggests that a norm of noninvolvement develops, by which one minds one's own business and does not pry into the behavior of others. It is not unusual to find individuals who have lived in an apartment house all their life, yet who have not met the family two doors down the hall. Such a life-style is completely appropriate in sections of our larger cities and should be viewed as an adaptive response to having many people around and needing some form of privacy.

(a)

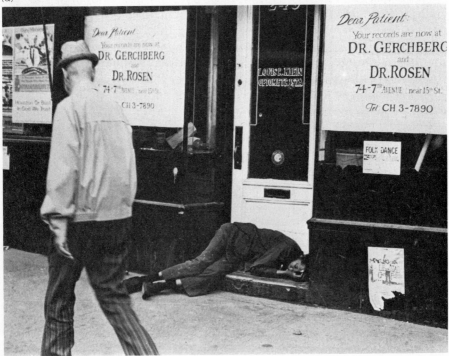

(b)

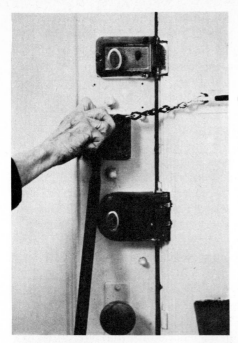

Figure 10-8. *Urban living has a great impact on social behavior, since the kind of person one becomes is affected by living in crowded situations. The frequently lonely, anonymous commuting (a) can leave one feeling forlorn and alienated. This capacity for ignoring others is depicted in extreme (and unfortunately typical) form by the failure to help the drunk asleep on the sidewalk (b). Another aspect of urban living has been the tremendous increase in crime; this door with many locks (c), an attempt at prevention, can cause a feeling of imprisonment. Concern for safety has led to the development of complex, sophisticated protection and security services. This guard (d) uses closed-circuit television to monitor all hallways and units in his building. Is he really so different from a prison guard?*

(d)

Anonymity: The prison. Another variable that has been related to urban life-styles is anonymity. If it is true that a norm of noninvolvement is developing, it would appear that outside one's own neighborhood, it would be adaptive to try to remain anonymous. As was mentioned in Chapter 6, anonymous urban settings lead to heightened vandalism (e.g., car-stripping), whereas in rural settings such behavior seems to occur at much lower rates.

It has been Philip Zimbardo's thesis that in large cities people are beginning to become prisoners of their own minds. Increasing numbers of urban residents wish to remain in their apartments. They are simply terrified of the possibilities of going out onto the street even in daylight. Delinquency and assault rates are so high that people are simply unwilling to take chances. The sales of weapons and locks have increased. Protection services have emerged wherein individuals escort clients from their apartments to waiting cars or cabs. As the sophistication and complexity of these services grow, Zimbardo [512] suggests that people are voluntarily creating a prison for themselves.

In a pilot study, Severy [394] described a new protection agency to a group of 100 college-age subjects. The protection service was supposedly the most sophisticated yet developed and took complete responsibility for the care of the individual. Actually, subjects listened to what amounted to a disguised description of a *real prison.* The urban apartment dweller would have handed over all keys for locks to the protection agency, and the agency would have been responsible for protecting the individual in the apartment, letting people out, and escorting them to their business or recreation and back to their apartments. Based on the client's willingness to pay $10 to $30, $40 to $60, or $70 to $100 per month for such a service, the agency promised to give service within an hour, within a half hour, or immediately. Amazingly, more than 80 percent of the subjects suggested that they would be willing to pay for such a service. Furthermore, about half of them were willing to pay the highest rate suggested. In terms of the difference between urban and rural backgrounds, 68 percent of those raised in urban settings were willing to pay the highest rate, whereas only 41 percent of those raised in rural settings so responded. Conversely, only one person from an urban setting saw through the cover story and identified the situation as a prison, while ten people from rural settings caught on to the project. Zimbardo may be correct in his hypothesis. Our social behavior and our personalities are being changed substantially by our changing environment.

Noise: Where's the beat? It is almost impossible to live in a large city without adapting to noise. There are country sounds and city sounds, but city sounds tend to be a good deal louder. Cars, trains, planes, people, ambulances, garbage trucks, and delivery trucks pound on and on, while factories on a large scale and machines on a smaller scale add to the intensity. The question becomes, Do urban dwellers really hear the sound? Does noise affect their performance, or do they seem to adapt?

Some answers are provided in a series of studies [182]. In different experiments, subjects worked on a variety of tasks while exposed to extremely loud sounds (108 decibels). Sometimes there was noise, sometimes quiet; sometimes the noise was intermittent, sometimes random, and sometimes regular. Subjects were found to adapt to constant or regularly intermittent noise rather well. In addition to physiological adaptation, performance was not seriously lessened except for tasks requiring continuous attention. On the other hand, when noise was unpredictable or uncontrollable, performance decreased. Subjects seemed to wait for, or prepare for, the noise, rather than work. When given a button to press that allowed subjects to control the noise, their performance was a lot better.

The implications are obvious. When urban dwellers adapt to a point of experiencing a city's noise as common, regular, or predictable, the sound will not bother them. This is probably the case for those who were born in a city and have always lived there. However, for those unaccustomed to a city's sounds, there is very likely to be a decrement in ability to function at optimal levels. This decrement will last as long as it takes an individual to become accustomed to city noise. Just as with Zimbardo's prisons, people change in response to their environment.

■ SUMMARY

This chapter began with a discussion of the world's growing population. An attempt was made to avoid moralizing about this development, and, in fact, it was suggested that problems are created from too few interactions as well as from too many. The conclusion appears to be that the social situation helps determine an appropriate "manning" level. After briefly noting that both field theory and ecological theory are relevant to discussion of social behavior in different environments, we concentrated on an individual's use of spatial concepts in social interaction. Specifically, "crowding" was discussed as a condition which exists when a person's desired space—generally known as personal space—exceeds what is available. Both concepts (crowding and personal space) play important roles in a variety of interpersonal situations. Territory was described as an area people claim responsibility for, as well as drawing identity from. Privacy is the concern for having the freedom to choose to be alone. Spatial distribution and the environment of others clearly affect social behavior.

Environments may affect behavior in other ways. Therefore, we reviewed how different natural environments and settings influence the social behaviors which are deemed appropriate. The important point is that as these environments affect our behavior and personalities. We might respond differently than we would have originally. For example, after a girl from Des Moines, Iowa, spends five years in Manhattan, she probably feels more "crowded" than she once did. In turn, she may be more competitive and aggressive. At any rate, both individual and environmental spatial variables will certainly affect her interpersonal style.

bibliography

1 Abelson, R., & Miller, J. Negative persuasion via personal insult. *Journal of Experimental Social Psychology,* 1967, **3,** 321–333.

2 Adair, J. G. *The human subject: The social psychology of the psychological experiment.* Boston: Little, Brown, 1973.

3 Adams, J. S. Inequity and social exchange. In L. Berkowitz (Ed.), *Advances in experimental social psychology.* Vol. 2. New York: Academic, 1965.

4 Adorno, T. W., Frenkel-Brunswik, E., Levinson, D., & Sanford, N. *The authoritarian personality.* New York: Harper, 1950.

5 Allen, V. I. (Ed.) Ghetto riots. *Journal of Social Issues,* 1970, **26** (Whole Issue).

6 Allen, V. I., & Levine, J. M. Social support and conformity: The role of independent assessment of reality. *Journal of Experimental Social Psychology,* 1971, **7,** 48–58.

7 Allport, F. H. The influence of the group upon association and thought. *Journal of Experimental Psychology,* 1920, **3,** 159–182.

8 Allport, G. W. *The nature of prejudice.* Reading, Mass.: Addison-Wesley, 1954.

9 Allport, G. W. *Pattern and growth in personality.* New York: Holt, 1961.

9a Allport, G. W., & Postman, L. *The psychology of rumor.* New York: Holt, 1947.

10 Altman, I. *The environment and social behavior: Privacy, personal space, territory, and crowding.* Monterey, Calif.: Brooks/Cole, 1975.

11 Altman, I., & Haythorn, W. W. The ecology of isolated groups. *Behavioral Science,* 1967, **12,** 169–182.

12 Ardrey, R. *African genesis.* New York: Delta Books, 1961.

13 Ardrey, R. *The territorial imperative.* New York: Atheneum, 1966.

14 Aronson, E. Dissonance theory: Progress and problems. In R. P. Abelson, E. Aronson, W. J. McGuire, T. M. Newcomb, M. J. Rosenberg, & P. H. Tannenbaum (Eds.), *Theories of cognitive consistency: A source book.* Chicago: Rand McNally, 1968. Pp. 5–27.

15 Aronson, E., & Mills, J. The effects of severity of initiation on liking for a group. *Journal of Abnormal and Social Psychology,* 1959, **59,** 177–181.

16 Aronson, E., Turner, J. A., & Carlsmith, J. M. Communicator credibility and communication discrepancy as a

determinant of opinion change. *Journal of Abnormal and Social Psychology,* 1963, **67,** 31–36.

17   Aronson, E., Willerman, B., & Floyd, J. The effect of a pratfall on increasing interpersonal attractiveness. *Psychonomic Science,* 1966, **4,** 157–158.

18   Asch, S. E. Forming impressions of personality. *Journal of Abnormal and Social Psychology,* 1946, **41,** 258–290.

19   Asch, S. E. Studies of independence and conformity: A minority of one against a unanimous majority. *Psychological Monographs,* 1956, **70** (9, Whole No. 416).

20   Asch, S. E. Effects of group pressures upon modification and distortion of judgments. In E. E. Maccoby, T. M. Newcomb, & E. L. Hartley (Eds.), *Readings in social psychology.* (3d ed.) New York: Holt, 1958. Pp. 174–183.

21   Associated Press, "Onlookers boo rescue, stone police." Sept. 27, 1973.

22   Associated Press, "Shot victim got no aid." Nov. 12, 1973.

23   Back, K. W. Influence through social communication. *Journal of Abnormal and Social Psychology,* 1951, **46,** 9–23.

24   Back, K. W., Festinger, L., Hymovitch, B., Kelley, H. H., Schachter, S., & Thibaut, J. W. The methodology of studying rumor transmission. *Human Relations,* 1950, **3,** 307–312.

24a   Bailey, K. G., Hartnett, J. J., & Glover, H. W. Modeling and personal space behavior in children. *Journal of Psychology,* 1973, **85,** 143–150.

25   Baldwin, A. L. *Theories of child development.* New York: Wiley, 1967.

26   Bales, R. F. How people interact in conferences. *Scientific American,* 1955, **192,** 31–35.

27   Bales, R. F. *Personality and interpersonal behavior.* New York: Holt, 1970.

28   Bales, R. F., & Slater, P. Role differentiation in small decision-making groups. In T. Parsons, R. F. Bales, et al. (Eds.), *Family, socialization and interaction process.* New York: Free Press, 1965.

29   Bandura, A. *Principles of behavior modification.* New York: Holt, 1969.

30   Bandura, A. *Social learning theory.* Morristown, N. J.: General Learning Press, 1971.

31   Bandura, A. *Aggression: A social learning analysis.* Englewood Cliffs, N.J.: Prentice-Hall, 1973.

32   Bandura, A., & Walters, R. H. *Social learning and personality development.* New York: Holt, 1963.

33   Bandura, A., Ross, D., & Ross, S. A. Transmission of aggression through imitation of aggressive models. *Journal of Abnormal and Social Psychology,* 1961, **63,** 575–582.

34   Barber, T. X., & Silver, M. J. Fact, fiction, and the experimenter bias effect. *Psychological Bulletin Monograph,* 1968, **70** (6 Pt. 2), 1–29.

35   Bardwick, J. Women's liberation: Nice idea, but it won't be easy. *Psychology Today,* 1973, **6,** 26–33.

36   Barker, R. G. Explorations in ecological psychology. *American Psychologist,* 1965, **20,** 1–14.

37   Barker, R. G., Dembo, T., & Lewin, K. Frustration and regression: An experiment with young children. *University of Iowa Studies in Child Welfare,* 1941, **18,** 1–314.

38   Baron, R. S. Anonymity, deindividuation and aggression. Unpublished doctoral dissertation. University of Iowa, 1970.

39   Baum, A., & Valins, S. Residential environments, group size and crowding. *Proceedings, 81st Annual Convention,* APA, 1973, 211–212.

40   Baumrind, D. Some thoughts on the ethics of research: After reading Milgram's "Behavioral Study of Obedience." *American Psychologist,* 1964, **19,** 421–423.

41   Baxter, J. C. Interpersonal spacing in natural settings. *Sociometry,* 1970, **33,** 444–456.

42   Bem, D. J. Self-perception: An alternative explanation of cognitive dissonance phenomena. *Psychological Review,* 1967, **74,** 183–200.

43   Bem, D. J. Self-perception theory. In L. Berkowitz (Ed.), *Advances in experimental social psychology.* Vol. 6. New York: Academic, 1972. Pp. 1–62.

44   Bem, S. L. Sex-role adaptability: One consequence of psychological androgyny. *Journal of Personality and Social Psychology,* 1975, **31,** 634–643.

45   Bem, S. L., & Bem, D. J. We're all nonconscious sexists. In D. J. Bem, *Beliefs,*

attitudes, and human affairs. Belmont, Calif.: Brooks, Cole, 1970.

46 Bem, S. L., & Bem. D. J. Sex-segregated want ads: Do they discourage female job applicants? In J. H. Hamsher & H. Sigall (Eds.), *Psychology and social issues.* New York: Macmillan, 1973.

47 Benedict, R. *Patterns of culture.* Boston: Houghton Mifflin, 1934.

48 Bennis, W. G., & Shephard, H. A. A theory of group development. *Human Relations,* 1956, **9,** 415–437.

49 Berkowitz, L. Group standards, cohesiveness, and productivity. *Human Relations,* 1954, **7,** 509–519.

50 Berkowitz, L. *Aggression: A social psychological analysis.* New York: McGraw-Hill, 1962.

51 Berkowitz, L. The concept of aggressive drive: Some additional considerations. In L. Berkowitz (Ed.), *Advances in experimental social psychology.* Vol. 2. New York: Academic, 1965. (a)

52 Berkowitz, L. Some aspects of observed aggression. *Journal of Personality and Social Psychology,* 1965, **2,** 359–396. (b)

53 Berkowitz, L. The contagion of violence: An S-R mediational analysis of some effects of observed aggression. In W. J. Arnold & M. M. Page (Eds.), *Nebraska symposium on motivation.* Lincoln: University of Nebraska Press, 1970.

54 Berkowitz, L., & Daniels, L. R. Affecting the salience of the social responsibility norm: Effects of past help on the response to dependency relationships. *Journal of Abnormal and Social Psychology,* 1964, **68,** 275–281.

55 Berkowitz, L., & Friedman, P. Some social class differences in helping behavior. *Journal of Personality and Social Psychology,* 1967, **5,** 217–225.

56 Berkowitz, L., & Geen, R. G. Film violence and the cue properties of available targets. *Journal of Personality and Social Psychology,* 1966, **3,** 525–530.

57 Berkowitz, L., & LePage, A. Weapons as aggression-eliciting stimuli. *Journal of Personality and Social Psychology,* 1967, **7,** 202–207.

58 Berkowitz, W. R., Nebel, J. C., & Reitman, J. W. Height and interpersonal attraction: The 1969 mayoral election in New York City. *Proceedings of the 79th Annual Convention of the American Psychological Association,* 1971.

59 Bermant, G. Never mind the birds and bees; regard the praying mantis. *Psychology Today,* 1969, **3,** 28–31.

60 Berscheid, E., & Walster, E. Physical attractiveness. In L. Berkowitz (Ed.), *Advances in experimental social psychology,* Vol. 7. New York: Academic, 1973.

61 Berscheid, E., Dion, K., Walster, E., & Walster, G. W. Physical attractiveness and dating choice: A test of the matching hypothesis. *Journal of Experimental Social Psychology,* 1971, **7,** 173–189.

62 Blau, P. M. *Exchange and power in social life.* New York: Wiley, 1964.

62a Blanchard, F. A., Adelman, L., and Cook, S. W. The effect of group success and failure upon interpersonal attraction in cooperating interracial groups. *Journal of Personality and Social Psychology,* 1975, **31,** 1020–1030.

62b Blanchard, F. A., Weigel, R. H., and Cook, S. W. The effect of relative competence of group members upon interpersonal attraction in cooperating interracial groups. *Journal of Personality and Social Psychology,* 1975, **32,** 519–530.

63 Bossard, J. H. S., & Boll, E. S. *The sociology of child development.* New York: Harper & Row, 1966.

64 Boulding, K. E. Am I a man or a mouse—or both? In M. F. A. Montagu (Ed.), *Man and aggression.* New York: Oxford, 1968.

65 Bramel, D. Interpersonal attraction, hostility, and perception. In J. Mills (Ed.), *Experimental social psychology.* New York: Macmillan, 1969. Pp. 1–120.

66 Brehm, J. W. Post-decision changes in desirability of alternatives. *Journal of Abnormal and Social Psychology,* 1956, **52,** 384–389.

67 Brehm, J. W. Increasing cognitive dissonance by a fait-accompli. *Journal of Abnormal and Social Psychology,* 1959, **58,** 379–382.

68 Brehm, J. W. *A theory of psychological reactance.* New York: Academic, 1966.

69 Brigham, J. C. Ethnic stereotypes. *Psychological Bulletin,* 1971, **76,** 15–38.

70 Brigham, J. C., & Cook, S. W. The influence of attitude on judgments of plausibility: A replication and extension.
*Educational and Psychological Mea-
surement,* 1970, **30,** 283–292.

71 Brigham, J. C., & Severy, L. J. An empir-
ically derived grouping of whites on the
basis of expressed attitudes toward
blacks. *Representative Research in
Social Psychology,* 1973, **4,** 48–55.

72 Brigham, J. C., & Severy, L. J. Personality and attitude determinants of voting behavior. *Social Behavior and Personality,* 1976, **4,** In press.

73 Brigham, J. C., & Weissbach, T. A.
(Eds.) *Racial attitudes in America:
Analyses and findings of social psychology.* New York: Harper & Row,
1972.

74 Brigham, J. C., Gunn, S. P., & Bloom,
L. M. Attitude change resulting from self-
feedback. Paper presented at American Psychological Association meeting, New Orleans, 1974.

75 Brinkley, W. Valley Forge GIs tell of
their brainwashing ordeal. *Life,* May
23, 1953, pp. 108ff.

76 Brock, T. C., & Becker, L. A. Debriefing
and susceptibility to subsequent
experimental manipulations. *Journal
of Experimental Social Psychology,*
1966, **2,** 314–323.

77 Bronfenbrenner, U. The mirror image
in Soviet-American relations: A social
psychologist's report. *Journal of
Social Issues,* 1961, **17,** 45–56.

78 Bronfenbrenner, U. Soviet methods of
character education: Some implications for research. *American Psychologist,* 1962, **17,** 550–564.

79 Brook, P. Filming a masterpiece.
Observer Weekend Review, July 26,
1964.

80 Broverman, I. K., Vogel, S. R., Broverman, D. M., Clarkson, F. E., & Rosenkrantz, P. S. Sex-role stereotypes: A
current appraisal. *Journal of Social
Issues,* 1972, **28,** 59–78.

81 Brown, R. *Social psychology.* New
York: Free Press, 1965.

82 Bryan, J. H., & Test, M. A. Models and
helping: Naturalistic studies in aiding
behavior. *Journal of Personality and
Social Psychology,* 1967, **6,** 400–407.

83 Burke, P. J. Leadership role differentiation. In C. G. McClintock (Ed.), *Experimental social psychology.* New York:
Holt, 1972.

84 Buss, A. H. *The psychology of aggression.* New York: Wiley, 1961.

85 Byrne, D. *The attraction paradigm.*
New York: Academic, 1971.

86 Calhoun, J. B. Population density and
social pathology. *Scientific American,*
1962, **206,** 139–148.

87 Cannon, W. B. *Bodily changes in pain,
hunger, fear, and rage.* (2d ed.) New
York: Appleton Century Crofts, 1929.

88 Carlsmith, J. M., & Gross, A. E. Some
effects of guilt on compliance. *Journal
of Personality and Social Psychology,*
1969, **11,** 232–239.

89 Carmichael, J. *The death of Jesus.* New
York: Macmillan, 1962.

90 Carmichael. S., & Hamilton, C. V. *Black
power: The politics of liberation in
America.* New York: Random House,
1967.

91 Cartwright, D., & Zander, A. (Eds.)
*Group dynamics: Research and the-
ory.* (3d ed.) New York: Harper & Row,
1968.

92 Chesler, P. Men drive women crazy.
Psychology Today, 1971, **5,** 18–27.

93 Chesney-Lind, M. Judicial enforcement
of the female sex role. *Issues in Criminology,* 1973, **8,** 51–69.

94 Clark, R. D., III, & Word, L. E. Why don't
bystanders help? Because of ambiguity? *Journal of Personality and Social
Psychology,* 1972, **24,** 392–400.

95 Clark, R. D., III, & Word, L. E. Where is
the apathetic bystander? Situational
characteristics of the emergency.
*Journal of Personality and Social Psy-
chology,* 1974, **29,** 279–287.

96 Clark, K. B. Desegregation: An
appraisal of the evidence. *Journal of
Social Issues,* 1953, **9** (4), 1–76.

97 Clark, K. B., & Clark, M. P. Racial identification and preference in Negro children. In T. M. Newcomb and E. L. Hartley (Eds.), *Readings in social psychology.* New York: Holt, 1947. Pp. 169–
178.

98 Clifford, M. M., & Walster, E. The effect
of physical attractiveness on teacher
expectation. *Sociology of Education,*
in press.

99 Cline, V. B. Interpersonal perception. In
B. A. Maher (Ed.), *Progress in experimental personality research.* Vol. 1.

New York: Academic, 1964. Pp. 221–284.

100 Club of Rome. *The limits to growth.* New York: Universe, 1972.

101 Cohen, A. R. Situational structure, self-esteem, and threat-oriented reactions to power. In D. Cartwright (Ed.), *Studies in social power.* Ann Arbor, Mich.: Institute for Social Research, 1959.

102 Cohen, D. J., Whitmyre, J. W., & Funk, W. H. Effect of group cohesiveness and training upon group thinking. *Journal of Applied Psychology,* 1960, **44,** 319–322.

103 *Colliers,* Nov. 27, 1953.

104 Collins, B. E., & Hoyt, M. F. Personal responsibility-for-consequences: An integration and extension of the "forced compliance" literature. *Journal of Experimental Social Psychology,* 1972, **8,** 558–593.

105 Collins, B. E., & Raven, B. H. Group structure: Attraction, coalitions, communication, and power. In G. Lindzey & E. Aronson (Eds.), *The handbook of social psychology.* Vol. 4. (2d ed.) Reading, Mass.: Addison-Wesley, 1969.

106 Cook, S. W. Motives in a conceptual analysis of attitude-related behavior. In W. J. Arnold & D. Levine (Eds.), *Nebraska Symposium on Motivation, 1969.* Lincoln: University of Nebraska Press, 1970. Pp. 179–231.

106a Cook, S. W. A comment on the ethical issues involved in West, Gunn, and Chernicky's "Ubiquitous Watergate: An attributional analysis. *Journal of Personality and Social Psychology,* 1975, **32,** 66–68.

107 Cook, S. W. & Selltiz, C. A. A multiple-indicator approach to attitude measurement. *Psychological Bulletin,* 1964, **62,** 36–55.

108 Cook, S. W., & Wrightsman, L. S. The factorial structure of "positive attitudes toward people." Symposium paper, Southeastern Psychological Association meeting, Atlanta, 1967.

109 Cooper, J., & Goethals, G. R. Unforeseen events and the elimination of cognitive dissonance. *Journal of Personality and Social Psychology,* 1974, **29,** 441–445.

110 Cooper, J., Darley, J. M., & Henderson, J. E. On the effectiveness of deviant- and conventional-appearing communi-cators: A field experiment. *Journal of Personality and Social Psychology,* 1974, **29,** 752–757.

111 Cronbach, L. J. Processes affecting scores on "understanding of others" and "assumed similarity." *Psychological Bulletin,* 1955, **52,** 177–193.

112 Cross, H. A., Halcomb, C. G., & Matter, W. M. Imprinting or exposure learning in rats given early auditory stimulation. *Psychonomic Science,* 1967, **7,** 233–234.

113 Crutchfield, R. S. Conformity and character. *American Psychologist,* 1955, **10,** 191–198.

114 Darley, J. M., & Latané, B. Bystander intervention in emergencies: Diffusion of responsibility. *Journal of Personality and Social Psychology,* 1968, **8,** 377–383.

115 Davis, J. H., & Restle, F. The analysis of problems and prediction of group problem solving. *Journal of Abnormal and Social Psychology,* 1963, **66,** 103–116.

116 Deaux, K. To err is humanizing: But sex makes a difference. *Representative Research in Social Psychology,* 1972, **3,** 20–28.

117 DeFleur, M. L., & Westie, F. R. Verbal attitudes and overt acts: An experiment on the salience of attitudes. *American Sociological Review,* 1958, **23,** 667–673.

118 Delgado, J. M. R. Social rank and radio-stimulated aggressiveness in monkeys. *Journal of Nervous and Mental Diseases,* 1967, **144,** 383–390.

119 de Rivera, J. H. *The psychological dimension of foreign policy.* Columbus, Ohio: Merrill, 1968.

120 Desor, J. A. Toward a psychological theory of crowding. *Journal of Personality and Social Psychology,* 1972, **21,** 79–83.

121 Deutsch, M. An experimental study of the effects of co-operation and competition upon group processes. *Human Relations,* 1949, **2,** 199–232.

122 Deutsch, M., & Collins, M. E. *Interracial housing: A psychological evaluation of a social experiment.* Minneapolis: University of Minnesota Press, 1951.

123 Deutsch, M., & Gerard, H. A study of normative and informational social influences on individual judgment.

Journal of Abnormal and Social Psychology, 1955, **51,** 629–636.

124 Deutsch, M., & Krauss, R. M. The effect of threat upon interpersonal bargaining. *Journal of Abnormal and Social Psychology,* 1960, **61,** 181–189.

125 Dicks, H. V. *Licensed mass murder: A socio-psychological study of some S.S. killers.* New York: Basic Books, 1972.

126 Dion, K. K. Physical attractiveness and evaluation of children's transgressions. *Journal of Personality and Social Psychology,* 1972, **24,** 207–213.

127 DiRenzo, G. J. *Personality and politics.* Garden City, N.Y.: Anchor Press, 1974.

128 Doland, D., & Adelberg, K. The learning of sharing behavior. *Child Development,* 1967, **38,** 695–700.

129 Dollard, J., Doob, L., Miller, N., Mowrer, O., & Sears, R. *Frustration and aggression.* New Haven: Yale University Press, 1939.

130 Driscoll, R. H., Davis, K. E., & Lipetz, M. E. Parental interference and romantic love: The Romeo and Juliet effect. *Journal of Personality and Social Psychology,* 1972, **24,** 1–10.

131 Driver, M. J. A structural analysis of aggression, stress, and personality in an inter-nation simulation. Paper No. 97, January 1965, Institute for Research in the Behavioral, Economic, and Management Sciences, Purdue University.

132 Druckman, D. Dogmatism, prenegotiation experience, and simulated group representation as determinants of dyadic behavior in a bargaining situation. *Journal of Personality and Social Psychology,* 1967, **6,** 279–290.

133 Duke, M. P., & Nowicki, S. A new measure and social-learning model for interpersonal distance. *Journal of Experimental Research in Personality,* 1972, **6,** 119–132.

134 Duke, M. P., & Wilson, J. The measurement of personal space and preferred inter-personal distance as a function of race and sex of stimulus in preschool children. Paper read at the Southeastern Psychological Association meetings, 1972.

134a Dunnette, M. D. People feeling: Joy, more joy, and the "slough of despond." *Journal of Applied Behavioral Science,* 1969, **5,** 25–44.

135 Dunnette, M. D., & Campbell, J. Effectiveness of T-group experiences in managerial training and development. *Psychological Bulletin,* 1968, **70,** 73–104.

136 Dunnette, M. D., Campbell, J., & Jaastad, K. The effect of group participation on brainstorming effectiveness for two industrial samples. *Journal of Applied Psychology,* 1963, **47,** 30–37.

137 Dutton, D. G., & Lennox, V. L. Effect of prior "token" compliance on subsequent interracial behavior. *Journal of Personality and Social Psychology,* 1974, **29,** 65–71.

138 Ehrlich, P. R. *The population bomb.* New York: Ballantine, 1968.

138a Eisenhower, M., et al. Commission statement on violence in television entertainment programs. Washington, D.C.: National Commission on the Causes and Prevention of Violence, 1969.

139 Ellison, C. D., & Flynn, J. P. Organized aggressive behavior in cats after surgical isolation of the hypothalamus. *Archives of Italian Biology,* 1968, **106,** 1–20.

140 Elms, A. C. Right-wingers in Dallas. *Psychology Today,* 1970, **3**(9), 27ff.

141 Elms, A. C. & Milgram, S. Personality characteristics associated with obedience and defiance toward authoritative command. *Journal of Experimental Research in Personality,* 1966, **2,** 282–289.

141a Ericksen-Paige, K. Women learn to sing the menstrual blues. *Psychology Today,* 1973, 7(4), 41–46.

142 Eron, L. D. Relationship of TV viewing habits and aggressive behavior in children. *Journal of Abnormal and Social Psychology,* 1963, **67,** 193–196.

143 Eron, L. D., Huessman, L. R., Lefkowitz, M. M., & Walder, L. O. Does television violence cause aggression? *American Psychologist,* 1972, **27,** 253–263.

144 Etzioni, A. *The hard way to peace.* New York: Collier, 1962.

145 Etzioni, A. The Kennedy experiment. *Western Political Quarterly,* 1967, **20,** 361–380.

146 Etzioni, A. A model of significant research. *International Journal of Psychiatry,* 1968, **6,** 279–280.

147 Fasteau, M. F. *The male machine.* New York: McGraw-Hill, 1974.

148 Fauls, L. B., & Smith, W. D. Sex-role learning of five-year-olds. *Journal of Genetic Psychology,* 1956, **89,** 105–117.

149 Feiss, C. Personal communication, 1975.

150 Feshbach, N. D. Cross-cultural studies of teaching styles in four-year-olds and their mothers. In A. D. Pick (Ed.), *Minnesota Symposium on Child Psychology: VII.* Minneapolis: University of Minnesota Press, 1973.

151 Feshbach, S. Dynamics and morality of violence and aggression: Some psychological considerations. *American Psychologist,* 1971, **26,** 281–292.

152 Feshbach, S., & Singer, R. D. *Television and aggression: An experimental field study.* San Francisco: Jossey-Bass, 1971.

153 Festinger, L. Informal social communication. *Psychological Review,* 1950, **57,** 271–282.

154 Festinger, L. A theory of social comparison processes. *Human Relations,* 1954, **7,** 117–140.

155 Festinger, L. *A theory of cognitive dissonance.* Stanford, Calif.: Stanford University Press, 1957.

156 Festinger, L., & Carlsmith, J. M. Cognitive consequences of forced compliance. *Journal of Abnormal and Social Psychology,* 1959, **58,** 203–210.

157 Festinger, L., Pepitone, A., & Newcomb, T. Some consequences of deindividuation in a group. *Journal of Abnormal and Social Psychology,* 1952, **47,** 382–389.

158 Festinger, L., Riecken, H., & Schachter, S. *When prophecy fails.* Minneapolis: University of Minnesota Press, 1956.

159 Festinger, L., Schachter, S., & Back, K. W. *Social pressures in informal groups.* New York: Harper, 1950.

160 Fiedler, F. E. A contingency model of leadership effectiveness. In L. Berkowitz (Ed.), *Advances in experimental social psychology.* Vol. 1. New York: Academic, 1964.

161 Fiedler, F. E. *A theory of leadership effectiveness.* New York: McGraw-Hill, 1967.

162 Fisher, J. D., & Nadler, A. The effect of similarity between donor and recipient on recipient's reactions to aid. Paper presented at the Midwestern Psychological Association meetings, 1973.

163 Foley, L. A. Personality and situational influences on changes in prejudice. Unpublished doctoral dissertation, University of Florida, 1974.

163a Forer, B. R. The fallacy of personal validation: A classroom demonstration of gullibility. *Journal of Abnormal and Social Psychology,* 1949, **44,** 118–123.

163b Frank, J. *Sanity and Survival: Psychological aspects of war and peace.* New York: Vintage Books, 1967.

164 Frankel, G. J. Self disclosure and personal space: Further clarification of the personal space concept. Paper presented at the Western Psychological Association meetings, 1973.

165 Fraser, S. C., Kelem, R. T., Diener, E., & Beamon, A. L. The Halloween caper: The effects of deindividuation variables on stealing. *Journal of Personality and Social Psychology,* in press.

166 Freedman, J. L., & Fraser, S. C. Compliance without pressure: The foot-in-the-door technique. *Journal of Personality and Social Psychology,* 1966, **4,** 196–202.

167 Freedman, J. L., Klevansky, S., & Ehrlich, P. The effect of crowding on human task performance. *Journal of Applied Social Psychology,* 1971, **1,** 7–25.

168 Freedman, J. L., Wallington, S. A., & Bless, E. Compliance without pressure: The effect of guilt. *Journal of Personality and Social Psychology,* 1967, **7,** 117–124.

169 Fried, M., & Gleicher, P. Some sources of residential satisfaction in an urban slum. In J. F. Wohlwill & D. H. Carson (Eds.), *Environment and the social sciences: Perspectives and applications.* Washington: American Psychological Association, 1972.

169a Fromm-Reichmann, F. Loneliness. *Psychiatry,* 1959, **22,** 1–15.

170 Fulbright, J. W. *The Pentagon propaganda machine.* New York: Liveright, 1970.

171 Gaertner, S. L. How do racial attitudes affect helping behavior? Paper pre-

sented at the Southeastern Psychological Association meetings, 1974.

172 Gaertner, S., & Bickman, L. Effects of race on the elicitation of helping behavior: The wrong number technique. *Journal of Personality and Social Psychology,* 1971, **20,** 218–222.

173 *Gainesville Sun,* Feb. 17, 1974.

174 Galle, O. R., Gove, W. R., & McPherson, J. M. Population density and pathology: What are the relationships for man? *Science,* 1972, **176,** 23–30.

175 George, A. L. Power as a compensatory value for political leaders. In G. J. DiRenzo (Ed.), *Personality and politics.* Garden City, N.Y.: Anchor Press, 1974.

176 Gerard, H. B., & Mathewson, G. C. The effects of severity of initiation on liking for a group: A replication. *Journal of Experimental Social Psychology,* 1966, **2,** 278–287.

177 Gerard, H., Wilhelmy, R., & Connolley, E. Conformity and group size. *Journal of Personality and Social Psychology,* 1968, **8,** 79–82.

178 Gergen, K. J. Social psychology as history. *Journal of Personality and Social Psychology,* 1973, **26,** 309–320.

179 Gergen, K. J., Gergen, M. M., & Meter, K. Individual orientations to prosocial behavior. *Journal of Social Issues,* 1972, **28,** 105–130.

180 Gillig, P. M., & Greenwald, A. G. Is it time to lay the sleeper effect to rest? *Journal of Personality and Social Psychology,* 1974, **29,** 132–139.

181 Gibb, C. A. Leadership. In G. Lindzey & E. Aronson (Eds.), *The handbook of social psychology.* Vol. 4. (2d ed.) Reading, Mass.: Addison-Wesley, 1969.

182 Glass, D. C., & Singer, J. E. *Urban stress.* New York: Academic, 1972.

183 Goldman, M. A comparison of group and individual performance where subjects have varying tendencies to solve problems. *Journal of Personality and Social Psychology,* 1966, **3,** 604–607.

184 Goodenough, E. W. Interest in persons as an aspect of sex difference in the early years. *Genetic Psychology Monographs,* 1957, **55,** 287–323.

185 Goranson, R. E., & Berkowitz, L. Reciprocity and responsibility reactions to prior help. *Journal of Personality and Social Psychology,* 1966, **3,** 227–232.

186 Graham, H. D., & Gurr, T. R. *The history of violence in America: A report to the National Commission on the Causes and Prevention of Violence.* New York: Bantam, 1969.

187 Granet, R. Unpublished study. Cited on pp. 92–93 by Darley, J., & Latané, B. Norms and normative behavior. In J. Macaulay & L. Berkowitz (Eds.), *Altruism and helping behavior.* New York: Academic, 1970.

188 Green, D. Dissonance and self-perception analysis of "forced compliance." When two theories make competing predictions. *Journal of Personality and Social Psychology,* 1974, **29,** 819–828.

189 Green, J. A. Attitudinal and situational determinants of intended behavior toward blacks. *Journal of Personality and Social Psychology,* 1972, **22,** 13–17.

189a Greenwald, H. J., & Oppenheim, D. B. Reported magnitude of self-misidentification among Negro children—Artifact? *Journal of Personality and Social Psychology,* 1968, **8,** 49–52.

190 Gross, A. E., Wallston, B. S., & Piliavin, I. M. Beneficiary attractiveness and cost as determinants of responses to routine requests for help. Unpublished paper, Ohio State University, 1973.

191 Gruder, C. L., & Cook, T. D. Sex, dependency, and helping. *Journal of Personality and Social Psychology,* 1971, **19,** 290–294.

192 Gurnee, H. A comparison of collective and individual judgments of facts. *Journal of Experimental Psychology,* 1937, **21,** 106–112.

193 Guthman, E. *We band of brothers.* New York: Harper & Row, 1971.

194 Hall, E. T. *The hidden dimension.* New York: Doubleday, 1966.

195 Haney, C., Banks, C., & Zimbardo, P. Interpersonal dynamics in a simulated prison. *International Journal of Criminology and Penology,* 1973, **1,** 69–97.

196 Hardyck, J. A., & Braden, M. Prophecy fails again: A report of a failure to replicate. *Journal of Abnormal and Social Psychology,* 1962, **65,** 136–141.

197 Harvey, O. J., Hunt, D. E., & Schroeder, H. M. *Conceptual systems and personality organization.* New York: Wiley, 1961.

198 Hastorf, A. H., Schneider, D. J., & Polefka, J. *Person perception.* Reading, Mass.: Addison-Wesley, 1970.

199 Hearn, G. Leadership and the spatial factor in small groups. *Journal of Abnormal and Social Psychology,* 1957, **54,** 269–272.

200 Heider, F. *The psychology of interpersonal relations.* New York: Wiley, 1958.

201 Hendricks, M., Cook, T. D., & Crano, W. D. Sex and prior favor as moderators of helping. Paper presented at the Midwestern Psychological Association meetings, 1973.

202 Hermann, M. G. Some personal characteristics related to foreign aid voting of Congressmen. Master's thesis, Northwestern University, 1963. Cited in Robinson, J. A., & Snyder, R. C. Decision-making in international politics. In H. Kelman (Ed.), *International behavior: A social-psychological analysis.* New York: Holt, 1965.

203 Hersey, J. *The Algiers Motel incident.* New York: Bantam, 1968.

204 Hess, E. H. Attitude and pupil size. *Scientific American,* 1965, **212,** 46–54.

205 Hess, E. H., & Polt, J. M. Pupil size as related to interest value of visual stimuli. *Science,* 1960, **132,** 349–350.

206 Hetherington, E. M. Effects of paternal absence on sex-typed behavior in Negro and white preadolescent males. *Journal of Personality and Social Psychology,* 1966, **4,** 87–91.

207 Hetherington, E. M., & Franke, G. Effects of parental dominance, warmth, and conflict on imitation in children. *Journal of Personality and Social Psychology,* 1969, **6,** 119–125.

208 Hoffman, L. W. Early childhood experiences and woman's achievement motives. *Journal of Social Issues,* 1972, **28,** 129–156.

209 Hokanson, J. E., Burgess, M., & Cohen, M. F. Effects of displaced aggression on systolic blood pressure. *Journal of Abnormal and Social Psychology,* 1963, **67,** 214–218.

210 Hollander, E. P. *Leaders, groups, and influence.* New York: Oxford, 1964.

211 Hollander, E. P., & Julian, J. W. Studies in leader legitimacy, influence, and innovation. In L. Berkowitz (Ed.), *Advances in experimental social psychology.* Vol. 5. New York: Academic, 1970.

212 Hollander, E. P., & Willis, R. Some current issues in the psychology of conformity and noncomformity. *Psychological Bulletin,* 1967, **68,** 62–76.

213 Holsti, O. R. The belief system and national images: A case study. *Journal of Conflict Resolution,* 1962, **6,** 244–252.

214 Homans, G. C. *Social behavior: Its elementary forms.* New York: Harcourt, Brace & World, 1961.

215 Horner, M. S. Sex differences in achievement motivation and performances in competitive and non-competitive situations. Unpublished doctoral dissertation, University of Michigan, 1968.

216 Horner, M. S. Achievement-related conflicts in women. *Journal of Social Issues,* 1972, **28,** 157–175.

217 Hornstein, H. A. The influence of social models on helping. In J. Macaulay & L. Berkowitz (Eds.), *Altruism and helping behavior.* New York: Academic, 1970.

218 Hovland, C. I., & Sears, R. R. Minor studies in aggression, VI: Correlation of lynchings with economic indices. *Journal of Personality,* 1940, **9,** 301–310.

219 Hovland, C. I., & Weiss, W. The influence of source credibility on communication effectiveness. *Public Opinion Quarterly,* 1951, **15,** 635–650.

220 Hraba, J., & Grant, G. Black is beautiful: A reexamination of racial preference and identification. *Journal of Personality and Social Psychology,* 1970, **16,** 398–402.

221 Huizinga, J. *Homo ludens: A study of the play element in culture.* Boston: Beacon Press, 1950.

222 Hutt, C., & Vaizey, M. Differential effects of group density on social behavior. *Nature,* 1966, **209,** 1371–1372.

223 Insko, C. A. Verbal reinforcement of attitude. *Journal of Personality and Social Psychology,* 1965, **2,** 621–623.

224 Iscoe, I., Williams, M., & Harvey, J. Age, intelligence, and sex as variables in the conformity behavior of Negro and white children. *Child Development,* 1964, **35,** 451–460.

225 Iwao, S. Internal versus external criticism of group standards. *Sociometry,* 1963, **26,** 410–421.

226 Janis, I. L. *Victims of groupthink: A psychological study of foreign-policy decisions and fiascoes.* Boston: Houghton Mifflin, 1972.

227 Jensen, A. R. The race × sex × ability interaction. Unpublished manuscript, University of California, Berkeley, 1970.

228 Johnson, P. B., Sears, D. O., & McConahay, J. B. Black invisibility, the press, and the Los Angeles riot. *American Journal of Sociology,* 1971, **76,** 698–721.

229 Johnson, R. C., & Medinnus, G. R. *Child pyschology: Behavior and development.* New York: Wiley, 1974.

230 Johnson, R. N. *Aggression in man and animals.* Philadelphia: Saunders, 1972.

231 Jones, E. E., & Davis, K. E. From acts to dispositions: The attribution process in person perception. In L. Berkowitz (Ed.), *Advances in experimental social psychology.* Vol. 2. New York: Academic, 1965. Pp. 219–266.

232 Jones, E. E., & Harris, V. A. The attribution of attitudes. *Journal of Experimental Social Psychology,* 1967, **3,** 1–24.

233 Jones, E. E., & Nisbett, R. E. The actor and the observer: Divergent perceptions of the causes of behavior. In E. E. Jones et al. (Eds.), *Attribution: Perceiving the causes of behavior.* Morristown, N.J.: General Learning Press, 1971. Pp. 79–94.

234 Jones, E. E., & Wortman, C. *Ingratiation: An attributional approach.* Morristown, N.J.: General Learning Press, 1973.

235 Jones, R., & Brehm, J. Persuasiveness of one- and two-sided communications as a function of awareness there are two sides. *Journal of Experimental Social Psychology,* 1970, **6,** 47–56.

236 Jones, S. E., & Aiello, J. R. Proxemic behavior of black and white first-, third-, and fifth-grade children. *Journal of Personality and Social Psychology,* 1973, **25,** 21–27.

237 Karnow, S. Calley, Eichmann, both obedient. *St. Petersburg Times,* Mar. 30, 1971.

238 Katz, D. The functional approach to the study of attitudes. *Public Opinion Quarterly,* 1960, **24,** 163–204.

239 Katz, D., & Stotland, E. A preliminary statement to a theory of attitude structure and change. In S. Koch (Ed.), *Psychology: A study of a science.* Vol. 3. New York: McGraw-Hill, 1959. Pp. 423–475.

240 Kelley, H. H. The warm-cold variable in first impressions of persons. *Journal of Personality,* 1950, **18,** 431–439.

241 Kelley, H. H. Two functions of reference groups. In G. E. Swanson, T. M. Newcomb, & E. L. Hartley (Eds.), *Readings in social psychology.* (2d ed.) New York: Holt, 1952.

242 Kelley, H. H., & Thibaut, J. W. Group problem solving. In G. Lindzey & E. Aronson (Eds.), *The handbook of social psychology.* Vol. 4. (2d ed.) Reading, Mass.: Addison-Wesley, 1969.

243 Kelman, H. C. (Ed.), *International behavior: A social-psychological analysis.* New York: Holt, 1965.

244 Kelman, H. C., & Hovland, C. I. "Reinstatement" of the communicator in delayed measurement of opinion change. *Journal of Abnormal and Social Psychology,* 1953, **48,** 327–355.

245 Kemeny, J. *A philosopher looks at science.* New York: Van Nostrand, 1959.

246 Kennan, G. F. The sources of Soviet conduct. *Foreign Affairs,* 1947, **25,** 566–582.

247 Kiesler, C. A., & Kiesler, S. B. *Conformity.* Reading, Mass.: Addison-Wesley, 1969.

248 Kleck, R. E., & Rubenstein, C. Physical attractiveness, perceived attitude similarity, and the interpersonal attraction in an opposite-sex encounter. *Journal of Personality and Social Psychology,* 1975, **31,** 107–114.

249 Kohlberg, L. The cognitive-developmental approach to socialization. In D. A. Goslin (Ed.), *Handbook of socialization theory and research.* Chicago: Rand McNally, 1969. Pp. 347–480.

250 Kohlberg, L., & Zigler, E. The impact of cognitive maturity on the development of sex-role attitudes in the years 4 to 8. *Genetic Psychology Monographs,* 1967, **75,** 89–165.

251 Korten, D. C. Situational determinants of leadership structure. *Journal of Conflict Resolution,* 1962, **6,** 222–235.

252 Krebs, D. L. Altruism: An examination of the concept and a review of the literature. *Psychological Bulletin,* 1970, **73,** 258–302.

253 Kuo, Z. Y. The genesis of the cat's responses to the rat. *Journal of Comparative Psychology,* 1930, **11,** 1–35.

254 Lagerspetz, K. M. J. Aggression and aggressiveness in laboratory mice. In S. Garattini & E. B. Sigg (Eds.), *Aggressive behavior.* New York: Wiley, 1969.

255 Lansing, J., & Hendricks, G. *Automobile ownership and residential density.* Ann Arbor: Institute for Social Research, University of Michigan, 1967.

256 LaPiere, R. T. Attitudes and actions. *Social Forces,* 1934, **13,** 230–237.

257 Latané, B., & Rodin, J. A lady in distress: Inhibiting effects of friends and strangers on bystander intervention. *Journal of Experimental Social Psychology,* 1969, **5,** 189–202.

258 Latané, B., & Darley, J. M. Group inhibition of bystander intervention in emergencies. *Journal of Personality and Social Psychology,* 1968, **10,** 215–221.

259 Laski, H. J. The dangers of obedience. *Harper's Monthly Magazine,* 1919, **159,** 1–10.

260 Laufer, R. S., Proshansky, H. M., & Wolfe, M. Some analytic dimensions of privacy. Presented at the 2d International Architectual Psychology Conference, University of Lund, Sweden, June 1973.

261 Laughlin, P. R., & Johnson, H. H. Group and individual performance on a complementary task as a function of initial ability level. *Journal of Experimental Social Psychology,* 1966, **2,** 407–414.

262 Lazarsfeld, P. F. The American soldier: An expository review. *Public Opinion Quarterly,* 1949, **13,** 377–404.

263 LeBon, G. *The crowd* (1st ed., 1895). New York: Viking, 1960.

264 Leeds, R. Altruism and the norm of giving. *Merrill-Palmer Quarterly,* 1963, **9,** 229–240.

265 Lerner, M. J. The desire for justice and reactions to victims. In J. Macaulay & L. L. Berkowitz (Eds.), *Altruism and helping behavior.* New York: Academic, 1970. Pp. 205–229.

266 Lerner, M. J., & Lichtman, R. R. Effects of perceived norms on attitudes and altruistic behavior toward a dependent other. *Journal of Personality and Social Psychology,* 1968, **9,** 226–232.

267 Lerner, R. M., Solomon, H., & Brody, S. Helping behavior at a busstop. *Psychological Reports,* 1971, **28,** 200.

268 Lett, E., Clark, W., & Altman, I. A propositional inventory of research on interpersonal distance. Naval Medical Research Institute, research report, 1969.

269 Leventhal, H. Findings and theory in the study of fear communications. In L. Berkowitz (Ed.), *Advances in experimental social psychology.* Vol. 5. New York: Academic, 1970, Pp. 119–186.

270 Levinger, G., & Snoek, J. D. *Attraction in relationship: A new look at interpersonal attraction.* Morristown, N.J.: General Learning Press, 1972.

271 Levitas, M. *America in crisis.* New York: Holt, 1969.

272 Lewin, K. Formalization and progress in psychology. In D. Cartwright (Ed.), *Field theory in social science.* New York: Harper, 1951. Pp. 1–29.

273 Liebert, R. M., Neale, J. M., & Davidson, E. S. *The early window: Effects of television on children and youth.* New York: Pergamon, 1972.

274 Lippitt, R., Polansky, N., Redl, F., & Rosen, S. The dynamics of power. *Human Relations,* 1952, **5,** 37–64.

275 Little, K. B. Personal space. *Journal of Experimental Social Psychology,* 1965, **1,** 237–247.

276 Loo, C. The effects of spatial density on the social behavior of children. *Journal of Applied Social Psychology,* 1972, **2,** 372–381.

277 Lorenz, K. *On aggression.* New York: Harcourt, Brace & World, 1966.

278 Lorge, I., & Solomon, H. Two models of group behavior in the solution of Eureka-type problems. *Psychometrika,* 1955, **20,** 139–148.

279 Lott, D. F., & Sommer, R. Seating arrangements and status. *Journal of*

Personality and Social Psychology, 1967, **7,** 90–95.

280 Lowe, R., & Ritchey, G. Relation of altruism to age, social class, and ethnic identity. *Psychological Reports,* 1973, **33,** 576–572.

281 Luce, R. D., & Raiffa, H. *Games and decisions.* New York: Wiley, 1957.

282 Luchins, A. S., & Luchins, E. H. Half-views and the autokinetic effect. *Psychological Record,* 1963, **13,** 415–444.

283 Machiavelli, N. *Discourses.* London: Routledge, 1950.

284 Mack, R. W. Do we really believe in the Bill of Rights? *Social Problems,* 1956, **3,** 264–269.

285 Mann, R. D. A review of relationships between personality and performance in small groups. *Psychological Bulletin,* 1959, **56,** 241–270.

286 *Marijuana and health.* Report issued by the National Institute of Mental Health. U.S. Government Printing Office, 1971.

287 Marsella, A. J., Escudero, M., & Gordon, P. The effects of dwelling density on mental disorders in Filipino men. *Journal of Health and Social Behavior,* 1970, **11,** 288–294.

288 Martindale, D. Territorial dominance behavior in dyadic verbal interactions. *Proceedings of the 79th Annual Convention of the American Psychological Association,* 1971, 305–306.

289 Masters, J. C. Effects of social comparison upon the imitation of neutral and altruistic behaviors by young children. Unpublished paper, University of Minnesota, 1974.

290 Mausner, B. The effect of prior reinforcement on the interaction of observer pairs. *Journal of Abnormal and Social Psychology,* 1954, **49,** 65–68.

291 McClintock, C. G. Personality syndromes and attitude change. *Journal of Personality,* 1958, **26,** 479–493.

292 McClosky, H. Consensus and ideology in American politics. *American Political Science Review,* 1964, **58,** 361–382.

293 McDougall, W. *An introduction to social psychology.* London: Methuen, 1908.

294 McGuire, W. J. Inducing resistance to persuasion. In L. Berkowitz (Ed.), *Advances in experimental social psychology.* Vol. 1. New York: Academic, 1964. Pp. 191–229.

295 McGuire, W. J. The nature of attitudes and attitude change. In G. Lindzey and E. Aronson (Eds.), *Handbook of social psychology.* Vol. 3. Reading, Mass.: Addison-Wesley, 1969. Pp. 136–314.

296 McNeil, E. B. *Human socialization.* Belmont, Calif.: Brooks/Cole, 1969.

297 Mead, M. *Male and Female.* New York: Morrow, 1949.

298 Meeker, R. J., & Shure, G. H. Pacifist bargaining tactics: Some "outsider" influences. *Journal of Conflict Resolution,* 1969, **13,** 487–493.

299 Melman, S. *Pentagon capitalism.* New York: McGraw-Hill, 1970.

300 Messé, L. A. Equity in bilateral bargaining. *Journal of Personality and Social Psychology,* 1971, **17,** 287–291.

301 Mettee, D. R., & Wilkins, P. C. When similarity "hurts": Effects of perceived ability and a humorous blunder on interpersonal attraction. *Journal of Personality and Social Psychology,* 1972, **22,** 246–258.

302 Meyer, T. Effects of viewing justified and unjustified real film violence on aggressive behavior. *Journal of Personality and Social Psychology,* 1972, **23,** 21–29.

303 Midlarsky, M., & Midlarsky, E. Additive and interactive status effects on altruistic behavior. Paper read at the American Psychological Association meetings, 1972.

304 Milgram, S. Behavioral study of obedience. *Journal of Abnormal and Social Psychology,* 1963, **67,** 371–378.

305 Milgram, S. Issues in the study of obedience: A reply to Baumrind. *American Psychologist,* 1964, **19,** 848–852.

306 Milgram, S. Some conditions of obedience and disobedience to authority. *Human Relations,* 1965, **18,** 57–76. (a)

307 Milgram, S. Liberating effects of group pressure. *Journal of Personality and Social Psychology,* 1965, **1,** 127–134. (b)

308 Milgram, S. The experience of living in cities: A psychological analysis. In F. F. Korten, S. W. Cook, & J. I. Lacey (Eds.), *Psychology and the problems of society.* Washington: American Psychological Association, 1970.

309 Milgram, S. *Obedience to authority.* New York: Harper & Row, 1974.

310 Miller, A. G. (Ed.) *The social psychology of psychological research.* New York: Free Press, 1972.

311 Mills, J., & Aronson, E. Opinion change as a function of the communicator's attractiveness and desire to influence. *Journal of Personality and Social Psychology,* 1965, **1**, 173–177.

312 Minard, R. D. Race relationships in the Pocahontas coal field. *Journal of Social Issues,* 1952, **3**, 29–44.

313 Minuchin, P. Sex-role concepts and sex typing in childhood as a function of school and home environment. *Child Development,* 1965, **36**, 1033–1048.

314 Montagu, M. F. A. (Ed.) *Man and aggression.* New York: Oxford, 1968.

315 Morris, D. *The naked ape.* New York: McGraw-Hill, 1967.

316 Mueller, D. J. Physiological techniques of attitude measurement. In G. F. Summers (Ed.), *Attitude Measurement.* Chicago: Rand McNally, 1970. Pp. 534–552.

317 Mulder, M., & Stemerding, A. Threat, attraction to group and need for strong leadership. *Human Relations,* 1963, **16**, 317–334.

318 Murstein, B. Physical attractiveness and marital choice. *Journal of Personality and Social Psychology,* 1972, **22**, 8–12.

319 Mussen, P., & Rutherford, E. Parent-child relations and parental personality in relation to young children's sex-role preferences. *Child Development,* 1963, **34**, 225–246.

320 Newcomb, T. M. An approach to the study of communicative acts. *Psychological Review,* 1953, **60**, 393–404.

321 Newcomb, T. M. Attitude development as a function of reference group: The Bennington study. In E. E. Maccoby, T. M. Newcomb, & E. L. Hartley (Eds.), *Readings in social psychology* (3d ed.) New York: Holt, 1958. Pp. 265–275.

322 Newcomb, T. M. *The acquaintance process.* New York: Holt, 1961.

323 Newcomb, T. M., Koenig, K. E., Flacks, R., & Warwick, D. P. *Persistence and change: Bennington College and its students after 25 years.* New York: Wiley, 1967.

324 *Newsweek,* Sept. 9, 1946; Jan. 17, 1961; Mar. 8, 1971; May 21, 1973; June 17, 1974.

325 *New York Times,* Mar. 28, 1964; Dec. 27, 1974.

326 *New York Times* staff. *The Watergate Hearings: Break-in and cover-up.* New York: Bantam, 1973.

327 Nisbett, R. C., & Schachter, S. Cognitive manipulation of pain. *Journal of Experimental Social Psychology,* 1966, **2**, 227–236.

328 Nisbett, R. E., Caputo, C., Legant, P., & Maracek, J. Behavior as seen by the actor and as seen by the observer. *Journal of Personality and Social Psychology,* 1973, **27**, 154–164.

329 Nord, W. Social exchange theory: An integrative approach to social conformity. *Psychological Bulletin,* 1969, **71**, 174–208.

330 North, R. C., Holsti, O. R., Zaninovich, M. G., & Zinnes, D. A. *Content analysis.* Evanston, Ill.: Northwestern University Press, 1963.

331 Nowicki, S., & Duke, M. P. A further test of the social learning model for interpersonal distance: The effects of age and race of stimulus. Paper presented at the Southeastern Psychological Association meetings, 1973.

332 Orne, M. On the social psychology of the psychological experiment: With particular reference to demand characteristics and their implications. *American Psychologist,* 1962, **17**, 776–783.

333 Osborn, A. F. *Applied imagination.* New York: Scribner, 1957.

334 Osgood, C. E. *An alternative to war or surrender.* Urbana: University of Illinois Press, 1962.

335 Osgood, C. E. *Perspectives in foreign policy.* (2d ed.) Palo Alto, Calif.: Pacific Books, 1966.

336 Oskamp, S., & Hartry, A. A factor-analytic study of the double standard in attitudes toward U.S. and Russian actions. *Behavioral Science,* 1968, **13**, 178–188.

337 Osmond, H. Function as a basis of psychiatric ward design. *Mental Hospitals,* 1957, **8**, 23–29.

338 Outdoor Recreation Resources Review Commission. *Wilderness and recreation: A report on resources, values, and*

problems. Report No. 3, Wildland Research Center, University of California. U.S. Government Printing Office, 1962.

339 Ovid, *The art of love* (republished). Bloomington: Indiana University Press, 1963.

340 Page, M. M., & Scheidt, R. J. The elusive weapons effect: Demand awareness, evaluation apprehension, and slightly sophisticated subjects. *Journal of Personality and Social Psychology,* 1971, **20,** 304–318.

341 Pandey, J., & Griffitt, W. Attraction and helping. Paper presented at the Midwestern Psychological Association meetings, 1973.

342 Pettigrew, T. F. *Racially separate or together?* New York: McGraw-Hill, 1971.

343 Pettigrew, T. F. Social psychology and desegregation research. *American Psychologist,* 1961, **16,** 105–112.

344 Pheterson, G. I., Kiesler, S. B., & Goldberg, P. A. Evaluation of the performance of women as a function of their sex, achievement, and personal history. *Journal of Personality and Social Psychology,* 1971, **19,** 114–118.

345 Phillips, N. E. Militarism and grassroots involvement in the military-industrial complex. *Journal of Conflict Resolution,* 1973, **17,** 625–655.

346 Piliavin, J. A. Discussion of "current perspectives in bystander intervention" at the Southeastern Psychological Association meetings, 1974.

347 Piliavin, J. A., & Piliavin, I. M. The effect of blood on reactions to a victim. *Journal of Personality and Social Psychology,* 1972, **23,** 253–261.

348 Piliavin, J. A., & Piliavin, I. M. *The good samaritan: Why does he help?* New York: MSS Modular Publications, 1975.

349 Piliavin, I. M., Rodin, J., & Piliavin, J. A. Good samaritanism: An underground phenomenon? *Journal of Personality and Social Psychology,* 1969, **13,** 289–299.

350 Pilisuk, M., Potter, P., Rapoport, A., & Winter, A. J. War hawks and peace doves: Alternative resolutions of experimental conflicts. *Journal of Conflict Resolution,* 1965, **9,** 491–508.

351 Pilisuk, M., & Skolnik, P. Inducing trust: A test of the Osgood proposal. *Journal of Personality and Social Psychology,* 1968, **8,** 121–133.

352 Plato. *Republic.* (Trans. by F. M. Cornford) New York: Oxford, 1945.

353 President's Commission on Law Enforcement and the Administration of Justice. *Drunkenness.* Task force report, U.S. Government Printing Office, 1967.

354 Prothro, J. W., & Grigg, C. W. Fundamental principles of democracy: Bases of agreement and disagreement. *Journal of Politics,* 1960, **22,** 276–294.

355 Pruitt, D. G., & Snyder, R. C. *Theory and research on the causes of war.* Englewood Cliffs, N.J.: Prentice-Hall, 1969.

356 Rabban, M. Sex-role identification in young children in two diverse social groups. *Genetic Psychology Monographs,* 1950, **42,** 81–158.

357 Rabbie, J. Differential preference for companionship under stress. *Journal of Abnormal and Social Psychology,* 1963, **67,** 643–648.

358 Rapoport, A., & Chammah, M. *Prisoner's Dilemma.* Ann Arbor: University of Michigan Press, 1965.

359 Raven, B. H., & Rietsema, J. The effects of varied clarity of group goal and group path upon the individual and his relation to the group. *Human Relations,* 1957, **10,** 29–44.

360 Regan, D. T. Effects of a favor and liking on compliance. *Journal of Experimental Social Psychology,* 1971, **7,** 627–639.

361 Ribal, J. E. Social character and meanings of selfishness and altruism. *Sociology and Social Research,* 1963, **47,** 311–321.

362 Richards, C. B., & Dobyns, H. F. Topography and culture: The case of the changing cage. *Human Organization,* 1957, **16,** 16–20.

363 Richardson, L. F. *The statistics of deadly quarrels.* Pittsburgh: Boxwood, 1960.

364 Robinson, J. P., & Shaver, P. R. *Measures of social psychological attitudes.* Ann Arbor, Mich.: Institute for Social Research, 1969.

365 Rohrer, J. H., Baron, S. H., Hoffman, E. L., & Swander, D. V. The stability of autokinetic judgments. *Journal of Abnormal and Social Psychology,* 1954, **49,** 595–597.

366 Rokeach, M. *The open and closed mind.* New York: Basic Books, 1960.

367 Rokeach, M. *Beliefs, attitudes, and values.* San Francisco: Jossey-Bass, 1968.

368 Rokeach, M. Faith, hope, bigotry. *Psychology Today,* 1970, **3**(11), 33ff.

369 Rosenhan, D., & White, G. M. Observation and rehearsal as determinants of prosocial behavior. *Journal of Personality and Social Psychology,* 1967, **5,** 424–431.

370 Rosenthal, R. Experimenter effects in behavioral research. New York: Appleton Century Crofts, 1966.

371 Rosenthal, R., & Jacobson, L. *Pygmalion in the classroom: Teacher expectation and pupils' intellectual development.* New York: Holt, 1968.

372 Rubin. Z. *Liking and loving: An invitation to social psychology.* New York: Holt, 1973.

373 Russell, B. *The scientific outlook.* New York: Norton, 1959.

374 Sanford, N. The roots of prejudice: Emotional dynamics. In P. Watson (Ed.), *Psychology and race.* Chicago: Aldine, 1973.

375 Sartre, J. *Anti-Semite and Jew.* New York: Grove Press, 1948.

376 Satow, K. L. The role of social approval in altruistic behavior. Paper read at the American Psychological Association meetings, 1973.

377 Sawyer, H. G. The meaning of numbers. Speech before the American Association of Advertising Agencies, 1961. Cited in E. J. Webb, D. T. Campbell, R. D. Schwartz, & L. Sechrest, *Unobtrusive measures: Nonreactive research in the social sciences.* Chicago: Rand McNally, 1966.

378 Schachter, S. Deviation, rejection, and communication. *Journal of Abnormal and Social Psychology,* 1951, **46,** 190–207.

379 Schachter, S. *The psychology of affiliation.* Stanford, Calif.: Stanford University Press, 1959.

380 Schachter, S. The interaction of cognitive and physiological determinants of emotional state. In L. Berkowitz (Ed.), *Advances in experimental social psychology.* Vol. 1. New York: Academic, 1964. Pp. 49–80.

381 Schachter, S. Some extraordinary facts about obese humans and rats. *American Psychologist,* 1971, **26,** 129–144.

382 Schachter, S., & Singer, J. Cognitive, social, and physiological determinants of emotional state. *Psychological Review,* 1962, **69,** 379–399.

383 Schachter, S., Ellertson, N., McBride, D., & Gregory, D. An experimental study of cohesiveness and productivity. *Human Relations,* 1951, **4,** 229–238.

384 Schafer, E. L., & Miety, J. Aesthetic and emotional experiences rate high with Northeast wilderness hikers. In J. F. Wohlwill & D. H. Carson (Eds.), *Environment and the social sciences: Perspectives and applications.* Washington: American Psychological Association, 1972.

385 Scheer, R. (Ed.) *Eldridge Cleaver: Post-prison writings and speeches.* New York: Random House, 1969.

386 Schein, E. H. The Chinese indoctrination program for prisoners of war. *Psychiatry,* 1956, **19,** 149–172.

387 Schlenker, B. R. Self-image maintenance and enhancement: Attitude change following counterattitudinal advocacy. *Proceedings of the 81st Annual Convention of the American Psychological Association,* Montreal, 1973.

388 Schlenker, B. R. Social psychology and science. *Journal of Personality and Social Psychology,* 1974, **29,** 1–15.

389 Schlesinger, A. M., Jr. *A thousand days.* Boston: Houghton Mifflin, 1965.

390 Schopler, J., & Thompson, V. D. Role of attribution processes in mediating amount of reciprocity for a favor. *Journal of Personality and Social Psychology,* 1968, **10,** 243–250.

391 Schramm, W. J., Lyle, J., & Parker, E. B. *Television in the lives of our children.* Stanford, Calif.: Stanford University Press, 1961.

392 Schwartz, S. H., & Clausen, G. T. Responsibility, norms and helping in an emergency. *Journal of Personality*

and *Social Psychology,* 1970, **16,** 299–310.

392a Sears, D. O. The paradox of de facto selective exposure without preference for supportive information. In R. P. Abelson et al. (Eds.) *Theories of cognitive consistency: A sourcebook.* Chicago: Rand McNally, 1968, 777–787.

393 Sears, R. R., Maccoby, E. E., & Levin, H. *Patterns of child rearing.* Evanston, Ill.: Row, Peterson, 1957.

394 Severy, L. J. Urban "prisons." Unpublished pilot study, University of Florida, 1973.

395 Severy, L. J. Personal space and population. Paper read at the Southeastern Psychological Association meetings, 1974.

396 Severy, L. J. Comment: On the essence of altruism. *Journal of Social Issues,* 1974, **30,** 189–194.

396a Severy, L. J., Brigham, J. C., & Harvey, O. J. Attitudes, personality characteristics, and voting behavior: Their relationship under differential conditions of involvement. Unpublished manuscript, 1972.

397 Severy, L. J., & Davis, K. E. Helping behavior among normal and retarded children. *Child Development,* 1971, **42,** 1017–1031.

398 Shaw, M. E., A comparison of individuals and small groups in the rational solution of complex problems. *American Journal of Psychology,* 1932, **44,** 491–504.

399 Shaw, M. E. Communication networks. In L. Berkowitz (Ed.), *Advances in experimental social psychology.* Vol. 1. New York: Academic, 1964.

400 Shaw, M. E. *Group dynamics: The psychology of small group behavior.* New York: McGraw-Hill, 1971.

401 Sherif, M. A study of some social factors in perception. *Archiva Psychologia,* 1935, **27**(187).

402 Sherif, M., & Hovland, C. I. *Social judgment.* New Haven: Yale University Press, 1961.

403 Sherif, M., Harvey, O. J., White, B. J., Hood, W. R., & Sherif, C. W. *Intergroup conflict and cooperation: The Robbers Cave experiment.* Norman: Institute of Group Relations, University of Oklahoma, 1961.

404 Sherif, C. W., Sherif, M., & Nebergall, R. E. *Attitude and attitude change.* Philadelphia: Saunders, 1965.

405 Shure, G. H., Meeker, R. J., & Hansford, E. A. The effectiveness of pacifist strategies in bargaining games. *Journal of Conflict Resolution,* 1965, **9,** 106–117.

406 Sigall, H., Aronson, E., & Van Hoose, T. The cooperative subject: Myth or reality. *Journal of Experimental Social Psychology,* 1970, **6,** 1–10.

407 Silverman, B. I. Consequences, racial discrimination, and the principle of belief congruence. *Journal of Personality and Social Psychology,* 1974, **29,** 497–508.

408 Silverman, I. Hedonistic considerations concerning altruistic behavior. Paper presented at the Southeastern Psychological Association meetings, 1974.

409 Singer, J. E., Brush, C. A., & Lublin, S. C. Some aspects of deindividuation: identification and conformity. *Journal of Experimental Social Psychology,* 1965, **1,** 356–378.

410 Sistrunk, F., & McDavid, J. W. Sex variable in conforming behavior. *Journal of Personality and Social Psychology,* 1971, **17,** 200–207.

411 Skinner, B. F. *Beyond freedom and dignity.* New York: Knopf, 1972.

412 Smith, F. *Man and his urban environment.* New York: Man and his urban environment project, 1972.

413 Smith, M. B. *Social psychology and human values.* Chicago: Aldine, 1969.

414 Smith, M. B., Bruner, J. S., & White, R. W. *Opinions and personality.* New York: Wiley, 1956.

415 Smith, R. E., Smythe, L., & Lien, D. Inhibition of helping behavior by a similar or dissimilar nonreactive bystander. *Journal of Personality and Social Psychology,* 1972, **23,** 414–419.

416 Snow, C. P. Either-or. *Progressive,* February 1961.

417 Sommer, R. *Personal space: The behavioral basis of design.* Englewood Cliffs, N.J.: Prentice-Hall, 1969.

418 Sommer, R. *Tight spaces: Hard architecture and how to humanize it.* Englewood Cliffs, N.J.: Prentice-Hall, 1974.

419 Sorensen, T. C. *Kennedy.* New York: Bantam, 1966.

420 Spiro, M. E. *Children of the kibbutz.*

Cambridge, Mass.: Harvard University Press, 1958.

421 *Sports Illustrated,* "Take me out to the old brawl game." June 17, 1974, p. 11.

422 Staines, G., Tavris, C., & Jayaraine, T. E. The queen bee syndrome. *Psychology Today,* 1974, **7**, 55–60.

423 Staub, E. A child in distress: The influence of age and number of witnesses on children's attempts to help. *Journal of Personality and Social Psychology,* 1970, **14**, 130–140.

424 Staub, E. Helping a person in distress: The influence of implicit and explicit "rules" of conduct on children and adults. *Journal of Personality and Social Psychology,* 1971, **17**, 137–144.

425 Stein, A. H., & Friedrich, L. K, The effects of aggressive and prosocial television programs on the naturalistic social behavior of preschool children. Paper presented at the Society for Research in Child Development meetings, 1971.

426 Stein, D. D., Hardyck, J. A., & Smith, M. B. Race and belief: An open and shut case. *Journal of Personality and Social Psychology,* 1965, **1**, 281–289.

427 Steinzor, B. The spatial factor in face-to-face discussion groups. *Journal of Abnormal and Social Psychology,* 1950, **45**, 552–555.

428 Stokols, D. A social-psychological model of human crowding phenomenon. *Journal of the American Institute of Planners,* 1972, **38**, 72–84.

429 Stokols, D. The relation between micro and macro crowding phenomena: Some implications for environmental research and design. *Man-environment Systems,* 1973, **3**, 139–149.

430 Stouffer, S. A. *Communism, conformity, and civil liberties.* New York: Doubleday, 1955.

431 Stouffer, S. A. Suchman, E. A., DeVinney, L. C., Star, S. A., & Williams, R. M., Jr. *The American soldier: Adjustments during army life.* Vol. 1 of *Studies in social psychology in World War II.* Princeton: Princeton University, 1949.

432 Stouffer, S. A., Lumsdaine, A. A., Lumsdaine, M. H., Williams, R. M., Jr., Smith, M. B., Janis, I. L., Star, S. A., & Cottrell, L. S., Jr. *The American soldier: Combat and its aftermath.* Vol. 2 of *Studies in social psychology in World War II.* Princeton: Princeton University, 1949.

433 Strauss, A. In B. J. Biddle, & E. J. Thomas (Eds.), *Role theory: Concepts and research.* New York: Wiley, 1966.

434 Stricker, L. J., Jacobs, P. I., & Kogan, N. Trait interrelations in implicit personality theories and questionnaire data. *Journal of Personality and Social Psychology,* 1974, **30**, 198–207.

435 Strodtbeck, F. L., & Hook, L. H. The social dimensions of a twelve man jury table. *Sociometry,* 1961, **24**, 397–416.

436 Suedfeld, P., Epstein, Y. M., Buchanan, E., & London, P. B. Effects of set on the "effects of mere exposure." *Journal of Personality and Social Psychology,* 1971, **17**, 121–123.

437 Sutton-Smith, B., & Rosenberg, B. G. *The sibling.* New York: Holt, 1970.

438 Sweet, W. H., Ervin, F., & Mark, V. H. The relationship of violent behavior to focal cerebral disease. In S. Garattini & E. Sigg (Eds.), *Aggressive behavior.* New York: Wiley, 1969.

438a Taft, R. The ability to judge people. *Psychological Bulletin,* 1955, **52**, 1–23.

439 Tagiuri, R. Person perception. In G. Lindzey and E. Aronson (Eds.), *Handbook of social psychology.* Vol. 3. Reading, Mass.: Addison-Wesley, 1969. Pp. 395–449.

440 Tavris, C., & Wexo, J. B. A game of confrontation: Woman and man. *Psychology Today,* 1971, **5**, 44–56.

441 Taylor, D. W., Berry, P. C., & Block, C. H. Does group participation when using brainstorming facilitate or inhibit creative thinking? *Administrative Science Quarterly,* 1958, **3**, 23–47.

442 Teague, B. Charlie doesn't even know his daily racism is a sick joke. In R. V. Guthrie (Ed.), *Being black: Psychological-sociological dilemmas.* New York: Harper & Row, 1970. Pp. 40–49.

443 Tedeschi, J. T., Bonoma, T. V., & Linskold, S. Threateners' reactions to prior announcement of behavioral compliance or defiance. *Behavioral Science,* 1970, **15**, 131–139.

444 Tedeschi, J. T., Lindskold, S., Horai, J., & Gahagan, J. Social power and the credibility of promises. *Journal of Per-*

sonality and Social Psychology, 1969, **13**, 253–261.

445 Tedeschi, J. T., Schlenker, B. R., & Bonoma, T. V. Cognitive dissonance. Private ratiocination or public spectacle? American Psychologist, 1971, **26**, 685–695.

446 Tedeschi, J. T., Schlenker, B. R., & Bonoma, T. V. Conflict, power, and games. Chicago: Aldine, 1973.

447 Tedeschi, J. T., Smith, R. B., III, & Brown, R. C. A reinterpretation of research on aggression. Psychological Bulletin, 1974, **81**, 540–562.

448 The Official Associated Press Almanac. Maplewood, N.J.: Hammond Almanac, 1974.

449 The Walker Report to the National Commission on the Causes and Prevention of Violence. New York: Bantam, 1968.

450 Thibaut, J. W. An experimental study of the cohesiveness of underprivileged groups. Human Relations, 1950, **3**, 251–278.

451 Thibaut, J. W., & Kelley, H. H. The social psychology of groups. New York: Wiley, 1959.

452 Thomas, W. I., & Znaniecki, F. The Polish peasant in Europe and America. Vol. 1. Boston: Badger, 1918.

453 Thompson, V. D. Personal communication, 1973.

454 Thurstone, L. L. Comment. American Journal of Sociology, 1946, **52**, 39–40.

455 Time, Jan. 14, 1961; Oct. 23, 1972; May 7, 1973.

456 Toch, H. Violent men. Chicago: Aldine, 1969.

457 Torrance, E. P. Some consequences of power differences on decision making in permanent and temporary three-man groups. In A. P. Hare, E. F. Borgatta, & R. F. Bales (Eds.), Small groups: Studies in social interaction. New York: Knopf, 1955.

458 Tresemer, D., & Pleck, J. Sex-role boundaries and resistance to sex-role change. Women's Studies, 1974, **2**, 61–78.

459 Triandis, H. C. Attitude and attitude change. New York: Wiley, 1971.

460 Triandis, H. C. A note on Rokeach's theory of prejudice. Journal of Abnormal and Social Psychology, 1961, **62**, 184–186.

461 Triplett, N. The dynamogenic factors in pacemaking and competition. American Journal of Psychology, 1897, **9**, 507–533.

462 Tulkin, S. R. Race, class, family, and school achievement. Journal of Personality and Social Psychology, 1968, **9**, 31–37.

463 Ulrich, R. E. Stachnik, D. J., & Stainton, N. R. Student acceptance of generalized personality interpretations. Psychological Reports, 1963, **13**, 831–834.

464 Underwood, B., Moore, B. S., & Rosenhan, D. L. The effect of mood on children's giving. Paper presented at the American Psychological Association meetings, 1972.

465 United Press International, "Girl tied to lamp post, beaten; Belfast residents watch silently." Feb. 23, 1973.

466 Valins, S. Cognitive effects of false heart-rate feedback. Journal of Personality and Social Psychology, 1966, **4**, 400–408.

467 Valins, S., & Baum, A. Residential group size, social interaction and crowding. Environment and Behavior, 1973, **5**, 421–439.

468 Van Hemel, P. E., & Meyer, J. S. Satiation of mouse killing by rats in an operant situation. Psychonomic Science, 1970, **21**, 129–130.

469 Vanneman, R. D., & Pettigrew, T. F. Race and relative deprivation in the urban United States. Race, 1972, **13**, 461–486.

470 Veroff, J. Development and validation of a projective measure of power motivation. Journal of Abnormal and Social Psychology, 1957, **54**, 1–8.

471 Vinacke, W. E. Variables in experimental games: Toward a field theory. Psychological Bulletin, 1969, **71**, 293–318.

472 Vreeland, R. Is it true what they say about Harvard boys? Psychology Today, 1972, **5**(8), 65–68.

473 Wagner, P. J., Ashton, N. L, Foley, L. A., & Yockey, J. M. Relative deprivation as predictive of voting for female candidates. Unpublished manuscript, University of Florida, 1974.

474 Walster, E. The temporal sequence of

post-decision processes. In L. Festinger, *Conflict, decision, and dissonance.* Stanford, Calif.: Stanford University Press, 1964. Pp. 112–127.

475 Walster, E. The effect of self-esteem on liking for dates of various social desirabilities. *Journal of Experimental Social Psychology,* 1970, **6,** 248–253.

476 Walster, E., & Berscheid, E. Adrenaline makes the heart grow fonder. *Psychology Today,* 1971, **5**(1), 46–50ff.

477 Walster, E., & Festinger, L. The effectiveness of "overheard" persuasive communications. *Journal of Abnormal and Social Psychology,* 1962, **65,** 395–402.

478 Walster, E., & Piliavin, J. A. Equity and the innocent bystander. *Journal of Social Issues,* 1972, **28,** 165–190.

479 Walster, E., Aronson, E., & Abrahams, D. On increasing the persuasiveness of a low prestige communicator. *Journal of Experimental Social Psychology,* 1966, **2,** 325–342.

480 Walster, E., Berscheid, E., & Walster, G. W. New directions in equity research. *Journal of Personality and Social Psychology,* 1973, **25,** 151–176.

481 Walster, E., Walster, G. W., Piliavin, J., & Schmidt, L. "Playing hard to get": Understanding an elusive phenomenon. *Journal of Personality and Social Psychology,* 1973, **26,** 113–121.

482 Ward, S. H., & Braun, J. Self-esteem and racial prejudice in children. *American Journal of Orthopsychiatry,* 1972, **42,** 644–647.

483 Watson, R. I., Jr. Investigation into deindividuation using a cross-cultural survey technique. *Journal of Personality and Social Psychology,* 1973, **25,** 342–345.

484 Webb, E., Campbell, D., Schwartz, R., & Sechrest, L. *Unobtrusive measures: Nonreactive research in the social sciences.* Chicago: Rand McNally, 1966.

485 Weber, M. *The Protestant ethic and the spirit of capitalism.* (Originally published, 1904–1905.) New York: Scribner, 1958.

486 Weigel, R. H., Vernon, D. T. A., & Tognacci, L. N. Specificity of attitude as a determinant of attitude-behavior congruence. *Journal of Personality and*

Social Psychology, 1974, **30,** 724–728.

487 Weisstein, N. Woman as nigger. *Psychology Today,* 1969, **3,** 20–22.

488 Wells, W. D. Television and aggression: Replication of an experimental field study. Unpublished manuscript, University of Chicago, 1971.

489 West, S. G., Gunn, S. P., & Chernicky, P. Ubiquitous Watergate: An attributional analysis. *Journal of Personality and Social Psychology,* 1975, **32,** 55–65.

490 Westin, A. *Privacy and freedom.* New York: Atheneum, 1967.

491 White, R. K. *Nobody wanted war: Misperception in Vietnam and other wars.* (Rev. ed.) New York: Anchor Books, 1970.

492 White, R. K., & Lippitt, R. *Autocracy and democracy: An experimental inquiry.* New York: Harper, 1960.

493 Wicker, A. W. Attitudes versus actions: The relationship of verbal and overt behavioral responses to attitude objects. *Journal of Social Issues,* 1969, **25,** 41–78.

494 Wicker, A. W. Undermanning theory and research: Implications for the study of psychological and behavioral effects of excess populations. *Representative Research in Social Psychology,* 1973, **4,** 185–206.

495 Williams, E. W. Help thy neighbor: A study of bystander intervention in emergencies. Unpublished doctoral dissertation, University of Florida, 1973.

496 Williams, E. W. The effect of attitudinal similarity and environmental familiarity on bystander intervention. Paper presented at the Southeastern Psychological Association meetings, 1974.

497 Williams, E. W., & Severy, L. J. Bystander intervention, similarity and existent justifiable reasons for not helping. Unpublished manuscript, University of Florida, 1974.

498 Williams, J. E., & Edwards, C. D. An exploratory study of the modification of color and racial concept attitudes in preschool children. *Child Development,* 1969, **40,** 737–750.

499 Wilner, D. M., Walkley, R., & Cook, S.

W. *Human relations in interracial housing: A study of the contact hypothesis.* Minneapolis: University of Minnesota Press, 1955.

500 Winch, R. F. *Mate selection: A study of complementary needs.* New York: Harper, 1958.

501 Winsborough, H. The social consequences of high population density. *Law and Contemporary Problems,* 1965, **30,** 120–126.

502 Wispe, L., & Freshley, H. B. Race, sex, and sympathetic helping behavior: The broken bag caper. *Journal of Personality and Social Psychology,* 1970, **17,** 59–65.

503 Woodmansee, J. J. The pupil response as a measure of social attitudes. In G. F. Summers (Ed.), *Attitude measurement.* Chicago: Rand McNally, 1970. Pp. 514–533.

504 Woodmansee, J. J., & Cook, S. W. Dimensions of verbal racial attitudes: Their identification and measurement. *Journal of Personality and Social Psychology,* 1967, **7,** 240–250.

505 World Health Organization. Wide research needed to solve the problem of mental health. *World Mental Health,* 1960, **12.**

506 Yablonsky, L. *The violent gang.* New York: Macmillan, 1962.

507 Yancey, W. L. Architecture, interaction, and social control: The case of a large-scale housing project. In J. F. Wohlwill, & D. H. Carson, (Eds.), *Environment and the social sciences: Perspectives and applications.* Washington: American Psychological Association, 1972.

508 Zajonc, R. B. Social facilitation. *Science,* 1965, **149,** 269–274.

509 Zajonc, R. B. Attitudinal effects of mere exposure. *Journal of Personality and Social Psychology,* 1968, **9**(2, part 2), 1–27.

510 Zehner, R. B. Neighborhood and community satisfaction: A report on new towns and less planned suburbs. In J. F. Wohwill, & D. H. Carson (Eds.), *Environment and the social sciences: Perspectives and applications.* Washington: American Psychological Association, 1972.

511 Zimbardo, P. G. The human choice: Individuation, reason, and order versus deindividuation, impulse, and chaos. In W. J. Arnold & D. Levine (Eds.), *Nebraska Symposium on motivation.* Lincoln: University of Nebraska Press, 1969.

512 Zimbardo, P. G. Personal communication, 1974.

513 Zimbardo, P. G., Haney, C., Banks, W. C., & Jaffe, D. The psychology of imprisonment: Privation, power, and pathology. Unpublished manuscript, Stanford, Calif.: Stanford University, 1973.

acknowledgments

A number of authors, publishers, and photographers have allowed us to use copyrighted material in this text. We wish to acknowledge these sources here.

Extracts and Tables

Page 9 Lazarsfeld, P. F. The American soldier—an expository review. *Public Opinion Quarterly,* 13, 377–404.

Pages 25–26 Oskamp, S., & Hartry, A. A factor-analytic study of the double standard in attitudes toward U.S. and Russian actions. Pages 181–182, copyrighted by and reprinted from *Behavioral Science,* Volume 13, No. 3, 1968, by permission of James G. Miller, M.D., Ph.D., Editor.

Pages 82–84 Festinger, L., Riecken, H., and Schachter, S. *When prophecy fails.* Minneapolis: University of Minnesota Press, 1956.

Page 103 Vanneman, R. D., and Pettigrew, T. F. Race and relative deprivation in the urban United States. *Race,* 1972, 13, 461–486. Institute of Race Relations, London.

Page 108 Carmichael, S., and Hamilton, C. V. *Black power: The politics of liberation in America.* New York: Random House, Inc., 1967.

Pages 110–111 Teague, B. Charlie doesn't even know his daily racism is a sick joke. *New York Times Magazine,* September 15, 1968. © 1968 by the New York Times Company.

Pages 113–114 Abridged from pp. 255–257, 327 (F-Scale) in *The authoritarian personality* by T. W. Adorno, Else Frenkel-Brunswik, Daniel J. Levinson, and R. Nevitt Sanford (Harper & Row, 1950).

Page 116 Sanford N. The roots of prejudice: Emotional dynamics. In P. Waston (Ed.), *Psychology and race.* Chicago: Aldine Press, 1973.

Pages 137–138 Reprinted from *Psychology Today,* July 1971. Copyright © 1971.

Ziff-Davis Publishing Company. All rights reserved.

Page 140 Broverman, I. K., Vogel, S. R., Broverman, D. M., Clarkson, F. E. and Rosenkrantz, P. S. Sex-role stereotypes: A current appraisal. *Journal of Social Issues,* 1972, 28, 59–78.

Page 143 Reprinted from *Psychology Today,* July 1969. Copyright © 1969. Ziff-Davis Publishing Company. All rights reserved.

Page 146 William Morrow & Company, Inc. *Male and female.* Copyright © 1949 by Margaret Mead.

Pages 158–161 Horner, M. S. Achievement-related conflicts in women. *Journal of Social Issues,* 1972, 28, 157–175.

Page 163 Adapted from *Psychology Today,* January 1974. Copyright © 1974. Ziff-Davis Publishing Company. All rights reserved.

Page 189 Kelley, H. H. The warm-cold variable in first impressions of groups. *Journal of Personality,* 1950, 18, 431–439. Duke University Press.

Pages 193–194 Ulrich, R. E., Stachnick, D. J., and Stainton, N. R. Student acceptance of generalized personality interpretations. *Psychological Reports,* 1963, 13, 831–834. Journal Press.

Page 200 Jones, E. E., and Nisbett, R. E. "The actor and the observer: Divergent perceptions of the causes of behavior," from *Attribution: Perceiving the causes of behavior,* page 79. © 1971, 1972, General Learning Corporation. Reprinted by permission of Silver Burdett Company.

Page 236 Reprinted from "The human choice," by P. G. Zimbardo in the *Nebraska Symposium on Motivation* (1969) by W. J. Arnold and D. Levine (Eds.) by permission of University of Nebraska Press. Copyright © 1970 by University of Nebraska Press.

Pages 245–246 Hornstein, H. A. The influence of social models on helping. In J. Macaulay and L. Berkowitz (Eds.), *Altruism and helping behavior.* Academic Press, 1970.

Page 255 Piliavin, J. A., and Piliavin, I. M. *The good samaritan: Why-does he help?* New York: MSS Modular Publications, 1975.

Page 264 Brook, P. "Filming a masterpiece," *The Observer,* London, July 26, 1964, p. 23.

Page 274 Johnson, R. N. *Aggression in man and animals.* Philadelphia: Saunders, 1972.

Page 284 Bandura, A., Ross, D., and Ross, S. Imitation of film-meditated aggressive models. *Journal of Abnormal and Social Psychology,* 1963, 66, 3–11. Copyright 1963 by the American Psychological Association. Reprinted by permission.

Pages 304–305 New York Times staff, *The Watergate hearings: Break-in and cover-up.* New York: Bantam Books, 1973.

Pages 307–308 Russell, B. *The scientific outlook.* New York: W. W. Norton, 1959.

Page 320 Excerpts from "Human beings fused together," *Time,* October 23, 1972. Reprinted by permission from TIME, The Weekly Newsmagazine; Copyright Time Inc.

Page 321 Zimbardo, P. G., Haney, D., Banks, W. C., and Jaffe, D. *The psychology of imprisonment: Privation, poverty, and pathology.* Unpublished manuscript, Stanford University, 1973.

Page 329 Milgram, S. *Obedience to authority: An experimental view.* New York: Harper and Row, 1974, page 200.

Page 336 Copyright 1929 by *Harper's* Magazine. Reprinted from the June 1929 issue by special permission.

Page 386 From "Population density and social pathology" by J. B. Calhoun. Copyright © 1962 by Scientific American, Inc. All rights reserved.

Page 405 Sommer, R. *Tight spaces.* Englewood Cliffs: Prentice-Hall, 1974.

Page 410 Festinger, Schacter, S., and Back, K. W. *Social pressure in informal groups.* Stanford University Press, 1950.

Art and Photographs

1-1 a Pictorial Parade/EPA
b United Press International
c Wide World Photos

1-2 J. Kemeny, *A philosopher looks at science.* © 1959 by Litton Educational Publishers, Inc., 1967. Reprinted by permission of Van Nostrand Reinhold Company.

1-3 a United Press International
b Wide World Photos

1-4 O. R. Holsti and R. C. North. The history of human conflict. In E. B. McNeil (ed.), *The nature of human conflict,* Prentice-Hall, Inc., Englewood Cliffs, N.J., 1965, p. 162.

1-5 M. Deutsch and R. M. Krauss, The effects of threat upon interpersonal bargaining. *Journal of Abnormal and Social Psychology,* 61, 1960, 181–189. Copyright 1960 by the American Psychological Association. Used with permission.

1-6 R. D. Luce and H. Raiffa. *Games and decisions.* New York: John Wiley and Sons, Inc., 1957.

1-7 a Dan O'Neill for Editorial Photocolor Archives
b Michael Tzovaras for Editorial Photocolor Archives
c Pictorial Parade/EPA
d Wide World Photos

2-1 a Adapted from J. J. Woodmansee and S. W. Cook, Dimensions of verbal racial attitudes: Their identification and measurement. *Journal of Personality and Social Psychology,* 1967, 7, 240–250.
b No credit
c No credit
d Joshua Tree Productions/EPA
e Michael Meadows for Editorial Photocolor Archives

2-2 G. W. Allport and L. Postman. *The psychology of rumor.* New York: Holt, Rinehart, and Winston, Inc., 1947.

2-3 a Pictorial Parade/EPA
b Dan O'Neill for Editorial Photocolor Archives

2-4 Adapted from P. M. Gillig and A. D. Greenwald. Is it time to lay the sleeper effect to rest? *Journal of Personality and Social Psychology,* 1974, 29, page 134.

2-5 No credit

2-6 a Dan O'Neill for Editorial Photocolor Archives
b American Cancer Society

2-7 Peter Vadnai for Editorial Photocolor Archives

3-1 a Culver Pictures
b Los Angeles County Museum of Natural History
c Abby Aldrich Rockefeller Folk Art Collection

3-2 a Bruce Anspach/EPA Newsphoto
b Andrew Sacks for Editorial Photocolor Archives

3-3 H. D. Graham and T. R. Gurr (eds.). *History of violence in america.* New York: Praeger Publishers, 1969.

3-4 P. B. Johnson, D. O. Sears, and J. B. McConahay, Black invisibility, the press, and the Los Angeles riot. *American Journal of Sociology,* 76, 1971, 698–721.

3-5 a Pictorial Parade/EPA
b Pictorial Parade/EPA
c Pictorial Parade/EPA
d Pictorial Parade/EPA
e Pictorial Parade/EPA

3-6 a Dan O'Neill for Editorial Photocolor Archives
b Dan O'Neill for Editorial Photocolor Archives
c Jan Lukas for Editorial Photocolor Archives

3-7 a Jan Lukas for Editorial Photocolor Archives
b London Daily Express

4-1 Adapted from *Human socialization* by E. B. McNeil. Copyright © 1969 by Wadsworth Publishing Company, Inc. Reprinted by permission of the publisher, Brooks/Cole Publishing Company, Monterey, Calif.

4-2 a Marion Bernstein for Editorial Photocolor Archives
b Daniel S. Brody for Editorial Photocolor Archives

4-3 a Culver Pictures
b Editorial Photocolor Archives

   c Courtesy of *Ms.* Magazine
   d Courtesy of Leo Burnett Agency

4-4 *a* Laima Turnley for Editorial Photocolor Archives
   b Dan O'Neill for Editorial Photocolor Archives

4-5 Laima Turnley for Editorial Photocolor Archives

4-6 Editorial Photocolor Archives

4-7 Dan O'Neill for Editorial Photocolor Archives

4-8 *a* Culver Pictures
   b Culver Pictures

4-9 Blair Seitz for Editorial Photocolor Archives

4-10 Laima Turnley for Editorial Photocolor Archives

5-1 Linda Rogers for Editorial Photocolor Archives

5-2 *a* Bruce Anspach/EPA Newsphoto
   b David R. Fosse for Editorial Photocolor Archives
   c Dan O'Neill for Editorial Photocolor Archives

5-3 Dan O'Neill for Editorial Photocolor Archives

5-4 Pictorial Parade/EPA

5-5 *a* Herb Taylor/EPA Newsphoto
   b Bruce Anspach/EPA Newsphoto

5-6 Editorial Photocolor Archives

5-7 G. Levinger and J. D. Snoek, *Attraction in relationship, a new look at interpersonal attraction,* page 5. © 1972 General Learning Corporation. Reprinted by permission of Silver Burdett Company.

6-1 *a* New York Daily News
   b Wide World Photos
   c United Press International
   d Wide World Photos

6-2 Wide World Photos

6-3 Wide World Photos

6-4 *a* Culver Pictures
   b Pictorial Parade/EPA

6-5 Editorial Photocolor Archives

6-6 Figure and text adapted from the Governor's Crime Prevention Committee, State of Florida, Tallahassee, Florida. Used with permission of J. W. Skeries, Director.

6-7 *a* United Press International
   b United Press International

7-1 *a* Culver Pictures
   b London Daily Express
   c Pictorial Parade/EPA
   d EDAHL/Editorial Photocolor Archives

7-2 United Press International

7-3 Courtesy of Professor Albert Bandura

7-4 *a* Culver Pictures
   b Culver Pictures

7-5 Reprinted from The contagion of violence, by L. Berkowitz, in the *Nebraska Symposium on Motivation.* Copyright © 1971 by the University of Nebraska Press. Used with permission.

7-6 United Press International

8-1 *a* United Press International
   b Wide World Photos
   c United Press International
   d Wide World Photos
   e United Press International
   f United Press International
   g United Press International
   h United Press International

8-2 No credit

8-3 *a* United Press International
   b United Press International
   c Pictorial Parade/EPA

9-1 *a* Henri Dauman from Pictorial Parade
   b Pictorial Parade/EPA
   c Pictorial Parade/EPA
   d Pictorial Parade/EPA
   e Pictorial Parade/EPA
   f Wide World Photos

9-2 Dan O'Neill for Editorial Photocolor Archives

9-3 Andrew Sacks for Editorial Photocolor Archives

9-4 *a* Culver Pictures
   b Culver Pictures
   c Pictorial Parade/EPA

9-6 *a* Henri Dauman from Pictorial Parade
   b London Daily Express
   c Pictorial Parade/EPA
   d Pictorial Parade/EPA
   e London Daily Express
   f Central Press/EPA
   g Central Press/EPA
   h Pictorial Parade/EPA
   i Dan Koblitz for Editorial Photocolor Archives

9-7 From R. F. Boles, *How people interact in conferences,* copyright © 1955 by Scientific American, Inc. All rights reserved.

10-2 Photo by Oscar Neuman, from *Defensible space, crime prevention through urban design.* New York: Macmillan, 1972.

10-3 A. W. Wicker, Undermanning theory and research: Implications for the study of psychological and behavioral effects of excess populations. *Representative Research in Social Psychology,* 4, 1973, 188–206.

10-4 Dan O'Neill for Editorial Photocolor Archives.

10-5 a Andrew Sacks for Editorial Photocolor Archives.

10-6 a Dan O'Neill for Editorial Photocolor Archives
b Bruce Anspach/EPA Newsphoto
c Editorial Photocolor Archives

10-7 a Dennis Brack/Black Star
b Daniel S. Brody for Editorial Photocolor Archives

10-8 a Michelle Stone for Editorial Photocolor Archives
b Laima Turnley for Editorial Photocolor Archives
c Jan Lukas for Editorial Photocolor Archives
d Bruce Anspach/EPA Newsphoto

name index

Page numbers in *italic* refer to text pages on which the reader will find numerical references to the Bibliography, pages 419–438.

Abelson, R., *69, 419*
Abrahams, D., 67, 437
Adair, J. G., *42, 419*
Adams, J. S., *12, 419*
Adelberg, K., *252, 424*
Adelman, L., 131, 421
Adorno, T. W., 112, 419
Aiello, J. R., *401, 428*
Allen, V. I., *101, 312, 419*
Allport, F. H., 419
Allport, G. W., *60,* 130, 419
Altman, I., *397, 401, 419, 429*
Ardrey, R., 269, 270, 419
Arnold, W. J., *421, 423, 438*
Aronson, E., *42, 65, 67, 71,* 81, *84, 213,* 419, 420, *423, 426, 428, 431, 434, 435, 437*
Asch, S. E., 189, 310–312, 337, 420
Ashton, N. L., *138, 436*

Back, K. W., *206–207, 356,* 359, *366, 410,* 420, 425
Bailey, K. G., *401, 420*
Baldwin, A. L., *166, 241, 420*
Bales, R. F., 377, 378, 420, 436
Bandura, A., 172, *269, 271, 272, 278, 279, 282, 284, 285, 289–292, 294–296,* 420
Banks, W. C., *237, 238, 321,* 332, 333, 426 438
Barber, T. X., *42, 420*
Bardwick, J., 420
Barker, R. G., *278, 389,* 420
Baron, R. S., *239, 420*
Baron, S. H., *310,* 433
Baum, A., *393, 420,* 436
Baumrind, D., *330,* 420
Baxter, J. C., *152, 401,* 420
Beamon, A. L., *239, 425*
Becker, L. A., *319, 422*
Bem, D. J., 86, *147,* 164, 420, 421
Bem, S. L., *147, 162,* 164, 420, 421
Benedict, R., 295, 421
Bennis, W. G., 360, 421
Berkowitz, L., *243, 247, 248,* 250–252, 279–281, 283, 289, *290, 314, 358,* 419–421, 425–428, 434
Berkowitz, W. R., *374,* 421
Berman, Edgar, 153
Bermant, G., *143,* 421
Berry, P. C., *355, 435*
Berscheid, E., *11, 12,* 210, *213,* 218, 421, 437
Bickman, L., 244, 245, 426

Biddle, B. J., *171,* 435
Blanchard, F. A., 131, 421
Blau, P. M., *182,* 421
Bless, E., *319,* 425
Block, C. H., *355,* 435
Bloom, L. M., 205, 422
Boll, E. S., *144,* 421
Bonoma, T. V., *48, 79,* 87, *285, 359,* 435, 436
Borgatta, E. F., 436
Bossard, J. H. S., *144,* 421
Boulding, K. E., 421
Braden, M., 84, 426
Bramel, D., *207, 213,* 421
Braun, J., *108,* 437
Brehm, J. W., *73, 77, 218,* 421, 428
Brigham, J. C., *57, 94,* 95, *104, 105,* 121, 126, 205, 421, 422, 434
Brinkley, W., *315,* 422
Brock, T. C., *319,* 422
Brody, S., *234,* 429
Bronfenbrenner, U., 23, *157,* 422
Brook, P., 264, 422
Broverman, D. M., *138,* 422
Broverman, I. K., 138–140, 422
Brown, H. Rap, 291
Brown, R. C., 116, *120, 279,* 292, 422, 436
Bruner, J. S., *54,* 434
Brush, C. A., *236,* 434
Bryan, J. H., 251, 422
Buchanan, E., *207,* 435
Burgess, M., *278,* 427
Burke, P. J., *378,* 422
Buss, A. H., *263,* 422
Byrne, D., *208, 213,* 422

Calhoun, J. B., 386–387, 422
Campbell, D. T., *21,* 433, 437
Campbell, J., *355,* 424
Cannon, W. B., *201,* 422
Caputo, C., *200,* 431
Carlsmith, J. M., 41, *65, 71,* 78, *319,* 419, 422, 425
Carmichael, J., 84, 422
Carmichael, S., 108, 422
Carson, D. H., *405, 408,* 410, 425, 438
Cartwright, D., 358, *375,* 422, 423, 429
Chammah, M., *40,* 432
Chernicky, P., *331,* 437
Chesler, P., 165, 422
Chesney-Lind, M., *152,* 422

Clark, K. B., 107, 130, 422
Clark, M. P., 107, 422
Clark, R. D., III, 233, 422
Clark, W., *401*
Clarkson, F. E., *138–140,* 422
Clausen, G. T., *234,* 433
Clifford, M. M., *212,* 422
Cline, V. B., *190,* 422
Cohen, A. R., *376,* 423
Cohen, D. J., *356,* 423
Cohen, M. F., *278,* 427
Collins, B. E., *79, 356, 357,* 423
Collins, M. E., *127,* 423
Connolley, E., *311,* 426
Cook, S. W., *56, 57, 95, 127,* 130, 131, *331,*
    421–423, 430, 437, 438
Cook, T. D., *246,* 426, 427
Cooper, J., *80,* 423
Correll, C., 96–97
Cottrell, L. S., Jr., *9,* 435
Crano, W. D., *246,* 427
Cronbach, L. J., *192,* 423
Cross, H. A., *207,* 423
Crutchfield, R. S., *333,* 423

Daniels, L. R., *250,* 421
Darley, J. M., 230–234, *252,* 423, 426, 429
Davidson, E. S., *289,* 429
Davis, J. H., *353,* 423
Davis, K. E., *197, 219, 253, 256,* 424, 428, 434
Deaux, K., *213,* 423
DeFleur, M. L., *57,* 423
Delgado, J. M. R., *273,* 423
Dembo, T., *278,* 420
deRivera, J. H., 27, 423
Desor, J. A., *389,* 423
Deutsch, M., 36–38, 41, *127, 308, 312, 356,*
    423, 424
Devinney, L. C., *127,* 435
Dicks, H. V., 332, 424
Diener, E., *239,* 425
Dion, K. K., *210, 211,* 421, 424
DiRenzo, G. J., *371,* 424, 426
Dobyns, H. F., *397,* 432
Doland, D., *252,* 424
Dollard, J., 277, 424
Doob, L., 277, 424
Driscoll, R. H., *219,* 424
Driver, M. J., *29,* 424
Druckman, D., *29,* 424
Duke, M. P., *400, 401,* 424, 431
Dunnette, M. D., *355, 361,* 424
Dutton, D. G., *94,* 424

Edwards, C. D., *106,* 437
Ehrlich, P. R., 384, *393,* 424, 425
Eisenhower, M., *289, 396,* 424
Ellerston, N., *358,* 433
Ellison, C. D., *273,* 424
Elms, A. C., *120, 333,* 424

Epstein, Y. M., *207, 435*
Erickson-Paige, K., 153, 424
Eron, L. D., *289,* 424
Ervin, F., *274,* 435
Escudero, M., *387,* 430
Etzioni, A., *48, 332,* 424

Fasteau, M. F., 166, 425
Fauls, L. B., *171,* 425
Feiss, C., 388, 425
Feshbach, N. D., *171,* 425
Feshbach, S., 288, 289, 425
Festinger, L., 41, *67,* 78, 80, 82, 184, *206–207,*
    235, *236, 356,* 359, *366, 410,* 420, 425,
    437
Fiedler, F. E., 376–378, *380,* 425
Fisher, J. D., *242,* 425
Flacks, R., *72,* 431
Floyd, J., *213,* 420
Flynn, J. P., *273,* 424
Foley, L. A., *131, 138,* 425, 436
Ford, G., 48
Forer, B. R., 193, 425
Frank, J., *43, 45,* 425
Franke, G., *157,* 427
Frankel, G. J., *402,* 425
Fraser, S. C., *239,* 314, 425
Freedman, J. L., 314, *319, 393,* 425
Frenkel-Brunswik, E., 112, 419
Freshley, H. B., *243,* 438
Freud, S., 137, 166, 168, 169, 175, 264–265,
    268, 270, 296
Fried, M., *408,* 425
Friedman, P., *247,* 421
Friedrich, L. K., *251,* 435
Fromm-Reichmann, F., 184, 425
Funk, W. H., *356,* 423

Gaertner, S., 242, 244, 245, 425, 426
Gahagan, J., *48,* 435
Galle, O. R., 385, 391, 413, 426
Garattini, S., 429, 435
Geen, R. G., *281,* 421
George, A. L., *370,* 426
Gerard, H. B., *82, 308, 311, 312,* 423, 426
Gergen, K. J., 15, *258,* 426
Gergen, M. M., 258, 426
Gibb, C. A., *371, 374, 375,* 426
Gillig, P. M., *68,* 426
Glass, D. C., *416,* 426
Gleicher, P., *408,* 425
Glover, H. W., *401,* 420
Goethals, G. R., *80,* 423
Goldberg, P. A., *161,* 432
Goldman, M. A., *354,* 426
Goodenough, E. W., *171,* 426
Goranson, R. E., *314,* 426
Gordon, P., *387,* 430
Gosden, F., 96–97
Goslin, D. A., 428

Gove, W. R., 385, 391, 413, 426
Graham, H. D., *262, 293,* 426
Granet, R., *252,* 426
Grant, G., *107,* 427
Green, D., *79,* 426
Green, J. A., *57,* 426
Greenwald, A. G., *68,* 426
Greenwald, H. J., 108, 426
Gregory, D., *358,* 433
Griffitt, W., *240,* 432
Grigg, C. W., 335, 432
Gross, A. E., *319, 422,* 426
Gruder, C. L., *246,* 426
Gunn, S. P., *205, 331, 422,* 437
Gurnee, H. A., *353,* 426
Gurr, T. R., *262, 293,* 426
Guthman, E., *343,* 426
Guthrie, R. V., 435

Halcomb, C. G., *207,* 423
Hall, E. T., 399, 426
Hamilton, C. V., *108,* 422
Hamsher, J. H., 421
Haney, C., *237, 238, 321, 332, 333,* 426, 438
Hansford, E. A., *46,* 434
Hardyck, J. A., 84, *103,* 426, 435
Hare, A. P., 436
Harrington, J., 224, 228, 231, 254
Harris, V. A., 195, 428
Hartley, E. L., 420, 422, 428, 431
Hartnett, J. J., *401,* 420
Hartry, A., 25, 431
Harvey, J., *148,* 427
Harvey, O. J., *44, 96,* 117, 121, 426, 427, 434
Hastorf, A. H., *191,* 427
Haythorn, W. W., 397, 419
Hearn, G., *396,* 427
Heider, F., 195, 427
Henderson, J. E., 423
Hendricks, G., *408,* 427, 429
Hendricks, M., *246,* 427
Hermann, M. G., *29,* 427
Hersey, J., *116,* 427
Hess, E. H., *60,* 427
Hetherington, E. M., *148, 157,* 427
Hoffman, E. L., *310,* 433
Hoffman, L. W., *147–149,* 427
Hokanson, J. E., *278,* 427
Hollander, E. P., *312, 371, 374,* 427
Holsti, O. R., 27, *32,* 427, 431
Homans, G. C., *182, 248,* 427
Hood, W. R., *44, 96,* 434
Hook, L. H., *396,* 435
Horai, J., *48,* 435
Horner, M. S., 158, 427
Hornstein, H. A., *99, 243, 251,* 427
Hovland, C. I., *65, 68, 71, 100, 278,* 427, 428, 434
Hoyt, M. F., *79,* 423
Hraba, J., *107,* 427
Huessmann, L. R., *289,* 424

Huizinga, J., 39, 427
Hunt, D. E., *117,* 426
Hutt, C., *393,* 427
Hymovitch, B., *366,* 420

Insko, C. A., 64, 427
Iscoe, I., *148,* 427
Iwao, S., *362,* 428

Jaastad, K., *355,* 424
Jacobs, P. I., *189,* 435
Jacobson, L., *212,* 433
Jaensch, E. R., 120, 121
Jaffe, D., *237, 238, 321, 332, 333,* 438
Janis, I. L., *9, 341,* 342, *346–348,* 428, 435
Jayaraine, T. E., *162,* 435
Jensen, A. R., *148,* 428
Johnson, H. H., *354,* 429
Johnson, P. B., 101, 428
Johnson, R. C., *147,* 428
Johnson, R. N., *270, 271, 273, 276, 290, 291, 293,* 295, 428
Jones, E. E., 195, *197, 200, 213,* 428
Jones, R., *73,* 428
Jones, S. E., *401,* 428
Julian, J. W., *371,* 427
Jung, C., 352

Karnow, S., 332, 428
Katz, D., *53, 54,* 428
Keitel, F. M., 318
Kelem, R. T., *239,* 425
Kelley, H. H., 189, *248, 308, 353, 366,* 420, 428, 436
Kelman, H. C., *68,* 427, 428
Kemeny, J., *10, 17,* 428
Kennan, G. F., 428
Kennedy, J., 396
Kiesler, C. A., *311,* 428
Kiesler, S. B., *161, 311,* 428, 432
Kleck, R. E., *211,* 428
Klevansky, S., *393,* 425
Koch, S., 428
Koenig, K. E., *72,* 431
Kogan, N., *189,* 435
Kohlberg, L., 169, 170, 175, *333,* 428
Korten, D. C., 380, 429
Korten, F. F., 430
Krauss, R. M., 36–38, 41, 424
Krebs, D. L., *258,* 429
Kuo, Z. Y., 272, 429

Lacey, J. I., 430
Lagerspetz, K. M. J., *272,* 429
Lansing, J., *408,* 429
LaPiere, R. T., 62, 429
Laski, H. J., 336, 429
Latané, B., 230–234, *252,* 423, 426, 429

Laufer, R. S., *398,* 429
Laughlin, P. R., *354,* 429
Lazarsfeld, P. F., 9, 429
LeBon, G., 234, 429
Leeds, R., *228,* 429
Lefkowitz, M. M., *289,* 424
Legant, P., *200,* 431
Lennox, V. L., *94,* 424
LePage, A., 283, 421
Lerner, M. J., *199, 248, 314,* 429
Lerner, R. M., *234,* 429
Lett, E., *401,* 429
Leventhal, H., *74,* 429
Levine, D., 438
Levine, J. M., *312,* 419, 423
Levinger, G., *219,* 429
Levinson, D., 112, 419
Levitas, M., *99,* 429
Lewin, K., *278,* 390, 420, 429
Lichtman, R. R., *314,* 429
Liebert, R. M., *289,* 429
Lien, D., *239,* 434
Lindzey, G., 423, 426, 428, 435
Linskold, S., *48,* 435
Lipetz, M. E., *219,* 424
Lippitt, R., *366,* 379, 429, 437
Little, K. B., *399,* 429
London, P. B., *207,* 435
Loo, C., *393,* 429
Lorenz, K., 265, 268–270, 278, 280, 296, 429
Lorge, I., *353,* 429
Lott, D. F., *366,* 429
Lowe, R., *243,* 430
Lublin, S. C., *236,* 434
Luce, R. D., 39, 430
Luchins, A. S., *309,* 430
Luchins, E. H., *309,* 430
Lumsdaine, A. A., 9, 435
Lumsdaine, M. H., 9, 435
Lyle, J., *289,* 433

Macaulay, J., *243, 248, 251, 252,* 426, 427
McBride, D., *358,* 433
McClintock, C. G., 123, 422, 430
McClosky, H., 335, 430
Maccoby, E. E., *286,* 420, 422, 431, 434
McConahay, J. B., *101,* 428
McDavid, J. W., *313,* 434
McDougall, W., 179, 430
McGuire, W. J., *70,* 89, 419, 430
Mack, R. W., 335, 336, 430
McNaughton, J., 166
McNeil, E. B., 141, 144, 146, 153, 430
McPherson, J. M., 385, 391, 413, 426
Maher, B. A., 422
Mann, R. D., *371,* 374, 430
Maracek, J., *200,* 431
Mark, V. H., *274,* 435
Marsella, A. J., *387,* 430
Martindale, D., *394,* 430

Masters, J. C., *251,* 430
Mathewson, G. C., *82,* 426
Matter, W. M., *207,* 423
Mausner, B., *312,* 430
Mead, M., 139, 144, 146, 430
Medinnus, G. R., *147,* 428
Meeker, R. J., *46,* 430, 434
Melman, S., *262,* 430
Messe, L. A., 12, 430
Meter, K., *258,* 426
Mettee, D. R., *213,* 430
Meyer, J. S., *270,* 436
Meyer, T., *286,* 430
Midlarsky, E., *258,* 430
Midlarsky, M., *258,* 430
Miety, J., *405,* 433
Milgram, S., 62, 323, 325–330, 332, 333, 337,
    413, 424, 430, 431
Miller, A. G., *42,* 431
Miller, J., *69,* 419
Miller, N., 277, 424
Mills, J., 81, 419, 421, 431
Minard, R. D., *104,* 430
Minuchin, P., *148,* 430
Montagu, M. F. A., 269, *271,* 431
Moore, B. S., *247,* 436
Moore, M. T., 150, 151
Morris, D., 269, 270, 431
Mowrer, O., 277, 424
Mueller, D. J., *61,* 431
Mulder, M., 380, 431
Murstein, B., *208,* 431
Mussen, P., *153,* 431

Nadler, A., *242,* 425
Neale, J. M., *289,* 429
Nebel, J. C., *374,* 421
Nebergall, R. E., *71,* 434
Newcomb, T. M., 72, 209, 235–236, *359,* 419,
    420, 422, 425, 428, 431
Newton, I., 15
Nisbett, R. E., *200, 204,* 428, 431
Nord, W., *313,* 431
North, R. C., 32, 431
Nowicki, S., *400, 401,* 424, 431

Oppenheim, D. B., 108, 426
Orne, M., 41, 431
Osborn, A. F., *354,* 431
Osgood, C. E., 46, 48, 431
Oskamp, S., 25, 431
Osmond, H., *402,* 431

Page, M. M., 284, 421, 432
Pandey, J., *240,* 432
Parker, E. B., *289,* 433
Parsons, T., 420
Pepitone, A., 235, *236,* 425
Perez, D., 231

Pettigrew, T. F., 98, 101, 104, 105, 130, 131, 432, 436
Pheterson, G. I., *161,* 432
Phillips, N. E., 34, 432
Piaget, J., 169
Pick, A. D., 425
Piliavin, I. M., *248,* 250, 254, 255, 426, 432
Piliavin, J. A., 215, *248–250,* 253–255, 432, 437
Pilisuk, M., *29, 48,* 432
Pleck, J., *158,* 436
Polansky, N., *366,* 429
Polefka, J., *191,* 427
Polt, J. M., *60,* 427
Porter, H. L., 305, 311, 312
Postman, L., *60,* 419
Potter, P., *29,* 432
Proshansky, H. M., *398,* 429
Prothro, J. W., 335, 432
Pruitt, D. G., *8, 32,* 432

Rabban, M., *146,* 432
Rabbie, J., *186,* 432
Raiffa, H., 39, 430
Rapoport, A., *29, 40,* 432
Raven, B. H., *356, 357, 376,* 423, 432
Redl, F., *366,* 429
Regan, D. T., *314,* 432
Reitman, J. W., *374,* 421
Restle, F., *353,* 423
Ribal, J. E., *258,* 432
Richards, C. B., *397,* 432
Richardson, L. F., *262,* 432
Riecken, H., 82, 425
Rietsema, J., *376,* 432
Ritchey, G., *243,* 430
Robinson, J. A., 427
Robinson, J. P., *113,* 432
Rockwell, G. L., 119
Rodin, J., *248, 252,* 429, 432
Rogers, G., 150, 151
Rohrer, J. H., *310,* 433
Rokeach, M., *103,* 116, *117, 199,* 433
Rosen, S., *366,* 429
Rosenberg, B. G., *157,* 435
Rosenberg, M. J., 419
Rosenhan, D. L., *247, 251,* 433, 436
Rosenkrantz, P. S., *138–140,* 422
Rosenthal, R., 42, *212,* 433
Ross, D., *284,* 420
Ross, S. A., *284,* 420
Rubenstein, C., *211,* 428
Rubin, Z., 217, 433
Russell, B., *307–308,* 433
Rutherford, E., *153,* 431

Sanford, N., 112, 116, 419, 433
Sartre, J., 112, 433
Satow, K. L., *252,* 433
Sawyer, H. G., 433

Schacter, S., 82, 185, 201, 202, 204, *206–207, 358,* 359, 362, 363, *366, 410,* 420, 425, 433
Schafer, E. L., *405,* 433
Scheer, R., *106,* 433
Scheidt, R. J., *284,* 432
Schein, E. H., *308, 315,* 316, 433
Schlenker, B. R., 15, *79,* 87, *285,* 359, 433, 436
Schmidt, L., 215, 437
Schneider, D. J., *191,* 427
Schopler, J., *314,* 433
Schramm, W. J., *289,* 433
Schroeder, H. M., *117,* 426
Schwartz, R. D., *21,* 433, 437
Schwartz, S. H., *234,* 433
Sears, D. O., 101, 428, 434
Sears, R. R., *100, 277–278, 286,* 424, 427, 434
Sechrest, L., *21,* 433, 437
Selltiz, C. A., *56,* 423
Severy, L. J., 95, 121, *228, 246, 253, 256, 402,* 416, 422, 434, 437
Shaver, P. R., *113,* 432
Shaw, M. E., *340, 353, 368, 369, 375,* 434
Shepard, H. A., *360,* 421
Sherif, C. W., *44, 71, 96,* 434
Sherif, M. A., 44, 71, 96, 309, 337, 434
Shure, G. H., *46,* 430, 434
Sigall, H., *42,* 421, 434
Sigg, E. B., 429, 435
Silver, M. J., *42,* 420
Silverman, B. I., *104,* 434
Silverman, I., 234, 258, 434
Singer, J. E., *202, 236, 416,* 426, 433, 434
Singer, R. D., *289,* 425
Sistrunk, F., *313,* 434
Skinner, B. F., 17, 434
Skolnik, P., *48,* 432
Slater, P., *377,* 420
Smith, F., *411, 412,* 434
Smith, M. B., *9, 54, 103,* 334, 434, 435
Smith, R. B., III, *279, 292,* 436
Smith, R. E., *239,* 434
Smith, W. D., *171,* 425
Smythe, L., *239,* 434
Snoek, J. D., *219,* 429
Snow, C. P., 320, 434
Snyder, R. C., *8, 32,* 427, 432
Solomon, H., *234, 353,* 429
Sommer, R., *366,* 396, 399, 403–404, 429, 434
Spiro, M. E., *157,* 434
Stachnik, D. J., 193, 436
Staines, G., *162,* 435
Stainton, N. R., 193, 436
Star, S. A., *9, 127,* 435
Staub, E., 253, 435
Stein, A. H., *251,* 435
Stein, D. D., *103,* 435
Steinzor, B., *396,* 434
Stemerding, A., 380, 431
Stokols, D., 391, 400, 435
Stotland, E., *53,* 428
Stouffer, S. A., *9, 127, 335,* 435

Strauss, A., *171,* 435
Stricker, L. J., *189,* 435
Strodtbeck, F. L., *396,* 435
Suchman, E. A., *127,* 435
Suedfeld, P., *207,* 435
Summers, G. F., 438
Sumner, W. G., 124
Sutton-Smith, B., *157,* 435
Swander, D. V., *310,* 433
Swanson, G. E., 428
Sweet, W. H., *274,* 435

Taft, R., *194,* 435
Tagiuri, R., *190, 192,* 435
Talmadge, H., 304
Tannenbaum, P. H., 419
Tavris, C., 137, *162,* 435
Taylor, D. W., 355, 435
Tedeschi, J. T., *48, 79,* 87, *279, 285, 292, 359,* 435, 436
Temple, S., 109
Test, M. A., *251,* 422
Thibaut, J. W., *248, 353, 366,* 420, 428, 436
Thomas, E. J., *171,* 435
Thomas, W. I., *52,* 435
Thompson, V. D., *314, 397,* 433, 436
Thurstone, L. L., *53,* 436
Toch, H., *293,* 436
Tognacci, L. N., *63,* 437
Torrance, E. P., 366, 436
Tresemer, D., *158,* 436
Triandis, H. C., *53, 103, 182–183,* 436
Triplett, N., 351, 436
Tulkin, S. R., *148,* 436
Turner, J. A., *65, 71,* 419

Ulrich, R. E., 193, 436
Underwood, B., *247,* 436

Vaizey, M., *393,* 427
Valins, S., *31,* 203, 393, 420, 436
Van Hemel, P. E., *270,* 436
Van Hoose, T., *42,* 434
Van Lawick-Goodall, J., 142
Vanneman, R. D., 98, *101,* 436
Vernon, D. T. A., *63,* 437
Veroff, J., *375,* 436
Vinacke, W. E., *40,* 436
Vogel, S. R., *138–140,* 422
Vreeland, R., *208,* 436

Wagner, P. J., *138,* 436
Walder, L. O., *289,* 424
Walker, F., 229
Walkley, R., *127,* 437
Wallington, S. A., *319,* 425
Wallston, B. S., 426

Walster, E., *11, 67, 77, 210, 212, 213,* 215, *218, 249,* 421, 422, 436, 437
Walster, G. W., *11, 210,* 215, 421, 437
Walters, R. H., *279, 282,* 420
Ward, S. H., *108,* 437
Warwick, D. P., *72,* 431
Watson, P., 433
Watson, R. I., Jr., *236,* 437
Webb, E. J., *21,* 433, 437
Weber, M., *334,* 437
Weigel, R. H., *63, 131,* 421, 437
Weiss, W., *65, 68,* 427
Weissbach, T. A., *104, 105, 126,* 422
Weisstein, N., 141, 437
Wells, W. D., *289,* 437
West, S. G., *331,* 437
Westie, F. R., *57,* 423
Westin, A., 397, 437
Wexo, J. B., 137, 435
White, B. J., *44, 96,* 434
White, G. M., *251,* 433
White, R. K., 28, 379, 437
White, R. W., *54,* 434
Whitmyre, J. W., *356,* 423
Wicker, A. W., *63,* 389–390, 437
Wilhelmy, R., *311,* 426
Wilkins, P. C., *213,* 430
Willerman, B., *213,* 420
Williams, E. W., *240, 246, 252, 397,* 437
Williams, J. E., *106,* 437
Williams, M., *148,* 427, 435
Williams, R. M., Jr., *9, 127,* 435
Willis, R., *312,* 427
Wilner, D. M., *127,* 437
Wilson, J., *401,* 424
Wilson, W., 370
Winch, R. F., *214,* 437
Winsborough, H., *385,* 438
Winter, A. J., *29,* 432
Wispe, L., *243,* 438
Wohlwill, J. F., *405, 408, 410,* 425, 438
Wolfe, M., *398,* 429
Woodmansee, J. J., *60, 95,* 438
Word, L. E., 233, 422
Wortman, C., *213,* 428
Wrightsman, L. S., *130,* 423

Yablonsky, L., *295,* 438
Yancey, W. L., *410,* 438
Yockey, J. M., *138,* 436

Zajonc, R. B., *207,* 351, 438
Zander, A., *358, 375,* 422
Zaninovich, M. G., *32,* 431
Zehner, R. B., *408,* 438
Zigler, E., *169, 170,* 428
Zimbardo, P. G., 235–238, 262, 279, 321, 330, 332, 333, 337, 416, 417, 426, 438
Zinnes, D. A., *32,* 431
Znaniecki, F., *52,* 436

subject index

Ability, liking and, 213
Abstract thinking, concrete thinking vs., 117, 120–122
Achieved status, 365
Active participation, brainwashing and, 317
Activity profile, 405
Adjustment, social: attitudes and, 54, 64
    conformity and, 104, 105
Advertisements:
    institutional racism and, 110–111
    sexism in employment and, 152
Affiliation, 178–186
    fear and, 185–187
    instinct and, 179–180, 182
    social comparison and, 184–186
    social exchange and, 182–184
    social rewards and, 182–184
    survival and, 182
Agape, 217
Age, helping behavior and, 253–256
Aggression, 260–297
    in animals, 265, 268–269
    athletics and, 279–280
    authoritarian, in F Scale, 113
    boxing and, 266
    control of, 280, 291, 296
        gun control, 283–284
    culture and, 295–296
    defining, 262–264, 292–293
    displaced, 277–278
    drugs and, 275–276

Aggression:
    genetics and, 271–272
    human nature and, 264–266, 269–271, 275–276
    inhibitions against, 268
    instincts and ethological approach to, 265, 268–271
    physiological bases of, 271–273
    psychoanalytical interpretation of, 264–265
    social and psychological bases of, 273, 276–295
        frustration, 276–282
        social influence approach, 291–295
        social learning theory, 282, 284–289
        violence and the mass media, 288–291
    status and, 294–295
Aggression center in brain, 272–273
Agonistic behavior, aggression and, 268*n.*
Agreement within groups, 361–363
    (*See also* Groupthink)
Agricultural societies, sexism in, 146
Airports, 403–404
Albertslund (Denmark), 388–389
Algiers motel incident (1968), 116
"All in the Family" (television series), 52, 54, 55, 67, 72, 87–90, 99
"Aloha week" study, 64
Alternatives, comparison level for, 183–184
Altruism, 222–259
    definitions of, 225, 228
    (*See also* Helping behavior)

Ambiguity, inability to tolerate, 29
Ambiguous stimuli, attitude measurement and, 56, 60
American Indians, 97
American Soldier, The (government-commissioned study), 9
"Amos 'n Andy" (radio and television series), 96, 109
Anal stage, 168
Analysis:
content and historical, 31–33
correlational, 33–35
of data, 33–35
Androgynous individuals, 162, 164
Anonymity, 398, 416
(*See also* Deindividuation)
Antecedents, as manipulated variables, 36
Anticonformity, 306, 308
Anti-intraception in *F* Scale, 113
Anti-Semitism, 111–112
Arapesh, study of sex roles among, 141
Archie (character in "All in the Family" series), 52, 54, 55, 67, 72, 87–90
Artifacts, evaluation of others and, 191
Ascribed status, 365
Assignment of subjects, random, 36, 38
Association, differential, 174–175
Athletics, aggression and, 279–280
Attachment, love and, 217
Attitude change, 63–91, 205
behavioral change and, 76–87, 124, 126–127
contact situations and, 127–132
legal change and, 124, 126
personality characteristics and, 130–131
persuasion and, 87–90
persuasive communication and, 65–76
audience characteristics, 74–76
message characteristics, 70–74
source characteristics, 65–70
prejudice and, 122–123, 127–132
reasons for, 64
resisting persuasion and, 87–90
step-by-step process of, 71, 72
Attitudes:
behavior and, correspondence between, 61–63
brainwashing techniques and, 315, 316
definition of, 52–53
functions of, 54–55
measurement of, 55–61
racial (*see* Prejudice, ethnic)
self-attributions about, 205
sexism and, 158–161
similarity of, liking others and, 208
(*See also* Attitude change)
Attraction, interpersonal (liking others), 206–216
ability as determinant of, 213
complementarity and, 214

Attraction, interpersonal (liking others):
physical attractiveness and, 210–213
propinquity and, 206–207
reciprocal, 213–214
similarity and, 207–209
Attractiveness:
of communicator, attitude change and, 65, 68–69
physical, liking others and, 210–213
Attribution theory, 195
Attributions, making, 194–205
factors affecting, 195–200
self-attributions, 201–205
Audience, persuasive communication and characteristics of, 65, 74–76
Authoritarian aggression in *F* Scale, 113
Authoritarian personality, 112–117, 119–122
conformity and obedience and, 333
Authoritarian submission in *F* Scale, 113
Authoritarianism, 112–117, 119–124, 379–380
child-rearing practices and, 115–116, 123–124
decline of, in America, 334, 336
(*See also* Dogmatism)
Authority:
obedience to (*see* Obedience)
relationships with, T-groups and, 360
Authority figure, immediacy of, 327
Autocratic leadership style, 379
Autokinetic effect, 309
Automation of experiments, 42
Availability, attraction and, 206–207
Awareness, unilateral, 219, 220
Aztecs, 295

Bargaining, comparison level for alternatives and, 184
Barriers, social, 106, 108
Bay of Pigs invasion (1961), 340–347, 349, 370
Behavior:
attitudes and, correspondence between, 61–63
attributions and expected, 196–197
change in: attitude change and, 76–87
reduction of prejudice, 124, 126–127
counterattitudinal, attitude change and, 79, 86
evaluation of (*see* Evaluation of other people)
group (*see* Group dynamics; Groupthink; Leadership)
helping (*see* Helping behavior)
socially desirable, expectations and, 196–197
(*See also specific topics*)
Behavior-engulfing-the-field effect, 195
Behavioral "laws," 15–17

Behavioral sinks, 386, 387
Beliefs:
    brainwashing and, 315, 316
    perceived dissimilarity in, 102–104, 131
    sexism and, 158–161
Bell Adjustment Inventory, 193
Bennington College, 72
Bias:
    in question construction, 22
    of respondents, 22
    sampling and, 24, 30
    social desirability, 22
Bill of Rights, 335–336
Black, symbolism of color, 106
Black-and-white thinking, 24, 27–29
Black-top image, 28
Blind studies, 42
Bob and Carol and Ted and Alice (film), 360
Bonnie and Clyde (film), 287, 288
Boomerang effect, attitude change and, 69
"Born leader," 370
Boxing, aggression and, 266
Brain, aggression and, 272–276
Brainstorming, 354–356
Brainwashing, compliance and, 315–317
Brotherhood, conflict resolution and appeals
    to, 43
Brown v. Board of Education, 107, 126
Bystander intervention, 229–230
    (*See also* Victim-bystander
        characteristics)

Candidates, political: personal
    characteristics of, voting behavior
    and, 371, 374
    race of, 101–102
    sex of, 136, 138
Caring, love and, 217
Categories in content analysis, 32
Catharsis, aggression and, 278, 289
Cause-effect relationship, 14
Causes, as manipulated variables, 36
Central Intelligence Agency (CIA), 341, 346
Central traits, evaluating others and, 189–
    190
Centralized communication networks, 367–
    369
Champion, The (film), 281, 288
Channels of communication in groups, 367–
    368
"Checkerboard" integration, 127–128
Chicago (Illinois), 1968 demonstrations in,
    14, 18–24, 30–34, 279
Child-rearing practices:
    authoritarianism and, 115–116, 123–124
    prejudice and, 123–124
China, 306, 308
Chinese Communists, 306, 308
    brainwashing techniques of, 314–317
Choices, 16

Christianity:
    institutional racism and, 108
    sexism in, 147
Church of the True Word, 83–84
CIA (Central Intelligence Agency), 341, 346
Civil rights movement, 129
Class, social: helping behavior and, 246–247
    sexism and, 146–147
Coaching, sex-role acquisition and, 171–172
Cognitive concreteness, abstractness vs., 29
Cognitive cues:
    self-attributions and, 201–204, 217
    in two-factor theory of emotional arousal,
        217–218
Cognitive-development approach to sex-role
    acquisition, 166, 169–170, 175
Cognitive dissonance theory, 80, 84, 86, 126
Cognitive overload in urban settings, 413
Cohesiveness of group, 356–363
    groupthink and, 347, 350
Color-coding, 106
Commitment, comparison level for
    alternatives and, 184
Committee to Re-Elect the President
    (CREEP), 300, 301, 305
Common goals, conflict resolution and, 44–
    45
Common sense, 5–10
Communication:
    attitude change and persuasive, 65–76
        audience characteristics, 74–76
        message characteristics, 70–74
        source characteristics, 65–70
    group, status and, 366, 367
    T-groups and, 360–361
Communication networks, 366–369
Community:
    failure of, 334, 336
    sexism and, 149, 152
Comparison, social, 184–186
Comparison conditions (control conditions),
    21
Comparison level, affiliation and, 182–184
Competence, attraction and, 213
Competition, ethnic prejudice and, 98–102
Complementarity, attraction and, 214
Compliance, 313–336
    brainwashing as example of, 315–317
    conformity and, 306
    definition of, 306
    Galileo's renunciation of his ideas as
        instance of, 307–308
    guilt and, 317–320
    reactance and, 318
    rewards and punishments and, 313–314
    states of the individual and, 314–318
    in today's society, 334–336
Compliments, attraction and, 213–214
Conceptual functioning, levels of, 121–122
Conclusions, persuasive communication
    and drawing of, 73

Concrete thinking (cognitive concreteness), abstract vs., 29, 117, 120, 121
Conflict:
   black-and-white thinking and, 24, 27–29
   definition of, 4–5
   double standards and, 24–27
   experiment on, 36–38
   games and study of, 36–41
   misperceptions and, 23–29
   racial, racial-conflict assumption, 131–132
   resolution or reduction of, 43–49
   role, 363
   self-fulfilling prophecies and, 28
   stereotyped images and, 28–29
Conformers, group reactions to, 361–363
Conforming personality, 333–334
Conformity, 306–313
   compliance and, 306
   definition of, 306
   early studies of, 309–311
   personality characteristics and, 333–334
   reasons for, 308–309
   social norms and, 104–106
   in today's society, 334–336
   variables affecting, 311–313
   Watergate scandal as instance of, 311–314, 330, 331, 336
Consciousness-raising groups, 163, 164
Consequences of behavior:
   attitude change and, 77, 79, 80
   modeling and, 284–285
Consequents, independent variables and, 36
Contact:
   intergroup, 44–45
   interracial, 124, 127–132
Contact prejudice, 96
Contact situations, attitude change and, 127–132
Content analysis, 31–33
Contingency model of leader effectiveness, 375–377
Continued interaction, expectations of, 207
Control:
   over others, need for, 375
   of variables, 36
Control condition (comparison condition), 21
Controlled settings, experimentation and, 35–43
Conventionalism in F Scale, 113
Cooperation:
   game-approach to conflict and, 40–41
   prejudice and, 130–131
   (See also Conflict)
Copernican system, 307
Correlation of data (correlational analysis), 33–35
Cost-reward considerations, helping behavior and, 247–250, 254–256
Counteractive phenomenon, 157

Counterattitudinal behavior, attitude change and, 79, 86
Cover stories, 41
Credibility of source, attitude change and, 65–70
"Credibility gap," 65
Crime, 388, 415, 416
   (See also Helping behavior)
Criminal justice system, 149, 152
Criterion problem in evaluating others, 190–191
Criticism, brainstorming and withholding of, 354
Crowding, 390–394
Crying, 196–197
Cuban missile crisis (1962), 48, 341, 342
Cues:
   aggressive instincts and external, 265, 268, 280–284
   cognitive: self-attributions and, 201–204, 217
      in two-factor theory of emotional arousal, 217–218
Culture (cultural forces):
   aggression and, 295–296
   sex-role socialization and, 144, 146–153
Cynicism in F Scale, 114

Dani society, 296–297
Darwinism, Social, 108–109
Data:
   analysis of, 33–35
   controlled settings and gathering of, 35–43
   validity and reliability of, 30–31
   (See also Evidence)
Dating:
   choosing a partner for, 210–211
   physical attractiveness and, 210–211
Decentralized communication networks, 367–369
Decision making, group, 340–350
Decisions, 16, 17
   bystander intervention and, 230
   groupthink and, 350
Deduction, 12, 13
Definition, operational, 12
Deindividuation, helping behavior and, 233, 235–240
Demand characteristics, 41–42, 320
Democrat, 379–380
Democratic National Convention (1968), 14, 20, 32–34, 279
Demographers, 384
Density, population, 391
   high, 385–387, 391, 392
   interpersonal, 385
   low, 387–389
   "right," 389–391
   social pathology and, 386–387
   structural, 385

Dependence:
    comparison level for alternatives and, 184
    helping behavior and, 250
Dependent variables, 36
Deprivation, competitive racism and, 101–103
Destructiveness in *F* Scale, 114
Determinism, fatalistic, 17–18
Detroit (Michigan), 1968 riots in, 116
Deviates, group reactions to, 361–365
Devil's advocate role, groupthink and, 348
Diabolical enemy image, 28
Diary of a Mad Housewife (film), 167
Differential accuracy, 192
Differential association, 174–175
Diffusion of responsibility, helping behavior and, 233–235, 239, 246
Directional influence, 34–35
Disagreement (*see* Conflict)
Discrimination, 94
    (*See also* Prejudice, ethnic; Racism; Sexism)
Displaced aggression, 277–278
Dissent (dissenting ideas):
    self-censorship of, in groupthink, 346
    tolerance for, in America, 334–336
Dissonance, cognitive, 80, 84, 86
Distortion of action, conformity and, 311
Distortion of judgment, conformity and, 311
Distortion of perception, conformity and, 311
Distribution of people, 407
    (*See also* Crowding; Personal space; Privacy; Territory)
Distributive justice, 248
Dogmatism, 116–117, 120, 121
Dolls, study of racial prejudice and, 106–108
Dominance hierarchies, aggression and, 268
Dominant responses, 351–352
"Doomsday Flight" (television show), 290–291
Double standards, 24–27
Drive-reduction model, 254
Drugs, aggression and, 275–276

Economic equality, prejudice and, 132
Ego, 166, 168
Ego-defense:
    attitudes and, 54, 55, 64
    conformity and, 104
Egoist deprivation, competitive racism and, 101, 103
"Eichmann, latent," 332
Electra complex, 169
Emergency, helping behavior and characteristics of, 230, 247–253
Emotional arousal, love and, 217–218
Emotions, "juke box" theory, 204
    (*See also specific topics*)
Encounter group movement, 360

Enemy:
    black-top image, 28
    diabolical image of, 28
Environment-person relationships, 412
Environmental forces, attributions as affected by, 195–196
Environmental settings, 402–417
    natural, 405, 407
    residential, 408–410
    urban, 410–417
        anonymity, 416
        cognitive overload, 413
        noise, 416–417
Equal Rights Amendment, 70, 71
Equal-status contact, interracial, 124, 127–132
Equality, prejudice and economic, 132
Equity, 10–12
    actual, 11
    psychological, 11–12, 248–249
Eros (Greek concept), 217
Eros (life instinct), 264–265
Ethnic groups, 94
Ethnic identity, helping behavior and, 242–246
Ethnic prejudice (*see* Prejudice, ethnic)
Ethnic separation, 131–132
    (*See also* Segregation)
Ethnic stereotypes, 95, 96, 130
Ethnocentrism, 112
Ethological approach to aggression, 265, 268–271
Evaluation of other people, 186, 188–194
    ability for accurate, 190–194
    attributions and (*see* Attributions, making)
    central traits and, 189–190
    generalizations and, 186, 188
    implicit personality theories and, 188–189
    physical attractiveness and, 211–212
    skill in, 192, 194
    (*See also* Attraction, interpersonal)
Evidence, getting, 14–33
    content analysis and, 31–33
    historical and content analysis and, 31–33
    observation of naturally occurring behaviors and, 14, 18–19, 21
    questionnaire-interview techniques and, 21–24, 30–31
    (*See also* Data; Information)
Expectations:
    attitude change and disconfirmed, 81–84
    attributions and, 196–197
    of continued interaction, attraction and, 207
Experimentation, 35–43
    definition of, 36
    demand characteristics and, 41–42
    experimenter effects and, 42–43
    field, 36
Experimenter-expectancy effects, 42–43

Expertise:
  of communication source, 65–66
  conformity and, 311
Exploitation, ethnic prejudice and, 96, 98, 100
Exposure of the individual, 336
Expression of values and attitudes, 54, 55, 64

F Scale, 112–117
Face-to-face interaction, helping behavior and, 253
Facts, social science and, 15, 16
Failure of community, 334, 336
Familiar Quotations (Bartlett), 217
Familiarity, attraction and, 207
Family, sexism and, 139, 141, 142, 148, 153, 155–157, 164, 171–172
Fascism, 112–115
Fatalistic determinism, 17–18
FBI (Federal Bureau of Investigation), 289, 290
Fear:
  affiliation and, 185–187
  persuasive communication and, 74
  of success, in women, 158–161
Federal Aviation Administration, 291
Federal Bureau of Investigation (FBI), 289, 290
"Feminine" behavior (see Sex roles; Sexism)
Feminism, 163
  (See also Women's Liberation)
Field experiments, 36, 244
Field theory, Lewin's, 390
Fighting, intraspecies, 268n.
  (See also Aggression)
"Flesh-colored" bandages, 109, 110
"Foot-in-the-door" technique, 314
Formal norms, 105
Fraternal deprivation, competitive racism and, 101–103
Free choice, attitude change and, 77–80, 86
Freedom:
  reactance as tendency to reestablish, 218, 219
  of speech, 335
Friendship, 213, 410
  (See also Attraction, interpersonal)
Frustration, aggression and, 276–282
Functional utility of area, 403

Games:
  conflict and, 36–41
  prisoner's dilemma, 39–40
  trucking, 36–38
Generalizations, 95, 186, 188
Genetics, aggression and, 271–272
Geocentric theory, 307
Germany, 379, 380

Gloria (character in "All in the Family"), 89, 90
Goals:
  aggression and, 263–264, 292, 293
  common, conflict resolution and, 44–45
  group cohesiveness and achievement of, 356
Graduate, The (Film), 404
Graduated Reciprocation in Tension-reduction (GRIT), 46–49
"Great man" theory of leadership, 370, 371
Gregariousness instinct, 180
Group dynamics, 338–381
  (See also Groups; Groupthink; Leadership)
"Group mind," 234
Group performance, 352–356
Group pressure:
  conformity and, 306, 310
  obedience experiment and, 328
Group therapy, 123
Groups:
  cohesiveness of, 347, 350, 356–363
    deviates and conformers, 361–363
    feelings and actions of members, 356–357
    group performance, 357–358
    social influence, 359, 361
  conformity and, 308–309, 311–313
  consciousness-raising, 163, 174
  definition of, 340
  ethnic, 94
    (See also Prejudice, ethnic)
  leadership of, 369–379
  person versus, 350–356
  size of, helping behavior and, 233–239
  social climate of, 350, 356–363
  structure of, 350, 363, 365–369
  T-, 360–361
Groupthink, 340–350, 362–363
  factors that increase, 347, 350
  prevention of, 348–349
  symptoms of, 343, 346–347
Guards, prisoners and, study on role requirements, 321, 323, 329, 330
Guilt, compliance and, 317–320
Gun-control, 283
Guns, aggression and, 283–284

Habits, sexism and, 164–166
Halo effect, 190
Hard to get, playing, 215–216
Hedonic relevance, 197–199
Heliocentric theory of solar system, 307
Helping behavior, 228–259
  age and, 253–256
  bystander intervention and, 229–230
  development of, 253–256
  emergency and, 230, 247–256
  mood and, 247
  motivation for, 254–256

Helping behavior:
  personality characteristics and, 256, 258
  race and, 242–246
  territory and, 252, 397
  victim-bystander characteristics and, 230–247
    ambiguity of victim's need, 231–233
    effects of group size, 233–239
    similarity, 239–247
Heretics, 361–363
Historical analysis, 31–33
House-Tree-Person (HTP) Test, 193
Housing, integration of, 127–128
Human nature, 143, 166
  aggression and, 264–266, 269–271, 275–276
  altruism and, 225, 228
Hunger, self-attribution of, 204–205
Hypothesis, 11, 13, 15–16

Id, 166, 168
Ideals, sexism and, 164
Identity, personal territory and, 397
Ignorance, pluralistic, 232
Image:
  diabolical enemy, 28
  self-, 28, 29
Imitation, helping behavior and, 251
  (See also Modeling)
Immigration system, 111
Implicit personality theories, 188–189
Impression management, theory of, 87, 88
Independence, 308
  groupthink and, 348
Independent variables, 36
Individual (person):
  exposure of the, 336
  socialization of, 143–144
Induction, 10–13
Influence, directional, 34–35
Informal norms, 105
Information:
  from authoritative sources, 8–9
  common sense as unevaluated, 5–9
  transmission of, communication networks and, 367, 369
  (See also Evidence)
Informational influence, conformity and, 309
Ingratiation effect, 246
Inquisition, the, 307
Instinct:
  affiliation and, 179–180, 182
  aggression and, 265, 268–271
  definition of, 179–180
Integration, racial, 126–130, 132–133
Intelligence:
  attraction and, 213
  of audience, persuasive communication and, 75, 76
  of leader, 374

Intention descriptions of altruism, 228
Intentions, aggression and, 263, 292
Interaction process analysis, 377
Intergroup contact, 44–45
International affairs, misperceptions in, 27–29
International perceptions, double standard in, 25–27
Interpersonal attraction (see Attraction, interpersonal)
Interpersonal density, 385, 387
Interpersonal relationships, 178
Interracial contact, 124, 127–132
Interrater reliability, 31
Interrogation, brainwashing and, 316
Interstitial behavior, 397
Interviewers, effects on respondents of, 22–23
Interviews, attitude measurement and, 56, 59
Intimacy (privacy), 398
  love and, 217
Intrapersonal reliability, 31
Invasion of personal space, 402
Invulnerability, groupthink and illusion of, 343
Islam, sexism, 147
Isolation, 389, 390
  groupthink and, 350

Japanese-Americans, 96
Judaism, sexism in, 147
Judgment, conformity and distortion of, 311
"Juke box" theory of emotion, 204
Justice, distributive, 248

Knowledge:
  attitudes and, 54
  sexism and, 162, 164
Korean War, 306, 308
  brainwashing techniques used in, 314–317
Ku Klux Klan, 240

Labels, modeling and, 286, 288
Lady in the Dark (film), 150–151
Laissez faire leadership style, 379
"Latent Eichmann," 332
Latent liberals, 105–106
Latitude of acceptance, 71
Latitude of noncommitment, 71
Latitude of rejection, 71
"Laws," behavioral, 15–17
Laws of nature, 16–17
  (See also Legal change)
Leader (leadership), 350, 368–380
  definition of, 369
  "great man" theory of, 370, 371
  personal characteristics of, 371–376
  relations-oriented, 376, 377

Leader (leadership):
    social forces theory of, 371
    styles of, 379–380
    task-oriented, 376, 377
    types of, 377–378
    (See also Groups)
Leader-effectiveness, contingency model of, 375–377
Leader-member relations within group, 376
Learning, observational (see Modeling)
Legal change, prejudice and, 124, 126–127, 129
Legitimacy, aggression and, 292
Levels of a relationship, 219–220
Liberals, latent, 105–106
Libido, 166
Liking others (see Attraction, interpersonal)
Limits to Growth Report, 384
Localism, 410
Lord of the Flies (Golding), 264, 266
Los Angeles riot (1965), 101, 102
Love:
    as emotion, 217–220
    nature of, 217
Lying, attitude change and, 78–80, 86, 87
Lynching, as displaced aggression, 278, 279

McGraw-Hill Book Company, 153–155
"Man and His Urban Environment"
    (Rockefeller Foundation Project), 411
Management of impressions, theory of, 87, 88
Manipulation of variables in experimentation, 36
Manning of environmental setting, 389, 390
Marriage:
    complementarity and, 214
    sex roles in, 164, 165
"Mary Tyler Moore Show, The" (television show), 150–151
"Masculine" behavior (see Sex roles; Sexism)
Masochism, 214
Mass media:
    prejudice and: institutional racism, 109–111
        reduction of, 122–124
    sexism and, 150–153
    violence and, 288–291
    (See also Aggression, modeling and)
Massachusetts Institute of Technology, 359
Measurement:
    of attitudes, 55–61
    unobtrusive and reactive, 21
Medical profession, sexism in, 160
Membership, group (see Groups)
Mental health, sexism and, 164–166
Message characteristics of communication, 65, 70–74
Mexican-Americans, 109

Mike (character in "All in the Family"), 52, 54, 55, 67, 72, 87–90
Mindguards in groupthink, 346–347
Mirror-image in perception, 23–24
Misperceptions in international affairs, 27–29
    (See also Perceptions)
Modeling (observational learning):
    aggression and, 282–288
    helping behavior and, 250–252
    labels and, 286, 288
    sex-role acquisition and, 172–175
Mood, helping behavior and, 247
Moral definitions of altruism, 228
Moral self-image, 28
Morality, groupthink and illusions of, 343, 346
Motion Picture Producers Association, 285
Motivation in leaders, 375
Motives, sexism and, 162
Movies:
    institutional racism and, 109
    sexism in, 150–152
Moving-light experiment, conformity and, 309–310
Mudugumor, study of sex roles among, 141
Mutuality, as level of relationship, 219–220
My Lai massacre (1968), 318, 322

National Broadcasting Company (NBC), 290–291
National Commission on the Causes and Prevention of Violence, The, 289
    Walker Report to, 14, 18–19, 21
National Institute of Mental Health, 165
National Organization for Women (NOW), 163
Native Americans (see American Indians)
Natural settings, 405, 407
Nature (natural order):
    laws of, 16–17
    sex roles and, 142–143
NBC (National Broadcasting Company), 290–291
Nearness (see Propinquity)
Neighborhood, 408–410
Networks of communication in groups, 366–369
New town (new city), 388, 411–412
New York City:
    mayoralty election (1969), 371, 374
    subway system of, 242, 248
"No better than the best" effect, 353
Noise, 416–417
Noncommitment, latitude of, 71
Nonviolence (see Pacifism)
Normative action, aggression and, 292
Normative influence, conformity and, 308–309

Norms:
    conformity and, 104–106, 308–309
    formal, 105
    informal, 105
    social-responsibility, 250
North Vietnam (see Vietnam war)
NOW (National Organization for Women), 163

Obedience, 320
    hurting-on-command experiment on, 323–326
        ethical considerations, 328–330
        other situational variables, 326–328
    implications of, 331–333
    personality character1stics and, 333–334
    situational forces and, 332–333
Obedient personality, 333–334
Obese persons, self-attribution of hunger by, 204–205
Observation:
    attitude measurement and, 56, 57, 59
    of naturally occurring behaviors, 14, 18–19, 21
    problems in interpreting data from, 19, 21
    unobtrusive and reactive measures and, 21
Observational learning (modeling):
    aggression and, 282–288
    sex-role acquisition and, 172–175
Observer, action as affected by, attributions and, 197–200
Oedipus complex, 168–169
On Aggression (Lorenz), 265
Operational definition, 12
Oral stage, 168
Orders, following, 331–332
    (See also Obedience)
Organization of group:
    cohesiveness and, 358–359
    (See also Groups, structure of)
Overdifferentiation of others, 192, 194
Overt behavior, attitude measurement and observation of, 56, 57, 59

Pacifism, 45–46, 296
"Pacing of demands" technique, 314, 317
Parental interference, love and, 218–219
Parents:
    as models of aggression, 286
    sex-role development and, 153, 155–157, 171–172
    socialization and, 153, 155–157
Pastoral societies, sexism in, 146
Peers:
    intimate relationships with, T-groups and, 360
    sex-role development and, 157, 159
    socialization and, 157, 159

Perceived belief dissimilarity, 102–104, 131
Perceived similarity, victim-bystander characteristics and, 239
Perceptions:
    conformity and distortion of, 311
    double standard in international, 25–27
    mirror-image in, 23–24
    (See also Misperceptions)
Person-environment relationships, 412
Personal characteristics of leader, 371–376
Personal forces, 195
Personal identity, territory and, 397
Personal space, 399–402
Personalism, 197–198
Personality (personality types):
    authoritarian, 112–117, 119–122
        conformity and obedience, 333
    conforming or obedient, 333–334
    ethnic prejudice and (see Prejudice, ethnic, personality characteristics and)
    socially oriented, 258
Personality characteristics (personality traits):
    attitude change and, 130–131
    attribution of causes of behavior to, 200
    of audience, persuasive communication and, 75–76
    central, evaluating others and, 189–190
    conformity and, 313, 333–334
    helping behavior and, 256, 258
    of leader, 370–376
    obedience and, 333–334
    prejudice and (see Prejudice, ethnic, personality characteristics and)
    sex and, 138–141, 158, 166
Personality theories, implicit, 188–189
Persuasibility, 130
Persuasion, resisting, attitude change and, 87–90
Persuasive communication, attitude change and, 65–76
    audience characteristics and, 74–76
    message characteristics and, 70–74
    source characteristics and, 65–70
Phallic stage, 168
Phenomenological model, 254
Physical attractiveness:
    dating and, 210–211
    liking others and, 208, 210–213
Physical characteristics of leader, 371, 374
Physiological arousal:
    love and, 217–218
    self-attributions and, 201–204, 217
    in two-factor theory of emotional arousal, 217–218
Physiological reactions, attitude measurement and, 56, 60–61
Physiology, aggression and, 271–273
Pittsburgh Press (newspaper), 152
Planning, residential, 410
    (See also Environmental settings)

Playing hard to get, 215–216
Plessy v. Ferguson (1896), 124, 126
Pluralistic ignorance, 232
Policy prejudice, 96, 105
Political candidates:
    race of, 101–103
    sex of, 136, 138
Pooling-of-abilities effect, 354
Population density (*see* Density)
    in random sampling, 24, 30
Population growth, 384
    (*See also* Crowding; Density)
Position advocated in messages, persuasive
    communication and, 70–73
Position power in groups, 376
Power:
    of communication source, 65, 69–70
    in *F* Scale, 113–114
    need for, leaders and, 375
Predatory behavior, aggression and, 268*n.*
Predictability, attraction and, 207
Predictions, scientific method and, 13, 14
Prejudice:
    definition of, 94
    ethnic, 94–133
        attitude change and, 122–123
        behavior change and, 124, 126–127
        causes of, 96–111
            belief dissimilarity, perceived, 102–
                104
            competition and exploitation, 96, 98–
                102
            conformity and social norms, 104–
                106
            cues from society, 106–111
        child-rearing practices and, 123–124
        equal-status contact and, 124, 127–132
        ethnic separation and, 131–132
        mass media and: institutional racism,
            109–111
            reduction of prejudice, 122–124
        personality characteristics and, 111–
            122, 130–131
            authoritarianism, 112–117, 119–122
            bias in typing personalities, 120, 122
            concrete versus abstract thinking,
                117, 120
            dogmatism, 116–117, 120, 121
        reduction of, 122–132
            changing attitudes, 122–123, 127–132
            changing behavior, 124, 126–127
            changing child-rearing practices,
               123–124
            economic equality and, 132
            equal-status contact, 124, 127–132
            therapy and, 123
        types of prejudicial attitudes, 95–96
        (*See also* Sexism)
Prejudiced personality, 111
    (*See also* Prejudice, ethnic, personality
        characteristics and)

President's Commission on Law
    Enforcement and the Administration of
    Justice, The, 149, 275
President's Executive Committee, 340–347,
    349
Prestige, group cohesiveness and, 356
Prison:
    deindividuation in, 237–239
    urban environment as, 416
Prisoners, guards and study on role
    requirements of, 321, 323, 329, 330
Prisoner's dilemma game, 39–40
Privacy, 397–398
Projectivity in *F* Scale, 114
Propinquity, attraction and, 206–207
Protestant Ethic, waning of, 334
Proximity of victim, obedience experiment
    and, 326–327
Psychoanalytical interpretation of
    aggression, 264–265
Psychodynamic approach to sex-role
    acquisition, 166, 168–169, 175
Psychological tension, attitude change and
    reduction of, 80, 84
Psychosexual development, stages of, 168
Ptolemaic system, 307
Punishments, compliance and rewards and,
    313–314
    (*See also* Rewards)
Puppets, study of racial prejudice and, 107–
    108
Pure stimulus effect, 246

"Queen bee" syndrome, sexism and, 162,
    163
Question construction, bias in, 22
Questionnaire-interview techniques:
    bias in question construction and, 22
    bias of respondents and, 22
    interviewer's effect on respondents and,
        22
    social desirability bias of respondents and,
        22
Quotas, immigration, 111

Race:
    helping behavior and, 242–246
    sexism and, 148
Racial attitudes, voting behavior and, 121–
    122
Racial-conflict assumption, 131–132
Racial inferiority, 131–132
Racism:
    institutional, 108–111
    relative deprivation and competitive, 100–
        103
    (*See also* Discrimination; Prejudice,
        ethnic)
Radicals, feminist, 163

Random assignment of subjects, 36, 38
Random sampling, 24, 30
Rape (rape victims):
  attributions regarding, 199–200
  helping behavior and, 249
Rationalizations of warnings in groupthink, 347
Reactance, 218, 219
  compliance and, 318
Reactive measurement, 21
"Real-life" (field) settings ("real world situations") in research, 244, 393
Reality, social, social comparison and, 184
Reinforcement, sex-role acquisition and, 170–171
Rejection, latitude of, 71
Relations-oriented leader, 376
Relationships:
  with authority, 360
  levels of, 219–220
  personal: with peers, 360
    prejudice and, reduction of, 130
Relative deprivation, competitive racism and, 100–103
Reliability of data, 30–31
Religion, sexism and, 147–148
Repetition, brainwashing and, 317
Representative sample, bias associated with obtaining, 24, 30
Research, methodological problems and, 114–115
Reserve (privacy), 398
Residential settings, 408–409
Respondents (see Interviews; Questionnaire-interview techniques)
Response acquiescence set, 115
Responses, dominant, 351–352
Responsibility:
  diffusion of, helping behavior and 233–235, 239, 246
  personal, helping behavior and, 230
Reward-cost definition of altruism, 225, 228
Rewards (rewards and punishments):
  attraction and, 213, 214
  brainwashing and, 317
Riots, 293
  Detroit (1968), 116
  Watts (Los Angeles, 1965), 101, 102
"Robber's Cave" study, 44–45, 98
Role conflict:
  group structure and, 363
  in women, 363
  (See also Sex roles; Sexism)
Roles:
  appropriateness of behavior and, 320–331
    hurting on command, Milgram's experiment on, 323–330
    prisoners and guards, 321, 323
  definition of, 300
  group structure and, 363, 365

Roles:
  of political campaign workers, 300–305
  sexual (see Sex roles; Sexism)
Romantic love, concept of, 217
  (See also Love)
Romeo and Juliet (Shakespeare), 218
Romeo and Juliet effect, 219
Russia (see Soviet Union)

Sadism, 214
Salespeople, compliance-inducing techniques of, 314
Sampling and estimation, comparison level for alternatives and, 184
Sampling techniques, 23–24, 30
Saturation of centralized communication network, 369
Scapegoats, racism and, 99–100
Schools (school system):
  institutional racism and, 109
  integration of, 125–130
  sexism and, 148–149
Scientific method, 9–14
  deduction and, 12
  induction and, 10–12
  summary of, 13–14
  testing and, 12–13
Segregation, 126–130
  (See also Integration; Separation, ethnic)
Selective exposure, 75
Self-assertiveness of leader, 374–375
Self-attributions, 201–205
  love and, 217–218
Self-censorship of dissenting ideas in groupthink, 346
Self-confidence of leader, 374–375
Self-criticism, brainwashing and, 316
Self-fulfilling prophecy, 28, 162
  physical attractiveness stereotype and, 211
Self-image:
  moral, 28
  virile, 29
Self-perception theory, 86–87, 126–127
Self-report measures of attitudes, 56, 58, 59
Sensitivity group, 360
Separation:
  ethnic, 131–132
  racial (see Separation, ethnic)
  (See also Segregation)
Separatism (see Separation, ethnic)
Separatists:
  black, 132
  white, 131–132
Sex:
  of audience, persuasive communication and, 75, 76
  in F Scale, 114
  helping behavior and, 246
Sex-role myths, game elucidating, 137–138
Sex-role stereotypes, 139–141, 158, 166, 167

Sex roles:
acquisition of: cognitive-developmental approach, 166, 169–170, 175
psychodynamic approach, 166, 168–169, 175
social learning approach, 170–175
androgynous individuals and, 162, 164
biology and, 141–143
in marriage, 164, 165
parents and development of, 153, 155–157, 171–172
peers and development of, 157, 159
(*See also* Sexism)
Sexism, 134–175
definition of, 136
effects of: on beliefs and attitudes, 158–161
on habits, 164–166
on ideals, 164
on knowledge, 162, 164
on motives and values, 162
on skills, 161–162
mass media and, 150–153
mental health and, 164–166
race and, 148
religion and, 147–148
schools and, 148–149
socialization and, 141, 143–158, 160, 166, 168–175
(*See also* Sex-role myths; Sex-role stereotypes)
Siblings:
sex-role development and, 157
socialization and, 157
"Sidedness" of message, 73
Similarity:
helping behavior and, 239–247
liking others and, 207–209
Sing Sing Prison, 238
Situation, leadership effectiveness and, 375–377
Situational forces, obedience and, 332–333
Skills, sexism and, 161–162
Sleeper effect, credibility of source and, 68
Social adjustment:
attitudes and, 54, 64
conformity and, 104, 105
Social barriers, 106, 108
Social class:
helping behavior and, 246–247
sexism and, 146–147
Social comparison, affiliation and, 184–186
Social conflict (*see* Conflict)
Social Darwinism, 108–109
Social debilitation effect, 351
Social desirability bias, 22
Social-distance scale, attitude measurement and, 56, 58, 59
Social exchange, affiliation and, 182–184
Social facilitation (social facilitation effect), 350–352

Social forces theory of leadership, 371
Social influence, groups and, 359, 361
Social influence approach to aggression, 291–295
Social learning theory (social learning approach):
of aggression, 282, 284–289
of sex-role acquisition, 170–175
Social norms (*see* Norms)
Social pressure of conforming, in groupthink, 346
Social psychologists, 4
Social psychology, as science or history, 15–18
Social reality, social comparison and, 184
Social-responsibility norm, 250
Social rewards, affiliation and, 182–184
Social science, laws and theories about behavior and, 15–17
(*See also specific social sciences*)
Social space, 399
Socialization:
definition of, 141
parents' role in, 153, 155–157
peers' role in, 157, 159
sexism and, 141, 143–158, 160, 166, 168–175
siblings' role in, 157
in Soviet Union, 157
Socially desirable behavior, expectations and, 196–197
Socially oriented personality, 258
Socioemotional specialist, 377–378
Sociofugal factors in environment, 402–404
Sociopetal factors in environment, 402
Solitude, 398
Source of communication, attitude change and, 65–70
Soviet Union, 27
socialization in, 157
United States and, 23–26, 34, 341
Space:
personal, 399–402
social, 399
Specialists, socioemotional, 377–378
Stanford Prison Experiment, 237–239
State University of New York at Stony Brook, 393
Status:
achieved, 365
aggression and achievement of, 294–295
ascribed, 365
in group structure, 365–367
Status prejudice, 96
Stereotype accuracy, 192, 193
Stereotypes (stereotyped images):
conflict and, 28–29
of enemy, in groupthink, 346
ethnic, 95, 96, 130
in *F* Scale, 113
physical attractiveness, 208, 211

Stereotypes (stereotyped images):
    sex-role, 139–141, 158, 166, 167
    (See also Generalizations)
Stimuli:
    ambiguous, attitude measurement and,
        56, 60
    modeling, 172
Structural density, 385
Structure, group, 350, 365–369
Submission, authoritarian, in F Scale, 113
Success, fear of, 158–161
Superego, 166, 168
Superstition in F Scale, 113
Surface-contact level of relationship, 219,
    220
Survival, affiliation and, 182
Symbolism, ethnic prejudice and, 106

T-groups, 360–361
Tahiti, 296
Task-oriented leader, 376, 377
Task performance, attitude measurement
    and, 56, 57
Task specialist, 378
Task structure in groups, 376
Tchambuli, study of sex roles among, 139,
    141
Teachers, physical attractiveness of children
    and, 211–212
Team players, Watergate scandal and, 304–
    305
Television:
    institutional racism and, 109–111
    sexism in, 150–152
    violence on, 288–291
    (See also Mass media)
Tension, attitude change and, 80, 84
Territorial control, aggression and, 268
Territoriality, helping behavior and, 252,
    397
Territory, 394, 396–397
Testing, scientific method and, 12–13
Thanatos (death instinct), 268
Theory, scientific method and, 12, 13
Therapist-patient relationship, sexism in,
    165–166
Therapy, reduction of prejudice and, 123
Tolerance for dissent, 334–336
"Toughness" in F Scale, 113–114
Trucking game, 36–38
Trustworthiness of communication source,
    65–67
Two-factor theory of emotional arousal, 217–
    218

Unanimity, groupthink and illusion of, 346
Unilateral-awareness level of relationship,
    219
United States Army, integration of, 127

Unobtrusive measurement, 21
Urban settings, 410–417

Valid communication, 360
Validity of data, 30–31
Value expressions, attitudes and, 54, 55, 64
Values:
    brainwashing and, 315, 316
    sexism and, 162
    similarity of, liking and, 208, 211
Variables, 11
    in analysis of data, 33–38
    control and manipulation of, in
        experiments, 36
    dependent, 36
    independent, 36
Vicarious consequences, 284–285
Victim, helping behavior and ambiguity of
    need of, 231–233
Victim-bystander characteristics, 230–247
Vietnam war, 6–8, 28, 29, 318, 320
    aggression and, 262, 263, 279, 291–292, 346
    sex-role socialization and, 166
Violence:
    brain disorders and, 274–275
    mass media and, 288–291
    observation of, 14, 18–19, 21
    (See also Aggression)
Voting behavior, 121–122
    personal characteristics of candidates
        and, 371, 374
    sexual identity and, 136, 138

Walker Report to the National Commission
    on the Causes and Prevention of
    Violence, 14, 18–19, 21
War, 270–271, 294, 296–297
Warnings, rationalizations of, 347
Watergate scandal, 300–306, 311–314, 330,
    331, 336
Watts (Los Angeles), 1965 riot in, 101, 102
Weapons, aggression and, 283–284
West End urban-renewal project (Boston),
    408, 410
Westgate (housing complexes), 359
White, symbolism of color, 106
Women (see Sex roles; Sexism)
Women's groups (consciousness-raising
    groups), 163, 164
Women's Liberation, 136
World Health Organization Expert
    Committee on Mental Health, 375
World War I, 31–33

Yale University, 326–328

Zero-contact level of relationship, 219, 220